Contemporary Authors®

ISSN 0010-7468

Contemporary Authors®

**A Bio-Bibliographical Guide to
Current Writers in Fiction, General Nonfiction,
Poetry, Journalism, Drama, Motion Pictures,
Television, and Other Fields**

volume **233**

THOMSON

GALE

Detroit • New York • San Francisco • San Diego • New Haven, Conn. • Waterville, Maine • London • Munich

THOMSON
™
GALE

Contemporary Authors, Vol. 233

Project Editor
Julie Mellors

Editorial
Katy Balcer, Michelle Kazensky, Joshua Kondek, Lisa Kumar, Tracey Matthews, Mary Ruby, Maikue Vang

Permissions
Lisa Kincade, Timothy Sisler

Imaging and Multimedia
Lezlie Light, Kelly A. Quin

Composition and Electronic Capture
Carolyn Roney

Manufacturing
Drew Kalasky

LIBRARY OF CONGRESS CATALOG CARD NUMBER 62-52046

ISBN 0-7876-7862-7
ISSN 0010-7468

Printed in the United States of America
10 9 8 7 6 5 4 3 2 1

Contents

Indexing note: All *Contemporary Authors* entries are indexed in the *Contemporary Authors* cumulative index, which is published separately and distributed twice a year.

As always, the most recent Contemporary Authors cumulative index continues to be the user's guide to the location of an individual author's listing.

v

Preface

Contemporary Authors (*CA*) provides information on approximately 115,000 writers in a wide range of media, including:

- Current writers of fiction, nonfiction, poetry, and drama whose works have been issued by commercial publishers, risk publishers, or university presses (authors whose books have been published only by known vanity or author-subsidized firms are ordinarily not included)

- Prominent print and broadcast journalists, editors, photojournalists, syndicated cartoonists, graphic novelists, screenwriters, television scriptwriters, and other media people

- Notable international authors

- Literary greats of the early twentieth century whose works are popular in today's high school and college curriculums and continue to elicit critical attention

A *CA* listing entails no charge or obligation. Authors are included on the basis of the above criteria and their interest to *CA* users. Sources of potential listees include trade periodicals, publishers' catalogs, librarians, and other users of the series.

How to Get the Most out of *CA*: Use the Index

The key to locating an author's most recent entry is the *CA* cumulative index, which is published separately and distributed twice a year. It provides access to *all* entries in *CA* and *Contemporary Authors New Revision Series* (*CANR*). Always consult the latest index to find an author's most recent entry.

For the convenience of users, the *CA* cumulative index also includes references to all entries in these Thomson Gale literary series: *Authors and Artists for Young Adults, Authors in the News, Bestsellers, Black Literature Criticism, Black Literature Criticism Supplement, Black Writers, Children's Literature Review, Concise Dictionary of American Literary Biography, Concise Dictionary of British Literary Biography, Contemporary Authors Autobiography Series, Contemporary Authors Bibliographical Series, Contemporary Dramatists, Contemporary Literary Criticism, Contemporary Novelists, Contemporary Poets, Contemporary Popular Writers, Contemporary Southern Writers, Contemporary Women Poets, Dictionary of Literary Biography, Dictionary of Literary Biography Documentary Series, Dictionary of Literary Biography Yearbook, DISCovering Authors, DISCovering Authors: British, DISCovering Authors: Canadian, DISCovering Authors: Modules* (including modules for Dramatists, Most-Studied Authors, Multicultural Authors, Novelists, Poets, and Popular/Genre Authors), *DISCovering Authors 3.0, Drama Criticism, Drama for Students, Feminist Writers, Hispanic Literature Criticism, Hispanic Writers, Junior DISCovering Authors, Major Authors and Illustrators for Children and Young Adults, Major 20th-Century Writers, Native North American Literature, Novels for Students, Poetry Criticism, Poetry for Students, Short Stories for Students, Short Story Criticism, Something about the Author, Something about the Author Autobiography Series, St. James Guide to Children's Writers, St. James Guide to Crime & Mystery Writers, St. James Guide to Fantasy Writers, St. James Guide to Horror, Ghost & Gothic Writers, St. James Guide to Science Fiction Writers, St. James Guide to Young Adult Writers, Twentieth-Century Literary Criticism, 20th Century Romance and Historical Writers, World Literature Criticism,* and *Yesterday's Authors of Books for Children.*

A Sample Index Entry:

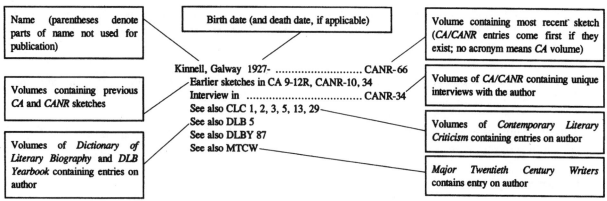

How Are Entries Compiled?

The editors make every effort to secure new information directly from the authors; listees' responses to our questionnaires and query letters provide most of the information featured in *CA*. For deceased writers, or those who fail to reply to requests for data, we consult other reliable biographical sources, such as those indexed in Thomson Gale's *Biography and Genealogy Master Index,* and bibliographical sources, including *National Union Catalog, LC MARC,* and *British National Bibliography.* Further details come from published interviews, feature stories, and book reviews, as well as information supplied by the authors' publishers and agents.

An asterisk (*) at the end of a sketch indicates that the listing has been compiled from secondary sources believed to be reliable but has not been personally verified for this edition by the author sketched.

What Kinds of Information Does An Entry Provide?

Sketches in *CA* contain the following biographical and bibliographical information:

- **Entry heading:** the most complete form of author's name, plus any pseudonyms or name variations used for writing

- **Personal information:** author's date and place of birth, family data, ethnicity, educational background, political and religious affiliations, and hobbies and leisure interests

- **Addresses:** author's home, office, or agent's addresses, plus e-mail and fax numbers, as available

- **Career summary:** name of employer, position, and dates held for each career post; resume of other vocational achievements; military service

- **Membership information:** professional, civic, and other association memberships and any official posts held

- **Awards and honors:** military and civic citations, major prizes and nominations, fellowships, grants, and honorary degrees

- **Writings:** a comprehensive, chronological list of titles, publishers, dates of original publication and revised editions, and production information for plays, television scripts, and screenplays

- **Adaptations:** a list of films, plays, and other media which have been adapted from the author's work

- **Work in progress:** current or planned projects, with dates of completion and/or publication, and expected publisher, when known

- **Sidelights:** a biographical portrait of the author's development; information about the critical reception of the author's works; revealing comments, often by the author, on personal interests, aspirations, motivations, and thoughts on writing

- **Interview:** a one-on-one discussion with authors conducted especially for *CA*, offering insight into authors' thoughts about their craft

- **Autobiographical essay:** an original essay written by noted authors for *CA*, a forum in which writers may present themselves, on their own terms, to their audience

- **Photographs:** portraits and personal photographs of notable authors

- **Biographical and critical sources:** a list of books and periodicals in which additional information on an author's life and/or writings appears

- **Obituary Notices** in *CA* provide date and place of birth as well as death information about authors whose full-length sketches appeared in the series before their deaths. The entries also summarize the authors' careers and writings and list other sources of biographical and death information.

Related Titles in the *CA* Series

Contemporary Authors Autobiography Series complements *CA* original and revised volumes with specially commissioned autobiographical essays by important current authors, illustrated with personal photographs they provide. Common topics include their motivations for writing, the people and experiences that shaped their careers, the rewards they derive from their work, and their impressions of the current literary scene.

Contemporary Authors Bibliographical Series surveys writings by and about important American authors since World War II. Each volume concentrates on a specific genre and features approximately ten writers; entries list works written by and about the author and contain a bibliographical essay discussing the merits and deficiencies of major critical and scholarly studies in detail.

Available in Electronic Formats

GaleNet. *CA* is available on a subscription basis through GaleNet, an online information resource that features an easy-to-use end-user interface, powerful search capabilities, and ease of access through the World-Wide Web. For more information, call 1-800-877-GALE.

Licensing. *CA* is available for licensing. The complete database is provided in a fielded format and is deliverable on such media as disk, CD-ROM, or tape. For more information, contact Thomson Gale's Business Development Group at 1-800-877-GALE, or visit us on our website at www.galegroup.com/bizdev.

Suggestions Are Welcome

The editors welcome comments and suggestions from users on any aspect of the *CA* series. If readers would like to recommend authors for inclusion in future volumes of the series, they are cordially invited to write the Editors at *Contemporary Authors*, Thomson Gale, 27500 Drake Rd., Farmington Hills, MI 48331-3535; or call at 1-248-699-4253; or fax at 1-248-699-8054.

Contemporary Authors Product Advisory Board

The editors of *Contemporary Authors* are dedicated to maintaining a high standard of excellence by publishing comprehensive, accurate, and highly readable entries on a wide array of writers. In addition to the quality of the content, the editors take pride in the graphic design of the series, which is intended to be orderly yet inviting, allowing readers to utilize the pages of *CA* easily and with efficiency. Despite the longevity of the *CA* print series, and the success of its format, we are mindful that the vitality of a literary reference product is dependent on its ability to serve its users over time. As literature, and attitudes about literature, constantly evolve, so do the reference needs of students, teachers, scholars, journalists, researchers, and book club members. To be certain that we continue to keep pace with the expectations of our customers, the editors of *CA* listen carefully to their comments regarding the value, utility, and quality of the series. Librarians, who have firsthand knowledge of the needs of library users, are a valuable resource for us. The *Contemporary Authors* Product Advisory Board, made up of school, public, and academic librarians, is a forum to promote focused feedback about *CA* on a regular basis. The six-member advisory board includes the following individuals, whom the editors wish to thank for sharing their expertise:

- **Anne M. Christensen,** Librarian II, Phoenix Public Library, Phoenix, Arizona.

- **Barbara C. Chumard,** Reference/Adult Services Librarian, Middletown Thrall Library, Middletown, New York.

- **Eva M. Davis,** Youth Department Manager, Ann Arbor District Library, Ann Arbor, Michigan.

- **Adam Janowski, Jr.,** Library Media Specialist, Naples High School Library Media Center, Naples, Florida.

- **Robert Reginald,** Head of Technical Services and Collection Development, California State University, San Bernadino, California.

- **Stephen Weiner,** Director, Maynard Public Library, Maynard, Massachusetts.

International Advisory Board

Well-represented among the 115,000 author entries published in *Contemporary Authors* are sketches on notable writers from many non-English-speaking countries. The primary criteria for inclusion of such authors has traditionally been the publication of at least one title in English, either as an original work or as a translation. However, the editors of *Contemporary Authors* came to observe that many important international writers were being overlooked due to a strict adherence to our inclusion criteria. In addition, writers who were publishing in languages other than English were not being covered in the traditional sources we used for identifying new listees. Intent on increasing our coverage of international authors, including those who write only in their native language and have not been translated into English, the editors enlisted the aid of a board of advisors, each of whom is an expert on the literature of a particular country or region. Among the countries we focused attention on are Mexico, Puerto Rico, Germany, Luxembourg, Belgium, the Netherlands, Norway, Sweden, Denmark, Finland, Taiwan, Singapore, Spain, Italy, South Africa, Israel, and Japan, as well as England, Scotland, Wales, Ireland, Australia, and New Zealand. The sixteen-member advisory board includes the following individuals, whom the editors wish to thank for sharing their expertise:

- **Lowell A. Bangerter,** Professor of German, University of Wyoming, Laramie, Wyoming.

- **Nancy E. Berg,** Associate Professor of Hebrew and Comparative Literature, Washington University, St. Louis, Missouri.

- **Frances Devlin-Glass,** Associate Professor, School of Literary and Communication Studies, Deakin University, Burwood, Victoria, Australia.

- **David William Foster,** Regent's Professor of Spanish, Interdisciplinary Humanities, and Women's Studies, Arizona State University, Tempe, Arizona.

- **Hosea Hirata,** Director of the Japanese Program, Associate Professor of Japanese, Tufts University, Medford, Massachusetts.

- **Jack Kolbert,** Professor Emeritus of French Literature, Susquehanna University, Selinsgrove, Pennsylvania.

- **Mark Libin,** Professor, University of Manitoba, Winnipeg, Manitoba, Canada.

- **C. S. Lim,** Professor, University of Malaya, Kuala Lumpur, Malaysia.

- **Eloy E. Merino,** Assistant Professor of Spanish, Northern Illinois University, DeKalb, Illinois.

- **Linda M. Rodríguez Guglielmoni,** Associate Professor, University of Puerto Rico—Mayagüez, Puerto Rico.

- **Sven Hakon Rossel,** Professor and Chair of Scandinavian Studies, University of Vienna, Vienna, Austria.

- **Steven R. Serafin,** Director, Writing Center, Hunter College of the City University of New York, New York City.

- **David Smyth,** Lecturer in Thai, School of Oriental and African Studies, University of London, England.

- **Ismail S. Talib,** Senior Lecturer, Department of English Language and Literature, National University of Singapore, Singapore.

- **Dionisio Viscarri,** Assistant Professor, Ohio State University, Columbus, Ohio.

- **Mark Williams,** Associate Professor, English Department, University of Canterbury, Christchurch, New Zealand.

CA Numbering System and Volume Update Chart

Occasionally questions arise about the *CA* numbering system and which volumes, if any, can be discarded. Despite numbers like " 29-32R," " 97-100" and "232," the entire *CA* print series consists of only 284 physical volumes with the publication of *CA* Volume 233. The following charts note changes in the numbering system and cover design, and indicate which volumes are essential for the most complete, up-to-date coverage.

CA First Revision

- 1-4R through 41-44R (11 books)
  Cover: Brown with black and gold trim.
  There will be no further First Revision volumes because revised entries are now being handled exclusively through the more efficient *New Revision Series* mentioned below.

CA Original Volumes

- 45-48 through 97-100 (14 books)
  Cover: Brown with black and gold trim.
  101 through 233 (133 books)
  Cover: Blue and black with orange bands.
  The same as previous *CA* original volumes but with a new, simplified numbering system and new cover design.

CA Permanent Series

- *CAP*-1 and *CAP*-2 (2 books)
  Cover: Brown with red and gold trim.
  There will be no further Permanent Series volumes because revised entries are now being handled exclusively through the more efficient *New Revision Series* mentioned below.

CA New Revision Series

- CANR-1 through CANR-138 (138 books)
  Cover: Blue and black with green bands.
  Includes only sketches requiring significant changes; **sketches are taken from any previously published CA, CAP, or CANR volume.**

If You Have:	You May Discard:
CA First Revision Volumes 1-4R through 41-44R and *CA Permanent Series* Volumes 1 and 2	*CA* Original Volumes 1, 2, 3, 4 Volumes 5-6 through 41-44
CA Original Volumes 45-48 through 97-100 and 101 through 233	**NONE:** These volumes will not be superseded by corresponding revised volumes. Individual entries from these and all other volumes appearing in the left column of this chart may be revised and included in the various volumes of the *New Revision Series*.
CA New Revision Series Volumes *CANR*-1 through *CANR*-138	**NONE:** The *New Revision Series* does not replace any single volume of *CA*. Instead, volumes of *CANR* include entries from many previous *CA* series volumes. All *New Revision Series* volumes must be retained for full coverage.

A Sampling of Authors and Media People Featured in This Volume

Ghadah al-Samman

Ghadah al-Samman, whose name is often transliterated as Ghada Samman, is one of the most notable female authors of the Arab world. Her novels, essays, and poetry often touch on political issues, including the role of women, but she also writes about such universal experiences as love and loss. Samman's work, with its frank and often satirical discussion of class and sex in the Arab world, has not been warmly received by the government in her native Lebanon. Because of this censorship, as well as the devastation caused by Lebanon's on-and-off sixteen-year civil war, Samman and her husband eventually moved to Paris, France. She has received the Award for Arabic Literature in Translation from the University of Arkansas Press for both *Beirut '75* and *The Square Moon: Supernatural Tales.*

Aaron Elkins

Elkins, the author of mystery novels, often sets his plots in foreign locations such as Egypt, Tahiti, Mexico, and Alaska. Though most famous for his "Gideon Oliver" series, about a forensic anthropologist who solves modern murders, Elkins also created the "Chris Norgren" series, featuring a retired museum curator whose sleuthing solves crimes. With his wife, Charlotte Elkins, he created the "Lee Ofstead" series, novels wherein crimes involve the sport of golf. Elkins is also the author of stand-alone crime novels including *Twenty Blue Devils, Loot,* and *Turncoat,* and his "Gideon Oliver" series was adapted as a television series in the late 1980s. For his work, Elkins has received several awards and honors, including an Edgar Allen Poe Award and Nero Wolfe Award, both for best mystery novel, and an Agatha Award for best short story. An autobiographical essay by Elkins is included in this volume of *CA.*

Nicholas Enright

At his death in 2003 at the age of fifty-two, Australian playwright Enright left behind a long list of acclaimed plays as well as many young thespians who remembered him as a dedicated drama teacher. Writing for television and radio in addition to the stage, Enright became most well known to American audiences as the coauthor, with medical doctor George Miller, of the Academy Award-nominated screenplay for the film *Lorenzo's Oil.* Enright's play *Black Rock,* about the death of a teenage girl in a New South Wales factory town, also eventually made it to film as well as onto Australian radio, and the stage musical *The Boy from Oz,* for which he wrote the book, was met with critical acclaim on Broadway and in

theaters around the world. In the last years before his death, Enright dedicated a significant portion of his time to teaching.

E. R. Frank

Frank has worked in prisons, day treatment centers, a middle school, and an outpatient mental health clinic. A clinical social worker who also established a psychotherapy practice in Manhattan, Frank has had many troubled youths pass her way; in fact, a full third of her caseload has been troubled adolescents. Frank brings her experience and expertise in the area of teen problems to bear in her novels about young New Yorkers at risk and dealing with trauma. Beginning with *Life Is Funny* and continuing in *America, Friction,* and *Wave,* Frank presents non-sensationalized yet haunting evocations of adolescents and teenagers confronted with daunting situations, including recognizing and surviving sexual abuse. Published in 2000, Frank's debut novel, *Life Is Funny* drew praise from critics, a trend that continued with her subsequent works.

Ron Hutchinson

British dramatist Hutchinson has built a diverse writing career that includes work for radio, stage, and screen. Hutchinson found success as a playwright in the 1970s, and in 1978 he was made a resident writer for the Royal Shakespeare Company, then based in London. From there he was able to make the leap to writing for television and film, and he eventually moved to Los Angeles in 1988. Much of Hutchinson's early writing, including the plays *Rat in the Skull* and *Says I, Says He,* reflects his Irish background, centering on both the political turmoil of the region and the experience of Irish characters away from their homeland. Upon moving to Los Angeles, he took up writing scripts for TV miniseries such as *Traffic, The Tuskegee Airmen,* and *The Burning Season,* all of which were nominated for Emmy Awards, and *Murderers Among Us: The Simon Wiesenthal Story,* which won that prestigious honor. In addition, Hutchinson wrote the screenplay for the feature film *The Island of Doctor Moreau.*

Chihiro Iwasaki

Japanese-born illustrator and author Iwasaki began studying art as a teenager, starting with sketches and oil painting. She mentored under a number of artists, including Saburosuke Okada and Tai Nakatani. During World War II she saw her family home destroyed in an air raid on Tokyo and was forced to flee to her grandmother's home in Nagano, where she joined the Japanese Communist

Party. Once the war was over, she resumed her artistic endeavors, and in 1946 became a writer/illustrator for the *Jimmin Shinbun* (People's Paper). Iwasaki's career developed further when she began work as an illustrator of children's books and magazines. Her artwork provided the framework for her own original stories as well as works by other authors, and she went on to illustrate more than seventy books, including well-known fairy tales by Hans Christian Andersen and the Brothers Grimm. Best known for her picture books centering on a small girl named Momoko, she received much critical acclaim, including the Fiera di Bologna graphics prize and a bronze medal from the Leipzig International Book Fair. Iwasaki died of liver cancer in 1974. In 1977, her house in Nerima-ku, Tokyo was transformed into the Chihiro Art Museum of Picture Books, and the majority of her work is now housed there.

Martin Meredith

An expert on South African history and politics, Meredith has authored numerous works on the postcolonial development of African nations, notably South Africa and Zimbabwe. He has also published biographies of anti-apartheid activists Nelson Mandela and Bram Fischer. Meredith has spent much of his life in Africa, beginning as a foreign correspondent for the London *Observer* and the London *Sunday Times,* then as an Oxford University research fellow and independent scholar. In

his work *The Past Is Another Country: Rhodesia, 1890-1979,* he traces the history of Rhodesia from inception to liberation and the country's ultimate renaming as Zimbabwe. Subsequent works by Meredith examine similarly important periods in Africa's history, touching on such topics as apartheid and Robert Mugabe, a former leader of Zimbabwe. In a departure from his political histories, he also published two books about the African elephant.

Jerry Stiller

Stiller and his wife, Anne Meara, have been entertaining Americans for over half a century, first through acting on stage and then through a stand-up comedy routine. They later took separate career paths, with Stiller continuing to act and Meara turning more to playwriting. Stiller's career has included frequent stints on *The Ed Sullivan Show* and many film roles, both credited and unacknowledged. He is also known for portraying the hilariously volatile character of Frank Costanza on the television show *Seinfeld,* a role that merited him an Emmy nomination. In addition to his screen appearances and comedy shows, Stiller has performed in many stage productions both on and off Broadway. In 2000 he published his memoir, *Married to Laughter: A Love Story Featuring Anne Meara,* relating the tale of his and Meara's career and life together in a surprisingly tender tone.

Acknowledgments

Grateful acknowledgment is made to those publishers, photographers, and artists whose work appear with these authors's essays. Following is a list of the copyright holders who have granted us permission to reproduce material in this volume of *CA*. Every effort has been made to trace copyright, but if omissions have been made, please let us know.

Photographs/Art

Elkins, Aaron: All photographs courtesy of Aaron Elkins. Reproduced by permission.

Spinrad, Norman: All photographs courtesy of Norman Spinrad. Reproduced by permission.

A

AARONS, Leroy (F.) 1933-2004

OBITUARY NOTICE— See index for *CA* sketch: Born December 8, 1933, in New York, NY; died of a heart attack November 28, 2004, in Santa Rosa, CA. Journalist, educator, and author. A respected journalist and newspaper editor, Aarons was also notable as a cofounder of the National Lesbian and Gay Journalists Association. Initially studying psychology at Brown University, where he earned a B.A. in 1955, he later switched to journalism and received a master's degree from Columbia University in 1958. At the time, he was still in the U.S. Navy Reserve, which he left, with the rank of lieutenant, in 1959. His first journalism job was with the New Haven, Connecticut, *Journal-Courier,* where he was a reporter and then city editor. Aarons joined the *Washington Post* in 1962 as an editor and became known as the "Silver Slasher" because of his editorial style and silver hair. Serving as a national correspondent from the mid-1960s through the early 1970s, Aarons covered a number of major stories, such as Senator Robert F. Kennedy's presidential campaign, Kennedy's later funeral after his assassination, and the 1967 Newark, New Jersey, riots. Leaving the *Post* in 1976, he joined the staff at the University of California at Berkeley, where he was involved with the summer program for minority journalists. A year spent in Israel as a freelance correspondent in 1982 was followed by a move to the *Oakland Tribune* in California where Aarons served as executive editor. Leading efforts to diversify the paper and boost circulation, he became the paper's senior vice president. Under his leadership, the *Tribune* won a Pulitzer Prize in 1990 for coverage of the Loma Prieta, California, earthquake. In 1991, Aarons returned to freelancing, publishing his book *Prayers for Bobby: A Mother's Coming to Terms with the Suicide of Her Gay Son* (1995), while also writing the radio docudrama *Top Secret: The Battle for the Pentagon Papers* (1991) and the libretto *Monticello* (2000). Aside from these later accomplishments, Aarons came into the limelight when he announced his homosexuality at a 1989 American Society of Newspaper Editors conference while presenting a paper about homosexual journalists. The next year, he and several other journalists founded the National Lesbian and Gay Journalists Association, for which he served as president until 1997. In 1999 he joined the University of Southern California faculty as a professor of journalism and director of the Annenberg School's sexual orientation issues-in-the-news program. At the time of his death, he was in the midst of writing a play about the South African Truth and Reconciliation Commission.

OBITUARIES AND OTHER SOURCES:

PERIODICALS

New York Times, November 30, 2004, p. A21.
Washington Post, November 30, 2004, p. B6.

*   *   *

ACUFF, Jerry 1949-

PERSONAL: Born 1949. *Education:* Graduated from Virginia Military Institute.

ADDRESSES: Office—Delta Point: The Sales Agency, 12196 East Sand Hills Rd., Scottsdale, AZ 85255.

CAREER: Hoechst-Roussel Pharmaceuticals, associated with company for twenty years, began as salesman, became vice president and general manager; JBI Associates (healthcare consulting firm), Morristown, NJ, founder, 1995-2001; Delta Point: The Sales Agency, Scottsdale, AZ, founder and principal. Former executive-in-residence, Amos Tuck School of Business, Dartmouth College.

WRITINGS:

(With Wally Wood) *The Relationship Edge in Business: Connecting with Customers and Colleagues When It Counts,* Wiley (Hoboken, NJ), 2004.

SIDELIGHTS: Sales consultant Jerry Acuff is co-author of *The Relationship Edge in Business: Connecting with Customers and Colleagues When It Counts.* The book, written with Wally Wood, provides "illuminating advice" for salespeople and for those who manage them, wrote *Business Week* reviewer Marilyn Harris.

In his book, Acuff argues that the most important thing for a salesperson to emphasize is not the features of his or her company's product, but the personal relationship with the client. Acuff explains how to go about building a lasting relationship with a potential client, starting by taking a genuine interest in him or her as a person. To get the client to open up, he suggests a list of "twenty questions"—all of which are about the other person—to start a conversation. These conversation starters break down into four categories, which can be remembered with the acronym FORM: family, occupation, recreation, and motivation. Then, once a salesman has learned something about his client as a person, he can use this information to carry out small, thoughtful gestures that keep him—and his firm—in the front of the client's mind, such as sending the client newspaper clippings about topics that interest him or her. However, Acuff emphasizes that these relationship-building techniques will only work if they come off as sincere and long term, not as merely short-term efforts to make a sale. That emphasis makes *The Relationship Edge in Business* "a refreshing break from the winner-take-all approach to salesmanship," remarked *Booklist* reviewer David Siegfried.

Acuff told *CA:* "I first became interested in writing from reading lots of books. My work is most influenced by my personal experiences, my analysis of them, and—of course—what I read and learn from so may others with expertise in my field.

"I write by talking stream-of-consciousness to my coauthor, and he helps put it together as a draft. We then make dozens of edits torturing every single word. I am surprised that people who are positively impacted by my book actually contact me and tell me what it has meant to them."

BIOGRAPHICAL AND CRITICAL SOURCES:

PERIODICALS

Booklist, May 1, 2004, David Siegfried, review of *The Relationship Edge in Business: Connecting with Customers and Colleagues When It Counts,* p. 1532.
Business Week, July 5, 2004, Marilyn Harris, review of *The Relationship Edge in Business.*
Daily Herald (Arlington Heights, IL), July 12, 2004, Jim Pawlak, review of *The Relationship Edge in Business,* p. 3.
HR, August, 2004, Leigh Rivenbark, review of *The Relationship Edge in Business,* p. 141.
Investor's Business Daily, April 2, 2004, Cord Cooper, review of *The Relationship Edge in Business,* p. A3; September 27, 2004, Cord Cooper, review of *The Relationship Edge in Business,* p. A3.
Publishers Weekly, April 19, 2004, review of *The Relationship Edge in Business,* p. 55.

ONLINE

BookPage.com, http://www.bookpage.com/ (November 1, 2004), Stephanie Swilley, review of *The Relationship Edge in Business: Connecting with Customers and Colleagues When It Counts.*
Delta Point: The Sales Agency Web site, http://www.relationshipedge.com/ (November 1, 2004).
National Association of Realtors Web site, http://www.realtor.org/ (September 1, 2004), Kelly Quigley, review of *The Relationship Edge in Business.*

*   *   *

ADAMS, Lorraine

PERSONAL: Female. *Education:* Princeton University, B.A., 1981; Columbia University, M.A., 1982.

ADDRESSES: Home—Washington, DC. *Agent*—c/o Author Mail, Knopf, 1745 Broadway, New York, NY 10019.

CAREER: Concord Monitor, Concord, NH, reporter, 1983-84; *Dallas Morning News,* Dallas, TX, reporter, 1984-92; *Washington Post,* Washington, DC, reporter, 1992-2003.

AWARDS, HONORS: Pulitzer Prize, 1992, for investigative reporting.

WRITINGS:

Harbor (novel), Knopf (New York, NY), 2004.

WORK IN PROGRESS: A novel.

SIDELIGHTS: Lorraine Adams is a Pulitzer Prize-winning journalist who has now turned to writing novels. When she worked for the *Washington Post* she was assigned at one point to cover the Federal Bureau of Investigation (FBI) and the Justice Department. One of the stories involved a terrorist plot planned by Algerians in Canada who sent one man over the border into Seattle with a trunk filled with explosives destined for the Los Angeles International Airport. Believing this action to be part of a much wider plot, the FBI launched what was at that time the largest counterterrorism investigation ever conducted in the United States. Adams said in a question-and-answer article on the Random House Web site's Borzoi Reader section that this "was to be an anatomy of a counterterrorism dragnet."

Adams examined how the FBI handled counterterrorism investigations, and she became involved with Algerian communities in the United States and Canada in order to assess the FBI's effectiveness and the impact of its investigations on Muslims. She found that while innocent people were scrutinized, the harder-to-track guilty went undetected. Adams had to earn the trust of the Muslim people to do her research. She took classes in Arabic and made herself visible in their communities. As a woman, she had to overcome prejudice, but word spread that she wanted to hear not only their stories connected to the FBI investigation, but also stories of why they left Algeria, which made

these people more receptive to her. Adams was contacted through calls from pay phones, restaurants, and from federal jails. Her experiences gave her the background and understanding that enabled her to write her first novel, *Harbor.*

The protagonist in *Harbor* is Aziz Arkoun, a young, bearded Muslim man who escapes terrorism in his own country by coming to the United States as a stowaway. He arrives in the late 1990s after enduring fifty-two days in the hold of a tanker. Aziz dives into Boston Harbor bleeding and wearing rags. He swims ashore to begin a life in Boston at a variety of jobs that include gas station attendant, dishwasher, house painter, and deli worker. His new friends include his roommate, Rafik, who plasters the walls of his apartment with Madonna posters, has an American girlfriend named Heather, deals in stolen goods, and introduces Aziz to the Boston nightlife, which they enjoy in shoplifted suits. Others in his group include Ghazi, an educated architect who washes dishes and suffers from depression, which he deadens by watching Al Pacino movies and reading the Koran. Aziz's brother, Mourad, obtains a green card, finds a good job, and begins to live the American dream. They are basically good men, but they are surrounded by others who are not, and who deal in drugs, smuggling, credit card theft, and fraud; their lives also intersect with those of the jihadists.

Neil Gordon noted in a review for the *New York Times* that it is understandable how Adams's experiences influenced her "meticulously constructed first novel." "What's harder to explain," continued Gordon, "is how Adams is able to draw so convincingly into the lived reality of her ensemble cast, a skill that derives less from the craft of journalism than the art of fiction. These characters are the product of a virtuoso act of the imagination, one that reminds us of fiction's deepest ambition—to understand the other. That the other is, in this case, a group that Americans have so long failed to understand makes Adams's novel not only engrossing but important." Gordon concluded by writing that Adams "vividly captures the humiliations that are so plentiful in the harsh life of illegal immigrants, conveying its painful anonymity." "*Harbor,*" he added, "is a remarkable act of artistic empathy. It takes us far beyond journalism to dramatize not just the awful nature of our strife-filled world but also the hopeless complexity of its ethical and cultural roots."

Joseph Finder wrote in *Washington Post Book World* that *Harbor* "is no apologia for terrorism. Adams is far less interested in the making of a terrorist than in exploring her characters' inner lives. The elegant architecture of her narrative is designed to illustrate the clash of cultures, the way we fail to understand Islamic immigrants just as surely as they're unable to understand us. In fact, it's barely a novel about terrorism at all. Instead, it is firmly rooted in the rich tradition of the immigrant novel, the novel of America as seen through alien eyes."

BIOGRAPHICAL AND CRITICAL SOURCES:

PERIODICALS

Booklist, July, 2004, Debi Lewis, review of *Harbor,* p. 1815.
Entertainment Weekly, August 20, 2004, Jennifer Reese, review of *Harbor,* p. 129.
Kirkus Reviews, June 1, 2004, review of *Harbor,* p. 503.
New York Times, September 5, 2004, Neil Gordon, "Under Surveillance," review of *Harbor.*
People, August 30, 2004, Margaux Wexberg, review of *Harbor,* p. 50.
Publishers Weekly, June 14, 2004, review of *Harbor,* p. 41.
U.S. News & World Report, September 13, 2004, Ulrich Boser, review of *Harbor,* p. 56.
Washington Post Book World, September 5, 2004, Joseph Finder, review of *Harbor,* p. 3.

ONLINE

Borzoi Reader, http://www.randomhouse.com/knopf/catalog/ (February 17, 2005), "Author Q & A."
Miami Herald Online, http://www.herald.com/ (August 29, 2004), Amy Driscoll, review of *Harbor.*
San Francisco Chronicle Online, http://www.sfgate.com/ (September 5, 2004), Tobin O'Donnell, review of *Harbor.**

* * *

AGRAWAL, Govind P. 1951-

PERSONAL: Born July 24, 1951, in Kashipur, India; son of Amar Nath (in business) and Sushila (a homemaker; maiden name, Devi) Agrawal; married, July 22, 1977; wife's name Anne (a tutor); children: Sipra Celine, Caroline Indu, Claire Kivan. *Ethnicity:* "Asian Indian." *Education:* University of Lucknow, B.S., 1969; Indian Institute of Technology, Delhi, M.S., 1971, Ph.D., 1974.

ADDRESSES: Office—Institute of Optics, University of Rochester, P.O. Box 270186, Rochester, NY 14627; fax: 716-244-4936. *E-mail*—gpa@optics.rochester.edu.

CAREER: École Polytechnique, Palaiseau, France, research assistant, 1974-76; City University of New York, research associate, 1977-80; Quantel S.A., Orsay, France, staff scientist, 1980-81; AT&T Bell Laboratories, Murray Hill, NJ, member of technical staff, 1982-88; University of Rochester, Rochester, NY, professor of optics, 1989—. South China Normal University, honorary professor, 1999; conference organizer.

MEMBER: Optical Society of America, Institute of Electrical and Electronics Engineers.

AWARDS, HONORS: Exceptional Contribution Award, AT&T Bell Laboratories, 1987; Distinguished Alumni Award, Indian Institute of Technology, 2000; grants from National Science Foundation, Research Office of the United States Army, State of New York, and National Aeronautics and Space Administration.

WRITINGS:

(With N. K. Dutta) *Long-Wavelength Semiconductor Lasers,* Van Nostrand Reinhold (New York, NY), 1986.
Nonlinear Fiber Optics, Academic Press (San Diego, CA), 1989, 3rd edition, 2001.
Fiber-Optic Communication Systems, Wiley Publishing Group (New York, NY), 1992, third edition, 2002.
(Editor, with R. W. Boyd, and contributor) *Contemporary Nonlinear Optics,* Academic Press (San Diego, CA), 1992.
(With N. K. Dutta) *Semiconductor Lasers,* Kluwer Academic (Boston, MA), 1993.
(Editor) *Semiconductor Lasers: Past, Present, and Future,* American Institute of Physics (New York, NY), 1995.
Applications of Nonlinear Fiber Optics, Academic Press (San Diego, CA), 2001.

(With Y. S. Kivshar) *Optical Solitons: From Fibers to Photonic Crystals,* Academic Press (San Diego, CA), 2003.

Editor of "Optics and Photonics" series, Academic Press (San Diego, CA), 1998-2002; member of editorial board, "Progress in Optics" series, 2001—. Contributor to books, including *Progress in Optics,* Volume 26, edited by E. Wolf, North-Holland (Amsterdam, Netherlands), 1988; *The Supercontinuum Laser Source,* edited by R. R. Alfano, Springer-Verlag (New York, NY), 1989; *Fundamentals of Fiber Optics in Telecommunication and Sensor Systems,* edited by B. P. Pal, Wiley Eastern (New Delhi, India), 1992; and *Nonlinear Science at the Dawn of the Twenty-first Century,* edited by P. L. Christiansen, M. P. Sørensen, and A. C. Scott, Springer-Verlag (New York, NY), 2000. Contributor to scientific and academic journals, including *Physics Teacher. Journal of the Optical Society of America,* topical editor, 1993-98, special-issue editor, 1999; *Optics Express,* special-issue editor, 1999, associate editor, 2001—; special-issue editor, *Fiber and Integrated Optics,* 2000, and *IEEE Journal of Selected Topics in Quantum Electronics,* 2002; member of editorial board, *Journal of the European Optical Society,* 1994-97, and *Microwave and Optical Technology Letters,* 1998—.

Agrawal's books have been translated into Chinese, Japanese, Russian, and Greek.

BIOGRAPHICAL AND CRITICAL SOURCES:

ONLINE

Govind Agrawal's Home Page, http://www.optics.rochester.edu (August 22, 2004).

*   *   *

AHRONS, Constance (Ruth) 1937-

PERSONAL: Born April 16, 1937, in New York, NY; daughter of Jacob Barnett and Estelle Katz (Golden) Ahrons; married (divorced) twice; children (first marriage): Geri Lynn, Amy Beth. *Education:* Upsala College, B.A., 1964; University of Wisconsin, M.S., 1967, Ph.D., 1973.

ADDRESSES: Home—San Diego, CA. *Agent*—c/o HarperCollins Publishers, 10 East 53rd Street, New York, NY 10022. *E-mail*—constance@ahrons.com.

CAREER: Professor and psychotherapist. Mental Health Associates, Madison, WI, associate, 1968-78; Wisconsin Family Studies Institute, Madison, family therapist, 1978-84; University of Wisconsin, Madison, assistant professor, 1974-81, associate professor, 1981-84; University of Southern California, Los Angeles, associate director of Human Relations Center, 1986, associate professor, 1986-87, professor of sociology, 1987, professor emerita, and former director of marriage and family therapy doctoral training program. Private practice in adult and family psychotherapy, Santa Monica, CA, 1984. Visiting scholar, University of Michigan, Ann Arbor, 1978. Council on Contemporary Families, founding co-chair and senior scholar. Lecturer, consultant. Divorce and Remarriage Consulting Associates, San Diego, CA, director. Television appearances include *Oprah* and *Good Morning America.*

MEMBER: American Psychological Association, American Family Therapy Association (member of executive board), American Sociological Association, International Sociological Association (member of committee on family research).

AWARDS, HONORS: Fellow, American Association of Marriage and Family Therapy; fellow, American Orthopsychiatric Association; Outstanding Achievement Award, Wisconsin Library Literary Association, 1995, for *The Good Divorce: Keeping Your Family Together When Your Marriage Comes Apart;* Radcliffe Institute fellow, 2000-01.

WRITINGS:

(With Roy H. Rodgers) *Divorced Families: A Multidisciplinary Developmental View,* W. W. Norton (New York, NY), 1987.
The Good Divorce: Keeping Your Family Together When Your Marriage Comes Apart, HarperCollins (New York, NY), 1994.
We're Still Family: What Grown Children Have to Say about Their Parents' Divorce, HarperCollins (New York, NY), 2004.

Also creator of the video *Making Divorce Work: A Clinical Approach to the Binuclear Family,* Guildford Press, 1995. Ahrons's writings have appeared in numerous professional journals.

SIDELIGHTS: Professor emerita from the University of Southern California, Constance Ahrons has researched families, divorce, and the effects of divorce for several decades. The results of such research are available in two popular volumes, *The Good Divorce: Keeping Your Family Together When Your Marriage Comes Apart* and *We're Still Family: What Grown Children Have to Say about Their Parents' Divorce.*

In *The Good Divorce,* Ahrons—herself twice divorced—presents evidence from families randomly selected to explore many of the concerns about the potential harmful effects of divorce. The ninety-eight families Ahrons studied were from Wisconsin, and her conclusion after two decades of research is that fully half of these had what she terms a "good divorce." She also proposes four models of divorced parents: "Fiery Foes," "Angry Associates," "Cooperative Colleagues," and "Perfect Pals," further arguing that what she labels the "binuclear," or two-household family, is more common in the modern industrial world than the traditional model of two parents and children living together in one household. Indeed, according to Ahrons, far from destroying a family, a well-handled divorce can be healthier for the children than a marriage filled with acrimony.

Mary Carroll, reviewing *The Good Divorce* in *Booklist,* called it a "landmark" study. Trudy Bush of the *Christian Century,* however, while acknowledging that Ahrons is "well-intentioned" in her study, also felt that the author's "vision seems utopian." As Bush pointed out, "binuclear," or blended families, "often do not function smoothly—which is one of the main reasons why second marriages end in divorce more frequently than first marriages."

Much of the criticism both for and against *The Good Divorce* was along the lines of progressives versus fundamentalists with regard to family values. Yet for Ahrons the truth of her conclusions lay in the people she studied. Thus in 2004 she returned to her original study sampling, contacting 173 children, or about three-fourths of the offspring of her original group, and conducted lengthy phone conversations with them.

Her results, published in *We're Still Family,* bolster her contention that divorce need not be destructive. Of those questioned, seventy-six percent did not wish that their parents were still together, seventy-nine percent felt their parents' decision to divorce was a good one, and seventy-eight percent felt they were better off or not affected at all by the divorce. However, twenty percent of those interviewed did feel lasting impact from their parents' divorce.

Such findings run counter to those of other researchers, such as Judith Wallerstein, whose book *What about the Kids?* warns of the lasting trauma divorce can bring children. *Library Journal*'s Kay Brodie felt that Ahrons's *We're Still Family* would thus be "a comforting and valuable resource for divorced and divorcing parents." Similarly, a reviewer for *Publishers Weekly* observed that "Ahrons's supportive guidebook should aid anyone trying to make a 'good divorce' better." And Joseph di Prisco, writing in the *San Francisco Chronicle,* praised Ahrons's "generous, wise and pragmatic" advice.

BIOGRAPHICAL AND CRITICAL SOURCES:

PERIODICALS

Booklist, October 15, 1994, Mary Carroll, review of *The Good Divorce: Keeping Your Family Together When Your Marriage Comes Apart,* p. 376.
Christian Century, January 31, 1996, Trudy Bush, review of *The Good Divorce,* p. 109.
Library Journal, June 15, 2004, Kay Brodie, review of *We're Still Family: What Grown Children Have to Say about Their Parents' Divorce,* p. 86.
People, July 12, 2004, Champ Clark, "Kids and Divorce: No Lasting Damage?" (interview), pp. 127-128.
Psychology Today, May, 1986, Elizabeth Stark, "Friends Through It All; It's Not Easy to Have a Friendly Relationship after Divorce. But Some People Do and Are Better off for It," p. 54.
Publishers Weekly, April 26, 2004, review of *We're Still Family,* p. 52.
San Francisco Chronicle, June 20, 2004, Joseph di Prisco, review of *We're Still Family.*
USA Today, June 7, 2004, Karen S. Peterson, "Families Split, but Kids Survive," p. D8.

ONLINE

Constance Ahrons Official Web site, http://constance ahrons.com (October 12, 2004).

HarperCollins Web site, http://www.harpercollins.com/ (October 12, 2004), "Constance Ahrons."

University of Southern California Web site, http://www.usc.edu/ (October 12, 2004), "Constance Ahrons."*

*   *   *

ALEXANDER, Alma
    See HROMIC, Alma A.

*   *   *

AL-SAMMAN, Ghadah 1942-
    (Ghada Samman)

PERSONAL: Born 1942, in Damascus, Syria; married. *Education:* Graduated from Damascus University; American University of Beirut, M.A.

ADDRESSES: Office—Manshurat Ghada Samman, P.O. Box 111813, Beirut, Lebanon. *Agent*—c/o Syracuse University Press, 621 Skytop Rd., Suite 110, Syracuse, NY 13244.

CAREER: Novelist, poet, and short story writer; journalist and translator. Manshurat Ghadah al-Samman, Beirut, Lebanon, founder and publisher; Damascus University, Damascus, Syria, teacher for two years; also worked in broadcasting.

AWARDS, HONORS: Award for Arabic literature in translation, University of Arkansas Press, 1995, for *Beirut '75,* and 1998, for *The Square Moon: Supernatural Tales.*

WRITINGS:

Layl al-ghuraba', Dar al-Adab (Beirut, Lebanon), 1966.

Hubb, Dar al-Adab (Beirut, Lebanon), 1973.

Bayrut '75 (novel), 1974, translation by Nancy N. Roberts published as *Beirut '75,* University of Arkansas Press (Fayetteville, AK), 1995.

Aynaka qadari (stories), Dar al-Adab (Beirut, Lebanon), 1975, Manshurat Ghadah al-Samman (Beirut, Lebanon), 2000.

La bahr fi Bayrut (stories), Dar al-Adab (Beirut, Lebanon), 1975, Manshurat Ghadah al-Samman (Beirut, Lebanon), 1993.

A'lantu 'alayka al-hubb (poems), 1976, Manshurat Ghadah al-Samman (Beirut, Lebanon), 1999.

Kawabis Bayrut, 1977, translation by Nancy N. Roberts published as *Beirut Nightmares,* Quartet Books (London, England), 1997.

Al-A'mal ghayr al-kamilah (selected works), 14 volumes, Manshurat Ghadah al-Samman (Beirut, Lebanon), Volume 1: *Zaman al-hubb al-akhar,* 1978, Volume 2:*Al-Jasad haqibat safar,* 1979, Volume 3: *Al-Sibahah fi buhayrat al-Shaytan,* 1979, Volume 4: *Khatm al-dhakirah bi-al-sham' al-ahmar,* 1979, Volume 5: *I'tiqal lahzah haribah,* 1979, Volume 6: *Muwatinah mutalabbisah bi-al-qira'ah,* 1980, Volume 7: *Al-Raghif yanbudu ka-al-qalb,* 1980, Volume 8: *'Gh. tatafarras,* 1980, Volume 9: *Saffarat indhar dakhil ra'si,* 1980, Volume 10: *Kitabat ghayr multazamah,* 1980, Volume 11: *Hubb min al-warid ilá al-warid,* 1980, Volume 12: *Al-Qabilah tastajwib al-qatilah,* 1981, Volume 13: *Bahr yuhakimu samakah,* 1986, Volume 14: *Tasakku' dakhil jurh,* 1988.

Ghurbah tahta al-sifr, Manshurat Ghadah al-Samman (Beirut, Lebanon), 1986.

Laylat al-milyar (novel), Manshurat Ghadah al-Samman (Beirut, Lebanon), 1986, translation by Nancy N. Roberts published as *The Night of the First Billion,* Syracuse University Press (Syracuse, NY), 2004.

Al-A'maq al-muhtallah, Manshurat Ghadah al-Samman (Beirut, Lebanon), 1987.

Raheel al-Marafi' al-Kadima (stories), Manshurat Ghadah al-Samman (Beirut, Lebanon), 1992.

Al-Qamar al-murabba': Qisas ghara'ibiyah, Manshurat Ghadah al-Samman (Beirut, Lebanon), 1994, translation by Issa J. Boullata published as *The Square Moon: Supernatural Tales,* University of Arkansas Press (Fayetteville, AR), 1998.

'Ashiqah fi mihbarah, Manshurat Ghadah al-Samman (Beirut, Lebanon), 1995.

Shahwat al-ajnihah, Manshurat Ghadah al-Samman (Beirut, Lebanon), 1995.

Rasa'il al-hanin ilá al-yasam, Manshurat Ghadah al-Samman (Beirut, Lebanon), 1996.

Al-Riwayah al-mustahilah: fusayfasa' Dimashqiyah (novel; title means "The Impossible Novel: Damascene Mosaics"), Manshurat Ghadah al-Samman (Beirut, Lebanon), 1997.

Al-Qalb nawras wahid, Manshurat Ghadah al-Samman (Beirut, Lebanon), 1998.

Al-Abadiyah lahzat hubb, Manshurat Ghadah al-Samman (Beirut, Lebanon), 1999.

Sahrah tanakkuriyah lil-mawtá (novel), Manshurat Ghadah al-Samman (Beirut, Lebanon), 2003.

Al-Raqs ma'a al-bum, Manshurat Ghadah al-Samman (Beirut, Lebanon), 2003.

Ra'shat al-hurriyah, Manshurat Ghadah al-Samman (Beirut, Lebanon), 2003.

Mouha Kamet Houb (collected works), Manshurat Ghadah al-Samman (Beirut, Lebanon), 2004.

Al Habeeb al Iftiradi (poems), Manshurat Ghadah al-Samman (Beirut, Lebanon), 2005.

Also author of novels, stories and poems.

Samman's books have been translated into ten different languages.

SIDELIGHTS: Ghadah al-Samman, whose name is often transliterated as Ghada Samman, is one of the most notable female authors of the Arab world. Her novels, essays, and poetry often touch on political issues, including the role of women, but she also writes about such universal experiences as love and loss. Samman's work, with its frank and often satirical condemnation of the problems of class and sex in the Arab world, has not been warmly received by the government in her native Lebanon. Because of this censorship, as well as the devastation caused by Lebanon's on-and-off sixteen-year civil war, Samman and her husband eventually moved to Paris, France.

One of Samman's early books was *Beirut '75,* a novel published in 1974. The book has been hailed by many for its prescient view of the class and sectarian divisions in Lebanese society that broke into the open during an extremely destructive civil war that began in April of 1975. These issues are depicted from the perspectives of five strangers who share a taxi from Damascus to Beirut. Each of the five are running away from or towards something: Farah seeks fame; Yasmeena, a teacher, hopes to escape from boredom; Abu'l-Malla, a poor father, needs to bring home money; Abu Mustafa hopes to bring home his son; and Ta'aan wants to escape from danger brought on by a clan rivalry. To each, Beirut, the glittering, seemingly modern capital of Lebanon, seems like the perfect place to realize their dreams, but each is soon disillusioned. Behind the city's modern facades, all the problems of pre-modern, rural Lebanon still exist.

"Each character's story is good, if abbreviated by the length of the novel," a *Publishers Weekly* critic stated. Calling *Beirut '75* a "frighteningly raw novel," Kim Jenson wrote in *Al Jadid* that the book provides "a short, yet harrowing exposé of the political reality of Beirut at the outset of the civil war."

The Square Moon: Supernatural Tales is a collection of semi-autobiographical short stories about Lebanese exiles who have fled to Paris, much as Samman herself did. In the stories, Samman uses the supernatural to emphasize the conflicts that occur when women from Arabic societies discover the freedoms offered in the West. Tensions often arise between these women and their men, who feel threatened or confused by the changes. Samman shows that conflicts can also within an individual woman, sometimes pushing someone into madness. Bonnie Johnston, in a *Booklist* review, claimed that "Samman shows the true complexity of this gender conflict without blaming either gender." In fact, Samman does not really place blame anywhere; as Christopher McCabe wrote in *Al Jadid,* "her concern for every woman's (and man's) plight is rooted in her overriding compassion for all human beings facing dilemmas not easily resolved." All her characters, both men and women, also struggle with memories of their old home and of old friends and loves. The ten stories are "narrated with wit, surprise endings, unexpected plot twists, and surrealistic and realistic details, all in a compelling style which does not leave the reader indifferent," wrote Evelyne Accad in a *World Literature Today* review of *The Square Moon.*

BIOGRAPHICAL AND CRITICAL SOURCES:

BOOKS

Buck, Claire, editor, *The Bloomsbury Guide to Women's Literature,* Prentice Hall General Reference (New York, NY), 1992.

Asfour, J. M., *When the Words Burn,* Cormorant Books (Toronto, Ontario, Canada), 1992.

Awwad, Hanan, *Arab Cause in the Fiction of Ghada Samman,* Edition Namaan (Montreal, Quebec, Canada), 1993.

Zeidan, J. T. *Arab Women Novelists,* State University of New York Press (Albany, NY), 1995.

Robinson, Lillian S., compiler and editor, *Modern Women Writers,* Continuum Publishing (New York, NY), 1996.

Bennani, Ben, *Shahrazad's Sisters,* Truman State University Press (Kirksville, MO), 2002.

PERIODICALS

Al Jadid, fall, 1999, Christopher McCabe, review of *The Square Moon: Supernatural Tales;* winter, 1999, Kim Jensen, review of *Beirut '75.*
Booklist, December 15, 1998, Bonnie Johnston, review of *The Square Moon,* p. 727.
Choice, November, 1999, L. K. MacKendrick, review of *The Square Moon,* p. 203.
Publishers Weekly, July 3, 1995, review of *Beirut '75,* p. 57.
World Literature Today, autumn, 1999, Evelyne Accad, review of *The Square Moon,* p. 811.

ONLINE

Arabic News Online, http://www.arabicnews.com/ (July 25, 1997), review of *Nostalgia Letters to Jasmine.*
Syria Times Online, http://www.teshreen.com/ (March 29, 2003).

* * *

ALTENBURG, Matthias 1958-
(Jan Seghers)

PERSONAL: Born 1958, in Fulda, West Germany (now Germany). *Education:* Attended University of Göttingen.

ADDRESSES: Home—Frankfurt, Germany. *Agent*—c/o Author Mail, Verlag Kiepenheuer und Witsch, Rondorfer Str. 5, 50968 Cologne, Germany.

CAREER: Freelance writer, journalist, critic, and essayist; formerly worked as kitchen help, a representative for a vacuum cleaner company, and a waiter. With guitarist Atilla Korap, creator and performer of "Ein kleiner Abend Glück," a musical performance of works by Martin Luther, Johann Wolfgang von Goethe, Heinrich von Kleist, Friedrich Hebbel, Heinrich Heine, Rosa Luxembourg, Bertolt Brecht, and Rolf Dieter.

AWARDS, HONORS: Marburger Literary Award, 1998.

WRITINGS:

(Editor) *Fremde Mütter, fremde Väter, fremdes Land: Gespräche mit Franz Josef Degenhardt, Gisela Elsner, Gerd Fuchs, Josef Haslinger, Hermann Peter Piwitt, E. A. Rauter, Michael Schneider, Guntram Vesper,* Konkret Literatur Verlag (Hamburg, Germany), 1985.
Die Liebe der Menschenfresser (novel), Piper (Munich, Germany), 1992.
Die Toten von Laroque (novella), Eichborn (Frankfurt am Main, Germany), 1994.
Alles wird gut (play; produced at Bremer Theater, 1997), Verlag der Autoren (Frankfurt am Main, Germany), 1995.
Landschaft mit Wölfen (novel), Kiepenheuer und Witsch (Cologne, Germany), 1997.
Zwei Entwürfe zum Holocaust-Denkmal in Berlin, Verlag für Moderne Kunst (Nurenburg, Germany), 2001.
Partisanen der Schönheit, Oktober-Verlag (Munster in Westfalen, Germany), 2002.
Irgendwie alles Sex, Kiepenheuer und Witsch (Cologne, Germany), 2002.
(As Jan Seghers) *Ein allzu schönes Mädchen* (crime novel), Wunderlich (Hamburg, Germany), 2004.

Also author of film scripts *Das Geheimnis von Wolfshagen* and (with Rolf-Bernhard Essig) *Tage und Nächte.*

Contributor to periodicals, including *Konkret, Spiegel, Die Zeit, Max, Financial Times Deutschland, Stern, SZ-Magazin, Frankfurter Allgemeine Sonntagszeitung, Frankfurter Rundschau, Süddeutsche Zeitung, Hörfunk,* and *Fernsehen.*

SIDELIGHTS: Matthias Altenburg has written several books, as well as a play, under his own name. However, it is as Jan Seghers, the pseudonym under which he published the crime novel *Ein allzu schönes Mädchen,* that Altenburg has won the most fame.

Ein allzu schönes Mädchen pays homage to the typical detective novel: it begins with a hard-boiled policeman, Robert Marthaler, examining the case of a man who was brutally murdered, and follows this rather average detective as he gets sucked deeper and deeper into the intrigue surrounding his current investigation, the new murders that follow it, and the related suicide of another person. The "all too beautiful girl" of the title is the prime suspect: she was seen in a car with the men who were murdered. The girl also has amnesia and other mental issues, the true nature of which are not revealed until the end of the book, which makes it challenging to figure out what her connection to the crimes could be.

Altenburg reads detective novels avidly and was inspired by the work of several classic American crime novelists, including Dashiell Hammett and Raymond Chandler, as well as that of Swedish writer Henning Mankell. As he explained in an interview on the *Jan Seghers* Web site, he did not attempt to mimic their stories directly, but instead to adapt the plots to German society and procedures. He did, however, consciously stick closely to the typical, straightforward language generally used in detective tales, and his fast-moving dialogue and sharp atmospheric descriptions were praised by *Zeit* reviewer Greiner Von Ulrich and others.

BIOGRAPHICAL AND CRITICAL SOURCES:

PERIODICALS

Allgemeine Zeitung, November 10, 2004, Inka Müller, "Die Melancholie des Eigenbrötlers: Lesung von Jan Seghers beim Krimiherbst."
Berliner Morgenpost, May 16, 2004, "Fünfundzwanzig Sonntagsfragen an Jan Seghers, Schriftsteller."
Frankenpost, March 22, 2004, review of *Ein allzu schönes Mädchen.*
Rheinischer Merkur, August 5, 2004, review of *Ein allzu schönes Mädchen.*
Times Literary Supplement, May 29, 1998, review of *Landschaft mit Wölfen,* p. 29.
Zeit, March 25, 2004, Greiner Von Ulrich, review of *Ein allzu schönes Mädchen.*

ONLINE

Bookinist, http://www.leser-service.de/ (November 20, 2004), Manuela Haselberger, review of *Ein allzu schönes Mädchen.*
Buchhandel.de, http://www.buchhandel.de/ (November 20, 2004), review of *Ein allzu schönes Mädchen.*
Crime Corner Web site, http://www.crime-corner.de/ (November 20, 2004), Ekkehard Knörer, review of *Ein allzu schönes Mädchen.*
Familie Contra Singles, http://www.single-generation.de/ (November 4, 2004), "Matthias Altenburg."
HR-online.de, http://www.hr-online.de/ (November 4, 2004), "Matthias Altenburg."
Jan Seghers Web site, http://www.janseghers.de (November 4, 2004).
Krimi-Couch, http://www.krimi-couch.de/ (November 4, 2004), "Jan Seghers (Matthias Altenburg)."
Krimi-Report 20, http://www.alligatorpapiere.de/ (August 10, 2004), Stefan Lichblau, review of *Ein allzu schönes Mädchen.**

*   *   *

AMEN, Daniel G.

PERSONAL: Male. *Education:* Attended University of Maryland, 1974-75; Orange Coast College, A.A., 1976; Southern California College (now Vanguard University), B.A., 1978; Oral Roberts University, M.D., 1982

ADDRESSES: Office—Mindworks Press, 4019 Westerly Place, Suite 100, Newport Beach, CA 92660.

CAREER: Psychiatrist, lecturer, and author. Founder of Amen Clinics, Inc., and Mindworks Press. Walter Reed Army Medical Center, intern, 1982-83, resident in psychiatry, 1983-85; Tripler Army Medical Center, HI, fellow in child and adolescent psychiatry, 1985-87; University of California, Irvine, assistant clinical professor in psychiatry and human behavior; Vanguard University, adjunct faculty in clinical psychobiology; nuclear brain imaging independent fellowship study, 1991-95; Medical Board of California medical expert reviewer, 1997—. Guest on various television and radio programs, including *The Today Show, CNN News, MSNBC News, 48 Hours, The Leeza Show, The View, Discovery Channel News: Inside the Mind of a Killer, Lifetime Television for Women's Speaking of Women's Health,* and UPN's *The Truth about Drinking* (educational television special; also producer). *Military service:* U.S. Army, combat field medic in West Germany, 1972-75; U.S. Army Reserves, 1975-78; U.S. Army, active duty physician, 1982-89, became major.

MEMBER: American Psychiatric Association, American Academy of Child and Adolescent Psychiatry, American Neuropsychiatric Association (member of research committee), Group for the Advancement of Psychiatry (Ginsberg fellow, 1984-86), Alpha Gamma Sigma.

AWARDS, HONORS: General William C. Menninger Memorial Award for best paper presented by a psychiatric resident at the annual General William C. Menninger Military Psychiatry Course, 1985, for "The Target Theory of Suicide: Ideas on Evaluating the Need for Hospitalization"; Emmy Award for best educational television special, 1999, for *The Truth about Drinking;* Outstanding Alumnus Award, Vanguard University, 2002.

WRITINGS:

Don't Shoot Yourself in the Foot: A Program to End Self-Defeating Behavior Forever, Warner Books (New York, NY), 1992.

Ten Steps to Building Values within Children, Mindworks Press (Newport Beach, CA), 1994.

The Most Important Thing in Life I Learned from a Penguin: A Story of How to Help People Change, Mindworks Press (Newport Beach, CA), 1994.

Mindcoach: Teaching Kids and Teens to Think Positive and Feel Good, Mindworks Press (Newport Beach, CA), 1994.

The Instruction Manual That Should Have Come with Your Children: New Skills for Frazzled Parents, Mindworks Press (Newport Beach, CA), 1994.

The Secrets of Successful Students, Mindworks Press (Newport Beach, CA), 1994.

(With Antony Amen and Sharon Johnson) *A Teenager's Guide to ADD,* Mindworks Press (Newport Beach, CA), 1995.

Healing the Chaos Within: The Interaction between ADD, Alcoholism, and Growing up in an Alcoholic Home, Mindworks Press (Newport Beach, CA), 1995.

A Child's Guide to ADD, Mindworks Press (Newport Beach, CA), 1996.

Would You Give Two Minutes a Day for a Lifetime of Love?, St. Martin's Press (New York, NY), 1996.

ADD in Intimate Relationships, Mindworks Press (Newport Beach, CA), 1997.

Firestorms in the Brain: An Inside Look at Violence, Mindworks Press (Newport Beach, CA), 1998.

Change Your Brain, Change Your Life: The Breakthrough Program for Conquering Anxiety, Depression, Obsessiveness, Anger, and Impulsiveness, Times Books (New York, NY), 1998.

Healing ADD: The Breakthrough Program That Allows You to See and Heal the Six Types of Attention Deficit Disorder, Putnam (New York, NY), 2001.

Healing the Hardware of the Soul: How Making the Brain-Soul Connection Can Optimize Your Life, Free Press (New York, NY), 2002.

Healing Anxiety and Depression, Putnam (New York, NY), 2003.

(With William Rodman Shankle) *Preventing Alzheimer's: Prevent, Detect, Diagnose, and Even Halt Alzheimer's Disease and Other Memory Loss,* Putnam (New York, NY), 2004.

Also author of *Which Brain Do You Want?* (DVD), and *Images of Human Behavior: A Brain SPECT Atlas,* 2001. Contributor to books, including *The Neuropsychology of Mental Disorders,* 1994; *Children and Adolescents: An Integrative Approach,* 1999; and *The Comprehensive Textbook of Psychiatry,* 2000. Contributor to periodicals, including *Neuropsychiatry Reviews, Molecular Psychiatry, Journal of Psychoactive Drugs, Primary Psychiatry, Journal of Neurotherapy, Diagnostic Imaging, Military Medicine, Resident and Staff Physician, General Hospital Psychiatry, Annals of Clinical Psychiatry, Men's Health, Journal of Nuclear Medicine, Journal of Neuropsychiatry,* and *Clinical Neurosciences.*

SIDELIGHTS: Daniel G. Amen is a psychiatrist and a pioneer in the use of brain scans in clinical practice. He utilizes a type of functional brain scan called single photon emission computerized tomography (SPECT) to examine which parts of his patients' brains are unusually active or inactive when they are concentrating on various topics or mental tasks. The resulting information helps Amen formulate appropriate diagnoses and treatment plans. Although the use of functional brain imaging has been common in psychological research for many years, its use in clinical practice is still very rare.

Amen has written many books that explain his findings to a lay audience and explain how to improve one's own mental health by applying his discoveries. In one such book, *Preventing Alzheimer's: Prevent,*

Detect, Diagnose, and Even Halt Alzheimer's Disease and Other Memory Loss, Amen and his coauthor, neurologist William Rodman Shankle, provide three basic steps for slowing mental deterioration: know the risk factors for dementia and reduce your risk if you can; test your memory regularly; and, once problems are noticed, get an accurate diagnosis and begin treatment as soon as possible. A *Publishers Weekly* reviewer commented that some of the extensive treatment information might be "too technical for lay readers" but praised the "extremely helpful" section listing caregiver resources and numerous "useful tables."

Many of Amen's books—among them *Healing ADD: The Breakthrough Program That Allows You to See and Heal the Six Types of Attention Deficit Disorder; A Child's Guide to ADD;* and *Healing the Chaos Within: The Interaction between ADD, Alcoholism, and Growing up in an Alcoholic Home*—focus on attention deficit disorder (ADD). Throughout these books, Amen argues that ADD is sorely misunderstood by most people within and outside of the medical establishment. Contradicting the many observers who believe that ADD is overdiagnosed and who worry that potent drugs are being prescribed to children who do not really need them, he claims that the disorder is actually underdiagnosed and undertreated. He also posits the existence of six different types of ADD, four more than are currently recognized. As in his other books, Amen backs up his theories with illustrations of the physical differences between healthy brains and brains with the various types of ADD.

BIOGRAPHICAL AND CRITICAL SOURCES:

PERIODICALS

Library Journal, December, 1998, Maria Uzdavinis, review of *Change Your Brain, Change Your Life: The Breakthrough Program for Conquering Anxiety, Depression, Obsessiveness, Anger, and Impulsiveness,* p. 134; March 15, 2002, Dale Farris, review of *Healing the Hardware of the Soul: How Making the Brain-Soul Connection Can Optimize Your Life,* p. 96.

Publishers Weekly, December 7, 1998, review of *Change Your Brain, Change Your Life,* p. 57; April 26, 2004, review of *Preventing Alzheimer's: Prevent, Detect, Diagnose, and Even Halt Alzheimer's Disease and Other Memory Loss,* p. 55.

ONLINE

Amen Clinic Web site, http://www.amenclinic.com/ (November 4, 2004).

BrainPlace.com, http://www.brainplace.com/ (November 4, 2004), "Daniel G. Amen, M.D."

Mindworks Press Web site, http://www.mindworks press.com/ (November 4, 2004).*

*   *   *

ARMBRUSTER, Ann

PERSONAL: Female. *Education:* Attended Justin Morrill College, Michigan State University.

ADDRESSES: Agent—c/o Author Mail, Franklin Watts/ Children's Press, 555 Broadway, New York, NY 10012.

CAREER: Children's writer and urban designer.

WRITINGS:

FOR CHILDREN

(With Elizabeth A. Taylor) *Tornadoes,* Franklin Watts (New York, NY), 1989.

(With Elizabeth A. Taylor) *Astronaut Training,* Franklin Watts (New York, NY), 1990.

The American Flag, Franklin Watts (New York, NY), 1991.

The United Nations, Franklin Watts (New York, NY), 1995.

The Life and Times of Miami Beach (general nonfiction), Knopf (New York, NY), 1995.

Lake Erie, Children's Press (New York, NY), 1996.

Lake Huron, Children's Press (New York, NY), 1996.

Lake Michigan, Children's Press (New York, NY), 1996.

Lake Ontario, Children's Press (New York, NY), 1996.

Lake Superior, Children's Press (New York, NY), 1996.

St. Lawrence Seaway, Children's Press (New York, NY), 1996.

Floods, Franklin Watts (New York, NY), 1996.

Wildfires, Franklin Watts (New York, NY), 1997.

SIDELIGHTS: Ann Armbruster is the author of books on science, history, and geography for young readers, as well as the author of the 1995 *The Life and Times of Miami Beach* for general readers. Working with Elizabeth A. Taylor, Armbruster authored her first two books, *Tornadoes* and *Astronaut Training,* both aimed at children in the fourth to seventh grades. *Tornadoes* offers a comprehensive look at twisters, from their formation and movement to the safety precautions one can take to avoid injury when caught in the path of such a weather pattern. The book is illustrated with color photographs, as are all of Armbruster's works, and has an extensive bibliography. *Booklist*'s Carolyn Phelan found *Tornadoes* a "useful resource for school projects or general interest." Similarly, Jonathan Betz-Zall, writing in *School Library Journal,* felt that the book "should appeal most to children living in tornado-affected areas, but will attract readers elsewhere, as well." *Astronaut Training* describes the selection and training of astronauts in a work that may, according to a *Kirkus Reviews* critic, "turn the thoughts of younger or less practiced middle readers towards careers in astronautics."

Armbruster's first solo book, *The American Flag,* is a "brief history of the Stars and Stripes," according to Marilyn Long Graham in *School Library Journal.* Graham also felt that Armbruster's "writing is clear and matter-of-fact." In the book Armbruster also deals with the manufacture of flags and the use of the flag "to symbolize both patriotism and protest," according to *Booklist*'s Stephanie Zvirin.

The Life and Times of Miami Beach examines that city from the turn of the twentieth century to the end of the millennium. The book surveys the glory days of the Florida town, filled with wealthy entrepreneurs, movie stars, and gangsters, all of whom came to Miami for some warmth and rest. Armbruster further traces the city's decline from the 1970s to the 1990s, and the contemporary attempts at rejuvenation. *Library Journal* reviewer Ann E. Cohen found the title a "delight for young and old," while Rebecca Ascher-Walsh, writing in *Entertainment Weekly,* called it a "thoroughly entertaining historical account."

In 1996 Armbruster returned to children's nonfiction with a series of titles in the "True Book" series on the Great Lakes and the St. Lawrence Seaway, all of which include history, sailing tales, and a look at the social and mercantile aspects of each body of water. She wrote *Floods* and *Wildfires,* two books in the "First Books" science series, each if which is "well researched, clearly and concisely written, and nicely organized," according to Lauren Peterson in *Booklist.* Both books offer historical perspectives on their respective subject and draw from sources such as myths as well as from scientific publications.

BIOGRAPHICAL AND CRITICAL SOURCES:

PERIODICALS

Booklist, December 1, 1989, Carolyn Phelan, review of *Tornadoes,* p. 740; July, 1991, Kathryn LaBarbera, review of *Astronaut Training,* p. 2043; January 1, 1992, Stephanie Zvirin, review of *The American Flag;* January 1, 1997, Lauren Peterson, review of *Floods* and *Wildfires,* p. 848.

Entertainment Weekly, January 12, 1996, Rebecca Ascher-Walsh, review of *The Life and Times of Miami Beach,* p. 52.

Kirkus Reviews, October 1, 2990, review of *Astronaut Training,* p. 1390.

Library Journal, September 15, 1995, Ann E. Cohen, review of *The Life and Times of Miami Beach,* p. 85.

New York Times, December 7, 1995, Mitchell Owens, review of *The Life and Times of Miami Beach,* p. C6.

Publishers Weekly, September 4, 1995, review of *The Life and Times of Miami Beach,* p. 61.

School Library Journal, December, 1989, Jonathan Betz-Zall, review of *Tornadoes,* p. 104; January, 1992, Marilyn Long Graham, review of *The American Flag,* p. 117.*

* * *

ARMSTRONG, Luanne (A.) 1949-

PERSONAL: Born June 15, 1949, in Creston, British Columbia, Canada; daughter of Robert William (a farmer) and Dorothy (a homemaker; maiden name, Klingensmith) Armstrong; children: Dorothy Woodend, Avril Woodend, Geronimo Morris, Naiches Morris. *Education:* University of Victoria, B.A. (with honors), 1972; University of British Columbia, M.F.A., 2001, and doctoral study.

ADDRESSES: Home—3476 Tupper St., Vancouver, British Columbia V52 3B7, Canada. *E-mail*—luannea@telus.net.

CAREER: Alberta Status of Women Action Committee, Edmonton, Alberta, Canada, researcher, writer, and provincial coordinator, 1986-88; Kamloops Women's Resource Centre, executive director, 1988-89; Nicola Valley Institute of Technology, Merritt, British Columbia, Canada, instructor in English, 1989-92; Kootenay Lake Environmental Information Project, research coordinator, 1993; consultant to *Eco-Sounder* (environmental magazine), Indonesia, 1994; British Columbia Library Trustees Association, publicity and newsletter coordinator, 1998-2000; writer and creative writing teacher at schools through western Canada, including College of the Rockies, Lanbara College of Continuing Education, Kootenay School of the Arts, Yukon Community College, Nelson Fine Arts Center, Okanagan School of the Arts, and Kaslo School of the Arts; workshop presenter. Editor for publishers Blue Lake Books and HodgePog Books, both beginning 1999; Berton House, writer-in-residence, 2000. Vancouver Public Library, board member, 2002-04. Creator and editor, *Other Voices,* 1988-90.

MEMBER: Writers Union of Canada (chair of writers in schools committee, 2003-04), Canadian Society of Children's Authors, Illustrators, and Performers, Federation of British Columbia Writers, Children's Writers and Illustrators, Art Starts in Schools.

AWARDS, HONORS: Grants from Canada Council and Canadian Research Institute for the Advancement of Women, both 1992; "Our Choice" selections, Canadian Children's Book Centre, 1995, for *Annie,* 1997, for *Arly and Spike,* and 2001, for *Jeannie and the Gentle Giants;* first prize, Winner's Circle Writing Contest, Canadian Authors Association, for "Tuning the Rig"; other awards including poetry award from Burnaby Writers Association.

WRITINGS:

Castle Mountain (poetry), Polestar Press (Nelson, British Columbia, Canada), 1981, reprinted, 2002.
(Editor) *From the Interior: A Kootenay Women's Anthology,* 1984.

Annie (novel), Polestar Press (Vancouver, British Columbia, Canada), 1995.
Bordering (novel), Gynergy Books (Charlottetown, Prince Edward Island, Canada), 1995.
The Woman in the Garden (poetry chapbook), Peachtree Press, 1996.
Arly and Spike (juvenile novel), HodgePog Press (Edmonton, Alberta, Canada), 1997.
The Colour of Water (novel), Caitlin Press (Prince George, British Columbia, Canada), 1998.
Maggie and Shine (young adult novel), HodgePog Books (Edmonton, Alberta, Canada), 1999.
Jeannie and the Gentle Giants (young adult novel), Ronsdale Press (Vancouver, British Columbia, Canada), 2001.
The Bone House (novel), New Star Books (Vancouver, British Columbia, Canada), 2002.
Into the Sun (young adult novel), illustrated by Robin Leurew, HodgePog Books (Edmonton, Alberta, Canada), 2002.
Breathing the Mountain (poetry chapbook), Leaf Books (Lantzville, British Columbia, Canada), 2003.
Pete's Gold (young adult novel), Ronsdale Press (Vancouver, British Columbia, Canada), in press.

Work represented in anthologies, including *Home: A Bioregional Anthology,* New Society Press; and *Resist,* Women's Press (Toronto, Ontario, Canada). Contributor of articles, short stories, and poetry to periodicals, including *Vancouver Sun, Western Living, Flare, Georgia Straight, Salon Online,* and *Herizons.* Editorial board member of periodicals *Educational Insights* and *Geist.*

WORK IN PROGRESS: Blue Valleys, a memoir.

SIDELIGHTS: Luanne A. Armstrong told *CA:* "I have spent most of my life in the Kootenay region of British Columbia, where I raised four children on an organic farm. I always wanted to be a writer from the time I first learned to read. I can't remember why, only that reading seemed to me so magical that writing must be equally magic. I now write in several genres: award-winning children's books, adult novels, and poetry. In my academic research, I am considering questions concerning memoir and autobiography.

"The most surprising thing I have learned as a writer is how financially unrewarding writing can be at times. My favorite book is always the one I am currently working on because I see so much potential in it. I have always worked at a variety of jobs, including coordinating women's groups, teaching at a First Nations college, and teaching in Indonesia with an environmental organization. I was also the editor for Blue Lake and HodgePog Books in Vancouver, which published literary and children's books before it folded.

"Finding the time and money to write is always difficult, but I am always working on at least two writing projects. I write about ideas, so I hope my books are both entertaining and thought provoking."

BIOGRAPHICAL AND CRITICAL SOURCES:

PERIODICALS

Herizons, fall, 2003, Noreen Shanahan, review of *The Bone House,* p. 33.
Resource Links, April, 2002, Veronica Allan, review of *Jeannie and the Gentle Giants,* p. 12; April, 2003, Victoria Pennell, review of *Into the Sun,* p. 11.

*   *   *

ARVIN, Reed

PERSONAL: Married. *Education:* Two degrees in music.

ADDRESSES: Home—Nashville, TN, and St. Petersburg, FL. *Agent*—Jane Dystel, Dystel & Goderich Literary Management, One Union Square West, New York, NY 10003. *E-mail*—info@reedarvin.com.

CAREER: Novelist and musician. Consultant to record companies; former musician and record producer; has performed with Amy Grant and toured the world with various artists.

WRITINGS:

The Wind in the Wheat, T. Nelson (Nashville, TN), 1994.
The Inside Track to—Getting Started in Christian Music, Harvest House (Eugene, OR), 2000.

The Will, Scribner (New York, NY), 2000.
The Last Goodbye, HarperCollins (New York, NY), 2004.

Also arranger of songs on *The CD Hymnal,* Crossfire Productions, 1994.

ADAPTATIONS: Paramount Pictures purchased the film rights for *The Will.*

WORK IN PROGRESS: A thriller, set in Nashville, about a prosecutor who accidentally convicts the wrong man of capital murder.

SIDELIGHTS: Reed Arvin had a successful career as a producer and musician in the world of Christian contemporary music before he turned to writing novels. His first book, *The Wind in the Wheat,* a semi-autobiographical story about a talented small-town boy who is discovered and exploited by a Nashville agent, was little noticed outside the world of Christian fiction. However, his secular legal thrillers *The Will* and *The Last Goodbye* have earned Arvin comparisons to best-selling author John Grisham.

The protagonist of *The Will,* Henry Matthews, originally planned a career in the ministry. However, before he completed his studies, his parents were killed by a drunk driver and Henry's faith died with them. He went to law school instead and became a rich and successful member of a large Chicago firm. He returns to his small hometown in Kansas to help execute the will of the late Tyler Crandall, the richest person in Council Grove. Instead of leaving his estate to family members or charitable causes, Crandall chose to give it to an apparently crazy, homeless man, Raymond Boyd. While Crandall's son Roger contests the will, some of the most powerful politicians in Kansas also get involved in trying to keep Boyd from getting the money—and from telling why Crandall chose to leave the money to him. *The Will* "is suspenseful from start to finish," wrote a *Publishers Weekly* critic, adding that its strongest point is Arvin's "portrait of Matthews, a complicated young man in turmoil over what he wants in life." *Denver Post* reviewer Tom Walker also praised Arvin's skill in working a deeper meaning into his tale. "Rather than getting the plot from point A to points B and C," Walker explained, "Arvin stops to smell the flowers," giving the reader "a sense of place and character."

The Last Goodbye pays homage to the classic detective-noir novels of Raymond Chandler. "Anyone with a taste for sultry, devious, adrenaline-boosting suspense stories may want to cancel a few appointments before opening this one," advised *New York Times* critic Janet Maslin. In the novel, attorney Jack Hammond is fired from his prestigious Atlanta firm and ends up working as a court-appointed lawyer for the poor. When his old college friend, Doug Townsend, is killed by an apparent drug overdose Jack suspects something more sinister. He discovers that Doug was investigating the deaths of patients with hepatitis C who were participating in clinical trials of an experimental drug. In Doug's apartment Jack also finds numerous photographs of a beautiful and famous African-American opera singer, Michele Sonnier. Coincidently, Michele's husband, Charles Ralston, is an executive with a pharmaceutical company.

"Arvin takes us into a lot of different worlds, all skillfully rendered with richly researched detail: housing projects bustling with predators, biotech firms doing complicated research, [and] the online underground where hackers do their work," noted *Atlanta Journal-Constitution* reviewer Phil Kloer in a review of *The Last Goodbye*. Moving through these worlds on both extremes of the social spectrum provides "Arvin ample fodder for exploring the lives, emotions and motives of his characters," Walker wrote, "and he takes full advantage of them, writing in an effortless style that moves the reader through the story all the while displaying talent to burn." *St. Louis Post-Dispatch* critic Harry Levins also thought that "Arvin seems to have the sociology of latter-day Atlanta down just right, a mixture of peach-tree affluence, bleak poverty and racial tiptoeing."

Although Arvin's books are ostensibly legal thrillers, the writer told a *ReadersRead.com* interviewer that "legal technicalities don't interest me as much as the things that drive and motivate my characters. The law is a great venue for drama, but at the end of the day, the human drama is the reason I became a writer."

BIOGRAPHICAL AND CRITICAL SOURCES:

PERIODICALS

Atlanta Journal-Constitution, March 7, 2004, Phil Kloer, review of *The Last Goodbye,* p. M8.

Booklist, December 15, 1994, John Mort, review of *The Wind in the Wheat,* p. 737; October 1, 2001, John Mort, review of *The Will,* p. 282; January 1, 2004, Wes Lukowsky, review of *The Last Goodbye,* p. 830.

Denver Post, November 19, 2000, Tom Walker, review of *The Will,* p. G2; February 29, 2004, Tom Walker, review of *The Last Goodbye,* p. F10.

Entertainment Weekly, December 8, 2000, review of *The Will,* p. 92; February 20, 2004, Jeff Labrecque, review of *The Last Goodbye,* p. 71.

Kirkus Reviews, January 1, 2004, review of *The Last Goodbye,* p. 3.

Knight Ridder/Tribune News Service, February 18, 2004, Harry Levins, review of *The Last Goodbye,* p. K0489; March 17, 2004, Oline H. Cogdill, review of *The Last Goodbye,* p. K2232.

Library Journal, November 15, 2000, Jane Jorgenson, review of *The Will,* p. 95; January, 2004, Jane Jorgenson, review of *The Last Goodbye,* p. 151.

New York Times, February 16, 2004, Janet Maslin, review of *The Last Goodbye,* p. E8.

Publishers Weekly, October 9, 2000, review of *The Will,* p. 72; December 8, 2003, review of *The Last Goodbye,* p. 44.

St. Louis Post-Dispatch, February 11, 2004, Harry Levins, review of *The Last Goodbye,* p. E3.

Student Lawyer, May, 2001, Matt Everett Lierman, review of *The Will,* p. 16.

ONLINE

AllReaders.com, http://www.allreaders.com/ (October 10, 2004), Harriet Klausner and Connie Rutter, review of *The Last Goodbye.*

BookBrowse.com, http://www.bookbrowse.com/ (October 10, 2004), interview with Arvin.

BookLoons.com, http://www.bookloons.com/ (October 10, 2004), Mary Ann Smyth, review of *The Last Goodbye.*

BookPage.com, http://www.bookpage.com/ (October 10, 2004), Edward Morris, interview with Arvin.

Bookreporter.com, http://www.bookreporter.com/ (February 20, 2004), interview with Arvin.

HarperCollins Web site, http://www.harpercollins.com/ (October 10, 2004), interview with Arvin.

ReadersRead.com, http://www.readersread.com/ (March, 2004), interview with Arvin.

Reed Arvin Home Page, http://www.reedarvin.com (October 10, 2004).

Watermark Books Web site, http://www.watermark books.com/ (October 10, 2004), Sarah Bagby, review of *The Last Goodbye.**

*　　*　　*

ATKINS, Charles

PERSONAL: Male.

ADDRESSES: Office—Atkins Unlimited, LLC, P.O. Box 833, Woodbury, CT 06798. *E-mail*—atkins unlimited@aol.com.

CAREER: Psychiatrist, author, and speaker. Yale University School of Medicine, New Haven, CT, member of clinical faculty in psychiatry; Waterbury Hospital, Waterbury, CT, director of behavioral health.

WRITINGS:

The Portrait, St. Martin's Press (New York, NY), 1998.
Risk Factor, St. Martin's Press (New York, NY), 1999.
The Cadaver's Ball, St. Martin's Press (New York, NY), 2005.

Contributor of short stories, articles, and essays to newspapers and magazines, including *American Medical News.* Consultant for Reader's Digest "Medical Breakthrough" series. Author, with Lisa Hoffmann, of column for *Waterbury Republican.*

SIDELIGHTS: Charles Atkins draws upon his experience as a psychiatrist, and on his love of thrillers, to write novels that feature protagonists struggling with mental illness, doctors struggling to aid their patients, and detectives struggling to solve murders. Through these tales, which have been praised for their suspense, Atkins also discusses such hot social topics as breakdowns in the mental health-care system and the root causes of teen violence.

The Portrait, Atkins's first detective novel, tells the story of Chad Greene, an artist who suffers from bipolar disorder and paranoia and is released from the psychiatric ward on the same day as the opening of his art exhibit at a New York gallery. Although Chad's psychiatrists work valiantly to help the artist keep his illness under control, Chad's medication leaves him feeling numb and incapable of real creativity; he takes himself off lithium and substitutes illicit drugs and alcohol whenever he feels a deep urge to paint. This behavior brings mixed blessings: it results in a successful art career, but a dreadful personal life. When Chad becomes the prime suspect in a murder, his paranoia kicks in hard, making him wonder whether he has been framed in a murder designed to raise the market value of his popular paintings.

Reviewers were generally impressed with Atkins's first novel, which a *Publishers Weekly* contributor called a "slick, assured debut" with a "satisfying conclusion." *Booklist* reviewer Whitney Scott singled out for praise Atkins's choice of "a riveting point of view—through the eyes of a creative psychotic, after all."

Risk Factor, a psychological thriller, deals with the issue of youth violence. The story is set in motion when a nurse is stabbed to death in the adolescent unit of the psychiatric ward at Boston Commonwealth Hospital. Fifteen-year-old Garret Jacobs, who suffers from schizophrenia, is the prime suspect. His doctor, Molly Katz, is consumed with guilt about her patient's apparently berserk episode; his previous behavior had not led her to suspect him to be capable of murder. When another nurse is killed while Garret is catatonic, the plot thickens. Dr. Katz devotes herself to solving the mystery and saving her patient from prison, but in the process, she puts herself and her own teenage children at risk.

Reviewers were impressed by the novel's competence in both the psychiatric and the thriller realms. *School Library Journal* contributor Carol DeAngelo called *Risk Factor* "compelling" and predicted that young-adult readers in particular are "sure to be fascinated by the symptomatology and care of teenaged psychiatric patients." A contributor to *Publishers Weekly* noted that, although Atkins's plot is sometimes subsumed in sociological, psychological, and political debates, "the chilling ending provides a shock that's more visceral than theoretical, which should satiate those who like their social psychology lesson laced with a measure of sinister suspense."

BIOGRAPHICAL AND CRITICAL SOURCES:

PERIODICALS

Booklist, May 15, 1998, Whitney Scott, review of *The Portrait,* p. 1592.
Journal of the American Medical Association, March 3, 1999, David W. Hodo, review of *The Portrait,* p. 851; April 12, 2000, David W. Hodo, review of *Risk Factor,* p. 1890.
Kirkus Reviews, May 1, 1998, review of *The Portrait,* p. 597.
Publishers Weekly, April 27, 1998, review of *The Portrait,* p. 44; September 6, 1999, review of *Risk Factor,* p. 82.
School Library Journal, March, 2000, Carol DeAngelo, review of *Risk Factor,* p. 264.

ONLINE

Charles Atkins Home Page, http://www.charlesatkins.com (October 20, 2004).*

* * *

ATKINS, E. Taylor 1967-

PERSONAL: Born May 4, 1967, in Murray, KY; son of Bill and Barbara (Bruce) Atkins; married August 31, 1991; wife's name, Zabrina; children: Gabriella, Annabelle. *Ethnicity:* "White." *Education:* University of Arkansas, B.A., 1989; University of Illinois, Ph.D., 1997. *Religion:* Baha'i. *Hobbies and other interests:* Cooking, music.

ADDRESSES: Office—Department of History, Northern Illinois University, DeKalb, IL 60115. *E-mail*—etatkins@niu.edu.

CAREER: University of Iowa, Iowa City, visiting assistant professor, 1997; Northern Illinois University, DeKalb, assistant professor, 1997-2003, associate professor of history, 2003—. University of California, Berkeley, visiting assistant professor, 2003.

MEMBER: American Historical Association, Association for Asian Studies, Association for Baha'i Studies, Midwest Japan Seminar.

AWARDS, HONORS: Mellon fellow, 1990; Fulbright fellow, 1993-95; John Whitney Hall Prize, 2003.

WRITINGS:

Blue Nippon: Authenticating Jazz in Japan, Duke University Press (Durham, NC), 2001.
(Editor) *Jazz Planet,* University Press of Mississippi (Jackson, MS), 2003.

WORK IN PROGRESS: A book on Korean performing arts under Japanese colonial occupation, 1910-45; research on Bahá'í critiques of colonialism.

BIOGRAPHICAL AND CRITICAL SOURCES:

PERIODICALS

Library Journal, July, 2001, James E. Perone, review of *Blue Nippon: Authenticating Jazz in Japan,* p. 92; December, 2003, William G. Kenz, review of *Jazz Planet,* p. 121.

B

BACKHOUSE, Janet 1938-2004

OBITUARY NOTICE— See index for *CA* sketch: Born February 8, 1938, in Corsham, Wiltshire, England; died November 3, 2004. Historian and author. Backhouse was an authority on medieval illuminated manuscripts and a longtime curator at the British Museum Library. Educated at Bedford College, London, and at the University of London Institute of Historical Research, she joined the British Museum Library in 1962, and remained there until her 1998 retirement. While there, she was part of the Department of Manuscripts, organizing exhibitions and creating outreach programs to help bring examples of medieval manuscripts to the public. As her particular field became increasingly popular among scholars and the general public alike, she also penned numerous books on the subject, including *The Lindisfarne Gospels* (1981), *The Isabella Breviary* (1993), and *Medieval Birds in the Sherborne Missal* (2001). Her last works, including *Illumination from Books of Hours* and a study on Jean Bourdichon, had not yet been published at the time of her death.

OBITUARIES AND OTHER SOURCES:

PERIODICALS

Times (London, England), December 29, 2004, p. 43.

* * *

BALLANTYNE, Andrew

PERSONAL: Male. *Education:* B.A., M.A., and Ph.D. degrees; diploma in architecture.

ADDRESSES: Office—School of Architecture, Planning, and Landscape, Claremont Tower, Room 315, University of Newcastle upon Tyne, Newcastle upon Tyne NE2 7RU, England. *E-mail*—a.n.ballantyne@ncl.ac.uk.

CAREER: University of Newcastle upon Tyne, Newcastle upon Tyne, England, professor of architecture. Also taught at universities of Sheffield and Bath; previously worked as a practicing architect.

MEMBER: Royal Institute of British Architects.

WRITINGS:

Architecture, Landscape, and Liberty: Richard Payne Knight and the Picturesque, Cambridge University Press (New York, NY), 1997.

Architecture: A Very Short Introduction, Oxford University Press (New York, NY), 2002.

(Editor) *What Is Architecture?,* Routledge (New York, NY), 2002.

(Editor) *Architecture: Modernism and After,* Blackwell (Malden, MA), 2004.

(Editor with Dana Arnold) *Architecture as Experience: Radical Changes in Spatial Practice,* Routledge (New York, NY), 2004.

Architecture Theory: Essential Writings in Philosophy and Culture, Continuum (New York, NY), 2004.

SIDELIGHTS: British educator Andrew Ballantyne has written and edited several books on architecture, including *Architecture, Landscape, and Liberty: Ri-*

chard Payne Knight and the Picturesque. In this book, Ballantyne profiles the accomplishments of Richard Payne Knight (1751-1824), an eccentric and wealthy English gentleman who pursued diverse scholarly interests. Knight designed his own home, Downton Castle, which broke with architectural tradition in its asymmetrical design. Knight's tastes were influenced by his admiration of ancient Greece, and he did not mind challenging popular trends and ideas. Ballantyne sifts through Knight's ideas and writings, which include the long poem "The Landscape," the prose work *Principles of Taste,* and a study of phallic worship, *The Worship of Priapus.*

In *Architectural Review* David Watkin called the book a "brilliant study, which should be read by all students of the Enlightenment." Watkin also noted that Ballantyne "convincingly reconciles the passionate paradoxes in Knight's intellectual career." According to Kerry Downes in the *Times Literary Supplement,* "Ballantyne argues that Knight's misfortune was never to manage to convey to the public his highly unconventional but consistent and complete world view." Downes suggested that, "For those without the leisure or the stomach for Knight's own writings, this book is a boon. It is long, and losing one's place or one's thread is easy enough. But it brings its subject vividly to life in ways not open to the best of painters."

What Is Architecture? is a collection of essays edited by Ballantyne, including his own work, "The Nest and the Pillar of Fire." In this introductory essay Ballantyne discusses how architecture is comprised of both the mundane and the extraordinary. Other contributors to the book include Robert Scruton, Demetri Porphyrios, Neil Leach, and David Goldblatt. *Times Literary Supplement* critic Robert Maxwell concluded, "the big question about how free an art architecture really is remains open, but Ballantyne has made an impressive assault on the initial uncertainties."

Reviewing *Architecture: A Very Short Introduction* for the *Times Literary Supplement,* Maxwell he described that book as "treating [architecture] as a subject open to culture, and definable only within culture." Rather than discussing or defining architectural styles, in this volume Ballantyne identifies the qualities that give buildings emotional and artistic impact.

BIOGRAPHICAL AND CRITICAL SOURCES:

PERIODICALS

Architectural Review, August, 1997, David Watkin, review of *Architecture, Landscape, and Liberty: Richard Payne Knight and the Picturesque,* p. 88.

Times Literary Supplement, May 1, 1998, Kerry Downes, review of *Architecture, Landscape, and Liberty,* p. 36; April 5, 2002, Robert Maxwell, review of *What Is Architecture?,* p. 31; January 17, 2003, Maxwell, review of *Architecture: A Very Short Introduction,* p. 29.*

*　　　　*　　　　*

BAPTIST, Edward E. 1970-

PERSONAL: Born January 3, 1970, in Cambridge, MA. *Education:* Georgetown University, B.S.F.S. (magna cum laude), 1992; University of Pennsylvania, Ph.D., 1997.

ADDRESSES: Office—Department of History, Cornell University, 450 McGraw Hall, Ithaca, NY 14850. *E-mail*—eebaptist@yahoo.com.

CAREER: University of Pennsylvania, Philadelphia, PA, lecturer, 1997-98; University of Miami, Miami, FL, Charlton W. Tebeau Assistant Professor, 1998-2003; Cornell University, Ithaca, NY, assistant professor of history, 2003—. Member of editorial board for *Florida Historical Quarterly* and *H-Carib* (online discussion network).

AWARDS, HONORS: Annenberg research awards, 1996, 1997; Orovitz Research Award, University of Miami, 1999, 2000; John Hope Franklin Center Research Award, Duke University, 2000; National Endowment for the Humanities fellowship, 2000-01; Southern Studies fellowship, University of North Carolina libraries, 2002; Remebert Patrick Award, Best Book in Florida history, Florida Historical Society, 2002.

WRITINGS:

Creating an Old South: Middle Florida's Plantation Frontier before the Civil War, University of North Carolina Press (Chapel Hill, NC), 2002.

WORK IN PROGRESS: Editing a book with Stephanie Camp titled *New Studies in American Slavery,* for University of Georgia Press.

SIDELIGHTS: Historian Edward E. Baptist specializes in the study of the antebellum Deep South and focuses particularly on the ways in which the plantation culture penetrated Florida. In *Creating an Old South: Middle Florida's Plantation Frontier before the Civil War,* Baptist shows that when plantation owners moved into middle Florida in the early nineteenth century, they brought with them a culture that discriminated, at first, against small yeoman farmers. They created institutions to help them separate themselves from local, poorer white yeomen, including a state bank. "According to Baptist," wrote Christopher Waldrep in the *Journal of American History,* the "transition [from opposition to yeomen farmers to an alliance with them] occurred after planters bungled their way into the Second Seminole War. After 1837 guerilla raids exposed the planters 'manly invulnerability' as a fraud; they suddenly seemed 'emasculated, submissive, unable to assert their invulnerability.'" The fact that a bank the planters had created crashed at this time also contributed to their social collapse.

By the mid-1800s the Florida planting class had incorporated the yeoman class into a new racial elite. The new social group, Baptist argued, rewrote the violent, conflict-ridden history of Middle Florida, presenting it as a story of "a mythological 'Old South,' . . . an extension of an old, stable Virginia society, made up of slaveholding squires, deferential yeomen, and grateful slaves," explained *Journal of the Early Republic* contributor J. William Harris. "This myth, Baptist concludes, helped Floridas white men convince themselves that their society was worthy of independence and sufficiently united to win it."

"This is essentially a story of how frontier conditions start out wild and unruly," stated Mary Waalkas in a review of *Creating an Old South* for the *Journal of Social History,* "and how various pressures work to alter class relationships." "Through impressive research," concluded Bradley G. Bond in the *Journal of Southern History,* "[Baptist] . . . has opened antebellum Florida to historians as never before."

BIOGRAPHICAL AND CRITICAL SOURCES:

PERIODICALS

Civil War History, June, 2003, A. James Fuller, review of *Creating an Old South: Middle Florida's Plantation Frontier before the Civil War,* p. 191.

Journal of American History, March, 2003, Christopher Waldrep, review of *Creating an Old South,* p. 1523.
Journal of Social History, winter, 2003, Mary Waalkes, review of *Creating an Old South,* p. 529.
Journal of Southern History, November, 2003, Bradley G. Bond, review of *Creating an Old South,* p. 906.
Journal of the Early Republic, fall, 2003, J. William Harris, review of *Creating an Old South,* p. 459.

*　　*　　*

BARRA, Allen

PERSONAL: Born in Birmingham, AL. *Education:* Attended University of Alabama at Birmingham.

ADDRESSES: Home—South Orange, NJ. *Office*—Wall Street Journal, 200 Liberty St., New York, NY 10281.

CAREER: Sports writer, columnist, and commentator. Frequently appears on Major League Baseball Radio.

WRITINGS:

(With George Ignatin) *Football by the Numbers, 1986,* Prentice Hall Press (New York, NY), 1986.
(With George Ignatin) *Football by the Numbers, 1987,* Prentice Hall Press (New York, NY), 1987.
(With Joe Glickman and Jesus Diaz) *That's Not the Way It Was: (Almost) Everything They Told You about Sports Is Wrong,* Hyperion (New York, NY), 1995.
Inventing Wyatt Earp: His Life and Many Legends, Carroll & Graf (New York, NY), 1999.
Clearing the Bases: The Greatest Baseball Debates of the Last Century, with a foreword by Bob Costas, T. Dunne Books (New York, NY), 2002.
Brushbacks and Knockdowns: The Greatest Baseball Debates of Two Centuries, T. Dunne Books (New York, NY), 2004.
Big Play: Barra on Football, Brassey's (Washington, DC), 2005.

Sports columnist for *Wall Street Journal;* contributor to periodicals and Web sites, including *New York Times, Village Voice, Slate,* and *Salon.com.*

SIDELIGHTS: "There are few who write [about sports] so entertainingly or instructively as [Allen] Barra," Paul Kaplan declared in *Library Journal*. Barra is probably best known for his sports columns for various newspapers and Web sites, including the *Wall Street Journal, New York Times,* and *Salon.com,* and his columns have been gathered into several book-length collections. Barra's writings are notable for the rigorous yet unorthodox ways in which he looks at athletics; as a *Publishers Weekly* critic wrote in a review of *Clearing the Bases: The Greatest Baseball Debates of the Last Century,* "It is a rare sportswriter who can cite [former Cardinals and Dodgers general manager] Branch Rickey and Irish writer/revolutionary Sean O'Faolain in the same work, but Barra does it with ease."

Barra's favorite subject is baseball, particularly its great debates. Was Mickey Mantle better than Willie Mays? (No.) Were Jackie Robinson and Babe Ruth as good as their current legendary status would suggest (Yes and no, respectively.) Who was the best baseball player of the twentieth century? (Mike Schmidt.) These questions and others are covered in what may be Barra's best-known book, *Clearing the Bases,* and a follow-up volume, *Brushbacks and Knockdowns: The Greatest Baseball Debates of Two Centuries.* Although Barra's writings cover the entire history of baseball, his "thesis—inasmuch as he can have one in a collection of articles such as this," *Nine* contributor Jan Finkel wrote of *Clearing the Bases,* "is that overall the best baseball ever played is being played today."

Barra makes his controversial argument, as well as other observations, through the intensive use of statistics. He consistently prefers provable facts to the anecdotal and impressionistic, and, as Jonathan Mahler explained in a *New York Times Book Review* critique of *Clearing the Bases,* "can work himself into a lather whenever a commentator declares that you just can't trust the numbers where so-and-so is concerned." However, Barra's "sheer enthusiasm for the sport ensures that he never lapses into the pedantic," as a *Publishers Weekly* contributor wrote in a review of *Brushbacks and Knockdowns.*

Barra is also the author of *Inventing Wyatt Earp: His Life and Many Legends,* a book that examines the process by which the frontier lawman's life was transformed into an enduring American myth. Many books have been written about Earp and his exploits,

but critics praised Barra's addition to the genre. This "well-researched, provocative study of the man and his legend offers us a welcome opportunity to consider what our several versions of Wyatt Earp tell us about ourselves," explained *New York Times Book Review* contributor Richard E. Nicholls, the critic adding that the work is "engaging, detailed and refreshingly pugnacious." *Wild West* reviewer Louis Hart praised Barra's "enthusiastic" tone in the book, while Charles V. Cowling noted in *Library Journal* that *Inventing Wyatt Earp* is not only "intriguing" but also "a well-written and carefully documented book."

BIOGRAPHICAL AND CRITICAL SOURCES:

PERIODICALS

Alberta Report, February 8, 1999, review of *Inventing Wyatt Earp: His Life and Many Legends,* p. 36.

BC Report, February 22, 1999, review of *Inventing Wyatt Earp,* p. 58.

Booklist, December 1, 1998, Jay Freeman, review of *Inventing Wyatt Earp,* p. 647; March 1, 2002, Wes Lukowsky, review of *Clearing the Bases: The Greatest Baseball Debates of the Last Century,* p. 1077.

Journal of American Culture, June, 2003, Hubert I. Cohen, review of *Inventing Wyatt Earp,* p. 204.

Kirkus Reviews, February 15, 2002, review of *Clearing the Bases,* p. 231.

Library Journal, September 1, 1986, William H. Hoffman, review of *Football by the Numbers, 1986,* p. 210; November 15, 1998, Charles V. Cowling, review of *Inventing Wyatt Earp,* p. 74; February 1, 2002, Paul Kaplan and Robert C. Cottrell, review of *Clearing the Bases,* p. 103; May 1, 2004, Paul Kaplan, review of *Brushbacks and Knockdowns,* p. 118.

New York Times Book Review, July 30, 1995, George Robinson, review of *That's Not the Way It Was: (Almost) Everything They Told You about Sports Is Wrong,* p. 14; April 18, 1999, Richard E. Nicholls, review of *Inventing Wyatt Earp,* p. 25; January 23, 2000, review of *Inventing Wyatt Earp,* p. 32; May 5, 2002, Jonathan Mahler, review of *Clearing the Bases,* p. 29.

Nine, spring, 2004, Jan Finkel, review of *Clearing the Bases,* p. 155.

Publishers Weekly, November 30, 1998, review of *Inventing Wyatt Earp,* p. 60; March 11, 2002, review of *Clearing the Bases,* p. 61; March 29, 2004, review of *Brushbacks and Knockdowns,* p. 50.

Roundup, December, 1999, review of *Inventing Wyatt Earp,* p. 25.

Tribune Books (Chicago, IL), May 9, 2004, Mark Luce, review of *Brushbacks and Knockdowns: The Greatest Baseball Debates of Two Centuries,* p. 4.

Wall Street Journal, March 19, 1999, Elizabeth Bukowski, review of *Inventing Wyatt Earp,* p. W13.

Western Report, February 8, 1999, review of *Inventing Wyatt Earp,* p. 36.

Wild West, June, 1999, Louis Hart, review of *Inventing Wyatt Earp,* p. 74.

ONLINE

Alabama Bound, http://www.alabamabound.org/ (November 4, 2004), "Allen Barra."

Beatrice, www.beatrice.com/ (April 4, 2004), interview with Barra.

Brassey's, Inc., http://www.brasseysinc.com/ (November 4, 2004), "Allen Bara."

Bronx Banter, http://www.all-baseball.com/ (November 4, 2004), interview with Barra.

CNN.com, http://www.cnn.com/ (July 9, 2002), Todd Leopold, review of *Clearing the Bases.*

Metroactive, http://www.metroactive.com/ (February 25, 1999), Michael S. Gant, review of *Inventing Wyatt Earp.**

*   *   *

BARRETT, (Denis) Cyril 1925-2003

PERSONAL: Born May 9, 1925, in Dublin, Ireland; died of cancer December 30, 2003, in Dublin, Ireland; son of Denis Barrett (an assistant police commissioner), stepson of Evelyn Barrett. *Education:* Attended University College, Dublin, University of London, and Warburg Institute. *Religion:* Roman Catholic.

CAREER: Priest, educator, and writer. Entered Society of Jesus (Jesuits); ordained Roman Catholic priest, 1956; taught in France; University of Warwick, Coventry, England, lecturer, 1965-67, senior lecturer,

1967-72, reader in philosophy, 1972-92; Campion Hall, Oxford University, Oxford, England, reader, beginning 1992.

WRITINGS:

(Editor) Ludwig Wittgenstein, *Lectures and Conversations on Aesthetics, Psychology, and Religious Belief,* University of California Press (Berkeley, CA), 1966.

(Editor) *Collected Papers on Aesthetics,* Barnes & Noble (New York, NY), 1966.

Op Art, Viking (New York, NY), 1970.

(Editor, with D. Petsch) Wladyslav Tatarkiewicz, *History of Aesthetics* (translation of *Historia estetyki*), three volumes, Mouton (The Hague, Netherlands), 1970–74.

An Introduction to Optical Art, Studio Vista (London, England), 1971.

(Editor) *Irish Art in the Nineteenth Century: An Exhibition of Irish Victorian Art at Crawford Municipal School of Art,* World Wide Books (Boston, MA), 1971.

The Crozier Memorial, Gifford & Craven (Ballycotton, Ireland), 1976.

(Author of text) *Michael Farrell: A Monograph,* Douglas Hyde Gallery (Dublin, Ireland), 1979.

(Author of text) Peter Sedgley, *Paintings, Objects, Installations: 1963-1980,* Kelpra-Studios (London, England), 1980.

(Editor, with Tom Winnifrith) *The Philosophy of Leisure,* St. Martin's Press (New York, NY), 1989.

Wittgenstein on Ethics and Religious Belief, Blackwell (Cambridge, MA), 1991.

(Editor, with Tom Winnifrith) *Leisure in Art and Literature,* Macmillan (Basingstoke, England), 1992.

(With Camille Souter and Gerry Walker) *Camille Souter,* Gandon Editions (Ireland), 1997.

Contributor to *The Tiger Rugs of Tibet,* edited by Mimi Lipton, Thames & Hudson (New York, NY), 1988. Contributor to periodicals.

SIDELIGHTS: The late Cyril Barrett was a Jesuit scholar of art and philosophy with numerous books and articles to his name. His best-known work was one of his first—*Lectures and Conversations on Aesthetics, Psychology, and Religious Belief,* a collection drawn from the notes of students of Austrian philosopher Ludwig Wittgenstein. The executors of Wittgenstein's estate—all former students of the philosopher—and other students had previously guarded this unpublished material extremely closely, and critics commended the fact that Barrett was allowed access to it. Near the other end of his career, Barrett published his own analysis of Wittgenstein, *Wittgenstein on Ethics and Religious Belief,* which Martin Warner described in a London *Independent* obituary as "long-awaited and sane."

Most of Barrett's books are about art, and he is remembered at the University of Warwick for his efforts to establish a modern art collection there. "As an art critic he was wide-ranging and formidable—his catalogue of nineteenth-century Irish Victorian Art is a classic of its kind—but also creative," noted a London *Times* contributor. Two of Barrett's best-known works of art criticism are *Op Art,* a book about the newly emerging style of art which Barrett championed, and an influential article titled "Are Bad Works of Art 'Works of Art'?"

Barrett was described as "a genuine polymath for whom everything provided a starting point for inquiry and reflection," by a Glasgow *Herald* contributor, the writer adding: "Beyond the loss of a particularly gifted individual, his death represents a further disconnection of philosophy from the wider world of humane learning and religious journeying. We may never see his like again."

BIOGRAPHICAL AND CRITICAL SOURCES:

PERIODICALS

Choice, October, 1992, C.G. Luckhardt, review of *Wittgenstein on Ethics and Religious Belief,* p. 314.
Ethics, January, 1991, Elizabeth Telfer, review of *The Philosophy of Leisure,* p. 429.
Journal of Religion, April, 1993, Charles Elder, review of *Wittgenstein on Ethics and Religious Belief,* p. 284.
Journal of Theological Studies, October, 1992, Fergus Kerr, review of *Wittgenstein on Ethics and Religious Belief,* p. 744.
Religious Studies, December, 1992, Brian R. Clack, review of *Wittgenstein on Ethics and Religious Belief,* p. 577.

Times Higher Education Supplement, May 1, 1992, Hans-Johann Glock, review of *Wittgenstein on Ethics and Religious Belief,* p. 25.
Times Literary Supplement, March 6, 1992, John Hyman, review of *Wittgenstein on Ethics and Religious Belief,* p. 25.

OBITUARIES

PERIODICALS

Herald (Glasgow, Scotland), January 23, 2004, p. 24.
Independent (London, England), February 25, 2004, p. 34.
Times (London, England), January 15, 2004, p. 36.

ONLINE

Warwick University Web site, http://www.warwick.ac.uk/ (November 5, 2004).*

* * *

BARSAMIAN, David

PERSONAL: Male.

ADDRESSES: Office—Alternative Radio, P.O. Box 551, Boulder, CO 80306. *E-mail*—dbarsamian@hotmail.com.

CAREER: Radio producer, journalist, lecturer, and author. Former program director for a bilingual community radio station, Alamosa, CO; *Alternative Radio,* Boulder, CO, founder, producer, and director, 1978—.

AWARDS, HONORS: Top Ten Media Heroes citation, Institute for Alternative Journalism; Upton Sinclair Award, American Civil Liberties Union, 2003.

WRITINGS:

Stenographers to Power: Media and Propaganda, Common Courage Press (Monroe, ME), 1992.

(With Noam Chomsky) *Chronicles of Dissent: Interviews with David Barsamian,* Common Courage Press (Monroe, ME), 1992.

(With Noam Chomsky) *The Prosperous Few and the Restless Many,* Odonian Press (Berkeley, CA), 1993.

(With Edward W. Said) *The Pen and the Sword: Conversations with David Barsamian,* Common Courage Press (Monroe, ME), 1994.

(With Noam Chomsky) *Keeping the Rabble in Line: Interviews with David Barsamian,* Common Courage Press (Monroe, ME), 1994.

(With Noam Chomsky) *Secrets, Lies, and Democracy,* Odonian Press (Tucson, AZ), 1994.

(With Noam Chomsky) *Class Warfare: Interviews with David Barsamian,* Common Courage Press (Monroe, ME), 1996.

(With Noam Chomsky) *The Common Good,* compiled and edited by Arthur Naiman, Odonian Press (Monroe, ME), 1998.

(With Howard Zinn) *The Future of History: Interviews with David Barsamian,* Common Courage Press (Monroe, ME), 1999.

Eqbal Ahmad, Confronting Empire: Interviews with David Barsamian, foreword by Edward W. Said, South End Press (Cambridge, MA), 2000.

(With Noam Chomsky) *Propaganda and the Public Mind: Conversations with Noam Chomsky,* South End Press (Cambridge, MA), 2001.

The Decline and Fall of Public Broadcasting, South End Press (Cambridge, MA), 2001.

Culture and Resistance: Conversations with Edward W. Said, South End Press (Cambridge, MA), 2003.

Louder than Bombs: Interviews from the Progressive Magazine, South End Press (Cambridge, MA), 2004.

The Checkbook and the Cruise Missile: Conversations with Arundhati Roy, South End Press (Cambridge, MA), 2004.

Speaking of Empire: Conversations with Tariq Ali, New Press (New York, NY), 2005.

Contributor of articles and interviews to periodicals, including *Nation, Progressive, Monthly Review, International Socialist Review,* and *Z* magazine.

SIDELIGHTS: During the course of his career, alternative-media journalist David Barsamian has interviewed many famous figures on the political left, including linguist Noam Chomsky, social theorist Edward W. Said, and feminist novelist and screenwriter Arundhati Roy. Many of these interviews are now available in print collections.

Critics have often praised Barsamian's collections of interviews as good introductions to the works of these thinkers. "Those who are intimidated by [Chomsky's] densely argued, exhaustively footnoted essays and books" will appreciate Barsamian's efforts at making Chomsky explain himself more simply in *Chronicles of Dissent,* explained a *Publishers Weekly* reviewer. Similarly, another *Publishers Weekly* contributor, reviewing a collection of interviews with Said titled *The Pen and the Sword,* described the work as "an accessible, engaging introduction to Said's thoughts." However, the collections of interviews are about more than simply explaining the thinkers' theories; "what sets this work apart from other reluctant messiahs who simply intellectualize suffering," a *Publishers Weekly* critic commented in a review of *Keeping the Rabble in Line,* "is that Barsamian and Chomsky discuss avenues for activism."

Barsamian had no formal background in journalism when he entered broadcasting by producing, hosting, and distributing his own world music show. He encourages others to take a similar "enormous leap of faith" and start their own programs and publications. "If you're thinking about obstacles, you'll come up with a million of them," he told *Alternative Press Review* interviewer Jason McQuinn, "and the people you're working with will come up with another two million. So, it's more about solutions. . . . To do something proactive is very empowering to you as well as to others."

BIOGRAPHICAL AND CRITICAL SOURCES:

PERIODICALS

Humanist, November-December, 1993, Brian Siano, review of *Chronicles of Dissent: Interviews with David Barsamian,* p. 45.

International Affairs, July, 2002, Bill Hayton, review of *Propaganda and the Public Mind: Conversations with Noam Chomsky,* p. 626.

Journal of Palestinian Studies, winter, 2001, Eric Hooglund, review of *Eqbal Ahmad: Confronting Empire,* p. 123.

Library Journal, April 15, 2004, Katherine E. Merrill, review of *The Checkbook and the Cruise Missile: Conversations with Arundhati Roy,* p. 106.

Middle East, December, 2003, Fred Rhodes, review of *Culture and Resistance: Conversations with Edward W. Said,* p. 64.

New Statesman & Society, November 27, 1992, Phil Edwards, review of *Chronicles of Dissent,* p. 43.

Political Studies, September, 2002, Tony Evans, review of *Propaganda and the Public Mind,* p. 893.

Publishers Weekly, December 14, 1992, review of *Chronicles of Dissent,* p. 52; August 29, 1994, review of *The Pen and the Sword: Conversations with David Barsamian,* p. 71; November 28, 1994, review of *Keeping the Rabble in Line: Interviews with David Barsamian,* p. 56.

Television Quarterly, spring, 2002, Ron Simon, review of *The Decline and Fall of Public Broadcasting,* p. 86.

ONLINE

Alternative Press Review Online, http://www.altpr.org/ (December 9, 2000), Jason McQuinn, "David Barsamian on Radio: Interviewing the Interviewer."

Alternative Radio Web site, http://www.alternative radio.org/ (October 21, 2004), "David Barsamian."

Subsol Web site, http://subsol.c3.hu/ (October 21, 2004), "David Barsamian (US)."

Washington Free Press Online, http://www.washington freepress.org/ (October 21, 2004), Colin Wright, "David Barsamian: Politics and the Media" (interview).

Z Online, http://www.zmag.org/ (October 21, 2004), "David Barsamian's ZNet Home Page."*

* * *

BATCHELOR, Stephen 1953-

PERSONAL: Born April 7, 1953, in Dundee, Scotland; married Martine Fages, 1985. *Education:* Studied with Geshe Ngawang Dhargyev (Dharamsala, India), 1972-75; studied with Geshe Rabten (Switzerland), 1975-79; studied Zen Buddhism with Kusan Sunim at Songgwangsa Monastery (South Korea), 1981-84. *Religion:* Buddhist.

ADDRESSES: Home—Aquitaine, France. *Agent*—Anne Edelstein Literary Agency, 20 West 22nd St., Suite 1603, New York, NY 10010.

CAREER: Writer, photographer, translator, teacher, and leader of Buddhist retreats. Buddhist monk, 1978-85. Worked as translator for Geshe Thubten Ngawang at Tibetisches Institut, Germany. Gaia House, Devon, England, guiding teacher, 1990-2000; Sharpham Trust, Devon, England, coordinator, beginning 1992; Sharpham College for Buddhist Studies and Contemporary Equity, cofounder, beginning 1996.

AWARDS, HONORS: Thomas Cook Guidebook Award, 1988, for *The Tibet Guide.*

WRITINGS:

(Translator) Acharya Shantideva, *A Guide to the Bodhisattva's Way of Life,* Library of Tibetan Works and Archives (Dharamsala, India), 1979.

Alone with Others: An Existential Approach to Buddhism, Grove (New York, NY), 1983.

(Translator) Geshe Rabten, *Echoes of Voidness,* Wisdom Publications (Boston, MA), 1983.

Flight: An Existential Conception of Buddhism (pamphlet), Buddhist Publication Society, 1984.

(Editor and author of introduction) Kusan Sunim, *The Way of Korean Zen,* translated by Matine Fages, Weatherhill (New York, NY), 1985.

(Editor and author of introduction) *The Jewel in the Lotus: A Guide to the Buddhist Traditions of Tibet,* Wisdom Publications (London, England), 1987.

The Tibet Guide, foreword by the Dalai Lama, Wisdom Publications (London, England), 1987, second edition, with Brian Beresford and Sean Jones, published as *The Tibet Guide: Central and Western Tibet,* 1998.

(Translator) Geshe Rabten, *Song of the Profound View,* Wisdom Publications (Boston, MA), 1989.

The Faith to Doubt: Glimpses of Buddhist Uncertainty, Parallax Press (Berkeley, CA), 1990.

(Translator) Geshe Rabten, *The Mind and Its Functions: A Textbook of Buddhist Epistemology and Psychology,* Rabten Choeling (Pélerin, Switzerland), 1991.

The Awakening of the West: The Encounter of Buddhism and Western Culture, Parallax Press (Berkeley, CA), 1994.

Buddhism without Beliefs: A Contemporary Guide to Awakening, Riverhead Books (New York, NY), 1997.

(Editor, with Gay Watson and Guy Claxton) *The Psychology of Awakening: Buddhism, Science, and Our Day-to-Day Lives,* Rider (London, England), 1999, S. Weiser (York Beach, ME), 2000.

Verses from the Center: A Buddhist Vision of the Sublime, Riverhead Books (New York, NY), 2000.

(Photographer) Martine Batchelor, *Meditation for Life,* Wisdom Publications (Boston, MA), 2001.

Living with the Devil: A Meditation on Good and Evil, Riverhead Books (New York, NY), 2004.

Contributor to anthologies, including *Space in Mind: East-West Psychology and Contemporary Buddhism,* edited by John Crook and David Fontana, Element (Shaftesbury, England), 1990; *Dharma Gaia: A Harvest of Essays in Buddhism and Ecology,* edited by Allan Hunt-Badiner, Parallax (Berkeley, CA), 1990; *Sharpham Miscellany,* edited by John Snelling, 1992; *Buddhism and Ecology,* edited by Martine Batchelor and Kerry Brown, Cassell (London, England), 1992; *For a Future to Be Possible,* Parallax (Berkeley, CA), 1993; *Religion in Europe: Contemporary Perspectives,* edited by Sean Gill, Gavin D'Costa, and Ursula King, Kok Pharos Publishing House (Kampen, the Netherlands), 1994; *The Buddhist Forum Volume IV: Seminar Papers 1994-1996,* edited by Tadeusz Skorupski, School of Oriental and African Studies, University of London, 1996; *Faith and Praxis in a Postmodern Age,* edited by Ursula King, Cassell (London, England), 1998; and *Buddhism in America: Proceedings of the First Buddhism in America Conference,* edited by Al Rapaport, Tuttle (Vermont), 1998.

Contributor of articles to magazines and journals, including *Tricycle, Middle Way, Interlink,* and *Inquiring Mind.* Contributing editor, *Tricycle,* 1992—.

Author's works have been translated into German, Dutch, French, and Italian.

ADAPTATIONS: Buddhism without Beliefs was adapted for audiocassette, 2002.

WORK IN PROGRESS: A book that will develop the concept of an agnostic Buddhism.

SIDELIGHTS: Born in Scotland and raised in England, Stephen Batchelor left home at age eighteen to travel to India and study Tibetan Buddhism. By 1978 he had become a Buddhist monk and was translating sacred texts. He went on to study Zen Buddhism in Korea, and "disrobed"—left the monastery—in 1985 when he married a former Buddhist nun. Batchelor has become an important voice of Buddhism in the West, both as a writer and as an editor of the magazine *Tricycle: The Buddhist Review.* He is also the author of several popular books on Buddhism, including *The Awakening of the West: The Encounter of Buddhism and Western Culture, Buddhism without Beliefs: A Contemporary Guide to Awakening, Verses from the Center: A Buddhist Vision of the Sublime,* and *Living with the Devil: A Meditation on Good and Evil.*

Writing in the *New York Times,* Kennedy Fraser noted that for the Buddhist community in the United States Batchelor is "a celebrity, albeit a somewhat controversial one. His skeptical views on karma and reincarnation, in particular, have been viewed with alarm" by some. Kennedy went on to note that Batchelor "is known as a translator of sacred texts and is steeped in Buddhist tradition. He respects history and lineage. He thinks that some popular American Buddhist centers may be in danger of trivializing the dharma and replacing spiritual inquiry with meditation and psychotherapy."

In *The Awakening of the West,* Batchelor "provides a clear overview," as Wesley Palmer noted in the *Whole Earth Review,* of the meeting of Buddhism and European civilization. Batchelor's treatment presents "the interconnectedness of the historical, psychological, and evolutionary changes in this fascinating but obscure relationship," Palmer further commented. Writing in the *Contemporary Review,* Chris Arthur called *The Awakening of the West* a "wide-ranging, thoughtful and well-informed account," and went on to observe that it is an "engaging book, written in an easy, accessible style, pleasingly unencumbered by technical vocabulary or distracting scholarly apparatus." In Palmer's opinion, "Batchelor is particularly adept at creating eye-catching cameo scenes which offer fascinating snapshots of Buddhism's Western presence and forcefully claim the reader's attention."

Batchelor's *Buddhism without Beliefs* explores, as a reviewer for *Publishers Weekly* noted, "the practical fundamentals of Buddhism and how they can be relevant to both religious and secular-minded Westerners." According to the same reviewer, Batchelor "deliberately eschews elitist, monastic Buddhist traditions," and makes the Buddhist tradition accessible to Westerners. With *Verses from the Center* he translates the verses of the second-century Indian philosopher and monk Nagarjuna, and makes extensive comments on them. A contributor for *Publishers Weekly* observed that "although this bracing, abstruse text has been lovingly translated for accessibility, it remains a demanding philosophical treatise geared for the serious student of Buddhism, not the dilettante."

In his 2004 title, *Living with the Devil,* Batchelor explores the Buddhist concept of evil. *Library Journal* critic Graham Christian noted that the author "draws deeply on traditional Buddhist insights as well as stories from the legends surrounding the Buddha's life" in this "moving and timely study." Similarly, a reviewer for *Publishers Weekly* felt that "Batchelor's genuine concern and desire for a better world come through clearly." For this work, Batchelor surveys not just Buddhist literature, but also Western texts, examining the struggles of the Biblical Job and of the French philosopher Pascal as they dealt with the reconciliation of the ego in the face of certain death.

Batchelor has also put his intimate knowledge of southern Asia to use in *The Tibet Guide,* first published in 1987 and brought out again in 1998. Harold M. Otness, writing in *Library Journal,* thought that Batchelor "goes far beyond conventional guidebooks" in this work, serving up chapters on history and religion and including a highly detailed description of Lhasa, the capital city of Tibet. Otness concluded that "this is a guide for serious travelers and is also an excellent reference source."

BIOGRAPHICAL AND CRITICAL SOURCES:

PERIODICALS

Contemporary Review, May, 1995, Chris Arthur, review of *The Awakening of the West: The Encounter of Buddhism and Western Culture,* p. 271.
Library Journal, March 15, 1998, Harold M. Otness, review of *The Tibet Guide,* p. 86; July, 2000, James R. Kuhlman, review of *Verses from the Center: A Buddhist Vision of the Sublime,* p. 99; May 1, 2004, Graham Christian, review of *Living with the Devil: A Meditation on Good and Evil,* p. 115.

New York Times, November 3, 1997, Kennedy Fraser, "Buddhism's Flowering in America: An Inside View," p. E2.
Psychology Today, November-December, 2001, review of *Meditation for Life,* p. 76.
Publishers Weekly, April 14, 1997, review of *Buddhism without Beliefs: A Contemporary Guide to Awakening,* p. 70; April 10, 2000, review of *Verses from the Center,* p. 94; May 10, 2004, review of *Living with the Devil,* p. 54.
Whole Earth Review, winter, 1994, Wesley Palmer, review of *The Awakening of the West,* p. 20.

ONLINE

Martine and Stephen Batchelor Web site, http://www.stephenbatchelor.com (November 3, 2004).

*　　*　　*

BATEMAN, Robert L. 1967-
(Matthew Brennan)

PERSONAL: Born April 17, 1967, in Bethlehem, PA; son of Robert (a research physicist) and Ursula (Veziné) Bateman; married Deborah A. (a fitness instructor), October 7, 1989; children: Morgan, Ryann, Connor. *Ethnicity:* "Caucasian." *Education:* University of Delaware, B.A., 1989; Ohio State University, M.A., 1998, and doctoral study.

ADDRESSES: Home—8 Brookstone Dr., Fredericksburg, VA 22405.

CAREER: U.S. Army, career infantry officer as airborne ranger, 1989—; present rank, major. Military assignments included rifle platoon leader for 25th Infantry Division, operations officer with multinational forces and observers in Sinai and Egypt, company commander of 2nd Battalion, 7th Cavalry, 1st Cavalry Division. U.S. Military Academy, West Point, NY, assistant professor of military history; military fellow, Center for Strategic and International Studies, Georgetown University, Washington, DC.

MEMBER: Association of the U.S. Army, U.S. Marine Corps Association, Armor Association, Infantry Association, Ranger Association, Mensa.

AWARDS, HONORS: Military: Meritorious Service Medal. *Other:* Named Military Author of the Year, Association of the U.S. Army, 1994; Golden Pen Award, 1st Cavalry Division Association, 1996.

WRITINGS:

(Editor) *Digital War: A View from the Front Lines,* Presidio Press (Novato, CA), 1999.
No Gun Ri: A Military History of the Korean War Incident, Stackpole Books (Mechanicsburg, PA), 2002.

Contributor to military periodicals. Some writings appear under the pseudonym Matthew Brennan.

WORK IN PROGRESS: Shifting Gears: The Interwar U.S. Army, 1919-1941.

SIDELIGHTS: Robert L. Bateman is an infantry officer and the author of several works of military history and analysis. In his books and articles he looks both backwards, at the history of the U.S. Army, and forward, to consider the paths that the armed forces might take in the future.

Bateman's first book is *Digital War: A View from the Front Lines,* a collection of essays by Bateman and others about the effect of the "digital revolution" upon the armed forces. The volume focuses on the Army in particular, but "there is a great deal in this book that will interest anyone following the debate over the shape of the U.S. military in the information age," Erik J. Dahl concluded in *Naval War College Review.* The "highly readable anthology" contains several "provocative, well-written essays," Ron Laurenzo wrote in *Defense Week,* and it also asks important questions about the future role of ground troops in the American military—will they be rendered obsolete, as proponents of increasingly accurate guided missiles and bombs suggest, or remain a crucial part of American tactics and strategy? Perhaps predictably, Bateman and his infantry and cavalry colleagues come down firmly on the latter side. "With all the hype in Washington about the promise" of air power, Laurenzo commented, "maybe *Digital War* will restore the balance somewhat in debates about the ultimate role of firepower."

In *No Gun Ri: A Military History of the Korean War Incident,* Bateman debunks a Pulitzer Prize-winning series of articles published in 1999 by three Associated Press reporters who claimed that American soldiers massacred several hundred South Korean civilians at a railroad bridge at No Gun Ri, Korea, on July 26, 1950. In fact, although one small group of soldiers did fire on a crowd of refugees threatening to force its way through U.S. lines to flee the fighting, the refugees who were hit numbered under three dozen. "Bateman meticulously traces the situation that led to the incident," David L. Snead explained on *H-Net: Humanities and Social Sciences Online,* including the poor training given to those troops and the chaotic situation on the ground at the time. "It is doubtful that anyone will ever describe the No Gun Ri incident in more detail or with more accuracy than Bateman," Snead concluded.

In addition to chronicling the actual history of the No Gun Ri incident, Bateman also "presents a compelling and conclusive case about how one man's war story can be spun into a national scandal," James H. Clifford explained in *Air and Space Power Journal;* "whether or not they are interested in this particular incident, people who consider themselves military historians should read *No Gun Ri.*" The book was recommended as "a required textbook for every journalism student—and an eye-opener for working reporters and editors," Robert Skole wrote in *Skeptical Inquirer.*

Bateman told *CA:* "As one of the most prolific soldier-writers (and aspiring scholars) of my generation, I found myself operating in circles I would never have foreseen at the beginning of my military career. With more than fifty works of military history, theory, and prognostication in professional military journals and magazines, I met several others of the small group of people who are both soldiers and published authors. Realizing that I stood at the epicenter of this unique group was the moment of genesis for my first book, the anthology on the future of war, *Digital War.*

"My second book, *No Gun Ri,* derived from work with veterans of Korea and the initial false reports of the media about the actions of fake combat veterans at No Gun Ri in the opening days of the Korean War. As a veteran of the same unit accused by the Associated Press of committing what others characterized as a 'war crime,' I was uniquely situated to conduct knowledgeable research into the military archives, and I had access which other writers did not to the veterans of my own unit.

"Currently I am a doctoral candidate in history at Ohio State University. My writings, both historical and theoretical, reflect my training as a U.S. Army Airborne Ranger and my classical academic training for the doctorate in history."

BIOGRAPHICAL AND CRITICAL SOURCES:

PERIODICALS

Air and Space Power Journal, fall, 2002, James H. Clifford, review of *No Gun Ri: A Military History of the Korean War Incident,* p. 113.
Defense Week, January 3, 2000, Ron Laurenzo, review of *Digital War: A View from the Front Lines.*
Journal of Military History, April, 2003, James I. Matray, review of *No Gun Ri,* pp. 622-623.
Naval War College Review, autumn, 2000, Erik J. Dahl, review of *Digital War,* p. 158.
Skeptical Inquirer, September-October, 2002, Robert Skole, review of *No Gun Ri,* p. 53.

ONLINE

History News Network, http://hnn.us/ (September 9, 2004), Bonnie Goodman, "The Face-Off: Bob Bateman vs. the Associated Press."
H-Net: Humanities and Social Sciences Online, http://www.h-net.org/ (March, 2004), David L. Snead, review of *No Gun Ri.*
Pritzker Military Library Web site, http://www.pritzkermilitarylibrary.org/ (October 21, 2004), "Front and Center: With John Callaway: The Debate over No Gun Ri."

*   *   *

BATESON, Catherine 1960-

PERSONAL: Born 1960; married; two children.

ADDRESSES: Home—Central Victoria, Australia. *Agent*—c/o Author Mail, University of Queensland Press, Staff House Rd., P.O. Box 6042, St. Lucia, Queensland 4067, Australia.

CAREER: Creative writing teacher and writer.

AWARDS, HONORS: Book of the Year designation, Children's Book Council of Australia (CBCA), for *Rain May and Captain Daniel;* CBCA Honour Book for Older Readers designation, and Australian Family Therapists' Award, both 2003, both for *Pained Love Letters;* New South Wales Premier's Literary Award, and Queensland Premier's Literary Award, both 2003, both for *Pained Love Letters,* and *Rain May and Captain Daniel;* John Shaw Neilson Award.

WRITINGS:

FOR YOUNG ADULTS

A Dangerous Girl, University of Queensland Press (St. Lucia, Queensland, Australia), 2000.
The Year It All Happened, University of Queensland Press (St. Lucia, Queensland, Australia), 2001.
Painted Love Letters, University of Queensland Press (St. Lucia, Queensland, Australia.), 2002.
Rain May and Captain Daniel, University of Queensland Press (St. Lucia, Queensland, Australia), 2002.
The Airdancer of Glass, 2004.

OTHER

Pomegranates from the Underworld (poetry), Pariah Press, 1990.
The Vigilant Heart (poetry), University of Queenland Press (St. Lucia, Queensland, Australia), 1998.

Also author of short fiction.

WORK IN PROGRESS: A junior fiction novel, *Millie and the Night Heron;* the young-adult novel *His Name in Fire;* a new volume of poetry.

SIDELIGHTS: Award-winning Australian author Catherine Bateson credits a childhood spent in a used bookstore with sparking her career as a poet and author of young-adult fiction. A published poet, Bateson made the transition to fiction by creating *A Dangerous Girl* and its sequel, *The Year It All Happened,* verse novels that reflect the concerns and speech of modern Australian teens.

In *Painted Love Letters* Bateson tells the story of Chrissie, a teen who must deal with the death of her mother to lung cancer and the tragedy's effect on other family members, while *Rain May and Captain Daniel* finds an inner-city mother and daughter adapting to platypus, fruit bats, and other quirks of life in rural Australia. In addition to writing novels and poetry, Bateston has worked as a creative writing teacher for over a decade. In her spare time she hosts writing workshops for students and appears at poetry and writing festivals.

BIOGRAPHICAL AND CRITICAL SOURCES:

ONLINE

Catherine Bateson Web site, http://www.catherine-bateson.com (October 22, 2004).
University of Queensland Press Web site, http://www.uqp.edu.au/ (July 23, 2004), "Catherine Bateson."*

*   *   *

BAZZANA, Kevin 1963-

PERSONAL: Born July 27, 1963, in Kelowna, British Columbia, Canada. *Education:* Attended University of Calgary and Okanagen College; University of Victoria, B.Mus., 1988; Stanford University, M.A., 1989; University of California at Berkeley, Ph.D., 1996.

ADDRESSES: Home—7227 Brentview Dr., Brentwood Bay, British Columbia V8M 1B9, Canada. *E-mail*—kevinbazzana@shaw.ca.

CAREER: Musicologist, writer, editor, and lecturer. *Beethoven Journal,* editorial assistant, 1990-92, 1999; University of Victoria, lecturer, 1993—;. *GlennGould* (magazine), editor, 1995—; Toronto Symphony Orchestra, program annotator, 1996—.

AWARDS, HONORS: Canada Council creative writing grants, 1998, 2003; Toronto Book Award for Nonfiction, 2004, for *Wondrous Strange: The Life and Art of Glenn Gould.*

WRITINGS:

Glenn Gould: The Performer in the Work—A Study in Performance Practice, Oxford University Press (New York, NY), 1997.
Wondrous Strange: The Life and Art of Glenn Gould, Oxford University Press (New York, NY), 2004.

Author's books have also been translated into Japanese, German, Italian, and French.

WORK IN PROGRESS: A biography of Hungarian pianist-composer Ervin Nyiregyházi (1903-87), tentatively scheduled for publication in 2006.

SIDELIGHTS: Kevin Bazzana is considered one of the foremost experts on the life and works of reclusive Canadian pianist Glenn Gould. The editor of *GlennGould* magazine, Bazzana has written two critically acclaimed works on the musician: *Glenn Gould: The Performer in the Work—A Study in Performance Practice,* published in 1997 and based on his Ph.D. dissertation, and *Wondrous Strange: The Life and Art of Glenn Gould,* published in 2004.

With *Glenn Gould,* Bazzana presents a detailed musicological study of Gould's performances, and in so doing, places Gould's career into a broader historical context. Bazzana not only examines the aesthetic philosophy that informed Gould's approach to music performance but also details specific features of his piano technique, drawing on the Glenn Gould archive at the Library and Archives Canada in Ottawa. *Booklist's* Alan Hirsch commended this aspect of the book, noting that the author "artfully describes each of Gould's techniques and how he used it to achieve his unique performance style." Timothy J. McGee, writing in *Library Journal,* called Bazzana's book a "detailed critical study" of the pianist and not simply "another biographical tribute." Tim Page, writing in the *Washington Post Book World,* deemed it a "fine" volume that explores, "with rare acuity, Gould's artistic philosophies and the manner in which they were put into practice." Page went on to observe that Bazzana "examines Gould's contradictions with a judicious mixture of sympathy and rigor."

Bazzana continues his investigations of Gould in the biography *Wondrous Strange,* the "most balanced" of the many biographies on the pianist, according to a critic for the *New Yorker.* Ivan Hewett, writing in *New Statesman,* called Bazzana's approach a "rounded portrait" by a person "eminently qualified to write [Gould's] biography." Bazzana deals with Gould's eccentricities, but also lays to rest some of the gossip about the pianist's sexuality. The *New Yorker* contributor called Bazzana a "keen deflator of myths" for this aspect of the book. Employing comprehensive interviews with friends and colleagues, as well as research in the archives, Bazzana "wisely and skillfully" follows a middle path in his biography, as Paul Griffiths wrote in *Nation,* by avoiding a caricature image of Gould as either "an inhibited homosexual or a hermetic straight man, a wonder or a clown, a tragedy or a triumph." For *Guardian Unlimited* contributor Edward Greenfield, "Bazzana's narrative and character study over a vast span reflects the allure of Gould himself." Greenfield went on to note that, "Very well documented, [*Wondrous Strange*] makes a compelling study even for the non-devotee." Likewise, a *Publishers Weekly* reviewer found Bazzana's work an "engaging biography that will captivate classical music lovers and casual listeners alike." More praise came from *Library Journal*'s Larry Lipkis, who commented that the "author's tone is sympathetic but by no means uncritical, and his prose is lively, witty, and often quite elegant." Lipkis concluded that this volume "will replace earlier biographies" of Gould.

BIOGRAPHICAL AND CRITICAL SOURCES:

PERIODICALS

Booklist, December 1, 1997, Alan Hirsch, review of *Glenn Gould: The Performer in the Work—A Study in Performance Practice,* p. 604; April 15, 2004, Alan Hirsch, review of *Wondrous Strange: The Life and Art of Glenn Gould,* p. 1415.

Gay & Lesbian Review Worldwide, July-August, 2004, John Mitzel, review of *Wondrous Strange,* p. 40.

Library Journal, December, 1997, Timothy J. McGee, review of *Glenn Gould,* p. 107; June 1, 2004, Larry Lipkis, review of *Wondrous Strange,* p. 136.

Nation, June 14, 2004, Paul Griffiths, review of *Wondrous Strange,* p. 15.

New Statesman, October 11, 2004, Ivan Hewett, review of *Wondrous Strange,* p. 53.

New Yorker, June 14, 2004, review of *Wondrous Strange,* p. 192.

Publishers Weekly, April 19, 2004, review of *Wondrous Strange,* p. 53.

Washington Post Book World, March 22, 1998, Tim Page, review of *Glenn Gould,* p. 8.

ONLINE

City of Toronto Web site, http://www.city.toronto.ca/ (November 9, 2004), "Toronto Book Awards, 2004."

Guardian Unlimited, http://books.guardian.co.uk/ (June 12, 2004), Edward Greenfield, review of *Wondrous Strange.*

Oxford University Press Web site, http://www.oup. com/ (November 9, 2004).

*   *   *

BEDARD, Anthony 1968(?)-
(Tony Bedard)

PERSONAL: Born c. 1968, in Puerto Rico; married to a personal trainer; children: one son.

ADDRESSES: Office—CrossGen Entertainment, Inc., 4023 Tampa Road, Suite 2400, Oldsmar, FL 34677.

CAREER: Comic-book writer and editor, 1992—. Valient/Acclaim Comics, New York, NY, executive editor and writer; Crusade Entertainment, senior editor; DC Comics, editor of Vertigo imprint; CrossGeneration Comics, Oldsmar, FL, writer, 2001—.

WRITINGS:

UNDER NAME TONY BEDARD

(With Karl Moline and John Dell) *Route 666: Highway to Horror,* CrossGeneration Comics (Oldsmar, FL), 2003.

Contributor to comic-book series, including "Negation," "Mystic," "Route 666," and "Kiss Kiss Bang Bang," all published by CrossGeneration Comics; "Shi," Crusade Entertainment; "Magnus Robot Fighter," "Solar: Man of the Atom," "Turok: Dinosaur Hunter," and "Shadowman," Valient/Acclaim; and series for Malibu and Broadway Comics. Editing includes work on "Aquaman," "Wonder Woman," and "Hourman" series, all published by DC Comics.

"NEGATION" SERIES; UNDER NAME TONY BEDARD

(With Mark Waid) *Negation 1: BOHICA!* (originally published in comic-book format), CrossGeneration Comics (Oldsmar, FL), 2002.

Negation 2: Baptism of Fire (originally published in comic-book format), CrossGeneration Comics (Oldsmar, FL), 2003.

Negation 3: Hounded (originally published in comic-book format), CrossGeneration Comics (Oldsmar, FL), 2003.

"MYSTIC" SERIES; UNDER NAME TONY BEDARD

(With Ron Marz) *Mystic 3: Siege of Scales,* CrossGeneration Comics (Oldsmar, FL), 2002.

Mystic 4: Out All Night, CrossGeneration Comics (Oldsmar, FL), 2003.

SIDELIGHTS: Anthony "Tony" Bedard explained that he "started editing for Valiant because I saw it as a route to writing, which was what I really wanted to do. Since then I learned that editing is actually very rewarding in its own way," as he told Christopher Allen in an interview for *Comic Book Gallery.* After working on a number of titles for Valiant, Bedard moved to DC Comics, where he got to work on perennial series favorites "Wonder Woman" and "Aquaman" as well as the newer "Hourman" series.

In 2001 Bedard fulfilled his original ambition, landing a position as a writer for CrossGeneration Comics in Florida, where he inherited the "Mystic" series from Ron Marz and launched the "Negation" series with Mark Waid. Drawing on comics from throughout the CrossGeneration universe, the "Negation" story line begins with the kidnapping of 100 characters by the soldiers of the Negation Empire, which seeks to put these heroes to the test, in order to discover the weaknesses of the various worlds and territories introduced in other CrossGeneration comics.

Reviewing the first book-length collection of this series, *Negation: BOHICA!* (which stands for "Bend Over, Here It Comes Again!"), a *Publishers Weekly* reviewer found that "the fugitives are a diverse bunch, and their interpersonal conflicts can be entertaining. Star Trek fans will be amused by the bumbling star-

ship crew that the escapees encounter." In the second collection, *Negation: Baptism of Fire,* the fugitives must rescue a baby girl kidnapped by the Negation's God-Emperor Charon. Led by Obregon Kaine, the escapees must sort out their own differences while battling Charon and his evil subordinates, Lawbringer Qztr and Komptin. For a *Publishers Weekly* reviewer, the "collection's later pages neatly balance wild, widescreen battles and the quiet enigma of a baby girl who's impervious to the Negation's power."

Beginning with issue eighteen, Bedard also started writing for the "Mystic" series, which features a story line set around a young woman named Giselle who inadvertently finds herself in possession of vast magical powers after a mysterious sigil appears on her hand. Unfortunately, the power has been snatched from some of the most powerful sorcerers on her planet, and they are none too happy about the new power arrangement. Throughout the series, Giselle is forced to master her newfound powers while avoiding the murderous vengeance of the Guild Masters. In *Mystic 3: Siege of Scales,* Giselle finds herself battling an old enemy, Animora, while striving to save her planet from the Demon Queen. "What follows is a battle both serious and humorous, with magic, technology, giant automatons, killer dragon scales, revealing costumes, and oversized monsters all playing a part," explained Douglas Davey in *School Library Journal.* In *Mystic 4: Out All Night,* Giselle finds herself saving corrupt cops from a demon, Mafioso, and seeking out the spirits of various mage guilds, including the primitive Shaman guild. "While there is an overall story arc, each of the issues that make up this book tells a separate, well-plotted story, which is satisfying, despite the fact that Giselle has not yet completed her quest," observed *School Library Journal* contributor Paul Brink.

Bedard's *Route 666: Highway to Horror* is centered around Cassandra "Cassie" Starkweather, an escaped mental patient who is convinced that she can see monsters where others cannot and who believes it her duty to slay them. As Cassie discovers, or perhaps imagines, there is a war going on in the world of the dead. The powerful Adversary has dispatched agents to kidnap the souls of those who die violently, including those murdered by those agents themselves while in human disguise. The series, with its ghosts and ghouls and other supernatural creatures set on a very Earth-like planet, was something of a departure for both Bedard and CrossGeneration Comics. As Bedard told Tim O'Shea on the *Orca* Web site, "I've tried very much to shift gears away from the pacing and style of an adventure comic. I'm trying to get more suspense and unsettling situations in this one." Reviewing *Route 666,* a *Publishers Weekly* contributor concluded that "this title looks like the start of an enjoyably creepy road trip."

BIOGRAPHICAL AND CRITICAL SOURCES:

PERIODICALS

Publishers Weekly, February 17, 2003, review of *Negation 1: BOHICA!,* p. 59; March 3, 2003, review of *Mystic 3: Siege of Scales,* p. 56; April 28, 2003, review of *Negation 2: Baptism of Fire,* p. 51; May 26, 2003, review of *Route 666: Highway to Horror,* p. 51; June 9, 2003, review of *Mystic 4: Out All Night,* p. 38.
School Library Journal, October, 2002, Susan Salpini, review of *Negation 1: BOHICA!,* p. 198; April, 2003, Susan Salpini, review of *Negation 2: Baptism of Fire,* p. 198; May, 2003, Douglas Davey, review of *Mystic 3: Siege of Scales,* p. 182; May, 2003, Paul Brink, review of *Mystic 4: Out All Night,* p. 181.

ONLINE

Comic Book Galaxy Web site, http://www.comicbook galaxy.com/ (November 29, 2003), Christopher Allen, "Negation Conversation: An Interview with Tony Bedard."
DigitalWebbing.com, http://www.digitalwebbing.com/ (November 29, 2003), Ian Ascher, reviews of "Negation" and "Route 666" series.
Orca Online, http://www.orcafresh.net/ (November 29, 2003), Tim O'Shea, "There's No Passing on Route 666."
Under Ground Online, http://www.ugo.com/ (June 16, 2004), David Weter, interview with Bedard.*

*   *   *

BEDARD, Michael

PERSONAL: Born in Windsor, Ontario, Canada.

ADDRESSES: Home—Los Angeles, CA. *Agent*—c/o Author Mail, Penguin Group, 375 Hudson St., New York, NY 10014.

CAREER: Artist. Co-founder of OXO ART Publishing, Topango Canyon, CA; executive producer of *Sitting Ducks* animated television series; creator of animated television film *The Santa Claus Brothers,* 2001.

AWARDS, HONORS: Emmy Award for *The Santa Claus Brothers,* 2001.

WRITINGS:

(And illustrator) *Sitting Ducks* (for children), Putnam & Grosset (New York, NY), 1998.

WORK IN PROGRESS: A collection called *Quatro Sightings,* using photographs taken by collectors of Bedard's sculpture of a character named Quatro.

SIDELIGHTS: After growing up in Windsor, Ontario, on the U.S.-Canada border, Michael Bedard moved to Los Angeles in the late 1960s and eventually became a popular poster artist. He is best known for his "Sitting Ducks" poster from the late 1970s, a darkly comical image of three ducks sunning themselves poolside with sunglasses and iced tea. One duck, however, has noticed bullet holes in the wall behind him and is curiously studying them. The poster is representative of Bedard's skill in using humor to highlight personal and social problems. "Sitting Ducks" was inspired by behaviors Bedard witnessed in ducks he was raising at his Topanga Canyon home, as well as by the death of Beatle John Lennon, who in 1980 was shot and killed by former mental patient Mark Chapman. The "Sitting Ducks" poster gave birth to several other projects, including a storybook, a video game, and a television series that aired in some fifty countries. Bedard, who has no formal art training, also won an Emmy Award for his animated film *The Santa Claus Brothers.*

For his book titled *Sitting Ducks,* Bedard crafted a story about ducks who are hatched at the Colossal Duck Factory and destined to become dinner for the local alligator population. When one duck escapes and makes friends with an alligator, he takes on the difficult task of saving his fellow ducks. The fowl live in ignorance in Ducktown, where they are encouraged to eat so much that they cannot save themselves by flying away. The illustrations expand on the colorful, sharply delineated artwork of the original poster. In an interview with *Los Angeles Times* writer Lynne Heffley, who described the work as "a fowl 'Soylent Green,'" Bedard remarked on the easy transition from one format to another: "I've always thought of the duck series more as story telling in a way than painting," he said. In a review for *Booklist*, Ilene Cooper observed that the "sassy text and singularly amusing art" contain laughs for adults as well as children. A *Publishers Weekly* critic described *Sitting Ducks* as possibly "a comment on Big Brother, vegetarianism or star-crossed lovers," adding further that the story compliments Bedard's "crisp, mechanical artwork." Karyn Miller-Medzon remarked in the *Boston Herald*, "Not only is this book a wonderfully imaginative (and perfectly silly) tale, but it's also a great lesson about friendship, accepting others despite their differences and the benefits of honesty."

BIOGRAPHICAL AND CRITICAL SOURCES:

PERIODICALS

Art Business News, July, 2003, Kevin Lo, "Ruffling Feathers: Artist Michael Bedard Uses Animation and Humor to Satirize His Perception of the World," pp. 54-55.

Booklist, December 1, 1998, Ilene Cooper, review of *Sitting Ducks*, p. 669.

Boston Herald, September 27, 1998, Karyn Miller-Medzon, "What a Duck Does When His Goose Is Cooked," p. 64.

Los Angeles Times, September 24, 1998, Lynne Heffley, "Fans Go Quackers for Bedard's Allegorical Art," p. 47.

Publishers Weekly, October 12, 1998, review of *Sitting Ducks*, p. 75.

ONLINE

ImageExchange.com, http://imageexchange.com/artists/ (March 31, 2004), Todd Bingham, "Michael Bedard."*

*　　*　　*

BEDARD, Tony
See BEDARD, Anthony

BEMBERG, María Luisa 1922-1995

PERSONAL: Born April 14, 1922, in Buenos Aires, Argentina; died of stomach cancer May 7, 1995, in Buenos Aires, Argentina; married (divorced); children: four. *Education:* Attended Lee Strasberg Institute.

CAREER: Film director and writer. Founder of Teatro del Globo (theater company).

AWARDS, HONORS: Academy Award nomination for Best Foreign Film, 1984, for *Camila*.

WRITINGS:

SCREENPLAYS

Cronica de una señora (title means "Chronicle of a Woman"), 1971.

El mundo de la mujer (short), 1972.

Triangulo de cuatro, 1975.

Juguetes (short), 1978.

(And director) *Momentos*, 1981.

(And director) *Señora de nadie* (title means "Nobody's Woman"), 1982.

(And director) *Camila*, 1984.

(And director) *Miss Mary*, 1987.

(And director) *Yo, la peor de todas* (title means "I, the Worst of Them All"), 1990.

(And director) *De eso no se habla* (title means "I Don't Want to Talk about It"), 1993.

SIDELIGHTS: María Luisa Bemberg entered filmmaking at the age of forty-six, after being married and divorced and raising her children. Despite her relatively late start as a director and screenplay writer, she quickly rose to become one of the most popular and important Argentinean directors, gaining acclaim in Europe and the United States as well.

Bemberg's first screenplay, *Cronica de una señora*, is a semi-autobiographical work that won praise as a contemporary domestic drama. It focuses on the way in which a regressive political system affects a female protagonist. After making this film, Bemberg was determined to exert more control over her screenplays.

To accomplish this she spent three months as an actress at the Lee Strasberg Institute in New York before returning to Argentina to direct.

In 1982 she caused a stir with *Señora de nadie,* which features a friendship between a gay man and a separated woman and challenges the sacred notions of marriage, family, and the Catholic Church. Released the same day Argentina invaded the Malvinas—Falkland Islands—the film's impact was somewhat overshadowed by political events as well as by censorship. At this point in time Argentina's government exerted so much control over the country's film industry that by the late 1970s only twelve films were being produced per year. The crumbling state of the military regime ultimately helped the film succeed, however. Hugely popular with female audiences, *Señora de nadie* provided an overtly feminist message to a culture crippled by its own repression and machismo.

After the overthrow of the military regime in Argentina, and the nation's humiliating defeat in the Falklands War, Bemberg continued to focus on conflicts involving the country's collective identity. She felt that her role as a filmmaker—and as a woman in a fiercely patriarchal society—was to explore political oppression by using it as a backdrop and context against which to depict intense interpersonal conflict. Her films explore Argentina's troubled past, and suggest that only by coming to terms with that history can the nation—and the individual—move foreward.

In 1984 Bemberg directed *Camila,* the first Argentinean film ever to break into the English-language market. Nominated for an Oscar for best foreign-language film, *Camila* is particularly notable because many directors had wanted to film this true story of illicit love between a priest and a young woman in 1847 but had been prevented from doing so by Argentinian censors. Though the two protagonists eventually acknowledge their forbidden love and find happiness together under assumed names, their union is short-lived. Pursued by the government, they are tracked down and executed. By casting the priest as a beautiful object of desire and Camila (historically portrayed as the innocent victim) as the temptress, Bemberg creates a passionate melodrama in which she consciously moves away from her harsh domestic dramas into a more emotional, lyrical sphere.

The historical basis of *Camila* also provides Bemberg with a mythical arena in which to explore very real contemporary political concerns. As Stanley Kauff-

mann wrote in a *New Republic* review, "Bemberg weaves into the film much of the caste rubbings in this society, a strong strand of political oppression, and some color of a passion that won't be stayed. The picture is slightly silly as well as moving, but then, so long as you're not personally involved, so are many heavy romances."

Miss Mary continues to focus on contemporary, political concerns, exploring the British influence on Argentina's upper class in the years before World War II. Rleated through a nanny's eyes, politics and history are expressed through family structures, sexuality, and human behavior. Female characters, even the repressed and unsympathetic nanny (played by Julie Christie), are portrayed with understanding. Although Miss Mary is a reactionary agent of oppression, the film explores *why* she is so, thereby analyzing the forces that have created her and the sick family for which she works.

Bemberg's last film before her death in 1995, *De eso no se habla,* is one of her most peculiar works. The story concerns a widow named Leonor, who refuses to acknowledge in any way that her daughter, Carlotta, is a dwarf. Leonor manages to accomplish this by convincing everyone in her town to treat her daughter like a person of normal height and by putting all her efforts into giving Carlotta an exceptional education that includes studying French and the piano. In this way, Carlotta becomes an extraordinary young woman who calls herself Charlotte instead of Carlotta. Though her mother continues to try to hide her daughter's dwarfism, Charlotte flaunts it and becomes an independent spirit who wins the love of a visiting Italian named Ludovico D'Andrea, whom she marries.

"The fetishization of the dwarf is an inevitable risk of a picture like this," remarked Karen Jaehne in a review of *De eso no se habla* for *Film Quarterly,* "and Bemberg steers a discreet course around it. She makes it quite clear that Charlotte herself is a sexual creature: the young girl prances before a mirror; we see flirtation in her eyes;. . . . Charlotte is a full, complete woman with a psyche as strong as an Amazon."

In the end, Leonor's plans to nurture her daughter into an extraordinary woman prove to be only too successful. Charlotte becomes so independent and confident that she is able to extricate herself from her mother's well-meaning control and become a fully realized individual. This realization includes acknowledging herself to be a dwarf, and at the end of the movie she joins a circus—the very place Leonor has forbidden her to go—where she can be with others who are like herself and who welcome her for what she is. Yet the filmmaker manages to avoid making this ending either farcical or melodramatic. As Jaehne pointed out, Bemberg "shows Charlotte riding away on her white horse, wearing a crown. The paradox is that the less said, the more metaphoric and less pathetic is the creature." Critics generally praised Bemberg's handling of her subject in *De eso no se habla*, Michael Sauter concluding in *Entertainment Weekly* that this "haunting love story . . . unfolds with exquisite grace."

Camila, Miss Mary, and *De eso no se habla* all depict characters being repressed by either society, the government, or family. This repression can be seen in other Bemberg films, such as *Yo, la peor de todas.* Set in Mexico during the seventeenth century, the heroine of the film is a nun whose thirst for knowledge eventually leads her to butt heads with her country's misogynistic archbishop. Some critics have felt that the repression of female characters in her work reflected Bemberg's own frustrations over postponing her career in film. Although she began making movies late in life, she nonetheless transcended the political and social forces in her country, and made some of Argentina's most acclaimed films.

BIOGRAPHICAL AND CRITICAL SOURCES:

PERIODICALS

Americas, March-April, 1994, Caleb Bach, "María Luisa Bemberg Tells the World."

Cineaste, Volume 14, number 3, 1986; Volume 16, number 1-2, Lynne Jackson and Karen Jaehne, "Eavesdropping on Female Voices: A Who's Who of Contemporary Women Filmmakers."

Entertainment Weekly, April 28, 1995, Michael Sauter, review of *I Don't Want to Talk about It,* p. 73.

Film Journal, September, 1994, "Bemberg's Late-blooming Career Thrives with Mastroianni Starrer."

Film Quarterly, winter, 1994, Karen Jaehne, review of *I Don't Want to Talk about It,* p. 52.

Guardian (London, England), December 10, 1982, Monika Maeckley, "Machismo Takes a Knock."

New Republic, April 15, 1985, Stanley Kauffman, review of *Camila,* p. 26.

Village Voice, February 10, 1987, B. Ruby Rich, "After the Revolutions: The Second Coming of Latin American Cinema."

OBITUARIES

PERIODICALS

Times (London, England), May 19, 1995; May 22, 1995.*

*   *   *

BERGER, Yves 1934-2004

OBITUARY NOTICE— See index for *CA* sketch: Born January 14, 1934, in Avignon, France; died of cancer November 16, 2004, in Paris, France. Educator, publisher, and author. Berger was the former literary director at French publishing house Grasset, as well as being a well-known novelist and essayist who typically wrote on American themes. Growing up in France during World War II, Berger became enamored by the idea of freedom and liberty as symbolized by the American forces that eventually helped to free that country from the Nazis. He read books by American authors and studied English literature at the University of Montpellier and the Sorbonne, where he graduated in 1956. He then started teaching at schools such as Lycée Pasteur and Lycée Lakanal, while also becoming a literary critic for periodicals, including *Nouvelle Revue Française, Express;* and *Le Monde.* In 1960 Berger was hired as editor-in-chief at Editions Bernard Grasset in Paris. Here he became an influential force in publishing, releasing award-winning works by such authors as Edmonde Charles-Roux, François Nourissier, and Marie-Claire Blais. Berger was also a prolific and successful author in his own right. An Americophile who was especially fascinated by the Old West of the United States, he regularly published essay collections and novels that celebrated American ideals. Among these are *Le sud* (1962), translated as *The South* (1963); *Le fou d'Amerique* (1976), translated as *Obsession: An American Love Story* (1978); *Les Indiens des plains* (1978); *L'attrapeur d'ombres* (1992); and *Santa Fe* (2000). His last book, published in 2003, was the extensive *Le dictionnaire amoureux de l'Amerique,* a "dictionary for lovers of America," that won the Renaudot prize for the essay. Although he was always interested in U.S. culture, Berger was also concerned about French culture and his nation's language; toward this end, he was a member of the Haut Comité de la Langue Française, a government-sponsored organization that championed the cause of keeping the French tongue unsullied by foreign—especially English—words and terminology.

OBITUARIES AND OTHER SOURCES:

PERIODICALS

Independent (London, England), January 13, 2005, p. 43.

* * *

BERTON, Pierre (Francis Demarigny) 1920-2004 (Lisa Kroniuk)

OBITUARY NOTICE— See index for *CA* sketch: Born July 12, 1920, in Whitehorse, Yukon Territory, Canada; died of heart failure November 30, 2004, in Toronto, Ontario, Canada. Journalist, editor, broadcaster, and author. Berton enjoyed a varied career as a magazine editor, television panelist, and author of books—often on history—for both adults and children. Graduating from the University of British Columbia with a B.A. in 1941, he worked briefly for the *Vancouver News Herald* before World War II, when he enlisted in the Canadian Army. After World War II ended, he returned to journalism, working for the *Vancouver Sun* for a year before joining the staff at *Maclean's* magazine, where he served in various editorial positions until 1958. With a growing family to support, Berton pursued careers as an author and television host to earn additional income. He hosted the *Pierre Berton Show* from 1957 until 1973 and was best remembered as a panelist on the Canadian game show *Front Page Challenge,* where he appeared for thirty-seven years, beginning in 1957. He also hosted *Heritage Theatre* from 1947 to 1958. Berton found success, too, as a prolific author of history books for adult and young readers. Among these are such award-winning books as *The Mysterious North* (1956), *The Klondike Fever*

(1958), the two-volume *The Great Railway* (1970, 1971), and *The Invasion of Canada, 1812-1813* (1977). A number of his books were adapted to television. One of these, *The Secret World of Og* (1961), was a children's book. Other notable books by Berton include *The Dionne Years: A Thirties Melodrama* (1977), *The Arctic Grail: The Quest for the North West Passage and the North Pole, 1818-1909* (1988), and the autobiography *My Times: Living with History, 1947-1995* (1995).

OBITUARIES AND OTHER SOURCES:

BOOKS

Berton, Pierre, *My Times: Living with History, 1947-1995,* Doubleday Canada (Toronto, Ontario, Canada), 1995.

PERIODICALS

New York Times, December 3, 2004, p. A21.
Washington Post, December 8, 2004, p. B6.

* * *

BEVANS, Stephen B(ennett) 1944-

PERSONAL: Born July 14, 1944, in Baltimore, MD; son of Bert Bennett (a patternmaker) and Bernadette (an administrative assistant; maiden name, O'Grady) Bevans. *Education:* Divine Word College, B.A.; Pontifical Gregorian University, Rome, S.T.L., M.A.; University of Notre Dame, Ph.D. *Politics:* Democrat. *Religion:* Roman Catholic.

ADDRESSES: Office—Catholic Theological Union, 5401 South Cornell Ave., Chicago, IL 60615. *E-mail*—sbevans@ctu.edu.

CAREER: Catholic Theological Union, Chicago, IL, 1986—, Louis J. Luzbetak SVD Professor of Mission and Culture, 1998—. Also spent nine years teaching theology at a diocesan seminary in the Philippines.

MEMBER: International Association for Mission Studies, American Society of Missiology, Catholic Theological Society of America.

WRITINGS:

John Oman and His Doctrine of God, Cambridge University Press (New York, NY), 1992.

Models of Contextual Theology, Orbis Books (Maryknoll, NY), 1992, revised and expanded edition, 2002.

(Editor, with Karl Mueller, Theo Sundermeier, and Richard Bliese) *Dictionary of Mission: Theology, History, Perspectives,* Orbis Books (Maryknoll, NY), 1997.

(Editor, with Roger Schroeder) *Word Remembered, Word Proclaimed: Selected Papers from Symposia Celebrating the SVD Centennial in North America,* Steyler Verlag (Nettetal, Germany), 1997.

(Editor, with James A. Scherer) *New Directions in Mission and Evangelization,* Orbis Books (Maryknoll, NY), 3 volumes, 1999.

(With Roger Schroeder) *Constants in Context: A Theology of Mission for Today,* Orbis Books (Maryknoll, NY), 2004.

Editor, *Mission Studies,* 1997-2004; contributing editor, *International Bulletin of Missionary Research.*

SIDELIGHTS: In his writings Roman Catholic theologian and missiologist Reverend Stephen B. Bevans examines questions surrounding ecumenical mission and the meaning of mission work in modern times. Works such as *Models of Contextual Theology, Dictionary of Mission: Theology, History, Perspectives,* and *New Directions in Mission and Evangelization* restructure mission in the modern world and reframe traditional theology within modern cultures. In the twentieth century Christian theology—traditionally a bastion of conservatism speaking for the rich and privileged of the world, according to Bevans—was transformed into a vehicle for radical political and religious expression among the poor of the world, especially Third-World populations. "Many contextual theologies have emerged from the perspectives of uprooted and oppressed people," explained *Ecumenical Review* contributor Cyris H. Moon in his assessment of *Models of Contextual Theology.* "Examples

include liberation theology in Latin America, black theology in the United States and Africa, minjung theology (Korea), third-eye theology (Taiwan), Dalit theology (India), people's power theology (Philippines) Pancha Sila theology (Indonesia) and so on." According to *Theological Studies* contributor Carl F. Starkloff, Bevan demonstrates in *Models of Contextual Theology* a need for a theology based on four principles: "the spirit and message of the gospel, the Christian tradition, the culture of the theologian, and social change in that culture."

Bevans continues to examine the relationship between mission and evangelization in his editorship of *New Directions in Mission and Evangelization.* The theologian and his co-editor, James A. Scherer, "have brought together some of the best writing on inculturation/contextualization that has appeared in the 1990s," stated Lawrence Nemer in the *International Bulletin of Missionary Research.* The three-volume work focuses on the question of how to reconcile cultural differences in Christian belief and practice with the universalism stressed in the Roman Catholic church. Similarly, Bevans's agenda in the *Dictionary of Mission* demonstrates a concern with a revised definition of mission—one that is not driven by Western cultural imperatives. This new definition, wrote contributor William J. Nottingham in the *International Review of Mission,* "reflects what Christian mission has become: a genuinely worldwide and ecumenical phenomenon," bringing Catholic and Protestant theologians together "in the spirit of Vatican II."

At the same time, however, Bevans bucks trends in modern theology that complain that contextual theology undermines the true calling of the Catholic Church. F. Dale Bruner, writing in the *International Bulletin of Missionary Research,* quoted Pope John Paul II in the papal letter *Redemptoris missio* as saying, "It is not right to give an incomplete picture of missionary activity, as if it consisted principally in helping the poor, contribution to the liberation of the oppressed, promoting development or defending human rights. The missionary Church is certainly involved on these fronts but her primary task lies elsewhere: the poor are hungry for God, not just for bread and freedom. Missionary activity must first of all bear witness to and proclaim salvation in Christ."

In Bevans's work, the theologian strives to create an ecumenical theology that provides dignity to all peoples and their diverse cultures while honoring the need to follow the teachings of Jesus.

BIOGRAPHICAL AND CRITICAL SOURCES:

PERIODICALS

Ecumenical Review, July, 1995, Cyris H. Moon, review of *Models of Contextual Theology,* p. 395.

International Bulletin of Missionary Research, July, 1998, F. Dale Bruner, "The Son of God Inside Out: A Response to Stephen B. Bevans, S.V.D.," p. 106; January, 2001, Lawrence Nemer, review of *New Directions in Mission and Evangelization: Volume 3: Faith and Culture,* p. 42.

International Review of Mission, October, 1998, William J. Nottingham, review of *Dictionary of Mission: Theology, History, Perspectives,* p. 571.

Journal of Theological Studies, April, 1994, Keith Ward, review of *John Oman and His Doctrine of God,* p. 424.

Theological Studies, March, 1993, Donald K. McKim, review of *John Oman and His Doctrine of God,* p. 198; September, 1994, Carl F. Starkloff, review of *Models of Contextual Theology,* p. 591.

*   *   *

BLASS, Thomas

PERSONAL: Born in Budapest, Hungary. *Education:* Yeshiva University, B.A., Ph.D., 1969.

ADDRESSES: Home—Baltimore, MD. *Office*—University of Maryland, Mathematics/Psychology 334, 3416 Olympia Ave., Baltimore, MD 21215. *E-mail*—blass@umbc.edu.

CAREER: Social psychologist. University of Maryland Baltimore County, professor of social psychology. G. Stanley Hall lecturer, American Psychological Association, 2001.

AWARDS, HONORS: J. R. Kantor fellowship, Archives of the History of American Psychology, 1998-99.

WRITINGS:

Contemporary Social Psychology: Representative Readings, F. E. Peacock (Itasca, IL), 1976.

(Editor) *Personality Variables in Social Behavior,* L. Erlbaum (Hillsdale, NJ), 1977.

(Editor) *Obedience to Authority: Current Perspectives on the Milgram Paradigm,* L. Erlbaum (Mahwah, NJ), 2000.

The Man Who Shocked the World: The Life and Legacy of Stanley Milgram, Basic Books (New York, NY), 2004.

Also contributor of chapters to numerous books on social psychology; contributor of articles to journals, including *Journal of Personality and Social Psychology, Psychology Today, Journal of Applied Social Psychology, Personality and Social Psychology Bulletin, Journal of Social Psychology, Personality & Individual Differences, Holocaust and Genocide Studies,* and *Teaching of Psychology.*

SIDELIGHTS: Thomas Blass is a professor of social psychology at the University of Maryland, Baltimore County, and is considered one of the foremost experts on the life and work of pioneering psychologist Stanley Milgram. Best known for his obedience studies undertaken during the early 1960s, Milgram also pioneered research in the social networks known as the "six degrees of separation," as well as the area of urban psychology.

Born in Budapest, Hungary, Blass grew up during World War II and witnessed the costs of blind obedience to authority. While he was a Holocaust survivor, over half a million other Hungarian Jews were not so lucky. Surviving the war, he went first to Austria, then to Canada, and from there to study in the United States, where he has since remained. He earned a doctorate in social psychology in 1969, and thereafter developed an interest in the work of Milgram. This interest led him to edit selected papers on Milgram and then to write a biography of the psychologist in *The Man Who Shocked the World: The Life and Legacy of Stanley Milgram.*

Published in 2004, *The Man Who Shocked the World* details Milgram's career, including his controversial 1961 experiment in which participants believed they were delivering electric shocks to other "participants" to enhance learning. In reality, the experiment was set up in order to see how far people would go in following orders, even if such orders cause real and visible pain to others. In the experiment, an authority figure would tell these "teachers" to increase the level of shock administered to "students," who visibly exhibited pain. Though no electric shock was being administered, the terrifying result of the experiments was the level to which people would obey authority, continuing to "shock" others despite their own conflicted feelings about the action required of them.

The high point of Milgram's career, this experiment likely cost the young psychologist his tenure at Harvard University, and though he went on to create other compelling studies, his obedience experiment remains the work for which he is best known. Milgram died at age fifty-one.

Robert Levine, writing in *American Scientist,* felt that Blass captures the complexities of Milgram's life and achievements in a "penetrating, thought-provoking biography." Danielle Max noted in the *Jerusalem Post* that *The Man Who Shocked the World* provides a "revealing glimpse into both the world of academia and the mind of a gifted scientist." Although a reviewer for *Publishers Weekly* commented that the book provides an "unsatisfyingly superficial portrait" of Milgram, the critic added, however, that Blass does a "workmanlike job of describing Milgram's research and its significance." *Choice* reviewer W. A. Ashton noted that Blass has "created an extremely readable book by combining an interesting biography with a thorough, but not technical, review of Milgram's work in social psychology." Cary Cooper concluded in the *Times Higher Education Supplement* that *The Man Who Shocked the World* "is well-written, with mountains of information, insights, discoveries, and reflections, and is a must-read for any behavioural scientist."

BIOGRAPHICAL AND CRITICAL SOURCES:

PERIODICALS

American Scientist, July-August, 2004, Robert Levine, review of *The Man Who Shocked the World: The Life and Legacy of Stanley Milgram,* p. 368.
Chicago Sun Times, August 1, 2004, Sandra G. Boodman, review of *The Man Who Shocked the World,* p. 14.
Choice, November, 2004, W. A. Ashton, review of *The Man Who Shocked the World,* p. 567.
Jerusalem Post, October 11, 2004, Danielle Max, review of *The Man Who Shocked the World.*
Journal of Social Psychology, June, 1996, Thomas Blass, "The Milgram Obedience Experiment," p. 407.
Library Journal, E. James Lieberman, review of *The Man Who Shocked the World,* p. 129.
Personnel Psychology, winter, 2004, Wayne Harrison, review of *The Man Who Shocked the World,* pp. 1081-1084.
Psychology Today, March-April, 2004, Erik Strand, review of *The Man Who Shocked the World,* p. 83.
Publishers Weekly, March 8, 2004, review of *The Man Who Shocked the World,* p. 65.
Spectator, June 12, 2004, Jonathan Sumption, review of *The Man Who Shocked the World,* p. 49.
Times Higher Education Supplement, October 1, 2004, Cary Cooper, review of *The Man Who Shocked the World,* p. 26.
Times Literary Supplement, December 10, 2004, John Darley, review of *The Man Who Shocked the World.*
Washington Post Book World, July 25, 2004, Sandra G. Boodman, review of *The Man Who Shocked the World,* p. T8.

ONLINE

Basic Books Web site, http://www.perseusbooksgroup.com/ (November 3, 2004), "Thomas Blass."
Official Stanley Milgram Web site, http://www.stanleymilgram.com (November 3, 2004).
UMBC Psychology Department Web site, http://www.umbc.edu/ (November 3, 2004), "Thomas Blass, Ph.D."

*   *   *

BLOCK, Cathy Collins 1948-

PERSONAL: Born December 11, 1948, in Madison, WI; daughter of Charles Douglas and Jo Ann (Jiru) Zinke; married Stanley Byron Block, June, 1991; children: Michael Donegan. *Education:* Lamar University, B.A. (magna cum laude), 1970; North Texas State University, M.S. (with honors), 1974; University of Wisconsin, Madison, Ph.D., 1976.

ADDRESSES: Office—School of Education, P.O. Box 297900, Texas Christian University, Fort Worth, TX 76129. *E-mail*—c.block@tcu.edu.

CAREER: Elementary classroom teacher in OK and TX, 1970-74; Southern Illinois University, Carbondale, assistant professor, 1976-77; Texas Christian University, Fort Worth, instructor, 1977-78, assistant professor, 1978-82, associate professor, 1982-90, professor of education, 1990—; University of Notre Dame, Notre Dame, IN, national faculty member, 1997—; educational advisor and consultant.

MEMBER: International Reading Association, American Educational Research Association, American Association for Supervision and Curriculum Development, National Council of Teachers of English, Kappa Delta Phi, Phi Delta Kappa.

AWARDS, HONORS: Named a Notable Woman of Texas, 1983; Paul A. Witty Award, National Reading Conference, 1997.

WRITINGS:

Time Management for Teachers: Techniques and Skills That Give You More Time to Teach, Parker Publishing Co. (West Nyack, NY), 1987.

(Editor, with John N. Mangieri) *Teaching Thinking: An Agenda for the Twenty-first Century,* L. Erlbaum Associates (Hillsdale, NJ), 1992.

126 Strategies to Build Language-Arts Abilities: A Month-by-Month Resource, illustrated by Ruben Olmos, Allyn and Bacon (Boston, MA), 1992.

Teaching the Language Arts: Expanding Thinking through Student-centered Instruction, Allyn and Bacon (Boston, MA), 1993, third edition, 2001.

(Editor, with John N. Mangieri) *Creating Powerful Thinking in Teachers and Students: Diverse Perspectives,* Harcourt Brace College (Fort Worth, TX), 1994.

(With Jo Ann Zinke) *Creating a Culturally Enriched Curriculum for Grades K-6,* Allyn and Bacon (Boston, MA), 1995.

(With John N. Mangieri) *Reason to Read: Thinking Strategies for Life through Literature,* two volumes, Innovative Learning Publications (Menlo Park, CA), 1995.

(With John N. Mangieri) *Power Thinking for Success,* Brookline Books (Cambridge, MA), 1996.

Literacy Difficulties: Diagnosis and Instruction, Harcourt Brace College (Fort Worth, TX), 1997, reprinted as *Literacy Difficulties: Diagnosis and Instruction for Reading Specialists and Classroom Teachers,* Allyn and Bacon (Boston, MA), 2003.

(With others) *Learning to Read: Lessons from Exemplary First-Grade Classrooms,* Guilford Press (New York, NY), 2001.

(Editor, with Michael Pressley) *Comprehension Instruction: Research-based Best Practices,* Guilford Press (New York, NY), 2001.

(Editor, with Linda Gambrell and Michael Pressley) *Improving Comprehension Instruction: Rethinking Research, Theory, and Classroom Practice,* Jossey-Bass (San Francisco, CA), 2002.

(With John N. Mangieri) *Exemplary Literacy Teachers: Promoting Success for All Children in Grades K-5,* Guilford Press (New York, NY), 2003.

(With John N. Mangieri) *Yale Assessment of Thinking: A Self-Assessment of Your Skill in the Areas of Reasoning, Insight, and Self-Knowledge,* Jossey-Bass (San Francisco, CA), 2003.

(With Lori L. Rodgers and Rebecca B. Johnson) *Comprehension Process Instruction: Creating Reading Success in Grades K-3* ("Solving Problems in the Teaching of Literacy" series), Guilford Press (New York, NY), 2004.

Teaching Comprehension: The Comprehension Process Approach, Pearson (Boston, MA), 2004.

(With John N. Mangieri) *Power Thinking: How the Way You Think Can Change the Way You Lead,* Jossey-Bass (San Francisco, CA), 2004.

Author and editor of and contributor to tests, test guides, booklets, educational Web sites, and CDs; contributor of chapters to books and to periodicals, including *Elementary School Journal, School Administrator, Reading Today, Reading Teacher, Journal of Reading,* and *Reading Horizons.* Serves on the editorial boards of publications including *Journal of Educational Psychology* and *Reading Teacher.*

SIDELIGHTS: Cathy Collins Block is an educator and the author or editor of a number of books that address education, particularly of elementary school children. She is a coauthor of *Learning to Read: Lessons from Exemplary First-Grade Classrooms,* which focuses on successful literacy teaching. The book explains teacher strategies that have resulted in outstanding performances by students, presented both through summaries and in chapters focusing on individual case studies. Donald J. Richgels wrote in *Reading Teacher* that Block's "general findings are easy to summarize. The essence of the book's message about exemplary first-grade literacy instruction, however, can be appreciated only from reading the case studies. Reading them is easy and enjoyable; they unequivocally justify this book-length presentation. These cases are rich with detail."

Block is also the editor, with Michael Pressley, of *Comprehension Instruction: Research-based Best Practices,* a volume that includes four sections, titled "Theoretical Foundations: New Directions for the Future," "Branching out and Expanding Our Horizons in the Twenty-first Century," "Comprehension Instruction in Preschool, Primary, and Intermediate Grades," and "Intensification of Comprehension Instruction throughout Middle School, High School, and College." "It is difficult in an ordinary review to provide even a snapshot of all this extraordinary book has to offer," wrote a contributor to *Education Oasis* online. "Here you will find research, insights, inspiration, questions, answers, critical examinations, suggestions, advice, and more."

Block serves as co-editor, with Linda Gambrell and Pressley, of *Improving Comprehension Instruction: Rethinking Research, Theory, and Classroom Practice,* a volume that addresses educational technology, lesson structure, and overcoming reading problems. A *Reading Today* reviewer noted that "issues of linguistic and cultural diversity, high-stakes testing, and critical literacy are addressed" in this volume.

BIOGRAPHICAL AND CRITICAL SOURCES:

PERIODICALS

Childhood Education, Volume 80, number 5, 2004, Angela S. Raines, review of *Improving Comprehension Instruction: Rethinking Research, Theory, and Classroom Practice,* p. 276.

Reading Teacher, May, 2003, Donald J. Richgels, review of *Learning to Read: Lessons from Exemplary First-Grade Classrooms,* p. 796.

Reading Today, August-September, 2002, review of *Improving Comprehension Instruction,* p. 35; June-July, 2003, Pat D. Cordero, "RAP conference touches magic," p. 29.

ONLINE

Education Book Reviews Online, http://www.lib.msu. edu/ (September 24, 2004), review of *Improving Comprehension Instruction.*

Education Oasis Web site, http://www.educationoasis. com/ (September 24, 2004), review of *Comprehension Instruction: Research-based Best Practices.*

*   *   *

BODANSKY, Yossef

PERSONAL: Male.

ADDRESSES: Office—International Strategic Studies Association, P.O. Box 20407, Alexandria, VA 22320; fax: 703-684-7476. *Agent*—c/o Author Mail, Regan Books, HarperCollins, 10 East 53rd St., Seventh Floor, New York, NY 10022. *E-mail*—ybodansky@ strategicstudies.org.

CAREER: U.S. House of Representatives, Congressional Task Force on Terrorism and Unconventional Warfare, director, 1988; International Strategic Studies Association, director of research; Freeman Center for Strategic Studies, Houston, TX, special consultant on international terrorism; U.S. Departments of State and Defense, senior consultant; Johns Hopkins University, visiting scholar, security studies program.

WRITINGS:

Target America: Terrorism in the United States, Spibooks (New York, NY), 1994.

Terror!: The Inside Story of the Terrorist Conspiracy in America, Spibooks (New York, NY), 1994.

Crisis in Korea: The Emergence of a New Nuclear Power, Spibooks (New York, NY), 1994.

Offensive in the Balkans: The Potential for a Wider War as a Result of Foreign Intervention in Bosnia-Herzegovina, International Media Corp. (London, England), 1995.

Some Call It Peace: Waiting for War in the Balkans, International Media Corp. (London, England), 1996.

Islamic Anti-Semitism as a Political Instrument, Freeman Center for Strategic Studies (Houston, TX), 1999.

Bin Laden: The Man Who Declared War on America, Prima Publishing (Rocklin, CA), 1999, 2nd edition, 2001.

The High Cost of Peace: How Washington's Middle-East Policy Left America Vulnerable to Terrorism, Forum (Roseville, CA), 2002.

The Secret History of the Iraq War, ReganBooks (New York, NY), 2004.

Contributor to books, including *International Military & Defense Encyclopedia.* Contributor to periodicals, including *Jane's Defense Weekly, Business Week, Defense and Foreign Affairs, Strategic Policy, Nativ,* and *Global Affairs.* Senior editor, *Defense & Foreign Affairs.*

ADAPTATIONS: Bin Laden: The Man Who Declared War on America was adapted for audiocassette by Blackstone Audiobooks (Ashland, OR), 2002.

SIDELIGHTS: Yossef Bodansky is an internationally renowned military and threat analyst and terrorism expert. His book *Bin Laden: The Man Who Declared War on America* is an account of the United States' most-wanted terrorist, Osama bin Laden. Bodansky explores bin Laden's life in depth, beginning with his status as a son and heir of a billionaire building contractor. The young bin Laden was "a barroom brawler and womanizer," commented James J. Moran in *Marine Corps Gazette,* who eventually "came to believe that exposure to western life would lead to the ultimate destruction of Islam and saw no solution but Islamic militancy." Bodansky explains bin Laden's role in resisting the 1979 Soviet invasion of Afghanistan, where his fearlessness earned him the respect of fellow Arab fighters. His willingness to give of his fortune, and of himself, made him a hero among the Afghans. Bodansky also explains bin Laden's pivotal role in the 1993 confrontation in Somalia between U.S. forces and a local Muslim warlord, a failed U.S. mission that resulted in eighteen deaths and the removal of U.S. troops from the country. He discusses in detail the terrorist network bin Laden developed to attack the United States. "The book is gripping but incredibly depressing—after a while, the reader is so sickened by the callousness, the inhumanity, the treachery and duplicity, the sheer worship of death and

destruction, the whole nest of vipers exposed here, that you want to just put the book down and go outside to breathe some fresh air," commented Sophie Masson in *Quadrant.*

Originally published in 1999, a paperback edition of *Bin Laden* was released shortly after the attacks on the United States of September 11, 2001. In hindsight, the work must have seemed prescient; two years before the attacks, Bodansky "eloquently articulates bin Laden's desire to launch 'spectacular' terrorist strikes against the United States," observed Gary Slater in *Leatherneck.* Reviewing the book for *Security Management,* James T. Dunne called the book "an interesting compilation of events surrounding the near-mythic bin Laden, but [it] should be considered neither the final analysis nor the gospel truth." *Human Events* reviewer Joseph A. D'Agostino wrote that "the well-researched and well-argued *Bin Laden* is a thorough history of the man and his ideological development." Slater called *Bin Laden: The Man Who Declared War on America* "Bodansky's masterwork, an exhaustive account of the rise and specter of the Islamic terror movement." Bodansky "has written a book we all should study," Moran commented. "As the war on terrorism continues, we can all benefit in gaining a deeper understanding of our enemy. This book is an excellent beginning."

In *The High Cost of Peace: How Washington's Middle-East Policy Left America Vulnerable to Terrorism,* Bodansky "charts a series of Middle East policy missteps that he claims antagonized al Qaeda into striking the United States," commented Mark Strauss in *Washington Post Book World.* Primary among them are former U.S. president Bill Clinton's attempts to broker a peace agreement between Palestine and Israel—an agreement that Palestinian leader Yasser Arafat never intended to honor, Bodansky asserts. He "believes that Clinton's pursuit of a legacy was precisely the problem," Strauss remarked. He "suggests that Clinton irresponsibly poked the Islamist hornet's nest with a stick when he fostered a flawed Middle East peace process" between Palestine and Israel during the Oslo peace negotiations, Strauss noted. *National Review* critic David Pryce-Jones called the book "a formidable and sustained attack on the Oslo peace process, presenting it from first to last as an exercise in wishful thinking." "The book's details are exceptional, with information from many sources, including data seemingly from Israeli intelligence," noted Herman Reinhold in *Military Review.* Gregory R. Copley, reviewing the book in *Defense & Foreign Affairs Strategic Policy,* called *The High Cost of Peace: How Washington's Middle-East Policy Left America Vulnerable to Terrorism* "one of the most powerful and persuasive books of the decade," and concluded that "it will influence policies."

The Secret History of the Iraq War explores the reasons behind going to war in Iraq to topple the regime of Saddam Hussein. It also provides "a sober and revealing assessment of why (despite the excellence of our forces) it has been so hard to win security and stability for postwar Iraq," noted a reviewer on the *Conservative Book Service* Web site. Bodansky explains "why there is simply no doubt that America had an urgent imperative to go to war against Iraq when it did," including collaboration between Iraq's intelligence services and Osama bin Laden's terrorist network, as well as Iraq's ongoing involvement in international terror and the activities of al Qaeda, the *Conservative Book Service* Web site critic commented. The same critic called the book "All inclusive, revelatory, and perceptive" in its analysis and conclusions.

BIOGRAPHICAL AND CRITICAL SOURCES:

PERIODICALS

Booklist, January 1, 2003, Karen Harris, review of *Bin Laden: The Man Who Declared War on America* audiobook, p. 920.

Defense & Foreign Affairs Strategic Policy, September, 20002, Gregory R. Copley, review of *The High Cost of Peace: How Washington's Middle East Policy Left America Vulnerable to Terrorism,* p. 10.

Human Events, August 20, 1999, Joseph A. D'Agostino, "Conservative Spotlight: Yossef Bodansky," p. 17; October 22, 2001, Joseph A. D'Agostino, review of *Bin Laden,* p. 14.

Jerusalem Report, December 20, 1999, Jael Haran, review of *Bin Laden,* p. 50.

Leatherneck, April, 2002, Gary Slater, review of *Bin Laden,* p. 56.

Library Journal, March 1, 2002, review of *The High Cost of Peace,* section S, p. 17; November 15, 2002, Joseph L. Carlson, review of *Bin Laden: The Man Who Declared War on America* audiobook, p. 119.

Marine Corps Gazette, November, 2001, Alfred B. Connable, review of *Bin Laden,* p. 85; July, 2003, James J. Moran, review of *Bin Laden,* p. 52.

Middle East Journal, spring, 2003, Duncan Clarke, review of *The High Cost of Peace,* p. 349.

Military Review, January-February, 2004, Herman Reinhold, review of *The High Cost of Peace,* p. 91.

National Review, December 9, 2002, David Pryce-Jones, review of *The High Cost of Peace,* p. 49.

Publishers Weekly, July 26, 1999, review of *Bin Laden,* p. 78; September 24, 2001, review of *Bin Laden,* p. 13; September 30, 2002, review of *The High Cost of Peace,* p. 61.

Quadrant, December, 2001, Sophie Masson, review of *Bin Laden,* p. 85.

Rapport, Volume 17, issue 6, 1994, Brian W. Firth, review of *Target America,* p. 30; Volume 18, issue 5, 1995, Brian W. Firth, review of *Crisis in Korea: The Emergence of a New Nuclear Power,* p. 34.

Security Management, March, 2000, James T. Dunne, review of *Bin Laden,* p. 118.

Washington Post Book World, October 20, 2002, Mark Strauss, "Reaping the Whirlwind," review of *The High Cost of Peace,* p. T3.

ONLINE

Ariel Center for Policy Research Web site, http://www.acpr.org.il/ (October 8, 2004), "Yossef Bodansky."

Conservative Book Service Web site, http://www.conservativebookservice.org/ (November 8, 2004), "What Really Happened (and Is Happening) in the Iraq War—And Why Victory over Global Terrorism Hangs in the Balance There Now."

Freeman Center for Strategic Studies, http://www.freeman.org/ (October 8, 2004), "Yossef Bodansky."

International Strategic Studies Association Web site, http://www.strategicstudies.org/ (October 8, 2004).*

*   *   *

BODEK, Richard 1961-

PERSONAL: Born February 4, 1961. *Education:* University of Michigan, Ph.D., 1990; also studied at Johns Hopkins University, University of Tübingen, and Free University of Berlin.

ADDRESSES: Office—College of Charleston, Department of History, 66 George St., Charleston, SC 29424. *E-mail*—bodekr@cofc.edu.

CAREER: Educator. College of Charleston, Charleston, SC, associate professor of history, 1990—.

AWARDS, HONORS: Grants from Fulbright Foundation, National Endowment for the Humanities, and German Academic Exchange Service.

WRITINGS:

Proletarian Performance in Weimar Berlin: Agitprop, Chorus, and Brecht, Camden House (Columbia, SC), 1997.

Contributor of articles to professional journals, including *Journal of Social History* and *Central European History,* and books, including *Elections, Mass Politics, and Social Change in Modern Germany,* edited by James Retallack and Larry Eugene Jones, Cambridge University Press, 1992.

WORK IN PROGRESS: Germany in the German-Jewish Literary Imagination.

SIDELIGHTS: Richard Bodek is an associate professor of history at the College of Charleston whose areas of interest include German history, modern European social and cultural history, and the cultural world of German Judaism in the first half of the twentieth century. In *Proletarian Performance in Weimar Berlin: Agitprop, Chorus, and Brecht,* he combines many of these interests in a "pithy book [that] is a path-breaking examination of Communist agitprop theater in late Weimar Berlin," as Donna Harsch described the work in *Journal of Social History.*

Investigating his subject from a variety of angles, including from the points of view of the avant garde dramatist Bertolt Brecht, the unemployed and under-employed youth of the era, and political parties of the left, Bodek attempts to demonstrate in his book a "cross-fertilization of high culture, left-wing cultural production, politics, and everyday life," as Harsch further explained. Dubbing this treatment "imaginative and effective," Harsch also found that "for scholars or

teachers of drama, the chapters on agitprop theatre and Brecht will be of special interest." Peter D. Smith, reviewing the title in *Journal of European Studies,* felt that Bodek's book "presents an alternative to the popular view of the 'Golden Twenties,'" though it does not, in Smith's opinion, "quite fulfill the high expectations that it raises." Nonetheless, Smith concluded, "Bodek's project is original and provides a valuable and stimulating insight into a complex period." Gerhard P. Knapp, writing in *Monatshefte,* also thought that Bodek does not totally prove his thesis of the underlying unity of Weimar culture, both high and low, partly because, as Knapp averred, "there was no such unity." However, the critic concluded that "all in all, this is a well-conceived and persuasively written study," and added that Bodek provides "a fascinating account of this unique period in cultural modernism." For Larry Peterson, writing in the *American Historical Review,* Bodek's book "provides a promising outline for future research."

BIOGRAPHICAL AND CRITICAL SOURCES:

PERIODICALS

American Historical Review, April, 1999, Larry Peterson, review of *Proletarian Performance in Weimar Berlin: Agitprop, Chorus, and Brecht,* p. 688.
Choice, May, 1998, E. Williams, review of *Proletarian Performance in Weimar Berlin,* p. 1538.
Journal of European Studies, December, 1998, Peter D. Smith, review of *Proletarian Performance in Weimar Berlin,* pp. 432-434.
Journal of Social History, fall, 1999, Donna Harsch, review of *Proletarian Performance in Weimar Berlin,* p. 215.
Modern Drama, summer, 1999, Kerstin Gaddy, review of *Proletarian Performance in Weimar Berlin,* pp. 292-294.
Monatshefte, winter, 1998, Gerhard P. Knapp, review of *Proletarian Performance in Weimar Berlin,* pp. 562-563.*

*   *   *

BORTOLOTTI, Dan 1969-

PERSONAL: Born July 27, 1969, in Toronto, Ontario, Canada. *Education:* University of Waterloo, B.A. (English; with honors), 1992.

ADDRESSES: Home—27 Twelve Oaks Dr., Aurora, Ontario, Canada L4G 6J5. *Agent*—Don Sedgwick, Transatlantic Literary Agency, 1603 Italy Cross Rd., Petite Riviere, Nova Scotia, Canada B0J 2P0. *E-mail*—dan@danbortolotti.com.

CAREER: Writer and journalist.

AWARDS, HONORS: Science in Society Book Award shortlist, both 2003, both for *Exploring Saturn* and *Panda Rescue.*

WRITINGS:

Exploring Saturn, Firefly Books (Buffalo, NY), 2003.
Panda Rescue: Changing the Future for Endangered Wildlife, Firefly Books (Buffalo, NY), 2003.
Tiger Rescue: Changing the Future for Endangered Wildlife, Firefly Books (Buffalo, NY), 2003.
Hope in Hell: Inside the World of Doctors without Borders (adult nonfiction), Firefly Books (Buffalo, NY), 2004.

SIDELIGHTS: Canadian journalist Dan Bortolotti is the author of several nonfiction books for young readers. His 2004 book, *Exploring Saturn,* helps readers position the sixth planet within the solar system, then examines the ringed planet's unique characteristics, including its many moons. Tracing the known history of Saturn for young researchers, Bortolotti follows human understanding about the planet, from the ancient models of Ptolemy to the photographs captured by modern space probes such as the Hubble satellite, and even up to the preparations for the 2004 Cassini-Hygens probe's trip into the Saturnian planetary system. In *Resource Links* Heather Empey described *Exploring Saturn* as a "fantastic" resource that is "absolutely packed with information" useful to amateur astronomers. Noting the timeliness of Bortolotti's book, John Peters predicted in *School Library Journal* that "serious students and casual browsers alike will have trouble putting this down."

Moving to earthbound studies, Bortolotti contributed *Panda Rescue* and *Tiger Rescue* to the "Firefly Animal Rescue" series, which focuses on wildlife trouble spots on our own planet. After profiling the animal under study, the author then discusses the factors that threaten each species, some involving long-held local customs and others a result of an expanding human population. With the threat to each species recognized, some conservation measures have already been enacted, and Bortolotti includes an overview of these programs, while also focusing on ways in which specific threats might also be averted. Praising Bortolotti's "engaging writing style" as well as the photographs in each book, *School Library Journal* contributor Kathy Piehl dubbed the series "fascinating" and "readable." In *Booklist* Gillian Engberg also noted the author's "accessible, lively language" and Bortolotti's inclusion of useful information and reference sources, while Linda Irvine praised both *Tiger Rescue* and *Panda Rescue* in a *Resource Links* review, citing their realistic depiction of animal species and the inclusion of information "on the cultural and economic issues around protection of species."

BIOGRAPHICAL AND CRITICAL SOURCES:

PERIODICALS

Booklist, December 1, 2003, Carolyn Phelan, review of *Exploring Saturn,* p. 674; January 1, 2004, Gillian Engberg, review of *Panda Rescue: Changing the Future for Endangered Wildlife,* p. 850; September 15, 2004, Donna Chavez, review of *Hope in Hell: Inside the World of Doctors without Borders,* p. 188.
Kliatt, January, 2004, Janet Julian, review of *Exploring Saturn,* p. 35.
Library Journal, October 1, 2004, Tina Neville, review of *Hope in Hell,* p. 103.
Publishers Weekly, August 9, 2004, review of *Hope in Hell,* p. 237.
Resource Links, February, 2004, Heather Empey, review of *Exploring Saturn,* p. 20; February, 2004, Linda Irvine, review of *Panda Rescue* and *Tiger Rescue,* p. 43.
School Library Journal, April, 2004, Kathy Piehl, review of *Panda Rescue:,* p. 166; May, 2004, John Peters, review of *Exploring Saturn,* p. 164.

*   *   *

BOSCHKEN, Herman L. 1944-

PERSONAL: Born June 12, 1944, in San Jose, CA; son of Herman Hoeft (a commercial banker) and Lutha (a homemaker; maiden name, Rossi) Boschken; married Irene Hartung (an educational administrator),

August 28, 1966; children: Steven F., David Rossi. *Ethnicity:* "White." *Education:* University of California, Berkeley, B.S., 1966, M.B.A., 1968; University of Washington, Seattle, Ph.D., 1972. *Hobbies and other interests:* Winemaking, skiing.

ADDRESSES: Office—Department of Organization and Management, San Jose State University, San Jose, CA 95192-0070. *E-mail*—boschken_h@cob.sjsu.edu.

CAREER: Ford Motor Co., Dearborn, MI, strategic financial analyst for product development group, 1967-69; San Diego State University, San Diego, CA, assistant professor of management, 1973-77; University of Southern California, Los Angeles, assistant professor of policy, planning, and development, 1977-81; University of California, Berkeley, visiting professor at Haas School of Business, 1981-82; San Jose State University, San Jose, CA, professor of organization and management, 1982—. University of New Brunswick, holder of Fulbright New Brunswick Distinguished Chair in Property Studies, 2000-01. Consultant to Vail Resorts, Scholastic Corp., and governments of Canada, Sweden, and South Africa.

MEMBER: American Political Science Association, American Society for Public Administration, Academy of Management.

AWARDS, HONORS: Federal sea grant, Department of Commerce, 1979-81; senior Fulbright scholar at University of Umea, 1983; Jeffrey Pressman Award for best article, *Policy Studies Review,* 1986, for "Public Enterprise, Economic Development, and the Impact of Environmental Regulation: The Experience of American Seaports on the Pacific Rim"; Charles H. Levine Award, Public Sector, Academy of Management, 1988; Herbert Kaufman Award, American Political Science Association, 1990, for "Analyzing Performance Skewness in Public Agencies: The Case of Urban Mass Transit"; Best Book of the Year, Public Sector, Academy of Management, 2002, for *Social Class, Politics, and Urban Markets: The Makings of Bias in Policy Outcomes;* grants from National Science Foundation, National Oceanic and Atmospheric Administration federal sea grant program, California Lottery Fund for University Research, American Political Science Association, Lincoln Foundation, and California Department of Real Estate.

WRITINGS:

Corporate Power and the Mismarketing of Urban Development, Praeger (New York, NY), 1974.

Port Authorities as Public Enterprises: Organizational Adjustment to Conflicting Demands, NOAA Sea Grant Program/University of Southern California (Los Angeles, CA), 1982.

Land Use Conflicts: Organizational Design and Resource Management, University of Illinois Press (Champaign, IL), 1982.

Strategic Design and Organizational Change: Pacific Rim Seaports in Transition, University of Alabama Press (University, AL), 1988.

Social Class, Politics, and Urban Markets: The Makings of Bias in Policy Outcomes, Stanford University Press (Stanford, CA), 2002.

Contributor to books, including *The Breakdown of Class Politics: A Debate on Post-Industrial Stratification,* edited by Terry N. Clark and Seymour Martin Lipset, Johns Hopkins University Press (Baltimore, MD), 2001; and *Strategic Management,* 6th edition, edited by Charles Hill and Gareth Jones, Houghton-Mifflin (Boston, MA), 2003. Contributor to academic journals, including *Administration and Society, Social Science Quarterly, Urban Affairs Review, Urban Studies, Journal of Public Administration Research and Theory, Public Works Management and Policy, Public Administration Review, Academy of Mangement Review, Journal of Management, Coastal Zone Management Journal,* and *Journal of Leisure Research.* Associate editor, *Political Research Quarterly,* 1978-82; editor, *Intermodal Fare,* 1994-98.

WORK IN PROGRESS: Impacts of the American Upper Middle Class and Government Structure on Global-City Development.

SIDELIGHTS: Herman L. Boschken told *CA:* "My writing has always been attendant to my deep interest in public-policy research. I write to articulate the complex concepts that I work with and to share the important and often provocative findings that I discover in the social sciences. Although my focus is specialized in urban affairs, transportation, and the environment, I direct my writings toward a broader audience—one that can see the larger practical implications of policy outcomes on society.

"Most writers are embedded in a small community of intellectuals sharing some common interests. Over the past thirty years, there have been several of these which have provided inspiration, support, and critical review. Early on, my policy focus was on land use and environmental policy. In those days, there was a small but geographically spread community that was interested in investigating environmental policymaking from the standpoint of American federalism and intergovernmental relations. My writing in this field resulted in several refereed articles and two books, *Land Use Conflicts: Organizational Design and Resource Management* and *Corporate Power and the Mismarketing of Urban Development.* Another community which I was part of in the 1980s jelled around the emergence of global transportation and the 'container revolution.' The nexus of this new inter-modal transportation system was in the Pacific Rim and facilitated the globalization of trade between Asia and the United States. Being a Californian from birth, I was particularly well-situated to appreciate the new developments which ultimately spawned Silicon Valley growth and the spreading of globalization across the country from its trans-Pacific origins. Ultimately, my research led me to publish several more articles and a book called *Strategic Design and Organizational Change: Pacific Rim Seaports in Transition.*

"My most recent research and writing began about 1990 and evolved around a community of scholars interested in the causes of bias in urban policy outcomes. For years, the literature was only interested in measuring policy performance from a single perspective, usually regarding whether outcomes were efficient or alternatively whether they were effectively delivered. But growing evidence suggested that in comparing public agencies, the impact of their policy-making was being skewed to benefit one 'public' at the expense of another. Bias varied from agency to agency, but the skewing of outcomes to favor certain interests over others was not well researched. Having enormous implications for equality and accountability, the subject piqued my interest. I organized an effort to evaluate social science literature to see what best explained the causes of bias in policy outcomes. What I found amazed a lot of people: the single most important factor implicated in the bias was social class and not the usual suspects of active politics, wealth and poverty, or the structure of the government. Specifically, the American upper-middle class, although a small proportion of the population, had come to be disproportionately represented, not by active

civic engagement, but by a symbolic icon or genre which influenced policymakers through what Clarence Stone calls 'systemic power.' With the collaboration of yet another small community of scholars, the research led to nearly a dozen refereed articles over the decade and the book *Social Class, Politics, and Urban Markets: The Makings of Bias in Policy Outcomes.*

"This work is leading me down a new path which looks at the causes that distinguish American global cities from their non-global counterparts. The major focus carries forward an interest in the upper-middle class genre in determining which cities become global, but it also will look at several other factors as well. The research promises to be important, because global cities appear to be emerging as city states, potentially replacing national governments (including that of the United States) in their power to provide for peace and security in a world of haves and have-nots. A concept article was published in the *Urban Affairs Review* in July, 2003."

BIOGRAPHICAL AND CRITICAL SOURCES:

PERIODICALS

American Planning Association Journal, winter, 1983, review of *Land Use Conflicts: Organizational Design and Resource Management.*

Annals of Regional Science, October, 1975, review of *Corporate Power and the Mismarketing of Urban Development.*

Journal of Economic Literature, March, 1975, review of *Corporate Power and the Mismarketing of Urban Development.*

Real Estate Review, winter, 1976, review of *Corporate Power and the Mismarketing of Urban Development.*

*   *   *

BOSWORTH, Sheila 1950-

PERSONAL: Born 1950, in New Orleans, LA; married; children: Allison, Charlotte Jane. *Education:* Sophie Newcomb College, Tulane University, B.A. *Hobbies and other interests:* Reading.

ADDRESSES: Home—Covington, LA. *Agent*—c/o Author Mail, Louisiana State University Press, P.O. Box 25053, Baton Rouge, LA 70894-5053.

CAREER: Writer.

WRITINGS:

Almost Innocent (novel), Simon and Schuster (New York, NY), 1984.
Slow Poison (novel), Knopf (New York, NY), 1992.

Contributor to *A World Unsuspected: Portraits of Southern Childhood,* Center for Documentary Photography/Duke University (Chapel Hill, NC), 1987.

SIDELIGHTS: Southern writer Sheila Bosworth writes novels set in her native territory of Louisiana. The 1984 *Almost Innocent* is a tale of a life-long love affair and uses Bosworth's hometowns—New Orleans and Covington, Louisiana—as settings. In her 1992 *Slow Poison,* Bosworth once again returns to New Orleans for a story of three sisters during the 1950s and 1960s. A contributor for *Contemporary Southern Writers* noted that both novels "create a world so enchanting that it is all the more heartbreaking when things go dreadfully wrong."

In *Almost Innocent* Constance Alexander elopes with her suitor, Rand Calvert, despite the protests of her judge father. Rand, a painter and liberal, is not the ideal of a southern gentleman that Judge Alexander had in mind for his daughter. The story of the long and unlikely love between Constance and Rand is narrated by their love child, Clay-Lee Calvert. As D. G. Myers noted in the *New York Times Book Review,* "she watches passion turn into need and then into worldly desire or into pity and then helplessness." Myer found this debut novel "graceful and understated," and wrote that Bosworth "writes with quiet assurance."

With *Slow Poison* Bosworth presents a "bitter-sweet episodic novel," according to a reviewer for *Publishers Weekly,* that "pierces Southern manners and mores with fierce tenderness." Writer Rory Cade is called back home to Covington, Louisiana, from her New York book tour with news that someone close to her is dying. Accompanying her on the journey is former lover and now famous journalist Johnny Killelea, who induces Rory to tell the turbulent story of her exotic family on the equally turbulent flight back to Louisiana. As *Time* critic Emily Mitchell noted, "the slow poison of the title is booze; it is also the ecstasy of love." The Cade family—three sisters and a father—has much of both in its history, and Rory recounts all of these tales as the flight progresses, and it is her voice that carries the novel, a sometimes risky technique. Jonathan Yardley, writing in the *Washington Post,* noted that "part of the risk is that Bosworth relies on little more than the strength of her own voice and intelligence to bring the reader to the tale and keep him there." For Yardley, however, reader patience "will be rewarded" with a "cast of characters that is interesting and appealing as a whole—as, that is, a family—and as discrete individuals."

Not all reviewers were equally charmed by this Southern atmosphere. Gene Lyons, for example, complained in *Entertainment Weekly* of the "hyperbolic Southern swamps" of some of the writing, and that "generically speaking, *Slow Poison* belongs to the Scamps & Tramps school of Southern fiction." Lyons further noted that though Bosworth has "a vivid style and an emotional intensity that often make up for her sins," still the novel "reads at times like satire, at other times like a Harlequin romance turned sour."

Other reviewers praised *Slow Poison* more highly. Mitchell felt that Bosworth "evokes her home state and its people with elegiac grace and gusts of humor," and that the author "measures out life's sorrow in equal proportion to its sweetness." Drawing parallels to the work of Southern writer Walker Percy, who also hailed from Covington, Louisiana, *Los Angeles Times Book Review* contributor Winston Groom observed that Bosworth "appears ready to take up the mantle of [Percy] . . . himself." Groom further noted that Bosworth "does a splendid job of irradiating the murky truths of an old southern family in a cautionary tale of love, hate, pathos and redemption that would make an old master like Percy pretty proud."

BIOGRAPHICAL AND CRITICAL SOURCES:

BOOKS

Contemporary Southern Writers, St. James Press (Detroit, MI), 1999.

PERIODICALS

Entertainment Weekly, April 17, 1992, Gene Lyons, review of *Slow Poison,* p. 52.
Los Angeles Times Book Review, March 15, 1992, Winston Groom, review of *Slow Poison,* p. 2.
New Orleans Magazine, August, 1995, "Persona: Sheila Bosworth," p. 15.
New York Times Book Review, December 30, 1984, D. G. Myers, review of *Almost Innocent,* p. 16.
Publishers Weekly, January 27, 1992, review of *Slow Poison,* p. 89.
Time, March 23, 1992, Emily Mitchell, review of *Slow Poison,* p. 67.
Washington Post, February 26, 1992, Jonathan Yardley, review of *Slow Poison,* p. C2.

ONLINE

Louisiana State University Press Web site, http://www.lsu.edu/ (November 3, 2004), "Sheila Bosworth."*

* * *

BOUDELANG, Bob
 See PELL, Ed(ward)

* * *

BREINER, Laurence A.

PERSONAL: Male. *Education:* Boston College, B.A.; Yale University, M.Phil., Ph.D.

ADDRESSES: Office—Department of English, Boston University, 236 Bay State Rd., Boston, MA 02215. *E-mail*—lbrei@bu.edu.

CAREER: Boston University, Boston, MA, professor of English and member of African-American studies faculty.

WRITINGS:

An Introduction to West Indian Poetry, Cambridge University Press (New York, NY), 1998.
Orality and Decolonization in West Indian Poetry: The Chemistry of Presence, Heinemann (Portsmouth, NH), 2005).

Contributor to books, including *The Art of Derek Walcott,* 1991; *Dictionary of Literary Biography,* Volume 125: *Twentieth-Century Caribbean and Black African Authors, Second Series,* 1993; *West Indian Literature,* 1995; and *Communities of the Air,* 2003. Contributor of scholarly works to periodicals, including *Journal of Commonwealth Studies, Journal of West Indian Literature, Modern Fiction Studies, Ariel, Isis,* and *Modern Language Quarterly;* contributor of poetry to *Agni, Paris Review,* and *Partisan Review;* reviewer for and contributor to periodicals, including *Commonweal.*

WORK IN PROGRESS: Orality and Decolonization in West Indian Poetry: The Chemistry of Presence.

SIDELIGHTS: Although the West Indian novel has prompted more studies than the poetry of the region, Laurence A. Breiner focuses more attention to the latter with his *An Introduction to West Indian Poetry.* The first chapter of the work focuses on role of the the writer in society, and Breiner notes the importance of local journals, poetry clubs, and scholarly organizations and conferences to West Indian poets and readers. He studies the cultural and geographic origins of various poets, including Edward Kamau Brathwaite, Derek Walcott, Jean Binta Breeze, Claude McKay, Michael Smith, and Linton Kwesi Johnson.

Keith Alan Sprouse, writing in *World Literature Today,* noted that in his book Breiner "situates the (anglophone) West Indies within the broader context of the hispanophone and francophone Caribbean, offering short sections on Afro-Cubanism, Negritude, and Haitian Indigenism, as well as some helpful allusions to U.S. African American writing of the period." Breiner establishes the relationship of West Indian poetry with that of Europe, Africa, and America and provides an analysis of how history from colonialism and resistance to decolonization are documented in poetry over time. A contributor to *Modern Language Studies* pointed out that one of the book's strengths "is the historical and social context of poetry in English written in the Caribbean."

BIOGRAPHICAL AND CRITICAL SOURCES:

PERIODICALS

Ariel, October, 1999, Stella Algoo-Baksh, review of *An Introduction to West Indian Poetry,* p. 157.

Choice, April, 1999, A. L. McLeod, review of *An Introduction to West Indian Poetry,* p. 1455.

Forum for Modern Language Studies, January, 2001, review of *An Introduction to West Indian Poetry,* p. 93.

World Literature Today, summer, 1999, Keith Alan Sprouse, review of *An Introduction to West Indian Poetry,* p. 577.

*   *   *

BRENNAN, Matthew
   See BATEMAN, Robert L.

*   *   *

BRESKIN, David

PERSONAL: Male.

ADDRESSES: Home—1061 Francisco St., San Francisco, CA 94109-1126.

CAREER: Music producer and freelance writer.

WRITINGS:

(With Cheryl McCall and Roger Hilburn) *We Are the World,* Perigee Books (New York, NY), 1985.
The Real Life Diary of a Boomtown Girl (novel), Viking (New York, NY), 1989.
Inner Views: Filmmakers in Conversation, Faber & Faber (Boston, MA), 1992, expanded edition, Da Capo Press (Cambridge, MA), 1997.
Fresh Kills (poetry), Cleveland State University Poetry Center (Cleveland, OH), 1997.

Contributor to periodicals, including *Rolling Stone, Esquire, Gentleman's Quarterly, New Yorker, TriQuarterly, Paris Review, Boulevard, Nimrod,* and *Salmagundi.*

SIDELIGHTS: Music producer and freelance writer David Breskin draws on his background in entertainment in his writings. His first book, *We Are the World,*

a collaborative effort with Cheryl McCall and Roger Hilburn, is about the singers and musicians who put together and performed the title song for the charitable cause of feeding the world's hungry. Written by Michael Jackson and Lionel Richie and produced by Quincy Jones, the song was also made a reality with the help of Breskin, who was involved in its production. *We Are the World* includes photographs and sheet music from the song and contains "all the nitty gritty" of how it was produced, according to a *People* contributor.

Breskin draws on his work for *Rolling Stone* in his collection of interviews published as *Inner Views: Filmmakers in Conversation.* Some of the conversations here include Francis Ford Coppola talking about *The Godfather Part III,* Oliver Stone on *JFK,* and Spike Lee analyzing *Do the Right Thing,* among many more movie director and producer heavyweights. Reviewing *Inner Views* for *Voice Literary Supplement,* Katherine Dieckmann noted an absence of female filmmakers, yet found Breskin's interviews to be "elegant, thorough, and dogged." Sybil Steinberg, writing in *Publishers Weekly,* felt some of Breskin's remarks to be "good," though "some of his critical judgments are questionable."

In addition to his nonfiction, Breskin has written a novel and a book of poetry. His novel, *The Real Life Diary of a Boomtown Girl,* which is set in Gillette, Wyoming, during the 1980s, "evokes" the "saloons, cocaine snorting, hot tubs, waterbeds, [and] rock 'n' roll dances" of the American West of the time, according to Steinberg in another *Publishers Weekly* review. The central character is nineteen-year-old Randi Bruce, who works in the oil fields and strip mines where the ratio of men to women is six to one. Prospering in the high-paying employment market, Randi keeps a diary that records her lusty lifestyle and progression of jobs that leads to a spot on the "first all-women blasting team in the country." The team is dubbed the "Boom-Boom Girls." While working one of her coal-moving jobs, Randi meets Derek Harper, a nice guy from North Dakota; they marry, but problems soon develop. Randi is also troubled by her parents' divorce and the fact that her sister is seeing a drug dealer. On top of it all, Randi becomes injured homebound, causing further strains on her marriage. A *Kirkus Reviews* critic complained that Randi is an "inarticulate narrator" who tries "the reader's patience." On the other hand, *Booklist* contributor Margaret Flanagan called the novel a "candid cultural chronicle of the modern American west."

BIOGRAPHICAL AND CRITICAL SOURCES:

PERIODICALS

Booklist, September 15, 1989, Margaret Flanagan, review of *The Real Life Diary of a Boomtown Girl,* p. 143.

Kirkus Reviews, August 1, 1989, review of *The Real Life Diary of a Boomtown Girl,* p. 1088.

People, May 6, 1985, review of *We Are the World,* p. 20.

Publishers Weekly, August 11, 1989, review of *The Real Life Diary of a Boomtown Girl,* p. 442; October 5, 1992, Sybil Steinberg, review of *Inner Views: Filmmakers in Conversation,* p. 65.

Voice Literary Supplement, February, 1993, Katherine Dieckmann, "Fame," p. 31.*

*   *   *

BRIGGS, Shirley Ann 1918-2004

OBITUARY NOTICE— See index for *CA* sketch: Born May 12, 1918, in Iowa City, IA; died of cardio-pulmonary failure November 11, 2004, in Derwood, MD. Naturalist, illustrator, and author. Briggs was an artist who became involved in nature conservation and was the former executive director of the Rachel Carson Council, which educates people about pesticides and other potentially hazardous chemicals. Studying art at the University of Iowa, where one of her professors was the famous "American Gothic" painter Grant Wood, she took a B.A. in 1939, followed by a master's degree in sculpture in 1940. After teaching art at North Dakota State College for two years and working as an illustrator for Glenn Martin Co. for another two years, she was hired by the U.S. Fish and Wildlife Service. Here she met Carson, the environmentalist famous for writing *Silent Spring,* and Briggs became involved in illustrating nature scenes. From 1948 until 1954 she was chief of graphics for the Bureau of Reclamation of the Department of the Interior, and she then worked as a painter for the Smithsonian Institute for a year and as a diorama artist for the National Park Service for another year. From 1947 until 1969 she was also the editor of *Atlantic Naturalist* magazine. Briggs taught natural history for the U.S. Department of Agriculture in the early 1960s, and around this time helped Carson research her famous book. After Carson died from cancer in 1964, Briggs helped found the Rachel Carson Council. Working with the council, she coauthored *Basic Guide to Pesticides* (1992), which won the Rachel Carson Award from the Environmental Protection Agency. A longtime member of the Audubon Society, Briggs was often involved in bird-counting surveys; she also edited and illustrated *The Trumpeter Swan* (1960) and *Landscaping for Birds* (1973), as well as illustrating such nature titles as *The Wonders of Seeds* (1956) and *Insects and Plants* (1963). Later in life Briggs was honored with several awards for her many accomplishments, including the Robert van den Bosch award and medal from the University of California at Berkeley in 1993 and the Distinguished Alumni Achievement award from the University of Iowa in 1995.

OBITUARIES AND OTHER SOURCES:

PERIODICALS

Washington Post, November 16, 2004, p. B7.

ONLINE

Rachel Carson Council Web site, http://members.aol.com/rccouncil/ (January 20, 2005).

*   *   *

BROCK, Rose
See HANSEN, Joseph

*   *   *

BROWN, (William) Larry 1951-2004

OBITUARY NOTICE— See index for *CA* sketch: Born July 9, 1951, in Oxford, MS; died of heart failure November 24, 2004, in Yocona, MS. Fireman and author. Brown was best known for his short stories and novels that often featured characters living deeply troubled lives in the American South. Not a bookish type, Brown struggled to pass his English class and complete high school. Graduating in 1969, he served in the U.S. Marines for two years and then worked a variety of odd jobs before finding work as a firefighter for the Oxford Fire Department in 1973. He eventually rose to the rank of captain in 1986, leaving four years later when he gained enough success as an author to pursue writing full time. A writer in the Southern tradition, Brown was greatly influenced by such authors as William Faulkner and Flannery O'Connor. Starting with short stories, he slowly taught himself writing skills through trial, error, and many rejection letters. Eventually, he began publishing in magazines, and by the late 1980s one of his stories caught the attention of an Algonquin Books editor. This led to his first short-story collection, *Facing the Music* (1987), which won an award from the Mississippi Institute of Arts and Letters in 1990. Other works followed, including the novels *Dirty Work* (1989), *Father and Son* (1996), and *The Rabbit Factory* (2003), as well as the memoir *Billy Ray's Farm* (2001). The 1990 story collection *Big Bad Love* was also adapted as a 2002 film staring Debra Winger.

OBITUARIES AND OTHER SOURCES:

BOOKS

Brown, Larry, *On Fire,* Algonquin Books (Chapel Hill, NC), 1994.
Brown, Larry, *Billy Ray's Farm,* Algonquin Books (Chapel Hill, NC), 2001.

PERIODICALS

Chicago Tribune, November 26, 2004, section 3, p. 7.
New York Times, November 26, 2004, p. C10.
Times (London, England), January 5, 2005, p. 53.
Washington Post, November 25, 2004, p. B6.

*   *   *

BROWNLEE, Donald E(ugene) 1943-

PERSONAL: Born December 21, 1943, in Las Vegas, NV; son of Donald Eugene and Geraldine Florence (Stephen) Brownlee; married Paula Szkody. *Education:* University of California—Berkeley, B.S., 1965; University of Washington, Ph.D., 1970.

ADDRESSES: Office—Department of Astronomy, University of Washington, P.O. Box 35158, Seattle, WA 98195-0001. *E-mail*—brownlee@bluemoon.astro.washington.edu.

CAREER: Astronomer and educator. University of Washington, Seattle, associate professor of astronomy, 1970-77; California Institute of Technology, Pasadena, associate professor of geochemistry, 1977-82; University of Washington, Seattle, professor of astronomy, 1989—. Consultant to National Aeronautics and Space Administration (NASA), 1976—; Enrico Fermi Institute, University of Chicago, distinguished visiting professor.

MEMBER: American Association for the Advancement of Science, International Astronomical Union, American Astronomical Association, Meteoritical Society.

AWARDS, HONORS: National Aeronautic and Space Administration grant, 1975; J. Lawrence Smith medal, National Academy of Sciences, 1994; Leonard Medal, Meteoritical Society.

WRITINGS:

(With Peter Douglas Ward) *Rare Earth: Why Complex Life Is Uncommon in the Universe,* Copernicus (New York, NY), 2000.
(With Peter Douglas Ward) *The Life and Death of Planet Earth: How the New Science of Astrobiology Charts the Ultimate Fate of Our World,* Times Books (New York, NY), 2003.

Contributor to scientific journals; *Meteorites,* associate editor; *Microbeam Analysis Journal,* member of editorial advisory board.

SIDELIGHTS: Donald E. Brownlee is a professor of astronomy who specializes in the study of extraterrestrial samples, comets, and the early solar system. He has served as the principal investigator of the National Aeronautic and Space Administration's Stardust mission, the purpose of which is to collect comet samples and return them to earth.

Brownlee collaborated with Peter Douglas Ward in the writing of *Rare Earth: Why Complex Life Is Uncommon in the Universe,* in which the co-authors put forth the theory that while microbial life may exist throughout the universe, only Earth possesses the conditions necessary for the development of complex life. Their "Rare Earth Hypothesis" is "the paradox that life may be nearly everywhere but complex life almost nowhere." They also predict the future of Earth, taking into account the effects of another ice age, global warming, and other trends that they feel will ultimately return Earth to a barren state. An *Economist* reviewer felt that "this carefully reasoned book makes a strong case for undoing at least some of the work of Copernicus, by accepting that the earth is special after all. It also makes the cosmos seem an even more vast and lonely place."

Brownlee and Ward write of the factors that have enabled life to flourish on Earth, including the fact that we are the right distance from our sun, enjoy a stable environment, and are not threatened by astronomical phenomena that could pour radiation down on our planet. They note that we have recently realized the effect Jupiter has in protecting Earth, pulling space debris into its atmosphere, so that it never reaches the smaller planet. The geology of Earth is also a factor: a collection of microenvironments, from lakes to deserts, in which a variety of animal life are able to survive. They list ten historical incidents for potential extinction that have threatened our planet and note that some forms of life managed to survive each, adding that there are no guarantees such luck will hold.

Skeptical Inquirer contributor Mark Wolverton wrote that "frankly, for those of us who have dreamed of great interstellar civilizations and encounters with other intelligences, it's all pretty depressing. But *Rare Earth* isn't trying to maliciously spoil our party. It's just trying to bring our expectations in line with what increasingly seems to be the way things are. Brownlee and Ward argue that simple life may be even more common in the universe than is currently believed. But a galaxy brimming with intelligent life is very unlikely. They may be out there, somewhere; if not in this galaxy, perhaps others."

Lawrence Krauss reviewed *Rare Earth* for *Physics Today Online*, writing that the authors "summarize clearly the developments over the past few decades that reveal the complexity of the evolution of advanced life forms on earth. However, demonstrating the complexity of a process is different from demonstrating that the end result is rare. If anything, Ward and Brownlee show clearly how much remains to be learned in the area NASA has named astrobiology—a combination of geology, paleontology, astronomy, and biology that pertains to understanding the evolution of life and its signatures." Krauss went on to note that the book "provides a great collection of diverse information brought together in one place and is very up-to-date." *American Science* reviewer Tim Tokaryk called *Rare Earth* "a stellar example of clear writing on a complex issue. For to ask 'What is life?' or about the astronomical and geological forces that helped or hindered life's origin requires patience with the intended audience."

In *The Life and Death of Planet Earth: How the New Science of Astrobiology Charts the Ultimate Fate of Our World* Brownlee and Ward restate their thesis from *Rare Earth* and continue to predict a future for Earth that ends in its destruction. The authors note that we are experiencing a brief interlude (11,000 years) between ice ages. Eventually, glaciers will again cover much of the planet, driving humans to the equator and spurring efforts to colonize in space. They predict that in a quarter of a billion years, the continents will come together to form a single desert-like continent and that the greenhouse effect will destroy, first, green plants, then most animal life. Several billion years later, earth would be incinerated by an expanding sun. A *Kirkus Reviews* critic called the book "far from cheerful, but fascinating," and *Booklist* contributor Gilbert Taylor wrote: "creative but scientifically grounded, the authors' prognostication of the ultimate environmental disaster is morbidly enthralling."

BIOGRAPHICAL AND CRITICAL SOURCES:

PERIODICALS

American Scientist, March, 2000, Tim Tokaryk, review of *Rare Earth: Why Complex Life Is Uncommon in the Universe,* p. 168.

Astronomy, August, 2000, Robert Naeye, review of *Rare Earth,* p. 105.

Booklist, December 15, 2002, Gilbert Taylor, review of *The Life and Death of Planet Earth: How the New Science of Astrobiology Charts the Ultimate Fate of Our World,* p. 715.

Economist, May 13, 2000, review of *Rare Earth,* p. 5.

Futurist, November-December, 2003, review of *The Life and Death of Planet Earth,* p. 61.

Kirkus Reviews, November 15, 2002, review of *The Life and Death of Planet Earth,* p. 1683.

Library Journal, November 15, 1999, Gloria Maxwell, review of *Rare Earth,* p. 96.

Nature, April 17, 2003, Norman H. Sleep, review of *The Life and Death of Planet Earth,* p. 663.

New Scientist, February 15, 2003, David Hughes, review of *The Life and Death of Planet Earth,* p. 50.

Perspectives in Biology and Medicine, winter, 2001, James F. Kasting, review of *Rare Earth,* p. 117.

Publishers Weekly, November 18, 2002, review of *The Life and Death of Planet Earth,* p. 53.

R & D, August, 2000, review of *Rare Earth,* p. 11.

Science, April 28, 2000, Christopher P. McKay, review of *Rare Earth,* p. 625; February 15, 2003, review of *The Life and Death of Planet Earth,* p. 111.

Skeptical Inquirer, November, 2000, Mark Wolverton, review of *Rare Earth,* p. 51.

ONLINE

Donald Brownlee Home Page, http://www.astro. washington.edu/brownlee (March 19, 2004).

Physics Today Online, http://www.aip.org/ (April 28, 2003), Lawrence Krauss, review of *Rare Earth.*

Pittsburgh Post-Gazette Online, http://www.post-gazette.com/ (January 19, 2003), Fred Bortz, review of *The Life and Death of Planet Earth.**

*   *   *

BURSTEIN, Michael A. 1970-

PERSONAL: Born 1970, in New York, NY; married, June 18, 1995; wife's name Nomi. *Education:* Harvard College, A.B. (physics), 1991; Boston University, M.A. (physics), 1993.

ADDRESSES: Home—Brookline, MA. *Office*—Public Library of Brookline, 361 Washington Street, Brookline, MA 02445. *E-mail*—librarytrustee@ brookline.mec.edu.

CAREER: Science-fiction writer and educator. Berkeley Carroll School, New York, NY, physics teacher, 1993-95; Cambridge School of Weston, Weston, MA, teacher, 1995-2001; Rashi School, Newton, MA, science coordinator and teacher, 2001—. Brookline Public Library, Brookline, MA, member of board of trustees. Worked as assistant coordinator of "Media in Transition" project and science-fiction lecture series, Massachusetts Institute of Technology (MIT), Cambridge.

MEMBER: Science Fiction and Fantasy Writers of America (secretary, 1998-2000), Lewis Carroll Society of North America, Horror Writers Association, New England Science Fiction Association (vice president, 1998-2000), American Association of Physics Teachers.

AWARDS, HONORS: Science Fiction Chronicle Reader Award, and Analytical Laboratory Award for best short story, *Analog,* both 1995, both for "TeleAbsence"; Reader Appreciation Award for best new writer, *Science Fiction Weekly,* 1996; John Campbell Award for best new writer, 1997; several Hugo Award nominations for stories; Nebula Award nomination and Sturgeon Award nomination, both for *Reality Check;* Nebula Award nomination for "Kaddish for the Last Survivor."

WRITINGS:

E-BOOKS

TeleAbsence, Fictionwise, 1995.

The Spider in the Hairdo, Fictionwise, 1997.

Cosmic Corkscrew, Fictionwise, 1998.

In Space, No One Can Hear, Fictionwise, 1998.

Hunger, Fictionwise, 1998.

(With Charles Ardai) *Nor through Inaction,* Fictionwise, 1998.

Vanishing Tears, Fictionwise, 1999.

The Quantum Teleporter, Fictionwise, 2000.

Escape Horizon, Fictionwise, 2000.

(With Lawrence D. Weinberg) *Debunking the Faith Healer,* Fictionwise, 2000.

Kaddish for the Last Survivor, Fictionwise, 2000.

Spaceships, Fictionwise, 2001.

The Great Miracle, Fictionwise, 2001.

The Cold Calculations, Fictionwise, 2001.

(With Shane Toutellotte) *Bug Out!,* Fictionwise, 2001.

In Her Image, Fictionwise, 2002.

(With Mike Resnick) *Reflections in Black Granite,* Fictionwise, 2002.

(With Jenny Bourne) *DSL: A Wiley Tech Brief,* Fictionwise, 2002.
Paying It Forward, Fictionwise, 2003.

"BROKEN SYMMETRY" SERIES; E-BOOKS

Broken Symmetry, Fictionwise, 1997.
Absent Friends, Fictionwise, 1998.
Reality Check, Fictionwise, 1999.

"PROBABILITY ZERO" SERIES; E-BOOKS

The Cure, Fictionwise, 1997.
Whose Millennium?, Fictionwise, 2000.
(With Joseph J. Lazzaro) *The Turing Testers,* Fictionwise, 2000.

Contributor of science fiction and nonfiction to periodicals, including *Analog, Absolute Magnitude, Science Fiction Weekly,* and *Mimosa.* Contributor to anthologies, including *Worldcon Guest of Honor Book* and *I, Alien,* edited by Mike Resnick, DAW, in press.

SIDELIGHTS: From the time his first published story, "TeleAbsence," was nominated for a Hugo Award, Michael A. Burstein has been a prominent fixture in the world of science fiction. He is known for drawing on his knowledge of science and physics, subjects he has taught in a number of secondary schools, which provides his stories with a verisimilitude that work in the genre often lacks. At the same time, in his writings Burstein questions the everyday consequences future technology or future discoveries might have on ordinary people. In "TeleAbsence," for instance, written at the beginning of the Internet explosion, a poor boy named Tony is forced to sneak into a private school and steal a pair of virtual reality glasses in order to enjoy the revolutionary educational opportunities that the middle-class students take for granted. As Burstein told *Boston Globe* correspondent Jennifer Peck, "I try to find something I really care about and often it's a social issue." Lucy Cohen Schmeidler, writing in *CyberCozen,* called "TeleAbsence" a "feel-good story." In his "Broken Symmetry" series, Burstein builds a trilogy around the superconducting supercollider, a massive, real-world project on hiatus because of a lack of congressional funding. When the abandoned structure starts "hiccupping," an explosion

creates a portal to another universe in which everyone has a double, and Burstein explores the emotional impact of this universe on those who seek the doubles of their lost loved ones. In addition to his own work, Burstein has nurtured future sci-fi writers through his work as a high school science and writing teacher and his active involvement with science fiction associations.

BIOGRAPHICAL AND CRITICAL SOURCES:

PERIODICALS

Analog, February, 1997, Jay Kay Klein, "Michael A. Burstein," p. 40.
Boston Globe, September 27, 1998, Jennifer Peck, "He Wonders and Then Writes: Teacher Has Burst onto Sci-Fi Scene."
CyberCozen, 1996, Lucy Cohen Schmeidler, "Michael Burstein: A Rising Star."
Jewish Advocate, May 21-28, 1999, Daniel M. Kimmel, "In the Tradition of Asimov: Michael Burstein."

ONLINE

Cybling.com, http://www.cybling.com/ (August 27, 2004), interview with Burstein.
Michael A. Burstein Home Page, http://www.mabfan.com (August 27, 2004).*

*   *   *

BURTON, Georganne B.

PERSONAL: Born in New York, NY; daughter of George and Anne (a homemaker; maiden name, Davies) Butler; married Orville Vernon Burton (an historian and educator); children: Joanna, Maya Burton Gouliard, Morgan Johnston, Beatrice, Carrah. *Education:* University of Illinois, M.A., 1971. *Politics:* Democrat. *Religion:* Baptist. *Hobbies and other interests:* Fishing, tennis, reading.

ADDRESSES: Home—605 West Washington, Urbana, IL 61801. *E-mail*—georg@ncsa.uiuc.edu.

CAREER: Writer and community activist.

WRITINGS:

(Editor, with Orville Vernon Burton, and coauthor of introduction) *"The Free Flag of Cuba": The Lost Novel of Lucy Pickens,* Louisiana State University Press (Baton Rouge, LA), 2002.

WORK IN PROGRESS: Research for a novel based on an 1850 murder case.

BIOGRAPHICAL AND CRITICAL SOURCES:

PERIODICALS

ANQ, winter, 2004, E. Irene Matthews, review of *"The Free Flag of Cuba": The Lost Novel of Lucy Pickens,* p. 51.

* * *

BUTLER, Linda 1946(?)-

PERSONAL: Born c. 1946.

ADDRESSES: Agent—c/o Author Mail, Stanford University Press, 1450 Page Mill Rd., Palo Alto, CA 94304-1124. *E-mail*—LBphoto@aol.com.

CAREER: Photographer and author. *Exhibitions:* Exhibitions include at Whitney Museum of American Art, Royal Ontario Museum, Yokohama Museum of Art, and Fondazione Querine-Stampalia, Venice, Italy. Work included in collections at Boston Museum of Fine Arts, Cleveland Museum of Art, Corcoran Gallery of Art, Cincinnati Art Museum, and San Francisco Museum of Modern Art.

WRITINGS:

(Photographer) June Sprigg, *Inner Light: The Shaker Legacy,* Knopf (New York, NY), 1985.

(And photographer) *Rural Japan: Radiance of the Ordinary* (essays), foreword by Donald Richie, Smithsonian Institution Press (Washington, DC), 1992.

(Photographer, with others) Delphine Hirasuna, *Presidio Gateways: Views of a National Landmark at San Francisco's Golden Gate,* afterword by Robert G. Kennedy, Chronicle Books (San Francisco, CA), 1994.

(And photographer) *Italy: In the Shadow of Time,* foreword by Naomi Rosenblum, Rizzoli (New York, NY), 1998.

(And photographer) *Yangtze Remembered: The River beneath the Lake,* foreword by Simon Winchester, Stanford University Press (Palo Alto, CA), 2004.

SIDELIGHTS: American photographer and author Linda Butler has published several critically acclaimed volumes of her photographs and essays. In her debut effort, *Inner Light: The Shaker Legacy,* written by June Sprigg, Butler uses her camera to capture the architecture and craftsmanship of various Shaker communities in the United States. (Shakers are members of a sect who live in celibate communities.) For her next two efforts, however, Butler traveled overseas. For her *Rural Japan: Radiance of the Ordinary,* she trekked through the remote Japanese islands of Honshu, Shikoku, and Kyushu to photograph ancient village life amid the encroaching industrialization of modern Japan. Then Butler, who specializes in still-life photography, published her lauded work *Italy: In the Shadow of Time.* "This is one of those exceptional books that will be deeply appreciated now and admired long into the future," *Library Journal* critic Raymond Bial wrote of *Italy,* comparing Butler's work in the book with that of such photographic masters as Ansel Adams. In addition to producing the photographs for each of the three books, Butler has also contributed the text in more recent endeavors.

Inner Light contains fifty-eight photographs depicting items created by Shaker artisans during the religious sect's heyday in the nineteenth century. The Shakers, who form a branch of the English Quakers, built up communities throughout eastern North America that were based on hard work and strict moral laws. Despite gaining some prominence, their numbers drastically declined by the dawn of the twentieth century, and very few members survived into the early twenty-first century. "Today, just two communities remain active," coauthor June Sprigg writes in the book's introduction, "with fewer than a dozen members combined, in Maine and New Hampshire. . . . There are still some buildings where Shakers dwell, rooms warm and full with the business of life. . . . It has been those other rooms, the quiet empty places, that have drawn us in the making of this book."

Butler found her subjects as she traveled to different Shaker communities and museums, including Shaker Village at Canterbury, New Hampshire, Shakertown in South Union, Kentucky, and the Shaker Museum located in Old Chatham, New York. While some of the photographs are of dwellings and larger objects such as a wooden fence or a doorway, many others are of normal, everyday items, including wooden kitchen bowls, milk buckets, brooms, and even gravestones. Butler chose each because they exemplify the Shaker aesthetic and reflect the group's attention to detail. "This is a soothing book. Looking through its pages is like praying," wrote critic Campbell Geeslin in *People*. *Choice* contributor P. D. Thomas called the work a "handsomely produced volume" and praised the photographs as "meticulously composed and carefully printed."

Butler's interest in Japan began in 1967 when, as a college student, she first traveled to that country and learned of its many ancient traditions. She returned to Japan in 1986 and spent three years moving from village to village, capturing what she refers to in *Rural Japan* as the "astonishing resilience" of the ancient cultures she encountered. In addition to the fifty-seven photographs that appear in *Rural Japan,* Butler includes fifteen short essays about her visits and experiences traveling throughout the coastal and mountain villages of the three islands. The photographic subjects include still lifes and landscapes, as well as a few portraits, including one of a seventy-year-old Buddhist nun. In the design of the book, Butler also includes some examples of haiku poetry, a Japanese verse form, to give the work a more authentic feel.

R. K. Dickson, writing in the *Bloomsbury Review,* was struck by what he called the work's "simplicity and grace." A contributor to *Publishers Weekly* called Butler's photographs in *Rural Japan* "exceptionally beautiful" and her text "charming and insightful." A contributor to the *Antioch Review* had a similar opinion, saying that "these beautiful photographs are remarkable in their authenticity."

Italy is a collection of sixty black-and-white photographs, none of which are human portraits. Instead, Butler concentrates on articles she felt had a timeless aura, such as wine bottles, ancient ruins, statues, fountains, and olive trees. She began the project in 1992 when she embarked on an eight-month tour of the ancient country, searching for unique subjects she hoped would capture the "distilled energy of artisans long dead." Many of her photographs come from the cities of Pompeii and Herculaneum, both of which had been destroyed, and subsequently preserved, by a volcanic eruption. The essay Butler contributes describes her adventures as she traveled the country, including the time she had to bribe a guard to photograph and gain access to a men's bathhouse in Pompeii. Critics were impressed with the effort. Calling the work "hauntingly beautiful," *Booklist* writer Ray Olson described Butler's work as "painstaking craftsmanship." "The stark, strong images imply the presence of humanity," wrote Sandra Mardenfeld in the *New York Times Book Review.*

Butler made eight trips to China from 2000 to 2003 to photograph the people, environment, and landscape of 1,500 cities, towns, and villages that disappeared when the Three Gorges Dam was opened in June, 2003, creating a reservoir the size of Lake Superior. Her *Yangtze Remembered: The River beneath the Lake* consists of before-and-after photographs accompanied by her commentary on the one million people who were moved and the new landscape and cities that are now springing up in the wake of the project.

BIOGRAPHICAL AND CRITICAL SOURCES:

PERIODICALS

Antioch Review, fall, 1992, review of *Rural Japan: Radiance of the Ordinary,* p. 781.
Bloomsbury Review, December, 1992, R. K, Dickson, review of *Rural Japan,* p. 18.
Booklist, October 15, 1998, Ray Olson, review of *Italy: In the Shadow of Time,* p. 390.
Choice, December, 1985, P. D. Thomas, review of *Inner Light: The Shaker Legacy,* p. 595; February, 1999, J. A. Day, review of *Italy,* p. 1049.
Kliatt, fall, 1985, Helen W. Coonley, review of *Inner Light,* pp. 44-45.
Library Journal, September 15, 1998, Raymond Bial, review of *Italy,* p. 70.
New York Times Book Review, October 4, 1998, Sandra Mardenfeld, review of *Italy,* p. 22.

People, May 6, 1985, Campbell Geeslin, review of *Inner Light,* p. 16.

Publishers Weekly, April 20, 1992, review of *Rural Japan,* p. 47.*

* * *

BUZZELL, Robert (Dow) 1933-2004

OBITUARY NOTICE— See index for *CA* sketch: Born April 18, 1933, in Lincoln, NE; died of complications from amyotrophic lateral sclerosis (Lou Gehrig's disease) November 6, 2004, in Arlington, VA. Educator, economist, and author. Buzzell was an influential expert on marketing best known for designing the Profit Impact of Marketing Strategies (PIMS) research program at Harvard University. Completing his undergraduate work at George Washington University in 1953, he earned his master's degree at the University of Illinois the next year, and his Ph.D. in business from Ohio State University in 1957. His first teaching job was at Ohio State, and in 1961 he joined the Harvard University School of Business faculty. He remained at Harvard until 1993, serving as executive director of the Marketing Science Institute from 1968 to 1972 and as chair of the marketing faculty from 1972 until 1977, eventually becoming Sebastian S. Kresge Professor of Business Administration. After leaving Harvard, he was a professor of marketing at George Mason University until 1998, and he also lectured at Georgetown University from 1998 until 2000. Always a forward-thinking, practical economist, Buzzell emphasized the importance of measurable business results and the necessity of research and development in large companies that wish to remain competitive, ideas that were a focus of the PIMS and explained in his book *The PIMS Principles: Linking Strategy to Performance* (1987), written with Bradley T. Gale. He also strongly believed in the necessity of businesses taking advantage of new technology. Among his other works are *Marketing: A Contemporary Analysis* (1972), the edited *Marketing in an Electronic Age* (1985), and the cowritten *The Marketing Challenge of Europe 1992* (1991).

OBITUARIES AND OTHER SOURCES:

PERIODICALS

Washington Post, November 11, 2004, p. B7.

ONLINE

Harvard Business School Web site, http://www.hbs. edu/ (November 9, 2004).

* * *

BYNUM, Sarah Shun-lien

PERSONAL: Married. *Education:* Brown University, received degree; Iowa Writers Workshop, University of Iowa, received degree.

ADDRESSES: Home—Brooklyn, NY. *Agent*—Bill Clegg, Burnes & Clegg, Inc., 1133 Broadway, Suite 1020, New York, NY 10010.

CAREER: Writer.

AWARDS, HONORS: Iowa arts fellowship; National Book Award finalist, 2004, for *Madeleine Is Sleeping.*

WRITINGS:

Madeleine Is Sleeping (novel), Harcourt (Orlando, FL), 2004.

Contributor to the anthology *The Best American Short Stories of 2004,* and to the periodicals *Alaska Quarterly Review* and *Georgia Review.*

SIDELIGHTS: Sarah Shun-lien Bynum won a coveted place as a finalist for the 2004 National Book Award for her debut novel, *Madeleine Is Sleeping,* "an allegory of adolescence," according to Heidi Jon Schmidt in *People.* The National Book Foundation, in announcing Bynum's place on the award's short list, described the novel as "part fairy tale, part coming-of-age story . . . [that] follows the real and surreal adventures of a girl from a small French village who falls into an unexpected triangle of desire and love."

Bynum's novel is filled with a cast of exotic characters, including an artist fashioned after the actual French performer Le Petomane, who made music by breaking wind, a woman who sprouts wings, and another who grows viola strings. A graduate of the Iowa Writers Workshop, Bynum explained to David Medaris in *DailyPage.com* that "a few of the characters probably began as a little piece of grit—a feeling of discomfort and anxiety (over fatness, hairiness, disfigurement)—and through heightening and re-imagining these grotesque attributes, I think I hoped to turn that discomfort into the source of something lustrous and remarkable and lovely."

Bynum's novel tells the adventures of Madeleine, who, upon falling into a deep sleep, dreams of joining a gypsy circus and there, as *Library Journal* critic Barbara Hoffert noted, "encounters love in all its manifestations." Bynum creates, as a contributor to *Publishers Weekly* observed, "a perverse revisitation" of Ludwig Bemelman's famous children's books about Madeleine. The same critic felt that Bynum "alternates deftly between reality and illusion" in this "remarkable debut." However, Caroline M. Hallsworth, writing in *Library Journal*, felt that "pervasive darkness and sexuality render the novel anything but light and childlike," and that Bynum's "multilayered story is complex and sometimes disconcerting." A critic for *Kirkus Reviews* similarly found "Madeleine Is Sleeping" to be a "self-consciously exquisite first novel." This reviewer further commented that though "Bynum is undoubtedly gifted with language and well-versed in literary allusion,. . . her first [novel] is almost unreadable and frankly sleep-inducing." A more positive evaluation came from Schmidt, who concluded that the reader will finish Bynum's novel "rediscovering how profound—and profoundly strange—adolescence is." And John Crowley, reviewing the novel in the *Washington Post Book World,* also had praise for Bynum's work, noting that "it's a tribute to

[Bynum's] talent that the lurid and excessive, nearly Gothic tale-telling seems neither crowded nor outrageous but instead delicate, grave and almost evanescent." Crowley further commended the "masterful way [Bynum] has kept her disappearing balls in the air."

BIOGRAPHICAL AND CRITICAL SOURCES:

PERIODICALS

Kirkus Reviews, July 1, 2004, review of *Madeleine Is Sleeping,* p. 589.
Library Journal, May 1, 2004, Barbara Hoffert, review of *Madeleine Is Sleeping,* p. 86; July, 2004, Caroline M. Hallsworth, review of *Madeleine Is Sleeping,* p. 67.
New York Times, October 17, 2004, Edward Wyatt, "New Novels, Big Awards, No Readers," section 4, p. 2.
People, September 20 2004, Heidi Jon Schmidt, review of *Madeleine Is Sleeping,* p. 61.
Publishers Weekly, June 7, 2004, review of *Madeleine Is Sleeping,* p. 29.
Washington Post Book World, October 3, 2004, John Crowley, review of *Madeleine Is Sleeping,* p. 7.

ONLINE

DailyPage.com, http://www.isthmus.com/ (November 3, 2004), David Medaris, "Sarah Shun-lien Bynum" (interview).
National Book Foundation Web site, http://www.nationalbook.org/ (November 3, 2004), "2004 National Book Award Finalist, Sarah Shun-lien Bynum."*

C

CACACI, Joe

PERSONAL: Male.

ADDRESSES: Agent—c/o The Alpern Group, 15645 Royal Oak Road, Encino, CA 91436.

CAREER: Writer, producer, and director. Provincetown Playhouse, producing director; American Premiere Stage, Boston, MA, producing director; East Coast Arts (theater company), New Rochelle, NY, beginning 1983; and Wildcliff Theatre, New Rochelle; directed *Concert Pianist,* Jewish Repertory Theater, New York, NY, 1997. Television series work includes: (creator) *The Trials of Rosie O'Neill,* CBS, 1990-92; (executive consultant) *John Grisham's The Client,* CBS, 1995; (executive producer) *The Hoop Life,* Showtime, 1999; and (executive producer) *The Education of Max Bickford,* CBS, 2001. Television film work includes: (executive producer) *The Bachelor's Baby,* CBS, 1996; (executive producer) *Indefensible: The Truth about Edward Brannigan* (also known as *A Father's Betrayal*), CBS, 1997; and (director) *Stranger in My House* (also known as *Total Stranger*), Lifetime, 1999.

WRITINGS:

TELEVISION MOVIES

Murder in New Hampshire: The Pamela Smart Story, CBS, 1991.
A Woman Scorned: The Betty Broderick Story (also known as *Till Murder Do Us Part*), NBC, 1992.
Her Final Fury: Betty Broderick, the Last Chapter (also known as *Till Murder Do Us Part II*), CBS, 1992.
Not in My Family (also known as *Shattering the Silence*), ABC, 1993.
(From draft) *In the Line of Duty: Hunt for Justice,* NBC, 1995.
The Bachelor's Baby, CBS, 1996.
Indefensible: The Truth about Edward Brannigan (also known as *A Father's Betrayal*), CBS, 1997.
(Story only) *Crime in Connecticut: The Story of Alex Kelly,* CBS, 1999.

TELEVISION EPISODES

L.A. Law, NBC, 1987.
The Trials of Rosie O'Neill, CBS, 1990–92.
John Grisham's The Client, CBS, 1995.
Gun, ABC, 1997.

PLAYS

Self Defense, produce in New Haven, CT, then New York, NY, 1987.
Old Business, produced at New York Shakespeare Festival, 1987.

SIDELIGHTS: Joe Cacaci began his directing career in the theatre—specifically, the Wildcliff Theatre, once a deteriorating mansion in New Rochelle, New York. In 1983, Cacaci, then a budding playwright, turned the building into a showcase for both established and up-and-coming authors. The renovation of the Wildcliff was slow, and the theatre opened in 1986 with *The Empty Room and Other Plays,* a work by writer-in-residence Shel Silverstein. Cacaci's own dramatic output includes the plays *Self Defense* and *Old Business.*

In subsequent years, Cacaci turned to writing television movies. His forte was the "based on" genre, do-cudramas centering on real events. He scripted the stories of Betty Broderick and Pamela Smart, the former the true story of a woman who shot her ex-husband and his second wife. The second installment of Broderick's tale, *Her Final Fury: Betty Broderick, the Last Chapter,* was, according to Ken Tucker of *Entertainment Weekly,* a "tedious courtroom drama"; the first installment was not only considered more dramatic, but also earned higher ratings. Cacaci also had the opportunity to create a series of his own, *The Trials of Rosie O'Neill.* Though the show did not last long, Cacaci established himself in episodic television. He served as executive producer of Showtime's ac-claimed *Hoop Life* before gaining a new assignment in 2001 by taking the creative reins of the CBS series *The Education of Max Bickford* after its creators stepped down.

The Education of Max Bickford, which premiered in October 2001, centers on a middle-aged male profes-sor at an all-female institution. In the series premiere Max confronts a turning point in his life after being passed over for a promotion. "Max realizes that he's an old-fashioned man in a modern world and that something has to change," as a *TV Tome* reviewer put it. "But he'll be damned if it's him."

Although the show boasted two Academy Award win-ners—Richard Dreyfus in the title role and Marcia Gay Harden as his professional foil—audiences rejected the series, which could feature as many as six storylines in a single episode. Some of the criticism was directed at the character of Max, originally portrayed as curmudgeonly, alcoholic, and downright bitter. Max needed a sense of humor, Dreyfus decided, and Cacaci was tapped to revamp the series. "We can get a little more fun out of Max's dilemmas," Cacaci told Kevin Williamson of the *Calgary Sun.* In a Pittsburgh *Post-Gazette* article by Rob Owen, Cacaci elaborated on his idea of streamlining the storylines: "With fewer stories, they each become more complex. You can only serve so many stories in 44 minutes. [The revamp] lets us go further in storytelling, and the audience can actually follow it, which is always a good thing."

Shot in Queens, New York, *The Education of Max Bickford* was one of several shows that made headlines following the terrorist attacks of September 11, 2001. According to a *Los Angeles Times Online* writer, production was suspended as film companies donated lighting trucks, electrical equipment, and other resources to the disaster scene. Accommodating the city under such circumstances was physically and emotionally draining, Cacaci recalled to the *Los Angeles Times Online* journalist, "but, really, that's a small price to pay. . . . When you look at the big picture, it's just a TV show."

Although the more up-beat approach to the series worked for a time, *The Education of Max Bickford* was finally cancelled in June, 2002. Cacaci once again teamed up with Dreyfuss in the 2004 television production of *Cop Shop,* part of the PBS series, *Holly-wood Presents.* As executive producer, he joined David Black, a writer for the popular series *Law & Order,* and Dreyfuss to present two forty-five-minute plays that take a more realistic approach to the lives of policemen. *Fear* and *Blind Date,* the two plays, present a different view of police work and the life of a cop after hours. The original concept of the two teleplays was to imitate a live television production by rehears-ing each story as a play and then shooting it straight through.

BIOGRAPHICAL AND CRITICAL SOURCES:

PERIODICALS

Calgary Sun, February 21, 2002, Kevin Williamson, "No More Mad Max."
Entertainment Weekly, October 30, 1992, Ken Tucker, review of *Her Final Fury: Betty Broderick, the Last Chapter,* p. 72.
Hollywood Reporter, October 23, 2001, Nellie Andre-eva, "'Bickford' Creators Pass the Baton," p. 97; October 6, 2004, Barry Garron, review of *Cop Shop,* p. 11.
New York Times, November 8, 1987, p. H6; January 23, 2997, Lawrence Van Gelder, review of "Con-cert Pianist," p. C18.
Post-Gazette (Pittsburgh, PA), February 23, 2002, Rob Owen, "Max Bickford Lightens up in Hope of Better Grade from Viewers."

ONLINE

Internet Movie Database, http://www.imdb.com/ (November 3, 2004), "Joe Cacaci."

Los Angeles Times Online, http://www.latimes.com/ (September 20, 2001), Meg James and Joseph Menn, "N.Y. Studios Help out by Redirecting Resources."

Tripod.com, http://members.tripod.com/Shel Silverstein/ (April 16, 2002), "The Empty Room and Other Plays."

TVTome.com, http://www.tvtome.com/ (April 16, 2002), "The Education of Max Bickford."*

*   *   *

CAPRIOLO, Paola 1962-

PERSONAL: Born 1962, in Milan, Italy.

ADDRESSES: Home—Milan, Italy. *Agent*—c/o Author Mail, Bompiani, Libreria Ambrosiana, 1, via Santo Clemente, 20122 Milan, Italy.

CAREER: Writer.

AWARDS, HONORS: G. Berto prize, 1988, for *La grande Eulalia;* Rapallo prize, 1991, for *Il nocchiero.*

WRITINGS:

NOVELS, EXCEPT AS NOTED

La grande Eulalia (short stories), Feltrinelli (Milan, Italy), 1988, second edition, 1990.

Il nocchiero, Feltrinelli (Milan, Italy), 1989.

Il doppio regno (title means "The Double Kingdom"), Bompiani (Milan, Italy), 1991, second edition, 1995.

La ragazza dala stella d'oro e altri racconti (short stories), illustrated by Gabriele Kutzke, Einaudi (Milan, Italy), 1991.

Vissi d'amore, Bompiani (Milan, Italy), 1992, translated by Liz Heron as *Floria Tosca,* Serpent's Tail (New York, NY), 1997.

La spettatrice, Bompiani (Milan, Italy), 1995, translated by Liz Heron as *The Woman Watching,* Serpent's Tail (New York, NY), 1999.

L'assoluto artificiale: Nichilism e mondo dell'espressione nell'opera saggistica di Gottfried Benn (nonfiction), Bompiani (Milan, Italy), 1996.

Un uomo di carattere, Bompiani (Milan, Italy), 1996, translated as *A Man of Character,* Serpent's Tail (London, England), 2000.

Con i miei mille occhi (includes CD-ROM), Bompiani (Milan, Italy), 1997.

Barbara, Bompiani (Milan, Italy), 1998.

Il sogno dell'agnello, Bompiani (Milan, Italy), 1999.

Una di loro, Bompiani (Milan, Italy), 2001.

Contributor to periodicals, including *Conjunctions* and *Review of Contemporary Fiction,* and to short-story collection *Il premio Berto: 1988-1993,* edited by Pasquale Russo, Monteleone, 1994. Also translator of works into Italian by Thomas Mann.

SIDELIGHTS: Writing in *World Literature Today,* Rocco Capozzi noted of Paola Capriolo that "of all the new writers who have emerged in the 1980s and 1990s in Italy, [she] stands unquestionably at the top of the list." Capozzi went on to state that "with each new novel [Capriolo] has shown great narrative skills, the ability to construct suspenseful stories, and a talent for unusual and colorful descriptions and original settings." In a dozen works, which include novels, short story collections, and literary criticism, Capriolo has established herself firmly in the European literary scene; and with several of her novels translated into English, her reputation is also growing in England and the United States.

Capriolo's 1995 novel, *La spettatrice,* was translated in 1998 as *The Woman Watching,* a "witty, psychologically astute gothic tale," according to a reviewer for *Publishers Weekly,* that "chronicles the ruin of two young actors in a provincial Italian theater troupe at the beginning of the century." The same reviewer went on to note that the book is both a "complex reworking of the Narcissus myth" as well as an "allegory of the fate of the theater under modernism." The story focuses on the actor Vulpius who becomes obsessed with a woman watching his performance in a play about the life of Casanova. Vulpius thereafter uses his long neglected lover Dora as his stand in, so that he might have the same view of himself that the anonymous and mysterious woman does. For Susann Cokal, writing in the *Review of Contemporary Fiction,* "the real power of [the novel] lies in Capriolo's tracing of the psychological effects of the ghost-muse woman's manifestation has on these two lives." Capozzi, writing in *World Literature Today,* commented that readers "have been treated to [Capriolo's] suspenseful stories, elegant style, unusual love relationships, solitary characters, rich symbolism, and metanarrative structures." Such readers will not be disappointed with *The Woman Watching*.

Capozzi also recommended the 2001 novel *Una di loro,* with its similarities to Thomas Mann, especially to his *Death in Venice* and the narrator Aschenbach's fixation on the young Tadzio. In Capriolo's novel, it is the unnamed, middle-aged critic narrator who becomes obsessed with Claudia in this novel of "self-awareness and metamorphosis," as Capozzi wrote.

Capriolo is also the author of *Un uomo di carattere,* translated into English as *A Man of Character*. This is the story of Erasmo Stiler, an engineer who inherits a rundown villa and, in the process of trying to create a private version of Versailles there, destroys himself. A cautionary tale of man's desire to tame chaos, the novel deals with large ideas, as do all the works of Capriolo. In this case she plumbs the relationship between art and nature, and investigates the importance of living one's life as a moral project. A further title translated into English is *Vissi d'amore,* published as *Floria Tosca,* "an exquisite melodrama which uses Puccini's *Tosca* as its palimpsest," according to Capozzi.

BIOGRAPHICAL AND CRITICAL SOURCES:

PERIODICALS

Publishers Weekly, August 24, 1998, review of *The Woman Watching,* p. 47.
Review of Contemporary Fiction, fall, 1998, Susann Cokal, review of *The Woman Watching,* p. 255.
World Literature Today, spring, 1999, Rocco Capozzi, review of *The Woman Watching,* p. 313; winter, 2002, Rocco Capozzi, review of *Una di loro,* p. 201.

ONLINE

TecaLibri, http://web.infinito.it/utenti/t/tecalibri/ (November 3, 2004), "Paola Capriolo: opere."
Words without Borders, http://www.wordswithout borders.org/ (November 3, 2004), "Paola Capriolo."*

CARLYLE, Liz
   See WOODHOUSE, S(usan). T.

                              *   *   *

CASEY, Don

PERSONAL: Married; wife's name Olga. *Education:* Graduated from University of Texas. *Hobbies and other interests:* Sailing, boat repair.

ADDRESSES: Home—Miami, FL. *Agent*—c/o Author Mail, International Marine Publishing, P.O. Box 220, Camden, ME 04843.

CAREER: Writer. Banker until 1983.

WRITINGS:

(With Lew Hackler) *Sensible Cruising: The Thoreau Approach,* International Marine Publishing (Camden, ME), 1988.
This Old Boat, International Marine Publishing (Camden, ME), 1991.
Sailboat Refinishing, International Marine Publishing (Camden, ME), 1996.
Sailboat Hull and Deck Repair, International Marine Publishing (Camden, ME), 1996.
Canvaswork and Sail Repair, International Marine Publishing (Camden, ME), 1996.
Inspecting the Aging Sailboat, International Marine Publishing (Camden, ME), 1997.
One Hundred Fast and Easy Boat Improvements, International Marine Publishing (Camden, ME), 1998.
Dragged Aboard: A Cruising Guide for the Reluctant Mate, illustrated by Don Almquist, W. W. Norton (New York, NY), 1998.
Sailboat Electrics Simplified, International Marine Publishing (Camden, ME), 1999.

Contributor to *Sail* and to other boating magazines. Author of "Ask Don Casey" column for *BoatUS.com* and monthly column for *SailNet.com.*

SIDELIGHTS: Although Don Casey was not the only successful banker who dreamed of getting away from it all in a sailboat, unlike many others, Casey actually made the move. In 1983 he quit his job, headed south, and embarked with his wife on a new life of freedom and adventure cruising the tropics. Determined to help others share his love of boats and sailing, Casey has published nearly a dozen books, as well as numerous magazine and Internet articles, on all aspects of the subject in clear, user-friendly prose that resonates with neophytes and lifelong sailors alike.

Casey's first book, *Sensible Cruising: The Thoreau Approach*, was a bestseller. "Its central premise," the author wrote on *SailNet.com*, "is that if you dream of going cruising, you almost certainly make an error if you postpone the pursuit of this dream while you earn the price of the 'perfect' boat." Casey reported that "over the years I have been approached by scores of sailors who tell me that reading *Sensible Cruising* enabled them to achieve their cruising dreams."

Another best seller, Casey's *This Old Boat,* is a long, fact-filled record of the renovation of a broken-down fiberglass sailboat with little money but lots of hard work and love. Meeting the needs of enthusiasts with a variety of technical books covering such topics as sails and sail repair, deck repair, refinishing, and electrical systems, Casey also addressed the needs of sailors' partners in *Dragged Aboard: A Cruising Guide for the Reluctant Mate.* In a review in the *San Francisco Chronicle,* Paul McHugh wrote that in *Dragged Aboard* "issues and solutions are defined, then defused with humor."

BIOGRAPHICAL AND CRITICAL SOURCES:

PERIODICALS

Booklist, July, 1998, Brenda Barrera, review of *Dragged Aboard: A Cruising Guide for the Reluctant Mate,* p. 1849.

Changing Times, January, 1988, review of *Sensible Cruising: The Thoreau Approach,* p. 104.

Cruising World, August, 1991, Nim Marsh, review of *This Old Boat,* p. 43; February 1999, Alison Langley, review of *Dragged Aboard,* p. 14.

San Francisco Chronicle, July 9, 1998, Paul McHugh, review of *Dragged Aboard,* p. E7.

Yacht, November, 1990, review of *Sensible Cruising,* p. 109.

ONLINE

SailNet.com, http://www.sailnet.com/ (November 11, 2004), Don Casey, "Less Is More."*

*   *   *

CHALKER, Dennis

PERSONAL: Male.

ADDRESSES: Home—Southern CA. *Agent*—c/o Author Mail, Avon Books/HarperCollins, 10 East 53rd Street, 7th Floor, New York, NY 10022.

CAREER: Retired Navy SEAL and author. Designed Chalker TAC weapon sling. *Military service:* U.S. Navy Basic Underwater Demolition/SEAL, command master chief, retired early 1990s. Previously U.S. Army paratrooper with 82nd Airborne Division.

WRITINGS:

(With Kevin Dockery) *The United States Navy SEALs Workout Guide: The Exercise and Fitness Programs Based on the U.S. Navy SEALs and BUD/S Training,* William Morrow (New York, NY), 1998.

(With Kevin Dockery) *One Perfect Op: An Insider's Account of the Navy SEAL Special Warfare Teams,* William Morrow (New York, NY), 2002.

(With Kevin Dockery) *Hell Week: SEALS in Training,* Avon Books (New York, NY), 2002.

SIDELIGHTS: Retired Command Master Chief Dennis Chalker, a former U.S. Navy SEAL (Sea, Land Air), has published several books revealing what it takes to become a member of this elite force. These works, written with military historian Kevin Dockery, tap more than twenty years of military experience. During the 1970s, Chalker served six years as a paratrooper in the U.S. Army's 82nd Airborne Division. He briefly returned to civilian life before volunteering for the SEALs, stealth commando units renowned for their daring and expertise. As a member of SEAL Team Six, Chalker participated in antiterrorist assignments including covert action in Grenada. He later joined one of the newly formed Red Cell units, which attempt to breach security at American military bases by entering and departing such facilities without detection.

Chalker's first book, *The United States Navy SEALs Workout Guide: The Exercise and Fitness Programs Based on the U.S. Navy SEALs and BUD/S Training,* shows readers how they can attain top physical conditioning—if they can hack it. It offers nine-week and twelve-week training programs including warm-ups and cool-downs, calisthenics, tips on aerobic training, nutrition, and motivation, and exercises devised for different climates. Chalker also shares anecdotes from true-life SEALs about the special ops that tested their hard-earned stamina.

Chalker delves deeper into the SEALs with *One Perfect Op: An Insider's Account of the Navy SEAL Special Warfare Teams.* The title refers to what the SEALs call a "perfect op"—a mission completed without being discovered and without the firing of a single shot. Chalker describes carrying out a perfect op in 1992, one of many experiences that are veiled by the need to maintain secrecy. A notable exception to this rule was in his discussion of the 1983 invasion of Grenada, where several of his friends were killed. Other episodes show how SEALs face considerable danger outside of war zones, including injuries and fatalities during exercises and horseplay. Readers will also find that during Chalker's service the strategy, tactics, and doctrine of the Navy SEALs would be modified in response to a changing world.

One Perfect Op was called "a quick but accurate glimpse into the training and life of a navy SEAL" by *Library Journal* critic David M. Alperstein. Given the book's highly personal and detailed subject matter, a *Publishers Weekly* reviewer advised that it is perfect reading for "special ops buffs" and does not serve as a general history. *One Perfect Op* reveals Chalker to be a practical joker and, as a *Kirkus Reviews* critic wrote, "a super-bad macho dude devoted to deadly weapons, fighting, and his buddies on the team." Writing for *Booklist,* Gilbert Taylor noted the book's relevance in wartime, calling it "a timely, adventuresome, and interesting account."

BIOGRAPHICAL AND CRITICAL SOURCES:

PERIODICALS

Booklist, January 1, 2002, Gilbert Taylor, review of *One Perfect Op: An Insider's Account of the Navy SEAL Special Warfare Teams,* p. 781.

Kirkus Reviews, November 15, 2001, review of *One Perfect Op,* p. 1592.
Library Journal, February 15, 2002, David M. Alperstein, review of *One Perfect Op,* p. 164.
Publishers Weekly, December 3, 2001, review of *One Perfect Op,* p. 47.*

*   *   *

CHANG, Iris 1968-2004

OBITUARY NOTICE— See index for *CA* sketch: Born March 28, 1968, in Princeton, NJ; died of an apparently self-inflicted gunshot wound November 9, 2004, near Los Gatos, CA. Activist and author. Chang is best remembered as the author of *The Rape of Nanking: The Forgotten Holocaust of World War II* (1997). After completing her B.A. in journalism at the University of Illinois at Urbana-Champaign in 1989, she worked briefly for the *Chicago Tribune* and the Associated Press. She then went back to school, receiving her master's degree from Johns Hopkins University in 1991. Chang's first book was the nonfiction *Thread of the Silkworm* (1995), but critical acclaim came with her second title, *The Rape of Nanking.* Chang spent two years researching the book after learning from her family that her grandparents survived the 1937 event in which, as the author reported, hundreds of thousands of Chinese were tortured, raped, and murdered by occupying Japanese forces. The book became a bestseller, earned the respect of contemporary historians, and spurred Chang's work as a social and civil rights activist. In 2003, she released *The Chinese in America: A Narrative History,* but while researching her fourth book, which concerned U.S. prisoners of war in the Philippines during World War II, Chang suffered a profound emotional breakdown. She was hospitalized for several months, but apparently not cured of her depression. Her body was found in her car along a highway near Los Gatos, California, where police speculated that the author shot herself.

OBITUARIES AND OTHER SOURCES:

PERIODICALS

Chicago Tribune, November 11, 2004, section 3, p. 11.
Los Angeles Times, November 11, 2004, p. B11.

New York Times, November 12, 2004, p. C9.
Times (London, England), November 15, 2004, p. 54.
Washington Post, November 12, 2004, p. B6.

* * *

CHEN, Ping

PERSONAL: Male. *Education:* University of Science and Technology, Beijing, China, B.S., 1968; University of Texas, Austin, Ph.D., 1987.

ADDRESSES: Office—University of Texas, C1609, Austin, TX 78712-1081; Peking University, Beijing 100871, China. *E-mail*—pchen@physics.utexas.edu; pchen@ccer.pku.edu.cn.

CAREER: Educator, scientist, and economist. Ilya Prigogine Center for Studies in Thermodynamics and Statistical Mechanics, University of Texas, Austin, research assistant, 1983-87, postdoctoral fellow, 1987-89, research associate and research scientist, 1989—; Peking University, Peking, China, professor at China Center for Economic Research, 1999—, codirector of Virtual Center for Complexity Science, 2001—.

MEMBER: American Economic Association, Chinese Economists Society in North America (founding senior fellow), American Physical Society, Chinese Young Economists Society (member, board of directors, 1986-87; president, 1987-88).

WRITINGS:

(Editor and contributor, with Richard Hollis Day) *Nonlinear Dynamics and Evolutionary Economics,* Oxford University Press (New York, NY), 1993.

Author and editor of volumes published in the Chinese language. Contributor to books, including *Self-Organization, Emerging Properties, and Learning,* edited by A. Babloyantz, Penguin, 1992; *Nonlinear Dynamics and Economics,* edited by W. A. Barnett and others, Cambridge University Press, 1996; and *Joint Time-Frequency Analysis,* by Shie Qian and Da-pang Chen, Prentice Hall, 1996. Contributor to journals, including *Journal of Economic Behavior &*

Organization, International Journal of Theoretical Physics, and *China Economic Review.* Member of editorial board, *China Economic Review.*

SIDELIGHTS: Ping Chen, an economist and physicist working in both the United States and China, has written and edited a number of volumes in Chinese and is a frequent contributor to English-language journals. The subjects of Chen's interest and research have included the empirical and theoretical evidence of monetary chaos from monetary indexes, time-frequency analysis in nonstationary time series analysis of business cycles, color chaos in the S&P 500 index and other macro indexes, fundamental limitations in equilibrium models of business cycles, the Adam Smith dilemma defined by George Stigler in 1951, a behavior model of corporate strategy in market-share competition, evolutionary economics, and understanding excess capacity and product cycles based on technology competition.

Chen and coeditor Richard Hollis Day published a collection of papers presented at a conference conducted at the University of Texas, Austin, in April 1989. *Nonlinear Dynamics and Evolutionary Economics* is divided into six sections, followed by the edited transcript of a roundtable discussion. Contributors include not only economists, but also physicists, ecologists, and anthropologists. Regarding Chen's own contribution, a discussion of estimation and inference. Carl Chiarella noted in *Economic Record* that the editor "reviews some of the techniques for distinguishing between randomly generated data and data generated by deterministic process, and some of the pitfalls in their use. He uses his earlier work on chaos in monetary aggregates to discuss the problems of inference with economic time series and also shows how a nonlinear differential equation can generate behavior that closely resembles the data."

Chiarella maintained that *Nonlinear Dynamics and Evolutionary Economics* "is less concerned with the intricacies of particular nonlinear economic models, but rather attempts to give the reader a feel for the broad sweep of the main ideas and issues of nonlinear and evolutionary economic dynamics." The critic cited the essays as "well written at a survey level and at the same time [able] to give a feel for and an introduction to the more intricate technicalities." Chiarella concluded by saying that "the reader who is uncomfortable with the dominance of the intertemporal utility maximizing paradigm as a basis for economic theory will find some insights into what is one possible future path for the evolution of economic theory" and dubbed the work "well worth reading."

BIOGRAPHICAL AND CRITICAL SOURCES:

PERIODICALS

Economic Journal, January, 1995, David Chappell, review of *Nonlinear Dynamics and Evolutionary Economics,* p. 244.

Economic Record, September, 1995, Carl Chiarella, review of *Nonlinear Dynamics and Evolutionary Economics,* p. 303.

ONLINE

Ping Chen Home Page, http://pchen.ccer.edu.cn (June 2, 2003).*

*   *   *

CHRISTENSEN, Kathleen E(lizabeth) 1951-

PERSONAL: Born May 25, 1951, in Madison, WI; daughter of Norbert Martin and Janet Cull Christensen; married John Joseph Murray III, May 25, 1990; children: Clare, Grace. *Education:* University of Wisconsin at Green Bay, B.S. (summa cum laude); Pennsylvania State University, M.S., 1979, Ph.D., 1981.

ADDRESSES: Office—Alfred P. Sloan Foundation, 630 Fifth Ave., Suite 2550, New York, NY 10111. *E-mail*—christensen@sloan.org.

CAREER: Urban Institute, Washington, DC, policy analyst, 1973-75; City University of New York, New York, NY, from assistant professor to professor of psychology, 1981-91, professor, 1991-99; Alfred P. Sloan Foundation, New York, director of family-work research program, 1995—. Consultant to businesses, federal agencies, and Congressional committees; member of advisory board, Boston Center for Work and Family, 1990-94.

MEMBER: American Association for the Advancement of Science, American Sociological Association, American Anthropological Association.

AWARDS, HONORS: Humanities fellowship, National Endowment for the Humanities, 1977-79; Danforth fellowship, Danforth Foundation, 1979-81; Mellon fellowship, Aspen Institute, 1982; Rockefeller Foundation fellowship.

WRITINGS:

(Editor) *The New Era of Home-based Work: Directions and Policies,* Westview Press (Boulder, CO), 1988.
Women and Home-based Work: The Unspoken Contract, Holt (New York, NY), 1988.
(Editor, with Irwin Altman) *Environment and Behavior Studies: Emergence of Intellectual Traditions,* Plenum Press (New York, NY), 1990.
Turbulence in the American Workplace, Oxford University Press (New York, NY), 1990.
(Editor, with Kathleen Barker) *Contingent Work: American Employment Relations in Transition,* ILR Press (Ithaca, NY), 1998.

SIDELIGHTS: Kathleen E. Christensen has been concerned with America's rapidly changing workplace, including such issues as women working at home, alternative work schedules, and the increasing practice of outsourcing work. One of her early books, *Women and Home-based Work: The Unspoken Contract,* emerged from a survey Christensen conducted of 14,000 women that appeared in *Family Circle* magazine. In this study, Christensen focuses mostly on married women who choose home-based work as a way to combine work and family life. Although many women work from their homes in an attempt to "have it all," Christensen asserts that the "unspoken contracts" of home life that still give women primary responsibility for child-rearing and housework keep them from feeling any real sense of professionalism. She argues that, in order for a woman's home-based job to be successful, spouses need to agree to discuss and evaluate these unspoken agreements, a process that would naturally require a level of openness and honesty that relatively uncommon.

According to Eileen Boris in a *Women's Review of Books* assessment of *Women and Home-based Work,* the author correctly points to a "hidden army of labor in a shadow economy" that often exploits women in the home. While the work middle-class women often do—everything from typing to running mail-order retail businesses—is not as demeaning and stressful as that done by women in Third-World countries or in city ghettoes, Christensen found that a sense of job satisfaction among those she studied was hindered by the constant tug-and-pull of home versus work responsibilities.

Christensen places some of the blame for home-based workers' dissatisfaction on employers who hire such women as "independent contractors" to avoid paying benefits or Social Security. Yet, according to Boris, Christensen also puts responsibility on the women themselves for buying into unspoken contracts with their domestic partners that create obstacles in their work life. The author says that a real solution would be "to recognize that the structure of work itself can be changed to benefit both parents and children." A *Kirkus Reviews* critic commented that Christensen "offers very little analysis, historical context, or practical suggestions" about the unspoken contracts accepted by the women she profiled and questioned why, when a survey for men was included, why the original survey of women on which the author based her findings was not. Boris concluded that studies done by Christensen and others help to reinforce the idea that "legal prohibition hasn't addressed why women do homework."

More recently, Christensen co-edited *Contingent Work: American Employment Relations in Transition* with Kathleen Barker. This book collects essays that address the outsourcing and hiring of temporary staff. Issues addressed include who the contingent workers are, how American businesses use contingent staffing, and what the human experiences of doing contingent work are. Divided into four sections, *Contingent Work* not only analyses the demographics involved and conditions in the modern workplace environment, but also offers case studies and analysis of current policies and changing labor practices. *Labor History* contributor Max Kirsch felt that the editors' premise that putting forth their book will stir debate and encourage the development of fair employment practices is naive. "The essential character of these corporations does not consider human costs," Kirsch asserted. "That said, there are some interesting pieces in this collection that provide data on the increase in contingent workers in the United States and their effect on families and com-

munities." Writing in *Industrial and Labor Relations Review,* Brenda A. Lautsch more optimistically felt that "this volume builds a thorough and convincing interdisciplinary portrait of the problems in contingent work and of potential solutions to them."

BIOGRAPHICAL AND CRITICAL SOURCES:

PERIODICALS

Berkeley Journal of Employment and Labor Law, summer, 1999, review of *Contingent Work: American Employment Relations in Transition,* p. 188.

Booklist, July, 1998, David Rouse, review of *Contingent Work,* p. 1840.

Comparative Labor Law & Policy Journal, spring, 1999, review of *Contingent Work,* p. 538.

Contemporary Sociology, January, 1990, Jean Stockard, review of *The New Era of Home-based Work: Directions and Policies,* p. 56; January, 2000, Ted Baker, review of *Contingent Work,* p. 250.

Gender & Society, June, 1990, Robin Leidner, review of *The New Era of Home-based Work,* p. 262.

Industrial and Labor Relations Review, April, 2000, Brenda A. Lautsch, review of *Contingent Work,* p. 525.

Industrial Relations, summer, 2000, Isik Urla Zeytinoglu, review of *Contingent Work,* p. 553.

Journal of American History, December, 1999, Judith Stein, review of *Contingent Work,* p. 1408.

Kirkus Reviews, November 1, 1987, review of *Women and Home-based Work: The Unspoken Contract,* pp. 1551-1552.

Labor History, November, 1999, Max Kirsch, review of *Contingent Work,* p. 568.

Labor Studies Journal, fall, 1990, Judi Catlett, review of *Women and Home-based Work,* p. 96.

Library Journal, December, 1987, Donna L. Nerboso, review of *Women and Home-based Work,* p. 106.

Los Angeles Times Book Review, December 27, 1987, Marjorie Marks, review of *Women and Home-based Work,* p. 4.

Mother Jones, January, 1988, Margie Frantz, review of *Women and Home-based Work,* p. 52.

New York Times, August 12, 1990, Deirdre Fanning, "Fleeing the Office, and Its Distractions: Almost Half of the Executives Who Work at Home Are Men, and Most Are Managers," p. F25.

Publishers Weekly, November 27, 1987, Genevieve Stuttaford, review of *Women and Home-based Work,* p. 73.

Signs, spring, 1991, Judith M. Gerson, review of *Women and Home-based Work,* p. 621.

Telecommuting Review: The Gordon Report, August 1, 1989, "Perched on the 'Slippery Slope': The Manager's View of Providing More Flexibility," p. 10.

Wall Street Journal, March 11, 1988, Amanda Bennett, review of *Women and Home-based Work,* p. 20.

Women's Review of Books, June, 1988, Eileen Boris, "Bringing It All Back Home," pp. 8-9.*

* * *

CLARKE, Anna (Emilia) 1919-2004

OBITUARY NOTICE— See index for *CA* sketch: Born April 28, 1919, in Cape Town, South Africa; died November 7, 2004, in Brighton, East Sussex, England. Author. Coming to the profession of fiction writer late in life, Clarke was a popular writer of detective novels. Earning a B.Sc. from London External in 1945 and a B.A. from Open University in 1973, she originally intended to be a mathematician, but a job as a secretary for the publisher Victor Gollancz in the late 1940s sparked her interest in the industry. She worked briefly as a secretary at the Eyre & Spottiswoode publishing company in London, and then for the British Association for American Studies from 1956 to 1962. Suffering from a severe illness and claustrophobia, Clarke had to leave her job and seek therapy for a time. When she had recovered, she found herself in need of an income and so tried her hand at writing. At first, she attempted to publish straight fiction, but she found no publishers for her more serious novels; therefore, she turned to mystery novels. Specializing in what are commonly referred to as "cozies," Clarke wrote stories with a distinct literary sensibility. Her series character Professor Paula Glenning is an intellectual who solves crimes with research, dialogue, and brains rather than muscles and violence. Among the over two dozen novels produced by Clarke are *The Darkened Room* (1968), *Legacy of Evil* (1976), *Soon She Must Die* (1984), and *The Case of the Anxious Aunt* (1996).

OBITUARIES AND OTHER SOURCES:

PERIODICALS

Independent (London, England), December 28, 2004, p. 33.

CLASON, Clyde B(urt) 1903-1987

PERSONAL: Born 1903, in Denver, CO; died 1987.

CAREER: Author. Also worked as an advertising copywriter and trade paper editor in Chicago, IL.

WRITINGS:

"THEOCRITUS LUCIUS WESTBOROUGH" SERIES; CRIME NOVELS

The Fifth Tumbler, Doubleday (New York, NY), 1936.
The Death Angel, Doubleday (New York, NY), 1936.
Blind Drifts, Doubleday (New York, NY), 1937.
The Purple Parrot, Doubleday (New York, NY), 1937.
The Man from Tibet, Doubleday (New York, NY), 1938.
The Whispering Ear, Doubleday (New York, NY), 1938.
Murder Gone Minoan, Doubleday (New York, NY), 1939, published as *Clue to the Labyrinth,* Heinemann (London, England), 1939.
Dragon's Cave, Doubleday (New York, NY), 1939.
Poison Jasmine, Doubleday (New York, NY), 1940.
Green Shiver, Doubleday (New York, NY), 1941.

OTHER

The Story of Period Furniture, Nutshell (Chicago, IL), 1925.
Ark of Venus (novel), Knopf (New York, NY), 1955.
Exploring the Distant Stars: Thrilling Adventures in Our Galaxy and Beyond, Putnam (New York, NY), 1959.
Men, Planets, and Stars (for children), Putnam (New York, NY), 1959.
I Am Lucifer: Confessions of the Devil (novel), Muhlenberg Press (Philadelphia, PA), 1960.
This Rock Exists, Davies (London, England), 1962.
The Delights of the Slide Rule, Crowell (London, England), 1964.

Also author of *Evolution of Architecture* and *How to Write Stories That Sell,* both for Nutshell (Chicago, IL).

SIDELIGHTS: Clyde B. Clason was in many ways a typical figure among traditional American detective novelists of the 1930s. The puzzle is very much the center of his novels, with most characters sketched just fully enough to be told apart. Beginning with his first novel, *The Fifth Tumbler,* he displayed an enthusiasm for the locked rooms and impossible crimes featured in the works of John Dickson Carr and Clayton S. Rawson. Clason's novels are often illustrated with maps of the murder scene. Like many American puzzle-makers of the 1930s, he was heavily influenced by the intellectual and informational content of S. S. Van Dine's "Philo Vance" novels, ahd thus offers a display of erudition on various arcane subjects relevant to the mystery at hand. Though Clason generally shunned footnotes, except to plug his earlier books, he went Van Dine's apparatus one better by including a three-page bibliography at the beginning of *The Man from Tibet.*

Clason's continuing sleuth, initially a Chicago resident but later pursuing crime in California, is elderly Roman Empire scholar Theocritus Lucius Westborough. The sleuth's police friend, Lieutenant John Mack, is notably rude when dealing with suspects, while Westborough is mild and likeable, a far cry from the abrasive intellect of Philo Vance or the irascible personalities of scholar-sleuths like John Rhode's Dr. Priestley or Jacques Futrelle's Thinking Machine. Speaking in an ornate and pedantic fashion when discussing crimes, despite his age Westborough is no armchair detective; he does not shun strenuous physical activity in the pursuit of truth.

Westborough solves his first case, *The Fifth Tumbler,* when impossible murder strikes among the inhabitants of the residential hotel where he lives. The novel's complicated plot is worked out in a way that plays fair with the reader. The same can be said for the subsequent Chicago case, *The Purple Parrot,* concerning a nutty will in which the only bequest to the decedent's granddaughter is the vanished bird of the title. In *The Man from Tibet* and *Dragon's Cave* Westborough is given the opportunity to display his erudition on Tibetan art and religion in the former and on puzzling out a cryptogram in the latter. With these stories, and many more, Clason became known for the elaborate puzzles in his plots, which often had to be solved with the dazzling ratiocinative powers of his sleuth, Westborough.*

CLENDINEN, Dudley

PERSONAL: Male.

ADDRESSES: Home—Baltimore, MD. *Office*—c/o New York Times, 229 West 43rd St., New York, NY 10036.

CAREER: Journalist. *Atlanta Journal-Constitution,* Atlanta, GA, features editor until 1988; *St. Petersburg Times,* St. Petersburg, FL, former reporter; *New York Times,* New York, NY, currently editorial writer.

AWARDS, HONORS: Finalist, New York Public Library Helen Bernstein Book Award for Excellence in Journalism, 2000, for *Out for Good: The Struggle to Build a Gay Rights Movement in America.*

WRITINGS:

(Editor) *The Prevailing South: Life and Politics in a Changing Culture,* Longstreet Press (Atlanta, GA), 1988.
Homeless in America, Acropolis Books (New York, NY), 1988.
(With Adam Nagourney) *Out for Good: The Struggle to Build a Gay Rights Movement in America,* Simon & Schuster (New York, NY) 1999.

SIDELIGHTS: Dudley Clendinen, an editorialist for the *New York Times,* wrote *Out for Good: The Struggle to Build a Gay Rights Movement in America* with *Times* reporter Adam Nagourney. He has also edited *The Prevailing South: Life and Politics in a Changing Culture,* a collection of sixteen essays on the past, present, and future of Southern politics and culture. The essays are written by Southern historians, novelists, and journalists.

Out for Good sprang from an article Clendinen wrote for the *New York Times* op-ed page during the 1992 presidential election campaign. A seven-year project, the book required researching press accounts and conducting more than seven hundred taped interviews. The resulting book is an account of the gay rights movement in the United States, beginning with the 1969 riot at Stonewall Inn, a gay bar in New York City, and ending with the founding of the AIDS Coalition to Unleash Power (ACT UP) in 1987. It focuses on many of the personalities who figure in the gay rights movement, which has long lacked cohesiveness.

Some reviewers argued that the book represents the most comprehensive work on the subject, given that the authors widen their focus beyond New York and San Francisco to include happenings in cities throughout the United States. Among the events reviewed are the campaign of Franklin Kameny, the first openly gay candidate for federal office in 1971, and Anita Bryant's opposition to a gay rights ordinance in Florida during the late 1970s.

While critics welcomed *Out for Good* as an expansion of the literature on the gay rights movement, some suggested areas that remained to be explored. According to *New York Times* writer Stephen O. Murray, for example, *Out for Good* "vividly reports the activism and intramural conflicts of the 1970's gay and lesbian movement," but does not fulfill its aim of being a larger history. *Lambda Book Report* critic Bob Summer viewed the book as an "obviously painstaking collaboration," but advised readers that the "chronologically episodic assemblage is far from the whole saga of the gay political movement's 'struggle,'" due to the fact that its focus does not extend past the late 1980s.

Questions about the book's perspective were raised by *Nation* reviewer Martin Duberman, who called the work a "vivid but determinedly untheoretical history." Duberman suggested that "the lack of sympathy for radical politics and analysis in *Out for Good* is subtle but pervasive," adding that inadequate attention is paid to race, lesbians, and being gay in non-urban areas. At the same time, the critic added, "What this ambitious volume does do, it does exceedingly well. . . . Clendinen and Nagourney . . . capture the essential, quirky characteristics of a remarkable set of characters. I may quarrel with their assorted anointments and omissions, but I admire the shrewdness with which they've constructed their narrative and the crisp, lean prose in which they've conveyed it."

The difficulty of shaping a comprehensive history was often noted. As Brad Hooper commented in *Booklist,* while *Out for Good* "is a big, long, epic narrative" the authors "sensibly bring it down to human proportions by focusing on individuals' tales of participation." In a review for the *Atlanta Journal-Constitution,* Shane Harrison admired how "the authors never allow the many disparate threads of the story to become tangled into outright incomprehensibility." Harrison concluded that the work serves as "an invaluable document, impressively researched, remarkably well-written and groundbreaking in its scope."

BIOGRAPHICAL AND CRITICAL SOURCES:

PERIODICALS

Atlanta Journal-Constitution, June 13, 1999, Shane Harrison, review of *Out for Good: The Struggle to Build a Gay Rights Movement in America,* p. L13.

Booklist, June 1, 1999, Brad Hooper, review of *Out for Good,* p. 1782.

Journal of Southern History, August, 1990, A. Cash Koeniger, review of *The Prevailing South: Life and Politics in a Changing Culture,* p. 568.

Lambda Book Report, July-August, 1999, Bob Summer, review of *Out for Good,* p. 29.

Library Journal, June 15, 1999, E. James Van Buskirk, review of *Out for Good,* p. 94.

Los Angeles Times Book Review, October 23, 1988, review of *The Prevailing South,* p. 4.

Mississippi Quarterly, fall, 1990, Albert J. Devlin, review of *The Prevailing South,* pp. 555-557.

Nation, June 14, 1999, Martin Duberman, "Uncloseted History," p. 51.

New York Times, September 25, 1988, Andrea Stevens, review of *Homeless in America,* p. 30; July 5, 1999, Stephen O. Murray, review of *Out for Good,* p. E13.

Publishers Weekly, April 12, 1999, review of *Out for Good,* p. 60.

Social Forces, June, 1990, review of *The Prevailing South,* p. 1368.

ONLINE

365Gay.com, http://www.365gay.com/ (November 24, 2001), review of *Out for Good.*

Independent Gay Forum Online, http://www.indegay forum.org/ (November 24, 2001), Stephen O. Murray, "Tracing the Rise of the Gay Movement."

Paula Gordon Show Web site, http://paulagordon.com/show/clendinen/ (November 3, 2004), "Honestly Out."

Public Broadcasting Service Web site, http://www.pbs.org/newshour/ (November 24, 2001), *News Hour* transcript, David Gergen, review of *Out for Good.**

*   *   *

CLOSE, Ajay

PERSONAL: Male.

ADDRESSES: Home—Glasgow, Scotland. *Office*—The Scotsman, 80 St. Vincent St., Glasgow G2 5UB, Scotland.

CAREER: Journalist and author. *Scotsman,* Glasgow, Scotland, reporter.

WRITINGS:

Official and Doubtful (novel), Secker & Warburg (London, England), 1996.

Forspoken (novel), Secker & Warburg (London, England), 1998.

Official and Doubtful has been translated into German.

SIDELIGHTS: Ajay Close, a journalist who lives and works in Scotland, is also a novelist. His first book, *Official and Doubtful,* takes place in postindustrial Glasgow. The main character, Nan Megratta, works in the post office, has the job of sorting letters in the "Official and Doubtful" department. One day, a threatening blackmail letter arrives from an unknown sender addressed to someone named "MacLeod," the only legible part of the addressee's name. Bored and seeking some type of adventure in her life, Nan decides to try and find out who may be threatened by the letter writer. Ultimately, she focuses on three potential targets: a politician, a fading feminist star, and a sleazy entrepreneur. Soon she is involved with all three of the MacLeods, and the reader learns that Nan also has a painful and violent past.

In a review for the *Richmond Review Online* Helena Mary Smith commented that Close "has given the city a fine novel." Although adding that the "plot occasionally creaks and groans," the reviewer noted, "*Official and Doubtful* is a tremendous first novel, passionate but never polemical, the painful theme of domestic violence undercut by wit and wonderful dialogue: Glasgow patter *par excellence.*"

Close's second novel, *Forspoken,* tells the story of thirty-nine-year-old Tracy Malleus, a bright and attractive woman who is in love with Drew Monzie. Unlike Tracy, however, Drew is overweight, pasty-skinned, and married. To complicate matters, Tracy's sister, Samantha, returns home after spending nearly two decades in America. Unlike Tracy, who is basically well grounded and happy with life, Samantha is an angry woman who cannot get over disappointments from childhood. Writing in the Manchester *Guardian,* Carrie O'Grady called *Forspoken* a "342-page monologue" and noted that the novelist "seems to be a little bit in love with Tracey himself: he gives us her every fleeting thought, and she is present in every single scene, thinking, talking, reflecting on life while brushing her teeth, and so on."

BIOGRAPHICAL AND CRITICAL SOURCES:

PERIODICALS

Guardian (Manchester, England), November 20, 1999, Carrie O'Grady, review of *Forspoken,* p. 11.

ONLINE

Richmond Review Online, http://www.richmondreview.co.uk/ (November 4, 2004), Helena Mary Smith, review of *Official and Doubtful.**

*   *   *

COARELLI, Filippo 1936-

PERSONAL: Born 1936, in Rome, Italy.

ADDRESSES: Agent—Riverside Book Company, 250 West 57th St., New York, NY 10107.

CAREER: Writer, editor, and educator. University of Perugia, Italy, professor of Greek and Roman antiquities.

WRITINGS:

Arte nel mezzogiorno, Editalia (Rome, Italy), 1966.

Loreficeria nellarte classica, Fabbri (Milan, Italy), 1966, published as *Greek and Roman Jewellery,* translated by D. Strong, Hamlyn (Feltham, England), 1970.

Roma, Mondadori (Milan, Italy), 1971, 4th edition, 2004, English translation published as *Rome,* foreword by Pier Luigi Nervi, Madison Square Press (New York, NY), 1972.

(Editor) *Il sepolcro degli Scipioni,* Assessorato per le antichit, belle arti e problemi della cultura (Rome, Italy), 1972.

Tesori delloreficeria, Fratelli Fabbri (Milan, Italy), 1973.

Arena di Verona, Ente autonomo Arena di Verona (Verona, Italy), c. 1973.

(With Luisanna Usai) *Guida archeologica di Roma,* photographs by Mauro Pucciarelli, A. Mondadori (Milan, Italy), 1974.

(With Francesca Boitani, Maria Cataldi, and Marinella Pasquinucci) *Etruscan Cities,* Putnam (New York, NY), 1975.

(Editor, with Annabella Rossi and Roberto Schezen) *Templi dellItalia antica,* photographs by Roberto Scheze, Touring Club Italiano (Milan, Italy), 1980.

(Editor, with Luisa Franchi DellOrto) Ranuccio Bianchi Bandinelli, *La pittura antica,* Editori Riuniti (Rome, Italy), 1980.

Dintorni di Roma, G. Laterza (Rome, Italy), 1981.

Lazio, G. Laterza (Rome, Italy), 1982.

Il foro romano, Quasar (Rome, Italy), 1983.

(With Mario Torelli) *Sicilia,* G. Laterza (Rome, Italy), 1984.

(With A. La Regina) *Abruzzo, Molise,* G. Laterza (Rome, Italy), 1984.

Italia centrale, G. Laterza (Rome, Italy), 1985.

(With René Ginouvés, Roland Martin, and others) *Dictionnaire méthodique de larchitecture grecque et romaine,* pictures by Jean-Pierre Adam and others, Ecole Française d'Athènes (Athens, Greece)/ Ecole Française de Rome (Rome, Italy), 1985–1998.

(Editor, with Pier Giorgio Monti) *Fregellae,* Quasar (Rome, Italy), 1986.

Roma repubblicana dal 270 A.C. alletà augustea, Quasar (Rome, Italy), 1987.

I santuari del Lazio in età repubblicana, La Nuova Italia Scientifica (Rome, Italy), 1987.

Il sepolcro degli Scipioni a Roma, F.lli Palombi (Rome, Italy), 1988.

Il foro boario: dalle origini alla fine della Repubblica, Quasar (Rome, Italy), 1988.

(Editor) *Minturnae,* NER (Rome, Italy), 1989.

(With Aldo Corcella and Pasquale Rossi) *Un angolo di mondo: i luoghi oraziani,* Osanna (Venosa, Italy), 1993.

Da Pergamo a Roma: i Galati nella città degli Attalidi, Quasar (Rome, Italy), 1995.

(Editor, with Giorgio Bonamente) *Assisi e gli umbri nellantichità: atti del convengo internazionale, Assisi, 18-21 dicembre 1991,* Societ . . . editrice Minerva (Assisi, Italy), 1996.

(Editor, with Vittorio Casale and Bruno Toscano) *Scritti di archeologia e storia dellarte in onore di Carlo Pietrangeli,* Quasar (Rome, Italy), 1996.

Revixit ars: arte e ideologia a Roma, dai modelli ellenistici alla tradizione repubblicana, Quasar (Rome, Italy), 1996.

Il campo Marzio: dalle origini alla fine della repubblica, Quasar (Rome, Italy), 1997.

(With others) *Il colosseo,* edited by Ada Gabucci, Electa (Milan, Italy), 1999, published as *The Colosseum,* translated by Mary Becker, J. Paul Getty Museum (Los Angeles, CA), 2001.

La colonna traiana, Editore Colombo/Istituto Archeologico Germanico (Rome, Italy), 1999.

Belli e lantico, with Fifty sonnets by Giuseppe Gioacchino Belli, L'Erma di Bretschneider (Rome, Italy), 2000.

(Editor with Corrado Fratini) *Archeologia e arte in Umbria e nei suoi musei,* Electa (Milan, Italy), 2001.

(Editor and author of text) *Pompei: la vita ritrovata,* photographs by Alfredo Foglia and Pio Foglia, Magnus (Udine, Italy), 2002, published as *Pompeii,* translated by Patricia A. Cockram, Riverside Book Co. (New York, NY), 2003.

Via Cavour: una strada della nuova Roma, edited by Giuseppe Cuccia, Palombi (Rome, Italy), 2003.

SIDELIGHTS: Antiquities expert and university professor Filippo Coarelli specializes in the relics and monuments of ancient Roman civilization. His book *Pompeii* is a compilation including essays on "distinguished Italian archaeologists and professors, the majority of whose work has not previously been available in English," explained *Library Journal* contributor Nancy J. Mactague. The volume sets out in formidable detail the story of the covering of the archaeological site when the Roman resort city near modern Naples was buried in the famous eruption of Mt. Vesuvius in southern Italy on August 24, 79 C.E. It also covers the rediscovery of the town in 1748, and the slow process of uncovering and placing in context the rich material culture of the Romans that was perfectly preserved by the volcanic ash. "It includes a sketch of the history of excavations, a brief account of what is known of the history of the city in antiquity," Larry Richardson wrote in the *Bryn Mawr Classical Review,* "and surveys of the public buildings and private houses." In addition, "Coarelli . . . [traces] Pompeii's profound influence on literature, history, art, music, and film," declared Donna Seaman in *Booklist,* "and [examines] the major role it has played in the evolution of archaeology."

BIOGRAPHICAL AND CRITICAL SOURCES:

PERIODICALS

Booklist, April 15, 2003, Donna Seaman, review of *Pompeii,* p. 1440.

Bryn Mawr Classical Review, March 30, 2003, Larry Richardson, review of *Pompeii.*

Library Journal, April 1, 2003, Nancy J. Mactague, review of *Pompeii,* p. 93.

*   *   *

COLLINS, Eamon 1954-1999

PERSONAL: Born 1954, in Newry, County Down, Ireland; murdered January 27, 1999, in Newry, County Down, Ireland.; son of Brian Collins (a border cattle and horse trader) and Kathleen Cumiskey. *Education:* Attended Queen's University, Belfast; degree in community education, Dublin. *Religion:* Catholic.

CAREER: Worked variously for the ministry of defense, London, England, as a border policeman, and as a customs officer; intelligence officer, Irish Republican Army (IRA).

WRITINGS:

(With Mick McGovern) *Killing Rage* (autobiography), Granta Books (London, England), 1997.

SIDELIGHTS: Eamon Collins was born in 1954 in Newry, County Down, Northern Ireland. The son of Roman Catholics, neither of whom were particularly political, he was raised on a horse and cattle farm until his parents separated when he was age five and his mother took him to live with his grandmother. In 1974 Collins was home on the family farm for a holiday from Belfast, where he was studying British law at Queen's University, when soldiers from the British Army's Parachute Regiment discovered what appeared to be explosives residue in his father's truck. They caught and abused Collins, beating him and threatening him with a gun. Once the "explosives" were proven to be creosote (a flammable tar created by wood smoke), he was released.

The incident turned Collins away from his studies; British law no longer seemed a valid subject to him. When the tentative peace between Catholics and Protestants crumbled in the wake of a strike by the Protestant paramilitaries, ending any hope of the two groups sharing political power, Collins began to consider the Irish Republican Army's (IRA) platform: that aggression was the only way to settle the situation. Jo Thomas, in a review for the *New York Times Book Review,* quoted Collins as saying that "only force would bring about justice for Catholics in this Protestant statelet. I can look back now and say that if power sharing had worked, I would not have ended up in the IRA."

In his autobiography, *Killing Rage,* Collins recounts his experiences as an intelligence officer for the IRA. Although he never killed anyone himself, he was responsible for the deaths of a number of people, marking them for assassination and calling in hit men to take care of the jobs. Some targeted individuals were policemen or off-duty soldiers, while others were people he knew, such as Ulster Defense Regiment (UDR) Major Ivan Toombs, whose funeral he attended. Still others were marked for death based on inaccurate information that Collins had obtained, as in the case of UDR member Norman Hanna, who was shot to death in front of his wife and children. It was later reported that Hanna had left the UDR six years earlier, which by IRA rules should have exempted him from becoming a target. Although Collins felt some guilt, he justified his actions as necessary for the greater good. Roane Carey, a reviewer for the *Nation,* quoted Collins, who stated that "I felt this savagery was the necessary price of our struggle to create a more just society. . . . We were involved in a war of attrition and even then I knew that my participation in that war changed me. . . . Every aspect of my life was dedicated to the purpose of death."

An arrest for a crime he did not commit ended Collins's IRA involvement. After five days of hard questioning and beatings by the police, he confessed to a number of crimes for which he was responsible, and turned state's witness. His family, however, convinced him to recant. While he was officially pardoned by the army according to IRA policy, Collins began to receive death threats, forcing a move from his home in Newry. Collins eventually returned and began speaking out against the army's publicly. Over a period of several years, IRA supporters burned Collins's car, attempted to hit him with a car, and set fire to his house. On January 27, 1999, his body was found by the side of the road near his home. Collins had taken his dogs for a walk and been attacked; his head was so badly beaten that police were not initially able to ascertain whether he had been shot as well.

Collins's book is his legacy, an explanation of the motivating factors behind a brutal situation from an insider's point of view. Kevin Toolis, a reviewer for the Manchester *Guardian,* commented that "*Killing Rage* is a document of an assassin; a descriptive guidebook on how to gather enough information to kill a man and an exposition of the moral cost that such deeds extract from the narrator's psyche." Thomas observed that "where *Killing Rage* succeeds— and it often does—is as an eyewitness account. Collins wanted to show the true horror of his experiences. He does."

BIOGRAPHICAL AND CRITICAL SOURCES:

BOOKS

Collins, Eamon, and Mick McGovern, *Killing Rage,* Granta Books (London, England), 1997.

PERIODICALS

Guardian (Manchester, England), April 5, 1997, Kevin Toolis, review of *Killing Rage,* p. T16; July 3, 1999, Kevin Toolis, "Eamon Collins," p. T16.
Nation, July 12, 1999, Roane Carey, "Republic of Pain," review of *Killing Rage,* p. 30.
New York Times, January 28, 1999, "Author of an Expose of IRA Is Slain, Apparently in Revenge," p. A7.
New York Times Book Review, November 21, 1999, Jo Thomas, "Defenders of the Faith," review of *Killing Rage,* p. 18.*

*   *   *

COLTON, James
See HANSEN, Joseph

*   *   *

COOLEY, Charles Horton 1864-1929

PERSONAL: Born August 17, 1864 in Ann Arbor, MI; died 1929, in Ann Arbor, MI; son of Thomas M. Cooley (a jurist). *Education:* University of Michigan, graduated 1887; pursued additional study in mechanical engineering and economics.

CAREER: Educator, sociologist, social psychologist, and writer. University of Michigan, teacher of politics and economics, 1892-1904, teacher of sociology, 1904-1929. Worked for the Civil Service Commission and the U.S. Census Bureau.

WRITINGS:

The Theory of Transportation, American Economics Association (Baltimore, MD), 1894.
Genius, Fame, and the Comparison of Race, American Academy of Political and Social Science (Philadelphia, PA), 1897.
Personal Competition; Its Place in the Social Order and Effect upon Individuals, with Some Considerations on Success, American Economic Association by Macmillan (New York, NY), 1899.

Human Nature and the Social Order, Charles Scribner's Sons (New York, NY), 1902, reprinted, introduction by Philip Rieff, foreword by George Herbert Mead, Transaction Books (New Brunswick, NJ), 1983.

Social Organization: A Study of the Larger Mind, Charles Scribner's Sons (New York, NY), 1909; reprinted, introduction by Philip Rieff, Transaction Books (New Brunswick, NJ), 1993.

Social Process, Charles Scribner's Sons (New York, NY), 1918, reprinted, introduction by Roscoe C. Hinkle, foreword by Herman R. Lantz, Southern Illinois University Press (Carbondale, IL), 1966.

Life and the Student: Roadside Notes on Human Nature, Society, and Letters, A. A. Knopf (New York, NY), 1927.

Sociological Theory and Social Research; Being Selected Papers of Charles Horton Cooley, introduction and notes by Robert Cooley Angell, Henry Holt & Co. (New York, NY), 1930; revised and expanded edition, A.M. Kelley (New York, NY), 1969.

(With Robert Cooley Angell and Lowell Juilliard Carr) *Introductory Sociology,* Charles Scribner's Sons (New York, NY), 1933.

Two Major Works: Social Organization, Human Nature and the Social Order, introduction by Robert Cooley Angell, Free Press (Glencoe, IL), 1956.

Contributor to periodicals, including *American Journal of Sociology, Quarterly Journal of Economics, Psychological Review, Psychological Bulletin, Political Science Quarterly, Journal of Applied Sociology, New Republic,* and *Journal of Political Economy.*

SIDELIGHTS: Psychologist, sociologist, and educator Charles Horton Cooley is known for demonstrating that "personality emerges from Social influences, and that the individual and the group are complementary aspects of human association," according to a biographer in *World of Sociology.*

Born in 1864 in Ann Arbor, Michigan, Cooley was the son of Judge Thomas M. Cooley. Educated at the University of Michigan, he studied mechanical engineering and then economics. In 1889, he took a job with the U.S. Civil Service Commission, then went to work for the Census Bureau. He taught political science and economics at the University of Michigan from 1892 to 1904, and was a professor of sociology from 1904 until his death in 1929.

The Theory of Transportation, Cooley's first major work, explored ideas in economic theory, the most notable being Cooley's conclusion that "towns and cities tend to be located at the confluence of transportation routes—the so-called break in transportation," the *World of Sociology* biographer noted. Later books undertook broader analysis of the interplay between social and individual processes. In *Human Nature and the Social Order* Cooley examines ways in which social responses influence normal social participation. In *Social Organization: A Study of the Larger Mind,* he outlines a comprehensive approach to society and its major processes. The beginning of *Social Organization* also contains what some have considered "a sociological antidote to Sigmund Freud," according to the *World of Sociology* writer. "In that much-quoted segment, Cooley formulates the crucial role of primary groups (family, play groups, and so on) as the source of one's morals, sentiments, and ideals. But the impact of the primary group is so great that individuals cling to primary ideals in more complex associations and even create new primary groupings within formal organizations."

In his last significant book, *Social Process,* published in 1918, Cooley addresses the "nonrational, tentative nature of social organization and the significance of social competition," the *World of Sociology* biographer remarked. Cooley saw modern difficulties as the conflict of primary group values, such as love, loyalty, and ambition, and institutional values, such as progress, Protestantism, and other impersonal ideologies. "As societies try to cope with their difficulties," the *World of Sociology* contributor commented, "they adjust these two kinds of values to one another as best they can."

BIOGRAPHICAL AND CRITICAL SOURCES:

BOOKS

Encyclopedia of World Biography, 2nd edition, Gale (Detroit, MI), 1998.

Palmisano, Joseph M., editor, *World of Sociology,* Gale (Detroit, MI), 2001.

Reiss, Albert J., Jr., *Cooley and Sociological Analysis,* introduction by Robert Cooley Angell, University of Michigan Press (Ann Arbor, MI), 1968.

PERIODICALS

American Journal of Legal History, April, 1992, Alan Jones, "Law and Economics v. a Democratic

Society: The Case of Thomas M. Cooley, Charles H. Cooley, and Henry C. Adams," pp. 119-138.

Radical History Review, winter, 2000, Jeff Sklansky, "Corporate Property and Social Psychology: Thomas M. Cooley, Charles H. Cooley, and the Ideological Origins of the Social Self," p. 90.*

*   *   *

CORNELIUS, Kay 1933-

PERSONAL: Born January 14, 1933, in Memphis, TN; married an aerospace contracts specialist; children: two. *Ethnicity:* "Caucasian." *Education:* George Peabody College of Vanderbilt University, B.A.; Alabama A & M University, M.Ed. *Politics:* Independent. *Religion:* Southern Baptist. *Hobbies and other interests:* Knitting, travel.

ADDRESSES: Agent—c/o Author Mail, Chelsea House Publishers, 1974 Sproul Rd., Ste. 400, Broomall, PA 19008. *E-mail*—kaycorn@hiwaay.net.

CAREER: Teacher in Huntsville, AL, 1956-86; teacher at a magnet school, 1986-90; writer.

MEMBER: Writers of America, Authors Guild, League of American PEN Women, Alabama Writers Conclave, Alabama Writers Forum, Phi Delta Kappa, Delta Kappa Gamma.

AWARDS, HONORS: Sullivan Award, Peabody College, 1952.

WRITINGS:

A Matter of Security, Barbour Publishing Co. (Ulrichsville, OH), 1995.

A Nostalgic Noel, Barbour Publishing Co. (Ulrichsville, OH), 1998.

Twin Willows, Barbour Publishing Co. (Ulrichsville, OH), 1999.

The Supreme Court, Chelsea House Publishers (Philadelphia, PA), 2000.

Francis Marion: The Swamp Fox, Chelsea House Publishers (Philadelphia, PA), 2001.

Chamique Holdsclaw, Chelsea House Publishers (Philadelphia, PA), 2001.

Edgar Allan Poe, Chelsea House Publishers (Philadelphia, PA), 2002.

Emily Dickinson, Chelsea House Publishers (Philadelphia, PA), 2002.

Pennsylvania, Barbour Publishing Co. (Ulrichsville, OH), 2002.

Love's Gentle Journey, Barbour Publishing Co. (Ulrichsville, OH), 2002.

Toni's Vow, Heartsong Presents (Uhrichsville, OH), 2003.

Anita's Fortune, Heartsong Presents (Ulrichsville, OH), 2004.

Mary's Choice, Barbour Publishing Co. (Ulrichsville, OH), 2004.

Contributor to periodicals, including *Alabama Heritage, Tennessee Historical Quarterly, Tennessee Encyclopedia of History, Alabama Writing Teacher, Alabama Writers' Forum, Journal of Doublespeak, Event, Daily Blessing, Peabody Post,* and *Alabama Alitcom.*

WORK IN PROGRESS: The Bell Witch Phenomenon.

SIDELIGHTS: Young-adult author Kay Cornelius has had a passion for words ever since she was a little girl growing up in the south. Today she is the author of novels for both adults and younger readers as well as works of nonfiction reflecting her interest in history. Her books include the juvenile biographies *Francis Marion: The Swamp Fox* and *Chamique Holdsclaw* as well as the historical novels *Love's Gentle Journey, Anita's Fortune,* and *Twin Willows,* all of which are Christian romances. Carolyn Janssen, writing in *School Library Journal,* praised *Francis Marion* for its "lively" narrative focusing on the man who led the British cavalry into the muck and mire of a South Carolina swamp during the American Revolution.

Prior to writing full time, Cornelius worked as an English teacher up until her retirement in 1990. As she once commented: "Like most authors, I was read to long before I started to school. Born Southern, I was surrounded by natural storytellers, and since my father ran the local 'picture show,' I also absorbed hundreds of movies. I loved working with words and finding new ways to express myself, so it was only natural that after winning a four-year college scholarship for a 750-word essay in a national contest, I should major in English and become a teacher.

"While I continued to write sporadically, my present writing career grew out of my participation in the National Writing Project at Auburn University in 1981. The intensive writing led me to combine my love of historical research and story-telling to produce my first novel, *Love's Gentle Journey.* Since its publication in 1985, it has been almost constantly in print. After I retired from teaching in 1990, I started writing full-time. I approach each new project with prospective readers in mind. I want my work to be entertaining as well as informative and inspiring.

"It's satisfying to conduct writing workshops and mentor authors. I tell them writing is hard work, but seeing their name in print on something that will live on after they are gone is well worth the effort."

BIOGRAPHICAL AND CRITICAL SOURCES:

PERIODICALS

Publishers Weekly, January 18, 1999, review of *Twin Willows,* p. 336.
School Library Journal, July, 2001, Carolyn Janssen, review of *Francis Marion: The Swamp Fox,* p. 118.

ONLINE

Heartsong Presents Web site, http://www.heartsong presents.com/ (October 22, 2004).

*   *   *

COULTON, James
 See HANSEN, Joseph

*   *   *

CRANNA, John 1954-

PERSONAL: Born 1954.

ADDRESSES: Agent—c/o Author Mail, Heinemann Reed, 39 Rawene Rd., Birkenhead, Auckland, New Zealand.

CAREER: Author.

AWARDS, HONORS: Commonwealth First Book Award and New Zealand Book Award, both 1990, both for *Visitors.*

WRITINGS:

Visitors (short stories), Heinemann Reed (Aukland, New Zealand), 1989.
Arena, Minerva (Aukland, New Zealand), 1992.

Contributor to *The Oxford Book of New Zealand Short Stories,* edited by Vincent O'Sullivan, Oxford University Press, 1993.

SIDELIGHTS: New Zealand author John Cranna received acclaim and awards for his first collection of short stories, *Visitors.* Although the eight stories in this collection are told in a realistic style and most often take place in the present, two of them are fantasies and one is a science-fiction tale. These works feature characters—mostly from the middle class and mix of white, Maori, and Polynesian—who are loners and try by various means to make sense of their world and lives. The themes include such subjects as the relationship between past and present, the struggle between man and nature, and the complexities of human sexuality. In a *World Literature Today* review, Bernard Gadd noted, "The style is one of clarity and ease of reading, with a care for telling details." Gadd added that Cranna's "great skill is in drawing the reader gently and persuasively into the odd worlds of his characters and in handling the process of time."

BIOGRAPHICAL AND CRITICAL SOURCES:

PERIODICALS

Gaurdian (Manchester, England), August 10, 1993, Michael Hulse, review of *The Oxford Book of New Zealand Short Stories.*
Times Literary Supplement, February 2, 1990, Freddie Baveystock, "Lost Worlds and Travellers' Tales," p. 122.
World Literature Today, winter, 1991, Bernard Gadd, review of *Visitors,* p. 191.*

*   *   *

CRAY, David
 See SOLOMITA, Stephen

CRONIN, Jeremy 1949-

PERSONAL: Born September 12, 1949, in South Africa; married; first wife's name, Anne Marie (deceased, 1977); second wife's name, Gemma. *Education:* Attended University of Cape Town; Sorbonne, University of Paris, M.A.

ADDRESSES: Agent—c/o Author Mail, David Philip Publications, 99 Garfield Rd., Claremont 7700, South Africa.

CAREER: University of Cape Town, Cape Town, South Africa, lecturer in political science, until 1976; imprisoned, 1976-83; exiled in London, England, then Lusaka, 1983-90; African National Congress, member of national executive committee 1991—; South African Communist Party, member of central committee and deputy secretary general, beginning 1989; member of South African Parliament.

AWARDS, HONORS: Ingrid Jonker Prize, 1984, for *Inside;* Sydney Clouts Memorial Prize for Poetry, for *Even the Dead: Poems, Parables, and a Jeremiad.*

WRITINGS:

(Editor, with Anthony de Crespigny) *Ideologies of Politics,* Oxford University Press (New York, NY), 1975.
Inside (poetry), Ravan Press (Johannesburg, South Africa), 1984.
(With Raymond Suttner and others) *Thirty Years of the Freedom Charter,* Ravan Press (Johannesburg, South Africa), c. 1985.
Even the Dead: Poems, Parables, and a Jeremiad, Mayaibuye Books (Bellville, South Africa)/David Philip Publishers (Cape Town, South Africa), 1997.
Inside and Out: Poems from Inside and Even the Dead, David Philip Publishers (Cape Town, South Africa), 1999.

Contributor of articles and poetry to anthologies, including *Against Forgetting: Twentieth Century Poetry of Witness,* Norton (New York, NY), 1993. Editor of *African Communist* and *Umsebenzi.*

SIDELIGHTS: Jeremy Cronin is a politician and poet whose writings are inextricably tied to his political activism. Born into a middle-class, white, English-speaking family in South Africa, Cronin grew up relatively insulated from the troubles of South African apartheid, which separated black and white in society. As a youth, he read primarily European and North American poetry and began writing his own poems when he was around fifteen years old. After entering university in 1968, he became involved in anti-apartheid political activism. Cronin told Helena Sheehan in an interview on the Dublin City University Web site that the assassination of the South African intellectual Rick Turner "really marked my entry into political intellectual activity and, quite quickly after that, organizational political activity as well."

In 1976 Cronin was arrested by South African security police for his participation in the then-outlawed African National Congress. He was sentenced to seven years in the Pretoria Maximum Security Prison. In the second year of his sentence, his wife died. "It was in prison that my first seriously sustained compulsive effort at writing poetry took place," Cronin told Barbara Harlow in an interview in *Alif.* He also told Sheehan that he began writing poetry "as a survival activity in prison without much sense of an audience."

The result of Cronin's writing efforts in prison was his first book of poetry, *Inside,* which was published in 1984, the year after his release. "*Inside,* These poems illegally recorded in prison and either smuggled out or memorized for later reworking, bears testimony in its strongest constituents to a surprising symbiosis of autobiography, lyricism, narrative, oral performance, and political commitment," noted a contributor to *Contemporary Poets.* The title of the volume clearly refers to Cronin's incarceration, but, as noted by the *Contemporary Poets* contributor, it also "refers to the autobiographical interiority of love poems written for the wife who died." Writing in *Research in African Literatures,* Rita Barnard noted that this "first collection emphasizes from the start the location of writing." She went on to comment that Cronin has often stated that prison gave him a sense of place from which he could speak, and wrote, "To claim prison as a privileged 'speaking place' is not to minimize the pain, frustration, and terror of incarceration—experiences which Cronin's poems movingly testify. They record also an acute sense of spatial disorientation, which the poet attributes to the paucity of visual stimuli in the gray, enclosed world 'inside.'"

It would be more than a decade before Cronin's next collection of poems was published. He wrote most of the poems appearing in *Even the Dead: Poems, Parables, and a Jeremiad* after South Africa held its first democratic elections in 1994. The poems in the collection range from the lyric to short narratives. They focus primarily on the complicated transition within South Africa following apartheid and pay special attention to giving justice to the present and the past. "*Even the Dead* argues on behalf of a narrative in lyric form that would re-tell the translations of the political struggle in and for South Africa from a national liberation movement in league with the internationalism of socialism to the new imperative of meeting the demands of globalization and the free-market economies," wrote Harlow in *Alif.* Harlow went on to note that "'Even the Dead,' the title poem, closes the volume with powerful admonitions against the collapse of amnesty in amnesia—syntagmatic or paradigmatic, CNN's globalised amnesia, the Gulf war's lobotomized amnesia, Third World structurally adjusted amnesia, Hollywood's milk of amnesia. Amnesia, 'even the dead' insists, 'has no cut-off date.'"

Inside and Out: Poems from Inside and Even the Dead is comprised of selections from Cronin's two previous volumes of poetry. Sharif Elmusa, who participated in the Harlow interview of Cronin for *Alif,* noted that in reading these selected poems "the reader notices a change of outlook or even of world-view" between the prison poems and Cronin's later poetry, which he penned as a free man.

Although Cronin's poetry gained international recognition through the publication of these three volumes, it has become better known through his public readings. He has read his poems in a variety of contexts, including political rallies, where oftentimes he read his poems over the din of police helicopters, the smell of tear-gas, and the din of a rambunctious audience. In *Alif* Cronin explained to Harlow the difference between reading his poems in book form and hearing the poet read or present them: "Poetry performance needs to be understood in part, in the social context of South Africa. There are very high levels of adult non-literacy in our society, but, on the other hand, there are strong oral performance traditions—singing, village meeting-place oratory, funeral speeches, and praise poetry."

The *Contemporary Poets* contributor noted that Cronin's poetic voice has been influenced "partly by international voices," but added that "its dexterity has more profoundly been coached by the many tongues of South Africa." The essayist also wrote: "Despite the dangers of sentimentalism and ideological dissimulation that might be expected to attend a project like Cronin's, dangers that do threaten some of the poems, the turning inside out, or metamorphoses, from isolation and despair to community and hope typically produce a remarkable record of resilience and beauty."

BIOGRAPHICAL AND CRITICAL SOURCES:

BOOKS

Attridge, Derek, and Rosemary Jolly, editors, *Writing South Africa: Literature, Apartheid, and Democracy, 1970-1995,* Cambridge University Press (Cambridge, England), 1998.
Contemporary Poets, seventh edition, St. James Press (Detroit, MI), 2001.
Nethersole, Reingard, editor, *Emerging Literatures,* Peter Lang (Bern, Switzerland), 1990.

PERIODICALS

Alif, 2001, Barbara Harlow, "A Chapter in South African Verse" (interview), p. 252.
Ariel, April, 1985, Sheila Roberts, "South African Prison Literature."
Index on Censorship, June, 1984, Stephen Gray, "Inside."
Monthly Review, December, 2002, John S. Saul, "Starting from Scratch? A Reply to Jeremy Cronin," p. 43.
Research in African Literatures, spring, 1994, David Schalkwyk, "Confessions and Solidarity in the Prison Writing of Breyten Breytenbach and Jeremy Cronin," p. 23; fall, 2001, Rita Barnard, "Speaking Places: Prison, Poetry, and the South African Nation," p. 155.

ONLINE

Dublin City University Web site, http://www.comms.dcu.ie/ (November 4, 2004), Helena Sheehan, interview with Cronin.*

*   *   *

CROW, Thomas E. 1948-

PERSONAL: Born 1948. *Education:* Pomona College, B.A., 1969; University of California, Los Angeles, M.A., 1975, Ph.D., 1978.

ADDRESSES: Office—University Park Campus, Getty Research Institute, University of Southern California, Los Angeles, CA 90089. *E-mail*—tcrow@getty.edu.

CAREER: California Institute of the Arts, Valencia, CA, instructor in critical studies, 1977-78; University of Chicago, Chicago, IL, assistant professor of history of art, 1978-80; Princeton University, Princeton, NJ, assistant professor of art and archaeology, 1980-86; University of Michigan, Ann Arbor, MI, associate professor of history of art, 1986-90; University of Sussex, Sussex, England, professor of history of art and chairman of department, 1990-96; Yale University, New Haven, CT, Robert Lehman Professor of the History of Art, 1996-2000, department chairman, 1997-2000; Getty Research Institute, University of Southern California, Los Angeles, director, 2000—. Lecturer at symposia on artists and art history.

MEMBER: American Academy of Arts and Sciences, American Society of Eighteenth-Century Studies.

AWARDS, HONORS: Mitchell Prize for the History of Art, 1986, for *Painters and Public Life in Eighteenth-Century Paris;* Michigan Society of Fellows senior fellow, 1987-90; National Endowment for the Humanities fellowship, 1988-89.

WRITINGS:

Painters and Public Life in Eighteenth-Century Paris, Yale University Press (New Haven, CT), 1985.
(With others) *Endgame: Reference and Simulation in Recent Painting and Sculpture,* MIT Press (Cambridge, MA), 1987.
Emulation: Making Artists for Revolutionary France, Yale University Press (New Haven, CT), 1995.
Modern Art in the Common Culture, Yale University Press (New Haven, CT), 1996.
The Rise of the Sixties: American and European Art in the Era of Dissent, Harry N. Abrams (New York, NY), 1996.
The Intelligence of Art, University of North Carolina Press (Chapel Hill, NC), 1999.

Contributor to books, including *Ross Bleckner,* Harry N. Abrams (New York, NY), 1995; Stephanie Barron, *Jasper Johns to Jeff Koons: Four Decades of Art from the Broad Collections,* Harry N. Abrams, 2001; Stephen Eisenman, *Nineteenth-Century Art: A Critical History,* Thames & Hudson (New York, NY), 1994. Contributing editor, *Art Forum,* 1993—.

SIDELIGHTS: Thomas E. Crow is an art historian and critic whose works defy easy summarization. His essays on issues involving the social and aesthetic aims of art works range widely, from the eighteenth century through the modern era. As Roger Malbert noted in the *Times Literary Supplement,* Crow's "exemplary texts are all firmly grounded in the empirical study of particular objects." Crow's first books concern the schools of painting in eighteenth-century France, specifically ofin the period prior to and including the French Revolution. More recently he has discussed the production of art in a cultural context, from the uses of art for political purposes in the 1960s to the commercial and social imperatives placed upon art in the modern world.

New York Times Book Review correspondent William Olander called Crow's *Painters and Public Life in Eighteenth-Century Paris* "the most comprehensive and valuable study of art and public life in that era now in print." Olander concluded: "The question of who is the audience for art, the viewer, the spectator, is a particularly vexing one, so obviously yet mysteriously is it linked to both production and consumption. Mr. Crow's book seems to suggest that little, if anything, has changed about that since the late 18th century. After reading it, one is almost tempted to agree."

P. N. Furbank, writing in the *London Review of Books,* described Crow's *Emulation: Making Artists for Revolutionary France* as "a history of the decline and fall, and amazing final reprieve, of history-painting in France." Furbank commented: "It is the fate of the ignorant amateur, like myself, to be convinced by whichever art-historian he happens to be reading at the time. But dazzled I certainly am, and, with the occasional sceptical twitch, also convinced, by Crow's book, which humanises and makes deeply involving a school of painting I used to consider chilly and remote."

Modern Art in the Common Culture "attacks the postmodern endeavor to blur the distinction between fine and popular art and to treat 'visual culture' as all of a piece," wrote Arthur C. Danto in the *Times Literary Supplement.* Danto felt that Crow's work "is set off by a discussion of the state of the field that makes this far and away the most searching and important book in the philosophy and history of art to have appeared in the past decade." *Art in America* essayist Marcia E. Vetrocq suggested that the book "resonates with Crow's determination to engage a community of writers and readers beyond academia, as well as with his pleasure at having become a new citizen of that larger community." Vetrocq also remarked that *Modern Art in the Common Culture* "remains a deeply compelling work which stands as a summons to fresh thinking."

Crow's *The Intelligence of Art* is a collection of four extended essays relating art to specific moments in the evolution of European capitalism, from the early stirrings of enterprise in the twelfth century to the studies of certain art historians in the twentieth century. In the *Art Bulletin,* David Summers found the work "a manifesto and an essay in method, in which case studies create the effect of close inference as works of art and exemplary scholarship are adapted to the author's developing thesis." In his review of the book, Malbert wrote: "Crow's dialectical skills are impressive. . . . This short but flawlessly written and intricately argued book offers a profoundly challenging critique of the current state of art history. It . . . should contribute to the revitalization of a discipline that Crow tactfully suggests has become increasingly 'complacent and inward-looking.'. . . Crow is an authoritative critic of contemporary art."

BIOGRAPHICAL AND CRITICAL SOURCES:

PERIODICALS

Art Bulletin, June, 2002, David Summers, review of *The Intelligence of Art,* p. 373.

Art in America, February, 1996, Garry Apgar, review of *Emulation: Making Artists for Revolutionary France,* p. 25; March, 1998, Marcia E. Vetrocq, review of *Modern Art in the Common Culture,* p. 37.

London Review of Books, August 3, 1995, P. N. Furbank, "Oppositional," p. 23.

Nation, October 14, 1996, Paul Mattick, review of *Modern Art in the Common Culture* and *The Rise of the Sixties: American and European Art in the Era of Dissent,* p. 33.

New Republic, July 3, 1995, Lynn Hunt, review of *Emulation,* p. 36.

New York Times Book Review, March 9, 1986, William Olander, review of *Painters and Public Life in Eighteenth-Century Paris,* p. 21.

Publishers Weekly, May 20, 1996, review of *The Rise of the Sixties,* p. 253.

Times Literary Supplement, November 8, 1996, Arthur C. Danto, "Why Modern Isn't Contemporary," pp. 14-15; November 5, 1999, Roger Malbert, review of *The Intelligence of Art,* p. 11.*

D

DARBY, Ann

PERSONAL: Female. *Education:* Attended Stanford University and University of California, Berkeley; Columbia University, B.A., M.F.A. *Hobbies and other interests:* Running.

ADDRESSES: Home—New York, NY. *Agent*—Emma Sweeney, Harold Ober Associates, Inc., 425 Madison Avenue, New York, NY 10017. *E-mail*—ann@anndarby.com.

CAREER: Writer. Former dancer; also worked variously as a waitress, secretary, corporate trainer, and instructor in business writing and presentation skills. Instructor, Riverside Writers' Group; teaching fellow, Columbia University; worked in science publishing at W. H. Freeman; instructor at writers' conferences.

AWARDS, HONORS: Bennett Cerf prize for short fiction.

WRITINGS:

Finny the Lovesick Frog, illustrated by Katia Karloff, Chalk Board Publications (Rancho Cucamonga, CA), 1996.
The Orphan Game, William Morrow (New York, NY), 1999.
(With Thomas P. Mauriello) *The Dollhouse Murders: A Forensic Expert Investigates Six Little Crimes,* PI Press (New York, NY), 2003.

Also author, with Laurie Swearingen, of performance-art piece *The Alice Boyd Story;* author of short stories; editor for *Scientific American Medicine* (textbook). Contributor to periodicals, including *Northwest Review, Malahat Review, Best of StoryQuarterly, Prairie Schooner, Scientific American Cancer Smart,* and *Scientific American Cancer Outlook.* Regular reviewer for *Publishers Weekly.*

WORK IN PROGRESS: The Sweet, Sad Songs of W. F. Pine, a novel.

SIDELIGHTS: Author Ann Darby was raised in southern California, the daughter of an attorney and a gym teacher. She attended the University of California, Berkeley, because it had a dance department. Her involvement in a summer dance workshop with the Merce Cunningham Company led her to relocate to New York City, where she arrived with just "sixty-five cents and one telephone number," as she remarked on her home page. While supporting herself waiting tables, Darby studied dance and performed in the city for twelve years. She returned to school to earn her B.A. and M.F.A. at Columbia University, and while she held various jobs over several years, worked on her first novel, *The Orphan Game,* which was published in 1999.

Set in southern California around 1965, *The Orphan Game* follows the travails of Maggie Harris, a pregnant sixteen year old whose older boyfriend has just joined the U.S. Army and may be sent to Vietnam. Maggie's home situation is precarious: her father plunges the family further and further into debt with his reckless real estate investments, while her mother tries to supplement their income by taking in sewing from the town's wealthy women. The parents fight a lot, Maggie's younger brother copes by skateboarding around the empty streets at night, and her younger sister attempts to be the model child. To cope, Maggie appeals to an eccentric aunt for emotional help and guidance.

Valerie Sayers wrote in the *New York Times Book Review:* "Darby's first novel is smart, sharply observant and—in its opening, at least—deceptively simple. In fact, its intricate pattern isn't entirely revealed until the story's last page." "*The Orphan Game* begins at a slow and deliberate pace," Sayers continued, "but quickly gains momentum. The novel's ending is startling, and it's a measure of Darby's skill that it also feels inevitable." An *Entertainment Weekly* contributor called the book a "thoughtful first novel," and a *Publishers Weekly* critic commented that Darby's prose is "tightly controlled . . . sometimes microscopically observant, sometimes musical. Her attention to every detail of the period is faultless." *The Orphan Game* became a *Los Angeles Times* bestseller.

For *The Dollhouse Murders: A Forensic Expert Investigates Six Little Crimes,* Darby teamed up with Thomas P. Mauriello, a former police officer, crime-scene investigator, and criminology professor at the University of Maryland. While teaching at the university, Mauriello created and used six tiny dioramas—or "dollhouses"—to show his students how to use forensic evidence in crime scene investigations. Darby lends her skill as a wordsmith to flesh out the prose for each of the book's six cases. Harry Charles, reviewing *The Dollhouse Murders* for *Library Journal,* called it "highly original" and commented that Darby presents the fictional crimes in "real-time narratives with sharp dialog and description."

BIOGRAPHICAL AND CRITICAL SOURCES:

PERIODICALS

Entertainment Weekly, May 28, 1999, review of *The Orphan Game,* p. 138.
Library Journal, April 1, 1999, Nancy Pearl, review of *The Orphan Game,* p. 128; October 1, 1999, review of *The Orphan Game,* p. 50; November 1,

2003, Harry Charles, review of *The Dollhouse Murders: A Forensic Expert Investigates Six Little Crimes,* p. 109.
New York Times Book Review, June 6, 1999, Valerie Sayers, review of *The Orphan Game,* p. 24.
Publishers Weekly, March 15, 1999, review of *The Orphan Game,* p. 44; July 5, 1999, Judy Quinn and Bob Summer, review of *The Orphan Game,* p. 31; October 6, 2003, review of *The Dollhouse Murders,* p. 73.

ONLINE

Ann Darby Home Page, http://anndarby.com (October 23, 2004).*

*   *   *

DAWSON, Geralyn

PERSONAL: Married; children: two sons, one daughter. *Education:* Attended Texas A&M University. *Hobbies and other interests:* Watching college football.

ADDRESSES: Agent—Pocket Books, 1230 Avenue of the Americas, New York, NY 10020. *E-mail*—g. dawson@genie.com.

CAREER: Author. Has worked in sales, advertising, and as a catalogue designer for a boating supply distributor. Member of advisory board, Making Memories Breast Cancer Foundation.

AWARDS, HONORS: National Readers' Choice Award, for *The Wedding Raffle;* Career Achievement Award, *Romantic Times.*

WRITINGS:

ROMANCE FICTION

The Texan's Bride, Bantam Books (New York, NY), 1993.
Capture the Night, Bantam Books (New York, NY), 1993.

The Bad Luck Wedding Dress, Bantam Books (New York, NY), 1993.

Tempting Morality, Bantam Books (New York, NY), 1993.

The Wedding Raffle, Pocket Books (New York, NY), 1996.

The Kissing Stars, Sonnet Books (New York, NY), 1999.

Simmer All Night, Sonnet Books (New York, NY), 1999.

Sizzle All Day, Sonnet Books (New York, NY), 2000.

The Bad Luck Wedding Night, Sonnet Books (New York, NY), 2001.

The Pink Magnolia Club, Pocket Books (New York, NY), 2002.

My Big Old Texas Heartache, Pocket Books (New York, NY), 2003.

My Long Tall Texas Heartthrob, Pocket Books (New York, NY), 2004.

Contributor to anthologies, including *Under the Boardwalk,* Sonnet Books (New York, NY), 1999, and *A Season in the Highlands,* Pocket Books (New York, NY), 2000.

SIDELIGHTS: Geralyn Dawson is an award-winning romance novelist. She started her career writing historical romances set in 1800s Texas, beginning with her 1993 novel, *The Texan's Bride.* In another Texas story, *The Wedding Raffle,* Dawson tells the story of Honor Duvall, a down-on-her-luck, thrice-widowed beauty who raffles off a horse to raise much-needed money. Luke Prescott, a Texas Ranger, wins the raffle but soon discovers that the horse is dead. Nevertheless, Luke remains true to his renown as a Texas hero and is soon defending Duvall against her father's demand that she marry a British lord. Readers learn of Luke's guilt over not being with his comrades when they died at the Alamo, as well as over the death of his own family as they tried to escape from Mexican General Santa Anna. A *Publishers Weekly* contributor complimented the historical accuracy of the story, the author's effective dialogue, and characters that are "funny, earthy and brave."

In *Tempting Morality* Dawson recounts the tale of Zach Burkett and Miss Morality Brown. Zach initially meets Morality when she is testifying at a revival meeting and he thinks she is a fraud who can help him wreak revenge on the people of Cottonwood Creek

who have betrayed him. Morality is not merely pretending to be holy, however, and Zach soon finds himself falling in love.

Dawson tells a story of love lost and then rediscovered in *The Kissing Stars.* Married as teenagers, lawman Gabe Montana and Tess Cameron are tragically separated for more than decade until they find each other again in 1889 Texas. Their rekindled love must then go through the catharsis of sorting out their past. Writing in *Publishers Weekly,* a reviewer enjoyed the author's "comic style," but felt that the intrusion of too many minor characters in *The Kissing Stars* makes for a "slow-moving plot."

Simmer All Night focuses on Christina Delaney, a rebel whose aristocratic San Antonio family sends her to Victorian England to visit her grandfather after she gets into trouble. Along for the ride is her friend Cole Morgan. Christina becomes engaged to be married but breaks off the engagement and ultimately turns to Cole as her one true love. A *Publishers Weekly* reviewer found parts of Dawson's novel "childish," but noted that "a dramatic twist adds some much-needed action."

In *The Bad Luck Wedding Night,* Nicholas and Sara marry only to experience what a *Booklist* reviewer called a "hilarious and disaster-filled wedding night" that results in their marriage going unconsummated. A decade later, however, Nicholas and Sara meet again, and Nicholas determines to make Sara his bride once again.

In some of her more recent books, Dawson leaves the historical romance genre for modern romance. For example, in *My Big Old Texas Heartache,* she tells about the love between Kate and former Cedar Dell high school football star Max Cooper. Max fathered a child with Kate when they were both teenagers but left Cedar Dell, Texas, only to return years later. *My Long Tall Texas Heartthrob* is also set in Cedar Dell and tells the story of Tess, who moves to Cedar Dell from Los Angeles to live in a trailer park and take care of her helpless sister's children. When she meets Nicholas Sutherland, she finds herself falling in love but wonders if an L.A. girl can live happily ever after with a Texas cowboy.

Dawson strays from the strict romance formula in her book *The Pink Magnolia Club.* Writing on her home page, she explained that she got the idea for the book after attending a wedding-gown sale held by the Making Memories Breast Cancer Foundation. Many of the wedding-gown donors included letters and pictures with the gowns. After reading the heart-rending letters that accompanied some of the donated dresses, Dawson's interest was piqued. "I found myself laughing over them and crying over them, sometimes both at the same time." The author went on, "My novel began to take shape. I knew it must be a story about three women: the woman who donates her wedding gown, the woman who buys it, and the woman whose wish will be partially funded by the sale of the club." The resulting story tells of the budding friendship between three women who are reaching turning points in their lives. Maggie Prescott has donated her gown to be auctioned after her husband forgets their twenty-fifth wedding anniversary. Grace Hardeman, who is volunteering at the sale, is about to celebrate her fiftieth wedding anniversary when she discovers she has cancer. And Holly Weeks buys a gown at the auction even though she has no desire to get married and refuses her boyfriend's proposal. Writing in *Publishers Weekly,* a reviewer chided Dawson for her "melodramatic" characters but added, "Still, there are a number of truly moving moments here."

BIOGRAPHICAL AND CRITICAL SOURCES:

PERIODICALS

Booklist, September 15, 1998, review of *The Wedding Raffle,* p. 211; September 15, 2001, review of *The Bad Luck Wedding Night,* p. 211.
Publishers Weekly, October 7, 1996, review of *The Wedding Raffle,* p. 69; March 1, 1999, review of *The Kissing Stars,* p. 66; November 29, 1999, review of *Simmer All Night,* p. 58; July 8, 2002, review of *The Pink Magnolia Club,* p. 36.

ONLINE

eReader.com, http://www.ereader.com/ (November 4, 2004), "Geralyn Dawson."
Geralyn Dawson Home Page, http://www.geralyndawson.com (November 4, 2004).
Romantic Times Online, http://www.romantictimes.com/ (November 4, 2004), "Geralyn Dawson."
WritePage.com, http://www.writepage.com/ (November, 4, 2004), "Geralyn Dawson."*

DAY, Cathy 1968-

PERSONAL: Born 1968, in Peru, IN. *Education:* De-Pauw University, B.A. (magna cum laude), 1991; University of Alabama, M.F.A., 1995.

ADDRESSES: Home—Ewing, NJ. *Office*—College of New Jersey, English Department, P.O. Box 7718, 129 Bliss Hall, Ewing, NJ 08628-0718. *E-mail*—dayc@tcnj.edu.

CAREER: Teacher and author. Minnesota State University, Mankato, workshop instructor, 1997-99; College of New Jersey, assistant professor of creative writing, 2000—.

MEMBER: Association of Writers and Writing Programs, Phi Beta Kappa.

AWARDS, HONORS: Teaching/Writing fellowship and graduate council fellowship, both University of Alabama, both 1994; faculty research grant, Minnesota State University, 1998; Bush artist fellowship, Bush Foundation, 1999; Tennessee Williams scholarship, Sewanee Writers' Conference, 2001; Discover Great New Writers selection, Barnes & Noble, and Best Books of 2004 Debut Fiction award, Amazon.com, both 2004, both for *The Circus in Winter.*

WRITINGS:

The Circus in Winter, Harcourt (Orlando, FL), 2004.

Short stories and articles have appeared in numerous periodicals, including *Antioch Review, Shenandoah, Southern Review, River Styx, Distillery: Artistic Spirits of the South, Cream City Review, Gettysburg Review, Story, Florida Review,* and *Quarterly West.* Short stories have appeared in the anthologies, *Walking on Water,* University of Alabama Press, 1996; *American Fiction,* volume ten, New Rivers Press, 1999; and *New Stories from the South,* Algonquin Books of Chapel Hill, 2000.

SIDELIGHTS: Cathy Day draws on her own past as a youth for her first novel *The Circus in Winter.* Day grew up in Peru, Indiana, which once served as the winter home for many circuses. The author boasts a great uncle who was known as the world's fastest ticket taker and another who was an elephant trainer. In her novel of eleven connected short stories, Day draws on the many stories she heard as a youth to tell the tale of Lima, Indiana, and the rise and fall of the fictional Great Porter Circus, which uses Lima as its winter home from 1884 to 1939. The stories, which meander back and forth in time, include an account of how Wallace Porter buys the circus as his wife nears death, how the erotic acrobat Jennie Dixianna takes and discards lovers and even has an affair with Porter, and how the death of an elephant trainer reverberates down through the years to his descendents.

Writing in the *New York Times Book Review,* Gary Krist praised Day for avoiding the trap of "giving us variations on certain trite and less-than-urgent truths" that many fiction writers fall into when focusing on circus life. Krist went on to note that the author "succeeds in appropriating much of the garish pungency of the world of freaks, geeks and sideshow Houdinis without succumbing to its ready banalities." In a review in the *Chicago Tribune,* Porter Shreve noted, "Foregoing the rising and falling action of traditional plot, Day has assembled instead a living museum of the town's history, a portrait gallery of its fascinating residents across time." The reviewer added that "Day employs a yarn-spinning voice that evokes the time and place without ever seeming quaint or overwrought." Wendy Smith, writing in the *Los Angeles Times,* praised how the author "draws her thematic threads together with impressive skill and lyrical warmth in the final chapter." A *Kirkus Reviews* contributor noted: "Funny and tough-minded, yet tender and touched with magic: this is a real find."

BIOGRAPHICAL AND CRITICAL SOURCES:

PERIODICALS

Booklist, July, 2004, Kaite Mediatore, review of *The Circus in Winter,* p. 1817.
Boston Globe, August 22, 2004, Caroline Leavitt, review of *The Circus in Winter,* p. F9.
Chicago Tribune, June 27, 2004, Porter Shreve, review of *The Circus in Winter,* p. 5.
Entertainment Weekly, June 25, 2004, Lisa Schwarzbaum, review of *The Circus in Winter,* p. 170.

Kirkus Reviews, April 15, 2004, review of *The Circus in Winter,* p. 346.
Library Journal, May 1, 2004, Beth E. Anderson, review of *The Circus in Winter,* p. 139.
Los Angeles Times, September 12, 2004, Wendy Smith, review of *The Circus in Winter,* p. R8.
New York Times Book Review, Gary Krist, July 18, 2004, review of *The Circus in Winter,* p. 21.
People, June 26, 2004, Lee Aitken, review of *The Circus in Winter,* p. 48.
Publishers Weekly, May 17, 2004, review of *The Circus in Winter,* p. 33.

ONLINE

Cathy Day Home Page, http://www.cathyday.com (January 11, 2005).
College of New Jersey Web site, http://www.tcnj.edu/ (November 4, 2004), "Cathy Day."

*   *   *

de BROCA, Philippe (Claude Alex) 1933-2004

OBITUARY NOTICE— See index for *CA* sketch: Born March 15, 1933, in Paris, France; died of cancer November 26, 2004, in Neuilly-sur-Seine, France. Film director, producer, and author. De Broca was a popular and critically acclaimed movie director well known for his farces and spoofs that nevertheless occasionally hid more serious themes. After studying at the École Nationale de Photographie et de Cinematographie, he learned the ropes of filmmaking from French directors François Truffaut and Claude Chabrol. After directing several shorts, his first big project was 1960's *Les jeux de l'amour.* The film was followed by dozens of other popular movies for the big screen and television, including *L'homme de Rio* (1963), *Le cavaleur* (1978), *La gitane* (1986), *Le bossu* (1997), and his last film, *Vipère au Poing* (2004). For several of his films, he served not only as producer but also as screenwriter or adapter. Some of his movies, such as *Le roi de coeur* (1966), which was released in the United States as *The King of Hearts,* became popular—even cult classic—hits in America. Hugely popular through the 1970s, de Broca suffered a decline in popularity in the 1980s and did not fully regain his footing until the 1997 release of *Le Bossu.*

OBITUARIES AND OTHER SOURCES:

PERIODICALS

Chicago Tribune, December 1, 2004, section 3, p. 10.
Guardian (London, England), December 2, 2004, p. 29.
Independent (London, England), November 29, 2004, p. 35.
International Herald Tribune, December 3, 2004, p. 2.
Los Angeles Times, December 13, 2004, p. 44.
New York Times, December 2, 2004, p. C11.
Washington Post, November 30, 2004, p. B7.

*   *   *

DELBANCO, Francesca

PERSONAL: Born in Bennington, VT; daughter of college instructors. *Education:* Harvard University, B.A.; University of Michigan, M.F.A.

ADDRESSES: Home—Los Angeles, CA. *Office*— Author Mail, W. W. Norton, 500 Fifth Ave., New York, NY 10110.

CAREER: Writer. *Seventeen* (magazine), staff member; University of Michigan, instructor.

WRITINGS:

Ask Me Anything, Norton (New York, NY), 2004, published in England as *Midnight in Manhattan,* Orion (London, England), 2004.

Contributor to periodicals and Web sites. Advice columnist, *Teen People.*

WORK IN PROGRESS: A novel.

SIDELIGHTS: Francesca Delbanco's debut novel, *Ask Me Anything,* follows a young woman as she struggles to make the transition from student life to true adulthood. The narrator, Rosalie Preston, is in her twenties, recently graduated from Harvard, and strug-
gling to get her life on track in Manhattan. Though she makes her living as an advice columnist for a teen magazine, Rosalie's true passion is acting. She and some of her friends from Harvard have formed a theater company, the First Borns, but even as they try to make the group cohere, the long-time companions are inevitably losing touch with each other. Some of the more talented members of the group are drawn away by better opportunities; others become absorbed in love. Rosalie feels estranged from her friends, and those feelings intensify when she begins an affair with Berglan Starker, a married man many years her senior. (Berglan is also the father of one of the other First Borns.) Rosalie keeps their relationship a secret from her friends, and her own situation becomes much more difficult to untangle than the ones she typically addresses in her advice column. Delbanco's narrator is "fully drawn, if not always fully sympathetic," noted Tania Barnes in *Library Journal.* Barnes considered *Tell Me Anything* a "wry, compelling, and keenly observed" story. *Booklist* contributor Kristine Huntley called Rosalie a "sharp, witty narrator" and added: "Delbanco's assured, insightful debut is a must-read for the twentysomething set."

BIOGRAPHICAL AND CRITICAL SOURCES:

PERIODICALS

Booklist, December 15, 2003, Kristine Huntley, review of *Ask Me Anything,* p. 725.
Kirkus Reviews, November 15, 2003, review of *Ask Me Anything,* p. 1326.
Library Journal, December, 2003, Tania Barnes, review of *Ask Me Anything,* p. 165.
Publishers Weekly, November 10, 2003, review of *Ask Me Anything,* p. 39.

ONLINE

Morning News Online, http://www.themorningnews. org/ (March 16, 2004), Robert Birnbaum, interview with Delbanco.*

*   *   *

de SOMOGYI, Nick

PERSONAL: Male. *Education:* Attended Dulwich College.

ADDRESSES: Agent—c/o Nick Hern Books, The Glasshouse, 49A Goldhawk Rd., Shepherd's Bush, London W12 8QP, England.

CAREER: Author. Globe Theatre, London, England, former curator for summer exhibition "Shakespeare and Love."

WRITINGS:

Jokermen and Thieves: Bob Dylan and the Ballad Tradition, Wanted Man (Bury, Lancashire, England), 1986.

Shakespeare's Theatre of War, Ashgate (Brookfield, VT), 1998.

(Editor) Thomas Dekker, *The Honest Whore,* Nick Hern Books (London, England), 1998.

(Editor) Thomas Middleton, *A Mad World, My Masters,* Globe Education and Theatre Arts Books/ Routledge (New York, NY), 1998.

(Editor) Barnabe Barnes, *The Devil's Charter: A Tragedy Containing the Life and Death of Pope Alexander the Sixth,* Theatre Arts Books/Routledge (New York, NY), 1999.

(Editor) John Fletcher and Philip Massinger, *The Custom of the Country,* Theatre Arts Books/ Routledge (New York, NY), 1999.

(Editor) William Shakespeare, *Twelfth Night: Twelfe Night; or, What You Will,* Nick Hern Books (London, England), 2001.

(Editor) William Shakespeare, *Henry V: The Life of Henry the Fifth,* Nick Hern Books (London, England), 2001.

(Editor) William Shakespeare, *Hamlet: The Tragedie of Hamlet, Prince of Denmarke,* Nick Hern Books (London, England), 2001.

(Editor) William Shakespeare, *Measure for Measure = Measvre, for Measure: The First Folio of 1623 and a Parallel Modern Edition,* Nick Hern Books (London, England), 2002.

(Editor) William Shakespeare, *Othello: The Tragedie of Othello, the Moore of Venice,* Nick Hern Books (London, England), 2002.

(Editor) William Shakespeare, *Richard III: The Tragedy of Richard the Third,* Nick Hern Books (London, England), 2002.

(Editor) William Shakespeare, *Macbeth: The Tragedie of Macbeth,* Nick Hern Books (London, England), 2003.

(Editor) William Shakespeare, *Richard II: The Life and Death of King Richard the Second,* Nick Hern Books (London, England), 2003.

(Editor) William Shakespeare, *As You Like It,* Nick Hern Books (London, England), 2003.

Contributing editor, *New Theatre Quarterly.* Contributor to periodicals, including *Literature Online.*

SIDELIGHTS: A Shakespearean scholar who has worked at London's Globe Theatre and who is also the editor of the "Shakespeare Folio" series published by Nick Hern, Nick de Somogyi is the author of *Shakespeare's Theatre of War.* In this book, de Somogyi presents evidence to illustrate how the military conflicts in Europe during the late sixteenth and early seventeenth centuries influenced the content of William Shakespeare's plays. "In this reconstructed context of protracted wartime and its attendant anxieties," wrote Jonathan Baldo in *Shakespeare Quarterly,* "characters such as Pistol and Osric, as well as entire plays, frequently acquire a new and often surprising dimension."

At the time Shakespeare was writing, England was involved in military conflicts with Spain and Ireland, and there was also strife across Europe, such as war in the Low Countries during the 1590s. Depictions of and references to war are therefore not surprising in Shakespeare's plays, but de Somogyi goes beyond the obvious to analyze how the Bard's plays, as well as those by contemporary writers such as Christopher Marlowe and Thomas Kyd, illuminate changing concepts about the world as perceived by English society. For example, Baldo noted, "the figures of knight and scholar, conceived as mutually exclusive in the Middle Ages, were fused in Elizabethan England." De Somogyi also "explores the theatrical dimensions of war on the home front" and notes the nostalgic power of war that evokes cultural memories for the audience, revealing how Shakespeare utilized this phenomena to good effect in his plays.

Although Baldo felt that de Somogyi could have offered a "more sustained discussion of the memory of war" and that he sometimes focuses "too narrowly on the relation between war and popular superstition," the critic concluded that the book provides "a valuable service to Shakespeareans by rounding out our awareness of the European conflicts that pressed upon the

English people of the time." Reviewing the book in *Renaissance Quarterly,* Clifford Davidson called it "exceptional."

BIOGRAPHICAL AND CRITICAL SOURCES:

PERIODICALS

Renaissance Quarterly, winter, 1999, Clifford Davidson, review of *Shakespeare's Theatre of War,* p. 1177; summer, 2000, "The Devil's Charter: A Tragedy Containing the Life and Death of Pope Alexander the Sixth," p. 616.

Shakespeare Quarterly, winter, 2000, Jonathan Baldo, review of *Shakespeare's Theatre of War,* p. 499.*

*   *   *

DIETZ, Steven 1958-

PERSONAL: Born June 23, 1958, in Denver, CO; father a railroad engineer; married Allison Gregory; children: Ruby. *Education:* University of Northern Colorado, Greeley, B.A., 1980.

ADDRESSES: Home—4416 Thackeray Northeast, Seattle, WA 98105. *Agent*—International Creative Management, 40 West 57th St., New York, NY 10019.

CAREER: Playwright and artistic director. Affiliated with Playwrights' Center, Minneapolis, MN, 1980-91; Quicksilver Stage, Minneapolis, cofounder, 1983-86; Midwest Playlabs, Minneapolis, artistic director, 1987-89; Sundance Institute, Sundance, UT, resident director, 1990; Contemporary Theatre, Seattle, WA, associate artist, 1990-91. Director of plays, including *Standing on My Knees,* 1982; *21-A,* 1984; *The Voice of the Prairie,* 1985; *Harry and Claire,* 1985; *A Country Doctor,* 1986; *Auguste Moderne,* 1986; *T Bone n Weasel,* 1986-87; *Lloyd's Prayer,* 1987; *The Einstein Project,* 1987 and 1992; *Saint Erik's Crown* (opera), 1989; *The Wild Goose Circus,* 1990; *Tears of Rage,* 1991; *New Business,* 1991; and *Home and Away,* 1992.

AWARDS, HONORS: Jerome Foundation fellowship, 1982, 1984; McKnight fellowship in directing, 1985, and playwriting, 1989; Theatre Communications Group fellowship in directing, 1987; Society of Midland Authors award, 1988; National Endowment for the Arts fellowship, 1989; Kennedy Center grants, for *Still Life with Iris* and *Fiction;* PEN award for *Lonely Planet;* and Lila Wallace/*Reader's Digest* award, for *The Rememberer.*

WRITINGS:

PLAYS

(With Roberta Carlson) *Brothers and Sisters* (musical), produced in Minneapolis, MN, 1982.

Railroad Tales, produced in Minneapolis, MN, 1983.

Random Acts, produced in Minneapolis, MN, 1983.

Carry On, produced in Minneapolis, MN, 1984.

(And director) *Wanderlust,* produced in Minneapolis, MN, 1984.

(With Greg Theisen) *Catch Me a Z* (musical), produced in Minneapolis, MN, 1985.

More Fun than Bowling (produced in St. Paul, MN, 1986; produced in New York, NY, 1992), Samuel French (New York, NY), 1990.

(With Gary Rue and Leslie Ball) *Painting It Red* (musical; produced in St. Paul, MN, 1986), Samuel French (New York, NY), 1990.

Burning Desire, produced in St. Paul, MN, 1987.

Foolin' around with Infinity (produced in Los Angeles, CA, 1987), Samuel French (New York, NY), 1990.

(With Eric Bain Peltoniemi) *Ten November* (musical; produced in Chicago, IL, 1987), Theatre Communications Group (New York, NY), 1987.

God's Country (produced in Louisville, KY, 1988; produced in New York, NY, 1992), Samuel French (New York, NY), 1990.

(With Eric Bain Peltoniemi) *Happenstance* (musical), produced in Seattle, WA, 1989.

After You (produced in Louisville, KY, 1990; produced in New York, NY, 1991), published in *More Ten-Minute Plays from Actor's Theatre of Louisville,* edited by Michael Dixon, Samuel French (New York, NY), 1992.

To the Nines (produced in Seattle, WA, 1991), published in *The Twentieth Century,* edited by Dan Fields, Rain City Press (Seattle, WA), 1991.

Halcyon Days (produced in Seattle, WA, 1991), Rain City Press (Seattle, WA), 1991.

Trust (two-act; produced in Seattle, WA, 1992), Rain City Press (Seattle, WA), 1992.

Lonely Planet (produced in Seattle, WA, 1992), Dramatists Play Service (New York, NY, 1994.

The Rememberer (produced in Seattle, WA, 1994), Rain City Projects (Seattle, WA), 1993.

The Nina Variations: A Play, Rain City Projects (Seattle, WA), 1996.

Dracula (adaptation of Bram Stoker's novel), Dramatists Play Service (New York, NY), 1996.

Private Eyes (produced in Louisville, KY, 1996), Dramatists Play Service (New York, NY), 1998.

Still Life with Iris: A Play (for children; produced in Seattle, WA), Rain City Projects (Seattle, WA), 1997.

Silence (adaptation of Shusaku Endo's novel), produced c. 1998.

Force of Nature (adaptation of Goethe's novella *Elective Affinities*), produced c. 1999.

Fiction (two-act), produced in Princeton, NJ, 2003.

Inventing Van Gogh, produced 2003.

Over the Moon (two-act; adapted from the work of P. G. Wodehouse), produced in Seattle, WA, 2003.

The Spot, produced in Louisville, KY, 2004.

Author of play *Rocket Man,* Dramatists Play Service (New York, NY), and of screenplay *The Blueprint,* 1992. Contributor to periodicals, including *American Theatre.* Works published in anthologies, including *Actor's Book of Gay and Lesbian Plays,* Penguin (New York, NY), 1995; and *Humana Festival '97: The Complete Plays,* edited by Smith and Kraus, 1997.

SIDELIGHTS: Although he never took a class in his craft, Steven Dietz has become one of the most successful playwrights of his generation to emerge from Colorado. His stage dramas, which include *More fun than Bowling, God's Country,* and *Private Eyes,* have been produced by theaters across the United States, as well as internationally, and range from satire to serious commentaries and adaptations of works by others. Calling Dietz "unique" due to his continued focus on politics, a *Contemporary Dramatists* essayist praised the playwright as "prolific and diverse, and he has a voice that is always changing and yet recognizable as his own." As Dietz himself commented in *Contemporary Dramatists:* "I believe that, at its best, the theatre can serve as a social forum, a place where members of a community can gather to confront those things which affect them. A place for reasoning and rage, laughter and loss, recognition and discussion."

Dietz was born in Denver, Colorado, the son of a career railroader. When he finished college, he moved to Minneapolis, Minnesota, and began an acting career. He wrote his first play out of necessity, when a production of the Children's Theatre Company in which he was cast was lacking a script. With this success, he authored more plays produced in Minneapolis, and also began directing plays by other writers. In more recent years, Dietz's plays have been produced in Seattle, Washington, where he now makes his home, although some have made debuts in cities such as San Diego, Washington, D.C., and Louisville, Kentucky.

Dietz's topics can sometimes be disturbing, as in *Foolin' around with Infinity,* wherein two men who work underground in a government nuclear weapons facility in Utah suffer from constant fear of the end of mankind, even as they guard the button that can make it happen. His plays are timely, and often incorporate actual news events or the politics of the day. *Ten November,* for example, is a retelling of the sinking of the *Edmund Fitzgerald* in Lake Superior in 1975.

In *God's Country,* Dietz replicates the 1984 murder of Denver-based talk-show host Alan Berg by The Order, a neo-Nazi, white supremacist group that was founded by Robert Matthews in 1983. Dietz provides background on how the group grew and increased its membership and power base prior to targeting Berg for death due to his constant attach on their ultra-conservative values. The downfall of The Order, whose members were charged with racketeering, is also covered in the play.

Dietz's *Trust* is about trust and how it is betrayed. *Back Stage West* critic Dany Margolies, who commented on a Hollywood production of the play, wrote that the drama is "carefully crafted in its structure and characters, ostensibly skewering L.A.'s music scene and mankind's pathetic attempts at enduring love."

The two main characters in *Lonely Planet* are the retiring Jody, who owns a map shop, and Carl, who spends most of his free time in Jody's store. "It's only as Dietz's leisurely paced script unfolds, however, and as Carl begins to clutter the shop with an assortment of chairs, that we better understand the bond these two share," noted Kristina Mannion in *Back Stage West.* The play recalls Eugene Ionesco's *The Chairs* in that by play's end, the set is filled with seating furniture, each chair representing a friend of the two protagonists who has died of AIDS. David Sheward wrote in *Back*

Stage that "the most refreshing part of *Lonely Planet* is its subtlety. The symbolism of the maps and the chairs is not heavy handed and the two men don't wear their emotions or preferences on their sleeves. Gay sexuality isn't even brought up until well into the second act."

Force of Nature is an adaptation of Goethe's novella *Elective Affinities,* and revolves around an aristocratic man and woman who, although married, each take another romantic partner. *Variety* reviewer Chris Jones called Dietz's play "one of those savvy period adaptations that provides an erudite evening of old-fashioned theater while simultaneously offering an audience a decent helping of contemporary relevance."

Fiction is about Michael and Linda, a writing couple who have been married for sixteen years. While Michael's work has not amounted to success, Linda's first novel, set in South Africa, gained her literary recognition and a faculty job at a university. When Linda is discovered to have a brain tumor that will end her life in three weeks, she asks only that Michael allow her to read his diaries. While she discovers that he had a month-long affair at a writers' colony, the question becomes whether what Michael has written is entirely fact, or perhaps contains a bit of fiction. When Abby, the other woman, shows up in the second act, having learned of Linda's illness, Linda realizes that she had also met her, and had appropriated a horrific real-life experience Abby had shared with her for her bestseller. "What we have here is a series of betrayals, a sense that nothing is quite as represented," wrote Stefan Kanfer in a review of *Fiction* for the *New Leader.* "Therein lies the appeal of *Fiction,* a narrative full of surprises as it traverses time and space."

After the birth of his daughter, Ruby, Dietz began to writing for children, and his *Still Life with Iris* was awarded a Kennedy Center grant. In an interview with *Denver Post* reviewer John Moore, Dietz said that writing for kids is "the hardest writing you will ever do. It's harder because kids take their imagination for granted. They are the most honest audience. . . . You can get through a lifetime in the 'adult American theater' and never really learn how to construct a story as a writer. When you write plays for kids, that's when you are tested. It's a gut-check."

BIOGRAPHICAL AND CRITICAL SOURCES:

BOOKS

Contemporary Dramatists, sixth edition, St. James Press (Detroit, MI), 1999.

PERIODICALS

American Theatre, December, 1995, John Istel, "Risking Sentiment," p. 38; November, 2002, Jim O'Quinn, "The Future of New Work," p. 17.

Back Stage, March 11, 1994, David Lefkowitz, review of *Lonely Planet,* p. 36; July 21, 1995, David Sheward, review of *Lonely Planet,* p. 40; June 7, 1996, Irene Backalenick, review of *God's Country,* p. 52.

Back Stage West, February 8, 2001, Kristina Mannion, review of *Lonely Planet,* p. 18; March 14, 2002, Dany Margolies, review of *Trust,* p. 18.

Chicago Sun-Times, August 18, 2004, Christopher Piatt, review of *Foolin' around with Infinity,* p. 76.

Commonweal, January 15, 1993, Gerald Weales, review of *Halcyon Days,* p. 20; November 20, 1998, Celia Wren, review of *Silence,* p. 20.

Daily Variety, March 21, 2002, Julio Martinez, review of *Trust,* p. 10.

Denver Post, March 7, 2003, John Moore, "Stage writing has taken Dietz around world," p. F1; April 7, 2004, review of *Inventing Van Gogh,* p. F1.

Nation, April 6, 1992, Hal Gelb, review of *God's Country,* p. 462.

New Leader, July-August, 2004, Stefan Kanfer, review of *Fiction,* "On Stage," p. 45.

Variety, April 26, 1999, Chris Jones, review of *Force of Nature,* p. 58; April 14, 2003, Robert L. Daniels, review of *Fiction,* p. 30; December 8, 2003, Lynn Jacobson, review of *Over the Moon,* p. 65.

ONLINE

TheatreScene.net, http://www.theatrescene.net/ (March 22, 2003), Simon Saltzman, interview with Dietz.*

* * *

DILLON, Sam(uel) 1951-

PERSONAL: Born 1951; married Julia Preston (a journalist).

ADDRESSES: Office—Farrar, Straus & Giroux, c/o Author Mail, 19 Union Square West, New York, NY 10003.

CAREER: Associated Press, chief of El Salvador bureau, 1981-82; *Miami Herald,* Miami, FL, San Salvador bureau chief, 1982-95, Nicaraguan bureau chief, 1987-89, South America bureau chief, 1990-92, Latin American correspondent, 1995-97; *New York Times,* New York, NY, metropolitan reporter, 1992-95, Mexico City bureau chief, 1995-2000, foreign and national correspondent, 2001.

AWARDS, HONORS: Pulitzer Prize, 1987, for reportage on Iran-Contra scandal, and 1998, for reportage on drug corruption in Mexico; Tom Wallace Award, Inter-American Press Association, 1988, for reportage on Nicaraguan civil war, and 1989, for a profile of Manuel Noriega's business empire; Alicia Patterson fellowship, 1989; MacArthur Foundation research and writing grant, 2000-01; Overseas Press Club Award for Best Book on Foreign Affairs.

WRITINGS:

Comandos: The CIA and Nicaragua's Contra Rebels, Henry Holt (New York, NY), 1991.
(With wife, Julia Preston) *Opening Mexico: The Making of a Democracy,* Farrar, Straus & Giroux (New York, NY), 2004.

SIDELIGHTS: Sam Dillon's news reportage from Latin America has been rewarded with numerous honors, including two Pulitzer prizes. He began his journalism career in 1981, when he reported on the civil war in El Salvador for the Associated Press. In 1987, Dillon was part of a team that won the Pulitzer for a series of stories on the Iran-Contra scandal, a situation in which the administration of U.S. president Ronald Reagan was accused of illegal arms dealings and negotiating for hostages. Dillon won his second Pulitzer for a series of articles on the effects of drug-related corruption in Mexico.

Dillon's book *Comandos: The CIA and Nicaragua's Contra Rebels* drew on his knowledge of the civil war in El Salvador, which pitted the contra rebels against the Sandinista government. *Comandos* shows some positive points about the contras as well as detailing their record of human-rights abuses, and also reveals the complicity of the Central Intelligence Agency (CIA) in their activities. Dillon focuses his account on Comandante Johnson, a contra leader who attempted to stop the abuses that were so commonplace among the rebel forces. "No one has written about the conduct of the contras on the battlefield with the insight and authority of Mr. Dillon," claimed a reviewer for the *Economist.* A different opinion was put forth by Brian Barger in *Washington Monthly,* however; he felt that "Dillon fails to offer the kind of critical perspective expected in a reporter's book. Nonetheless, he provides a significant contribution to the body of knowledge about the latter years of the contra war."

Opening Mexico: The Making of a Democracy describes how the election of Vicente Fox in 2000 brought an end to seven decades of government control by the Institutional Revolutionary Party (IRP). The IRP was an authoritarian ruling party, despite Mexico's claim of democracy. Dillon and coauthor Julia Preston "brilliantly" tell a significant story, according to a *Foreign Affairs* reviewer. They discuss how the authoritarian history of Mexican rule compounded the problem of establishing true democracy in that country. Scott W. Helman, a contributor to the *Houston Chronicle,* stated that the writers "paint a moving portrait of a people fighting great odds to force democracy on a country that had long been democratic in name only." *New York Times Book Review* critic Michele Wucker believed that readers might want a more "analytical elaboration," but added that "Preston and Dillon more than make up for this minor shortcoming with their classic, nuanced storytelling." Walter Russell Mead, evaluating the book for the *New York Times,* found *Opening Mexico* somewhat flawed in its lack of a more critical examination of the IRP, but concluded: "The story of how the perfect dictatorship came unglued is one of the most fascinating stories of our time, and the authors tell their story well."

BIOGRAPHICAL AND CRITICAL SOURCES:

PERIODICALS

Columbia Journalism Review, November-December, 2002, Jay Cheshes, "A Drug Reporter's Strange Brew," p. 62.
Economist, February 15, 1992, review of *Comandos: The CIA and Nicaragua's Contra Rebels,* p. 104.
Foreign Affairs, March-April, 2004, Kenneth Maxwell, review of *Opening Mexico: The Making of a Democracy.*

Houston Chronicle, March 12, 2004, Scott W. Helman, review of *Opening Mexico.*

New York Times, March 26, 2004, Walter Russell Mead, review of *Opening Mexico.*

New York Times Book Review, March 28, 2004, Michele Wucker, review of *Opening Mexico.*

Publishers Weekly, August 23, 1991, review of *Comandos,* p. 52.

Village Voice, May 24-30, 2000, Cynthia Cotts, "Mouth of the Border: Mexico City Gets a New Bureau Chief."

Washington Monthly, January-February, 1992, Brian Barger, review of *Comandos,* p. 55.

ONLINE

Book Passage Web site, http://www.bookpassage.com/ (October 4, 2004), interview with Dillon.

Narco News Bulletin, http://www.narconews.com/ (May 28, 2000), Al Giordano, "*Times* Dumps Dillon."*

*   *   *

DIXON, Franklin W.
    See LANTZ, Francess L(in)

*   *   *

DOCKERY, Kevin

PERSONAL: Male. *Education:* Attended Oakland University.

ADDRESSES: Agent—c/o Author Mail, Berkley Books, Penguin Group Publicity, 375 Hudson St., New York, NY 10014.

CAREER: Worked in President's Guard under U.S. Presidents Richard Nixon and Gerald Ford and as a grade-school teacher, radio broadcaster, gunsmith, and historian. Co-creator of role-playing game The Morrow Project, 1980. *Military service:* U.S. Army, infantry; served in Operation: Desert Storm.

WRITINGS:

The Armory: A Compendium of Weaponry for Gamers and Students of Ordnance, edited by Elaine Abbrecht and Bob Shroeder, Firebird Ltd. (Ann Arbor, MI), 1983.

SEALs in Action, Avon Books (New York, NY), 1991.

(With James Watson) *Point Man: Inside the Toughest and Most Deadly Unit in Vietnam by a Founding Member of the Elite Navy SEALs,* Morrow (New York, NY), 1993.

Special Warfare: Special Weapons: The Arms and Equipment of the UDT and SEALs from 1943 to the Present, Emperor's Press (Chicago, IL), 1996.

(With James Watson) *Walking Point: The Experiences of a Founding Member of the Elite Navy SEALs,* Morrow (New York, NY), 1997.

(Editor, with Bill Fawcett) *The Teams: An Oral History of the U.S. Navy SEALs,* Morrow (New York, NY), 1998.

(With Dennis C. Chalker) *The United States Navy SEALs Workout Guide: The Exercise and Fitness Programs Based on the U.S. Navy SEALs and BUD/S Training,* Morrow (New York, NY), 1998.

Free Fire Zones: SEALs Missions, HarperCollins (New York, NY), 2000.

Navy SEALs: A History of the Early Years, Berkley Books (New York, NY), 2001.

(With Dennis C. Chalker) *Hell Week: SEALs in Training,* Avon Books (New York, NY), 2002.

(With Dennis C. Chalker) *One Perfect Op: An Insider's Account of the Navy SEALs' Special Warfare Teams,* Morrow (New York, NY), 2002.

Navy SEALs: A History Part II: From Vietnam to Desert Storm, Berkley Books (New York, NY), 2002.

Navy SEALs: A History Part III: Post-Vietnam to the Present, Berkley Books (New York, NY), 2003.

(With Elaine Abbrecht) *Special Forces in Action: Missions, Ops, Weapons, and Combat, Day by Day,* Citadel Press (New York, NY), 2004.

(With Dennis C. Chalker) *The Home Team: Undeclared War* (novel), Avon Books (New York, NY), 2004.

Weapons of the Navy SEALs, Berkley Books (New York, NY), 2004.

Also co-author of History Channel documentary about the Navy SEALs, 2000. Contributor to *Hunters and Shooters,* edited by Bill Fawcett, Morrow (New York, NY), 1995; and *Mercs: True Stories of Mercenaries in Action,* edited by Bill Fawcett, Avon Books (New York, NY), 1999.

SIDELIGHTS: An expert on both modern combat and the U.S. Navy's elite, covert fighting unit call the Navy SEALs (Sea, Air, Land), Kevin Dockery has written numerous books on both topics. Dockery collaborated with James Watson, one of the founders of the SEALs, to write *Point Man: Inside the Toughest and Most Deadly Unit in Vietnam by a Founding Member of the Elite Navy SEALs*. The book, which is the first published autobiography by an enlisted member of the SEALs team, recounts Watson's twenty years in the service, including his time in the SEALs unit and three tours in Vietnam between 1967 and 1970. A *Publishers Weekly* contributor found that Watson and Dockery provided a "narrative . . . replete with seemingly exaggerated anecdotes glorifying the pluck of the enlisted man." However, the reviewer also noted that the story is "highly entertaining."

Dockery also collaborated with Watson to write *Walking Point: The Experiences of a Founding Member of the Elite Navy SEALs*. This time, the authors recount Watson's involvement in covert missions around the world, including assignments involving the arming of a "baby" A-bomb and training recruits. Writing in the *Library Journal*, Michael Coleman commented, "The work is packed with excitement that will please military enthusiasts."

In *The Teams: An Oral History of the U.S. Navy SEALs,* Dockery and Bill Fawcett collect stories of six Navy SEALs who served in the Vietnam War. Told in the first person, the stories recount feats of endurance during training and exploits in the field, including the story of James Janos, who later became professional wrestler Jess "the Body" Ventura and governor of Minnesota. Writing in *Booklist*, Roland Green noted, "None of these half-dozen testimonies is dull, nor are the men who give them." A *Publishers Weekly* contributor called the book an "engaging tribute."

Dockery collaborated with U.S. Navy SEAL Command Master Dennis C. Chalker for Chalker's memoir *One Perfect Op: An Insider's Account of the Navy SEALs' Special Warfare Teams*. Chalker, who joined the SEALs in 1977, recounts both his training and his work as part of the team's secret antiterrorism unit. The book also focuses on Chalker's experiences with Navy politics and with his colleagues, as well as his exploits drinking and fighting. "Despite the lack of world-shaking events, Chalker's life makes good reading," wrote a *Kirkus Reviews* contributor. In *Publishers Weekly,* a reviewer called the book a "timely, adventuresome, and interesting account."

In *Navy SEALs: A History of the Early Years,* Dockery recounts how the SEALs developed from five different units established during World War II, including the Naval Combat Demolition Units and the Underwater Demolition Teams that also played a role in the Korean War. The SEAL force was created during President John F. Kennedy's term in office in the early 1960s, under the guidance of Admiral Arleigh Burke. Dale Andrade wrote in the *Journal of Military History* that "the book's most significant contribution" is its examination of "the bureaucratic trail that led to the formation of the modern SEALs." Andrade added, "Dockery effectively portrays this evolution and ties it in with the coming conflict in Vietnam." In a review in *Booklist,* Roland Green noted that "Dockery blends oral history and conventional narrative with consummate skill, making the book exceptionally accessible to casual readers as well as serious students."

Dockery continues to explore the history of the SEALs with *Navy SEALs: A History Part II: From Vietnam to Desert Storm* and *Navy SEALs: A History Part III: Post-Vietnam to the Present*. In his history of the SEALs' efforts in Vietnam, Dockery draws on interviews conducted by Bud Brutsman to provide an oral account of the SEAL team members' numerous exploits, including the small SEALS group that first went to Vietnam in 1962, before the war became front-page news in America, and the subsequent SEAL platoons that arrived in 1966. The book contains details on the Phoenix program, which was designed to counter the Viet Cong's clandestine political infrastructure, and Operation Thunderhead, in which SEAL teams were to enter North Vietnam to rescue American prisoners of war. Andrade, writing in the *Journal of Military History,* found that "the book provides only a narrow glimpse into the history of the SEALs in Vietnam" and wrote that the book's interview format "simply does not work." A *Kirkus Reviews* contributor praised *Navy SEALs: A History Part II,* however, noting that the "collection captures the SEAL teams' can-do spirit." The reviewer also called it an "entertaining and informative volume."

Although Dockery specializesin military history, he teamed up once again with Chalker to write the 2004 novel *The Home Team: Undeclared War.* The story focuses on SEAL Chief Ted "Grim" Reaper, who is forced to retire after disobeying a direct order while on assignment in Bosnia. At home with his family, Reaper is suddenly faced with his past when he refuses to accept an illegal shipment of weapons into his gun shop, which leads to his wife and son being kidnapped. When the police prove to be of no help, Reaper gathers together his team to save his family.

BIOGRAPHICAL AND CRITICAL SOURCES:

BOOKS

Chalker, Dennis C., and Kevin Dockery, *One Perfect Op: An Insider's Account of the Navy SEALs' Special Warfare Teams,* Morrow (New York, NY), 2002.

Watson, James, and Kevin Dockery, *Point Man: Inside the Toughest and Most Deadly Unit in Vietnam by a Founding Member of the Elite Navy SEALs,* Morrow (New York, NY), 1993.

PERIODICALS

Booklist, March 15, 1997, Roland Green, review of *Walking Point: The Experiences of a Founding Member of the Elite Navy SEALs,* p. 1209; February 1, 1998, Roland Green, review of *The Teams: An Oral History of the U.S. Navy SEALs,* p. 884; August, 2001, Roland Green, review of *Navy SEALs: A History of the Early Years,* p. 2058; January 1, 2002, Gilbert Taylor, review of *One Perfect Op: An Insider's Account of the Navy SEALs' Special Warfare Teams,* p. 781; August, 2002, Roland Green, review of *Navy SEALs: A History Part II: From Vietnam to Desert Storm,* p. 1896.

Journal of Military History, April, 2003, Dale Andrade, review of *Navy SEALs,* p. 624; January, 2003, Dale Andrade, review of *Navy SEALs: A History Part II,* p. 303.

Kirkus Reviews, November 15, 2001, review of *One Perfect Op,* p. 1592; June 15, 2002, review of *Navy SEALs: A History Part II,* p. 853.

Library Journal, April 1, 1997, Michael Coleman, review of *Walking Point,* p. p. 108; January, 1998, Michael Coleman, review of *The Teams,* p. 118; February 15, 2002, David M. Alperstein, review of *One Perfect Op,* p. 164.

Publishers Weekly, June 21, 1993, review of *Point Man: Inside the Toughest and Most Deadly Unit in Vietnam by a Founding Member of the Elite Navy SEALs,* p. 92; January 5, 1998, review of *The Teams,* p. 48; December 3, 2001, review of *One Perfect Op,* p. 47.

ONLINE

Wes's Home Page, http://home.earthlink.net/~kywess/ (November 4, 2004), interview with Dockery.*

DORMAN, Daniel

PERSONAL: Male. *Education:* Received medical degree.

ADDRESSES: Home—Los Angeles, CA. *Agent*—c/o Author Mail, Other Press LLC, 307 Seventh Ave., Suite 1807, New York, NY 10001.

CAREER: University of California School of Medicine, Los Angeles, assistant clinical professor. Has also taught psychotherapy for more than thirty years.

WRITINGS:

Dante's Cure: A Journey out of Madness, Other Press (New York, NY), 2003.

SIDELIGHTS: Daniel Dorman, whose background is in family medicine, psychoanalysis, and neurophysiology, has written *Dante's Cure: A Journey out of Madness,* a book documenting one of his most successful cases, which began in the 1970s. Dorman was a young doctor when he first met Catherine Penney, a nineteen-year-old woman suffering from schizophrenia. With a family background in depression and alcoholism, she was first hospitalized at age seventeen, when she heard voices that suggested she commit suicide and murder. She was prescribed tranquilizers and released, but she developed a tolerance for the drugs, and the voices returned. Becoming anorexic, she weighed only eighty-five pounds when Dorman first met her.

Dorman was convinced that Penney's condition was the result of her family history rather than a chemical imbalance, and he chose to treat her without using medications. He was encouraged because she kept her daily appointments with him and spoke openly. The voices stopped, she gained weight, and after seven years of therapy, she was able to rejoin society. Penney returned to college, became a psychiatric technician, and then a registered nurse. She worked in psychiatric units where she adopted Dorman's policy on medications. A *Kirkus Reviews* contributor noted that Penny's "refusal as a psychiatric nurse to administer drugs to mental patients has entangled her in job disputes, which Dorman chronicles with relish." A *Publishers Weekly* reviewer wrote that Dorman's "advocacy of a humanist approach that emphasizes patient-doctor collaboration and the growth of soul will be welcomed by all those who value the psychotherapeutic tradition."

BIOGRAPHICAL AND CRITICAL SOURCES:

PERIODICALS

Booklist, March 15, 2004, Donna Chavez, review of *Dante's Cure: A Journey out of Madness,* p. 1252.
Kirkus Reviews, February 1, 2004, review of *Dante's Cure,* p. 117.
Publishers Weekly, February 9, 2004, review of *Dante's Cure,* p. 67.

ONLINE

Desert Sun Online, http://www.thedesertsun.com/ (May 2, 2004), Kelly O'Connor, review of *Dante's Cure.**

*   *   *

DORRIL, Stephen

PERSONAL: Male.

ADDRESSES: Office—Department of Media and Journalism, University of Huddersfield, Queensgate, Huddersfield HD1 3DH, England. *Agent*—Andrew Lownie Literary Agency, 17 Sutherland St., London SW1V 4JU, England; fax: 0717 8287608. *E-mail*—s. dorril@hud.ac.uk.

CAREER: Journalist, writer, and educator. University of Huddersfield, Queensgate, Huddersfield, England, senior lecturer in print journalism; *Lobster,* founder, former editor, and writer, 1983—. Has appeared on numerous television and radio programs as a security and intelligence expert.

WRITINGS:

(With Anthony Summers) *Honeytrap: The Secret Worlds of Stephen Ward,* Coronet Books (London, England), 1987.

(With Robin Ramsay) *Smear!: Wilson and the Secret State,* Fourth Estate (London, England), 1991.
The Silent Conspiracy: Inside the Intelligence Services in the 1990s, Mandarin (London, England), 1994.
MI6: Inside the Covert World of Her Majesty's Secret Intelligence Service, Free Press (New York, NY), 2000, published as *MI6: Fifty Years of Special Operations,* Fourth Estate (London, England), 2000.
Gladio: MI6 and the European Stay-behind Networks, 1945-1990, 2000.
Blackshirt: Mosley and the Rise of Fascism, Viking (London, England), 2005.

Contributor to newspapers and other periodicals, including *Mail, Observer, Guardian,* and *Sunday Times.*

SIDELIGHTS: Stephen Dorril is a journalist, consultant, and researcher whose main interests—security and intelligence issues—have resulted in several books focusing on British and European intelligence. *Smear! Wilson and the Secret State,* which Dorril coauthored with Robin Ramsay, was described as "impressive and important" by Philip Knightley in the *London Review of Books.* The book describes several plots against Harold Wilson, who became prime minister of the United Kingdom in 1964. According to Bernard Porter in the *Times Literary Supplement,* the plots involved "various groups of people, including MI5 and MI6, the CIA, BOSS, financiers, ex-Army officers, the New Right, Gaitskellites, and even, at one early stage, a very famous woman romance novelist." The purpose of these plots varied, from bringing down Wilson's Labour Party government to simply removing Wilson and replacing him with someone else. Dorril and Ramsay examine each of these plots in detail. Porter commented that "the proof is here: masses of it, set out in fascinating detail, judiciously weighed, scrupulously footnoted" and that this "is easily the best and most credible account of the Wilson and related plots." In *Spectator,* Paul Foot wrote, "Anyone who wants to know how the British secret service works owes a huge debt to Stephen Dorril and Robin Ramsay."

In *The Silent Conspiracy: Inside the Intelligence Services in the 1990s,* Dorril describes the British intelligence services: MI6, which spies on people outside Britain; MI5, which spies on people within Britain; and GCHQ, which "spies massively on both," according to Stuart Weir in a review for *New States-man & Society*. Dorril describes how the intelligence services have resisted efforts to place them under parliamentary control and oversight, and along the way discusses mistakes, scandals, and botched missions and schemes. He believes that these organizations would not be able to resist reform so effectively if they did not have allies in the British government. As Weir noted, if the government is not directly responsible for the activities of the secret services, then it is free to encourage, in secret, illegal activities that would not be tolerated if the government was made to account for them. Dorril's "engrossing study (deprived by the censors of a few names) has convinced me that we need root-and-branch reform of our largely autonomous state," Weir stated. "Secrecy is the root of all the evils, powers, and inefficiencies of our secret services, as of the civil service and governments." Weir commented that "anyone who is not a conspiracy theorist is likely to become one" after reading this "dense and fascinating" book.

MI6: Inside the Covert World of Her Majesty's Secret Intelligence Service is a compendium of information on the secret service and how it works. A reviewer for the *Economist* remarked that Dorril was faced with great difficulty in writing it, because "his subject [the secret service] is officially non-existent, providing no reports, granting no interviews, answering no questions—just breaking surface briefly here and there." To gain information, Dorril scoured thousands of sources, ranging from pieces of common knowledge, to published reports, even obituaries. He relied on reasonable inference as well as speculation. When the book was serialized before publication in the London *Sunday Times* in 2000, "British authorities raided the publisher to seize files and computers, and sought by a series of legal maneuvers to suppress the book," reported Martin Walker in the *Wilson Quarterly*. "They failed, thanks less to the robust state of civil liberties in Britain than to the fact that the author was able to show that he had used open and public sources." Through fifteen years of painstaking research, correlating declassified documents in Eastern Europe, quoted materials found in documents obtained through the American Freedom of Information Act, and minimal resources available in Britain, Dorril "produced a book that amounts to a genuine breakthrough," Walker remarked. Despite all attempts to derail it, the book saw publication in England, under the title *MI6: Fifty Years of Special Operations*.

Among Dorril's documented findings are suggestions that "British intelligence helped bring about the Cold

War by starting hostile operations against the Soviets in 1943, almost as soon as Stalingrad had shown that the Soviet Union would survive," Walker remarked. The organization botched plans to assassinate rival leaders such as Slobodan Milosevic. Intelligence sources failed to anticipate the invasion of the Falklands, the fall of the Berlin Wall, and Iraq's invasion of Kuwait. Dorril even suggests that Nelson Mandela served as an agent for MI6, providing information on the Libyan financing of the IRA, a charge Mandela has vigorously denied. After "burrowing through an immense amount of material, the author has emerged with a picture of an organization highly skilled in bureaucratic maneuvering and self-protection but rather less effective at the stated object of the exercise: finding out what the other fellows are up to," observed Andrew Cockburn in the *Los Angeles Times*. Still, despite controversial claims and unflattering findings, "his book does not set out to be hostile, merely encyclopedic," noted a reviewer in the *Economist*.

"Dorril's new book on MI6 is an astonishing piece of work," commented Francis Wheen in the Manchester *Guardian*. "What Dorril has done, rather brilliantly, is to collate all these disparate details into a coherent, detailed biography of British intelligence and its motives, its character, and its behavior." *Library Journal* reviewer Ed Goedeken called *MI6* "richly detailed," while the *Publishers Weekly* reviewer remarked that through Dorril's examination, "MI6 is no longer the precision-tuned organization of legend, but appears far more American in its tendency to blunder its way through important missions." "Given its ambitious scope, though, this is a remarkable achievement and an encyclopedic post-war history which any student of the secret world should read," concluded critic Mark Hollingsworth in the Manchester *Guardian*. A reviewer for *Booklist* called the work "invaluable for readers who want to separate spy fact from spy fiction."

BIOGRAPHICAL AND CRITICAL SOURCES:

PERIODICALS

Booklist, June 1, 2000, David Pitt, review of *MI6: Inside the Covert World of Her Majesty's Secret Intelligence Service,* p. 1795.
Chicago Sun-Times, October 8, 2000, T. R. Reid, review of *MI6,* p. 19.

Economist, May 30, 1987, "Do You Know the Puffin Man?" p. 88; July 15, 2000, review of *MI6,* p. 7.

Guardian (Manchester, England), March 23, 2000, Anthony Sampson, "Mandela Mocks Idea He Was MI6 Man, Such Claims Show 'a Contempt for Africa,' Says Anti-Apartheid Leader after Spy-Book Allegations," p. 16; March 29, 2000, Francis Wheen, review of *MI6: Fifty Years of Special Operations,* p. 5; April 8, 2000, Mark Hollingsworth, review of *MI6,* p. 10; February 17, 2001, John Dugdale, review of *MI6,* p. 11.

Journal of Peace Research, February, 1995, review of *The Silent Conspiracy: Inside the Intelligence Services in the 1990s,* p. 124.

Library Journal, September 15, 1991, p. 120; July, 2000, Ed Goedeken, review of *MI6,* p. 119.

London Review of Books, October 10, 1991, Phillip Knightley, "Cowboy Coups," p. 5.

Los Angeles Times, September 10, 2000, Andrew Cockburn, review of *MI6,* p. 6.

New Statesman & Society, September 13, 1991, p. 37; June 18, 1993, Stuart Weir, review of *The Silent Conspiracy,* p. 39.

Observer (London, England), September 15, 1991, p. 63; November 22, 1992, p. 64.

Publishers Weekly, June 12, 2000, review of *MI6,* p. 64.

Spectator, November 16, 1991, Paul Foot, "A Wronged Man Need Not Be a Good Man," p. 52.

Times Literary Supplement, August 30, 1991, Bernard Porter, "Doing the Dirty on the Left," p. 7.

Wilson Quarterly, summer, 2000, Martin Walker, review of *MI6,* p. 136.

ONLINE

Andrew Lownie Literary Agency Web site, http://www.andrewlownie.co.uk/ (November 8, 2004).

Lobster Online, http://www.lobster-magazine.co.uk/index.php/ (November 15, 2004).

University of Huddersfield Web site, http://www.hud.ac.uk/ (November 15, 2004).*

*   *   *

DOVAL, Teresa de la Caridad 1966-
(Teresa Dovalpage)

PERSONAL: Born 1966, in Havana, Cuba; immigrated to United States, 1996; married Hugh Page (an author, psychologist, professor, and chaplain), 1994. *Educa-*tion:* University of Havana, B.A. (English literature), 1990; University of New Mexico, doctoral student.

ADDRESSES: Home—Albuquerque, NM. *Agent*—c/o Author Mail, Soho Press, 853 Broadway, New York, NY 10003. *E-mail*—info@dovalpage.com.

CAREER: Taught English at University of Havana and Havana Dentist School, Havana, Cuba; taught Spanish in community colleges and at University of California, San Diego Extension.

WRITINGS:

A Girl like Che Guevara (young adult novel), Soho Press (New York, NY), 2004.

(Under name Teresa Dovalpage) *Posesas de la Habana* (novel; title means "The Possessed of Havana"), Pureplay Press (Los Angeles, CA), 2004.

WORK IN PROGRESS: Two works of fiction, one in English, one in Spanish.

SIDELIGHTS: Teresa de la Caridad Doval, who publishes using the combination of her maiden and married names, Dovalpage, is the author of the novel *A Girl like Che Guevara.* Born in Havana, Cuba, and a graduate of the University of Havana, she taught in Cuba and met her husband while translating for him at a Silent Quaker meeting in Havana. They married, and two years later they traveled to San Diego, California, where Doval taught English in community colleges and at the University of California, San Diego Extension.

In San Diego, Doval was frequently asked about life in Cuba, and she began to write down her experiences. She adapted these to her debut young adult novel, which is set in 1982. During this era Communist revolutionary Che Guevara is a hero to all, including the protagonist. Lourdes Torres is a sixteen-year-old girl who must leave her comfortable urban home to serve for four months in a government work camp in the tobacco fields of the western province of Pinar del Rio. She is of mixed race, and her maternal grandmother practices the rites of Santeria to protect the girl, while her mother sticks pins in a doll clothed in scrap from her mother-in-law's dress.

Lourdes, who calls herself a skinny *mulatica* (mulatto), feels that no one will ever be attracted to her, but the work camp provides the opportunity for experimentation, first with boys, then with the voluptuous Aurora, with whom Lourdes shares a bed. Aurora becomes pregnant, and Lourdes, who is herself in a relationship with a boy, continues to have a crush on her. But she knows her hero, Guevara, would not have approved, since homosexuality was not tolerated by the Cuban government.

Several reviewers noted a certain stiffness to the prose as well as the slow pace exhibited by the first-time author. However, a *Publishers Weekly* contributor wrote that Duval's "sensitive characterizations and rich picture of Havana and the beguiling Cuban landscape redeem her story." *Booklist* contributor Gillian Engberg described Lourdes's voice as "vulnerable, [and] believable," while *St. Louis Post-Dispatch* writer Thomas Crone felt that, "without an uplifting finale, Doval seems to make clear that being raised in an impoverished nation takes a toll on multiple levels. The youths of *A Girl like Che Guevara* are lacking more than material goods and the simply joys of leisure time. They're essentially being robbed of their late childhoods."

In 2002, Doval and her husband moved to Albuquerque, New Mexico, where she enrolled in the doctoral program in the Spanish and Portuguese department. During her first year there, she wrote her Spanish-language novel, *Posesas de la Habana,* which was published by Pureplay Press, a Los Angeles publisher dedicated to preserving the culture and history of Cuba.

The four women protagonists in *Posesas de la Habana* are members of one family, and the novel relates their experiences and recollections during a government-programmed blackout in 2000. In a press release posted at the publisher's Web site, Doval explained that "when different generations live under one roof, disputes will surely break out. When four out of five family members are female, with ages ranging from eleven to ninety, the estrogen building up in a two-bedroom apartment reaches dramatic proportions. The characters of *Posesas de la habana,* thanks to endless economic problems and political asphyxia, live not merely at the edge but in the middle of a constant nervous breakdown. Can these women find hope on an island where the sea appears as the only route to salvation?"

BIOGRAPHICAL AND CRITICAL SOURCES:

PERIODICALS

Booklist, February 1, 2004, Gillian Engberg, review of *A Girl like Che Guevara,* p. 949.
Kirkus Reviews, February 1, 2004, review of *A Girl like Che Guevara,* p. 98.
Library Journal, February 15, 2004, Mary Margaret Benson, review of *A Girl like Che Guevara,* p. 159.
O, April, 2004, review of *A Girl like Che Guevara,* p. 172.
Publishers Weekly, March 1, 2004, review of *A Girl like Che Guevara,* p. 48.
St. Louis Post-Dispatch, May 23, 2004, Thomas Crone, "Cuban Teen Tests Limits on Farm Growing Tobacco and Communists," p. F13.

ONLINE

Pureplay Press Online, http://www.pureplaypress.com/ (August 14, 2004).
Teresa Doval Home Page, http://www.dovalpage.com (August 14, 2004).*

*   *   *

DOVALPAGE, Teresa
   See DOVAL, Teresa de la Caridad

*   *   *

DOW, James R(aymond) 1936-

PERSONAL: Born January 2, 1936 in D'Lo, MS. *Education:* Attended Tougaloo College, 1956-57; Mississippi College, B.A., 1957; attended Guteberg Universität, 1957-59; attended Middlebury College, 1959; University of Iowa, M.A., 1961, Ph.D., 1966; attended Indiana University, 1968; attended University of California, Los Angeles, 1970-71.

ADDRESSES: Home—503 Lafayette Ave., Story City, IA 50248-1421. *Office*—Iowa State University, Department of Foreign Languages and Literatures, 300 East Pearson, Ames, IA 50011-2205. *E-mail*—jrdow@ iastate.edu.

CAREER: Educator and scholar. University of Iowa, Iowa City, instructor in German, 1964-66; University of Wyoming, Laramie, assistant professor of German, 1966-70; Iowa State University, Ames, assistant professor, 1971-74, associate professor, 1974-80, professor of German, 1980—, chair of department of foreign languages and literatures, 1991-97, chair of linguistics program, 1998-2004. Visiting professor in Millstatt, Austria, 1973; St. Radegund, Austria, 1977, 1979, 1981, 1983, and 1985; Universität Essen, Germany, 1990; and Universität Bremen, Germany, 2003. Modern Language Association, chair of advisory committee to *MLA International Bibliography,* 1989-92 and 1993.

AWARDS, HONORS: Grant, Skaggs Foundation, 1988; named distinguished foreign-language alumnus, Mississippi College, 1995; Iowa Regents' Award for faculty excellence, 2003.

WRITINGS:

(Translator) Mark Azadovskii, *Eine Sibirische Märchenerzählerin,* introduction by Robert A. Geroges, University of Texas, (Austin, TX), 1974.

(Editor and translator, with Hannjost Lixfield) *German Volkskunde: A Decade of Theoretical Confrontation, Debate, and Reorientation (1967-1977),* Indiana University Press (Bloomington, IN), 1986.

Language and Ethnicity, J. Benjamins Publishing (Philadelphia, PA), 1991.

(Editor, with Thomas Stolz and others) *Sprachminoritüten/Minoritätensprachen,* N. Brockmeyer (Bochum, Germany), 1991.

(Editor, with Michèle Wolff) *Languages and Lives: Essays in Honor of Werner Enninger,* P. Lang (New York, NY), 1991.

(Editor, with Olaf Bockhorn) Reinhard Schmook, *"Gesunkenes Kulturgut—primitive Gemeinschaft": Der Germanist Hans Naumann (1886-1951) in seiner Bedeutung für die Volkskunde,* Riegelnik (Vienna, Austria), 1993.

(Editor and translator, with Hannjost Lixfield) *The Nazification of an Academic Discipline: Folklore in the Third Reich,* Indiana University Press (Bloomington, IN), 1994.

(Editor, with Werner Enninger and Joachim Raith) *Old and New World Anabaptists: Studies on the Language, Culture, Society, and Health of the Amish and Mennonites,* Universität Essen (Essen, Germany), 1994.

(Editor and translator) Hannjost Lixfield, *Folklore and Fascism: The Reich Institute for German Volkskunde,* Indiana University Press (Bloomington, IN), 1994.

(Editor, with Wolfgang Jacobeit, Hannjost Lixfeld, and Olaf Bockhorn) *Völkische Wissenschaft? Gestalten und Tendenzen in der deutschen und österreichischen Volkskunde in der ersten Hälfte des 20. Jahrhunderts,* Böhlau (Vienna, Austria), 1994.

(Editor) Anthony S. Mercatante, *The Facts on File Encyclopedia of World Mythology and Legend,* 2nd edition, Facts on File (New York, NY), 2003.

(With Olaf Bockhorn) *The Study of European Ethnology in Austria,* Ashgate (Burlington, VT), 2004.

Editor of *Internationale Volkskundliche Bibliographie,* 1978-88. Guest editor of *International Journal of the Sociology of Language,* Volume 68, number 6 and Volume 69, number 1; and jubilee edition of *Asian Folklore Studies,* Volume 50, number 1. Contributor to books, including *Culture and Civilization of the German-speaking States,* edited by Gerhard Weiss, University of Northern Iowa Press (Cedar Falls, IA), 1975; and *Encyclopedia of Modern German History,* edited by Dieter K. Buse and Jürgen Doerr, Garland Press (New York, NY), 1998. Contributor to periodicals, including *Asian Folklore Studies, Journal of American Folklore,* and *Keystone Folklore Quarterly.* Contributor of scholarly articles to periodicals, including *Keystone Folklore Quarterly, New York Folklore Quarterly, Tennessee Folklore Society Bulletin, International Folklore Review,* and *International Journal of the Sociology of Language.*

WORK IN PROGRESS: Editing *A Cymbrian Grammar,* by Bruno Schweizer.

SIDELIGHTS: James R. Dow, a professor of German at Iowa State University, has published extensively on European and American folklore, particularly German folklore. Dow is the coeditor and cotranslator of *The Nazification of an Academic Discipline: Folklore in the Third Reich,* and he edited and translated *Folklore and Fascism: The Reich Institute for German Volkskunde.* Dow also served as editor for the second edition of *The Facts on File Encyclopedia of World Mythology and Legend,* published in 2003.

Both *The Nazification of an Academic Discipline* and *Folklore and Fascism* examine the role of folklorists during the Third Reich. According to Richard F. Szippl in *Asian Folklore Studies,* the thesis of the books is that German folklore "was hijacked by National Socialism," thus subverting its scholarly and ethical principles. "This flies directly in the face of the commonly held notion that there were two distinct folklores in Nazi Germany—a legitimate, scholarly folklore coexisting alongside an ideologically perverted, methodologically compromised National Socialist folklore," Szippl added. "The strength of this notion . . . made it possible for the discipline of folklore in the German-speaking countries to largely avoid coming to terms with the relationship of folklore and National Socialism." Szippl praised the essays in *The Nazification of an Academic Discipline,* stating, "The publication of these translations will go a long way towards opening the debate to English-reading circles."

The Facts on File Encyclopedia of World Mythology and Legend includes entries of "nearly 3000 myths and legends from around the world," wrote *Library Journal* reviewer Richard K. Burns. First published in 1988, the work was expanded to two volumes by Dow, who added new entries, cross-references, and bibliographic citations. According to *School Library Journal* contributor Ann G. Brouse, the revised version of the book "takes on a fresh face and shape" under Dow's editorship.

BIOGRAPHICAL AND CRITICAL SOURCES:

PERIODICALS

Asian Folklore Studies, October, 1996, Richard F. Szippl, review of *The Nazification of an Academic Discipline: Folklore in the Third Reich,* p. 329.

Booklist, July, 2004, review of *The Facts on File Encyclopedia of World Mythology and Legend,* p. 1863.

Journal of Modern History, March, 1998, Suzanne Marchand, review of *Folklore and Fascism: The Reich Institute for German Volkskunde,* p. 108.

Library Journal, April 15, 2004, Richard K. Burns, review of *The Facts on File Encyclopedia of World Mythology and Legend,* p. 75.

School Library Journal, August, 2004, Ann G. Brouse, review of *The Facts on File Encyclopedia of World Mythology and Legend,* p. 58.

ONLINE

Iowa State University Web site, http://www.iastate.edu/ (October 22, 2004), "James R. Dow."*

DOWELL, Frances O'Roark

PERSONAL: Female. *Education:* Wake Forest University, B.A.; University of Massachusetts, M.F.A.

ADDRESSES: Home—8 Briarfield Rd., Durham, NC 27713. *E-mail*—fdowell@mindspring.com.

CAREER: Worked variously as paralegal, college English instructor, and arts administrator. Former editor and copublisher of *Dream/Girl* (arts magazine for girls).

AWARDS, HONORS: Edgar Allan Poe Award for Best Juvenile Novel, 2001, and William Allen White Award, 2003, both for *Dovey Coe.*

WRITINGS:

FOR CHILDREN

Dovey Coe, Atheneum (New York, NY), 2000.
Where I'd Like to Be, Atheneum (New York, NY), 2003.
The Secret Language of Girls, Atheneum (New York, NY), 2004.
Chicken Boy, Atheneum (New York, NY), 2005.

Contributor of poetry to periodicals, including *Poetry East, Shenandoah,* and *New Delta Review.*

WORK IN PROGRESS: Two novels.

SIDELIGHTS: Frances O'Roark Dowell's novels for young adult readers explore issues of growing up, family and friend relationships, and overcoming adversity. Reviewing her novels, which include *Dovey Coe* and *The Secret Language of Girls,* critics have praised her well-developed and believable protagonists. While Dowell's subjects range from the ordinary to the dramatic, the female protagonists at the center of her stories are girls to whom teen readers can relate.

Dowell's acclaimed debut novel *Dovey Coe* features a spunky young heroine who is outspoken, assertive, and protective of her family. Dovey does not like Parnell, her older sister's suitor, particularly the way he disrespects her family, and she is not afraid to say so. When Parnell takes her dog one night and threatens to kill it, Dovey tries to save her dog by attacking Parnell and is knocked unconscious. When she wakes up, both her dog and Parnell are dead, and Dovey must face a courtroom battle to prove her innocence. Betsy Fraser, writing in *School Library Journal,* noted that the novel "maintains a very fast pace, and Dovey is an original character," adding, "The background and characters are carefully developed and appealing." *Booklist* contributor Frances Bradburn added that "Dowell has created a memorable character in Dovey, quick-witted and honest to a fault."

In an interview for *DreamGirl* online, Dowell answered questions about the inspiration behind *Dovey Coe.* "The reasons I wanted to set a book in the past is because I'm very interested in folklore and folkways—the ways people lived before we had so many time-saving devices and big grocery stores and all of our modern conveniences. I had been reading a lot of books about life in the Blue Ridge mountains in earlier times, and I thought it would be fun to write a book using some of the knowledge I'd picked up." As for critics who draw comparisons between *Dovey Coe* and Harper Lee's classic novel *To Kill a Mockingbird,* Dowell commented, "It's a little embarrassing, to be honest. . . . Don't get me wrong, I like my own book a lot, but nothing will ever truly compare to *To Kill a Mockingbird.* There are similarities, it's true. Both Scout, the narrator of *To Kill a Mockingbird,* and Dovey are tomboys, they're both outspoken and honest, and they're both loyal to the people they love."

Where I'd Like to Be is set in a home where orphaned children await foster homes. The protagonist is a girl named Maddie who makes the best of her bad situation and has a strong sense of herself. When a new girl, Murphy, arrives, Maddie is captivated by the other girl's story as well as her imaginative personality. In the novel Dowell creates a cast of diverse children who create a family among themselves as they dream of becoming part of a permanent family. In *Booklist,* Linda Perkins wrote that Maddie's "voice and views are consistently those of a perceptive eleven-year-old," and added that the novel provides "ample discussion possibilities." The characters in the novel were particularly impressive to Faith Brautigam of *School Library Journal,* who commented that "the foster children's backgrounds are believable, diverse, and

engaging," creating "unique and memorable characters." A contributor to *Kirkus Reviews* also praised Dowell's characterizations, concluding: "The talky pie-in-the-sky resolution mars the tightness of the narrative that precedes it, but taken as a whole, this is a lovely, quietly bittersweet tale of friendship and family." And a *Publishers Weekly* reviewer deemed *Where I'd Like to Be* "a celebration of friendship and the powers of the imagination."

The way teenage girls grow apart from their friends is the subject of *The Secret Language of Girls.* Kate and Marilyn have been friends since childhood, but as they enter the sixth grade, their paths diverge. While Marilyn gains access to the popular crowd, becomes a cheerleader, and is interested in make-up and boys, Kate worries about her father's health and shies away from being noticed by her peers. In the end, the two girls find that their different lifestyles have not forced them as far apart as they thought. Martha P. Parravano, reviewing the novel for *Horn Book,* observed that "Dowell's development of this familiar situation is refreshingly nonjudgmental," and noted that the thoughtful tone of the novel is balanced by "supersonic pacing—a perspective that swings freely between Kate and Marylin, and vivid characterization." A *Publishers Weekly* reviewer described the book as a "perceptive slice-of-life novel" that will leave readers feeling "encouraged by the author's honest and sympathetic approach." B. Allison Gray wrote in *School Library Journal* that *The Secret Language of Girls* will ring true to young readers because of "excellent characterization, an accurate portrayal of the painful and often cruel machinations of preteens, and evocative dialogue."

BIOGRAPHICAL AND CRITICAL SOURCES:

PERIODICALS

Booklist, April 15, 2000, review of *Dovey Coe,* p. 1537; May 15, 2003, Linda Perkins, review of *Where I'd Like to Be,* pp. 1660-1661.
Horn Book, July-August, 2004, Martha P. Parravano, review of *The Secret Language of Girls,* p. 450.
Kirkus Reviews, March 1, 2003, review of *Where I'd Like to Be,* p. 382.
Publishers Weekly, February 24, 2003, review of *Where I'd Like to Be,* p. 73; May 31, 2004, review of *The Secret Language of Girls,* p. 74.

School Library Journal, May, 2000, review of *Dovey Coe,* p. 171; April, 2003, Faith Brautigam, review of *Where I'd Like to Be,* p. 158; May, 2004, B. Allison Gray, review of *The Secret Language of Girls,* p. 146.

ONLINE

DreamGirl Online, http://www.dgarts.com/ (February 2, 2005), interview with Dowell.

*   *   *

DUIKER, K. Sello 1974-

PERSONAL: Born April 13, 1974, in Orlando West, Soweto, South Africa. *Education:* Rhodes University, B.A. (journalism and art history).

ADDRESSES: *Home*—Johannesburg, South Africa. *Agent*—c/o Author Mail, Kwela Books, P.O. Box 6525, Roggebaai 8012, South Africa.

CAREER: Writer. Netherlands Institute for Advanced Study in the Humanities and Social Sciences (NAIS), writer-in-residence, 2003-04. Has also worked as an advertising copywriter for Harrison Human, Johannesburg, South Africa; and as a scriptwriter for Endemol Productions, London, England.

MEMBER: Seeds Poetry Society (founder).

AWARDS, HONORS: Commonwealth Writers Prize for best first book, Africa Region, 2001, for *Thirteen Cents;* Herman Charles Bosman Prize for English literature, 2001, for *The Quiet Violence of Dreams.*

WRITINGS:

Thirteen Cents (novel), David Phillips (Claremont, South Africa), 2000.
The Quiet Violence of Dreams (novel), Kwela Books (Cape Town, South Africa), 2001.

Contributor to the short story anthology *In the Rapids,* Kwela Books (Cape Town, South Africa), 2003. Contributor to *Backstage.*

WORK IN PROGRESS: A novel about reconciliation in the new South Africa.

SIDELIGHTS: South African author K. Sello Duiker received recognition with the 2000 publication of his debut novel, *Thirteen Cents.* A year later, Duiker's second novel, *The Quiet Violence of Dreams,* was published and also received wide critical attention. Both works explore the multicultural, economically stratified life in Cape Town, South Africa. Many of Duiker's characters reside on the fringes of society and are refugees of South Africa's unsettled history.

Duiker lived with the street kids of Cape Town to gather material for *Thirteen Cents,* which is set in the poorer parts of the city, where violence is common. The novel follows an adolescent named Azure (pronounced Ah-zuh-ray) who comes of age as he works odd jobs to survive. Although his environment is tough, Azure is strong and defiant as he faces obstacles that are no longer based on his race but a new inequality based primarily on class.

Sue Valentine, writing in the Johannesburg *Sunday Times,* stated that the author presents a "gritty and real" story that does not "gloss over the crude realities of life on the streets." Bafana Khumalo, also writing in the *Sunday Times,* noted that in *Thirteen Cents* "one can see a young writer who is still maturing as he tries to communicate something close to his heart."

In *The Quiet Violence of Dreams,* Duiker tells the story of Tshepo, a young man whose somewhat privileged life and upbringing are shattered when his mobster father murders his mother. The incident destroys Tshepo's mental well being, and he turns to drug use as a way to hide from his problems. Tshepo eventually is locked up in a psychiatric hospital and realizes he has to come to grips with who he really is, including accepting his own homosexuality. "But certainly the novel is about more than this," Duiker told Dunton in a *Mail and Guardian Online* interview. "Tshepo's questions about his sexuality engage him in a bigger journey about what it means to be black, educated. Can the West and Africa be reconciled?" Another primary character in the novel is Tshepo's female friend Mmabatho, who walks between the white and black, as well as the modern and traditional, Cape Town. Duiker told Dunton: "Mmabatho to me serves as a bridge between two worlds. She tries to integrate her own African culture with that of Cape Town and everything that is perceived as outside African culture. In a way, she's her own tapestry." Dunton called *The Quiet Violence of Dreams* an "ambitious book, both thematically and in terms of its length." Khumalo noted that Duiker finds his voice in *The Quiet Violence of Dreams,* "and he lets it bellow out in its entire glory."

BIOGRAPHICAL AND CRITICAL SOURCES:

PERIODICALS

New York Times, June 24, 2002, Rachel L. Swarns, "South Africa's Black Writers Explore a Free Society's Tensions," p. E1.
Sunday Times (Johannesburg, South Africa), July 9, 2000, Sue Valentine, "Two Tales of One City," review of *Thirteen Cents;* May 31, 2002, Bafana Khumalo, "Seeking Other Selves" (interview).

ONLINE

Commonwealth Writers Web site, http://www. commonwealthwriters.com/ (November 7, 2002), "Commonwealth Writers Prize 2001."
Contemporary Africa Database, http://people. africadatabase.org/ (August 25, 2004), "K. Sello Duiker."
Mail & Guardian Online (Johannesburg, South Africa), http://www.mg.co.za/ (November 7, 2001), Chris Dunton, "With Many Voices," author interview.
Netherlands Institute for Advanced Study in the Humanities and Social Sciences Web site, http:// www.nias.knaw.nl/ (August 25, 2004), "K. S. Duiker."
Q-online, http://www.q.co.za/ (August 25, 2004), Victor Lakay, "I'm a Travelling Salesman" (interview with Duiker).*

*   *   *

DUNCAN, Otis Dudley 1921-2004

OBITUARY NOTICE— See index for *CA* sketch: Born December 2, 1921, in Nocona, TX; died of prostate cancer November 16, 2004, in Santa Barbara, CA. Social scientist, educator, and author. Duncan was a quantitative sociologist who was the first to study the importance of socioeconomic status of a person's parents as a determining factor for passing down educational success and social status to the next generation. With his B.A. earned from Louisiana State University in 1941, he went on to receive his M.A. from the University of Minnesota in 1942 before serving in the U.S. Army during World War II. After the war, he completed his Ph.D. at the University of Chicago in 1949. Brief teaching jobs at Pennsylvania State University and the University of Wisconsin—Madison were followed by a longer period spent at the University of Chicago. Here, Duncan was a professor of sociology in the early 1950s and a professor of human ecology in the late 1950s and early 1960s. He also served as associate director of Chicago Community Inventory in the early 1950s and associate director of Population Research and Training Center from 1953 to 1956. From 1962 until 1973, he was on the faculty at the University of Michigan, where he taught sociology and directed the Population Studies Center from 1967 to 1968. Duncan then moved to Tucson to teach at the University of Arizona from 1973 until 1983, spending the last years of his academic career at the University of California at Santa Barbara, until he retired in 1987. As a researcher, Duncan was interested in using statistical analysis to study populations and social trends. He was particularly interested in finding out how important it is in determining one's own future success to have a parent who is well educated and of high social standing. He discovered that parents' schooling only partially influences how well their children do in school, a finding he discussed in *The American Occupational Structure* (1978), written with Peter Blau. In other research, Duncan also found that it is more difficult for African Americans to pass down their social gains to their children than it is for whites. Social status was also a concern of Duncan's in other books he wrote or coauthored, including *Occupations and Social Status* (1961) and *Socioeconomic Background and Achievement* (1972). Among his many other books are *The Negro Population of Chicago* (1957), *An Examination of the Problem of Optimum City Size* (1980), and *Notes on Social Measurement* (1984).

OBITUARIES AND OTHER SOURCES:

PERIODICALS

Chicago Tribune, November 29, 2004, section 1, p. 11.
New York Times, November 27, 2004, p. A16.

DUQUETTE, David A. 1949-

PERSONAL: Born May 22, 1949, in Nashua, NH; son of Albert C. (a journeyman printer) and Rolande (in retail sales; maiden name, Chomard) Duquette; married Ann F. Romenesko (in inventory control); August 11, 2001. *Ethnicity:* "Caucasian." *Education:* University of New Hampshire, B.A. (political science), 1971; Rensselaer Polytechnic Institute, M.S. (philosophy), 1976; University of Kansas, M.Phil. (philosophy), 1981, Ph.D. (philosophy), 1985. *Religion:* "Baptized and raised Roman Catholic."

ADDRESSES: Home—720 North Broadway, De Pere, WI 54115. *Office*—St. Norbert College, 100 Grant St., De Pere, WI 54115; fax: 920-403-4086. *E-mail*—david.duquette@snc.edu.

CAREER: St. Norbert College, De Pere, WI, professor of philosophy, 1985—, coordinator for philosophy discipline, 1994-96. Guest lecturer at other institutions, including University of Wisconsin at Green Bay.

MEMBER: International Association for Philosophy of Law and Social Philosophy (American section), North American Society for Social Philosophy, American Philosophical Association, Hegel Society of America (member of executive committee, 1992-96; vice president, 1998-2000), Southwestern Philosophical Society, Wisconsin Philosophical Association.

WRITINGS:

(Editor) *Hegel's History of Philosophy: New Interpretations,* State University of New York Press (Albany, NY), 2003.

Contributor to books, including *The Social Power of Ideas,* edited by C. Peden and Yeager Hudson, Edwin Mellen Press (Lewiston, NY), 1995; *Rending and Renewing the Social Order,* edited by Yeager Hudson, Edwin Mellen Press (Lewiston, NY), 1996; *Hegel's Phenomenology of Spirit: A Reappraisal,* edited by Gary K. Browning, Kluwer Academic Press (New York, NY), 1997; *Memory, History, and Critique: European Identity at the Millennium* (CD-ROM), edited by Frank Brinkhuis and Sascha Talmor, MIT

Press (Cambridge, MA), 1998; and *Universal Human Rights: Moral Order in a Divided World,* edited by Mortimer Sellars, New York University Press (New York, NY). Contributor of articles and reviews to periodicals, including *Review of Politics, Owl of Minerva, Southwest Philosophy Review,* and *Philosophy of the Social Sciences.* Assistant editor, *Auslegung: Journal of Philosophy.*

WORK IN PROGRESS: Research on theory and practice in the history of political thought.

SIDELIGHTS: David A. Duquette told *CA:* "My primary motivation for writing is to give expression to ideas for self-clarification and to engage critically in the community of academic scholarship in philosophy and political thought. Academic writing is largely about communication, clarification, and argument, but it also involves creative thinking. A passion for the creativity of ideas is a central impetus for me, as well as the urge to perfect my thinking and writing skills.

"My earliest influences are the college mentors who inspired me to pursue the academic life, who taught me how to think and to write, particularly in my areas of interest and specialty. My mature professional work has been inspired to a great extent by the thought of G. W. F. Hegel and Karl Marx, both of whom have had a significant impact on the development of the thought of late modernity. More broadly, I have an abiding interest in the history of ideas and a desire to make sense of the history of human thought, particularly in philosophy and political theory. I'm convinced that there is much continuity and connectedness in the course of philosophical and political ideas, and that a careful study of their development can bring insights into human nature and the human condition.

"My writing emerges from wrestling with philosophical issues and problems with the wish to contribute intellectually and professionally to their ongoing discussion and debate. Given the responsibilities that go with a position at an academic institution where teaching is given the highest priority, I cannot write on a consistent and regular basis. Hence, my strategy is to set short-term goals and to commit myself in advance to scholarly contributions in books, journals, et cetera, in order to establish deadlines for myself.

"Publishing a book on Hegel is one significant way of expressing my commitment to the furthering of Hegel studies. In particular, a volume on Hegel's *History of Philosophy* has intrinsic connection to my larger philosophical interests. Moreover, Hegel was a philosopher of the 'big picture,' of a system of philosophy intended to be fully comprehensive and all encompassing, and while it would take a genius like him to accomplish anything of this magnitude and scale, those of us with lesser talents can still partake of such a project through scholarly examination, explication, and critical review."

E

ELKINS, Aaron 1935-

PERSONAL: Born July 24, 1935, in Brooklyn, NY; son of Irving Abraham (a machinist) and Jennie (Katz) Elkins; married Toby Siev, 1959 (divorced, 1972); married Charlotte Trangmar (a writer), 1972; children: (first marriage) Laurence, Robin. *Education:* Hunter College (now of the City University of New York), B.A., 1956; graduate study at University of Wisconsin—Madison, 1957-59; University of Arizona, M.A., 1960; California State University, Los Angeles, M.A., 1962; University of California, Berkeley, Ed.D., 1976.

ADDRESSES: Home—Sequim, WA. *Agent*—Lisa Vance, The Aaron Priest Agency, 708 Third Ave., 23rd Floor, New York, NY 10017.

CAREER: Government of Los Angeles County, CA, personnel analyst, 1960-66; Government of Orange County, CA, training director, 1966-69; Santa Ana College, Santa Ana, CA, instructor in anthropology and business, 1969-70; Ernst & Whinney, Chicago, IL, management consultant, 1970-71; Government of Contra Costa County, CA, director of management development, 1971-76, 1980-83; University of Maryland at College Park, European Division, Heidelberg, West Germany, lecturer in anthropology, psychology, and business, 1976-78, lecturer in business, 1984-85; U.S. Office of Personnel Management, San Francisco, CA, management analyst, 1979-80; writer, 1984—. Lecturer at California State University, Hayward and Fullerton, and at Golden Gate University.

MEMBER: Mystery Writers of America.

AWARDS, HONORS: Edgar Allan Poe Award for best mystery novel, Mystery Writers of America, 1988, for *Old Bones;* (with Charlotte Elkins) Agatha Award for

Aaron Elkins

best short story, Malice Domestic Ltd., 1992, for "Nice Gorilla"; Nero Wolfe Award for best mystery novel, 1993, for *Old Scores.*

WRITINGS:

NOVELS

"GIDEON OLIVER" SERIES

Fellowship of Fear, Walker & Co. (New York, NY), 1982.

The Dark Place, Walker & Co. (New York, NY), 1983.

Murder in the Queen's Armes, Walker & Co. (New York, NY), 1985.

A Deceptive Clarity, Walker & Co. (New York, NY), 1987.

Old Bones, Mysterious Press (New York, NY), 1987.

Curses!, Mysterious Press (New York, NY), 1989.

Icy Clutches, Mysterious Press (New York, NY), 1990

Make No Bones, Mysterious Press (New York, NY), 1991.

Dead Men's Hearts, Mysterious Press (New York, NY), 1994.

Twenty Blue Devils, Mysterious Press (New York, NY), 1997.

Skeleton Dance, William Morrow (New York, NY), 2000.

Good Blood, Berkley Prime Crime (New York, NY), 2004.

Where There's a Will, Berkley Prime Crime (New York, NY), 2005.

"CHRIS NORGREN" SERIES

A Glancing Light, Scribner (New York, NY), 1991.

Old Scores, Scribner (New York, NY), 1993.

"LEE OFSTEAD" SERIES; WITH WIFE, CHARLOTTE ELKINS

A Wicked Slice, St. Martin's Press (New York, NY), 1989.

Rotten Lies, Mysterious Press (New York, NY), 1995.

Nasty Breaks, Mysterious Press (New York, NY), 1997.

Where Have All the Birdies Gone?, Severn House Publishers (Sutton, Surrey, England), 2004.

OTHER

Loot (novel), William Morrow (New York, NY), 1999.

Turncoat (novel), William Morrow (New York, NY), 2002.

Contributor to literary journals and anthologies.

ADAPTATIONS: The "Gideon Oliver" books were adapted for television by American Broadcasting Companies, Inc. (ABC), 1989.

SIDELIGHTS: Aaron Elkins, the author of mystery novels, often sets his plots in foreign locations such as Egypt, Tahiti, Mexico, and Alaska. Though most famous for his "Gideon Oliver" series, about a forensic anthropologist who solves modern murders, Elkins also created the "Chris Norgren" series, featuring a retired museum curator whose sleuthing solves crimes, and, with his wife, Charlotte Elkins, the "Lee Ofstead" series, novels wherein crimes involve the sport of golf. Elkins is also the author of stand-alone crime novels including *Twenty Blue Devils, Loot,* and *Turncoat,* and his "Gideon Oliver" series was adapted as a television series in the late 1980s.

According to a writer in the *St. James Guide to Crime and Mystery Writers,* "Elkins writes exactly the kind of mysteries that have become so enormously popular with readers. . . . His books are neither cozy nor hard-boiled . . . but instead fall into that large middle area of the genre that most mystery fans, male and female, now seem to prefer." The writer continued, "Elkins is a superb craftsman, whose plots are ingenious, with every piece fitting perfectly together with every other piece, whose prose is perfectly polished but also perfectly simple and natural, so that each word or turn of phrase seems exactly right—and he does it all so smoothly and unobtrusively that he makes it look easy."

The "Gideon Oliver" series is set all over the world, due to Gideon's occupational need for travel. Several of his adventures begin while he is supposed to be vacationing in an exotic locale. When the series begins in *Fellowship of Fear,* Gideon is in Germany, and is still in the process of grieving for his late wife, who died in a car accident two years before the novel opens. Through the first several books, Gideon travels through Italy, Spain, Washington state, England, France, and the Yucatan; over the course of the early novels, Gideon realizes he no longer wants to be alone, and in *The Dark Place,* he meets Julie, the woman who will later become his second wife.

In *Old Bones,* the fourth novel in the series, Gideon Oliver, known as the "skeleton detective," is in France to attend a conference on forensic anthropology. While there, Guillaume du Rocher, a World War II hero of the French Resistance, drowns, and a dismembered human skeleton is unearthed from the cellar of du Rocher's chateau. Local police believe the skeleton is that of a Nazi SS officer du Rocher killed in 1942, but

Oliver does not agree. A *Publishers Weekly* critic complimented the "intricate plot" and "a thrilling final scene" that "gallops along as fast and compelling as the tide itself," while Sharon Miller of the *Seattle Post-Intelligencer* called *Old Bones* "witty and well-plotted."

The fifth "Gideon Oliver" mystery, *Skeleton Dance,* was described as "an entertaining and informative excursion through the prehistory and cuisine of rural France," by George Needham in *Booklist.* In this book Oliver is traveling in France with Julie, conducting research for a book about scientific hoaxes. He is in the process of interviewing five scientists at the Institut de Préhistoire, a renowned archeological institute, about a hoax carried out by a former director when he is called on by the local police to help identify some human bones that have been unearthed. Forensic examination determines that the bones are not prehistoric fossils, as supposed, but the remains of someone murdered within the last five years and with possible ties to the institute. As Gideon uncovers information about it, he is persuaded that the hoax is connected to the bones. A *Publishers Weekly* contributor praised the novel's "mischievous wit" and "fascinating erudition," together with "a gorgeous setting redolent with Gitanes and goose liver," all of which result in "an exceptionally delectable treat."

Good Blood takes Gideon and Julie to Italy to visit a friend who is a tour guide. However, their friend's extended family is more than disfunctional, and when one of the children is kidnapped and the ten-year-old remains of the family's patriarch are discovered under a construction site, Gideon teams up with local police officer Colonnello Tullio Caravale to solve the crime. Calling the series "noteworthy for its witty dialogue and clever plotting," Wes Lukowsky added in a review for *Booklist* that "Elkins delivers on both counts here," wrote Ann Forister, in her *Library Journal* review, complimented the "well-drawn supporting character, lovely scenery, and a bit of interesting science," while a reviewer for *Publishers Weekly* commented that "the forensic facts Elkins chooses to include and the brisk pace of the plot make for a total success." Pam Johnson in *School Library Journal* praised, "Weaving complications into the exotic setting, spicing it up with details of forensic pathology, and adding memorable characters make for an enticing story."

Gideon's next intersection with crime takes place in Hawaii, and is the focus of *Where There's a Will.* An old family mystery is uncovered when a plane that mysteriously crashed into the ocean in 1994 is discovered by divers. The plane's passenger was one Magnus Torkelsson, whose brother had been murdered on the same night of the crash all those years before. It seems that all the Torkelsson heirs have a motive for making sure both brothers died: teh fortune would be passed along to them. With such old tracks, it's up to Gideon and FBI agent (and returning series character) John Lau to discover the truth. "Elkins provides a fabulous 'A' quality level forensic investigative tale," praised Harriet Klausner in her online review for *MBR Bookwatch.*

Though not as well known as his "Gideon Oliver" series, the "Lee Ofstead" novels Elkins writes with his wife, Charlotte, have also developed a following. Lee is a professional golfer who always seems to find herself involved in a mystery, though her concerns are primarily focused on improving her game, financing her pro-golf career, and furthering her budding romance with policeman Graham Sheldon. In *A Wicked Slice,* the authors provide a behind-the-scenes view of life on tour, as well as bringing to light the difficult negotiation sessions that finance a successful golf career. In *Where Have All the Birdies Gone?* Lee is on the American team playing for the Stewart Cup, a competition against British golfers. Things go terribly wrong, however, when the American captain's caddy is found dead, and Lee's caddy and Peg, Lee's biggest fan, both seem to know more than they're willing to tell. "What a pleasure . . . [to] watch two genre veterans work their way around a mystery plot and a golf course without any disasters," praised Bill Ott in *Booklist.* A *Kirkus Reviews* critic noted, "It's true: No caddie would miss a pro golfer's tee time unless he was dead."

Loot is a stand-alone mystery that begins in 1945 Germany as the crumbling Nazi regime works furiously to hide stole works of art. In the confusion a truckload of the stolen art disappears. Fifty years later a Velazquez painting, part of the missing shipment, turns up in a Boston pawnshop, and then the pawnshop owner turns up dead. Retired art curator Benjamin Revere, moonlighting with the police, sets out to solve the murder of the pawnshop owner and to discover the whereabouts of the missing art. Reviewing *Loot* in *Publishers Weekly,* a reviewer wrote that as a character "Revere's combination of high intellect and low pretense makes him an engaging sleuth." In solving the mystery, Revere travels to Europe to find out why pieces of the missing loot are turning up and who is murdering people to find them. *Library Journal*'s Susan Clifford commented that Elkins combines "personably erudite central characters, and historically intriguing plot to enthrall readers." Jenny McLarin, writing in *Booklist* called *Loot* "manna for those who love art and just plain irresistible."

Elkin's novel *Turncoat* is a "thriller that probes wartime guilt from multiple angles," according to a *Publishers Weekly* writer. Set in Brooklyn in 1963, *Turncoat* features Peter Simon, a history professor, and Peter's wife Lilly. One night Lily has an argument with a stranger who turns out to be her father; he is not dead as Lilly had told Peter. Her father has an old film he wants her to look at, but before Lilly can do so, her father is murdered, and thieves attempt to steal the film. As Peter investigates he makes disturbing discoveries about Lilly's family. A *Publishers Weekly* review called the characters "sketchy" and commented that the book has "an ending that ties up matters rather too neatly," but concluded that *Turncoat* "captivates" and that "Pete's voice, a garlicky mix of France and Brooklyn, always sound just right."

Elkins once told *CA:* "I have been a voracious reader of fiction since I was eleven or twelve, but it never occurred to me that I could be a writer myself until a few years ago. Until then, I had classed novelists with opera singers, or baseball players, or movie stars—extraordinary people who inhabited some other world than mine.

"In 1978, at the age of forty-four, I returned from two years in Europe, with no likely job prospects in sight. I had been teaching anthropology for the University of Maryland's Overseas Division, on assignments that took me to NATO bases in England, Germany, Holland, Spain, Sicily, and Sardinia. I had kept a journal of my observations, and I thought I might be able to use it in writing a book. With considerable trepidation, I began a novel involving (of all things) an anthropology professor who moved through Europe, teaching at U.S. military bases."

AUTOBIOGRAPHICAL ESSAY: Aaron Elkins contributed the following autobiographical essay to *CA:*

My father, Irving Abraham Elkins, came to America from Minsk in 1911, when he was twenty-one.

Or maybe it was Pinsk. Possibly he was nineteen, not twenty-one, at the time, and it may well be that his actual year of immigration was 1909, when he was seventeen (or nineteen).

This is by way of saying that I may have a little trouble with this essay. A bent for candid, straightforward autobiography is not part of my heritage. It certainly wasn't that I never asked Dad about his early life. I asked him, all right; I just got different answers, or more often, a flap of the hand, a shrug, and a bemused "What do you want to know that stuff for?" All frequently without looking up from his after-dinner New York *Daily News* or *Daily Forward*.

In the thirties and forties, immigrants were still looking ahead, not back. America was all-important, the Old Country was something to forget as thoroughly as possible. Besides, it wasn't a good idea to talk too much, especially if you were not just an immigrant but a Jewish immigrant. American anti-Semitism, taking life from Hitler's successes, was thriving. The proudly pro-Nazi German-American Bund was holding mass rallies in Madison Square Garden, the Christian Front had "Buy Christian" as its slogan and was mounting a boycott of Jewish businesses, and the vicious Father Charles Coughlin, perhaps the most popular radio personality in America, was spouting out-and-out anti-Semitism to enthusiastic radio audiences nationwide. No, you never knew what the future held, you never knew what *they* could use against you. Roosevelt was wonderful, but every American wasn't Roosevelt. It happened in Russia, it happened in Germany, it could happen here.

And so they learned to muddy the waters, to obscure their pasts, to cover their tracks, and after a while it became a habit. And then they found they couldn't get the facts straight themselves anymore. At least I think that's the way it worked. In any case, the upshot was prevarication, gaps, holes, and "What do you want to know that stuff for?"

It wasn't any different with my friends' fathers. In the Brooklyn of the 1940s, in the six-story tenements on Blake Avenue and Amboy Street, everybody's parents were immigrants, or so it seemed to me then (and seems to me now). We were all the children of foreigners who had fled from Eastern Europe to escape the pogroms, the cossacks, the wretched poverty. A

Aaron with his mother, Long Island, New York, about 1937

grown-up without an accent was something you noticed. Throughout my young life I envied my friend Lyle, whose father could talk so knowledgeably about the Dodgers and the Giants, and who spoke—and walked, and laughed—like a native-born American. (He wasn't.)

Whatever Dad did before he left Minsk (Pinsk?), I never did learn. He must have gone to school, because he could read and write and do numbers. Here in America, he worked as a machinist at the Brooklyn Navy Yard while I was growing up and, when he could, he puttered away at inventions that were bound to make us rich someday. Some of them he patented. The story was that, years before, he had invented the bicycle coaster brake and sold it for four hundred dollars to Schwinn, who made millions with it. I don't know if it's true or not. The inventions I do remember were less exciting. There was a question-and-answer game called The Wise Old Owl, in which a cutout of a (surprise) wise, old owl was manipulated to point with its beak at answers to hundreds of educational questions about arithmetic, geography, history, and spelling.

He really believed kids would go wild for it. He was working the night shift at the Navy Yard at the time, and for months he spent his weary days walking all over New York City with an increasingly beat-up cardboard prototype, carrying it to every Woolworth's and Kresge, trying to get them interested. You can imagine how they queued up for it.

And then there was the Elkins Handy Holdall, another winner. I was eleven or twelve then, and I remember it more clearly than any of the others because on many a grim weekend, while my friends were out in the sunny streets—I could hear their shouts and laughter—I was at a makeshift wooden contraption in our storefront apartment, sulkily working the foot treadle that stapled strong, flat rubber bands to glossy, 81/2-by-11-inch photographs of neatly arranged pens, pencils, rulers, and compasses. Protractors too, I think. That's what the Elkins Handy Holdall was: a colored photograph of school implements on cardboard, punched with three holes along one side so that it could be inserted at the front of a loose-leaf notebook. The rubber bands were designed to make pockets into which you were supposed to stick your otherwise hard-to-carry implements. The ruler went right over the picture of the ruler, the pencil went where the pencil photograph was, and so on. Children would no longer have to carry ruler boxes.

Dad was so sure he was going to make it big with this one that he borrowed a thousand dollars on it from Mr. Goldberg, the tailor across the street, so that he could hire someone to help him peddle it to the stores. He advertised for a salesman in the *New York Times,* as I recall, and those had to have been tough times for salesmen, because we must have gotten fifty responses—confident, bragging letters, lists of references, three-page resumes (and these were the days before Xerox)—all in hopes of what was manifestly a shabby, scrambling, footslogging job. Most were handwritten. Many were from other immigrants.

I can remember Dad sitting at the kitchen table with a dozen letters spread out in front of him, slowly shaking his head. I thought he was having a hard time picking his man, but it wasn't that at all.

"Oy, *kinder,*" he said, and he really sounded sad, "I wish I could give you all a job."

I spent a lot of miserable weekends stapling those things, and Dad worked himself to exhaustion with them, and I suppose the salesman—a red-faced man named Jake who smelled of cloves and looked like a salesman—did his best. A few stationery stores accepted some, and Jake actually talked Woolworth into taking a few gross on consignment (what a day that was). But of course the customers wouldn't buy it in the stores, and the thing went bust.

I remember that it took a long time to pay back Mr. Goldberg, and that Mom was bitter over it and Dad was depressed, and I think that was the end of his career as an inventor.

But I remember a success story too. This was a little earlier, during the Second World War, when he developed a mechanism to safely jettison a burning airplane engine. The Navy had no use for it, so he offered it to the Army Air Force and received a gold-rimmed certificate with a big *E* on it—for Excellence?—over which he wept with pride, and laughed, and then put up on the wall, Where it was still hanging when I went away to graduate school in 1957. I don't know if the Army ever put his invention to use or not. Dad never got any cash for it, of course.

Mom, Jennie Beatrice Katz, was born in New York of Russian immigrant parents, and she had learned from them to be as tight-lipped about her past as Dad was. I was nine or ten before I found out that my sister Sonia was actually my half sister, the offspring of my mother's previous marriage—which in itself was staggering news to me. Even then, I didn't find out from Mom (or Sonia, for that matter), but only through some remark I wasn't meant to overhear. And I was well into my thirties, maybe my forties, before I finally learned Mom's earlier married name (Pastelnick), also without any help from her. Mom died in 1992, at the age of eighty-nine, and in all her long life, I. never wormed out of her what Mr. Pastelnick did for a living, or where they lived, or what *his* first name was. But then I don't know what her father's name was either, or what relationship the mysterious, seedy old man named Hennoch (Was that his first name? His last name?), who seemed to live on and off in my maternal grandmother's apartment, was to the Katz family.

There were plenty of other mysteries on both sides of the house; things that were never, ever talked about and things that broke the surface occasionally, precipitating wild arguments. My mother would cry, and scream, and break dishes; my father would put his fist through the wall or literally tear out his hair. These were no more than once-a-year occurrences in an otherwise subdued relationship, but they were so terrifying and unsettling that I stopped asking questions. I was starting to see deep, unexplained tensions and undercurrents between my parents, even in the quiet times, and to tell the truth, I stopped wanting to know any more than I already did.

I spent a lot of time outside in those days, playing stickball and punchball with my friends, or making our first fumbling advances to the girls in the neighborhood, or just exploring the run-down streets on our own. I remember it as fun. I remember how sincerely we wished that we could all stay twelve forever, that nothing would ever force us to move out of Brooklyn or, more specifically, out of our beloved Brownsville section of Brooklyn.

It was a childhood made for a writer, I suppose, filled with grist for the mill. Plenty of novelists have since turned similar grist into gold, both literary and commercial. Coming-of-age-in-New York has become a respectable genre all to itself. Perhaps if I had realized a bit earlier than I eventually did that I was going to end up as a writer, I might have tried to join that crowd. But I was long, long out of New York before that ever happened.

This brings up a point that is addressed in every writer's biography or autobiography, and now would seem to be the time to raise it: When did I first know that I was meant to be a writer? One of the things to be learned from authors' accounts of their lives is that the writing impulse tends to come early. Over and over one finds phrases like "The urge burnt in me from earliest times," or "Certainly, by the time I was eleven, I knew that I was meant. . . . "

Well, here is mine: The urge to be a writer first entered my mind at the tender age of forty-three. And even then, somebody else had to put it there.

But this is to anticipate a little.

Why I never seriously entertained thoughts of writing as a boy I'm not sure. But wanting to be an author would have been presumptuous and unrealistic, like wanting to be a baseball player, or a film actor, or an opera singer. People like that lived in a different world, and it was a world that tenement kids from Brooklyn could never hope to get into. As a matter of fact, kids from Brooklyn were getting into it all over the place, and had been for years. I just didn't know it.

But I was a great reader as a boy and had from somewhere formed an enormous respect for writers. I can remember once when someone—I'm not sure, but I think it was a now-obscure mystery writer named Bruno Fischer—was pointed out to me in a cafeteria, and I spent the rest of my meal sneaking fascinated, surreptitious glances at him to try and read his expression. What deep thoughts was he thinking as he chewed away on his veal cutlet? What perceptions was he forming and honing from the lively scene around him?

Now I'm a writer myself, and I know better.

*

My first taste of literary acclaim came when I was ten. I was home from school for a day, sick in bed with something, and for a reason I no longer remember I decided to try writing a poem; possibly it was a class assignment. Anyway, I remember approaching it in earnest. I spent most of the day on it, and I thought the finished product was dandy. I copied it carefully into one of those piebald composition books and read it aloud to my class. It was called "The Boogeyman."

My teacher thought it was a dandy too, and for months to come I did the fifth-grade equivalent to dining out on it. If there was a school recital, there was little Aaron Elkins on the stage reading "The Boogeyman." If there was a PTA night, there was little Aaron Elkins and his damned "Boogeyman." I gobbled up the adulation, of course, and in a way it was surprising that I didn't see that there might be something in a literary career after all, but I didn't.

I always have wanted to see it in print, however, so now, to that end, I am going to take advantage of the nice people of *Contemporary Authors Autobiography Series.*

Here then is my earliest work—published in these pages for the first time:

THE BOOGEYMAN

Every night when the lights are turned down low,

I hear and see the boogeyman come in and say hello.

I huddle under the blankets in fear

And wonder—is he there or is he . . . *here?*

Then I run like a mad fool,

And then my mother wakes me up—'cause it's time to go

To school!

Looking at it now, one can certainly see why it was such a hit. It has everything: a sympathetic protagonist, gut-wrenching suspense, a twist at the end, and a clean, punchy resolution. Why wasn't it even more successful? Why did it take so long to get into print? Who can say? Possibly, the meter is not everything it might have been. But whatever the reason, this promising beginning was followed by a four-decade hiatus in my literary career.

Those thirty-seven intervening years were, all in all, a pretty uneventful interlude and not likely to be of much interest to anyone out there. Inasmuch as I wasn't writing or thinking about becoming a writer, they do not have even the dubious virtue of being a "writer's life," so if you don't mind, I think I'll merely sketch them in, without going into a lot of detail.

In other words, what do you want to know that stuff for?

In grade school and junior high school I was a pretty good student, but in the last year of high school my grades plummeted, not for want of trying. For reasons I never have understood, the mathematics and science that had always come so easily to me was suddenly impenetrable. I managed to graduate, but barely. "Good luck to a boy who means well," was what my algebra teacher, Miss Sibley, wrote in my autograph book, and it makes a perceptive if double-edged epitaph for my high school phase.

In Brooklyn, New York, about 1944

It had been determined years before that I was going to go to college, and the only school that had ever come into consideration was Brooklyn College. about a twenty-minute bus ride from home and more important—overwhelmingly important—free. But now it turned out that my average wasn't good enough to get me in. Nor was it good enough for entrance to City College in Manhattan, about a forty-minute subway ride. It was good enough for Hunter College in the Bronx, a then brand-new campus of what is now called the City University of New York.

Hunter was a full hour-and-a-half subway journey from home; three hours a day on the BMT and IRT, with two transfers each way. Five days a week, ten months a year, from 1952 to 1956. The subways were better then than they are now, but they weren't much fun. If only I'd been a writer at the time, I would have had plenty of time for thinking deep thoughts and polishing and honing my perceptions. Mostly, however, I read other people's novels—Louis Bromfield, Irwin

Shaw, John P. Marquand, Jerome Weidman—or stared out the window at the tunnel.

I came close to flunking out in my first year, but then I wandered dubiously into an anthropology course and suddenly remembered how exciting education could be. I had a major, and my grades became respectable again.

When I informed my parents that I planned to be an anthropologist, something they could never have heard of before, a kitchen-table conference was called. "Can you," my father solemnly asked, "earn six thousand dollars a year at this?" I said I was sure I could (I had no idea), and the matter was settled.

By the time I finished at Hunter in 1956, my grades had improved enough so that I got a small scholarship in physical anthropology to the University of Arizona. I made ends meet by boxing professionally, of all things, under the name Al Blake, and even managed to put together a winning record, but when I got knocked out for the third time in a row, I decided to hang up the gloves while I still had some brain cells left. By that time I had my master's degree and had won a more substantial graduate assistantship at the University of Wisconsin. But I ran into personal and personality problems (you don't want to know) and left after two years without ever getting a doctorate.

What I did get in Madison, Wisconsin, however, was a wife. I met Toby Siev, an occupational therapy student at the university, in 1957, and we were married in 1959. The marriage produced two children, Laurence and Robin, and lasted ten years, nine of which I remember as wonderful and one as miserable; not a bad record, if you look at it the right way. We separated in 1970 and were divorced in 1972.

Early in that marriage I started on a meandering, aimless sort of dual career—in government and teaching—that lasted almost twenty years. There was nothing shady or irresponsible about it, you understand. Never was there a time when I couldn't support my family or come up with the mortgage payments on the new suburban house we bought in Orange County, California. Never was there a time when I didn't have an eminently respectable job, and most of the time I had more than one. But there was an awful lot of

As a graduate student in Arizona, 1956

bouncing around from one eminently respectable job to another eminently respectable job, and not in any kind of career progression that I or anybody else could apprehend.

In those twenty years I taught at ten different colleges and universities, mostly evening classes but occasionally full-time, in three different subjects: anthropology, psychology, and management. And I worked full-time, mostly as an administrator, for seven different organizations, most of them governmental. It was even more frenetic than it sounds, because I left several of those organizations only to return again later for a second or even a third stint. And then there was a two-year period when I worked during the day, taught a course or two at night, and completed a second master's degree, this time in psychology.

It was hectic but not unpleasant; I was never fired or asked to leave, and my employment records are stuffed with positive evaluations. But it wasn't satisfying either. The thing was, I could never figure out what I was doing serving as the safety and training director of Orange County, or teaching theories of management at California State University, or, for that matter, spending my weekends in the southern California sunshine applying leaf polish to our variegated *Aucuba japonica* hedge.

It was a very nice life, and I knew it; it just didn't seem like *my* life.

*

The big turnabout came when I married Charlotte—Charlotte Marie Trangmar—in 1972, just one day after my divorce from Toby became final. (I have been known to say, when attempting to be amusing, that I tried being single for a whole day before I decided I didn't like it. The truth of the matter is that I had been living alone, with Toby and the children in faraway Texas, since 1970. So the truth is that I tried being single for a whole two years before I decided I didn't like it.)

When we married, I was the chief of employee development for Contra Costa County in northern California and an evening lecturer in anthropology and supervision at Golden Gate University. Charlotte was an artist selling her sculptures through several San Francisco galleries. That seemed right for her, but my life didn't seem right for me, and she agreed with me on that. It was time, she made me see, to take my life into my own hands and get it moving again, even if I didn't quite know in what direction.

The encouragement took. By 1976 I had started and finished a doctorate in adult education at Berkeley—seventeen years after quitting the doctorate at Wisconsin—I had resigned from my job at Contra Costa County, and I had accepted a two-year, dream position in Europe as a lecturer with the University of Maryland's Overseas Division, moving every eight weeks to a new country and a new assignment.

It was the first bold thing I'd done in decades, and it felt wonderful. Two years later, however, my contract was about to run out, and it was time to come home again. But there was nothing to come back to. I had burnt my bridges behind me, and I didn't want to be a chief of employee development anymore anyway. And I certainly couldn't live on part-time teaching.

We had mailed applications and resumes from Europe to dozens of American universities, but none of them had come to anything. We were winding up an assignment in Munich at the time, and I had begun to wonder gloomily how hard it would be to unburn some of those bridges. Then, out of nowhere one morning, while I was at the dining room table grading a pile of papers on human evolution, Charlotte uttered the Eight Words That Changed Everything.

"Well," she said, "you could always try writing a book."

The seed, thus cast, did not alight on fertile ground. What kind of book was I supposed to write, I demanded to know, and not very enthusiastically either.

"A thriller," she said decisively. This from a woman who had read perhaps three thrillers in her life. "I think you'd be good at that."

I didn't. My most exciting publication to date had been "An Anthropological Analysis of the Skeletal Remains from CK-44, the Smullins Site," published as the second lead article in the *Oklahoma Journal of Anthropology* in October 1959. I wasn't a writer, I was a—well, I wasn't sure what I was, but I certainly wasn't a novelist. I'd never even written a short story. My last serious literary endeavor had been "The Boogeyman."

But by that afternoon, lacking reasonable alternatives, or any alternatives at all, I was mulling over the idea. It was over a dinner of bratwurst and liver-dumpling soup in Munich's Marienplatz that I mutteringly brought the subject up again.

I didn't know what to write about, I told her. "Write about what you know," she said sensibly.

"You want me to write a thriller about Pleistocene hominid evolution?"

She saw how that might present a problem and suggested that perhaps I might write about my adventures as an anthropology professor.

"You're kidding," I said.

"All right," Charlotte said, "use your imagination a little. Write about the adventures that *might* have happened to you."

By now you may be wondering about my ability to recall verbatim a conversation of fifteen years ago. But this was a pivotal conversation, the starting point of a transformation, and I was aware of it even then. To be honest, I've told the story a lot of times, and retelling has probably condensed things a little and sharpened them up. But not much.

Before that week was out, I had begun *The Need-to-Know Principle,* about the European adventures of Gideon Oliver, a likable, intelligent, witty, attractively quirky anthropology professor (whose real-life model I have never divulged to anyone). Interestingly, there turned out to be all sorts of adventures I might have had. The writing flowed, the characters developed, the plot thickened. But after a few chapters, I began to lose focus. I felt the book needed something different, something offbeat. So in the midst of what I can now see were rather conventional goings-on, I produced a burned car with a few charred skeletal fragments: a tiny piece of the jaw, a bit of tibia, a little chunk of the occiput. Then I put them into Gideon's hands and wrote a long, detailed description of how a forensic anthropologist would go about analyzing them.

Why not? I was supposed to write about what I knew, and what I knew were bones. If they were so fascinating to me, why shouldn't they be at least passably interesting to others?

In any case, after twenty-one densely packed pages, Gideon was ready to make his report to the police. The minuscule fragments, he announced, had belonged to a muscular, thirty-eight-year-old, Oriental male who was five-feet-five-inches in height and weighed 145 pounds.

The police, of course, are smugly skeptical; can this crack-brained, ivory-towered professor seriously expect them to believe that he has deduced all this from a literal handful of bones, and a small handful at that? Damn right, says an irritated Gideon, and for good measure he tells them that the person was left-handed and smoked a pipe.

Mystery devotees will not be surprised to find out that he turns out to be right in every detail, much to the astonishment of the police but not of the reader, who has been at Gideon's shoulder every step of the way.

I finished writing the book after returning to the United States, bought a copy of *Writer's Market,* and began sending query letters to those publishers listed as having an interest in mysteries. Walker and Company, the first publisher to agree to look at the manuscript—after twelve negative responses from other houses—bought it. Ruth Cavin, the senior editor who telephoned me to express their interest, said they would be happy to publish it and would, in fact, be pleased to consider publishing future novels about Gideon Oliver. (This was in response to my original letter, in which I had recklessly and not altogether truthfully said that I had a second such book well under way.) However, Ruth would prefer that the first one be shortened a bit, and that a few patently Ludlumesque elements be deleted as being out of character with the rest of the story. Would that be all right with me?

What a question. There was nothing that wouldn't have been all right with me, as long as they didn't change their mind about publishing it.

In addition, she was not overly keen on *The Need-to-Know Principle* as a title (neither was I) and decided, with my willing agreement, to change it. As a result, my first novel was published in September 1982 as *Fellowship of Fear.* Perhaps, Ruth suggested hopefully (or was it wistfully?) people might confuse it with *The Ministry of Fear.*

To my knowledge, no one did confuse me with Graham Greene, but the reviews were uniformly good, and the sales were as good as was to be hoped from an unpromoted first mystery novel—which is to say modest, but not embarrassingly so.

There were, as I recall, sixteen newspaper reviews that came to my attention, every one of them positive, which, in my middle-aged naivete was welcome but hardly surprising. What *was* a surprise, however, was how much most of them—and most of the letters from readers—expressed a. liking for the skeletal analysis. I had made Gideon Oliver a physical anthropologist because a protagonist has to be something, and inasmuch as that's what I was, that's what he was. The anthropology had been intended as backdrop, not center-stage material. The business with the muscular, thirty-eight-year-old, left-handed Oriental man who smoked a pipe had been put in simply as a bit of "business," a one-time tour de force.

But the reviews and letters made me think again. I was on to something, I realized. Without trying to, I had created what every new mystery writer dreams of: a niche of my own, all to myself, with an appreciative audience and no likely competitors. Under those conditions, one's ingenuity is stimulated. I began to see all kinds of interesting and unusual plots that might involve bits of bone, and from then on, Gideon's skeletal detective work, and the field of anthropology in general, became a continuing and critical part of the series.

*

I had sold my first novel without an agent, but I knew I would need one if I was going to try to earn a living from writing. Among my strengths, such as they are, business acumen does not figure prominently, and I was going to require help in contract negotiations and the like. But not knowing how one went about acquiring an agent, I asked my editor to recommend one. This is not an approach I would suggest to other writers; agents on close terms with editors or publishers are not necessarily the best people to represent authors. In this case, however, I was well served. Ruth recommended her old college friend Victor Chapin, an agent in the small John Schaffner Agency in New York. My association with Victor was a good one, but sadly it lasted only a few months before Victor died without my ever having met him. My account was dumped into the lap of Barney Karpfinger, a young agent on the Schaffner staff.

After a somewhat rocky beginning (Barney was overloaded with his own clients and Victor's as well), we hit it off. When he moved to the Aaron M. Priest Literary Agency I went with him, and when a year or two later he opened his own agency, I was the first client for whom he wrote a book contract. In the decade that has passed since then, I have never once even thought about changing agents, and I don't know how many writers can say that.

For the second "Gideon Oliver" book, I had in mind a plot involving a small band of ancient people that had managed to survive twelve thousand years, unknown to the modern world, in the Neolithic cave complexes of the Dordogne region of France. I didn't see how I could write it without revisiting the Dordogne, but with our financial situation what it was, I couldn't

Aaron with his father and mother on a trip around Manhattan, 1958

bring myself to risk spending the money to make the trip, certainly not on the remote possibility that I was actually going to make a career of writing.

At the moment, that possibility was extremely remote. Writing was still a spare-time affair for me, something I did from 5:00 A.M. to 6:30 A.M. most mornings. *Fellowship of Fear* had earned me a two-thousand-dollar advance (about average for a first mystery) and further royalties that were, as they say in the business, in the low three figures. These were not living wages, even in 1982. As a result, I had repaired some old bridges and was back working for Contra Costa County. That was another reason the trip to France was out. I hadn't yet built up enough vacation to let me take off more than a few days.

Further thought suggested that I might get by with a plot involving a band of presumably extinct Indians

that had managed to survive unknown to the modern world not for twelve thousand years, but for sixty or seventy years, as a band of Yahi Indians had in fact done in California at the beginning of the century. The question was: Where could I set it? Where could it credibly happen in 1983? Not California, obviously. Was there anyplace within a two-or three-day drive of the Bay Area?

And so *The Dark Place* takes place eight hundred miles north of the San Francisco Bay Area, in the rain forests of Washington State's Olympic Peninsula, the rugged, uncrowded thumb of land that forms the northwest corner of the United States. It took two or three research trips, all of them made with Charlotte, to get the details right, and by the time we were done the place had gotten to us. In another year, when the books were doing well enough to support us, it was where we moved, and we still live there.

Like *Fellowship of Fear, The Dark Place* came out to warm reviews—all except the *New York Times,* which had been generous to the first book. This time it was merciless. "Panning" doesn't begin to do it justice. "Crucifixion" is nearer the mark.

Smart writers do not let negative reviews affect them adversely. In that regard, I am a smart writer; negative reviews don't bother me. But in 1983 I wasn't smart yet. I was devastated. I had just come from an optometric examination in which drops that blurred my vision had been placed in my eyes. I was driving slowly home (I shouldn't have been driving at all) when I passed the library. It was a Thursday, the day the *New York Times Book Review* arrived, and I had been going to the library for the last several weeks hoping to find a review of *The Dark Place* in it, so I stopped in.

The *Book Review* was in, and squinting at the mystery page, 1 was able to see that *The Dark Place* was the lead mystery review, and a longish one at that. I borrowed a magnifying glass and sat down in a cubicle practically panting with anticipation. My eyes were tearing and blinking. I could barely focus. I was able to make out phrases, but not complete sentences, and I kept losing my place. I saw some nice words— something about the spooky rain forest setting and the action scenes—and then, sitting all by itself, a brief, one-sentence paragraph:

"But, oh, the writing."

If I were the sort of novelist who wrote about people's blood freezing, that's what I'd put in here. I couldn't believe that sentence meant what it seemed to mean. But the following paragraphs made it clear that it did. My first negative review, and not only was it a lulu, but it was from the *Times.* It was the worst moment of my life as a writer. I didn't sleep most of that night. My self-confidence, never overwhelming, evaporated. The new book I had begun, set near Mont-Saint-Michel, lost what steam it had and went into a desk drawer while I pottered uncertainly among other writing projects. It was weeks before I got my confidence back.

Had I foolishly been expecting never to get anything but positive reviews? I don't know. I hadn't thought about it. They'd all been good so far; that was all I

Sister Sonia and Mother, 1958

knew. Do other writers react as strongly to their first negative review? Yes, many do. But, assuming that one keeps writing, more of the same are certain to follow, and the others tend not to be as painful as the first, and after a while a kind of protective scar tissue forms that makes them easier to take. Besides, by then you have often had the fun of seeing your friends and colleagues similarly skewered, which helps a lot.

People who are not writers might think that authors would be well-advised to read their negative reviews with particular attention rather than letting a protective skin form. Reviews are, in a sense, free advice. Isn't there something to be learned from the thoughtful analyses of intelligent and knowledgeable critics? Maybe, but I don't know a professional writer who takes them seriously, and I know a lot of writers.

One reason they don't is that reviewers do not prepare their columns for writers. They write them, as they should, with readers in mind, and that is a different thing. More importantly, a successful writer—successful enough to be reviewed in major newspapers—is no longer a student trying to learn how to write. He or she writes, sentence by sentence and paragraph by paragraph, from the personal conviction that this is the way to say what he or she is trying to say. It can very likely be improved, yes, but not by following someone else's advice on the way it should have been done in the first place. Once you start writing what other people think you should be writing, the issue of just whose book it is arises. And a writer who writes any book but his or her own is heading for trouble—is already *in* trouble.

There are a few authors, of course, who simply cannot ignore negative reviews, and they fire letters back to the newspapers pointing out the errors, oversights, ignorances, and biases of their reviewers. No doubt there is a certain amount of catharsis to be gained from this, but I find it simpler and more soothing to leave the reviewers—who are, after all, only earning their living, as I am mine—to their jobs while I get on with my own work, tranquil and unruffled.

How do I manage to maintain this constructive and magnanimous attitude? Easy. I don't read negative reviews of my books. My publishers don't send them to me, and if Charlotte spots one, she keeps it to herself. Every now and then one sneaks through anyway, but it is no longer enough to bother me. Besides, the reviews, knock on wood, continue to be overwhelmingly positive.

On the other hand, how would I know if they weren't?

*

A book called *Murder in the Queen's Armes,* set in England, followed, after which I had one of my recurring crises of confidence. It seemed to me that the "skeleton detective" series, while enjoyable to write, well received, and doing moderately well, had run its course. How many plots can you construct, after all, that revolve around solving murders from little bits of bone? And how long can you go on doing it without repeating yourself, or seeming to repeat yourself, which amounts to the same thing as far as readers are concerned?

So, casting about for another subject that might provide an interesting and challenging milieu in which to set a mystery, I settled on art, not at all sure that I was doing the right thing. Friends in the publishing field shook their heads: art mysteries were out of fashion (if they were ever in) and unsellable. But I had gotten deeply involved in the research by then and had come up with what seemed to me to be a nifty plot, and I saw it cheerfully if not always confidently through.

A Deceptive Clarity, featuring a curator of Baroque and Renaissance art named Chris Norgren, turned out to be very much an art mystery; that is, the story centered on some technical, fascinating (to me) aspects of Old Master paintings and forgery, much as the "Gideon Oliver" books had centered on the technical aspects of forensic anthropology.

Alas, my friends were essentially right. The manuscript did sell, but not for very much. On publication the reviews were scant, and for the first time, there was no sale of paperback rights; indeed, *A Deceptive Clarity* was not to appear in paperback until 1993, six years later.

There was a bright spot: a magazine reviewer read a galley of *A Deceptive Clarity* and liked it enough to want to do a major interview piece on me. The interview was duly conducted by telephone, I was at my brightest and wittiest, and the resulting article was published a few months later. But someone at the printer's, never having heard of Aaron J. Elkins, concluded that the interviewer had a better-known author in mind and corrected the title on his own. The piece was published as "An Interview with Stanley Elkin."

I sincerely hope it did Mr. Elkin some good.

A word about "Aaron J. Elkins," who vanished from sight with *A Deceptive Clarity* to be replaced by the simpler "Aaron Elkins." This small transformation continues to create minor confusion for *Books in Print,* the Library of Congress, and numerous lesser libraries, and to them I apologize. Actually, "Aaron J. Elkins" never was my name. I was born "Aaron Elkins" and was content with it until my late twenties, when I published my first paper in anthropology. Everyone else putting out academic papers seemed to have at least one middle initial, some had two or even three, and I decided I needed one of my own.

Acting on something I read that said one could change one's name simply by changing it, without going to court or filling out papers (if this isn't true, please don't tell me now), I added an initial of my own: *P.* The name I had in mind was Aaron Paul Elkins, which to my ears had a ring both scholarly and friendly. But before it showed up in print, a far-thinking colleague

With Charlotte in the Tucson Mountains, about 1975

alluded delicately to the potential for unwelcome drollery that lay in wait for a physical anthropologist whose initials were APE.

I promptly changed it to *J* (for Joseph) and used it for the next twenty years for business and academic dealings. I never had it in mind for my novels, but my original letter to Walker had been signed with it (more distinguished, don't you know), and they put it on the books. It took me four publications to get around to having it removed.

Back to the writing. Chastened by *A Deceptive Clarity*'s nonreception, and in a decidedly gloomy frame of mind, I concluded that I might have been a little hasty in retiring Gideon Oliver, so I went back to the desk drawer in which, three years earlier—in another gloomy frame of mind—I had stowed the unfinished manuscript of the Mont-Saint-Michel book. Seeing the title, "Legacy of Death," was enough to make my teeth ache, but the work itself, unlooked at all this time, now seemed salvageable. Retitling it *Old Bones,* I got back to work on it, a complex story of death on the tideflats, bones in the cellar, and buried familial hatreds going back to the days of the Nazi occupation.

When it was finished, I was still in a generally negative frame of mind. The lack of critical attention to *A Deceptive Clarity* had scared me. Most mystery novelists get a fair amount of attention from reviewers for their first book, or two, or three. But then interest withers. Mysteries, after all, tend to be somewhat repetitive and predictable simply by virtue of being mysteries. (You know someone is going to get killed, you know someone else—the protagonist—will try to solve the murder, you know the protagonist will follow many false leads and face many obstacles, and you know that in the end he or she will solve it.) And those of any individual writer are bound to be even more alike than mysteries in general. What a reviewer might say about book number seven by a given writer is likely to be similar, on the whole, to what he or she said about book number two. Thus, better to be on the lookout for new and different writers, of whom there are always plenty, about whom something new and different can be said. Only a relatively small group of authors becomes well-regarded enough, or well-known enough, to continue to be reviewed, book after book. And without reviews, writers fade away. The publishers lose interest and the readers, even if interested, can't find the books.

The sum total of three reviews for *A Deceptive Clarity* had me wondering if I had reached that cutoff point and failed to get by it. I thought of *Old Bones* as my last try at establishing a place as a credible mystery writer. I was over fifty; a long apprenticeship was not in the cards. If this book, hauled from the refuse pile, was just one more unnoticed mystery among the four hundred or so published every year in the United States, I was ready to throw in the towel and look for something else to do.

But things went wonderfully from the beginning. First, the book was bought by Otto Penzler's Mysterious Press, arguably the best of the mystery publishers, and I acquired another superb editor, Sara Ann Freed, who continues to edit my novels till this day, knock on wood.

And then, to my intense surprise, *Old Bones* won the 1988 Edgar—the Mystery Writers of America Edgar Allan Poe Award—as the year's best mystery. That did it. I became an instant celebrity, and I can prove it: at the International Congress of Crime Writers held in New York that May there was an event called the celebrity luncheon, where honest-to-goodness writing celebrities such as Donald Westlake, Evan Hunter (a. k.a. Ed McBain), Mary Higgins Clark, and Isaac Asimov joined mystery fans and aspiring writers for lunch and then participated in a panel or writing. The fans, of course, paid for the privilege. Had I reserved a place at this affair ahead of time I would have been charged thirty-five dollars like anybody else. But as it happened, it was held on the day after the Edgar awards ceremony at the Sheraton Centre.

And by then, of course, I was a celebrity. Early that morning I was pressed into service to join the other celebrities on view, which I did with pleasure. Well, to be candid, it was an emergency, one of the advertised attractions having found it impossible to be there, but all the same, there I was at the celebrity luncheon, a certified celebrity.

The point was brought forcefully home in the course of the afternoon, when I gave my jacket to a shivering attendee in a thin dress and I heard a nearby woman whisper to a companion: "Won't *this* be something for her to remember!"

Clearly, I was in for some heady times.

When Gabriel García Márquez won the Nobel Prize for literature in 1982 he was so overwhelmed by the attendant publicity that he had no time for work. For a year, he said, he had to give up writing and simply be the Nobel laureate, like a reigning beauty queen. So it was for me. There were interviews, appearances, book signings, and congratulatory letters to be answered. All of it was welcome, but it kept me from concentrating on my current novel, and it made for a self-puffery that I hadn't known was there and didn't like. Fortunately, it lasted not for a year, but only for about two weeks (thereby empirically establishing that an Edgar carries one twenty-sixth the cachet of a Nobel Prize), after which I was able to settle down to my writing again.

*

And settled down to my writing I have remained for the past five years. My life at last has become a "writer's life," enormously satisfying to me, but not so easy to write about. Simply put, writers do not make very good biographical subjects. Flannery O'Connor, expressing comparable thoughts, says somewhere that the story of her own life would consist mainly of walking from the house to the barn and back again. Except

for my having a study instead of a barn, that about says it for me too. Readers of biographies who expect anything very novelistic in the lives of novelists are going to be routinely disappointed and certainly will be in my case. Like most other novelists, I spend most of my time sitting quietly in a room in front of a word processor, making up stories.

In other words, here is where, if I don't watch myself, this is going to turn into a series of six more "And then I wrote. . . . " Rather than finish on that dreary route, I thought I might make some remarks about what I write and why I write it.

I am a mystery writer. I am not on my way to grander things. My first book was a mystery, all of my books since then have been mysteries, and I will be very surprised if my last book isn't one. Basically, the reason that I write mysteries and nothing else is that you can write them without having anything to say.

When I say that at a writers conference or in an interview, it's usually treated as an attempt at humor or disingenuousness, but I mean it sincerely. I really do love being a writer. I love the fun and anguish of wrestling with plot and character, of trying to make the words say what I mean. But I don't have anything in particular to *say:* no solutions to the problems of society, no comprehensive grasp of the root causes of the world's evils, no insights into personality and character that millions of others (well, thousands) don't have too. The mystery novel is precisely the vehicle I need: a form with structure, with point, and with a ready readership, but with no need for an overarching message or theme.

As I see it, I am following in the wake of an old and glorious tradition. The mystery, surely more than any other fiction genre, can boast a long, honorable history of works that are primarily entertainments and diversions—but diversions of high literary merit—by authors such as Edgar Allan Poe, Wilkie Collins, Arthur Conan Doyle, G. K. Chesterton, and Dorothy Sayers.

Some of my fellow writers—and too many of the academics now writing about mystery writing—feel otherwise. They view the contemporary mystery novel as a means of putting forward important political,

"A celebrity at last." The author (far right) with Evan Hunter (a.k.a. Ed McBain) and Donald Westlake at a celebrity luncheon, May 1988

social, and environmental agendas, of raising consciousness. I don't see it that way at all. Here I am in the middle of my twelfth novel, and I've yet to go out of my way to take on an environmental issue, or a social issue, or just about any other kind of issue. They show up in my books from time to time because the books are set in today's world, but having them show up is different from taking them on. If any reader has ever figured out from my books where I stand on Brazilian rain forests, or overpopulation, or the problems of the homeless, or the plight of the spotted owl, he or she has done it without my help.

There is more involved here than personal preference. I think that issues and mysteries make edgy bedfellows. For one thing, they're an awkward combination for the author. Writing mysteries is tricky business. Writing cogently on issues is tricky business too, but of a different kind, requiring different techniques if it's going to be done well. (High school English teachers have good reason to try to drum into their students' heads the critical difference between narrative and exposition.) Besides, there are other forums, easier and more effective ones, for sounding off on issues. Mysteries have more than enough constraints—the placement and ordering of clues and red herrings, the hiding and holding back of information until the novelistically right time—as it is. Of course it's possible,

yes, to weave significant messages into mystery fiction; what I don't understand is why anyone tries to do it.

More than that, the reader that I have in mind as I write doesn't turn to a mystery at the end of a workday or on a rainy Sunday afternoon to have his or her consciousness raised about all the terrifying, patently insoluble problems that grow more threatening and further out of control every day. I worry about a lot of things, but one of them is not a shortage of stress-inducers and frustration-makers, of critical needs crying out for urgent action before it's too late, of simmering problems that will surely mean the end of the world as we know it (and probably the end of the world, period). Television programming and daily newspapers do very well at maintaining general agitation levels without the help of mysteries.

On the contrary, I think that the sweetest, best function of the mystery novel or story is as a decompressant, a consciousness-lowering interlude for the intelligent reader. This is nothing to be sneezed at.

"Holmes," Christopher Morley once wrote about Conan Doyle's great detective, "is pure anesthesia." He said it lovingly and meant it as praise. Not anesthesia in the sense of unconsciousness or dullness of perception, of course, but in the sense of relief from pain, worry, and uneasiness. It's still why most readers come to mystery fiction, in my opinion. They come for comfort, for security, for a welcome dose of order in a disorderly and changing world.

Moral issues are a different matter. The mystery is, I think, the most moral of all forms of popular fiction. At least in traditional, "classic" detective fiction, which is what I try to write, there are certain predictabilities (which is where the comfort and security come from): actions beget consequences. People get what's coming to them. The good guys win, the bad guys lose, and they pay for what they did. Virtue triumphs, if not in every particular, then for the most part.

When I read a mystery myself, I like to do it in a good chair with a long, leisurely evening before me and a glass of wine or a cup of coffee at my side. And I don't do it to confront the implacable issues of world ecology and human society, I do it to get away from the damn things. I think that's why most other readers do it too.

I must admit some trepidation about confessing to all this, that is, to not being a Serious Writer of Meaningful Fiction. Anthony Trollope's reputation suffered famously when he acknowledged something similar in his autobiography. What will happen to mine? Who knows, would I have been invited to write this memoir for the *Autobiography Series* if the people at Gale Research had known so much about me before? (If you are reading this, it would appear to mean that at least they didn't have a change of heart about publishing it.)

Time will tell, I guess. In the meantime I have continued to write Gideon Oliver novels and Chris Norgren novels with literate entertainment as my primary aim. For as far ahead as I can see, that's what I will keep doing. The one departure was to collaborate on a novel—a mystery, of course—with Charlotte, but it's unlikely that there will be any more of those. Our marriage comes before our joint literary career.

I have discovered that autobiography is more difficult to write than biography, at least in one respect: It's hard to know quite when to stop, or even how. One

feels almost as if one should have the decency to die immediately on completion. That dangling, expectant hyphen on the first page (Aaron Elkins, 1935–) gives one an edgy and peculiar feeling.

Like waiting for the other shoe to drop.

Aaron Elkins contributed the following update to *CA* in 2005:

So far so good. Here it is, more than a decade later, and the shoe has yet to drop. Another eleven years have gone by, and another ten Aaron Elkins books have hit the shelves.

Now there's a funny thing right there—the amount of time it takes to turn out a book, at least in my case. All those years ago, when I first began, I used to do my writing in the mornings, from 5:30 A.M. to 7 A.M., before I went off to whichever of several jobs I was holding down. This wasn't easy for me. I wasn't a morning person back then (I've turned into one since), but writing in the evenings, which I'd tried first, simply didn't work; for three hours I would sit, to paraphrase Gene Fowler, staring at a blank sheet of paper until little drops of blood formed on my forehead. So those morning hours were all I had. Then I'd generally put in another half-day or so on the weekend: a total of about twelve hours a week, sometimes a little more. It took me thirteen months to write that first book, *Fellowship of Fear*. Now that I have the good fortune to be able to do it full-time, I typically work about seven hours a day (six for writing, and one for research, cogitation, and generally second-guessing myself over knotty problems of character, plot, motive, and especially—this will come as a surprise to the non-writer—logistics, i.e., getting my characters from one place to another and accounting for their whereabouts when they're not onstage). I usually do another four or five hours over the weekend if Charlotte lets me get away with it. In total, that's roughly forty hours a week, more than three times what I was able to devote to my first book.

So how long did *Where There's a Will,* my most recent novel, take me to write? Thirteen months. On the button. And if you divide ten books into eleven years, you get an average of . . . guess. On the surface, this seems pretty strange. Does it really mean that my output doesn't depend on the number of hours I sit at

Aaron in his workroom, 1992

the computer, it simply depends on the number of months that that go by on the calendar once I get started, regardless of how much or how little I work?

Well . . . yes, pretty much. I've talked to other writers about this, and although they take differing lengths of time to turn out a book—most mystery writers are a lot faster than I am, most mainstream novelists a lot slower—they generally agree that, whatever it is that determines the volume of output, it isn't the volume of input. All of us have learned to our disappointment that doubling or tripling the time one slogs away at the computer doesn't double or triple one's production.

It's as if you had only so much psychic energy to put into the tremendous project of writing a book. You can increase your working hours as much as you want, but you can't up the psychic energy level. Or maybe it's creativity. Or the ability to hold the threads of your

story together and keep them all in mind, something that gets harder and harder as you get further into a book.

Whatever it is, it makes most of us who earn a living as writers of popular fiction turn out our books at a steady and predictable pace, which happens to be the way our publishers like it anyway, so maybe it's all for the good. Agatha Christie suggested that we were like sausage machines: whenever one sausage popped out of the business end of the machine, there was another one right behind it, ready to push on out at a nice, even rhythm. Others have used a digestive metaphor that is more imaginative but less flattering, but either way, that seems to be the way it works.

*

Re-reading my original essay, now more than a decade old, has been an interesting experience. Generally speaking, the author of that piece still sounds a lot like me to me, but a couple of the observations that I made—predictions, really—turned out to have been fired a little too quickly from the hip. For one thing, back then I made rather a big point of saying that I wrote mysteries because, while I loved working with words and ideas, and it was a pleasure to think that I was actually entertaining, maybe even enlightening, many thousands (well, thousands) of people, I had nothing very profound or meaningful to say, and I didn't see much prospect of anything changing.

But four or five years later, as it turned out, I did have something meaningful to say, after all, or at least something that I wanted to say. The mid-nineties was a time in which the cruelties and injustices associated with the Holocaust came under greatly increased public scrutiny. I don't mean the atrocities of the Nazis, but the duplicity and greed displayed by supposedly upright nations, institutions and individuals long after the end of the war: the Swiss stonewalling when it came to releasing to their impoverished owners the money and possessions that had been stolen from them by the Nazis and Nazi sympathizers and deposited in unnumbered accounts in Zurich or Geneva, for example; or the impossible requirements the post-war Austrian government placed on those who tried to reclaim art objects and other precious possessions that had been confiscated during the thirties and forties and had somehow or other wound up in the great and stately museums of Vienna; or the dug-in reluctance of French museums, including the Louvre, to return similar stolen, confiscated, or "Aryanized" paintings.

I found the stories fascinating and moving. Although several recent nonfiction books had come out on the subject, I knew of no detailed, serious fictional treatment. After quite a bit of self-examination, including a good dollop of self-doubt—after all, I had never written anything but series-mysteries—I girded my loins and plunged into this dismal chapter of human avarice and venality. I read the available books; I went to the National Archives to look at old Nazi manifests; I visited the Alt Aussee salt mine in Austria, where hundreds of looted Old Master paintings had been stored; I went to Vienna and to St. Petersburg; I visited with one of the few surviving members of MFA&A, the famed American military unit tasked with getting stolen art objects back to their original owners in the early postwar years. And then I sat down to write

Aaron and Charlotte, 2004

Loot, a multi-tiered novel about a Nazi-appropriated Velazquez painting that disappears at war's end and drops from sight until it shows up fifty years later in a seedy Boston pawnshop.

This one was an exception. There was just too much to it for my usual thirteen months. It took me a full two years: two of the most absorbing, thoughtful, stimulating years of my writing life. Reviews were excellent, sales were good, and my publisher—by this time it was William Morrow—was eager for another. But I'd had my say (I thought), and I was ready to return to adventuring with my old friend Gideon Oliver, the Skeleton Detective; my first-born, so to speak. The result was *Skeleton Dance,* set among the prehistoric ruins and wonderful little villages of France's Dordogne. But when I turned it in (after thirteen months) and began to push along the next little sausage, I found my plotting for Gideon disrupted. There were, it appeared, a few more meaningful things about the dark side of human nature rattling around in my brain and clamoring to get out.

Turncoat said them. The novel takes place in the 1960s, but its subject is French collaboration during the war, a bitter, complex morass of an issue that continues to pit Frenchman against Frenchman to this day. Like *Loot*, *Turncoat* humbled me, wholly absorbed me, opened my eyes to a great deal I hadn't understood . . . and was fun, at least in the writer's sense of fun, which involves very little laughing, but quite a lot of vacillating, agonizing, and self-doubt.

When it was done I found myself more than ready to get back to the ordered, morally unambiguous world of mystery fiction. Since then, with Berkley (Penguin-Putnam) as my publisher, I've produced two more "Gideon Olivers"—*Good Blood* and *Where There's a Will*—and am working on a third. I've learned from what I wrote here eleven years ago to be less cocksure with my self-predictions, but from where I sit at the moment it looks as if I'll be chronicling Professor Oliver's adventures and misadventures for some time to come, a happy prospect. Once again, I've been tremendously lucky on the editing front, acquiring one of the great ladies of editing and publishing, Leona Nevler, as my editor. I've already asked her if she would edit my books in my next life as well, and, thank God, she said yes.

The other big thing I got wrong eleven years ago was my saying that collaborating on one book with Charlotte was quite enough, thank you, and our joint literary career was at its end. I really meant it, too, but here we are now, working on our fifth novel about female golfer Lee Ofsted. Most people understand, correctly enough, that novel-writing is about as solitary an occupation as there is, and we are often asked just how two people go about writing a book together. Our answer is that we don't write it together, we write it separately; although we have frequent consultations, we are never working on the same section at the same time. Charlotte, as the idea-person of the team, conceives the basic plot and gets input on it from me, usually minimal. Then she writes a draft of the first section and turns it over to the word-person on the team (me). I polish the draft and usually add a few ideas and some color. Charlotte waits to see what I've done with the material before going on to the next section, which she drafts and gives to me for polishing and expansion. And so on. As collaboration goes, it's pretty painless: no arguments over the breakfast table, no hashing out of divergent ideas, no gnashing of teeth over one another's editorial presumptions. But it's not *totally* painless, and it is not an exercise either of us would recommend to other married couples.

And so we've pretty much decided that the work in progress, *Fringe Behavior,* will be our final joint contribution to world literature. No more Lee Ofsteds. This time I mean it. Really.

BIOGRAPHICAL AND CRITICAL SOURCES:

BOOKS

St. James Guide to Crime and Mystery Writers, St. James Press (Detroit, MI), 1996.

PERIODICALS

Booklist, December 1, 1998, Jenny McLarin, review of *Loot,* p. 165; March 15, 2002, George Needham, review of *Skeleton Dance,* p. 1332; January 1, 2004, Wes Lukowsky, review of *Good Blood,* p. 830; November 15, 2004, Bill Ott, review of *Where Have All the Birdies Gone?,* pp. 564-565.

Kirkus Reviews, December 1, 2003, review of *Good Blood,* p. 1383; December 1, 2004, review of *Where Have All the Birdies Gone?,* p. 1120; February 15, 2005, review of *Where There's a Will,* p. 200.

Library Journal, January, 1999, Susan Clifford, review of *Loot,* p. 165; January, 2004, Ann Forister, review of *Good Blood,* p. 166.

MBR Bookwatch, March, 2005, Harriet Klausner, review of *Where Have All the Birdies Gone?*

New York Times, February 6, 1983, review of *Fellowship of Fear,* p. 20; January 19, 1997, Marilyn Stasio, review of *Twenty Blue Devils,;* section 7, p. 22; March 7, 1999, Marilyn Stasio, *Loot,* section 7, p. 20.

Publishers Weekly, October 30, 1987, review of *Old Bones;* January 4, 1999, review of *Loot,* p. 77; April 17, 2000, review of *Skeleton Dance,* p. 56; May 6, 2002, review of *Turncoat,* p. 37; January 26, 2004, review of *Good Blood,* p. 234; February 21, 2005, review of *Where There's a Will,* pp. 160-161.

School Library Journal, July, 2004, review of *Good Blood,* p. 131.

Seattle Times/Seattle Post-Intelligencer, July 3, 1988, Sharon Miller, review of *Old Bones.*

Washington Post Book World, June 19, 1988.

ELLIS, Mary Relindes 1960-

PERSONAL: Middle name is pronounced "Ree-*lin*-des"; born February 4, 1960, in Glidden, WI; daughter of Harold Conrad and Relindes Catherine (Alexander) Berg. *Ethnicity:* "White." *Education:* University of Minnesota, B.A., 1986.

ADDRESSES: Agent—Marly Rusoff, Marly Rusoff and Associates, 811 Palmer Rd., Suite AA, Bronxville, NY 10708.

CAREER: Writer. Guest on media programs; gives readings and lectures.

AWARDS, HONORS: Grant from Minnesota State Arts Board, 1995.

WRITINGS:

The Turtle Warrior (novel), Viking (New York, NY), 2004.

Work represented in anthologies, including *The Year's Best Fantasy and Horror,* edited by Ellen Datlow and Terri Windling, St. Martin's Press (New York, NY), 1994; *Bless Me Father: Stories of Catholic Childhood,* edited by Amber Coverdale Sumrall and Patrice Vecchione, Penguin Books (New York, NY), 1994; and *Gifts from the Wild,* edited by Faith Conlon, Ingrid Emerick, and Jennie Goode, Seal Press, 1998. Contributor of essays, short stories, and reviews to periodicals, including *Milwaukee Journal, Wisconsin Academy Review, Bellingham Review,* and *Glimmer Train Press.*

WORK IN PROGRESS: Geese, a novel.

SIDELIGHTS: Mary Relindes Ellis told *CA:* "I have never taken a course in fiction writing. Beyond the basic composition requirements in college, I moved onto courses in reading and writing poetry. I think that learning to write poetry is very difficult but very rewarding. And of course imagery is at the heart of great poetry and prose. Writing poetry also makes one pay attention to each word, to the cadence of speech, and the pause for a necessary breath. An oral storyteller knows how important those fundamentals are to telling an engaging story.

"I was and am influenced by those writers who can tell a story with lyricism, who use language skillfully to inform, amaze, and educate. I also gravitate toward writers (as a reader and a writer) who are not afraid to tackle issues that are difficult or painful or hidden, using a variety of techniques (including humor) skillfully. Leslie Marmon Silko's writing never fails to engage me and her first novel, *Ceremony,* remains pivotal for its extraordinary look at human evil and the need to conquer despair.

"Outside of Silko, there isn't a specific 'who' that influences me. I read many writers for pleasure and instruction. I read both female and male writers, and writers from other cultures. I am not fond of pulp fiction or pulp writing. I don't like to see language 'dummied' down. On the other hand, I don't care for writing that is so grandiose that it is unreadable. I had a demanding professor for freshman composition who told me never to use a fifty-cent word when I could use a twenty-five-cent one. He did not mean that I should write like a simpleton, only that I should use my fifty-cent words sparingly and when they carried the necessary impact and understanding to the writing.

"I honestly can't nail down when I became interested in writing to a single moment. It was a slow revelation upon my transitioning from writing poetry and wanting to carry an image onto a large 'frame.' I had a vivid imagination as a child. I was also read to from my earliest memory. I grew up listening to oral stories, told from the male and female perspective, a rural and urban perspective, and an immigrant past. Yet so much was not said, at that time, from a woman's perspective.

"I think it was Toni Morrison who said something to the effect of, 'If the book you want to read hasn't been written, then write it.' I had a rich, if somewhat difficult, childhood in a region of the United States that has been overlooked. I wanted to write about the interior life of that region.

"Although I may be the writer and hence the creator of the characters in my short stories and my novel, they become their own people—so much so that at some point, I cannot have a character behave in a certain way or do something because it would not be in their nature to do so. I have to pause then and think and often do some research because in a strange way, my character is asking a question of me—such as 'who do you think I am?'"

BIOGRAPHICAL AND CRITICAL SOURCES:

PERIODICALS

Booklist, November 15, 2003, Keir Graff, review of *The Turtle Warrior,* p. 574.
Kirkus Reviews, November 1, 2003, review of *The Turtle Warrior,* p. 1286.
Kliatt, July, 2004, Nola Theiss, review of *The Turtle Warrior,* p. 57.
Library Journal, November 15, 2003, Marc Kloszewski, review of *The Turtle Warrior,* p. 96.
Publishers Weekly, December 1, 2003, review of *The Turtle Warrior,* p. 41.
School Library Journal, August, 2004, Pat Bender, review of *The Turtle Warrior,* p. 146.

ONLINE

Marly Rusoff and Associates Web site, http://www.rusoffagency.com/ (June 21, 2004), "Mary Relindes Ellis."
Mary Relindes Ellis Home Page, http://www.maryrelindesellis.com (January 27, 2005).

*   *   *

EMMONS, Didi 1963-

PERSONAL: Born February 13, 1963, in Stamford, CT; daughter of Harry I. (a realtor) and Rosamond (an artist; maiden name, Lehrer) Emmons. *Ethnicity:* "White." *Education:* New York University, B.S., 1985; La Varenne École de Cuisine, diploma.

ADDRESSES: Home—110 Rockview St., Boston, MA 02130.

CAREER: Center Street Café, Boston, MA, dinner chef; editor and assistant to chef and food writer Steven Raichlen, 1988-92; Blue Room, Cambridge,

MA, pastry chef, 1994-95; DeLux Café, Boston, head chef, 1995-98; Pho Republique (French-Vietnamese restaurants), startup chef, co-owner, and consultant in Cambridge and Boston, 1998-2000; Veggie Planet (vegetarian restaurant), Cambridge, co-owner and chef, 2001—. La Varenne École de Cuisine, Paris, France, apprentice and translator, 1989-90; worked at Boston-area restaurants such as Hamersley's Bistro and Cambridge House Inn. Guest on television programs, including those airing on cable Food Network.

AWARDS, HONORS: Award from International Association of Culinary Professionals, 2004, for *Entertaining for a Veggie Planet.*

WRITINGS:

Vegetarian Planet: 350 Big-Flavor Recipes for Out-of-This-World Food Every Day, Harvard Common Press (Cambridge, MA), 1997.
Entertaining for a Veggie Planet: 250 Down-to-Earth Recipes, Houghton Mifflin (New York, NY), 2003.

Author of "On the Chef's Plate," a weekly column in Boston area newspapers, 1995.

SIDELIGHTS: Didi Emmons told *CA:* "I write because it lets me hone my thoughts—sculpting them for greater accuracy and amusement. That is satisfying.

"I write cookbooks because cooking is my primary passion. I grin and bear the mundane technicalities that writing two or three hundred recipes demands. But what makes up for it is in the writing the head-note—the paragraph right before the recipe that describes the dish or tells a story about it.

"I'm a pretty neurotic writer. I need my cat near, a blanket on my lap, something good to drink, like hot cocoa or cappucino, and then I can get some work done. Often I go to a coffee shop or library, and this helps my focus. I've made the mistake of writing a book with a publisher without really knowing the company well. In my last book, I saw my vision crumble because we didn't see eye to eye, especially on the title and cover. I'll be more careful next time."

BIOGRAPHICAL AND CRITICAL SOURCES:

PERIODICALS

Booklist, May 15, 1997, Mark Knoblauch, review of *Vegetarian Planet: 350 Big-Flavor Recipes for Out-of-This-World Food Every Day,* p. 1551.

Houston Chronicle, July 16, 1997, Ann Criswell, review of *Vegetarian Planet,* p. 1.

Library Journal, June 15, 1997, Judith C. Sutton, review of *Vegetarian Planet,* p. 90; May 15, 2003, Judith C. Sutton, review of *Entertaining for a Veggie Planet: 250 Down-to-Earth Recipes,* p. 118.

Publishers Weekly, May 5, 1997, review of *Vegetarian Planet,* p. 203; May 19, 2003, review of *Entertaining for a Veggie Planet,* p. 70.

San Francisco Chronicle, July 23, 1997, Angela Hwang, review of *Vegetarian Planet.*

* * *

ENGLISH, Sharon 1965-

PERSONAL: Born December 15, 1965, in London, Ontario, Canada; daughter of J. Douglas Land (a journalist) and Shirleyan (a journalist; maiden name, Grieve) English. *Education:* University of Western Ontario, B.A. (English literature, with honors), M.A. (English literature).

ADDRESSES: Office—Writing Center, Innis College, University of Toronto, 2 Sussex St., Toronto, Ontario, Canada M5S 1A1.

CAREER: University of Toronto, Toronto, Ontario, Canada, instructor in writing, 2000—.

WRITINGS:

Uncomfortably Numb (short stories), Porcupine's Quill (Erie, Ontario, Canada), 2002.

WORK IN PROGRESS: Zero Gravity, a collection of short stories.

* * *

ENRIGHT, Nicholas (Paul) 1950-2003
(Nick Enright)

PERSONAL: Born December 22, 1950, in Newcastle, New South Wales, Australia; died of melanoma March 31, 2003, in Sydney, New South Wales, Australia. *Education:* Attended St. Ignatius College, 1962-67; Sydney University, B.A., 1972; New York University School of the Arts, M.F.A., 1977.

CAREER: Playwright, drama teacher, and actor. State Theatre Company of South Australia, Adelaide, associate director, 1978-81, teacher of acting, 1978, 1989-92, head of acting, 1982-84; teacher at National Institute of Dramatic Art, Sydney, New South Wales, Australia, West Australian Academy of Performing Arts, and Australian Theatre for Young People; host and narrator of symphony and opera presentations for stage and television; actor in television films, including *Breaking Up,* 1985, and *Brotherhood of the Rose,* 1989.

AWARDS, HONORS: New South Wales Premier's play award, 1983; Australia Council grants, 1975-76, 1984, 1991; Australia Writers' Guild award, 1990; Academy Award nomination for best original screenplay, Motion Picture Academy of Arts and Sciences, 1992, for *Lorenzo's Oil.*

WRITINGS:

PLAYS

(Adaptor, with Frank Hauser) Sophocles, *Electra,* produced in Melbourne, New South Wales, Australia, 1978.

(With Ron Blair) *The Servant of Two Masters* (adaptation of the play by Carlo Goldoni), produced in Adelaide, South Australia, Australia, 1978.

Oh, What a Lovely War, Mate! (adaptation of Australian scenes in the play created by Joan Littlewood), produced in Adelaide, South Australia, Australia, 1979.

The Venetian Twins (adaptation of the play by Carlo Goldoni), music by Terence Clarke, produced in Sydney, New South Wales, Australia, 1979, revised version produced in Brisbane, Queensland, Australia, 1990.

King Stag (adaptation of a play by Carlo Gozzi), produced in Adelaide, South Australia, Australia, 1980.

On the Wallaby (produced in Adelaide, South Australia, Australia, 1980), Currency Press (Sydney, New South Wales, Australia), 1982.

Music (for children), produced in Adelaide, South Australia, Australia, 1981.

Fatal Johnny (for children), produced in Adelaide, South Australia, Australia, 1982.

First Class Women, produced in Sydney, New South Wales, Australia, 1982.

Variations, music by Terence Clarke, produced in Sydney, New South Wales, Australia, 1982.

The Marriage of Figaro (adaptation of the play by Beaumarchais), produced in Adelaide, South Australia, Australia, 1983.

Summer Rain, music by Terence Clarke, produced in Sydney, New South Wales, Australia, 1983, revised version, 1989.

Don Juan (adaptation of the play by Molière; produced in Adelaide, South Australia, Australia, 1984), Currency Press (Sydney, New South Wales, Australia), 1984.

The Snow Queen (adaptation of the story by Hans Christian Andersen), music by Graham Dudley, produced in Adelaide, South Australia, Australia, 1985.

Daylight Saving (produced in Sydney, New South Wales, Australia), 1989), Currency Press (Sydney, New South Wales, Australia), 1990.

Carnival of the Animals, music by Saint-Saëns (produced in Sydney, New South Wales, Australia, 1989), ABC Publications (Sydney, New South Wales, Australia), 1991.

Mongrels, produced in Sydney, New South Wales, Australia, 1991.

St. James Infirmary (produced in Penrith, New South Wales, Australia, 1991), Currency Press (Sydney, New South Wales, Australia), 1992.

A Property of the Clan, produced in Newcastle, New South Wales, Australia, 1991.

(Under name Nick Enright) *Good Works* (produced in Queensland, Australia, 1995; produced in Bristol, England, 1997), Currency Press (Sydney, New South Wales, Australia), 1995.

Black Rock (also see below; produced in Sydney, New South Wales, Australia, 1995), Currency Press (Sydney, New South Wales, Australia), 1996.

The Way I Was, produced in Sydney, New South Wales, Australia, 1995.

Miracle City, music by Max Lambert, produced in Sydney, New South Wales, Australia, 1995.

The Voyage of Mary Bryant, produced in Perth, Western Australia, Australia, 1996.

The Female Factory, produced in Sydney, New South Wales, Australia, 1997.

(Author of book, under name Nick Enright) *The Boy from Oz* (musical), music and lyrics by Peter Allen, produced in Sydney, New South Wales, Australia, 1998.

(Under name Nick Enright; with Justin Monjo) *Cloudstreet* (adaptation of the novel by Tim Winton; produced in Sydney, New South Wales, Australia, 1998), Currency Press (Sydney, New South Wales, Australia), 1999.

Chasing the Dragon, produced in Sydney, New South Wales, Australia, 1998.

A Man with Five Children, produced in Sydney, New South Wales, Australia, 2002.

Also writer of *The Quartet from Rigoletto,* produced 1995.

RADIO PLAYS

Ship without a Sail (documentary), 1985.
(Adaptor) Euripedes, *The Trojan Women,* 1989.
Watching over Israel, 1990.
St. James Infirmary, 1992.
Black Rock, 1997.

OTHER

The Maitland and Morpeth String Quartet (for children; based on a radio series), illustrated by Victoria Roberts, David Ell Press (Sydney, New South Wales, Australia), 1980.

(And actor; with Lisa Benyon) *Come in Spinner* (television; adapted from the novel by F. James and D. Cusack), 1989.

(Under name Nick Enright; with George Miller) *Lorenzo's Oil* (screenplay), Universal, 1992.

Adapted *The Maitland and Morpeth String Quartet* as an animated television series. Contributor to periodicals, including Sydney *Morning Herald, Australian, National Times, Theatre Australia,* and *Vogue Australia.* Reviewer for ABC Radio, *Books and Writing,* and *First Edition.*

Recordings include *The Venetian Twins,* Larrikin Records (Sydney, New South Wales, Australia), 1981, and *Carnival of the Animals* with *Peter and the Wolf,* music by Saint-Saëns, Polygram Records, 1989.

ADAPTATIONS: Black Rock was adapted for film, 1997. The book of the musical *The Boy from Oz* was adapted for Broadway production by Martin Sherman, 2003.

SIDELIGHTS: At his death in 2003, at the age of fifty-two, Australian playwright Nicholas Enright left behind a long list of acclaimed plays as well as many young thespians who remembered him as a dedicated drama teacher. Writing—sometimes under the name Nick Enright—for television and radio in addition to the stage, Enright became most well known to American audiences as the coauthor, with medical doctor George Miller, of the Academy Award-nominated screenplay for the film *Lorenzo's Oil*. The film is based on the true story of Augusto Odone (Nick Nolte) and his wife, Michaela (Susan Sarandon), who fought to save the life of a son who has been diagnosed with adrenoleukodystrophy, or ALD, an incurable disease of the brain. The film follows the quest of these parents to understand and deal with their son's illness; ALD is passed from mother to son, leaving Michaela with feelings of guilt as well as fear regarding her son's Lorenzo's fate. In 2004 the real-life Lorenzo was still enjoying a vital life, although Michaela had passed away.

Lorenzo's Oil follows the parents as they discover and refine a combination of plant oils that lessen their son's symptoms, all the while fighting the medical establishment and fielding objections from parents of other ALD sufferers. As James Berardinelli commented for *Movie-Reviews* online, "in the final analysis, when *Lorenzo's Oil* is stripped to the bare story, it's about the war for knowledge and the victory of hope through perseverance." *Commonweal* reviewer Richard Alleva called the script "superb," adding that it "doesn't confine itself to illustrating one theme but allows many connected themes to be developed in the course of the story. The limitations of sheer professionalism vs. the less informed but suppler efforts of the amateur, the contracting responses of people similarly afflicted, the way catastrophe can both solidify and blast human relationships: these and many other human matters are more than merely touched upon by this splendid film."

Enright's play *Black Rock,* about the death of a teenage girl in a New South Wales factory town, also eventually made it to film, as well as onto Australian radio. *The Boy from Oz,* which enjoyed its original Australian run with a book by Enright, follows the life of Peter Allen, who died of AIDS in 1992. Allen, an entertainer, was one of the first to introduce gay camp to mainstream audiences. With its book rewritten by Martin Sherman, *The Boy from Oz* eventually came to Broadway, with actor Hugh Jackman as its star; other characters include entertainer Lisa Minnelli, Allen's wife for a very brief period of time, and Minnelli's mother, Judy Garland, who had discovered the Australian in Hong Kong and mentored him for many years.

Enright was a popular figure in the United States, especially after the release of *Lorenzo's Oil.* In a *Variety* tribute to the late playwright, it was noted that toward the end of his life Enright dedicated a significant portion of his time to teaching. Of his drama students Enright was quoted as commenting: "You learn more from them, their life experiences and their view of the world. They bring passion and joy that is often lacking in young professionals."

BIOGRAPHICAL AND CRITICAL SOURCES:

BOOKS

Contemporary Dramatists, sixth edition, St. James Press (Detroit, MI), 1999.

PERIODICALS

Commonweal, March 12, 1993, Richard Alleva, review of *Lorenzo's Oil,* p. 14.
New York Times, October 17, 2003, Ben Brantley, review of *The Boy from Oz.*

ONLINE

Movie-Reviews, http://www.movie-reviews.colossus.net/ (October 9, 2004), James Berardinelli, review of *Lorenzo's Oil.*
TalkinBroadway.com, http://www.talkinbroadway.com/ (October 16, 2003), Matthew Murray, review of *The Boy from Oz.*
Z Review, http://www.thezreview.co.uk/ (October 9, 2004), Betty Jo Tucker, review of *Lorenzo's Oil.*

OBITUARIES

PERIODICALS

Daily Variety, April 10, 2003.
Variety, April 1, 2003.

ONLINE

Australian Broadcasting Corporation Web site, http://
www.abc.net.au/7.30/ (March 31, 2003).*

* * *

ENRIGHT, Nick
   See ENRIGHT, Nicholas (Paul)

* * *

ERDMAN, Charles R(osenbury) 1866-1960

PERSONAL: Born July 20, 1866, in Fayetteville, NY;
died May 10, 1960, in Princeton, NJ; son of William
Jacob (a Presbyterian minister) and Henrietta (Rosen-
bury) Erdman; married Mary Estelle Pardee, June 1,
1892; children: four. *Education:* Princeton University,
graduated, 1886; also attended Princeton Theological
Seminary, 1887-91.

CAREER: Schoolteacher in Germantown (now part of
Philadelphia), PA, c. 1866-87; ordained Presbyterian
minister, 1891; pastor of Presbyterian churches in
Philadelphia, PA, 1891-97, and Germantown, PA,
1897-1905; Princeton Theological Seminary, Princeton, NJ, chair of practical theology, c. 1906-36. First
Presbyterian Church, Princeton, NJ, pastor, 1924-34.
General Assembly of the Presbyterian Church, modera-
tor, 1925; Presbyterian Board of Foreign Missions,
president, 1926.

WRITINGS:

The Gospel of John: An Exposition, Westminster Press
   (Philadelphia, PA), 1917, published with preface
   by Earl F. Zeigler, 1966.
The Gospel of Mark: An Exposition, Westminster Press
   (Philadelphia, PA), 1917, published with preface
   by Earl F. Zeigler, 1966.
The General Epistles: An Exposition, Westminster
   Press (Philadelphia, PA), 1918, published with
   preface by Earl F. Zeigler, 1966.
The Acts: An Exposition, Westminster Press (Philadel-
   phia, PA), 1919.

The Gospel of Matthew: An Exposition, Westminster
   Press (Philadelphia, PA), 1920, published with
   preface by Earl F. Zeigler, 1966.
The Gospel of Luke, Westminster Press (Philadelphia,
   PA), 1921, published as *The Gospel of Luke: An
   Exposition,* preface by Earl F. Zeigler, 1966.
*Within the Gateways of the Far East: A Record of
   Recent Travel,* Fleming H. Revell (New York,
   NY), 1922.
The Return of Christ, George H. Doran (New York,
   NY), 1922.
The Pastoral Epistles of Paul: An Exposition, West-
   minster Press (Philadelphia, PA), 1923, published
   with preface by Earl F. Zeigler, 1966.
The Work of the Pastor, Westminster Press (Philadel-
   phia, PA), 1924.
*The Lord We Love: Devotional Studies in the Life of
   Christ,* George H. Doran (New York, NY), 1924.
*The Spirit of Christ: Devotional Studies in the
   Doctrine of the Holy Spirit,* George H. Doran
   (New York, NY), 1926.
D. L. Moody: His Message for Today, Fleming H. Rev-
   ell (New York, NY), 1928.
*Paul's Hymn of Love, First Corinthians Thirteen: An
   Interpretation,* Fleming H. Revell (New York,
   NY), 1928.
*The First Epistle of Paul to the Corinthians: An
   Exposition,* Westminster Press (Philadelphia, PA),
   1928, published with preface by Earl F. Zeigler,
   1966.
*The Second Epistle of Paul to the Corinthians: An
   Exposition,* Westminster Press (Philadelphia, PA),
   1929, published with preface by Earl F. Zeigler,
   1966.
The Epistle of Paul to the Galatians: An Exposition,
   Westminster Press (Philadelphia, PA), 1930.
(Editor) William Jacob Erdman, *Notes on the Revela-
   tion,* Fleming H. Revell (New York, NY), 1930.
The Epistle of Paul to the Ephesians: An Exposition,
   Westminster Press (Philadelphia, PA), 1931,
   published with preface by Earl F. Zeigler, 1966.
The Epistle of Paul to the Philippians: An Exposition,
   Westminster Press (Philadelphia, PA), 1932,
   published with preface by Earl F. Zeigler, 1966.
*The Epistles of Paul to the Colossians and to
   Philemon: An Exposition,* Westminster Press
   (Philadelphia, PA), 1933, published with preface
   by Earl F. Zeigler, 1966.
The Epistle to the Hebrews: An Exposition, Westmin-
   ster Press (Philadelphia, PA), 1934, published with
   preface by Earl F. Zeigler, 1966.

The Epistles of Paul to the Thessalonians, Westminster Press (Philadelphia, PA), 1935, published as *The Epistles of Paul to the Thessalonians: An Exposition,* preface by Earl F. Zeigler, 1966.

The Revelation of John, Westminster Press (Philadelphia, PA), 1936, published as *The Revelation of John: An Exposition,* preface by Earl F. Zeigler, 1966.

The Book of Exodus: An Exposition, 1949.

Your Bible and You, John C. Winston (Philadelphia, PA), 1950.

The Book of Genesis: An Exposition, Fleming H. Revell (New York, NY), 1950.

The Book of Leviticus: An Exposition, Fleming H. Revell (New York, NY), 1951.

The Book of Numbers: An Exposition, Fleming H. Revell (Westwood, NJ), 1952.

The Book of Deuteronomy: An Exposition, Fleming H. Revell (Westwood, NJ), 1953.

The Pentateuch: A Concise Commentary on Genesis, Exodus, Leviticus, Numbers, and Deuteronomy (contains *The Book of Genesis: An Exposition, The Book of Exodus: An Exposition, The Book of Leviticus: An Exposition, The Book of Numbers: An Exposition,* and *The Book of Deuteronomy: An Exposition*), Fleming H. Revell (Old Tappan, NJ), 1953.

The Book of Isaiah: An Exposition, Fleming H. Revell (Westwood, NJ), 1954.

The Book of Jeremiah and Lamentations: An Exposition, Fleming H. Revell (Westwood, NJ), 1955.

The Book of Ezekiel: An Exposition, Fleming H. Revell (Westwood, NJ), 1956.

Remember Jesus Christ, Eerdmans (Grand Rapids, MI), 1958.

Author of shorter works, including "The Epistle to the Romans," Westminster Press (Philadelphia, PA), 1925. Contributor to series "The Fundamentals," between 1910 and 1915. Contributor to periodicals, including *Princeton Seminary Bulletin.* Editorial consultant, *Scofield Reference Bible.*

Erdman's books have been published in foreign translation.

Erdman's papers are collected in the Speer Library, Princeton Theological Seminary, Princeton, NJ.

BIOGRAPHICAL AND CRITICAL SOURCES:

BOOKS

Religious Leaders of America, 2nd edition, Gale (Detroit, MI), 1999.

PERIODICALS

Christian Herald, November, 1926.

OBITUARIES

PERIODICALS

New York Times, May 10, 1960, p. 37.
Princeton Seminary Bulletin, November, 1960.*

*   *   *

ERI, Vincent Serei 1936-1993

PERSONAL: Born September 12, 1936, in Moveave, Papua New Guinea; died May 25, 1993, in Port Moresby, Papua New Guinea; married Margaret Karulaka; children: two daughters, four sons. *Education:* University of Papua New Guinea, B.A., 1970, additional study, 1970-71.

CAREER: Schoolteacher, 1956-66; Education Department, Port Moresby, Papua New Guinea, chief of operations, 1972-73; Information Department, Port Moresby, director, 1973-74; Papua New Guinea Foreign Service, consul general in Sydney, Australia, 1975-76, high commissioner in Canberra, Australia, 1976-79; Department of Transport and Civil Aviation, Port Moresby, director, 1980; Department of Defense, Port Moresby, director, 1981-82; Harrisons & Crosfield Ltd., personnel director, c. 1982-89; governor general of Papua New Guinea, 1990-91. People's Action Party (political party), cofounder, 1986, president, 1986-90. National Provident Fund Board, employers' representative, 1984; University of Papua New Guinea, chair of finance committee, 1984-90.

AWARDS, HONORS: Knighted, 1990.

WRITINGS:

The Crocodile (novel), Jacaranda Press (Milton, Queensland, Australia), 1970.

BIOGRAPHICAL AND CRITICAL SOURCES:

BOOKS

Contemporary Novelists, 5th edition, St. James Press (Detroit, MI), 1991.

OBITUARIES

PERIODICALS

New York Times, May 27, 1993.

*   *   *

EVANS, Gary P. 1942-

PERSONAL: Born September 1, 1942, in Buffalo, NY; son of Miller (a grain miller) and Katherine (Struble) Evans; children: Meredith. *Ethnicity:* "Caucasian." *Education:* William Carey College, B.A. (cum laude), 1969; Southern Baptist Theological Seminary, M.C.M., 1971, D.M.A., 1976. *Hobbies and other interests:* Piano, composition, art.

ADDRESSES: Home—226 Arthur Cir., Ferrum, VA 24088. *Office*—Ferrum College, 150 Wiley Drive, Ferrum, VA 24088. *E-mail*—gevans@ferrum.edu.

CAREER: Ferrum College, Ferrum, VA, professor of music, 1978—. Franklin County Chorus, member.

MEMBER: Association for Recorded Sound Collections.

AWARDS, HONORS: Award for best research in general discography and history of recorded sound, Association for Recorded Sound Collections, 2003, for *Music Inspired by Art: A Guide to Recordings.*

WRITINGS:

Music Inspired by Art: A Guide to Recordings, Scarecrow Press (Lanham, MD), 2002.

SIDELIGHTS: Gary P. Evans told *CA:* "As a teacher of interdisciplinary fine arts, I attempt to research and develop books that will serve as resources for educators in this field."

F

FALLON, Jennifer

PERSONAL: Born in Carlton, Victoria, Australia; children: Amanda, Tracy, David.

ADDRESSES: Home—Alice Springs, Northern Territory, Australia. *Agent*—c/o Australian Literary Management, 2A Booth St., Balmain, New South Wales 2041, Australia. *E-mail*—info@jenniferfallon.com.

CAREER: Author and trainer. Accredited workplace trainer; former gymnastics coach and judge; founder of Anzac Hill Gymnastics Club. Also worked as a store detective, a shop assistant, a youth worker, an advertising sales representative, car rental manager, and an executive secretary.

WRITINGS:

"HYTHRUN CHRONICLES"

Medalon (book one of "Demon Child" trilogy), Voyager (Pymble, New South Wales, Australia), 2000, Tor Books (New York, NY), 2004.

Treason Keep (book two of "Demon Child" trilogy), Voyager (Pymble, New South Wales, Australia), 2001, Tor Books (New York, NY), 2004.

Harshini (book three of "Demon Child" trilogy), Voyager (Pymble, New South Wales, Australia), 2001.

Wolfblade, Voyager (Pymble, New South Wales, Australia), 2004.

Warrior, Voyager (Pymble, New South Wales, Australia), 2005.

Warlord, Voyager (Pymble, New South Wales, Australia), 2005.

"SECOND SONS" TRILOGY

The Lion of Senet, Voyager (Pymble, New South Wales, Australia), 2002, Bantam Spectra (New York, NY), 2004.

Eye of the Labyrinth, Voyager (Pymble, New South Wales, Australia), 2003, Bantam Spectra (New York, NY), 2004.

Lord of the Shadows, Voyager (Pymble, New South Wales, Australia), 2003, Bantam Spectra (New York, NY), 2004.

WORK IN PROGRESS: "Tide Lords" series.

SIDELIGHTS: Australian Jennifer Fallon is the author of the popular "Hythrun Chonicles" fantasy series. A former store detective, secretary, and youth worker, Fallon vowed to become a published author by the age of forty. Three weeks before her fortieth birthday, she received word that her novel *Medalon* would be published. Since then, Fallon has completed three more works in the "Hythrun Chonicles," as well as the "Second Sons" trilogy. As she told Dorothy Grimm in the *Alice Springs News,* "Writing is an obsession, life gets in the way."

The first three works of the "Hythrun Chronicles"—*Medalon, Treason Keep,* and *Harshini*—were originally published in Australia as the "Demon Child" trilogy. In *Medalon* Fallon "conjures a viable, richly detailed world and its disparate societies," wrote *Booklist* critic Sally Estes. The country of Medalon is ruled by the Sisters of the Blade, a harsh matriarchy that has banned religious worship. The novel's protagonists, eighteen-year-old R'shiel Tenragen and her half-brother Tarja, flee their home after their mother, Joyhina, ascends to power. R'shiel and Tarja join a rebel group fighting against the Sisterhood, and R'shiel is revealed to be the Demon Child, a half-human descended from a magical race who is destined to lead the struggle against an evil god. A critic in *Publishers Weekly* stated that *Medalon* is "stocked with well-developed characters with clear motivations that carry them through a series of byzantine plots and counterplots," and *Entertainment Weekly* contributor Nisha Gopalan called the work "an intriguing soap opera of espionage and family revelations."

Treason Keep, the second volume in Fallon's "Hythrun Chronicles," follows the adventures of R'sheil and Tarja after their successful rebellion against the Sisterhood. A badly wounded R'sheil recovers at Sanctuary, the homeland of the magical Harshini, while Tarja prepares for an attack from the forces of Karien, a neighboring kingdom. According to a critic in *Kirkus Reviews,* Fallon "builds a fast-moving tale full of Machiavellian schemes, extreme character conflict, sudden reverses of fortune, and capricious interventions of gods whose power waxes and wanes in proportion to the number of their human followers." "Convoluted intrigues, rivalries, and romance provide an entertaining tangle" in *Treason Keep,* wrote a *Publishers Weekly* contributor.

BIOGRAPHICAL AND CRITICAL SOURCES:

PERIODICALS

Alice Springs News, July 19, 2000, Dorothy Grimm, "Harry Potter, Move over, Alice Springs' *Medalon* Is Coming!"

Booklist, May 15, 2004, Sally Estes, review of *Medalon,* p. 1604.

Entertainment Weekly, April 30, 2004, Nisha Gopalan, review of *Medalon,* p. 166.

Kirkus Reviews, March 1, 2004, review of *Medalon,* p. 206; September 15, 2004, review of *Treason Keep,* p. 896.

Library Journal, April 15, 2004, Jackie Cassada, review of *Medalon,* p. 129.

Publishers Weekly, March 15, 2004, review of *Medalon,* p. 59; September 6, 2004, review of *Treason Keep,* p. 50.

ONLINE

Jennifer Fallon Home Page, http://www.jenniferfallon. com (October 23, 2004).

*   *   *

FENNELLY, Beth Ann 1971-

PERSONAL: Born May 22, 1971, in NJ; married Tom Franklin (a writer); children: Claire. *Education:* University of Notre Dame, B.A. (English; magna cum laude), 1993; University of Arkansas, M.F.A. (creative writing), 1998.

ADDRESSES: Home—Oxford, MS. *Office*—University of Mississippi, Department of English, C 135 West Bondurant, University, MS 38677. *E-mail*—bafennel@ olemiss.edu.

CAREER: Poet, author, and educator. Knox College, Galesburg, IL, assistant professor of English; University of Mississippi, University, currently assistant professor of English.

AWARDS, HONORS: Chapbook Breakthrough Award, *Texas Review,* 1997, for *A Different Kind of Hunger;* Diane Middlebrook postdoctoral fellowship, University of Wisconsin, 1999; Pushcart Prize, 2001, for *The Impossibility of Language;* Illinois Arts Council grant, 2001; *Kenyon Review* Prize for Poetry, 2001, for *Open House;* New Writers Award for Poetry, Great Lakes College Association, 2003; Wood Award for Distinguished Writing, *Carolina Quarterly;* Academy of American Poets Prize; National Endowment for the Arts grant; Sewanee Writers' Conference, Tennessee Williams scholarship; MacDowell residency; University of Arizona summer residency; Lily Peter fellowship; Bread Loaf Writers' Conference fellowship.

WRITINGS:

A Different Kind of Hunger (chapbook), Texas Review Press (Huntsville, TX), 1998.

Open House (poems), Zoo Press (Lincoln, NE), 2002.
Tender Hooks (poems), W. W. Norton (New York, NY), 2004.

Contributor of poems to volumes such as *The Best American Poetry 1996,* edited by Adrienne Rich, Scribner (New York, NY), 1997; *Thirteen Ways of Looking for a Poem: A Guide to Writing Poetry,* edited by Wendy Bishop, Longman Publishing Group, 1999; and *The Pushcart Prize: Best of the Small Presses XXV,* edited by Bill Henderson, Pushcart Press, 2001. Contributor to periodicals such as *TriQuarterly, Shenandoah, Michigan Quarterly Review, Poetry Ireland Review, American Scholar,* and *Kenyon Review.*

WORK IN PROGRESS: Essays in volumes such as *Fourth Genre* and *The Writer's Chronicle;* poems in anthologies such as *Line Drives: 100 Contemporary Baseball Poems.*

SIDELIGHTS: Poet Beth Ann Fennelly has achieved recognition for her talent with a multitude of awards ranging from a National Endowment for the Arts grant to the Pushcart Prize and the Academy of American Poets prize. She has been awarded fellowships to prestigious writers' conferences such as Bread Loaf and the Sewanee Writers' Conference, and has received awards from publications such as *Kenyon Review, Texas Review,* and *Carolina Quarterly.*

Born in New Jersey, Fennelly was raised in the Chicago suburb of Lake Forest, Illinois. In an interview with Katherine Montgomery on the *Starksville High School* Web site, the poet described her younger self as "a very bookish kid, so I've always done well in school." After completing her M.F.A., Fennelly attended the University of Wisconsin under a Diane Middlebrook postdoctoral fellowship. An assistant professor of English at "Ole Miss"—the University of Mississippi—Fennelly has also been an assistant professor of English at Knox College in Galesburg, Illinois.

Fennelly's poetry collection *Open House* won the *Kenyon Review* Prize in Poetry in 2001, and "marks the debut of a poet with both a broad canvas and an acute eye for detail," commented a reviewer in the *Virginia Quarterly Review.* Fennelly herself appears as a character in many of these poems, joining notables such as Carl Sagan, Michelangelo, Frank Lloyd Wright, and Moses in her poetic musings. The long poem "From L'Hotel Terminus Notebooks" introduces Fennelly's alter ego and inner critic, Mr. Daylater, who alternates criticism of Fennelly the poet with encouragement and advice. Mr. Daylater's counsel, like that of all doubting inner voices, should be taken with caution, however—his chiding of the poet for using the word "palimpsest," for example, "is a signal that Mr. Daylater . . . is not as smart as the poet," observed Robert Hass in *Kenyon Review.* The poem, Hass concluded, "advances with a determination to keep the author interested and alive to her materials; in places, amused with itself and hopscotching, in places veering into unexpected depths, it is an immensely lively performance."

Fennelly's collection *Tender Hooks* explores the intense, sometimes contradictory emotions, sensations, and physical reactions to first-time motherhood, and is based on the poet's experiences during the birth and early years of her daughter, Claire. Many of the poems in the book were written while Fennelly was teaching at Knox College, noted David Kirby in the *Atlanta Journal-Constitution,* and they cover topics such as baby worship, the unexpectedly vigorous physical efforts of a breastfeeding child, grief at an earlier miscarriage, and the feelings of sheer, total love for her daughter. Fennelly describes "the experience of motherhood . . . more convincingly and intimately that any other poet who comes to mind," remarked Ray Olson in *Booklist.* "Fennelly doesn't flinch from showing the darker side of mothering, not just the can't-see-straight exhaustion and the anxiety of new parenthood, but the fury of both infant and mother," observed a *Publishers Weekly* reviewer. Olson called the work "awesome, humanly humbling poetry," while Ellen Kaufman, writing in *Library Journal,* concluded that *Tender Hooks* is a "smart and vivacious book."

BIOGRAPHICAL AND CRITICAL SOURCES:

PERIODICALS

Atlanta Journal-Constitution, April 18, 2004, David Kirby, "As Good as Their Word, Poetry Collections That Stand out from the 'Wallpaper' Pack," p. M4.
Booklist, March 1, 2004, Ray Olson, review of *Tender Hooks,* p. 1127.

Journal Star (Peoria, IL), p. C5.

Kenyon Review, summer-fall, 2001, Robert Hass, "Losing Mr. Daylater: A Note on Beth Ann Fennelly," p. 28.

Library Journal, March 15, 2004, Ellen Kaufman, review of *Tender Hooks,* p. 82.

Publishers Weekly, April 26, 2004, review of *Tender Hooks,* p. 58.

Virginia Quarterly Review, autumn, 2002, review of *Open House,* p. 137.

ONLINE

College of Wooster Web site, http://www.wooster.edu/ (August 6, 2004), "Beth Ann Fennelly."

National Endowment for the Arts Web site, http://www.nea.gov/ (August 6, 2004), "Beth Ann Fennelly."

Starkville High School Web site, http://shs.starkville.k12.ms.us/ (August 6, 2004), Katherine Montgomery, interview with Fennelly.

University of Illinois Department of English Web site, http://www.english.uiuc.edu/ (August 6, 2004), "Beth Ann Fennelly."

University of Mississippi Web site, http://www.olemiss.edu/ (August 5, 2004), "Beth Ann Fennelly."

Zoo Press Web site, http://www.zoopress.org/ (August 6, 2004).*

*   *   *

FISHER, Catherine 1957-

PERSONAL: Born 1957, in Wales.

ADDRESSES: Home—Newport, Wales. *Agent*—Lesley Pollinger, Pollinger Ltd., 9 Staple Inn, Holborn, London WC1V 7QH, England.

CAREER: Writer. Worked as a school teacher, archaeologist, broadcaster, and adjudicator. University of Glamorgan, Glamorgan, Wales, visiting professor of children's literature.

AWARDS, HONORS: Welsh Arts Council Young Writers' Prize, and Cardiff International Poetry Competition prize, both 1989, both for poetry; Smart-

ies Book Prize shortlist, 1990; Tir na n'Og Prize, 1995, for *The Candle Man* and shortlist, 2003, for *Corbenic;* Whitbread Prize shortlist, 2003, for *The Oracle.*

WRITINGS:

Immrama (poetry), Seren (Bridgend, Wales), 1988.

The Conjuror's Game, Bodley Head (London, England), 1990.

Fintan's Tower, Bodley Head (London, England), 1991.

Saint Tarvel's Bell, Swift Children's (London, England), 1992.

The Snow-Walker's Son (first volume in trilogy; also see below), Bodley Head (London, England), 1993.

The Unexplored Ocean (poetry), Seren (Bridgend, Wales), 1994.

The Hare and Other Stories, Pont Books (Llandysul, Wales), 1994.

The Candleman, Bodley Head (London, England), 1994.

The Empty Hand (second volume in trilogy; also see below), Bodley Head (London, England), 1995.

The Soul Thieves (third volume in trilogy; also see below), Bodley Head (London, England), 1996.

Scared Stiff: Stories, Dolphin Books (London, England), 1997.

Belin's Hill, Red Fox (London, England), 1998.

The Relic Master, Bodley Head (London, England), 1998.

Altered States (poetry), Seren (Bridgend, Wales), 1999.

The Interrex, Bodley Head (London, England), 1999.

Magical Mystery Stories, Red Fox (London, England), 1999.

The Lammas Field, Hodder Children's (London, England), 1999.

Flain's Coronet, Bodley Head (London, England), 2000.

Darkwater Hall, Hodder Children's (London, England), 2000.

The Margrave, Red Fox (London, England), 2001.

Old Enough and Other Stories, Cló Iar-Chonnachta, (Indreabhán, Conamara, Wales), 2002.

The Snow-Walker Trilogy (includes *The Snow-Walker's Son, The Empty Hand,* and *The Soul Thieves*), Red Fox (London, England), 2003, Greenwillow Books (New York, NY), 2004.

Folklore (poetry) Smith/Doorstep Books (Wakefield, England), 2003.

The Oracle (first volume of trilogy), Hodder Children's Books (London, England), 2003, published as *The Oracle Betrayed,* Greenwillow Books (New York, NY), 2004.

The Archon (second volume in trilogy), Hodder Children's Books (London, England), 2004.

Corbenic, Greenwillow Books (New York, NY), 2005.

Darkhenge, Greenwillow Books (New York, NY), 2005.

The Sphere of Secrets, Greenwillow Books (New York, NY), 2005.

Also author of *The Book of the Crow,* for Hodder Children's Books (London, England). Contributor to poetry anthologies, including *Twentieth-Century Anglo-Welsh Poetry,* Seren (Bridgend, Wales); *Oxygen,* Seren (Bridgend, Wales), and *The Forward Book of Poetry, 2001.*

SIDELIGHTS: Catherine Fisher lives and works in Wales, but her fantasy adventures for children reach to wider sources for their inspiration. Fisher's *The Snow-Walker Trilogy,* published in America in a single volume, creates an icy world based upon old Norse myths and legends, while the Whitbread Award-nominated "Oracle" trilogy is set in desert countries reminiscent of ancient Egypt and Greece. In addition to her trilogies, Fisher has authored a number of stand-alone fantasies for children and young adults, including *Corbenic,* winner of Wales's Tir na n'Og Prize. Amanda Craig, in the London *Times,* said that Fisher is "a writer who has thought deeply not just about re-alising the supernatural, but about the extreme loneliness of being different."

By inclination a poet, Fisher first published verses and won several awards in Wales for her work. She moved into children's fiction in the early 1990s and has since released at least one book every year. Even so, she has not abandoned poetry. A *Publishers Weekly* critic felt that the pieces in *The Unexplored Ocean* convey "a reverence for the physical world." In a *Booklist* review of *Altered States,* Patricia Monaghan commended Fisher's verse for its "classic dignity" and added that the author provides "a sterling presence in poetry."

Among Fisher's best-known works for children are her two trilogies, *The Snow-Walker* and "The Oracle." In *The Snow-Walker,* an evil queen named Gudrun uses magic to control her subjects and monsters to threaten her enemies. Her son Kari opposes her, and with a small band of allies escapes his imprisonment to journey into Gudrun's icy northern kingdom. There, despite his anxieties about becoming too similar to his evil mother, he sparks a showdown for rule of the kingdom. *Horn Book* contributor Anita L. Burkam felt that Kari's human struggle with his self-doubt "gains readers' sympathies." Burkam also called the work "another winner."

The Oracle, published in the United States as *The Oracle Betrayed,* presents another fully imagined fantasy world. The citizens of the two lands struggle with a terrible drought that has left them starving and parched. They seek help from the aging Archon, a holy man who converses with the gods as an oracle. The Archon is under siege, however, from one of the ambitious priestesses who serves him. Only the youngest of the priestesses, Mirany, can help the dying Oracle find his replacement before a false Archon is installed. Mirany is shy and, worse, skeptical about the Archon's real power. She must overcome her own faults and, with the help of the Archon's musician and a crafty criminal, find the new Archon in time to save the kingdoms and alleviate the drought. A *Publishers Weekly* correspondent deemed *The Oracle Betrayed* "a fascinating cosmology, doubly so because of the gravity [Fisher] grants it." In her review of the second volume, *The Archon,* Craig concluded: "As a novel about the conflict between religious belief and scepticism it could all collapse into dreadful rubbish. But the toughness and realism underlying all Fisher's fantasies is what makes them believable as well as wholly absorbing and aesthetically pleasing."

BIOGRAPHICAL AND CRITICAL SOURCES:

PERIODICALS

Booklist, June 1, 2000, Patricia Monaghan, review of *Altered States,* p. 1839; February 15, 2004, Carolyn Phelan, review of *The Oracle Betrayed,* p. 1059; September 1, 2004, Cindy Dobrez, review of *The Snow-Walker,* p. 106.

Horn Book, March-April, 2004, Anita L. Burkam, review of *The Oracle Betrayed,* p. 181; September-October, 2004, Anita L. Burkam, review of *The Snow-Walker,* p. 581.

Publishers Weekly, June 26, 1995, review of *The Unexplored Ocean,* p. 102; January 19, 2004, review of *The Oracle Betrayed,* p. 77.

School Library Journal, March, 2004, Margaret A. Chang, review of *The Oracle Betrayed,* p. 210.

Times (London, England), February 21, 2004, Amanda Craig, "Mad Magician in Search of Rain," p. 17.

Western Mail (Cardiff, Wales), November 14, 2003, Karen Price, "Welsh Writer Shortlisted for Book Award," p. 8.

ONLINE

Catherine Fisher Home Page, http://www.geocities. com/catherinefisheruk (October 13, 2004).*

*   *   *

FLEISCHMAN, Harry 1914-2004

OBITUARY NOTICE— See index for *CA* sketch: Born October 3, 1914, in New York, NY; died of cancer November 1, 2004, in New York, NY. Socialist and author. Fleischman was a former officer of the Socialist Party U.S.A. who later directed the American Jewish Committee's National Labor Service. After attending the City College for two years, he became involved in the fledgling Socialist Party when he attempted to organize a union at the clothes-hangar factory where he worked. Fired from that job for his union activities, he next worked at a window-blind factory and put together an effective labor strike. By 1942, Fleischman had risen to the position of national secretary for the Socialist Party U.S.A., and in 1944 and 1948 he served as campaign manager for his party's presidential candidate, Norman Thomas, about whom he would later write in *Norman Thomas: A Biography* (1964; third edition, 1969). After resigning his post at the Socialist Party, Fleischman worked as the labor editor for the *Voice of America* from 1951 until 1953; he then was named director of the National Labor Service of the American Jewish Committee, a post he held until 1979. In 1963, he became vice president of the Workers Defense League (WDL). An avid opponent of communism, Fleischman found himself struggling against not only the extreme left but also labor union leaders who staunchly resisted allowing their organizations to become racially integrated. Toward this end, in his role with the WDL, Fleischman was the driving force in getting New York City unions integrated, but an apprenticeship training program he worked on for minorities was taken over by the U.S. Labor Depart-

ment in partnership with the AFL-CIO, rendering them largely ineffective. Seeing that the American labor movement was on the decline, Fleischman tried to work more within the system in later life, assisting with the Democratic Socialists of America party, and serving as executive director of the National Alliance for Safer Cities in the 1970s. In addition to the Thomas biography, he was also the author of *Let's Be Human* (1960).

OBITUARIES AND OTHER SOURCES:

PERIODICALS

Guardian (London, England), November 16, 2004, p. 29.

New York Times, November 7, 2004, p. A35.

*   *   *

FLEMING, Anne Taylor 1950-

PERSONAL: Born 1950, in CA; married Karl Fleming (a journalist).

ADDRESSES: Agent—c/o Author Mail, Hyperion Books, 77 West 66th St., 11th Fl., New York, NY 10023.

CAREER: Journalist, author, radio and television commentator. Essayist, *Newshour with Jim Lehrer,* PBS; contributor to *News Night,* CNN.

WRITINGS:

(With husband, Karl Fleming) *The First Time,* Simon and Schuster (New York, NY), 1975.

Motherhood Deferred: A Woman's Journey, G. P. Putnam's Sons (New York, NY), 1994.

Marriage: A Duet (two novellas), Hyperion (New York, NY), 2003.

Contributor to periodicals, including the *Los Angeles Magazine, New York Times, New Yorker, Redbook, Vogue,* and *Newsweek.*

SIDELIGHTS: Freelance writer and media commentator Anne Taylor Fleming documents her struggle to conceive a child in *Motherhood Deferred: A Woman's Journey.* Fleming was one of many feminists who put off having a family in favor of furthering her career, and when she did decide to become a mother, found that conception was impossible. Her memoir is of this failure and of her life leading up to it.

According to Fleming, she and her sister were born into a privileged family, the daughters of successful Hollywood actors who were able to provide them with a comfortable life and private education. Fleming writes that her parents divorced "with rare grace, and we were never batted around between them or made pawns in any leftover business of theirs." When she was sixteen, Fleming met her husband-to-be, a married writer twice her age and the father of four sons. He divorced, and when she graduated college, they married. Inspired by feminist writers like Betty Friedan (*The Feminine Mystique*) and Simone de Beauvoir (*The Second Sex*), Fleming pursued her writing career.

Fleming writes that she was influenced in her decision not to begin a family by the "sacrificial generation" of women who put off having children. *Newsweek* reviewer Laura Shapiro wrote that "this is sticky stuff. It badly misrepresents the women's movement, which did a lot more agitating for day care than issuing decrees against childbearing." Shapiro called "genuinely gripping" the second half of the book, where Fleming turns to the rounds of disappointment and hope through which she cycled, and said it "captures the sadness of her plight."

When Fleming failed to conceive, she underwent all of the available procedures. *Commentary* reviewer Rachel Abrams wrote that "every encounter with a syringe, a petrie dish, a scanner, and a stirrup, each drop of sperm in the seemingly endless stream supplied by her obliging husband, then washed and counted and mounted via laparoscope, every failure of every mechanically fertilized embryo to implant itself in her uterus, Mrs. Fleming faithfully, one is tempted to say lovingly, records."

Booklist contributor Alice Joyce recommended *Motherhood Deferred* "for baby boomers who have reached a point of reassessment in their own lives." A *Publishers Weekly* contributor felt that most readers "will appreciate her [Fleming's] hard-won insights."

Marriage: A Duet comprises two novellas, the plots of which revolve around marital infidelity. In *A Married Woman,* Caroline Betts dyes her hair in the bathroom of her husband's hospital room as he lays dying, and she recalls an affair he had with a young friend of their daughter some fifteen years earlier and the long period of repair to their damaged marriage that followed. Shannon Bloomstran noted for *Mostly Fiction* online that Caroline is a very private person who thinks rather than says what she is feeling, "and so we are privy to her every erudite and elegantly icy thought about the affair."

The second novella, *A Married Man,* is a story of successful businessman whose wife reveals that she had a one-night stand with a party guest in the back seat of a car. David, the devoted husband and father, is dragged by his wife to a television "forgiveness" therapist, and it is during these sessions that most of the humorous lines appear. Bloomstran described David as a "snarky adolescent, unwilling or unable to let go of his humiliation. David is so sexually attracted to his wife that he's willing to forsake her and their children because someone else has touched her." Bloomstran wrote that this novella "is much more graphic, digging up a more raw and unsophisticated grief than the first, and ties in all sorts of ruminations about male and female roles." *Booklist*'s Donna Seaman said that Fleming "evinces remarkable insights into intimacy and betrayal" and "writes with extraordinary exactitude about sex, family life, loss, sorrow." A *Publishers Weekly* contributor called Fleming "a thoughtful, intelligent writer whose arch humor and dead-on dialogue suggest great potential for subsequent novels."

BIOGRAPHICAL AND CRITICAL SOURCES:

BOOKS

Fleming, Anne Taylor, *Motherhood Deferred: A Woman's Journey,* G. P. Putnam's Sons (New York, NY), 1994.

PERIODICALS

Booklist, April 15, 1994, Alice Joyce, review of *Motherhood Deferred: A Woman's Journey,* p. 1482; November 15, 2002, Donna Seaman, review of *Marriage: A Duet,* p. 568.

Commentary, November, 1994, Rachel Abrams, review of *Motherhood Deferred,* p. 74.

Kirkus Reviews, October 15, 2002, review of *Marriage,* p. 1493.

Library Journal, November 1, 2002, Robin Nesbitt, review of *Marriage,* p. 131.

Los Angeles Magazine, February, 2003, Robert Ito, review of *Marriage,* p. 112.

Newsweek, June 20, 1994, Laura Shapiro, review of *Motherhood Deferred,* pp. 68-70.

Publishers Weekly, May 2, 1994, review of *Motherhood Deferred,* p. 293; January 13, 2003, review of *Marriage: A Duet,* p. 41.

ONLINE

MostlyFiction.com, http://www.mostlyfiction.com/ (January 9, 2003), Shannon Bloomstran, review of *Marriage.**

*   *   *

FLETCHER, Charlotte Goldsborough 1915-

PERSONAL: Born December 11, 1915, in Cambridge, MD; daughter of Frederick H. (a lawyer) and Mary Henry (Gould) Fletcher. *Ethnicity:* "American-Anglo." *Education:* Hollins College, A.B., 1935; Columbia University, B.S., 1939. *Politics:* Democrat. *Religion:* Episcopalian.

ADDRESSES: Agent—c/o Author Mail, University Press of America, 4501 Forbes Blvd., Suite 200, Lanham, MD 20706.

CAREER: Writer.

AWARDS, HONORS: Honorary M.A., St. John's College, 1969.

WRITINGS:

Cato's Mirania: A Life of Provost Smith, University Press of America (Lanham, MD), 2002.

FOREMAN, George 1949-

PERSONAL: Born January 10, 1949, in Marshall, TX; son of J. D. and Nancy Foreman; married, wife's name: Mary; children: George Jr., George III, George IV, George V, George VI, Michi, Freeda George, Georgetta, Natalie, Leola. *Religion:* Christian.

ADDRESSES: Agent—c/o Author Mail, Simon & Schuster, 1230 Avenue of the Americas, New York, NY 10020. *E-mail*—george@biggeorge.com.

CAREER: Boxer, preacher, and author. U.S. Job Corps, affiliated, beginning 1965; professional boxer, beginning 1969; ordained minister, Church of the Lord Jesus Christ, 1977; George Foreman Youth and Community Center, founder, 1984; television boxing commentator for HBO; television infomercial salesman.

AWARDS, HONORS: Olympic Gold Medal, 1968, for heavyweight boxing; World Heavyweight Champion, 1973-74, 1994-95.

WRITINGS:

(With Joel Engel) *By George: The Autobiography of George Foreman,* Villard (New York, NY), 1995.

(With Cherie Calbom) *George Foreman's Knock-out-the-Fat Barbeque and Grilling Cookbook,* Villard (New York, NY), 1996.

(With Connie Merydith) *George Foreman's Big George Rotisserie Cookbook,* Pascoe Publishing (Cincinnati, OH), 1999.

(With Barbara Witt) *George Foreman's Big Book of Grilling, Barbecue, and Rotisserie: More than Seventy-five Recipes for Family and Friends,* Simon & Schuster (New York, NY), 2000.

(Author of foreword) *And the Fans Roared: The Sports Broadcasts That Kept Us on the Edge of Our Seats,* Sourcebooks (Naperville, IL), 2000.

(With Connie Merydith) *The George Foreman Lean Mean Fat-reducing Grilling Machine Cookbook,* Pascoe Publishing, (Rocklin, CA), 2000.

(With Linda Kulman) *George Foreman's Guide to Life: How to Get up off the Canvas When Life Knocks You Down,* Simon & Schuster (New York, NY), 2002.

SIDELIGHTS: World heavyweight boxing champion George Foreman was one of seven children born to J. D. and Nancy Foreman. He grew up in Marshall, Texas, where, in his teens, he became rebellious and misdirected. By age fifteen, Foreman was a mugger and alley fighter, until an ad for the Job Corps program caught his attention. Foreman joined the Corps 1965, and there learned the sport that would make him famous. After winning sixteen of eighteen fights as an amateur boxer, he qualified for the U.S. Olympic boxing team. Foreman won a gold medal in Mexico City's 1968 Olympic Games and turned professional the following year. He went on to win two world heavyweight championships, first in 1973 and again in 1994, when at age forty-five he became the oldest fighter ever to win the title.

Foreman tells his story in *By George: The Autobiography of George Foreman,* beginning with his troubled youth and documenting his rise to boxing fame. The book recounts some of his biggest fights, including his 1973 defeat of Joe Frazier, which earned Foreman his first heavyweight championship, and his historic fight against Muhammad Ali in Zaire, Africa, in which Ali knocked out Foreman after eight rounds, resulting in one of the greatest upsets in sports history.

Forman's autobiography also explores how, after losing to Jimmy Young in a twelve-round decision in 1977, he experienced a "religious awakening" which changed his life and inspired him to retire from boxing. After leaving the sport Foreman became an ordained minister, founded his own church, counseled prisoners, and in 1984 used the money he had saved during the eight years of his retirement to found the George Foreman Youth and Community Center. When an accountant warned him that investing any more of his own money in the center would leave him broke, he shocked the sports world by returning to boxing after a ten-year absence and winning twenty-four consecutive comeback fights.

In 1991 Foreman found himself contending for his second championship title against Evander Holyfield. Although he lost the fight by decision, he earned great respect from the boxing community for his unprecedented comeback. Finally, in 1994, Foreman earned the title of World Heavyweight Champion for a second time, twenty-one years after winning his first title, by defeating reigning champion Michael Moorer. The win earned Foreman the distinction of being the oldest heavyweight boxing champion in history.

William Plummer wrote in a review of *By George* for *People* that the book is "Foreman's fascinating act of reparation," and that he "spins a wonderful tale with characteristic humor."

Foreman is also the pitchman for the "Lean, Mean, Fat-reducing Grilling Machine," a kitchen appliance. The success of the grilling machine has inspired a number of grilling cookbooks that bear Foreman's name. A *Publishers Weekly* reviewer called *George Foreman's Big Book of Grilling, Barbecue, and Rotisserie: More than Seventy-five Recipes for Family and Friends* a "happy-go-lucky collection of . . . recipes inspired by his salad days of boxing all over the world" that include meat dishes, salads, and vegetable dishes. The reviewer noted that the "exotic concoctions are superior to the more domestic efforts, the most worrisome of which is an American version of Indonesian chicken satay with a peanut sauce made of peanut butter, ketchup, Worcestershire sauce, honey and vinegar."

Foreman also shares his wisdom in *George Foreman's Guide to Life: How to Get up off the Canvas When Life Knocks You Down,* a small volume filled with practical advice. Foreman "shares his life lessons here, showing how to turn hardship to happiness . . . and achieve fulfillment no matter what life brings," according to a writer for *Library Journal.* A *Publishers Weekly* reviewer deemed it a "slim but wise book," noteworthy for its "simplicity, its directness and the vast pool of personal experience that Foreman calls upon." "With its hard-won lessons and congenial tone," the reviewer concluded, "this book can be of real use to many."

BIOGRAPHICAL AND CRITICAL SOURCES:

BOOKS

Foreman, George, and Joel Engel, *By George: The Autobiography of George Foreman,* Easton Press (Norwalk, CT), 1995.

Foreman, George, and Linda Kulman, *George Foreman's Guide to Life: How to Get up off the Canvas When Life Knocks You Down,* Simon & Schuster (New York, NY), 2002.

PERIODICALS

Library Journal, November 1, 2002, review of *George Foreman's Guide to Life: How to Get up off the Canvas When Life Knocks You Down,* p.115.

People Weekly, June 12, 1995, William Plummer, review of *By George: The Autobiography of George Foreman,* p. 28

Publishers Weekly, September 4, 2000, review of *George Foreman's Big Book of Grilling, Barbecue, and Rotisserie: More than Seventy-five Recipes for Family and Friends,* p. 102; January 6, 2003, review of *George Foreman's Guide to Life,* p. 54.

ONLINE

Big George Foreman's Place, http://www.biggeorge. com (June 19, 2003).

Healthy-Grill.com, http://www.healthy-grill.com/ (June 19, 2003).

Simon & Schuster Web site, http://www. simonandschuster.com/ (June 19, 2003).

OTHER

When We Were Kings (documentary film), Polygram, 1996.*

*   *   *

FRANCIS, C. D. E.
    See HOWARTH, Patrick (John Fielding)

*   *   *

FRANK, E(mily) R. 1967-

PERSONAL: Born 1967, in Richmond, VA; married. *Education:* College graduate; attended writing class at New School of Social Research (now New School University).

ADDRESSES: Home—Montclair, NJ. *Agent*—Charlotte Sheedy Literary Agency, 65 Bleecker St., New York, NY 10012.

CAREER: Psychotherapist and clinical social worker in New York, NY; author of young adult novels.

AWARDS, HONORS: Quick Picks for Reluctant Young Adult Readers selection, American Library Association (ALA), 2001, for *Life Is Funny;* Best Books for Young Adults selection, ALA, and *Los Angeles Times* Book Award finalist, both 2003, both for *America;* Best Books for Young Adults selection, ALA, 2004, for *Friction.*

WRITINGS:

Life Is Funny, DK Ink (New York, NY), 2000.
America, Atheneum (New York, NY), 2002.
Friction, Atheneum (New York, NY), 2003.
Wave, Atheneum (New York, NY), 2005.

Contributor to *Rush Hour.*

SIDELIGHTS: E. R. Frank has worked in prisons, day treatment centers, a middle school, and an outpatient mental health clinic. A clinical social worker who also established a psychotherapy practice in Manhattan, Frank has had many troubled youths pass her way; in fact, a full third of her caseload has been troubled adolescents. Frank brings her experience and expertise in the area of teen problems to bear in her novels about young New Yorkers at risk and dealing with trauma.

Beginning with *Life Is Funny,* and continuing in *America, Friction,* and *Wave,* Frank presents non-sensationalized yet haunting evocations of adolescents and teenagers confronted with daunting situations, including recognizing and surviving sexual abuse. "All of my characters are complete fiction," Frank assured Holly Atkins in an interview for the *St. Petersburg Times.*

Although inspired by the experiences she has had as a clinical psychologist, the author maintains that "the characters in those books are not based on any one person." Rather they are a composite of many of the adolescents she has worked with over the years. Speaking with Jean Westmoore in the *Buffalo News,* Frank reiterated this point: "I do not write or talk about my clients at all. After so many years of working with kids, adolescents, [and] adults within the criminal justice system, I had this cumulative emotion of so many people who had been lost in the system and hadn't had the one kind of relationship that might have saved them."

Born into a family of "voracious readers," as Jason Britton noted in a *Publishers Weekly* profile of the author, Frank gravitated to writing at an early age. She spent a lot of time during her childhood around her grandfather, writer Gerold Frank, author of *The Boston Strangler, American Death,* and *Judy.* "When I was very young, it was because of [my grandfather] . . . that I realized that a writing career was a possibility," Frank told Britton. A clinical social worker who sometimes used writing as a form of therapy with her clients, Frank finally began writing herself in 1996.

Frank did not have a particular audience in mind when composing her first book, a tale of eleven kids that is composed of interlocking stories. Her young protagonists narrate their misadventures over a seven-year period, each in his or her distinctive voice. When she was finished with the manuscript, Frank took the advice of friends and submitted it to a literary agent who liked the story and sent it on to Richard Jackson at DK Ink. Jackson also appreciated the story and gave Frank a call, during which he began the editorial process. "It was like a dream come true," Frank told Britton. "I felt honored to be working with him."

Published in 2000, Frank's debut novel, *Life Is Funny,* drew praise from critics. Alice Casey Smith, writing in *School Library Journal,* called the book a "choral piece of writing that sings of coming-of-age in a multiracial Brooklyn community." Dysfunctional families, racism, drugs, violence, divorce, death, molestation, violence, and abandonment all mar the lives of the book's seven adolescents, but they greet their predicaments with more than anger. As Smith noted, the characters "are boisterous and full of laughter, because after all is said and done, life is funny, isn't it?" According to *Booklist* critic Hazel Rochman, "Each chapter, each vignette within a chapter, builds to its own climax, and the stories weave together to surprise you." More praise came from a contributor for *Publishers Weekly,* who remarked that "the language is gritty, and some of the story lines will be intense for young readers, but this is ultimately an uplifting book about resilience, loyalty and courage." Paula Rohrlick, reviewing the title in *Kliatt,* pronounced *Life Is Funny,* "an arresting, accomplished first novel."

Frank continues her gritty investigations of adolescence and young adulthood with 2002's *America,* a "heartbreaking story of survival, forgiveness, and redemption," in the opinion of *School Library Journal* contributor Jennifer Ralston. In the book Frank tells the story of America, a confused fifteen-year-old boy of mixed race who is lost in the labyrinthine system of foster care and hospitalization. So damaged is America by abandonment and abuse that he has tried to kill himself. When he becomes a patient in a residential psychiatric program, he is lucky enough to meet up with Dr. B, who slowly teaches him the lessons of survival.

Frank's second book was greeted with wide critical acclaim. A contributor for *Kirkus Reviews* called *America,* a "wrenching tour de force" as well as a "work of sublime humanity," while *Booklist* reviewer Gillian Engberg found it a "piercing, unforgettable novel." Kathleen Isaacs, writing in *School Library Journal,* felt that Frank's "control of this story is impressive." For *Horn Book* contributor Jennifer M. Brabander, "it's the strong, deeply felt connection created between protagonist and audience that makes this such a moving novel." Kristen R. Crabtree, writing in the *Journal of Adolescence and Adult Literacy,* commented that *America* "is not for the immature reader" because its complex plot makes it "sophisticated in delivering disturbing experiences." Crabtree went on to note, though, that mature "adolescents will find a connection to [America's] voice and self-acceptance. America is worth finding and getting to know."

In *Friction* Frank again deals with teen trauma and abuse. In this novel, she focuses on an eighth-grade classroom, a microcosm in which friction can arise between students and teacher and between individual students. The book is told in the present tense from the point of view of twelve-year-old Alex, a student in an alternative school. A happy tomboyish kid on the cusp of adolescence, Alex loves soccer, her buddy, Tim, and her teacher, Simon, who she considers to be the best teacher in the school. Simon has managed, in fact, to win over the entire class with his unorthodox teaching style and his friendliness. But all this changes with the arrival of a new student in class, Stacy. The new girl has real attitude and at first Alex is drawn to her. But soon Stacy begins spreading rumors that Simon has more than a friendly interest in Alex. Stacy accuses the teacher of being a "pervert," and soon the whole class, including Alex, is double-thinking their relationship with him. The police enter the picture, and Alex is confused when they ask her if Simon has ever touched her. Ultimately, through the intercession of Alex's psychiatrist father, things are straightened out, and it becomes apparent that in fact it is Stacy's father who is doing the abusing.

Again reviewers responded warmly to Frank's hard-hitting theme. A reviewer for *Publishers Weekly* noted that the author "insightfully addresses topics of teen sexuality and child abuse" in this "provocative novel" that is "sure to spark heated discussions." *Kliatt*'s Rohrlick also observed that Frank "doesn't shy away from difficult topics," and that *Friction* serves as an "excellent way for teachers, counselors, and parents to open up discussions of what constitutes sexual abuse." Rohrlick also thought the novel would be a "gripping read for younger adolescent girls." A critic for *Kirkus Reviews* praised Frank for a "subtly done" approach to a "combustible" subject, and *Horn Book* reviewer Bridget T. McCaffrey commended Alex's narrative voice as "genuine" and "believable."

Speaking with Westmoore, Frank summed up her approach to writing for young adults. "I don't write to make a point," she noted. "If people read [one of my novels] and take away from it some new information or feelings about action they want to take, that would be wonderful." In her interview with Atkins, Frank commented that she does not write with an "agenda." Instead, "what's important to me is that readers are moved or touched in some way and that when they finish a book, they feel they've been transported into the world of the characters for a short while."

BIOGRAPHICAL AND CRITICAL SOURCES:

PERIODICALS

Book, May-June, 2002, review of *America,* p. 29.
Booklist, February 15, 2001, Hazel Rochman, review of *Life Is Funny,* p. 1152; February 15, 2002, Gillian Engberg, review of *America,* p. 1013; July, 2003, Gillian Engberg, review of *Friction,* p. 1886; January 1, 2004, Lolly Gepson, review of *Friction* (audiobook), p. 893.
Buffalo News, February 11, 2002, Jean Westmoore, "The Story of a Boy Named 'America,'" p. A7.
Horn Book, May, 2000, Jennifer M. Brabander, review of *Life Is Funny,* p. 313; March-April, 2002, Jennifer M. Brabander, review of *America,* pp. 211-212; July-August, 2003, Bridget T. McCaffrey, review of *Friction,* p. 455; March-April, 2004, Kristi Elle Jemtegaard, review of *America* (audiobook), p. 199.
Journal of Adolescent and Adult Literacy, September, 2002, Kristen R. Crabtree, review of *America,* p. 83.

Kirkus Reviews, December 1, 2001, review of *America,* p. 1684; May 1, 2003, review of *Friction,* p. 676.
Kliatt, January, 2002, Paula Rohrlick, review of *America,* pp. 5-6; July, 2002, Paula Rohrlick, review of *Life Is Funny,* p. 18; May, 2003, Paula Rohrlick, review of *Friction,* p. 8; November, 2003, Sherri F. Ginsberg, review of *Friction* (audiobook), p. 48.
New York Times, May 19, 2002, Mary Harris Russell, "Lost Boy," p. L24.
Publishers Weekly, March 13, 2000, review of *Life Is Funny,* p. 85; June 26, 2000, Jason Britton, "E. R. Frank," p. 32; January 7, 2002, review of *America,* p. 66; April 7, 2003, review of *Friction,* p. 68; June 16, 2003, review of *Friction* (audiobook), p. 25.
St. Petersburg Times (St. Petersburg, FL), February 16, 2004, Holly Atkins, interview with Frank, p. E6.
School Library Journal, May, 2000, Alice Casey Smith, review of *Life Is Funny,* p. 172; March, 2002, Kathleen Isaacs, review of *America,* p. 230; October, 2003, Lynn Evarts, review of *Friction* (audiobook), p. 91, and Jennifer Ralston, review of *America,* p. 99.*

* * *

FRANKLIN, Lance
See LANTZ, Francess L(in)

* * *

FREEDMAN, Jessica B(lackman) 1954(?)-2002

PERSONAL: Born c. 1954; died of congestive heart failure July 20, 2002, in Alexandria, VA; daughter of Norman S. Blackman; married Bruce Freedman. *Education:* Syracuse University, master's degree; Western New England College, J.D.; doctoral study at American University. *Religion:* Jewish.

CAREER: Advice columnist with twin sister, Alison Blackman Dunham, as "The Advice Sisters." Legislative assistant in Washington, DC, late 1970s; freelance writer and editor, beginning mid-1980s. Northern Virginia Community College, adjunct professor of writing and literature for twelve years; also adjunct professor at American University and George Mason University.

WRITINGS:

(With Alison Blackman Dunham) *Recruiting Love: Using the Business Skills You Have to Find the Love You Want,* Cyclone Books (Los Angeles, CA), 1998.

Author of several e-books. Creator of a five-part audio tape series "Making New Connections." Editor and ghostwriter of speeches and film scripts. Contributor to periodicals.

BIOGRAPHICAL AND CRITICAL SOURCES:

ONLINE

Advice Sisters—Relationship Tools for Winners Web site, http://www.advicesisters.net (January 2, 2003).

OBITUARIES

PERIODICALS

Washington Post, July 28, 2002, p. C6.*

*   *   *

FREY, James N.

PERSONAL: Male.

ADDRESSES: Office—James N. Frey Events, P.O. Box 7427, Berkeley, CA 94707. *E-mail*—jnfrey@ jamesnfrey.com.

CAREER: Author and educator. Lecturer and workshop presenter at schools and conferences in the United States and internationally, including Squaw Valley Community of Writers Conference, Oregon Writers Colony, Santa Barbara Writers Conference, Heartland Writers, University of California Extension, and California Writers Club.

AWARDS, HONORS: Edgar Allen Poe Award nomination, Mystery Writers of America, for *The Long Way to Die.*

WRITINGS:

How to Write a Damn Good Novel, St. Martin's Press (New York, NY), 1987.
A Killing in Dreamland (novel), Bantam Books (New York, NY), 1988.
Came a Dead Cat, St. Martin's Press (New York, NY), 1991.
Winter of the Wolves, Henry Holt (New York, NY), 1992.
How to Write a Damn Good Novel, II: Advanced Techniques for Dramatic Storytelling, St. Martin's Press (New York, NY), 1994.
The Key: How to Write Damn Good Fiction Using the Power of Myth, St. Martin's Press (New York, NY), 2000.
How to Write a Damn Good Mystery: A Practical Step-by-Step Guide from Inspiration to Finished Manuscript, St. Martin's Press (New York, NY), 2004.

Also author of novel *The Long Way to Die.*

SIDELIGHTS: James N. Frey is an author and writing workshop instructor who has also written several books on his craft, beginning with 1987's *How to Write a Damn Good Novel.* Frey's *The Key: How to Write Damn Good Fiction Using the Power of Myth* draws on Joseph Campbell's *The Power of Myth* and uses romance novels as an example of how readers are willing to read the same stories again and again. In the first half of the book, Frey examines mythic structure in such works as *Beowulf,* Peter Bencheley's novel *Jaws,* and the story of Robin Hood.In the second half, he includes a novella, *The Blue Light,* as an example of using myth in writing. *Library Journal* reviewer Lisa J. Cihlar called *The Key* a "well-written and witty how-to."

In his *How to Write a Damn Good Mystery: A Practical Step-by-Step Guide from Inspiration to Finished Manuscript,* Frey guides writing readers through the steps necessary to complete a novel, detailing the art of creating compelling characters and constructing a plot line that will increase suspense. He concludes by offering advise on finding an agent and getting published. *Booklist* contributor David Pitt called Frey's approach "eminently practical and rich in details, a must for budding crime-fiction authors."

BIOGRAPHICAL AND CRITICAL SOURCES:

PERIODICALS

Booklist, January 1, 2004, David Pitt, review of *How to Write a Damn Good Mystery: A Practical Step-by-Step Guide from Inspiration to Finished Manuscript,* p. 809.

Library Journal, June 1, 2000, Lisa J. Cihlar, review of *The Key: How to Write Damn Good Fiction Using the Power of Myth,* p. 148; February 1, 2004, Ann Schade, review of *How to Write a Damn Good Mystery,* p. 103.

Publishers Weekly, April 27, 1992, review of *Winter of the Wolves,* p. 250.

ONLINE

James N. Frey Home Page, http://www.jamesnfrey. com (October 10, 2004).*

*   *   *

FRIEDMAN, Andrew 1967-

PERSONAL: Born in 1967; married. *Education:* French Culinary Institute, "La Technique" program graduate.

ADDRESSES: Home—New York and Chatham, NY *Agent*—c/o Author Mail, Wiley Publishing, 111 River St., 5th Floor, Hoboken, NJ 07030

CAREER: Cookbook author and publicist for restaurants and corporations, including Starbucks and Gotham Bar and Grill.

WRITINGS:

(With Alfred Portale) *Alfred Portale's 12 Seasons Cookbook,* photographs by Gozen Koshida, Broadway Books (New York, NY), 2000.

Chef on a Shoestring: More Than 120 Delicious, Easy-on-the-Budget Recipes from America's Best Chefs, Simon & Schuster (New York, NY), 2001.

(With Silvano Marchetto and Scott Haas) *Da Silvano Cookbook: Simple Secrets From New York's Favorite Italian Restaurant,* foreword by Nick Tosches, photographs by Robert DiScalfani, Bloomsbury (New York, NY), 2001.

(With Tom Valenti) *Welcome to My Kitchen: A New York Chef Shares His Robust Recipes and Secret Techniques,* HarperCollins (New York, NY), 2002.

(With Tom Valenti) *Tom Valenti's Soups, Stews, and One-Pot Meals: 125 Home Recipes from the Chef-Owner of New York City's Ouest and 'Cesca,* Scribner (New York, NY), 2003.

(With Pino Luongo and Marta Pulini) *La Mia Cucina Toscana: A Tuscan Cooks in America,* photographs by Michele Tabozzi, Broadway Books (New York, NY), 2003.

(With Laurent Tourondel) *Go Fish: Fresh Ideas for American Seafood,* John Wiley (Hoboken, NJ), 2004.

(With Bill Telepan) *Inspired by Ingredients: Market Menus and Family Favorites from a Three-Star Chef,* Simon & Schuster (New York, NY), 2004.

(With Alfred Portale) *Alfred Portale Simple Pleasures: Home Cooking from Gotham Bar and Grill's Acclaimed Chef,* Morrow (New York, NY), 2004.

(With Michael Lomonaco) *Nightly Specials: 125 Recipes for Spontanious, Creative Cooking at Home,* HarperCollins (New York, NY), 2004.

(With David Walzog) *The New American Steakhouse Cookbook: It's Not Just Meat and Potatoes Anymore,* Broadway Books (New York, NY), 2005.

(With Terrance Brennan) *Artisanal Cooking: A Chef Shares Hiks Passion for Handcrafting Great Meals at Home,* John Wiley (Hoboken, NJ), 2005.

(With Kimberly Witherspoon) *Don't Try This At Home: Kitchen Disasters and Memorable Mishaps from the World's Greatest Cooks and Chefs,* Bloomsbury, 2005.

SIDELIGHTS: Andrew Friedman is best known for the many cookbooks he has co-authored with well-known chefs, such as Michael Lomonaco, Bill Telepan, and David Walzog. Friedman wrote two books, including his first, with the celebrated chef and restauranteur Alfred Portale, owner of Gotham Bar and Grill in New York City. Despite Portale's reputation for haute cuisine, the books had a down-to-earth tone. *Publishers Weekly* wrote of *Alfred Portale's 12 Seasons Cook-*

book that "many recipes are simple, yet sublimely accented." Some of the recipes, the reviewer wrote, are complex, but "not beyond the reach of enthusiastic cooks." All in all, the review called the book "a winning, personal take on seasonal cooking from a Northeastern perspective." The authors' other joint effort was *Alfred Portale Simple Pleasures: Home Cooking from the Gotham Bar and Grill's Acclaimed Chef*, which according to *Publishers Weekly* focuses on "home-style foods rather than dishes that require a team of [assistant] chefs to be executed properly."

Friedman also wrote two books with New York chef Tom Valenti, who is recognized "for hearty, flavorful cooking," according to Judith Sutton in a *Library Journal* review of *Welcome to My Kitchen: A New York Chef Shares His Robust Recipes and Secret Techniques*. Sutton wrote that the authors "have adopted a relaxed tone, suitable for the comfort food Valenti likes so much." The pair's second effort, *Tom Valenti's Soups, Stews, and One-Pot Meals: 125 Home Recipes from the Chef-Owner of New York City's Ouest and 'Cesca*, is a "uniformly tight and well-written" work, according to a *Publishers Weekly* critic who, nevertheless, believed some of the dishes themselves disappointed.

A more recent work by Friedman goes beyond recipes and food. Published in 2004 with chef Bill Telepan, *Inspired by Ingredients: Market Menus and Family Favorites from a Three-Star Chef*, also offers "portraits of some of the farmers and other purveyors" that Telepan has used, according to Judith Sutton in *Library Journal*. Sutton praised the book's "engaging, personable style.". But Sutton, in the same periodical, said "the recipe headnotes and text" in Friedman's other 2004 effort, *Go Fish: Fresh Ideas for American Seafood*, "are somewhat pedestrian."

Aside from the dozen cookbooks Friedman coauthored, as of 2005 the only title for which Friedman is credited as the sole author is his second book, *Chef on a Shoestring: More Than 120 Delicious, Easy-on-the-Budget Recipes from America's Best Chefs*. In a way, however, this 2001 publication is also a collaboration. *Chef on a Shoestring* is based on a series of television appearances by noted chefs shopping for and cooking a three-course, four-person meal for $20 or less. Friedman worked with the chefs before translating their segments into print. "The book," according to Michelle Moran in *Gourmet Retailer* that "captures the essence

of the show, providing readers with shopping tips, recipes, and personalities."

BIOGRAPHICAL AND CRITICAL SOURCES:

PERIODICALS

Booklist, October 1, 2004, Mark Knoblauch, review of *Alfred Portale Simple Pleasures: Home Cooking from the Gothan Bar and Grill's Acclaimed Chef*, p. 291.

Gourmet Retailer, January 2001, Michelle Moran, review of *Chef on a Shoestring: More Than 120 Delicious, Easy-on-the-Budget Recipes from America's Best Chefs*, p. 164.

Library Journal, September 15, 2000, Judith Sutton, review of *Alfred Portale's 12 Seasons Cookbook*, p. 107; December 2000, Judith Sutton, review of *Chef on a Shoestring*, p. 178; February 15, 2002, Judith Sutton, review of *Welcome to My Kitchen: A New York Chef Shares His Robust Recipes and Secret Techniques*, p. 173; October 15, 2003, Judith Sutton, review of *Tom Valenti's Soups, Stews, and One-Pot Meals: 125 Home Recipes from the Chef-Owner of New York City's Ouest and 'Cesca*, p. 93; October 15, 2004, Judith Sutton, reviews of *Inspired by Ingredients: Market Menus and Family Favorites from a Three-Star Chef* and *Go Fish: Fresh Ideas for American Seafood*, pp. 82 and 83.

People Weekly, November 10, 2003, review of *Tom Valenti's Soups, Stews, and One-Pot Meals*, p. 68.

Publishers Weekly, August 21, 2000, review of *Alfred Portale's 12 Seasons Cookbook*, p. 67; July 7, 2003, review of *La Mia Cucina Toscana: A Tuscan Cooks in America*, p. 68; September 1, 2003, review of *Tom Valenti's Soups, Stews, and One-Pot Meals*, p. 81; September 27, 2004, reviews of *Inspired by Ingredients* and *Alfred Portale Simple Pleasures*, p. 51.*

*   *   *

FROST, Helen 1949-

PERSONAL: Born 1949, in Brookings, SD; married; children: two sons. *Education:* Syracuse University, B.A. (elementary education); Indiana University, M.A., 1994. *Hobbies and other interests:* Hiking, cross-country skiing, kayaking, raising and releasing monarch butterflies.

ADDRESSES: Home—Fort Wayne, IN *Agent*—Capstone Press, 151 Good Counsel Dr., P.O. Box 669, Mankato, MN 56002. *E-mail*—helenfrost@comcast.net.

CAREER: Educator and author. Kilquhanity House School (boarding school), Scotland, teacher; elementary school teacher in Telida, AK, for three years, then Ketchican, AK; Indiana University; Purdue, instructor. Fort Wayne Dance Collective, member of inderdisciplinary program, beginning 1994; actively involved in YWCA and teen youth groups.

AWARDS, HONORS: Michael Printz Honor Book designation, American Library Association, 2004, for *Keesha's House.*

WRITINGS:

JUVENILE FICTION

Keesha's House, Frances Foster Books (New York, NY), 2003.
Spinning through the Universe: A Novel in Poems from Room 214, Farrar, Straus & Giroux (New York, NY), 2004.

"BIRDS" SERIES: JUVENILE NONFICTION

Bird Nests, Pebble Books (Mankato, MN), 1999.
Baby Birds, Pebble Books (Mankato, MN), 1999.
Bird Families, Pebble Books (Mankato, MN), 1999.

"BUTTERFLIES" SERIES: JUVENILE NONFICTION

Butterfly Eggs, Pebble Books (Mankato, MN), 1999.
Caterpillars, Pebble Books (Mankato, MN), 1999.
Butterfly Colors, Pebble Books (Mankato, MN), 1999.
Monarch Butterflies, Pebble Books (Mankato, MN), 1999.

"DENTAL HEALTH" SERIES: JUVENILE NONFICTION

Your Teeth, Pebble Books (Mankato, MN), 1999.
Going to the Dentist, Pebble Books (Mankato, MN), 1999.

Food for Healthy Teeth, Pebble Books (Mankato, MN), 1999.
Brushing Well, Pebble Books (Mankato, MN), 1999.

"FOOD GROUP PYRAMID" SERIES; JUVENILE NONFICTION

The Fruit Group, Pebble Books (Mankato, MN), 2000.
Eating Right, Pebble Books (Mankato, MN), 2000.
The Vegetable Group, Pebble Books (Mankato, MN), 2000.
The Dairy Group, Pebble Books (Mankato, MN), 2000.
Fats, Oils, and Sweets, Pebble Books (Mankato, MN), 2000.
Drinking Water, Pebble Books (Mankato, MN), 2000.
The Grain Group, Pebble Books (Mankato, MN), 2000.
The Meat and Protein Group, Pebble Books (Mankato, MN), 2000.

"WATER" SERIES: JUVENILE NONFICTION

Keeping Water Clean, Pebble Books (Mankato, MN), 2000.
The Water Cycle, Pebble Books (Mankato, MN), 2000.
Water as a Solid, Pebble Books (Mankato, MN), 2000.
Water as a Liquid, Pebble Books (Mankato, MN), 2000.
Water as a Gas, Pebble Books (Mankato, MN), 2000.
We Need Water, Pebble Books (Mankato, MN), 2000.

Author's titles have been translated into Spanish.

"NATIONAL HOLIDAYS" SERIES; JUVENILE NONFICTION

Memorial Day, Pebble Books (Mankato, MN), 2000.
Independence Day, Pebble Books (Mankato, MN), 2000.
Martin Luther King, Jr., Day, Pebble Books (Mankato, MN), 2000.
Presidents' Day, Pebble Books (Mankato, MN), 2000.

"SENSES" SERIES; JUVENILE NONFICTION

Your Senses, Pebble Books (Mankato, MN), 2000.
Smelling, Pebble Books (Mankato, MN), 2000.
Touching, Pebble Books (Mankato, MN), 2000.

Tasting, Pebble Books (Mankato, MN), 2000.
Seeing, Pebble Books (Mankato, MN), 2000.
Hearing, Pebble Books (Mankato, MN), 2000.

"EMOTIONS" SERIES; JUVENILE NONFICTION

Feeling Sad, Pebble Books (Mankato, MN), 2001.
Feeling Angry, Pebble Books (Mankato, MN), 2001.
Feeling Scared, Pebble Books (Mankato, MN), 2001.
Feeling Happy, Pebble Books (Mankato, MN), 2001.

"HUMAN BODY SYSTEMS" SERIES; JUVENILE NONFICTION

The Circulatory System, Pebble Books (Mankato, MN), 2001.
The Respiratory System, Pebble Books (Mankato, MN), 2001.
The Nervous System, Pebble Books (Mankato, MN), 2001.
The Muscular System, Pebble Books (Mankato, MN), 2001.
The Skeletal System, Pebble Books (Mankato, MN), 2001.
The Digestive System, Pebble Books (Mankato, MN), 2001.

"LOOKING AT SIMPLE MACHINES" SERIES: JUVENILE NONFICTION

What Are Inclined Planes?, Pebble Books (Mankato, MN), 2001.
What Are Levers?, Pebble Books (Mankato, MN), 2001.
What Are Screws?, Pebble Books (Mankato, MN), 2001.
What Are Wedges?, Pebble Books (Mankato, MN), 2001.
What Are Wheels and Axles?, Pebble Books (Mankato, MN), 2001.
What Are Pulleys?, Pebble Books (Mankato, MN), 2001.

"OUR WORLD" SERIES: JUVENILE NONFICTION

A Look at France, Pebble Books (Mankato, MN), 2002.
A Look at Kenya, Pebble Books (Mankato, MN), 2002.
A Look at Russia, Pebble Books (Mankato, MN), 2002.
A Look at Japan, Pebble Books (Mankato, MN), 2002.
A Look at Canada, Pebble Books (Mankato, MN), 2002.
A Look at Australia, Pebble Books (Mankato, MN), 2002.
A Look at Mexico, Pebble Books (Mankato, MN), 2002.
A Look at Egypt, Pebble Books (Mankato, MN), 2003.
A Look at Cuba, Pebble Books (Mankato, MN), 2003.
A Look at Germany, Pebble Books (Mankato, MN), 2003.
A Look at Vietnam, Pebble Books (Mankato, MN), 2003.

"ALL ABOUT PETS" SERIES; JUVENILE NONFICTION

Cats, Pebble Books (Mankato, MN), 2001.
Fish, Pebble Books (Mankato, MN), 2001.
Hamsters, Pebble Books (Mankato, MN), 2001.
Dogs, Pebble Books (Mankato, MN), 2001.
Rabbits, Pebble Books (Mankato, MN), 2001.
Birds, Pebble Books (Mankato, MN), 2001.

"INSECTS" SERIES; JUVENILE NONFICTION

Praying Mantises, Pebble Books (Mankato, MN), 2001.
Walkingsticks, Pebble Books (Mankato, MN), 2001.
Water Bugs, Pebble Books (Mankato, MN), 2001.
Moths, Pebble Books (Mankato, MN), 2001.
Wasps, Pebble Books (Mankato, MN), 2001.
Cicadas, Pebble Books (Mankato, MN), 2001.

"RAIN FOREST ANIMALS" SERIES; JUVENILE NONFICTION

Jaguars, Pebble Books (Mankato, MN), 2002.
Boa Constrictors, Pebble Books (Mankato, MN), 2002.
Gorillas, Capstone Press (Mankato, MN), 2002.
Tree Frogs, Pebble Books (Mankato, MN), 2002.
Tarantulas, Pebble Books (Mankato, MN), 2002.
Parrots, Capstone Press (Mankato, MN), 2002.
Lemurs, Pebble Books (Mankato, MN), 2003.
Chimpanzees, Pebble Books (Mankato, MN), 2003.
Leaf-cutting Ants, Pebble Books (Mankato, MN), 2003.
Tigers, Pebble Books (Mankato, MN), 2003.

"COMING TO AMERICA" SERIES; JUVENILE NONFICTION

German Immigrants, 1820-1920, Blue Earth Books (Mankato, MN), 2002.

Russian Immigrants, 1860-1949, Blue Earth Books (Mankato, MN), 2003.

"FAMOUS AMERICANS" SERIES; JUVENILE NONFICTION

John F. Kennedy, Pebble Books (Mankato, MN), 2003.

Sojourner Truth, Pebble Books (Mankato, MN), 2003.

Betsy Ross, Pebble Books (Mankato, MN), 2003.

"LET'S MEET" SERIES; JUVENILE NONFICTION

Let's Meet Jackie Robinson, Chelsea Clubhouse (Philadelphia, PA), 2004.

Let's Meet Booker T. Washington, Chelsea Clubhouse (Philadelphia, PA), 2004.

Let's Meed Ida B. Wells-Barnett, Chelsea Clubhouse (Philadelphia, PA), 2004.

"WEATHER" SERIES; JUVENILE NONFICTION

Ice, Capstone Press (Mankato, MN), 2004.

Fog, Capstone Press (Mankato, MN), 2004.

Snow, Capstone Press (Mankato, MN), 2004.

Wind, Capstone Press (Mankato, MN), 2004.

"DINOSAURS AND PREHISTORIC ANIMALS" SERIES; JUVENILE NONFICTION

Woolly Mammoth, Capstone Press (Mankato, MN), 2004.

Tyrannosaurus Rex, Capstone Press (Mankato, MN), 2004.

Triceratops, Capstone Press (Mankato, MN), 2004.

Sabertooth Cat, Capstone Press (Mankato, MN), 2004.

Allosaurus, Capstone Press (Mankato, MN), 2004.

Stegosaurus, Capstone Press (Mankato, MN), 2004.

"HELPERS IN OUR COMMUNITY" SERIES; JUVENILE NONFICTION

We Need Auto Mechanics, Capstone Press (Mankato, MN), 2004.

We Need Plumbers, Capstone Press (Mankato, MN), 2004.

We Need School Bus Drivers, Pebble Books (Mankato, MN), 2004.

We Need Pharmacists, Capstone Press (Mankato, MN), 2005.

FOR ADULTS

(Editor) *Season of Dead Water* (poetry and prose anthology), Breitenbush Books (Portland, OR), 1990.

Skin of a Fish, Bones of a Bird: Poems, Ampersand Press (Bristol, RI), 1993.

When I Whisper, Nobody Listens: Helping Young People Write about Difficult Issues, Heinemann (Portsmouth, NH), 2001.

SIDELIGHTS: In addition to her work as a teacher—she has taught students in Scotland, Alaska, and the American Midwest—poet, and playwright, Helen Frost is a prolific author of nonfiction and fiction for young readers. Her contributions to informative series for elementary-grade students reflect her interest in science and biology, and include books in Capstone Press's "Water," "Rainforest Animals," "All about Pets" and "Looking at Simple Machines" series, while her fictional works include the award-winning young-adult novel *Keesha's House* and the novel *Spinning through the Universe: A Novel in Poems from Room 214.* In addition to her work for young people, Frost is also the author of *When I Whisper, Nobody Listens: Helping Young People Write about Difficult Issues,* a book which, according to *Journal of Adolescent and Adult Literacy* contributor M. P. Cavanaugh, is designed to "prepare teachers to work with students on sensitive issues and to provide nonviolent solutions to some of their problems."

A novel-in-verse for older readers, *Keesha's House* focuses on seven inner-city teens whose lives are currently in turmoil and who find refuge in a home owned by a caring adult named Joe. Dubbed "Keesha's House" in honor of the first person to be welcomed there, the home becomes a haven for pregnant teen Stephie; Katie, who is escaping her stepfather's sexual molestation; gay teen Harris, whose parents do not accept his sexual orientation; unhappy foster child Dontay; Carmen, who is battling an addiction to drugs; high school basketball star Jason, who struggles between college and his responsibility as the father of Stephie's baby; and Keesha herself. Praised as a "moving" work containing "dramatic monologues that are personal, poetic, and immediate," by *Booklist* contributor Hazel Rochman, *Keesha's House* features sonnet and sestina verse forms that reflect actual speech, making the book easy going for those unfamiliar with poetry. In *Publishers Weekly* a reviewer found the work "thoughtfully composed and ultimately touching," while Michele Winship wrote in *Kliatt* that the poems in *Keesha's House* "weave together stories that depict the harsh reality of teenage life."

A book that "brings to life the voices and spirit of a fifth-grade classroom," according to a *Publishers Weekly* contributor, *Spinning through the Universe* contains poems that reflect the dreams, worries, enthusiasms, and day-to-day lives of Mrs. Williams's twenty-two fifth graders, each of whom composes a poem in a different poetic form. The fictional preteen writers wax poetic about subjects ranging from a lost bicycle to the death of a parent, in what the *Publishers Weekly* critic described as "brief, deceptively casual poetic monologues" that Frost follows with a concluding chapter about reading and writing verse. Forms include haiku, blank verse, sonnets, sestinas, rondelets, and other less-familiar schemes; an entire section devoted to acrostics prompted *School Library Journal* contributor Lee Bock to note that "readers will enjoy decoding them to reveal an additional thought about each character." Bock dubbed *Spinning through the Universe* a "boon for poetry classes," while in *Kirkus Reviews* a critic wrote that Frost's use of "original imagery and understated, natural voices make these poems sensitive and insightful."

Many of Frost's series nonfiction are short books presenting basic facts and information in a minimal text well-illustrated with photographs, maps, diagrams, and other artwork. With approximately twenty sentences per book, volumes such as *A Look at France* in the "Our World" series and *What Are Levers?* in the "Looking at Simple Machines" series are designed for beginning scholars, and incorporate large print and a simple vocabulary to convey rudimentary information. More detail is provided in Frost's contributions to the "Coming to America" series, designed for older readers. Praising Frost's research in *German Immigrants, 1820-1920* as "solid," *Booklist* reviewer Rochman added that the book serves young readers of German and Scandinavian descent as "a good place to start researching family history."

BIOGRAPHICAL AND CRITICAL SOURCES:

PERIODICALS

Booklist, October 15, 2001, Hazel Rochman, review of *German Immigrants, 1820-1920,* p. 406; March 1, 2003, Hazel Rochman, review of *Keesha's House,* p. 1192; April 1, 2004, Hazel Rochman, review of *Spinning through the Universe: A Novel in Poems from Room 214,* p. 1363.
Journal of Adolescent & Adult Literacy, November, 2002, M. P. Cavanaugh, review of *When I Whisper, Nobody Listens: Helping Young People Write about Difficult Issues,* p. 275.
Kirkus Reviews, March 1, 2004, review of *Spinning through the Universe,* p. 221.
Kliatt, March, 2003, Michele Winship, review of *Keesha's House,* p. 10.
Publishers Weekly, May 25, 1990, Penny Kaganoff, review of *Season of Dead Water,* p. 54; April 21, 2003, review of *Keesha's House,* p. 63; April 5, 2004, review of *Spinning through the Universe,* p. 63.
School Library Journal, August, 2000, Pamela K. Bombay, review of *Martin Luther King, Jr. Day,* p. 169; October, 2000, Carolyn Jenks, review of *Drinking Water,* p. 147; January, 2001, Judith Constantinides, review of *Feeling Angry,* p. 117; April, 2001, Dona J. Helmer, review of *The Circulatory System,* p. 130; August, 2001, Blair Christolon, review of *What Are Levers?,* p. 168; September, 2001, Karey Wehner, review of *Moths,* p. 214; December, 2001, Elizabeth Talbot, review of *A Look at Russia,* p. 121; June, 2002, Ann W. Moore, review of *A Look at France,* p. 120; October, 2002, Linda Ludke, review of *A Look at Canada,* p. 144; October, 2003, Jennifer Ralston, review of *Keesha's House,* p. 99; November, 2003, Michele Shaw, review of *Betsy Ross,* p. 125; April, 2004, Lee Bock, review of *Spinning through the Universe,* p. 154; April, 2004, review of *Keesha's House,* p. 64.

ONLINE

Helen Frost Web site, http://home.att.net/~frost-thompson (December 30, 2004).*

FURTADO, Celso (Monteiro) 1920-2004

OBITUARY NOTICE— See index for *CA* sketch: Born July 26, 1920, in Pombal, Paraíba, Brazil; died November 20, 2004, in Rio de Janeiro, Brazil. Economist and author. Furtado was an influential economist who was the key author of Brazil's economic policies during the 1950s and early 1960s. After earning a law degree at the Federal University of Rio de Janeiro in 1944, he went to Europe, where he fought with the Allies as part of the Brazilian Expeditionary Force in Italy. After the war, Furtado completed a Ph.D. degree in economics at the Sorbonne in 1948. The next year, he joined the United Nations Economic Commission for Latin America in Santiago, Chile, serving as an economist there until 1957. During this time, Furtado was greatly influenced by the structuralist school of development, which favored government-directed economies and advocated fair-trade policies between North and South America. In 1958, Furtado became president of the Brazilian Bank of Economic Development, which led to his idea for the formation of the Superintendencia de Desenvolvimento do Nordeste (Sudene). The Sudene was a federal institution that Furtado headed until 1964. He also became Brazil's planning minister in 1962 and as such was largely responsible for developing Brazilian economic policy. But in 1964, the Brazilian government was overthrown by a military coup, and Furtado was forced into exile. During this time, he taught at French and American universities, including Yale and the Sorbonne. In 1979 Furtado became active in politics again as part of the New York City-based United Nations committee for development, and from 1980 until 1985 he was director of associated studies at the École des Hautes Études en Sciences Sociales in Paris. As the government in Brazil returned to democracy, Furtado was allowed to end his exile. He became a member of the Brazilian Democratic Movement's (PMDB) national executive committee, and from 1985 to 1986 was ambassador to the European Community in Brussels. President José Sarney selected him to be the country's culture minister from 1986 until 1988. But Furtado disagreed with the economic course Brazil was taking as it became more and more capitalistic. Instead of staying involved in Brazilian politics, he spent much of the 1990s in international posts. He was a member of UNESCO's world commission on culture and development and a member of the international bioethics committee. After Luis Inacio Lula da Silva was elected Brazil's president in 2002, Furtado was happy to see the reestablishment of Sudene. In 2003, Furtado was elected to the Brazilian Academy of Sciences and nominated for a Nobel prize in economics. He was the author of numerous books about economics, including *Development and Underdevelopment* (1964), *Obstacles to Development in Latin America* (1970), and *No to Recession and Underemployment: An Examination of the Brazilian Economic Crisis* (1985).

OBITUARIES AND OTHER SOURCES:

PERIODICALS

Independent (London, England), November 23, 2004, p. 35.
New York Times, November 27, 2004, p. A16.
Times (London, England), December 15, 2004, p. 52.

G

GABRIEL, Michael P. 1962-

PERSONAL: Born February 23, 1962, in Pittsfield, MA; son of Frederick R. (a radiologist) and Elizabeth B. (a registered nurse) Gabriel; married Sandra Longworth (a magnetic resonance imaging technologist), May 31, 2003. *Education:* Clarion University, B.S., 1984; St. Bonaventure University, M.A., 1988; Pennsylvania State University, Ph.D., 1996. *Politics:* Republican. *Religion:* Roman Catholic. *Hobbies and other interests:* Travel, reading, tennis.

ADDRESSES: Office—Department of History, Kutztown University, Kutztown, PA 19530.

CAREER: University of Pittsburgh—Bradford, Bradford, PA, instructor in history, 1992, 1993-94; Kutztown University, Kutztown, PA, instructor, 1994-96, assistant professor, 1996-2001, associate professor, 2001-04, department chair, 2002—, professor of history, 2004—. National Council on Public History, member.

MEMBER: Organization of American Historians, Pennsylvania Historical Society, New York State Historical Association, Kutztown Area Historical Society (board member, 1997—), First Defenders Civil War Round Table (cofounder).

AWARDS, HONORS: Research fellow, David Library of the American Revolution; research grant, James A. and Ruth B. Neff Historical Foundation.

WRITINGS:

Major General Richard Montgomery, Fairleigh Dickinson University Press (Madison, NJ), 2002.
(Editor, with S. Pascale Dewey) *Quebec during the American Invasion, 1775-1776,* Michigan State University Press (East Lansing, MI), 2005.

Contributor to books, including *History in Dispute: The American Revolution,* Gale (Detroit, MI), 2003. Contributor to periodicals, including *Connecticut Historical Society Bulletin.*

WORK IN PROGRESS: Research on the American Revolution in northern New York and the Battle of Bennington.

SIDELIGHTS: Michael P. Gabriel told *CA:* "I have always loved history. This was given to me by my parents and six older brothers and sisters. Over time, my interests began to focus primarily on United States history, especially the period between 1750 and 1865. Many important developments and issues unfolded during this time, and collectively they helped shape the United States, and continue to do so.

"For me, history is a story, almost like literature, and I think that others find it compelling when that's how it is presented. I try to do this in my writing. I want my students and readers to understand that history is not only important, but it's also really interesting. I hope that they'll want to read more history books and learn new things. I have been influenced by the works of such historians as Francis Parkman, James M. McPherson, Stephen E. Ambrose, and Bernard Bailyn."

*   *   *

GAGLIANI, William D. 1962(?)-

PERSONAL: Born c. 1962, in Kenosha, WI; son of Gilberto Gagliani. *Education:* University of Wisconsin at Milwaukee, M.A., 1986. *Hobbies and other interests:* Progressive rock music, exotic weapons, history.

ADDRESSES: Home—Milwaukee, WI. *Agent*—Jack Byrne, Sternig & Byrne Literary Agency, 2370 South 107th Street, Apt. 4, Milwaukee, WI 53227-2036. *E-mail*—wdg@williamdgagliani.com; tarkusp@execpc.com.

CAREER: Writer. University of Wisconsin at Milwaukee, creative writing and composition teacher, 1985-88; Marquette University, Raynor Memorial Libraries, Milwaukee, stacks supervisor, 1988—.

MEMBER: Horror Writers Association.

AWARDS, HONORS: Darrell Award, Memphis Science-Fiction Association, 1999, for short story "Until Hell Calls Our Names"; Bram Stoker award finalist for outstanding achievement in a first novel, 2004, for *Wolf's Trap.*

WRITINGS:

Wolf's Trap, Yard Dog Press (Alma, AZ), 2003.

Author of numerous book reviews, articles, interviews, and short stories that have appeared in publications, including *Milwaukee Journal Sentinel, Cemetery Dance, Chiaroscuro, Hellnotes, Flesh & Blood, Crimespree, BookPage, Booklovers, Scream Factory, Bare Bones,* and *Horror.* Work included in anthologies, such as *Robert Bloch's Psychos,* Pocket Books; *More Monsters from Memphis,* Hot Biscuit; *Extremes 3: Terror on the High Seas,* and *Extremes 4: Darkest Africa,* both Lone Wolf Publications; *The Asylum,* Volume 2:

The Violent Ward, Dark Tales Publications; *The Black Spiral: Twisted Tales of Terror,* Cyberpulp; *Bubbas of the Apocalypse,* Yard Dog Press; *More Stories That Won't Make Your Parents Hurl,* Yard Dog Press; *The Midnighters Club,* Alphabeta Soup Media; *Tooth and Claw 2,* Lone Wolf Publications; *The Red Red Robin Project,* Lone Wolf; and *Midnight Journeys,* Ozark Triangle Press. Also author of *Shadowplays* (e-book story collection). Author of "Writing Life" column for *Iguana Informer.*

Some of Gaglianai's works have been translated into Italian and Japanese.

WORK IN PROGRESS: Three novels.

SIDELIGHTS: Horror and dark fantasy/noir writer William D. Gagliani told *CA:* that he "prefers writing short stories exploring the dark side of human nature." On his Home Page, Gagliani noted that he has "always appreciated the mores visceral approach to storytelling." He went on to explain his attraction this way: "Partly, the realization that true horror can be the fact that your neighbor is Jeffrey Dahmer. We horror writers don't have to make up that much stuff anymore—it's all out there. We need to reflect it. The randomness of horror. The disgruntled guy with the gun. The child-killer. The molesting priest. The government's games. All this stuff is out there, and we don't need the supernatural to provide us with horror. I like having a supernatural streak . . . but it doesn't have to provide the horror aspect. People do that well enough on their own!"

While Gagliani's short stories have appeared in numerous publications and anthologies over the years, his first novel was published in 2003. *Wolf's Trap* deals with a blend of traditional and Native American lycanthrope mythology and focuses on the story of a werewolf who roams the streets of Milwaukee and the city's northern countryside. The two main characters are Nick Lupo, a tough Milwaukee cop who is also a werewolf, and Martin Stewart, a serial killer who has come to Milwaukee seeking revenge on Lupo, who Stewart thinks killed his sister. Because Stewart is psychotic, simply destroying Lupo is not enough. Instead, Stewart intends to play cat-and-mouse with the detective, murdering a good friend and others before kidnapping a woman Lupo loves in order to lure the detective into the woods for a final showdown.

As for Lupo, he attempts to cope with his lycanthropy partially by barricading himself inside his sound-proofed city apartment or fleeing to a rented cabin in the north woods. Nevertheless, he is not in complete control because stress can bring about his change into the beast, and as a cop he faces stress daily. An adult-oriented novel, *Wolf's Trap* explores themes of duality using characters whose dual natures cripple their lives in various ways.

In an article on *CNN.com,* James Argendeli recommended that readers "tear into . . . Gagliani's first novel," calling it "a hirsute werewolf story that will grab you by the reading jugular and keep you clawing the pages until the story's exciting conclusion." Argendeli, however, warned that the book is not for the young "due to some 'R'-rated adult themes." A *Dark-Echo* online reviewer commented that the book is "written like a screenplay: quick cuts between different points of view, rapid scenes, short chapters, and a tendency toward snappy dialogue." The reviewer felt the book has "some strengths" but thought that it does not achieve either the "depth of character" or the "tight plotting" needed to make it "a strong book." On the other hand, Don D'Ammassa, writing in the *Science Fiction Chronicle,* noted that Gagliani does a "good job of making us care about his protagonist" and recommended the book as a "small press title worth chasing down."

Gagliani told *CA:* "As a child growing up in Italy, my father's sea-faring life opened my eyes to knowledge of the world that I wouldn't have had otherwise. He brought back tales and toys, souvenirs and photographs that piqued my interest in exploration and adventure. Also, I began reading early, before the age of four, and by the time I turned seven I was a life-long fan of Jules Verne and his brand of adventure story. Eventually, more modern science fiction captured my interest, but even now I have a soft spot for the kind of grand adventure Verne wrote.

"Later, the Universal monster movies would make an impact—chief among them *Dracula, The Wolf-Man,* and (believe it or not) *Abbott and Costello Meet Frankenstein.* By 1976 I had certainly read my share of adventurous fiction. Favorites were the works of Ian Fleming, Alistair MacLean, Duncan Kyle, Harry Patterson (Jack Higgins), and Desmond Bagley, among others. On television, I steeped myself in *Kolchak: The Night Stalker, Night Gallery, The Twilight Zone,*

Ghost Story, and every horror-tinged Movie of the Week I could manage to watch. Then a stranger by the name of Stephen King came along. I read *Salem's Lot* during a dark and dreary winter and it scared me thoroughly—yet I couldn't get enough. I had always written short stories in school, some of them so well-received that they were read aloud, but now I knew that I wanted to explore some of the same themes as King.

"In the Eighties, I would read works by more visceral writers of horror such as Richard Laymon, Ray Garton, Jack Ketchum, John Skipp and Craig Spector, Joe Lansdale, David Schow, and Edward Lee, as well as quieter purveyors of the fantastic such as Charles L. Grant, Peter Straub, Matthew J. Costello, and Robert Bloch (author of *Psycho*). I also read a great number of mysteries and crime tales, including those of Lawrence Block, Donald Westlake, Dashiell Hammett, Raymond Chandler, and many other authors in the noir universe. I found that I preferred my mysteries as dark as possible.

"I feel that my style has been to blend the quieter elements of horror along with the more visceral, and then add a dash of high adventure. Indeed, many of my short stories tend to cross genre lines. From the visceral group, however, I learned that horror doesn't have to be supernatural. That we are most afraid of pain and bodily harm, and that evil seems to manifest itself not so much through so-called monsters, but through the monstrous characteristics of other humans: serial killers, mass murderers, abusive relatives, murderous neighbors, and even playground bullies. The 'crossroads' for all these elements is what interests me most, and what I try to write about most.

"The most surprising thing I have learned from being a writer is that creativity is simply not valued in our society. We say it is, but most creative people I know have to struggle to make ends meet. And most cannot make a living being creative. I feel a great sadness when I think about it.

"Like most horror writers, I hope my work will terrify. I hope readers will be taken aback by some of what I write, because I don't believe art should be safe. I feel creative works should elicit a response, even if it's disagreement or even disgust. But I want readers to find themselves thinking about deeper themes, about motivation, and about the dark side within them. I want people to realize that we all have a capacity for evil and hatred, for causing others pain, and I want to explore the reasons human cruelty exists. I want my work to entertain, too, but often I want it to come with a price. I hope people will see layers in my work, but I also hope I'm posing questions worth asking, about what it means to be human—and inhuman."

BIOGRAPHICAL AND CRITICAL SOURCES:

PERIODICALS

Science Fiction Chronicle, December, 2003, Don D'Ammassa, review of *Wolf's Trap,* p. 44.

ONLINE

Allscifi.com, http://allscifi.com/ (November 5, 2004), review of *Wolf's Trap.*
AuthorsDen.com, http://www.authorsden.com/ (November 5, 2004), "William D. Gagliani."
CNN.com, http://www.cnn.com/ (December 15, 2003), James Argendeli, review of *Wolf's Trap.*
DarkEcho.com, http://www.darkecho.com/ (November 5, 2004), review of *Wolf's Trap.*
William D. Gagliani Home Page, http://www. williamdgagliani.com (November 5, 2004).

*   *   *

GANGEMI, Joseph 1970-
(J. G. Passarella, a joint pseudonym)

PERSONAL: Born 1970, in Wilmington, DE; companion of Stacey Himes. *Education:* Swarthmore, B.S., 1992.

ADDRESSES: Home—Philadelphia, PA. *Agent*—Theresa Park, Sanford J. Greenburger and Associates, 55 Fifth Ave., New York, NY 10003. *E-mail*—joegangemi@comcast.net.

CAREER: Independent screenplay writer and novelist, 1998—. Worked variously as a waiter, grant writer, translator, typist, receptionist, and communications consultant for DuPont and Conoco.

AWARDS, HONORS: Bram Stoker Award for first novel (with John Passarella), c. 1999, for *Wither.*

WRITINGS:

(With John Passarella, under joint pseudonym J. G. Passarella) *Wither* (novel), Pocket Books (New York, NY), 1999.
Inamorata (novel), Viking (New York, NY), 2004.

Contributor of short story to fiction anthology *Full Spectrum II,* Bantam Doubleday (New York, NY), 1989.

SCREENPLAYS

(With Jon Cohen) *Crossover,* Interscope Films, 1995.
Black Ice, New Line Cinema, 1997.
Eliza Graves, Icon Productions, 2004.
Into the Mirror, Twentieth Century-Fox, 2004.

Also author of screenplay based on *Salem's Lot,* by Stephen King.

SIDELIGHTS: Joseph Gangemi has become successful both as a screenwriter and novelist. After graduating from Swarthmore College, Gangemi worked at a number of different jobs: translator, receptionist at a detective agency, typist, grant writer, and communications consultant for industry. In 1995, at the suggestion of friend Jon Cohen, he collaborated on the screenplay *Thriller.* Within two years Gangemi had given up his day job to concentrate on writing.

Since he had been an avid science-fiction reader as a child, it comes as no surprise that Gangemi's first novel was a genre piece, the gothic novel *Wither,* which he penned with John Passarella under the joint pseudonym J. G. Passarella. Although Don D'Ammassa, writing in *Science Fiction Chronicle,* complained of the uneven pacing and lack of surprises and a *Publishers Weekly* contributor called the plot "derivative," other reviewers praised the novel. Among its enthusiasts, *Booklist* reviewer Roberta Johnson remarked on its "appealing characters," and *Library Journal* critic Jackie Cassada deemed the book "a good choice for most horror collections." *Wither* won the Bram Stoker award for first novel.

In the early 2000s, while browsing in a Philadelphia gift shop, Gangemi happened across a book on the history of spiritualism in America. This title sparked the idea for his novel *Inamorata,* which centers on spiritualism in the 1920s, in particular the offer by the editors of *Scientific American* of a $5,000 prize to anyone who could find "conclusive psychic manifestations." Gangemi's first-person narrator, Finch, wants to disprove the so-called psychic abilities of Mrs. Crawley, an affluent Philadelphian. Finch finds his efforts thwarted, however, when he falls in love with this would-be medium.

Inamorata elicited qualified praise from reviewers. Although Charles Matthews of the *Chicago Tribune* found the characters underdeveloped and the plot scattered, and Douglas Wolk called Gangemi's similes "ridiculous," other reviewers were more appreciative. *Library Journal* critic Wendy Bethel found Finch's capture of false psychics both "fascinating" and "plain funny," and a *Kirkus Reviews* contributor dubbed *Inamorata* a "more-than-competent first novel." "While the narrative suffers from occasional lapses into a creaky Edwardian prose style and the odd discursive passage in which the author gives in to the temptation to show off his erudition, such peccadilloes are easily forgiven in this otherwise flawless maiden voyage," concluded *Artforum* reviewer Thomas D'Adamo. "Readers footing for an entertaining historical probably won't be disappointed," predicted Jeff Zaleski in *Publishers Weekly.*

By 2004 Gangemi had written a handful of screenplays for a variety of production companies. Regarding the process of becoming a screenplay writer, he told Elizabeth Redden in the *Swarthmore College Bulletin Onlin:* "I'm convinced it takes ten years. . . . It just takes time to figure out what you have to say and develop your craft so you have the ability to say it." He added, "It doesn't really matter what medium you write in. My novel writing has made me a better screenwriter, and my screenwriting has made me a better novel writer."

BIOGRAPHICAL AND CRITICAL SOURCES:

PERIODICALS

Artforum, spring, 2004, Thomas D'Adamo, review of *Inamorata,* p. 51.

Booklist, February 15, 1999, Roberta Johnson, review of *Wither,* p. 1048.
Chicago Tribune, February 3, 2004, Charles Matthews, "Spirts Willing, but Novel's Text Weak," p. 2.
Kirkus Reviews, January 1, 1999, review of *Wither,* p. 13; November 15, 2003, review of *Inamorata,* p. 1328.
Library Journal, February 15, 1999, Jackie Cassada, review of *Wither,* p. 188; February 1, 2004, Wendy Bethel, review of *Inamorata,* p. 122.
Los Angeles Times February 8, 2004, Mark Rozzo, review of *Inamorata,* p. R10.
New York Times Book Review, February 22, 2004, Douglas Wolk, review of *Inamorata,* p. 16.
Publishers Weekly, January 4, 1999, review of *Wither,* p. 74; December 1, 2003, Jeff Zaleski, review of *Inamorata,* p. 39.
Science Fiction Chronicle, April-May, 1999, Don D'Ammassa, review of *Wither,* p. 44.
Washington Post, February 29, 2004, Daniel Stashower, "When the Spirit Moves," p. T8.

ONLINE

BookBrowser.com, http://www.bookbrowse.com/ (September 27, 2004), "Joseph Gangemi Interview."
Joseph Gangemi Home Page, http://www. josephgangemi.com (September 27, 2004).
Swarthmore College Bulletin Online, http://www. swarthmore.edu/bulletin/ (September 27, 2004), Elizabeth Redden, "Storyteller."*

*   *   *

GENIZI, Haim 1934-

PERSONAL: Born August 24, 1934, in Budapest, Hungary; son of Jacob and Sima (Friedman) Genizi; married Elisheva Aharoni (a chemist), January 1, 1960; children: Sima, Shlomit, Jacob, Aaron. *Education:* Bar-Ilan University, B.A. (history), 1960, M.A., 1962; City University of New York, Ph.D., 1968.

ADDRESSES: Home—1 Aluf Simchoni St., Bne-Beraq 51586, Israel; fax: 972-3-677-3204. *Office*—c/o Department of History, Bar-Ilan University, Ramat Gan 52900, Israel. *E-mail*—genizih@mail.biu.ac.il.

CAREER: Bar-Ilan University, Ramat Gan, Israel, senior lecturer, 1972-82, associate professor, 1982-87, professor of general history and American history, 1987-2002, professor emeritus, 2002—, department chair, 1978-81, director of Begin Institute for the Study of Underground and Resistance Movements, 1984-88. Visiting professor at Hebrew University of Jerusalem, 1978-80, Brooklyn College of the City University of New York, 1990-91, and York University, 1995, 1998-99, 2001. High school history teacher in Israel, 1960-88. *Military service:* Nachal-Infantry, Israel, 1953-55.

MEMBER: World Union of Jewish Studies, Israel Association for American Studies, Israel Association for Canadian Studies.

AWARDS, HONORS: Grants from Israeli National Academy of Science, 1973-74, 1975-76, 1978-80, and Memorial Foundation of Jewish Culture, 1985-86; Annual Award for Religious Zionist Literature, 1993; award from Canadian Faculty Enrichment Program, 1994.

WRITINGS:

American Apathy: The Plight of Christian Refugees from Nazism, Bar-Ilan University Press (Ramat Gan, Israel), 1983.

Yoetz Umekim: The Advisor on Jewish Affairs to the American Army and the DPs, 1945-1949 (in Hebrew), Moreshet, Sifriat Hapoalim (Tel Aviv, Israel), 1987.

America's Fair Share: The Admission and Resettlement of the DPs, 1945-1952, Wayne State University Press (Detroit, MI), 1993.

(With Naomi Blank) *Underground for the Sake of Rescue: Bne Akiva in Hungary during the Holocaust* (in Hebrew), Bar-Ilan University Press (Ramat Gan, Israel), 1993.

(Editor) *Religion and Resistance in Mandatory Palestine* (in Hebrew), Moreshet, Sifriat Hapoalim (Tel Aviv, Israel), 1995.

The Rehabilitation of Survivors of Holocaust Children in Hungary: The History of a Religious Youth Village in the Diaspora at Deszk (in Hebrew), Nir Galim, 1998.

The Holocaust, Israel, and Canadian Protestant Churches, McGill-Queen's University Press (Montreal, Quebec, Canada), 2002.

Contributor to books, including *American Experience,* edited by Arnon Gutfeld, Tel Aviv University (Tel Aviv, Israel), 1986; *Remembering for the Future,* Pergamon Press (Oxford, England), 1989; *The Netherlands and Nazi Genocide,* edited by G. Jan Colijn and Marcia S. Littell, Edwin Mellen Press (Lewiston, NY), 1992; *What Have We Learned? Telling the Story and Teaching the Lessons of the Holocaust,* edited by Franklin H. Littell, Alan L. Berger, and H. G. Locke, Edwin Mellen Press (Lewiston, NY), 1993; and *America, American Jews, and the Holocaust,* edited by Jeffrey S. Gurock, Routledge (New York, NY), 1998. Contributor of articles and reviews to periodicals in the United States, Canada, England, and Israel, including *Journal of American Studies, Canadian Journal of History, Labor History, American Jewish History, Jewish Social Studies, Holocaust and Genocide Studies,* and *Journal of Negro History.*

WORK IN PROGRESS: Research on Christian-Jewish dialogue in Canada, 1945-2000.

*   *   *

GHOSE, Indira

PERSONAL: Female. *Education:* Free University of Berlin, Ph.D., 1996.

ADDRESSES: Office—Free University of Berlin, Gosslerstr. 2-4, 14195 Berlin, Germany. *E-mail*—indiraghose@aol.com.

CAREER: Writer and educator. Free University of Berlin, Germany, professor of English.

WRITINGS:

(Editor) *Memsahibs Abroad: Writings by Women Travellers in Nineteenth-Century India,* Oxford University Press (New York, NY), 1998.

Women Travellers in Colonial India: The Power of the Female Gaze, Oxford University Press (New York, NY), 1998.

(Editor and author of introduction and notes, with Sara Mills) Fanny Parkes Parlby, *Wanderings of a Pilgrim in Search of the Picturesque,* Manchester University Press (Manchester, England), 2001.

Editor of *India,* volumes 3 and 5, Pickering and Chatto (London, England), 2002 and 2003 respectively.

SIDELIGHTS: Indira Ghose is an English professor with a strong interest in the writings of "memsahibs," European (mostly English) women who lived and/or traveled in India during its colonial period, when it was ruled by Great Britain. She is the editor of *Memsahibs Abroad: Writings by Women Travellers in Nineteenth-Century India,* which presents the writings of English women who wanted to see the "real India." She also coedited and provided notes and the introduction to *Wanderings of a Pilgrim in Search of the Picturesque,* a book by noted travel writer, diarist, and memsahib Fanny Parkes Parlby.

Ghose turns a critical eye toward the travel writing of memsahibs in her book *Women Travellers in Colonial India: The Power of the Female Gaze.* In the book she writes that her aims are "to help displace the stereotype of the memsahib" and "to draw attention to the contribution these women travellers have made to the genre of travel writing." In the process, Ghose explores gender differences by discussing the different aspects of Indian life that women focused on, as opposed to their male counterparts. The scholarly book also explores concepts of race and empire within the British and Indian context. Among the writers whose work she discusses are well-known travelers such as Emily Eden, Fanny Parks Parlby, and Mary Carpenter, but Ghose also explores the writings of lesser-known women travelers such as Anne Elwood and Frances Isabella Duberly.

Writing in *Victorian Studies,* Ali Behdad felt that in *Women Travellers in Colonial India* Ghose's aims are much more than the author states, namely that she has "a desire to make a theoretically broader claim: that the 'plurality of female gazes' sheds light on the ambivalent web of colonial power relations." Behdad went on to note, "Ghose's book is a contribution to the field of colonial historiography and points to the need for further exploration of the political implications of colonialism's cultural ambivalences." *Journal of Asian Studies* contributor Durba Ghosh commented that the "book charts the complex ways in which European women in India alternately transgressed and maintained gender norms while sustaining and contesting the imperial cause in various ways." Ghosh also noted, "The strength of the book lies in the analysis of the more obscure authors and its extensive quotations of written texts."

BIOGRAPHICAL AND CRITICAL SOURCES:

BOOKS

Ghose, Indira, *Women Travellers in Colonial India: The Power of the Female Gaze,* Oxford University Press (New York, NY), 1998.

PERIODICALS

Journal of Asian Studies, February, 2001, Durba Ghosh, review of *Women Travellers in Colonial India: The Power of the Female Gaze,* p. 264.
Victorian Studies, spring, 2001, Ali Behdad, review of *Women Travellers in Colonial India,* p. 522.

*   *   *

GILBERT, Sheri L.

PERSONAL: Married; children: one son.

ADDRESSES: Home—AZ. *Agent*—c/o Author Mail, Knopf Publishing Group, Random House, 299 Park Avenue, New York, NY, 10171-0002. *E-mail*—sheril gilbert@qwest.net.

CAREER: Writer.

WRITINGS:

The Legacy of Gloria Russell, Alfred A. Knopf (New York, NY), 2004.

SIDELIGHTS: Beginning her authorial career after dedicating several years to her family, Sheri L. Gilbert approached the craft of writing children's books seriously. She studied, wrote, and connected with other writers, ultimately publishing her first book, *The Legacy of Gloria Russell,* in 2004.

Taking place in the Ozarks of Missouri, Gilbert's debut recounts the affect small-town's prejudice has on an unfortunate outsider with the Eastern European last name Satan. After twelve-year-old Billy James Wilkins' best friend, Gloria Russell, dies of an aneurysm, Billy decides to follow the outgoing girl's example and befriends Mr. Satan, a reclusive wood-carver who had also been a friend of Gloria's prior to her death. While his friendship is at first motivated by curiosity as much as anything, Billy gradually comes to appreciate his new friend, as Gloria did, and defends the foreign-born craftsman when suspicions start to circulate among neighbors. "Billy James' grief over the loss of his friend is palpable, and young readers will admire his determination" to defend his friend's memory, stated *Booklist* reviewer Jennifer Mattson, while a *Publishers Weekly* reviewer praised Gilbert's prose as "skillful." In a review for *School Library Journal,* Connie Tyrrell Burns praised the book as an effective coming-of-age novel, adding that *The Legacy of Gloria Russell* is "lyrically written."

BIOGRAPHICAL AND CRITICAL SOURCES:

PERIODICALS

Booklist, May 1, 2004, Jennifer Mattson, review of *The Legacy of Gloria Russell,* p. 1559.

Kirkus Reviews, April 1, 2004, review of *The Legacy of Gloria Russell,* p. 329.

Publishers Weekly, April 5, 2004, review of *The Legacy of Gloria Russell,* p. 62.

School Library Journal, April, 2004, Connie Tyrrell Burns, review of *The Legacy of Gloria Russell,* p. 154.

ONLINE

Sheri L. Gilbert Web site, http://www.sherigilbert.com (January 25, 2005).

*   *   *

GILKEY, Langdon (Brown) 1919-2004

OBITUARY NOTICE— See index for *CA* sketch: Born February 9, 1919, in Chicago, IL; died of meningitis November 19, 2004, in Charlottesville, VA. Theologian, educator, and author. A humanist and pacifist, Gilkey was a leading Protestant theologian who often wrote on issues involving the secularism-versus-religion debate in the modern era. Earning his undergraduate degree from Harvard University in 1940, he was greatly influenced by the beliefs of Reinhold Niebuhr, whom he heard speak at the chapel at Harvard. Traveling to China to teach English in 1940, he was caught off guard the next year by the Japanese invasion. Captured, he spent the next five years in a Japanese interment camp. He later wrote about his experience there in his *Shantung Compound: The Story of Men and Women under Pressure* (1966). With the war over, he went back to school to study international law. Finding the subject not to his taste, however, he switched to theology and completed a Ph.D. at Columbia University in 1954. During the early 1950s, he was a philosophy and religion instructor at Union Theological Seminary in New York City, as well as a lecturer in religion at Vassar College. He then joined the Vanderbilt University faculty as a professor in the Divinity School until 1963. The last phase of his academic career was spent at the University of Chicago, where he was Shailer Matthews Professor of Theology until his 1989 retirement. Liberal-minded, Gilkey was interested in social activism, the civil rights movement, and Eastern religions and philosophies; in the debate between religion and secularism he felt there was no reason why science and religion could not coexist. He was unsympathetic toward people who wished to impose their particular beliefs on school curricula, a movement that was particularly strong in the "Bible Belt" South. Gilkey published numerous thought-provoking theology studies during his lifetime, including *Religion and the Scientific Future: Reflections on Myth, Science, and Theology* (1970), *Society and the Sacred: Toward a Theology of Culture in Decline* (1981), *Creationism on Trial: Evolution and God at Little Rock* (1985), and *Nature, Reality, and the Sacred: The Nexus of Science and Religion* (1993).

OBITUARIES AND OTHER SOURCES:

PERIODICALS

Chicago Tribune, November 22, 2004, section 1, p. 13.

New York Times, November 26, 2004, p. C10.

Washington Post, November 22, 2004, p. B7.

GLENN, Evelyn Nakano 1940-

PERSONAL: Born August 20, 1940, in Sacramento, CA; daughter of Makoto (in business) and Haru (a homemaker; maiden name, Ito) Nakano; married Gary Glenn (a writer), 1962; children: Sara, Antonia, Patrick. *Ethnicity:* "Japanese American." *Education:* University of California at Berkeley, B.A. (psychology, with high honors), 1962; Harvard University, Ph.D. (social psychology), 1971. *Religion:* Buddhist.

ADDRESSES: Home—957 Peralta Ave., Albany, CA 94706. *Office*—Department of Women's Studies, University of California at Berkeley, Berkeley, CA 94720. *E-mail*—englenn@socrates.berkeley.edu.

CAREER: Abt Associates, Cambridge, MA, senior researcher, 1970-71; Boston University, Boston, MA, lecturer, 1971-72, assistant professor of sociology, 1972-84; Florida State University, Tallahassee, associate professor of sociology, 1984-86; State University of New York at Binghamton, professor of sociology, 1986-90; University of California at Berkeley, professor of ethnic studies and women's studies, 1990—, chair, department of women's studies, 1993-95, director, Beatrice Bain Research Group, 2000-02, founding director, Center for Race and Gender, 2001—, humanities research fellow, 1998-99, member of chancellor's committee on raculty renewal in ethnic studies, 1999-2000. Harvard University, lecturer in Extension Division, 1971-73, research affiliate at Radcliffe Institute, 1974; University of Hawaii at Manoa, visiting assistant professor, 1983; Memphis State University, faculty member at Center for Research on Women, 1986; Radcliffe College, visiting research scholar at Murray Research Center, 1989-90; guest speaker at other institutions, including University of Wisconsin at Madison, Cornell University, Wellesley College, Rhode Island College, and University of São Paulo; guest on media programs. Japanese American History Museum, San Francisco, CA, humanist scholar, 1988-89; Japanese American National Museum, Los Angeles, CA, member of board of scholars, 1989—. Massachusetts Office of Science and Technology, member of state advisory board, 1988-90; University of Maryland, member of advisory board for Center for African American Women's Labor Studies, 2001—; Stanford University, member of advisory board for Center for Comparative Studies in Race and Ethnicity, 2001—; Center for Women's Policy Studies, Washington, DC, member of research advisory board; consultant to documentary filmmakers.

MEMBER: American Sociological Association (council member-at-large, 1991-94; chair of Asia and Asian America Section, 2001-02), Society for the Study of Social Problems (chair of editorial and publications committee, 1982-83; member of board of directors, 1984-87; president, 1998-99), Association for Asian American Studies (member of council, 1987-89), Sociologists for Women in Society (national first vice president, 1975-76), Sociological Society for Asia and Asian Americans, Eastern Sociological Society, Massachusetts Sociological Association (president, 1979-80).

AWARDS, HONORS: Grants from National Institute of Mental Health, 1974, 1977-79, 1979-82, Ford Foundation, 1980-82, and American Sociological Association, 1983-84; Letitia Woods Brown Memorial Article Prize, Association of Black Women Historians, 1993, for "From Servitude to Service Work: Historical Continuities in the Racial Division of Paid Reproductive Labor"; Outstanding Alumna Award, Japanese Women Alumnae of University of California—Berkeley, 1994; Nikkei of the Biennium Award for Contributions to Education, Japanese American Citizens League, 1994.

WRITINGS:

(With Christine Bose, Roslyn Feldberg, and Natalie Sokoloff) *Hidden Aspects of Women's Work,* Praeger (New York, NY), 1987.

Issei, Nisei, Warbride: Three Generations of Japanese American Women in Domestic Service, Temple University Press (Philadelphia, PA), 1986.

(Editor, with Grace Chang and Linda Forcey, and contributor) *Mothering: Ideology, Experience, and Agency,* Routledge (New York, NY), 1994.

Unequal Freedom: How Race and Gender Shaped American Citizenship and Labor, Harvard University Press (Cambridge, MA), 2002.

Contributor to books, including *Making an Americas: Immigration, Race, and Ethnicity in the United States, Past and Present,* edited by Sylvia Pedraza and Ruben G. Rumbaut, Wadsworth Press (Belmont, CA), 1995;

America's Women: A Documentary History, 1600 to the Present, edited by Rosalyn Blaxendall and Linda Gordon, W. W. Norton (New York, NY), 1996; *Revisioning Gender,* edited by Judith Lorber, Beth Hess, and Myra Marx Ferree, Sage Publications (Beverly Hills, CA), 1999; *Readings in Black Political Economy,* edited by John Whitehead and Cobie Kwasi Harris, Kendall/Hunt Publishing (Dubuque, IA), 1999; and *The Critical Study of Work: Labor, Technology, and Global Production,* edited by Rick Baldoz, Charles Koeber, and Philip Kraft, Temple University Press (Philadelphia, PA), 2001. Contributor to periodicals, including *Ethnicity, Journal of Marriage and the Family, Review of Radical Political Economy, Stanford Law Review, Signs, Feminist Sociology, Social Science History,* and *Social Problems.* Editor, *Feminist Studies,* 1999—; deputy editor, *American Sociological Review,* 1999—; member of editorial board, *Race and Society,* 1996—, and *Contemporary Sociology,* 1997-2000; advisory editor, *Gender and Society,* 1986-90, and *Frontiers,* 1991—; newsletter editor, Sociologists for Women in Society, 1975-76.

*   *   *

GOLDBERG, Harold

PERSONAL: Male.

ADDRESSES: Agent—c/o Author Mail, William Morrow/HarperCollins, 10 East 53rd St., New York, NY 10022.

CAREER: Journalist.

WRITINGS:

(With Helen Morrison) *My Life among the Serial Killers: Inside the Minds of the World's Notorious Murderers,* William Morrow (New York, NY), 2004.

Contributor to periodicals, including *New York Times Book Review, Vanity Fair,* and *Entertainment Weekly.*

SIDELIGHTS: Harold Goldberg cowrote *My Life among the Serial Killers: Inside the Minds of the World's Most Notorious Murderers* with Helen Morri-

son, a forensic psychiatrist who has worked with law enforcement in solving some of the most gruesome and bloody criminal cases of our time. She shares the details of eighty of these, including the most notorious.

They include Richard Otto Macek, dubbed the "Mad Biter," who chewed on his victims' body parts, Atlanta child killer Wayne Williams, and rapist turned murderer Bobby Joe Long. Other criminals include Rosemary and Fred West, of England, who killed girls and women, and Brazilian child killer Marcelo Costa de Andrade. Morrison also interviewed Ed Gein, who was film director Alfred Hitchcock's inspiration for *Psycho,* just before Gein's death.

Morrison feels that a serial killer is destined to commit his crimes from the time he/she begins to form as a fetus. She notes that John Wayne Gacy, who killed thirty-three males, had the emotional development of an infant. Gacy asked Morrison to take his brain after he was executed, which she did, along with other organs, for study. Pathologists found nothing extraordinary about Gacy's brain, which Morrison keeps locked in her basement. A *Kirkus Reviews* contributor called the book "a scary piece of work, with even scarier implications."

BIOGRAPHICAL AND CRITICAL SOURCES:

PERIODICALS

Kirkus Reviews, March 15, 2004, review of *My Life among the Serial Killers: Inside the Minds of the World's Most Notorious Murderers,* p. 260.
Library Journal, April 15, 2004, Tim Delaney, review of *My Life among the Serial Killers,* p. 103.
Publishers Weekly, April 5, 2004, review of *My Life among the Serial Killers,* p. 56.

ONLINE

Nthposition Online, http://www.nthposition.com/ (November 5, 2004), Seamus Sweeney, review of *My Life among the Serial Killers.**

*   *   *

GORE, Patrick Wilson 1938-
(Rob Wilson)

PERSONAL: Born May 27, 1938; son of Geoffrey (a schoolmaster) and Margaret (Wilson) Gore; married (divorced); children: Louise, Richard. *Education:* University of Oxford, B.A., 1962; M.A., 1966.

ADDRESSES: Office—P.O. Box 573, Perth, Ontario K7H 3K4, Canada.

CAREER: Writer and journalist. Associated Press, Columbus, OH, editor, 1968-69; Humber College, Toronto, Ontario, Canada, assistant chairman, 1969-73; North Frontier Communications, Perth, Ontario, president, 1971-87. *Military service:* Commissioned in British and Canadian forces Royal Air Force, Royal Marine Commando Reserve; paratrooper; Green Beret.

MEMBER: Canadian Intelligence and Security Association, Canadian Institute of Strategic Studies, National Defence College Association.

WRITINGS:

(As Rob Wilson) *Escape from Marrakesh,* Simon & Pierre (Toronto, Ontario, Canada), 1983.
(As Rob Wilson) *Frame-up in Belize,* Simon & Pierre (Toronto, Ontario, Canada), 1985.
And Death in Erin, Writers Club Press (Lincoln, NE), 2000.
Bolivar's Right Hand, Writers Club Press (Lincoln, NE), 2001.
In the Month of Muharram, Writers Club Press (Lincoln, NE), 2001.
Jango Says, Writers Club Press (Lincoln, NE), 2001.
Staggerbush: A Story of the New Millenium, Writers Club Press (Lincoln, NE), 2001.
The Gold Miner of Magadan, Writers Club Press (Lincoln, NE), 2001.

SIDELIGHTS: Patrick Wilson Gore told *CA:* "My main interest is in what George Orwell called 'unofficial history.' I bring to bear the skills of an Oxford-trained historian, honed by years in military intelligence and international journalism, to produce accounts of what may have happened in those shady areas where the laws of libel and the reticence KGB and CIA alike make the work of the conventional historian impossible. While my primary task is to entertain the reader, I hope that the information and insights I share may broaden his understanding of what is really going on in the world. I am a citizen of three countries. I have travelled in fifty countries and lived and worked in three continents."

BIOGRAPHICAL AND CRITICAL SOURCES:

PERIODICALS

Canadian Book Review Annual, 1982.

GRAHAM, Dominick S(tuart) 1920-

PERSONAL: Born July 24, 1920, in Somerset, England; son of Fergus Reginald Winsford and Egeria Marion Spottiswood (Baker) Graham; married Mary Lady Bell, September 16, 1991; children: Anita Caroline, Patricia Robin. *Education:* University of New Brunswick, B.A., M.A., 1962; University of London, Ph.D., 1969. *Hobbies and other interests:* Skiing, sailing, travel, gardening, chess.

ADDRESSES: Home—The Hollis, East Rounton, Northallerton, North Yorkshire DL6 2LG, England.

CAREER: St. John High School, St. John, New Brunswick, Canada, mathematics teacher; University of New Brunswick, New Brunswick, military history professor, 1964-86, department of national defense chair for military studies, 1971-86, founder of Centre for Conflict Studies, 1980, professor emeritus, 1986—. Visiting lecturer at Canadian and U.S. military colleges. Member of history advisory committee, U.S. Air Force. Participated in 1956 Winter Olympics in cross country skiing. *Military service:* British Armed Forces, 1939-58; during World War II served in Battle of Britain, Norway, Normandy, and the Rhineland; prisoner of war, 1942-43; awarded Military Cross.

MEMBER: Army and Navy Club, Pall Mall Club.

AWARDS, HONORS: Norwegian Ski Council Award, Canadian Ski Marathon, 1986.

WRITINGS:

Cassino, Ballantine Books (New York, NY), 1971.
(With Shelford Bidwell) *Fire-Power: British Army Weapons and Theories of War, 1904-1945,* Allen & Unwin (Boston, MA), 1982.
(With Shelford Bidwell) *Tug of War: The Battle for Italy, 1943-1945,* St. Martin's (New York, NY), 1986.
(With Shelford Bidwell) *Coalitions, Politicians, and Generals: Some Aspects of Command in Two World Wars,* Brassey's (London, England), 1993.
The Price of Command: A Biography of General Guy Simmonds, Stoddart (Toronto, Ontario, Canada), 1993.

Against Odds: Reflections on the Experiences of the British Army, 1914-1945, St. Martin's (New York, NY), 1999.

SIDELIGHTS: Dominick S. Graham began his military career at the age of nineteen when he joined the British army. Serving during World War II, he participated in the Battle of Britain and became a prisoner of war in 1942, escaping the following year. Twice wounded, his heroics during the war earned him the Military Cross. Retiring from military service in 1958, Graham went on to study military history. While working toward his doctorate, he began a professional association with the University of New Brunswick that has lasted through much of his academic career. Teaching undergraduate and graduate courses in history, he also became director of the university's military and strategic studies program in the 1970s, founded its Centre for Conflict Studies, and published a number of academic works on military history.

Graham's *Tug of War: The Battle for Italy, 1943-1945,* written with Shelford Bidwell, explores the contentious relationships between British and American commanders during the Allied campaign against Italy in World War II. The authors analyze the personalities and styles of Dwight D. Eisenhower, the leader of the Allied forces in Europe, and Sir Harold Alexander, the British commander in chief. Pointing out the men's shared qualities, the authors comment that "neither could make a military plan and stick to it through political and military vicissitudes." In presenting their theories, Graham and Bidwell cite a wide range of documentary sources, including German war diaries, recorded interviews with German generals, and the previously unpublished journal of General Kirkman of the 13th Corps. Reviewing *Tug of War* for the *Times Literary Supplement,* Raleigh Trevelyan wrote, "Their exhaustive researches give a good idea of how no battle can follow textbook rules, and how so much depends on the unexpected, and indeed on the caliber of ordinary fighting men."

Coalitions, Politicians, and Generals: Some Aspects of Command in Two World Wars, also written with Bidwell, is a collection of essays that touch on the subject of technology's influence on military decision making during the period 1914 to 1945. One notable piece, "Logistics: Neglect and Mischief," focuses on the topics of the interplay of politics and logistic mistakes

experienced by American commanders during World War II. Theodore A. Wilson, a reviewer for the *Journal of Military History,* cited both positive and negative aspects of this collection, writing that it "is marked by penetrating observation, occasional disregard for the context in which policies developed, [and] arguments skewed by dependence on a limited range of archival documents, and well-aimed salvos of vituperation."

In *Against Odds: Reflections on the Experiences of the British Army, 1914-1945,* Graham presents a critical reflection from the distance of some fifty years on the actions of the British army during the two world wars. Glyn Harper commented in the *Journal of Military History* that while the "factual framework unfortunately contains many errors that spoil the book's overall worth . . . there are many things to like about the book," adding that Graham's "reflections on the Montgomery/Eisenhower/Bradley relationship should promote further debate and this is to be welcomed."

BIOGRAPHICAL AND CRITICAL SOURCES:

BOOKS

Graham, Dominick S., and Shelford Bidwell, *Tug of War: The Battle for Italy, 1943-1945,* St. Martin's (New York, NY), 1986.

PERIODICALS

American Historical Review, February, 1989, M. Van Crevel, review of *Tug of War: The Battle for Italy, 1943-1945,* p. 78.
Journal of Military History, January, 1996, Theodore A. Wilson, review of *Coalitions, Politicians, and Generals: Some Aspects of Command in Two World Wars,* pp. 167-169; January, 2000, Glyn Harper, review of *Against Odds: Reflections on the Experiences of the British Army, 1914-1945,* p. 219.
Library Journal, June 15, 1986, Dennis Showalter, review of *Tug of War,* p. 66.
New York Times, August 17, 1986, Hal Goodman, review of *Tug of War,* p. 23.
New York Times Book Review, August 17, 1986, Hal Goodman, review of *Tug of War,* p. 23.

Publishers Weekly, June 13, 1986, Genevieve Stuttaford, review of *Tug of War,* p. 229.

Times Literary Supplement, January 23, 1987, Raleigh Trevelyan, review of *Tug of War,* p. 78.*

*   *   *

GRANT, Michael Johnston 1961-

PERSONAL: Born April 27, 1961, in Sidney, NE; son of Martin (a farmer) and Frances (a homemaker; maiden name, Johnston) Grant. *Ethnicity:* "White." *Education:* University of Nebraska, Lincoln, B.A., 1983; University of Kansas, M.A., 1993, Ph.D., 1999. *Politics:* Democrat. *Religion:* Catholic. *Hobbies and other interests:* Cycling, hiking, biking, gardening, reading.

ADDRESSES: Office—Kentucky Department of Agriculture, 500 Mero St., Seventh Floor, Frankfort, KY 40601. *E-mail*—michaeljgrant@yahoo.com.

CAREER: Kentucky Department of Agriculture, Frankfort, affiliate. Worked for both state and federal government agencies; instructor in history; public speaker; consultant on grant-writing. Also community volunteer.

MEMBER: National Grant Managers Association, Phi Alpha Theta.

WRITINGS:

Down and out on the Family Farm: Rural Rehabilitation in the Great Plains, 1929-1945, University of Nebraska Press (Lincoln, NE), 2002.

Contributor to multimedia teaching curricula. Contributor to *Kansas History.*

WORK IN PROGRESS: Research on the role of agriculture in global power and stability.

SIDELIGHTS: Michael Johnston Grant told *CA:* "I write about agricultural history because I have a deep love for rural America and what makes it unique. For decades the number of farm families has decreased, and the proportion of national income and work force related to agricultural life has declined in the United States. The impact of farm life on national culture has receded. Still, agricultural and rural America are very relevant to the nation, and I try to express and explore their importance.

"I admire writers such as Donald Worster and Wendell Berry for the questions they ask. They challenge readers to question the moral significance of modern-day United States agriculture and rural life. They recognize that America has been blessed by rich environmental resources and ask questions such as: what have we done with such wealth in natural resources? Particularly they ask: what kind of world have farmers, ranchers, and agribusiness built in modern America?

"I also admire historical insights on the interplay between culture, religion, and politics by Lawrence Levine, Catherine M. Stock, and of course, Richard Hofstadter. Finally, I appreciate the high level of scholarship by multi-disciplinary historians of the American frontier such as John Mack Faragher and Richard White."

BIOGRAPHICAL AND CRITICAL SOURCES:

PERIODICALS

Journal of American History, June, 2004, Catherine McNicol Stock, review of *Down and out on the Family Farm: Rural Rehabilitation in the Great Plains, 1929-1945,* p. 285.

*   *   *

GRAY, Robert (Curtis) 1945-

PERSONAL: Born February 23, 1945, in Coffs Harbour, New South Wales, Australia.

ADDRESSES: Agent—c/o Author Mail, Angus & Robertson, 1/1 Talavera Road, North Ryde, New South Wales 2113, Australia.

CAREER: Poet and writer. Has worked variously as a book shop salesperson, advertising copy writer, magazine writer and editor, and reviewer. Worked for

Sydney Morning Herald, Sydney, New South Wales, Australia; writer-in-residence at universities in Australia and at Meiji University, Tokyo, Japan.

AWARDS, HONORS: Literature Board of Australia, senior fellowships; Marten Bequest traveling scholarship, 1982; Adelaide Arts Festival National Poetry Award, New South Wales Premier's Award for poetry, and Grace Leven Poetry Prize, all 1986, all for *Selected Poems, 1963-1983;* Patrick White Award, 1990; Victorian Premier's Literary Award, for *Certain Things;* Poetry Book of the Year, *Age,* and Victorian Premiers Prize for Poetry, both 2002, both for *Afterimages.*

WRITINGS:

POETRY

Introspect, Retrospect, Lyre-Bird Writers (Sydney, New South Wales, Australia), 1970.

Creekwater Journal, University of Queensland Press (St. Lucia, Queensland, Australia), 1974.

Grass Script, Angus & Robertson (Sydney, New South Wales, Australia), 1978.

The Skylight, Angus & Robertson (Sydney, New South Wales, Australia), 1983.

Selected Poems, 1963-1983, Angus & Robertson (North Ryde, New South Wales, Australia), 1985, revised and expanded version published as *Selected Poems* ("Modern Poets" series), 1990.

Piano, Angus & Robertson (North Ryde, New South Wales, Australia), 1988.

Certain Things, William Heinemann Australia (Port Melbourne, Victoria, Australia), 1993.

New and Selected Poems ("Poetry" series), William Heinemann Australia (Port Melbourne, Victoria, Australia), 1995.

Lineations, Duffy & Snellgrove (Potts Point, New South Wales, Australia), 1996.

New Selected Poems, Duffy & Snellgrove (Potts Point, New South Wales, Australia), 1998.

Afterimages, Duffy & Snellgrove (Potts Point, New South Wales, Australia), 2002.

EDITOR

(With Geoffrey Lehmann) *The Younger Australian Poets* (anthology), Hale & Iremonger (Sydney, New South Wales, Australia), 1983.

(With Graeme Sturgeon and Christopher Gentle) *Alun Leach-Jones,* Craftsman House (Roseville, New South Wales, Australia), 1988.

(With Geoffrey Lehmann) *Australian Poetry in the Twentieth Century,* William Heinemann Australia (Port Melbourne, Victoria, Australia), 1991.

(With Vivian Smith) *Sydney's Poems: A Selection on the Occasion of the City's One Hundred and Fiftieth Anniversary 1842-1992,* Primavera Press (Leichhardt, New South Wales, Australia), 1992.

(And author of introduction) John Shaw Neilson *Selected Poems* ("Modern Poets" series), Angus & Robertson (Pymble, New South Wales, Australia), 1993.

SIDELIGHTS: Australian poet Robert Gray employs a broad range of styles, from haiku-like three-line poems to his free verse tributes to nature and spiritualism. In his poem "A Testimony," he writes that there is "a substance to things, which is ungraspable, unbounded. It is divided and passed on, like a secret inheritance." Gray captures precise images, supple rhythms, humanity, and warmth in his poems, which are now enjoyed outside of his native Australia.

Gray grew up on the coast of New South Wales and moved to Sydney in the 1960s. He has worked at many jobs, nearly all of which are writing-related, while creating his poetry and editing and collecting the works of others. In addition to his poems of nature, he has written critically acclaimed narratives such as "Flames and Dangling Wire," about a trip to the dump, and "Diptych," which paints a portrait of his parents.

A *Contemporary Poets* contributor noted that "Gray's interest in Eastern religions is embodied in poems written directly about historical figures." These include "To the Master Dogen Zenji." "Other poems infuse Buddhism and Taoism into the Australian landscape," continued the writer. "An example is the long poem 'Dharma Vehicle' from *Grass Script,* in which episodes of landscapes merge with quotations or incidents from the lives of sages."

Writing in *Quadrant,* as quoted on the *Duffy & Snellgrove* Web site, Jamie Grant called "Flames and Dangling Wire" "an exceptional achievement. Few poets could have taken such an unpromising setting and drawn from it a connected sequence of ideas which takes in the theory of evolution, aspects of theology, nineteenth-century painting, and ideas about the future, before returning to the poignantly realised scene, somewhere in the unnamed person's past, which the final stanza sketches with deft economy."

In an interview with *Southerly* contributor Barbara Williams, also reprinted on the *Duffy & Snellgrove* Web site, Gray commented on "Diptych," revealing that his parents, "like the panels of a diptych, were forever separated while in proximity. In a way I was fortunate they were so different: I was able to see the inadequacies of both their extreme temperaments. Maybe that's the origin of the underlying attitude of my poems, which I've realized is a dialectical one." "I admire some things about both my parents," continued Gray. "All through my poems there is, subtly I hope, a consciousness of the interdependence of opposites, and an acceptance or reconciling of these. I will leave it to the critics, however, to discover the extent and the significance of this."

In reviewing *New Selected Poems* in *Quadrant,* Stephen McInerney named eight poems by Gray that he considers "as among the finest written in English in the last fifty years." They include "A Day at Bellingen," "Bringing the Cattle," "Bondi," "Curriculum Vitae," "The Life of a Chinese Poet," and "A Sight of Proteus." McInerney noted that the last "is an allegory of Gray's own life and work; it exemplifies and describes those qualities that will endear him to poetry lovers for generations."

With *New Selected Poems,* Gray has assembled individual collections, including *The Skylight,* which McInerney considered to be one of the greatest collections of poetry to be published in three decades. In a review of *The Skylight* for the *Sydney Morning Herald,* reprinted on the *Duffy & Snellgrove* Web site, Kevin Hart wrote of the underlying philosophy of this collection. Hart said that Gray's Taoism (a Chinese religious and philosophical system) brings "him to the view that the ego is an illusion, and that true happiness is to be found only 'in the contemplation of matter,' a position he associates with [Communist founder Karl] Marx."

McInerney commented on Gray's influence on the work of fellow poets Jamie Grant, Philip Hodgins, and Jemal Sharah, "though it seems unlikely that any poet attentive to natural landscapes in the future, be that landscape Australian or not, will be able to completely free himself from the echo of Gray's voice. Robert Gray is part of the landscape, like a pool of water that contains the landscape it is contained by."

BIOGRAPHICAL AND CRITICAL SOURCES:

BOOKS

Contemporary Poets, St. James Press (Detroit, MI), 2001.
Spurr, Barry, *The Poetry of Robert Gray,* Pascal Press (Glebe, New South Wales, Australia), 1995.

PERIODICALS

Quadrant, March, 2002, Stephen McInerney, review of *New Selected Poems,* p. 84.

ONLINE

Duffy & Snellgrove Web site, http://www.duffyandsnell grove.com.au/ (November 8, 2004), "Reading Group and Teachers' Notes: The Poetry of Robert Gray."

*   *   *

GREENWALD, Marilyn S. 1954-

PERSONAL: Born September 15, 1954, in Cleveland, OH; daughter of Louis (an employee of East Ohio Gas Co.) and Dorothy (a writer and newspaper columnist) Greenwald; married Timothy Doulin, August 6, 1988. *Education:* Ohio State University, B.A., 1975, M.A., 1984, Ph.D., 1991. *Hobbies and other interests:* Running, film.

ADDRESSES: Office—E. W. Scripps School of Journalism, Scripps Hall, Room 230, Ohio University, Athens, OH 45701. *E-mail*—greenwal@ohio.edu.

CAREER: Journalist and educator. *Telegraph,* Painesville, OH, copy editor, entertainment editor, 1976-78; *Columbus Citizen-Journal,* Columbus, OH, business and news reporter, 1978-85; *Columbus Dispatch,* Columbus, business reporter, 1986-87; Ohio University, Athens, professor of journalism, 1987—.

MEMBER: Society of Professional Journalists, Association for Education in Journalism and Mass Communication.

AWARDS, HONORS: Awards from Ohio Newspaper Women's Association, Ohio UPI, and Scripps Howard newspapers, 1980-86; Ohio State University Women's Studies Center grant, 1989; Ohio University Challenge grant, and College of Communications matching grant, 1991; Freedom Forum grant, 1996; Distinguished Service Award, Central Ohio chapter, Society of Professional Journalists, 1998; Ohioana Library Book Award, 1999; Sigma Delta Chi Award for Research in Journalism, 2001.

WRITINGS:

(With Ralph Izard) *Public Affairs Reporting: The Citizen's News,* William C. Brown (Dubuque, IA), 1991.
A Woman of the Times: Journalism, Feminism, and the Career of Charlotte Curtis, Ohio University Press (Athens, OH), 1999.
(Editor, with Joseph Bernt) *The Big Chill: Investigative Reporting in the Current Media Environment* (anthology), Iowa State University Press (Ames, IA), 2000.
The Secret of the Hardy Boys: Leslie McFarlane and the Stratemeyer Syndicate, Ohio University Press (Athens, OH), 2004.

Contributor to books, including *Communication, Value, and the Public Interest,* Ablex, 1991. Contributor to periodicals, including *Journalism History, Newspaper Research Journal, Longterm View,* and *CompuServe* magazine.

WORK IN PROGRESS: Research of representation of women in newspapers, representation of gays and lesbians in newspapers, role of gays and lesbians in the newsroom, and status of investigative reporting in journalism today.

SIDELIGHTS: Journalist and educator Marilyn S. Greenwald is the author of several volumes, including *A Woman of the Times: Journalism, Feminism, and the*

Career of Charlotte Curtis. Curtis (1928-1987) was first a society reporter with the *New York Times,* then rose to become editor of the op-ed page. She was the first woman to appear on the newspaper's masthead and was often the only woman in a room full of men. At the peak of her career, she was considered one of the most powerful women in America. Greenwald studies /curtis's rise to prominence, and ultimately her fall, when her responsibilities were narrowed to writing a weekly column. *Washington Monthly* writer Emily Yoffe wrote that "one of the best parts of the book is the portrait of the early life of Curtis's mother, Lucile, who was a suffragist and the first woman foreign service officer."

At the age of twenty five, the Vassar educated Curtis ended her unsatisfactory marriage to concentrate on her career, writing for the women's pages of the *Columbus Citizen* in Ohio. Ten years later, she followed a colleague with whom she was having an affair to New York and found a job as a home furnishings writer with the *New York Times.* Although she had wanted to write news, she became a society writer, covering the glamorous New York scene.

When the landmark sex discrimination suit was filed against the *Times,* Curtis did not join, citing the fact that she was now in management, but many of the women concluded that her promotion to op-ed editor was a reward for her decision. Curtis, who had broken her own ground, was ambivalent about the feminist movement, which cost her friendships and the respect of female colleagues. But although she was a successful female journalist, Greenwald demonstrates that management was stingy with its compliments and rewards for the "New Journalism" style Curtis brought to their pages. She was forbidden from writing about politics in her final column, and she instead concentrated on profiling business leaders and entrepreneurs. *Columbia Journalism Review* editor James Boylan wrote that Curtis, who died from breast cancer, told a young Anna Quindlen, "You will only have as much power as they wish you to have. . . . Do the best you can for yourself and for other women and don't blame yourself if that's not enough." *Library Journal's* Kay Meredith Dusheck praised *A Woman of the Times* not only as a biography but because it "offers a glimpse of journalism and workplace attitudes in historical perspective."

Greenwald and Joseph Bernt coedited *The Big Chill: Investigative Reporting in the Current Media Environ-*

ment. The collection suggests that investigative reporting is being excluded from contemporary journalism. In another *Columbia Journalism Review* piece, James Boylan felt that the articles with the most value "are those that address specific legal threats facing investigative reporters."

In *The Secret of the Hardy Boys: Leslie McFarlane and the Stratemeyer Syndicate,* Greenwald documents the origination of the book series. The named author, Franklin W. Dixon, was in fact a fiction; Canadian journalist Leslie McFarlane wrote the first sixteen novels using formulaic outlines supplied by New Jersey book packager Edward Stratemeyer, who wished to market to adolescent boys. McFarlane, who aspired to becoming a novelist, considered this hack writing, and consequently never sought or received remuneration of a level that was appropriate to the popularity of the series. He eventually found success in broadcast writing and directing. Stratemeyer expanded his empire with other series that included "Nancy Drew" and the "Bobbsey Twins." *Booklist* contributor Bill Ott called *The Secret of the Hardy Boys* "a fascinating slice of publishing history and a lease on life for Franklin W. Dixon fans."

Greenwald told *CA:* "I became interested in women's biography after doing initial research into representation of women in the media. Almost by chance, I read of the death of Charlotte Curtis, a prominent woman editor at the *New York Times,* and knew she was from Ohio, where I live. After some initial research, I found she had been a pioneering journalist and editor—one of the earliest women to be a news manager at the *Times.* She had such an interesting life that the biography I wrote of her nearly wrote itself.

"I learned that, indeed, fact is frequently more interesting than fiction, and to always have faith in the subjects of my writing. If subjects appear to be interesting to you, they will be interesting to readers.

"I also learned that writing is a laborious process and it usually cannot be hurried. I spent several hours a day for many months writing the biography of Curtis, and even more time writing and rewriting. I usually ran out of steam after about four hours each day. If I continued after that, my writing became labored and forced. But, ultimately, I believe my patience was rewarded."

BIOGRAPHICAL AND CRITICAL SOURCES:

PERIODICALS

Booklist, May 15, 1999, Vanessa Bush, review of *A Woman of the Times: Journalism, Feminism, and the Career of Charlotte Curtis,* p. 1644; May 1, 2004, Bill Ott, review of *The Secret of the Hardy Boys: Leslie McFarlane and the Stratemeyer Syndicate,* p. 503.
Charlotte Observer, August 20, 2004, Mark I. West, review of *The Secret of the Hardy Boys.*
Chronicle of Higher Education, August 13, 2004, Kendra Nichols, review of *The Secret of the Hardy Boys.*
Cleveland Plain Dealer, October 31, 2004, James F. Sweeney, review of *The Secret of the Hardy Boys.*
Columbia Journalism Review, May, 1999, James Boylan, review of *A Woman of the Times,* p. 67; March, 2000, James Boylan, review of *The Big Chill: Investigative Reporting in the Current Media Environment,* p. 71.
Columbus Dispatch, July 20, 2004, Margaret Quamme, review of *The Secret of the Hardy Boys.*
Library Journal, April 15, 1999, Kay Meredith Dusheck, review of *A Woman of the Times,* p. 108.
National Review, November 8, 2004, S. T. Kanick, review of *The Secret of the Hardy Boys.*
New Yorker, November 8, 2004, Meghan O'Rourke, review of *The Secret of the Hardy Boys.*
Nieman Reports, fall, 1999, Maria Henson, review of *A Woman of the Times,* p. 67.
Publishers Weekly, April 12, 1999, review of *A Woman of the Times,* p. 68; May 31, 2004, review of *The Secret of the Hardy Boys,* pp. 63-64.
Washington Monthly, September, 1999, Emily Yoffe, review of *A Woman of the Times,* p. 51.
Wisconsin Bookwatch, September, 2004, review of *The Secret of the Hardy Boys.*

*   *   *

GRIEST, Stephanie Elizondo 1974-

PERSONAL: Born 1974. *Education:* University of Texas, Austin, received degrees in journalism and post-Soviet studies, 1997.

ADDRESSES: Agent—c/o Author Mail, Random House, 1745 Broadway, New York, NY 10019. *E-mail*—stephanie@aroundthebloc.com.

CAREER: Former editor and journalism instructor for *China Daily;* Associated Press, Austin, TX, former political reporter; former reporter for *Odyssey* (nonprofit education Web site); Youth Free Expression Network, New York, NY, former coordinator; Free Expression Project, former spokesperson.

MEMBER: Phi Beta Kappa.

AWARDS, HONORS: Honors and scholarships from *El Andar, USA Today,* National Forum of Hispanic Journalists, Freedom Forum, Network of Hispanic Communicators, Headliners Foundation, Pan-American Golf Writer's Association, Scripps-Howard, National Hispanic Scholarship Fund, and University of Texas, Austin School of Journalism; Ragdale Foundation residency, 2003.

WRITINGS:

Around the Bloc: My Life in Moscow, Beijing, and Havana, Villard (New York, NY), 2004.

Contributor to periodicals, including *Washington Post, Latina, New York Times, Seattle Post-Intelligencer,* and *Texas Triangle,* and to "Travelers' Tales" guides.

SIDELIGHTS: Stephanie Elizondo Griest has written for newspapers and magazines on such subjects as belly dancing, filmmaking, and religious cults, and she also traveled through forty-two states gathering history for the nonprofit, educational Web site *Odyssey.* Beginning in 1996, Griest pursued her dream to become a foreign correspondent by traveling to Moscow with a group of students; there she learned the language and began her four-year tour of twenty-one countries, twelve of them in the Communist bloc. She went to Beijing, where she worked for the English-language version of *China Daily,* and on another occasion, she visited Cuba.

In *Around the Bloc: My Life in Moscow, Beijing, and Havana,* Griest writes primarily of the three cities of the title. "The value of all this comes down to Griest getting off the beaten track, which she does often enough to keep the pages turning," noted a *Kirkus Reviews* writer. She recalls her experience as a journalist in China and about the care taken in writing about controversial subjects. She worked in a children's shelter in Moscow, and learned about the consumption habits of alcohol and food in each country. In Cuba, she focused on the culture, particularly the dances. A *Publishers Weekly* contributor said that Griest "doesn't flinch from depicting the brutal effects of authoritarianism and economic decline, or how her experiences hastened her political and emotional maturity."

Steven E. Alford wrote in the *Houston Chronicle* that this is "definitely a young person's book, chronicling as it does boyfriends, nights of drunkenness, and lots of dancing. Readers may also be struck by Griest's capacity to empathize with peoples we've been instructed to hate. But therein lies the charm of the story: a smart, daring, accomplished single woman ready to thoughtfully explore other countries and draw her own independent conclusions." *Booklist* contributor Janet St. John felt that Griest "is a fine observer, open to experiences and frank in expression, and she certainly is entertaining."

BIOGRAPHICAL AND CRITICAL SOURCES:

PERIODICALS

Booklist, March 1, 2004, Janet St. John, review of *Around the Bloc: My Life in Moscow, Beijing, and Havana,* p. 1127.
Houston Chronicle, April 4, 2004, Steven E. Alford, review of *Around the Bloc,* p. 18.
Kirkus Reviews, January 1, 2004, review of *Around the Bloc,* p. 23.
Library Journal, March 1, 2004, Alison Hopkins, review of *Around the Bloc,* p. 96.
Publishers Weekly, January 5, 2004, review of *Around the Bloc,* p. 48.

ONLINE

Stephanie Elizondo Griest Home Page, http://www.aroundthebloc.com (August 22, 2004).*

*   *   *

GRIFFIN-PIERCE, Trudy 1949-

PERSONAL: Born December 27, 1949, in Spartanburg, SC; daughter of Benjamin Tillman, Jr. (a military officer) and Trudy (a homemaker; maiden name, Owens) Griffin; married A. Keith Pierce (a solar astronomer), December 27, 1979. *Ethnicity:* "Native

American." *Education:* Florida State University, B.F.A., 1970; University of Arizona, Ph.D., 1987. *Politics:* Democrat. *Religion:* Unity. *Hobbies and other interests:* Hiking, sewing, painting.

ADDRESSES: Office—Department of Anthropology, University of Arizona, Tucson, AZ 85721.

CAREER: Indian Pueblo Cultural Center, Albuquerque, NM, curator, 1975; Kitt Peak National Observatory, curator, 1976-77; University of Arizona, Tucson, adjunct faculty, 1987-2002, assistant professor of anthropology, 2003—. Gives readings from her works; consultant on Native American art.

MEMBER: American Anthropological Association, American Association of Museums.

AWARDS, HONORS: Longan Award, 2000, for *Native Peoples of the Southwest.*

WRITINGS:

Earth Is My Mother, Sky Is My Father: Space, Time, and Astronomy in Navajo Sandpainting, University of New Mexico Press (Albuquerque, NM), 1992.
The Encyclopedia of Native America, Penguin (New York, NY), 1995.
Native America: Enduring Cultures and Traditions, Metro Books (New York, NY), 1996.
Native Peoples of the Southwest, University of New Mexico Press (Albuquerque, NM), 2000.

Contributor to books, including *Peoples of the World,* National Geographic Society (Washington, DC), 2001.

WORK IN PROGRESS: Indians of the Southwest, for Columbia University Press (New York, NY); editing and writing a chapter for *Time, Self, and Society: The Cross-Cultural Embodiment of Time in Illness and Health,* University of Arizona Press (Tucson, AZ); research on traditional Navajo beliefs and practices and the conflict with "biomedicine."

SIDELIGHTS: Trudy Griffin-Pierce told *CA:* "I cannot imagine a life without writing, and I cannot remember a time when I did not write. I began keeping a journal

after my mother died when I was sixteen, although this connection did not register in my mind until much later. In many ways, we were more like sisters, and the sudden death of the person who was my whole world shattered my core beliefs about reality and sent me searching for meaning. The only things in my life to which I was truly connected were writing and the Navajo Indians.

"Born in South Carolina, I am part Catawba Indian, but the Navajos captured my heart and my imagination from an early age. Since early childhood—I was a military nomad who grew up in Hawaii, California, England, Florida, and Illinois—I had always known that someday I would live with the Navajos. Two years after my mother died, I wrote to Navajo Tribal Chairman Raymond Nakai, asking him 'to find a traditional family that I could join as a daughter.'

"And so I came to live with a non-English-speaking older couple who lived in a hogan between Many Farms and Round Rock, Arizona. Without electricity or running water, we got up at dawn to chop firewood, fix breakfast, and pack food for lunch before we ushered a flock of sheep and goats out of their corral and over the hill. All day long we herded them, occasionally resting beneath the spotty shade of a lone juniper, where my Navajo mother spun carded wool into yarn with her wooden spindle. We returned home with just enough sunlight to chop firewood and prepare dinner; I usually finished drying the dishes by the light of an oil lamp.

"After I returned to Florida State to complete my final semester, I moved to Arizona for good to be close to my Navajo parents and began graduate school at the University of Arizona. At the time, I did not really know where I was going, but I knew that I had begun. I was only following what sustained me and what was most alive in me; little did I dream that the Navajos would lead me to a career of writing and university teaching in anthropology."

BIOGRAPHICAL AND CRITICAL SOURCES:

PERIODICALS

American Indian Quarterly, winter, 1994, Stephen C. McCluskey, review of *Earth Is My Mother, Sky Is My Father: Space, Time, and Astronomy in Navajo Sandpainting,* p. 137.

Booklist, September 1, 1995, review of *The Encyclopedia of Native America,* p. 106.
Library Journal, April 15, 2001, review of *Native Peoples of the Southwest,* p. 106.

* * *

GRILLEY, Robert (L.) 1920-

PERSONAL: Born November 14, 1920, in Lancaster, WI; son of Robert Earl and Ella Louise (a school-teacher; maiden name, Cruger) Grilley; married Shirley Gene Miller, January, 1945 (marriage ended); married Ei Terasawa (a scientist), June 7, 1955; children: (first marriage) Rinelda, Robert G. Dorian; (second marriage) Juneko. *Ethnicity:* "Irish-German." *Education:* University of Wisconsin—Madison, B.S., 1942, M.F.A., 1946. *Politics:* Democrat. *Hobbies and other interests:* Flying his own plane.

ADDRESSES: Home—2802 Ridge Rd., Madison, WI 53705.

CAREER: Educator and figurative painter. University of Wisconsin—Madison, professor of art, 1945-87, professor emeritus, 1987—, department chair, 1960-65. *Exhibitions:* Work exhibited at Wichita Museum, 1987. *Military service:* U.S. Army Air Forces, navigator during World War II; served in Europe; received Distinguished Flying Cross, Air Medal with three oak leaf clusters, and Presidential Unit Citation.

WRITINGS:

Return from Berlin: The Eye of a Navigator (memoir), University of Wisconsin Press (Madison, WI), 2003.

WORK IN PROGRESS: Where Late the Sweet Birds Sang, a memoir of childhood.

SIDELIGHTS: Robert Grilley told *CA:* "Writing is for me a form of visual expression. It is closely akin to my life's work as a figurative painter. Literary works that I love most involve visual metaphor as we see in Shakespeare's sonnets. My long-term memory is

primarily visual, and since I am an old man, the things I write about come from a world of introspective remembrance, virtual reality with a touch of educated invention.

"My only published work, *Return from Berlin: The Eye of a Navigator,* has profound visual contrasts—the look of a dense barrage of flak bursts, a B-17 wrapped in orange flame, trailing smoke, the sun-bleached, tiny white hairs on the arm of a child, the tall cumulus in late afternoon, whiter on its western side than anything else in the world.

"Also the book contrasts the excitement of battle, which has no counterpart in ordinary existence, with the before-and-after speculation about how and why young men can be persuaded to do such unreasonable things. No one was drafted to fly. In looking back through the long tunnel of time, I speculate what death in combat could be like, but survival was the winning number on my lottery ticket, a new one for each mission. Finally, when I came back to the U.S.A. unscathed, I wondered why.

"In a very different vein, I, as an artist, saw a symbol for life as it should be, the real intention of nature in Elizabeth, a going-on-nine-year-old girl who lived at Yokehill Farm, the site of my squadron billeting. I made many landscape drawings with her included."

BIOGRAPHICAL AND CRITICAL SOURCES:

BOOKS

Grilley, Robert, *Return from Berlin: The Eye of a Navigator,* University of Wisconsin Press (Madison, WI), 2003.

* * *

GRONDAHL, Paul 1959-

PERSONAL: Born 1959; married; wife's name, Mary (a college dean of admissions); children: Sam, Caroline. *Education:* University of Puget Sound, B.A.; State University of New York, Albany, M.A.

ADDRESSES: Office—Times Union, News Plaza, Box 15000, Albany, NY 12212.

CAREER: Worked in New York State senate; *Times Union,* Albany, NY, reporter.

AWARDS, HONORS: Mental Health Media Award, Mental Health Association, New York State, 2003, for series "The New Asylums: Mental Illness behind Bars."

WRITINGS:

Mayor Erastus Corning: Albany Icon, Albany Enigma, Washington Park Press (Albany, NY), 1997.
(With Mary Ann LoGiudice) *That Place Called Home: A Very Special Love Story,* Charis, Servant Publications (Ann Arbor, MI), 2000.
I Rose like a Rocket: The Political Education of Theodore Roosevelt, Free Press (New York, NY), 2004.

Contributor to periodicals, including *New York Times Book Review* and *Newsday*

SIDELIGHTS: Paul Grondahl is an award-winning journalist whose series "The New Asylums: Mental Illness behind Bars," published in the Albany *Times Union,* was honored with the Mental Health Media Award by the New York State Mental Health Association. In announcing the award, President and C.E.O. Joseph A. Glazer said that Grondahl's articles "have helped change how the public and policymakers look at the overlap between criminal justice and mental health," according to the Mental Health Association in New York State Web site.

Grondahl's first book, *Mayor Erastus Corning: Albany Icon, Albany Enigma,* is a biography of the man who set a record for tenure in American political history, having been elected mayor of Albany eleven times to serve forty-two years. The author reports that Corning was a charming, philandering, brilliant man who led the powerful, all-inclusive Democratic Party that was formed in 1921, and which was comprised of members of both the working class and the wealthy. Grondahl conducted more than two hundred interviews and searched archival sources in writing the story of Corning, for whom New York State named its tallest building north of New York City. The author also documents Corning's family background, his years at Yale University, his political ties, war service, interactions with Rockefeller, Dewey, and the media, his retreat to Maine, and his ultimate decline and death.

Grondahl's next book, *That Place Called Home: A Very Special Love Story,* grew out of story he was researching about a home for pregnant teens. Sister Mary Ann LoGiudice, who ran the program, asked Grondahl not to include the fact that she had an adopted eight-year-old daughter who was HIV positive, because the child's health status was not public knowledge. He agreed, but several years later, when the girl died of AIDS, LoGiudice asked Grondahl to help her tell her story. A *Publishers Weekly* contributor called *That Place Called Home* a "heart-breaking first-person account of the transforming love of a child."

Another *Publishers Weekly* contributor commented that in *I Rose like a Rocket: The Political Education of Theodore Roosevelt* Grondahl "does an outstanding job of documenting Theodore Roosevelt's evolution from brash young political reformer to shrewd and pragmatic political operator." The volume covers Roosevelt's life from his birth to his presidency after the assassination of William McKinley, and concentrates on Roosevelt's "political education," including his years as a twenty-something assemblyman in the state legislator, beginning in 1882. It was then that he first learned how to deal with the powerful figures within the party, including John McManus, Boss Tweed, Roscoe Conkling, and Richard Croker.

Roosevelt served as civil service commissioner in Washington during the late 1880s and early 1990s. He became police commissioner of New York City from 1895 to 1897, assistant secretary of the U.S. Navy, commander of the Rough Riders, governor of New York, vice president, and finally president. *Library Journal* critic William D. Pederson wrote that Grondahl "makes a significant contribution to the Roosevelt literature" and added that his "writing is so engaging that readers won't want to put the book down."

BIOGRAPHICAL AND CRITICAL SOURCES:

PERIODICALS

Booklist, May 1, 2004, George Cohen, review of *I Rose like a Rocket: The Political Education of Theodore Roosevelt,* p. 1539.
Kirkus Reviews, April 1, 2004, review of *I Rose Like a Rocket,* p. 310.
Library Journal, May 1, 2004, William D. Pederson, review of *I Rose Like a Rocket,* p. 125.

Publishers Weekly, May 29, 2000, review of *That Place Called Home: A Very Special Love Story,* p. 78; March 15, 2004, review of *I Rose like a Rocket,* p. 61.

ONLINE

Mental Health Association in New York State Web site, http://www.mhanys.org/ (September 15, 2003).*

H

HAILEY, Arthur 1920-2004

OBITUARY NOTICE— See index for *CA* sketch: Born April 5, 1920, in Luton, Bedfordshire, England; died of a stroke November 24, 2004, on Lyford Cay, New Providence, Bahamas. Author. Hailey was the best-selling author of suspense novels such as *Hotel* and *Airport*. Born in a working-class family, his first desire was to become a journalist, but his lack of higher education prevented him from getting a job. Instead, he found work at a real estate company before he enlisted in the Royal Air Force during World War II. While in the military, he began trying his hand at writing, and he managed to publish some short fiction and other works. After the war, Hailey moved to Canada, where he continued work as a realtor briefly before becoming an editor for *Bus and Truck Transport* magazine in Toronto. From 1953 until 1956, he was a sales promotion and advertising manager for Canadian Trailmobile Ltd. By the mid-1950s Hailey's screenplay *Flight to Danger* was sold to the Canadian Broadcasting Corp. This led to his being hired as a television writer for a variety of networks. Wary of his continued success in entertainment, however, he also founded an advertising agency for financial security. But he need not have bothered with this precaution, since, beginning with his first novel *The Final Diagnosis* (1959), Hailey would enjoy a successful writing career for the rest of his days. Creating a formula that offered nonstop suspense to his readers, Hailey was often criticized by reviewers for his predictable plots; however, his novels sold millions of copies and were published around the world in over three dozen languages. Among his early successes were *Hotel* (1965), *Airport* (1968), and *Wheels* (1971), all of which were adapted as successful movies. *The Money-changers* (1975) was turned into a television series, as was *The Final Diagnosis,* which was adapted as *The Young Doctors*. Other more recent books by Hailey include *Strong Medicine* (1984) and his last novel, *Detective* (1997).

OBITUARIES AND OTHER SOURCES:

PERIODICALS

Chicago Tribune, November 26, 2004, section 3, p. 8.
New York Times, November 26, 2004, p. C10.
Times (London, England), November 27, 2004, p. 80.
Washington Post, November 27, 2004, p. B4.

* * *

HAMILTON, Richard 1943-

PERSONAL: Born December 19, 1943, in Bryn Mawr, PA; married, 1965; children: two. *Education:* Harvard University, A.B., 1965; University of Michigan, Ph.D. (classics), 1971.

ADDRESSES: Office—Department of Greek, Latin, and Classical Studies, Bryn Mawr College, 101 North Merion Ave, Bryn Mawr, PA 19010-2899. *E-mail*—rhamilto@brynmawr.edu.

CAREER: Bryn Mawr College, Bryn Mawr, PA, began as assistant professor, became associate professor, 1971-88, Paul Shorey Professor of Greek, 1988—. Founder, "Bryn Mawr Commentaries" series.

MEMBER: American Philological Association.

AWARDS, HONORS: National Endowment for the Humanities senior fellow, 1994.

WRITINGS:

Epinikion: General Form in the Odes of Pindar, Mouton (The Hague, Netherlands), 1974.
The Architecture of Hesiodic Poetry, Johns Hopkins University Press (Baltimore, MD), 1989.
Choes and Anthesteria: Athenian Iconography and Ritual, University of Michigan Press (Ann Arbor, MI), 1992.
Treasure Map: A Guide to the Delian Inventories, University of Michigan Press (Ann Arbor, MI), 2000.

Also annotator of numerous texts in "Bryn Mawr Commentaries" series of texts in Greek and Latin.

SIDELIGHTS: Richard Hamilton, a scholar of ancient Greek literature at Bryn Mawr College with specialties in Greek literature, religion, and iconography, has published a number of interpretations of the works of the lyric poets Pindar and Hesiod as well as studies of Greek vase art and inventories of gifts to the Greek gods. He is also the founder of the "Bryn Mawr Commentaries" series, which publishes intermediate texts in both Greek and Latin with annotations.

In *The Architecture of Hesiodic Poetry* Hamilton focuses on Hesiod's *Theogony* and *Works and Days,* which have long intrigued scholars who like a riddle. As he states in *The Architecture of Hesiodic Poetry,* Hamilton set out to investigate "the poorly understood parts of each poem, the digressions of the *Theogony* and the second half of the *Works and Days,* to see how they contribute to the form of the whole." After reviewing the interpretations of previous scholars, particularly those of M. L. West, Hamilton launched into his own close reading and discussion of the poems, particularly their narrative structure.

Reviewing *The Architecture of Hesiodic Poetry* in *Religious Studies Review,* Jon Solomon felt that "the book will be difficult for the Greekless reader." More

positive was the assessment of Minna Skafte Jensen, writing in *Classical Review,* who called the work a "sober, serious" study, one that takes "into proper account earlier theories and recapitulat[es] them loyally." Jensen also remarked, however, that Hamilton's method of analysis "clearly rings of New Criticism," yet it does not meet the expectations of that critical method. "Important terms (such as digression, extension, structural device and distinctive repetition) are defined loosely or not all," Jensen reported. "These inconsistencies are serious flaws in an otherwise imaginative and attractive whole," she concluded.

In *Choes and Anthesteria: Athenian Iconography and Ritual* Hamilton studies the most important Athenian festival through its representation on vases. For Brian P. Sparkes, writing in *Joint Association of Classical Teachers Review,* Hamilton manages to forge meaning out of minutiae: He "has made what had always seemed to be intractable data intelligible, and has carried out a painstaking study that will be used as a reference book for anyone studying the workings of the religious machinery on Delos and elsewhere."

In *Treasure Map: A Guide to the Delian Inventories* Hamilton takes a look at the gifts Greeks offered to their gods through a careful examination of marble inscriptions of such "inventories" on the sacred island of Delos. The Athenians began making such inscriptions as early as the fourth century B.C.E., and over the millennia they became badly damaged. Hamilton's is the first English translation of these inventories of goods in this religious precinct; he also details such specifics as how the goods were weighed and listed, and how daily life was lived on the island. As such, *Treasure Map* provides a resource for researchers on Greek history, religion, politics, and economics.

BIOGRAPHICAL AND CRITICAL SOURCES:

BOOKS

Hamilton, Richard, *The Architecture of Hesiodic Poetry,* Johns Hopkins University Press (Baltimore, MD), 1989.

PERIODICALS

American Journal of Archaeology, July, 1993, Mark W. Padilla, review of *Choes and Anthesteria: Athenian Iconography and Ritual,* p. 578.

Classical Philology, January, 1991, Robert Mondi, review of *The Architecture of Hesiodic Poetry,* p. 64; October, 1994, T. H. Carpenter, review of *Choes and Anthesteria,* p. 372.

Classical Review, Volume 40, issue 2, 1990, Minna Skafte Jensen, review of *The Architecture of Hesiodic Poetry,* pp. 213-214.

Classical World, May, 1991, p. 406.

Greece and Rome, October, 1990, N. Hopkinson, review of *The Architecture of Hesiodic Poetry,* p. 232.

Joint Association of Classical Teachers Review, summer, 2001, Brian P. Sparkes, review of *Choes and Anthesteria.*

Journal of Hellenic Studies, Volume 116, 1996, B. A. Sparkes, review of *Choes and Anthesteria,* p. 220.

Mnemosyne, November, 1993, W. Kassies, review of *The Architecture of Hesiodic Poetry,* p. 549.

Religious Studies Review, January, 1991, Jon Solomon, review of *The Architecture of Hesiodic Poetry,* p. 63.

ONLINE

Bryn Mawr Graduate Group in Archaeology, Classics and History of Art Web site, http://www.brynmawr.edu/ (August 9, 2004), "Richard Hamilton."

University of Michigan Press Web site, http://www.press.umich.edu/ (August 9, 2004).*

*   *   *

HANSEN, Joseph 1923-2004
(Rose Brock, James Colton, James Coulton)

OBITUARY NOTICE— See index for *CA* sketch: Born July 19, 1923, in Aberdeen, SD; died of heart failure November 24, 2004, in Laguna Beach, CA. Author. Hansen is best remembered as the creator of series character Dave Brandstetter, the first homosexual detective to appear as a hero in American crime fiction. The author's grew up in Depression-era South Dakota, until his father lost his shoe store shop and the family moved to California to work a small citrus tree farm. Hansen, who never attended college, was interested in writing early in life but did not find much success until 1952, when the *New Yorker* published one of his poems. He continued to write poems and fiction with homosexual themes, often publishing them pseudonymously as James Colton, or, in one book, Coulton. He also published a gothic novel under the name Rose Brock called *Tarn House* (1971). During the 1960s, Hansen, who did not conceal his sexual orientation, worked on the staff of the gay and lesbian magazine *One,* and in 1965 cofounded another magazine, *Tangents,* which he worked on until 1970. In another venture, he produced a radio program in Los Angeles called *Homosexuality Today* in 1969, and in 1970 he was responsible for organizing the first gay pride parade in Hollywood. But his biggest claim to fame came through his "Dave Brandstetter" series. Long a fan of detective fiction, and also upset with the unfair portrayal of homosexual characters in novels, Hansen decided to create a protagonist who happened to be gay but whose sexuality was just one aspect of his complex personality. Hansen finished his debut book, *Fadeout,* in 1967 but could not find a publisher until 1970. When the novel finally did appear, it received considerable positive fanfare and critical attention. The success of the "Brandstetter" series continued for several more books, including *Troublemaker* (1975), *Gravedigger* (1982), *Early Graves* (1987), and the last in the series, *A Country of Old Men* (1991). Hansen continued publishing for many years, releasing such books as *Living Upstairs* (1993), *Jack of Hearts* (1995), and *Bohannon's Women: Mystery Stories* (2002).

OBITUARIES AND OTHER SOURCES:

PERIODICALS

New York Times, December 7, 2004, p. A20.
Times (London, England), February 2, 2005, p. 54.
Washington Post, December 7, 2004, p. B6.

*   *   *

HARGREAVES, Harry 1922-2004

OBITUARY NOTICE— See index for *CA* sketch: Born February 9, 1922, in Manchester, England; died of cancer November 12, 2004, in Yeovil, Somerset, England. Cartoonist, illustrator, and author. Hargreaves was a popular British cartoonist who regularly contributed to magazines such as *Punch*. He created the cartoons "The Bird" and "Hayseeds," and was also an animator and book illustrator. Beginning his cartooning career while still at Chorlton high school, he created a strip for the school magazine and had a cartoon accepted by the *Manchester Evening News* when he was just fourteen years old. After school, he received design and engineering training at the Lawn & Howarth Co., a home furnishings company, and at Ford Motor Co., and he attended the Manchester School of Art. With the start of World War II, Hargreaves enlisted in the Royal Air Force signal corps. Assigned to duty in Asia, he also did illustrations for *Blighty* and RAF publications. After the war, the cartoonist joined an animation studio called Gaumont British Animation, which was directed by former Disney director David Hand. Unfortunately, the studio went under in 1950, and Hargreaves became a freelance cartoonist. He created many original and popular strips, such as "Harold Hare," "The Alley Cat," "Don Quickshot," and the television cartoon "Terry the Troubador." Beginning in 1953, the cartoonist worked for Amsterdam's Toonder Film Studios and took over the strip "Little Panda" from Martin Toonder; it had a successful run until 1961. In the 1950s, he also sold strips to many periodicals, including *The Cricketer* and London's *Daily Telegraph*. During the 1960s, Hargreaves saw his characters appear in television cartoons, including *Go-Go the Fox* and *Crater Critters*. In 1968, the cartoonist found success yet again with another strip called "The Hayseeds," which ran in the London *Evening News* until 1980. Hargreaves also illustrated children's books, most notably contributing art to the Paddington Bear stories by Michael Bond and to the 1983 edition of *The Wind in the Willows* by Kenneth Grahame. He also enjoyed a healthy career illustrating greeting cards. Many of his cartoons have been collected in books, including *How's That* (1959), *Strictly for the Bird* (1967), *Hayseeds* (1971), and *Hayseeds 2* (1972). More recently, he published *Canny Curlew* (1988) and, with Ross Mallock, *Botanic Verses* (1993). Interested in wildlife conservation throughout his life, Hargreaves was made an honorary life fellow of the Wildfowl and Wetland Trust; he was also made an honorary member of the Army Air Corps Association. Exhibits of his artwork have been held at the National Portrait Gallery, the Musée des Hommes in Montreal, Canada, and the Center for the Study of Cartoons and Caricature at Kent University

OBITUARIES AND OTHER SOURCES:

PERIODICALS

Daily Telegraph (London, England), November 20, 2004.
Guardian (London, England), December 8, 2004, p. 27.
Independent (London, England), November 22, 2004, p. 35.
Times (London, England), December 1, 2004, p. 58.

*   *   *

HARMON, Daniel E(lton) 1949-
(Dan Harmon)

PERSONAL: Born December 6, 1949, in Lexington, SC; son of Harvey J. (a law enforcement officer) and Mertie K. (a waitress) Harmon; married; wife's name Patricia C. (a social worker), August, 1976 (divorced, July, 2002); married June 6, 1997; second wife's name Sherie C. (a respiratory therapist); children: Courtney. *Education:* University of South Carolina, B.A. (journalism), 1972. *Religion:* Associate Reformed Presbyterian. *Hobbies and other interests:* Folk music, nautical history, correspondence chess.

ADDRESSES: Office—Hornpipe Publications, P.O. Box 18428, Spartanburg, SC 29318. *E-mail*—d@daniel eltonharmon.com.

CAREER: Author and editor. *Sandlapper: The Magazine of South Carolina,* Lexington, SC, assistant editor, 1971-73, associate editor and art director, 1989—; Dispatch-News, Lexington, reporter and editor, 1973-83; RPW Publishing Corp, Lexington, editor, 1983-97; freelance editor, beginning 1997.

AWARDS, HONORS: Excellence in Technology Communications Award, Acer Group/Computer Museum, 1989; awards from Computer Press Association and South Carolina Press Association; various other press awards.

WRITINGS:

FOR CHILDREN

(Editor, under name Dan Harmon) Edwin P. Booth, *Martin Luther: The Great Reformer,* Barbour Publishers (Uhrichsville, OH), 1995.

(Under name Dan Harmon) *Civil War Generals,* Chelsea House Publishers (Philadelphia, PA), 1997.

The Tortured Mind: The Many Faces of Manic Depression, Chelsea House Publishers (Philadelphia, PA), 1998.

(Under name Dan Harmon) Fighting Units of the American War of Independence, Chelsea House Publishers (Philadelphia, PA), 1999.

(Under name Dan Harmon) *Life out of Focus: Alzheimer's Disease and Related Disorders,* Chelsea House Publishers (Philadelphia, PA), 1999.

(Under name Dan Harmon) Anorexia Nervosa: Starving for Attention, Chelsea House Publishers (Philadelphia, PA), 1999.

(With Tamela Hancock Murray; under name Dan Harmon) *More Clean Jokes for Kids,* Barbour Publishers (Uhrichsville, OH), 1999.

(Under name Dan Harmon) *Juan Ponce de Leon and the Search for the Fountain of Youth,* Chelsea House Publishers (Philadelphia, PA), 2000.

Nigeria: 1880 to the Present: The Struggle, the Tragedy, the Promise, Chelsea House Publishers (Philadelphia, PA), 2000.

Schizophrenia; Losing Touch with Reality, Chelsea House Publishers (Philadelphia, PA), 2000.

West Africa, 1880 to the Present: A Cultural Patchwork, Chelsea House Publishers (Philadelphia, PA), 2001.

The FBI, Chelsea House Publishers (Philadelphia, PA), 2001.

Jacques Cartier and the Exploration of Canada, Chelsea House Publishers (Philadelphia, PA), 2001.

Egypt: 1880 to the Present: Desert of Envy, Water of Life, Chelsea House Publishers (Philadelphia, PA), 2001.

La Salle and the Exploration of the Mississippi, Chelsea House Publishers (Philadelphia, PA), 2001.

The U.S. Armed Forced, Chelsea House Publishers (Philadelphia, PA), 2001.

(Under name Dan Harmon) *The Titanic,* Chelsea House Publishers (Philadelphia, PA), 2001.

The Attorney General's Office, Chelsea House Publishers (Philadelphia, PA), 2001.

Sudan: 1880 to the Present: Crossroads of a Continent in Conflict, Chelsea House Publishers (Philadelphia, PA), 2001.

Jolliet and Marquette: Explorers of the Mississippi River, Chelsea House Publishers (Philadelphia, PA), 2002.

Lord Cornwallis: British General, Chelsea House Publishers (Philadelphia, PA), 2002.

The Food and Drug Administration, Chelsea House Publishers (Philadelphia, PA), 2002.

The Environmental Protection Agency, Chelsea House Publishers (Philadelphia, PA), 2002.

Davy Crockett, Chelsea House Publishers (Philadelphia, PA), 2002.

Defense Lawyers, Chelsea House Publishers (Philadelphia, PA), 2003.

OTHER

(Editor, under name Dan Harmon) S. D. Gordon, *Life after Death,* Barbour Publishers (Uhrichsville, OH), 1998.

The Chalk Town Train, and Other Tales (first volume of "Harper Chronicles"), Trafford Publishing, 2001.

Bible Challenge: Small Facts from the Big Book, CrossAmerica Books, 2002.

(With others) *Taught to Lead: The Education of the Presidents of the United States,* Mason Crest Publishers, 2004.

Editor, *The Lawyer's PC,* 1983—.

WORK IN PROGRESS: Biographies for "Amazing Americans" series; Volume 2 of the "Harper Chronicles."

SIDELIGHTS: Daniel E. Harmon once commented: "At about age thirteen, I determined to become a professional writer. School career counselors directed me to obtain a journalism degree, which led to ten agonizing years as a newspaper journalist after college. Although I hated the work, journalism matured my writing and taught me much about the publishing industry.

"Eventually, the Lord gave me more agreeable writing and editing work to do and, in 1994, opened the door to authoring books. After compiling several joke books and performing abridgement projects for Barbour Publishing, I was engaged by Chelsea House in 1997 to begin authoring educational books for different grade levels. The subjects were gloriously diverse, from history to foreign culture. Today I have the privilege of researching and writing books for several juvenile publishers.

"Meanwhile, as time permits, I relish crafting historical mystery short stories, the kind of writing I REALLY wanted to do from the very beginning, forty years ago. I continue to enjoy my long-term work on the editorial staff of *Sandlapper: The Magazine of South Carolina.* Since 1983, I've also edited *The Lawyer's PC,* a national technology newsletter now published by Thomson/West.

BIOGRAPHICAL AND CRITICAL SOURCES:

PERIODICALS

School Library Journal, February, 2001, Daniel Mungai, review of *Nigeria: 1880 to the Present: The Struggle, the Tragedy, the Promise,* p. 132; March, 2002, Genevieve Gallagher, review of *Egypt: 1880 to the Present: Desert of Envy, Water of Life,* p. 251; April, 2002, review of *Defense Lawyers,* p. 172; October, 2003, review of *The Environmental Protection Agency,* p. 43.

ONLINE

Daniel Harmon Web site, http://www.danieleltonharmon.com (January 3, 2005).

*   *   *

HARMON, Dan
    See HARMON, Daniel E(lton)

*   *   *

HENNESSEY, Thomas W.

PERSONAL: Male. *Education:* Holds a Ph.D.

ADDRESSES: Office—History Department, Canterbury Christ Church University College, North Holmes Road, Canterbury, Kent CT1 1QU, England.

CAREER: Author and educator. Canterbury Christ Church University College, Canterbury, England, currently professor of history. Previously taught at Queen's University, Belfast, Ireland, and served as a research fellow at Centre for the Study of Conflict, University of Ulster, Ulster, Ireland.

WRITINGS:

A History of Northern Ireland, 1920-1996, St. Martin's Press (New York, NY), 1997.
Dividing Ireland: World War I and Partition, Routledge (New York, NY), 1998.
The Northern Ireland Peace Process: Ending the Troubles?, Gill and Macmillan (Dublin, Ireland), 2000.

SIDELIGHTS: Author and educator Thomas Hennessey is a professor of history and politics at Canterbury Christ Church University College in Canterbury, England, where his teaching responsibilities include British imperial and commonwealth history, nineteenth-century European history, and Irish history centering on the political troubles surrounding Ulster after 1800. Hennessey's primary areas of research interest are the Northern Ireland conflict, concepts of national identity in Britain, the Great Powers in the nineteenth and twentieth centuries, and the Northern Ireland peace process.

Hennessey's first book, *A History of Northern Ireland, 1920-1996,* addresses the political conflict surrounding the division of the country. Hennessey examines the situation from both sides, striving to achieve a balance between the Nationalist and Unionist points of view. Fred Barbash, writing in the *Washington Post Book World,* felt that Hennessey's efforts to avoid taking sides result in a book that is "numbingly neutral." In the book, Hennessey starts with an explanation of Ulster's origins following World War I and continues on through the failed Irish Republican Army cease-fire and the violence of the mid-nineties. A contributor to the *Economist* noted that "his history is, inevitably, overshadowed by the troubles of the past three decades, and this makes it a study of the gathering storm rather than a rounded account of the province." The reviewer went on to call the book "a closely argued account [that] offers not only shrewd analysis but also copious extracts from key documents, and some interesting statistics."

Many critics felt that Hennessey's book is well argued and well presented. *Library Journal* contributor Robert C. Moore wrote that the author's "fatalistic assessment of the future of the peace process is supported painfully well by his text," and John F. Quinn, reviewing for the *Catholic Historical Review,* commented that "Hennessey provides a painstakingly thorough and dispassionate chronicle of the successive crises that have plagued Northern Ireland." Quinn noted that "some readers may . . . be frustrated by Hennessey's writing," calling it "very dry reading at times," but added that "the substance of the work is such that readers interested in the history of Northern Ireland will find it well worth their time."

In *Dividing Ireland: World War I and Partition* Hennessey strives to prove his theory that the division of the nation can be traced back to a conflict of national identity. He explains that while Britain claimed to encourage an inclusive sense of nationalism that allowed a certain amount of individuality, Ireland cited the blatant discrimination toward them by other members of the United Kingdom and chose to stand apart. The division between Nationalists and Unionists was highlighted strongly at the start of the war when support of other nations potentially fell along lines of religious solidarity, Catholics supporting Catholic Belgium while Protestants favored Protestant Germany. D. George Boyce, in the *English Historical Review,* referred to Hennessey's work as "a more nuanced interpretation of the initial stages of the war, which are often seen as showing a real possibility of reconciling the two traditions in a common British-Irish enterprise."

The Northern Ireland Peace Process: Ending the Troubles? considers the complicated political situation in Ireland, chronicling the peace process from the early 1970s through the Belfast Agreement in 1998, and explaining the positions of the parties involved. *Political Science Quarterly* contributor Jeffrey M. Togman commented that "Hennessey's study is a history of elite negotiations, not of the cultural, social, or economic dynamics of the conflict. The author covers the give and take of multiparty bargaining with aplomb, describing each side's interests and strategies in their own terms." Togman went on to note that Hennessey's conclusions are slight in relation to the length of the volume, remarking that "it is disappointing that someone who obviously knows so much would offer so little," but overall called the book

"indispensable for anyone interested in the Troubles." J. J. N. McGurk, writing in *Contemporary Review,* wrote that "this is important contemporary history illustrating that in the most notably turbulent corner of the island of Ireland, where so many contrary streams of history have converged, democratic peacemaking is not only possible but is the only alternative for the two communities to co-exist in the same political and geographical entity."

BIOGRAPHICAL AND CRITICAL SOURCES:

PERIODICALS

Booklist, March 15, 1998, Mary Carroll, review of *A History of Northern Ireland, 1920-1996,* pp. 1197-1198.

Canadian Journal of History, August, 2001, Brian Jenkins, review of *Dividing Ireland: World War I and Partition,* p. 377.

Catholic Historical Review, October, 2000, John F. Quinn, review of *A History of Northern Ireland, 1920-1996,* p. 700.

Contemporary Review, June, 2001, J.J. N. McGurk, "Solving the Troubles of Northern Ireland," review of *The Northern Ireland Peace Process: Ending the Troubles?,* p. 369.

Economist, January 24, 1998, "Bloody Ireland," review of *A History of Northern Ireland, 1920-1996,* pp. 81-82.

English Historical Review, September, 1999, D. George Boyce, review of *Dividing Ireland,* p. 1018.

History: Review of New Books, spring, 2001, Todd Lee, review of *A History of Northern Ireland, 1920-1996,* p. 112.

Journal of Church and State, summer, 1999, James W. Vardaman, review of *A History of Northern Ireland, 1920-1996,* p. 613.

Journal of Modern History, June, 2000, Graham Walker, review of *A History of Northern Ireland, 1920-1996,* p. 524.

Library Journal, March 15, 1998, Robert C. Moore, review of *A History of Northern Ireland, 1920-1996,* p. 82; November 1, 1998, Robert C. Moore, review of *Dividing Ireland,* p. 109.

Political Science Quarterly, spring, 2002, Jeffrey M. Togman, review of *The Northern Ireland Peace Process,* p. 159.

Times Literary Supplement, September 25, 1998, Eunan O'Halpin, "Two States, Two Parts," review of *A History of Northern Ireland, 1920-1996,* p. 30.

Washington Post Book World, April 19, 1998, Fred Barbash, "All the Folly of a Fight," review of *A History of Northern Ireland, 1920-1996,* p. X6.

ONLINE

Canterbury Christ Church University, Humanities Department Web site, http://arts-humanitites.cant.ac.uk/ (September 23, 2004), "Thomas Hennessey."*

*   *   *

HERSHON, Joanna (Brett)

PERSONAL: Daughter of Stuart J. (an orthopedic surgeon) and Judith (an attorney) Hershon; married George Derek Buckner (an artist), July 24, 1999. *Education:* Graduate of University of Michigan; Columbia University, M.A. (fiction writing).

ADDRESSES: Agent—c/o Author Mail, Ballantine Books/Random House, 1745 Broadway, New York, NY 10019.

CAREER: Writer.

WRITINGS:

Swimming (novel), Ballantine Books (New York, NY), 2001.
The Outside of August (novel), Ballantine Books (New York, NY), 2003.

Contributor of short stories to periodicals, including *One Story.*

SIDELIGHTS: In Joanna Hershon's debut novel, *Swimming,* Vivian Silver is a free spirit who settled down in the 1960s with the staid Jeb Wheeler on his New Hampshire acreage. Here their lives and the lives of their children become closely linked to their hand-built house and a nearby pond, a murky pool that witnesses the darkest of family secrets.

The tension that has always existed between the successful and handsome Aaron and his volatile younger brother, Jack, reaches the breaking point when Aaron brings his girlfriend, Suzanne, home from college. Late one night after a party, Jack and Suzanne go swimming alone, and when Jack comes back to shore naked, Aaron is waiting for him. Their confrontation ends in tragedy, a Cain and Able tale that results in Aaron leaving home. The story then moves forward ten years, and Lila, who adored her older brothers, is now teaching English in New York City. She sees their faces everywhere as she searches for Aaron, the brother who disappeared from her life, and the truth about what happened on that fateful weekend. "Hershon's carefully worked prose aspires to hothouse perfection," said a *Publishers Weekly* contributor. And *Library Journal* critic Yvette Olson said Hershon "has an eye for place, an ear for dialog, and true feeling for character." Kristine Huntley concluded in a *Booklist* review that *Swimming* "is an engrossing tale of love, redemption, and second chances."

Hershon's second novel, *The Outside of August,* is also the story of an unhappy family. Marie Hashima Lofton commented in a review for *Bookreporter.com* that it is "written in a very descriptive style" and said that Hershon "successfully creates a mood and atmosphere throughout the book that matches the story line." In this story, Alan and Charlotte Green are a professor of neurobiology and artist, respectively, who have raised their two children, August and Alice, on Long Island. Charlotte is emotionally and physically unavailable to her children much of the time because she takes unannounced and extended trips that last up to several months at a time. Alan is physically present but absorbed by long hours of work. As teens, August becomes rebellious, and when their mother dies in a fire, August, who now has a rich, orphaned girlfriend named Cady, leaves home to travel around the world. Alice, who narrates the story, cares for her widower father until his death; then she travels to Baja, where August is living as a surfer. When she finds him and attempts to learn what he is hiding from her, a family secret surfaces that explains her mother's absences and August's anger. A *Publishers Weekly* reviewer found the characters of Alice and Cady "particularly satisfying," while *Library Journal* contributor Reba

Leiding felt that Charlotte "is by far the most compelling character, charming one moment, disconsolate and self-destructive the next."

BIOGRAPHICAL AND CRITICAL SOURCES:

PERIODICALS

Booklist, November 15, 2000, Kristine Huntley, review of *Swimming*, p. 621.

Kirkus Reviews, June 15, 2003, review of *The Outside of August*, p. 824.

Library Journal, December, 2000, Yvette Olson, review of *Swimming*, p. 188; March 15, 2003, Reba Leiding, review of *The Outside of August*, p. 114.

Publishers Weekly, February 5, 2001, review of *Swimming*, p. 69; April 21, 2003, review of *The Outside of August*, p. 35.

Washington Post Book World, March 12, 2001, Chris Bohjalian, "Finding Her Stroke," p. C02.

ONLINE

Bookreporter.com, http://www.bookreporter.com/ (November 8, 2004), Marie Hashima Lofton, review of *The Outside of August*.

*   *   *

HILL, Ingrid

PERSONAL: Born in New York, NY; children: Christopher, Hope, Leif, Eli, Benjamin and Luke (identical twins), Hilary, Annika and Britt (fraternal twins), Amos, Zachary, and Maria. *Education:* University of Iowa, Ph.D.

ADDRESSES: Home—Iowa City, IA. *Agent*—c/o Author Mail, Workman Publishing, 708 Broadway, New York, NY 10003.

CAREER: Writer.

AWARDS, HONORS: Two grants from National Endowment for the Arts; Great Lakes Book Award, and Best Novel designation, *Washington Post Books World*, both 2004, and Michigan Notable Book designation, 2005, all for *Ursula, Under.*

WRITINGS:

Dixie Church Interstate Blues, Viking (New York, NY), 1989.

Ursula, Under, Algonquin Books of Chapel Hill (Chapel Hill, NC), 2004.

Author of over thirty short stories. Work represented in anthologies; contributor of short stories to literary journals, including *Black Warrior Review, Southern Review,* and *Shenandoah.*

WORK IN PROGRESS: The Ballad of Rappy Valcour (and More New Orleans Stories).

SIDELIGHTS: Ingrid Hill was born in New York City and spent much of her childhood in New Orleans. Except for three years in Washington State, she has spent half of her adult life in the university communities of Ann Arbor, Michigan and Iowa City, Iowa, where she earned her doctorate. Hill, who has twelve children, including two sets of twins, began her writing career as a short story writer. Her first published book is a collection of these stories titled *Dixie Church Interstate Blues.*

Hill's debut novel, *Ursula, Under,* spans more than 2,000 years and the lives of the ancestors of one family. *Times-Picayune* reviewer Susan Larson wrote that reading it "is a bit like opening up a treasure chest; the reader is drawn in by the shining brightness, and keeps digging to find more beauty beneath. The riches just keep on coming." The central figure in the story is two-year-old Ursula, daughter of Justin Wong and Annie Maki, both of whom suffered traumatic childhoods, and who struggle to raise their daughter in a trailer on Michigan's Upper Peninsula. Justin is a half Chinese, half Polish laborer and musician. Annie, whose injuries from a childhood bike accident have led to her dependence on a walker, is searching for her roots in Michigan's mining towns, one of which was the site of a cave-in that took her Finnish grandfather's life

On one such trip, toddler Ursula, who loves the color purple, slips away from her parents and falls into a mine shaft, instantly becoming national news. Hill takes the reader in another direction, however, exploring the ancestors from whom the child is descended, including third-century Chinese alchemist Qin Lao, the female companion of an eighteenth-century Finnish queen, and Chen Bing, a nineteenth-century mollusk collector living in California. Larson remarked that Hill "is like Scheherezade, dancing the reader along through one magical landscape after another in stories of Ursula's ancient ancestors." A *Kirkus Reviews* critic commented that "the cumulative impact of all those ancestors' stories adds an epic grandeur and surprising emotional punch to the finale."

One of the present-day characters is wealthy Jinx Muhlenberg, who caused Annie's childhood injuries when she hit her while driving drunk. Now Jinx wonders what all the fuss is about over a "goddamn half-breed, trailer-trash kid." Another is Ursula's grandmother, Mindy Ji, who senses the power of the ancestors, "as if everything here were incredibly fragile—all these meld together in a tissue of hope, suddenly. Life is persistent. Ursula will live."

Washington Post Book World reviewer Michael Anft felt that "some of the characters would work as main players in novels of their own" and concluded: "ultimately, Hill embraces a crucial Big Novel component. Her book asks, and at length answers, a Big Question: What is a life worth? The miracle of *Ursula, Under* is that it reminds us that while a good story—told with all the weight of the world and through skeins of time—might not be as indispensable as a beloved child, it can relate the value of that child, and through its narrative gift help us recall why life is worth the trouble."

Hill told *CA:* "Audience response to the size of my old-fashioned family tends both to distract from the text at hand and to reinforce the undeniable source of my fiction, for which I am very grateful.

"There is a magical-realist tilt to a good bit of my work—just as Gabriel García Márquez explained, that orientation in his fiction (perhaps a bit tongue in cheek) is an effort to replicate faithfully the experiences of his childhood in a colonial Latin-American culture suffused with superstitious religious practice and a tropical climate. I believe my own tilt proceeds from a variety of surreal life experiences which could be accurately represented no other way. I write as a woman, first and undeniably. My artistic influences are diverse, from the nineteenth-century novel to Imagist poetry to Asian and European immigrant oral histories to the contemporary personal essay to metafiction. Always I write from a life model."

BIOGRAPHICAL AND CRITICAL SOURCES:

PERIODICALS

Booklist, Deborah Donovan, review of *Ursula, Under,* p. 1544.
Kirkus Reviews, April 1, 2004, review of *Ursula, Under,* p. 287.
Library Journal, May 1, 2004, Ann H. Fisher, review of *Ursula, Under,* p. 140.
People, June 21, 2004, Margaux Wexberg, review of *Ursula, Under,* p. 52.
Times Picayune (New Orleans, LA), July 13, 2004, Susan Larson, review of *Ursula, Under,* "Living," p. 1.
Washington Post Book World, August 22, 2004, Michael Anft, review of *Ursula, Under,* p. T5.

ONLINE

San Diego Union-Tribune Online, http://www. signonsandiego.com/ (June 27, 2004), Wendy L. Smith, review of *Ursula, Under.*

*　　*　　*

HODGES, C(yril) Walter 1909-2004

OBITUARY NOTICE— See index for *CA* sketch: Born March 18, 1909, in Beckenham, Kent, England; died November 26, 2004, in Moretonhampstead, Devon, England. Illustrator and author. Hodges was an award-winning illustrator of children's books whose love of history and the theater were often evident in his work. After attending Dulwich College, he studied for three years at Goldsmith's College of Art. Always interested in the theater, when he completed school he found work as a costumes and scenery designer for the Everyman Theatre in Hampstead. This work did not pay well, unfortunately, and so Hodges found employment at an advertising agency. His first success as an illustrator came when the *Radio Times* began publishing his work in 1931. Hodges would continue to contribute to the publication over the next four decades. His first book, *Columbus Sails,* was released in 1939; it would be the first of many titles for young readers that he would produce. However, his career was interrupted by World War II, during which Hodges was a captain for the British Army and participated in the Normandy invasion. After the war, Hodges resumed his career as a book illustrator and worked for a number of theaters, such as the Mermaid Theatre in the early 1950s and the St. George's Theatre in 1976. He also lectured at the Brighton Polytechnic School of Art and Design, beginning in 1959. In addition to his artwork, Hodges also wrote many of the children's books he worked on, including the fiction works *The Namesake* (1964), *The Overland Launch* (1970), and *Plain Lane Christmas* (1978). His love of history and Shakespeare led to such nonfiction books for children as *Shakespeare's Theatre* (1964), *Magna Carta* (1966), *The English Civil War* (1972), and *The Battlement Garden: Britain from the Wars of the Roses to the Age of Shakespeare* (1980). He also illustrated books on Shakespeare for adult readers, such as *Shakespeare's Second Globe: The Missing Monument* (1973), and illustrated books by such children's authors as Kenneth Macfarlane, E. Nesbit, Ian Serraillier, William Mayne, and Richard Armstrong. His last book to be published in his lifetime was *Enter the Whole Army: A Pictorial Study of Shakespearean Staging* (1999). Hodges, who as a Shakespeare scholar had served as a design consultant for the Globe Theatre Reconstruction project at Wayne State University, was working on illustrating the *New Cambridge Shakespeare* at the time of his death.

OBITUARIES AND OTHER SOURCES:

PERIODICALS

Independent (London, England), December 1, 2004, p. 34.
Times (London, England), December 7, 2004, p. 54.

* * *

HODGSON, Barbara L. 1955-

PERSONAL: Born 1955, in Edmonton, Alberta, Canada; daughter of Stanley and Beatrice Theresa Hodgson. *Education:* Simon Fraser University, B.A., 1977; Capilano College, diploma in graphic design, 1982. *Hobbies and other interests:* Painting, photography, travel.

ADDRESSES: Office—Barbara Hodgson Design, 404-402 West Pender, Vancouver, British Columbia, Canada V6B 1T6.

CAREER: Douglas & McIntyre (publisher), Vancouver, British Columbia, Canada, worked as assistant, then book designer and art director for Trade Publishing Division, 1982-89; Barbara Hodgson Design, Vancouver, principal, 1991—. Byzantium Books (book packaging company), founding partner, 1993—. Simon Fraser University, sessional instructor, 1990, and lecturer in book design; Emily Carr School of Art and Design, instructor, 1990-93. Also worked as museum artifact illustrator and exhibit curator; gives readings from her works, including appearances at Harbourfront Centre and North Shore Writers Festival; guest on media programs.

AWARDS, HONORS: Studio magazine awards, 1986, 1989, 1995, 1996; GDC Awards, three awards, 1987, two awards, 1991, two awards, 1995, three awards, 1997, one award, 2000; Gilbert Paper Letterhead Award, 1988; Alcuin Society, two awards, 1989, two awards, 1990, two awards, 1994, and, Award for Excellence in Book Design in Canada, prose fiction category, 2002, for *Hippolyte's Island; Applied Arts* magazine awards, 1997, two awards, 1999, two awards, 2000.

WRITINGS:

(Designer) Samuel Taylor Coleridge, *Kubla Khan: A Pop-up Version of Coleridge's Classic,* illustrated by Nick Bantock, Viking (New York, NY), 1994.
(And illustrator) *The Tattooed Map,* Chronicle Books (San Francisco, CA), 1995.
(With Nick Bantock and Karen Elizabeth Gordon) *Paris out of Hand,* Chronicle Books (San Francisco, CA), 1996.
(Compiler) *The Rat: A Perverse Miscellany,* Ten Speed Press (Berkeley, CA), 1997.
(And illustrator) *The Sensualist* (novel), Chronicle Books (San Francisco, CA), 1998.
Opium: A Portrait of the Heavenly Demon, Chronicle Books (San Francisco, CA), 1999.
In the Arms of Morpheus: The Tragic History of Laudanum, Morphine, and Patent Medicines, Firefly Books (Richmond Hill, Ontario, Canada), 2001.

(And illustrator) *Hippolyte's Island,* Chronicle Books (San Francisco, CA), 2001.

No Place for a Lady: Tales of Adventurous Women Travelers, Ten Speed Press (Berkeley, CA), 2002.

Good and Evil in the Garden (essays), Heavenly Monkey (Vancouver, British Columbia, Canada), 2003.

(And illustrator) *The Lives of Shadows* (novel), Chronicle Books (San Francisco, CA), 2004.

SIDELIGHTS: A book designer and illustrator, Barbara L. Hodgson founded Byzantium Books with Nick Bantock, author of the hugely popular, mixed format "Griffin & Sabine" series, with whom she collaborated on *Kubla Khan: A Pop-up Version of Coleridge's Classic* and *Paris out of Hand.* She is well known in her own right as a novelist and illustrator, with such books to her credit as *The Lives of Shadows* and *Hippolyte's Island,* which combine text, drawings, maps, and handwritten notes to tell unusual, often mysterious tales. Hodgson has also published a number of nonfiction books on subjects including opium and morphine, rats, and women travelers.

Her first solo effort, *The Tattooed Map,* takes the form of a journal written by Lydia, an inveterate traveler and collector who awakes one morning in Morocco to discover a series of flea bites on her wrist. Eventually, these bites take the form of a map, invisible to all but Lydia and a mysterious Moroccan man. When Lydia disappears, her traveling companion Christopher finds the journal, as well as the photos, maps, and ticket stubs that are included in the book and play an integral part in the mystery. Christopher takes up the tale at this point, chronicling his attempts to find Lydia. "The prose as 'written' by each of the characters resounds, each with its own individual voice, and the manner in which Hodgson lays out her plot, while unorthodox in terms of most novels, becomes a fascinating and gripping journey the reader will not want to end," concluded *Fantasy & Science Fiction* contributor Charles DeLint. Similarly, *Hippolyte's Island* uses old maps, sketches of plants and animals, and numerous other illustrations to tell the story of reporter Hippolyte Webb's journey to find the mysterious Aurora Islands, which appear on ancient maps of the South Atlantic but are unknown to modern geographers. "The real fun begins when Webb's footloose existence clashes with the precise, ordered world of Marie Simplon, his New York editor," noted a *Publishers Weekly* contributor. The reviewer added, "Hodgson, using her talents as both writer and artist, once again displays her gift for bringing charmingly idiosyncratic characters to life."

In her first nonfiction book, *The Rat: A Perverse Miscellany,* Hodgson again mixes media, editing a combination of text with medieval engravings, comics, and movie stills to reveal mankind's mixture of fascination and repulsion for this small, but sometimes devastating, creature. The result is "a book whose charm is not unlike that of a favorite frightening movie scene lovingly seen and recalled again and again," commented *Booklist* reviewer Mike Tribby.

Two other Hodgson titles illustrate humanity's love/hate relationship with narcotics. In *Opium: A Portrait of the Heavenly Demon* she brings together woodcuts, photographs, and stills from silent movies with first-person accounts, pulp fiction excerpts, and poetry to tell the history of this drug. Some critics, though, were put off by the seeming glamorization of opium. With its "ill-informed text and endless, lavish illustrations of silk-clad maidens and wise, wizened old Chinamen lost to their dreams," maintained Julian Keeling in the *New Statesman,* "this book seeks to present opium in the best possible light, as if it were a lengthy advert-[izement] sponsored by some opium growers association." In contrast, *Toronto Star* reviewer Len Gasparini called *Opium* "a rich pipeful of so many fascinating facts, photographs, anecdotes and colour illustrations that the reader can open the book to any page and experience vicariously the intoxication of Hodgson's brilliant research."

In the Arms of Morpheus: The Tragic History of Laudanum, Morphine, and Patent Medicines again portrays the history of a once-ubiquitous, perfectly legal narcotic in "a creative mixture of narrative, literary excerpts, photographs, and illustrations," in the words of *Library Journal* contributor Kathy Arsenault. Here, Hodgson reveals facts such as that Otto von Bismarck habitually used a shot of morphine to calm his nerves before addressing the German Reichstag, and that artists, doctors, and housewives alike prized the drug for its soothing qualities. The author also includes an "Opium at the Movies" filmography, which further illustrates the drug's one-time popularity.

Hodgson has also produced a history that harks back to the exotic voyages of her fictional characters. In *No Place for a Lady: Tales of Adventurous Women Travel-*

ers, she draws on diaries, letters, and memoirs to bring to life the seventeenth-, eighteenth-and nineteenth-century ladies who traveled throughout Asia and Africa by horse, camel, or foot. "The charm of this book lies not only in quotations or intriguing anecdotes, but also in the lavish illustrations," noted *Herizons* contributor Claire Helman. Some of these women traveled out of necessity, including Lady Elizabeth Craven, who was essentially tossed out of England "for adulterous behavior." Others simply refused to accept domestic restrictions, as was the case for Lady Hester Stanhope, who became the first Western woman since the Roman empire to visit the lost capital of Queen Zenobia and who ultimately settled in the wild mountainous region of Lebanon. Still others went to learn. Lady Mary Wortley Montague, for one, became the first European to describe the hidden world of the Turkish harem. But all the women travelers in Hodgson's book showed a thirst for adventure, and many donned men's clothes in order to visit even more dangerous places. *Toronto Star* contributor Nancy Wigston concluded that "Hodgson's book, thoroughly researched, meticulously annotated, remains a seductive introduction to the world of traveling women."

BIOGRAPHICAL AND CRITICAL SOURCES:

PERIODICALS

Booklist, August, 1997, Mike Tribby, review of *The Rat: A Perverse Miscellany,* p. 1862; September 15, 1999, Mike Tribby, review of *Opium: A Portrait of the Heavenly Demon,* p. 201; September 15, 2001, Whitney Scott, review of *Hippolyte's Island,* p. 190; November 15, 2001, Mike Tribby, review of *In the Arms of Morpheus: The Tragic History of Laudanum, Morphine, and Patent Medicines,* p. 527.

Boston Globe, January 31, 2002, Julie Hatfield, "'Island' Takes Readers on a Delightful Adventure," p. C4.

Chicago Tribune, January 8, 2003, Anne Stein, "Discovering Those Who Paved Way for Women Travelers Today," Women's News, p. 3.

Fantasy & Science Fiction, June, 1996, Charles DeLint, review of *The Tattooed Map.*

Herizons, winter, 2004, Claire Helman, review of *No Place for a Lady: Tales of Adventurous Women Travelers,* p. 38.

Library Journal, January, 2002, Kathy Arsenault, review of *In the Arms of Morpheus,* p. 141.

New Statesman, December 4, 2000, Julian Keeling, "The Drugs Don't Work," p. 52.

New York Times Book Review, January 17, 1999, Eric Burns, "A Box of Wonders," section 7, p. 20; October 17, 1999, Carolyn T. Hughes, "Perils of the Poppy," section 7, p. 23.

Publishers Weekly, August 19, 1996, review of *Paris Out of Hand,* p. 50; August 2, 1999, review of *Opium,* p. 66; August 13, 2001, review of *Hippolyte's Island,* p. 286.

School Library Journal, March, 1998, review of *The Rat.*

Times (London, England), November 22, 2000, "In Xanadu," p. 18.

Toronto Star, January 30, 2000, Len Gasparini, "Tokin' Offerings," Entertainment, p. 1; August 17, 2003, Nancy Wigston, "Fabled Femmes," p. D16.*

*   *   *

HOFF, Mary (King) 1956-

PERSONAL: Born August 16, 1956; daughter of Harold and Delores (Reinecke) King; married Paul Hoff; children: Tony, Kate, Daniel. *Education:* University of Wisconsin, B.S., 1978; University of Minnesota, M.A., 1984.

ADDRESSES: Agent—c/o Author Mail, Creative Education, Inc., 123 South Broad St., Mankato, MN 56001.

CAREER: Author. Freelance communicator specializing in science and medical communication.

WRITINGS:

Our Endangered Planet: Atmosphere, Lerner Publications (Minneapolis, MN), 1995.

Living Together, Creative Education (Mankato, MN), 2003.

Pollination, Creative Education (Mankato, MN), 2003.

Mimicry and Camouflage, Creative Education (Mankato, MN), 2003.

Migration, Creative Education (Mankato, MN), 2003.

Metamorphosis, Creative Education (Mankato, MN), 2003.

Life at Night, Creative Education (Mankato, MN), 2003.

Handling Heat, Creative Education (Mankato, MN), 2003.

Coping with Cold, Creative Education (Mankato, MN), 2003.

Communication, Creative Education (Mankato, MN), 2003.

Swans, Creative Education (Mankato, MN), 2004.

Tigers, Creative Education (Mankato, MN), 2004.

Monkeys, Creative Education (Mankato, MN), 2004.

Polar Bears, Creative Education (Mankato, MN), 2004.

Koalas, Creative Education (Mankato, MN), 2004.

Also contributor to periodicals.*

* * *

HOPCRAFT, Arthur 1932-2004

OBITUARY NOTICE— See index for *CA* sketch: Born November 29, 1932 (one source says November 30), in Shoeburyness, Essex, England; died November 22, 2004, in London, England. Journalist and author. Hopcraft was a well-known sports writer who later became a successful author of television screenplays. His journalism career began at the age of fifteen, when he left school to write for various local newspapers. During the 1950s, '60s, and '70s, he wrote for such papers as the *Guardian, Daily Mirror,* and *Observer,* often traveling the world to report on such serious issues as world hunger and poverty, a subject about which he wrote in his first book, *Born to Hunger* (1968). His favorite topic, however, was soccer (or football, as it is known in England and Europe), and he became well-established as a sports journalist. His second book, *The Football Man: People and Passions in Soccer* (1968; revised edition, 1971), was a critical and popular success. By the 1970s, however, Hopcraft was becoming increasingly plagued by claustrophobia, which hampered his ability to attend crowded sporting events for his reports. He found a solution when a chance meeting with someone who worked at the Stables Theatre led to his writing his first play, *Cyril and the Sex Kittens.* This was followed by other early plays, including *The Mosedale Horseshow* (1971) and the teleplays *The Reporters.* (1972) and *The Nearly Man* (1975). By the mid-1970s, Hopcraft had built a

successful television writing career, to which he added adaptations of books by such writers as Charles Dickens and John le Carré. The winner of the 1985 British Academy of Film and Television Arts award, his more recent works for television include *Hostage* (1992) and *Rebecca* (1997); he also published the autobiographical *The Great Apple Raid* (1970), and the book *Mid-Century Man* (1982).

OBITUARIES AND OTHER SOURCES:

PERIODICALS

Guardian (London, England), November 26, 2004, p. 31.

Independent (London, England), November 26, 2004, p. 42.

Times (London, England), November 27, 2004, p. 82.

* * *

HORN, Miriam

PERSONAL: Female. *Education:* Graduate of Williams College and Harvard University.

*ADDRESSES: Office—*U.S. News and World Report, 1050 Thomas Jefferson St. NW, Washington, DC 20007.

CAREER: U.S. News and World Report, Washington, DC, senior writer.

WRITINGS:

Rebels in White Gloves: Coming of Age with Hillary's Class, Wellesley '69, Times Books (New York, NY), 1999.

SIDELIGHTS: Miriam Horn's *Rebels in White Gloves: Coming of Age with Hillary's Class, Wellesley '69* is a study of the 420 members of former first lady Hillary Rodham Clinton's graduating class at the prestigious liberal arts college. She writes about the characteristics of these women, how their years at Wellesley shaped their character and politics, and what happened to them after 1969, based on her interviews with individual members.

Hillary Rodham is the most well-known graduate of her class, and Horn writes not only of her life at and after Wellesley, but also of her relationships with her classmates. She writes of other women who "have dropped acid, cheated on their husbands, had abortions, struggled to get pregnant, run away with the stableman, run away to be a Buddhist nun, made fortunes, lost fortunes, taken Prozac, started menopause, pushed a stroller through their twenty-fifth reunion parade." She also comments on those who have become respected doctors, lawyers, politicians, teachers, wives, and mothers, and, of course, on the one who became wife of a president and, after the book's publication, senator from the state of New York. Horn notes the significant social changes that have occurred in these women's lifetimes. While at Wellesley, they were taught how to stay physically appealing, talk to their husband's boss, gracefully exit a car's back seat while wearing heels, and how to pour tea. And, of course, they were taught that white gloves were mandatory when socializing after dinner. The idea of sex before marriage was associated with social ruin, and questions about sex and orgasm went unanswered. Although a Wellesley education at the all-woman college was top-notch during the late 1960s, the school was, in many ways, a finishing school.

Rodham spoke at graduation, discarding her prepared speech to urge her classmates to make a difference in the world, to protest and "question basic assumptions." She received a seven-minute standing ovation, after which classmate Nancy Wanderer told her mother that Hillary Rodham "will probably be the president of the United States someday."

Wanderer was the first in her class to marry and have a child. She later became a lawyer and had a female life partner. Kris Olson became the first U.S. attorney in Oregon, a Clinton appointment. While living in her Wellesley dorm, Martha McClintock observed that the menstrual periods of women who lived together tended to synchronize. She became a behavioral scientist and researcher. Janet McDonald, one of only five black members of the class, became a consultant and married Yale football player Calvin Hill, who later played

for the Dallas Cowboys. Their son, Grant, became a National Basketball Association rookie of the year and played for the Detroit Pistons. Advertising executive Chris Osborne, who supported draft resisters during the Vietnam conflict, has smoked dope every day since 1965 and supports legalization. Lorna Rinear is the classmate who ran off with the stableman, divorced, raised her family, and earned a Ph.D. in women's history. Several of the women did become full-time mothers.

As Horn told Bob Levey in an interview for the *Washington Post Online,* "when they entered college in 1965, the women of Hillary's class were, like their parents, mostly Republican conservatives. By the time they graduated, most were liberal Democrats, and most of them have remained both. Very few entered business school or professions in the corporate world; most are in teaching, medicine, or law, and even the lawyers are often involved in public advocacy. Only a few subscribe to conservative politics today, and I would guess that applies to fiscal policies as well."

One third of the women in Horn's group portrait admitted that they have had abortions, and an equal number claim to have been sexually harassed. Eighty percent identify themselves as feminists, and the women of their generation had fewer children than any previous generation. Twenty-three percent have none. Of those who married, forty-two percent provide half or more of their household income. Jill Abramson noted in the *New York Times Book Review* that Horn's book mirrors "the struggle of a generation to test-drive a new set of gender and cultural road rules."

Carolyn G. Heilbrun wrote in *Women's Review of Books* that *Rebels in White Gloves* "is an excellent example of the effect of the modern women's movement on so-called privileged women—Virginia Woolf called them the daughters of educated men—because, unlike so many other group studies, it combines an intelligent presentation of the revolutionary forces at work in 1969 with a skillful use of interviews and individual case studies. Miriam Horn has read the books this class read, and studied later interpretations of female identity and feminist politics. . . . She "has used personal stories with great discretion, making their different parts relevant to the cultural dilemma she is portraying."

BIOGRAPHICAL AND CRITICAL SOURCES:

PERIODICALS

Atlantic Monthly, June, 1999, Wendy Kaminer, review of *Rebels in White Gloves: Coming of Age with Hillary's Class, Wellesley '69,* pp. 134-137.

Booklist, April 15, 1999, Ilene Cooper, review of *Rebels in White Gloves,* p. 1491.

Entertainment Weekly, June 18, 1999, Gillian Flynn, review of *Rebels in White Gloves,* p. 72.

Library Journal, May 15, 1999, Julie Still, review of *Rebels in White Gloves,* p. 113.

New York Times Book Review, May 23, 1999, Jill Abramson, review of *Rebels in White Gloves,* p. 12.

People, May 17, 1999, Francine Prose, review of *Rebels in White Gloves,* p. 53.

Publishers Weekly, April 26, 1999, review of *Rebels in White Gloves,* p. 67.

Times-Picayune (New Orleans, LA), June 20, 1999, Dayna Harpster, review of *Rebels in White Gloves,* p. D7.

Women's Review of Books, May, 2000, Carolyn G. Heilbrun, review of *Rebels in White Gloves,* p. 8.

ONLINE

Washington Post Online, http://www.washingtonpost. com/ (June 1, 1999), Bob Levey, "Q & A with Miriam Horn."*

*   *   *

HORNSCHEMEIER, Paul 1977-

PERSONAL: Born 1977. *Education:* Earned degree in philosophy.

ADDRESSES: Office—Forlorn Funnies, 2324 West Walton, 3F, Chicago, IL 60622. *Agent*—c/o Author Mail, Dark Horse Comics, 10956 SE Main Street, Milwaukie, OR 97222. *E-mail*—feedback@sequentialcomics.com.

CAREER: Comic-book artist and author.

WRITINGS:

Stand on a Mountain, Look Back: Sequential Book Seven, Last Gasp (San Francisco, CA), 2001.

Mother, Come Home, introduction by Thomas Tennant, Dark Horse Comics, (Milwaukie, OR) 2003.

The Collected Sequential, AdHouse Books (Richmond, VA), 2004.

Return of the Elephant, AdHouse Books (Richmond, VA), 2004.

Contributor to volumes such as *Autobiographix,* Dark Hose Comics (Milwaukie, OR) 2003. Writer and illustrator of "Forlorn Funnies" and "Sequential" comics series.

WORK IN PROGRESS: A New Decade for Eli Guggenheim, Planet, and *Life with Mr. Dangerous,* all graphic novels.

SIDELIGHTS: Comics artist and writer Paul Hornschemeier is the creator of the comic-book series "Sequential" and "Forlorn Funnies." *"Sequential* was Hornschemeier's first, self-published attempt at a regular comic book series," noted Alan David Doane on the *Comic Book Galaxy* Web site. Doane added, "Over the course of its seven issues, *Sequential* demonstrated an emerging talent eager to assay the parameters and possibilities of his chosen artform." "Forlorn Funnies," a more recent, "and artistically more mature work," is a series that "stuns with its sheer dedication to its creator's joy of cartooning," Doane stated.

Hornschemeier has no problems with the term "comic book" to describe what he does, when many of his colleagues prefer to refer to such work as graphic novels or sequential art. "I think comic book is fine because, like any name, its definition is dictated by its use," Hornschemeier said in an interview with Julie Lain on the *Loyola Phoenix* Web site. "I have met people who are pretentious enough to never want to call a movie a 'movie,' they only call it 'film.'" "We can all put on berets and smoke clove cigarettes later."

Hornschemeier finds mixed benefit in the ongoing interest in comic book properties by Hollywood studios. "I think, unfortunately, that's one of the ways things are validated in American culture," he remarked in the interview with Lain. "A movie was made of it! Therefore it must be something of consequence. I think it's having an effect [on the comics industry], a positive effect, but I wish it didn't need that sort of thing to be validated."

"Forlorn Funnies" contains the original story that Hornschemeier has collected and published in graphic-novel format as *Mother, Come Home*. As the story opens, seven-year-old Thomas Tennant has lost his mother to cancer. His father, a professor, retains a tenuous grip on his emotions and struggles to cope with his own loss while providing as well as he can for Thomas. Gradually, the pair's roles reverse, with Thomas becoming more of the caretaker and caregiver, cleaning up the house, taking care of his mother's garden and grave, and making excuses to his father's colleagues when he misses classes or appointments. Thomas finds his strength in a lion mask and superhero cape he wears to symbolically transform himself into a powerful individual with the ability to cope with his problems and his father's as well. Eventually, Thomas loses his father, too, when the grief-crippled man checks himself into a residential-care center for psychiatric treatment. While living with an aunt and uncle, Thomas retreats into a cheerful cartoonish fantasy world where everything is perfect and just the way he wants it. Thomas's fantasies remain at the forefront as he "rescues" his father in the story's emotional climax.

In *Mother, Come Home* "Hornschemeier shows the utmost compassion for both father and son, who react to their grief the only way they know how," wrote *Library Journal* reviewer Khadija Caturani. The "book's greatest strength is the story itself and the lessons it offers for life, loss, and, most importantly, how to move on," commented *School Library Journal* reviewer Matthew L. Moffett. "The plot is a real three-hanky weeper, but Hornschemeier leverages some of the heaviness into bittersweet absurdity," observed a *Publishers Weekly* reviewer. *Entertainment Weekly* reviewer Jeff Jensen declared that *Mother, Come Home* "is deserving of the word masterpiece without reservation."

BIOGRAPHICAL AND CRITICAL SOURCES:

PERIODICALS

Booklist, February 1, 2004, Roy Olson, review of *Mother, Come Home,* p. 964.

Entertainment Weekly, February 13, 2004, Jeff Jensen, review of *Mother, Come Home,* p. L2T20.
Library Journal, March 1, 2004, Khadijah Caturani, review of *Mother, Come Home,* p. 62.
Publishers Weekly, February 16, 2004, review of *Mother, Come Home,* p. 154.
School Library Journal, Matthew L. Moffett, review of *Mother, Come Home,* p. 182.

ONLINE

Comic Book Galaxy Web site http://www.comicbookgalaxy.com/ (August 30, 2004), Alan David Doane, "Floating with Paul."
Loyola Phoenix Online, http://www.loyolaphoenix.com/ (March 17, 2004), Julie Lain, "Hornschemeier Draws on Tragedy for 'Funnies'" (nterview).
Margo Mitchell Media Web site, http://www.margomitchell.com/ (August 30, 2004), review of "Sequential."*

*   *   *

HOWARTH, Patrick (John Fielding) 1916-2004 (C. D. E. Francis)

OBITUARY NOTICE— See index for *CA* sketch: Born April 25, 1916, in Calcutta, India; died of cancer November 12, 2004, in Sherborne, Dorset, England. Public relations executive, journalist, and author. Though he spent many years in public relations for the Royal National Lifeboat Institution (RNLI), Howarth is best remembered as the author of histories, biographies, travel books, and poetry. Born in India while his father worked for the New Zealand Insurance Company, he returned to England for his education, earning a master's degree from St. John's College, Oxford, in 1937. Howarth was determined to become a journalist, and he moved to Poland to edit a publication for the Baltic Institute. Fleeing the country just as World War II was beginning, he enlisted in the British Army, where he was in charge of controlling the actions of British secret agents in Europe. After the war, he returned to Poland, working as a press attaché for the British Embassy in Warsaw until 1947. He then returned to England and obtained a job with the British Home Civil Service, working for the Ministry of Town and Country Planning and the Ministry of Housing and Local Government. Howarth grew frustrated with the bureaucracy and left government work in 1953. Several eclectic business ventures followed, including growing bananas in Fiji and organizing expeditions to the North Pole. He then found his niche with the RNLI, for which he served as public relations officer and editor of the magazine *Lifeboat* until 1979. The security of a steady job allowed Howarth to write a number of books, including fictional works such as *The Dying Ukrainian* (1953), the satirical *A Matter of Minutes* (1953), and the detective novel *Portrait of a Killer* (1957), which was written under the pen name C. D. E. Francis. Howarth also wrote histories such as *Questions in the House* (1956) and *Lifeboats and Lifeboat People* (1974), as well as biographies like *Squire: Most Generous of Men* (1963) and *Intelligence Chief Extraordinary: The Life of the Ninth Duke of Portland* (1986). The poetry he had been so fond of writing back at university—he almost won the Newdigate Poetry Prize—reemerged as well, and his 1974 verse memoir *Playback a Lifetime* was broadcast on the BBC. He continued writing poetry almost until the day he died, often hearing his poems aired on BBC Radio programs. Among his last publications were *My God, Soldiers!* (1989) and *Attila, King of the Huns* (1994).

OBITUARIES AND OTHER SOURCES:

PERIODICALS

Independent (London, England), November 19, 2004, p. 42.
Times (London, England), December 7, 2004, p. 56.

* * *

HOZIC, Aida (A.) 1963-

PERSONAL: Born April 29, 1963, in Belgrade, Yugoslavia (now Serbia and Montenegro); daughter of Arfan (a sculptor) and Nadezda (a professor; maiden name, Cuperlovic) Hozic. *Education:* University of Sarajevo, B.A., 1985; Johns Hopkins School of Advanced International Studies, M.A., 1989; University of Virginia, Ph.D., 1997.

ADDRESSES: Office—234 Anderson Hall, University of Florida, Gainesville, FL 32611. *E-mail*—hozic@ yahoo.com.

CAREER: University of Florida, Gainesville, assistant professor, 2001—.

WRITINGS:

Hollywood: Space, Power, and Fantasy in the American Economy, Cornell University Press (Ithaca, NY), 2001.

BIOGRAPHICAL AND CRITICAL SOURCES:

PERIODICALS

American Journal of Sociology, September, 2002, Jan Lin, review of *Hollywood: Space, Power, and Fantasy in the American Economy,* p. 489.

* * *

HROMIC, Alma A. 1963-
(Alma Alexander)

PERSONAL: Born 1963, in Novi Sad, Yugoslavia (now Serbia); married R. A. Deckert (a journalist and editor), June, 2000. *Education:* University of Cape Town, South Africa, M.Sc. (microbiology), 1987.

ADDRESSES: Home—506 Sudden Valley, Bellingham, WA 98229. *Agent*—c/o Author Mail, 7th Floor, HarperCollins Publishers, 10 East 53rd St., New York, NY 10022.

CAREER: Writer, editor, and microbiologist. Allergy Society, South Africa, editor of scientific journal; editor for an educational publisher in New Zealand; literary critic.

AWARDS, HONORS: Finalist, Sir Julius Vogel Award, 2002, and Award of Excellence, WordWeaving, both for *Changer of Days.*

WRITINGS:

Houses in Africa (memoir), David Ling Publishing Limited (Auckland, New Zealand), 1995.

The Dolphin's Daughter and Other Stories, Longman (London, England), 1995.

(With R. A. Deckert) *Letters from the Fire* (novel), HarperCollins (Auckland, New Zealand), 2000.

Changer of Days (fantasy series), Volume 1 and 2, HarperCollins/Voyager (Auckland, New Zealand), 2001–02.

(As Alma Alexander) *The Secrets of Jin-Shei* (novel), HarperCollins (New York, NY), 2004.

Also contributor of short fiction and nonfiction to magazines in South Africa, New Zealand, and the United Kingdom.

Hromic's work has been translated into Dutch, Italian, and German.

WORK IN PROGRESS: A novel dealing with the Anasazi Indians of the American Southwest, cybermagic, and a race of elves.

SIDELIGHTS: Born in Yugoslavia, writer Alma A. Hromic was raised in various countries of Africa where her father, employed by international aid agencies, was posted. She was trained in microbiology in South Africa, but writing about science overtook her desire for lab and research work. From South Africa, Hromic moved to New Zealand, where she published her first book-length work, *Houses in Africa,* a memoir of the twenty years she spent in Zambia, Swaziland, and South Africa. She also published a collection of three fables in New Zealand in 1995, the best-selling *The Dolphin's Daughter and Other Stories.*

In 1999, with the beginning of NATO air strikes against Serbia, Hromic witnessed from afar the destruction of her native town, Novi Sad. Desperate to be somehow involved from the distance of her home in Auckland, New Zealand, she began a series of e-mail correspondences with a friend she had met online, Florida journalist R. A. Deckert. The result of this correspondence was the collaboration of *Letters from the Fire,* a "cyber-romance novel set in the political context of the NATO bombings," as Margie Thomson described the book in a *New Zealand Herald Review.* Composed in real time as the two watched the unfolding of events in Serbia from both New Zealand and Florida, the novel tells of the growing love of Dave, a liberal American opposed to the war, and

Sasha, a Serb in Novi Sad undergoing NATO bombings. For Vasili Stavropoulos, reviewing *Letters from the Fire* in Australia's *Sydney Morning Herald,* the novel "makes an important contribution to our understanding of the Kosovo crisis, bringing it back from the abstractions of international relations to the minutiae of ordinary life." The fictional romance between Dave and Sasha found reality in the lives of the book's coauthors, who were married in 2000 and moved to the state of Washington.

The versatile Hromic next ventured into fantasy literature, publishing two volumes of *Changer of Days* in 2001 and 2002. The volumes tell the story of nine-year-old Anghara Kir Hama, who loses her powerful father and loving mother, and also her royal name and her home at Miranei, mountain capital of the land of Roisinan. She is forced into hiding by her greedy half-brother Sif, who not only steals her kingdom but also seeks her death to secure his hold on the future of the Kir Hama dynasty. Anghara must act with a maturity far beyond her years in order to survive; she develops her powers of sight as she flees to the safety of Sanctuary, but even there she finds betrayal. Finally escaping to the harsh desert, she finds allies and a new strength to battle Sif. Victoria Strauss, writing on *SF Site.com,* called the work an "epic fantasy."

Hromic discovered science fiction and fantasy when she was a teen growing up in Africa. Speaking with interviewer Chris Przybyszewski for *SF Site.com,* Hromic noted that once she discovered the works of writers such as Ursula K. LeGuin, Roger Zelazny and J. R. R. Tolkien, "I never looked back." The work of LeGuin in particular influenced her 2004 novel, *The Secrets of Jin-Shei,* written under the name Alma Alexander. According to *Booklist* reviewer Nancy Pearl, this "fast-paced, imaginative, and thoroughly engrossing fantasy explores the meaning of friendship and loyalty among eight women."

Set in a mythical Chinese kingdom where mothers have passed down to their daughters a secret language and the ability to create special friendships, *The Secrets of Jin-Shei* focuses on the young poet Tai, daughter of a seamstress. Tai finds her special friendship, her jin-shei, in the form of the oldest daughter of the emperor, and this friendship changes not only Tai's life but also the fate of the entire realm. Pearl noted that this was the first of Hromic's novels to be published in the United States and prophesied that it "will surely whet readers' appetites for more." A *Kirkus Reviews* critic described the novel as the events of an "ancient sisterhood [who] fight, die, and practice sorcery for one another as they struggle to survive." For this critic the novel is "more episodic than epic," but Jennifer Baker, writing in *Library Journal,* had higher praise, calling *The Secrets of Jin-Shei* a "perfect genre-buster: romance, political intrigue, adventure, horror, magic, suspense—and enough anthropological detail to create a believable alternate history." And Strauss found the same work both "vivid and involving . . . an exotic journey into the imagination, and a graceful exploration of the heart."

Hromic told *CA:* "Reading is the first thing that got me interested in writing. As a child I read the way other people breathed or ate—it was as much a part of my existence as my heartbeat. After that, it was just a matter of time. In particular, though, I have to single out the influence of my poet grandfather, who taught me to love language when I was barely a toddler. It was thanks to this man and his beautiful spirit that I felt able to spread my own literary wings. I owe him more than I can possibly say.

"I read widely and voraciously. In the mainstream arena (and I include historical fiction in this bracket), I would single out an eclectic mixture of contemporary and more venerable writers like Louis de Bernieres, Pearl Buck, Howard Spring, Oscar Wilde, Shakespeare, John Glasworthy, Isabel Allende, Sharon Penman, Ivo Andric (Nobel prize winner from Yugoslavia), and a bunch of poets including, but not limited to, Neruda, Rimbaud, Pushkin, and my grandfather (Stevan Mutibaric). In the speculative fiction arena (fantasy and science fiction), I would like to mention Neil Gaiman, Guy Gavriel Kay, Charles de Lint, Judith Tarr, Michael Moorcock, Arthur C. Clarke, Ursula K. le Guin, and the list goes on. A writer cannot be a writer unless the reading net is cast far and wide.

"My writing process is, in a word, chaotic. I seldom, if ever, write from synopsis and frequently find out what happens next in a story at the time as my readers would—by writing that next scene. I never know what my characters might get up to from one chapter to the next, and I am often utterly taken by surprise when they change the track I thought they were on and disappear to pursue their own agendas. Somehow, though, it always works out.

"The most surprising thing I have learned as a writer is that it is possible to live in many worlds and love them all."

BIOGRAPHICAL AND CRITICAL SOURCES:

PERIODICALS

Booklist, March 1, 2004, Nancy Pearl, review of *The Secrets of Jin-Shei,* p. 136.

Kirkus Reviews, February 1, 2004, review of *The Secrets of Jin-Shei,* pp. 95-96.

Library Journal, March 1, 2004, Jennifer Baker, review of *The Secrets of Jin-Shei,* p. 106.

New Zealand Herald, October 2, 1999, Margie Thomson, review of *Letters from the Fire.*

Sydney Morning Herald (Sydney, Australia), December 24, 1999, Vasili Stavropoulos, "We Shall Create a Desert and Call It Peace."

ONLINE

Alma A. Hromic Home Page, http://www.almahromic.com (July 5, 2004).

SF Site.com, http://www.sfsite.com/ (April, 2004), Chris Przybyszewski, "A Conversation with Alma Alexander"; (July 5, 2004) Victoria Strauss, review of *The Secrets of Jin-Shei.*

WordWeaving.com, http://www.wordweaving.com/ (July 5, 2004).

*   *   *

HURVITZ, Yair 1941-1988

PERSONAL: Born 1941, in Tel Aviv, Israel; died from heart failure 1988, in Tel Aviv, Israel.

CAREER: Poet. Worked as a typesetter and proofreader.

WRITINGS:

Shirim min ha-katseh ha-namukh, Manu shir (Tel Aviv, Israel), 1962.

Shirim le-Lu'is (title means "Poems to Louise"), 'Akshav (Jerusalem, Israel), 1963, reprinted, 1988.

Salviyon, 'Akshav (Jerusalem, Israel), 1966.

Be-'ir she-reki'im lah en u-margo'ah mahseh, Gog (Tel Aviv, Israel), 1968.

'Onat ha-mekhashefah (title means "Season of the Witch"), Daga (Tel Aviv, Israel), 1969.

Yonaikah, 'Eked (Tel Aviv, Israel), 1970.

Narkisim le-malkhut madmenah; shirim, Sifriyat po'alim (Merhavyah, Israel), 1972.

Shirim: 1960/1973 (title means "Poems: 1960-1973"), Mif'alim universita'iyim (Tel Aviv, Israel), 1975.

Be-shivti levadi, Mif'alim universita'iyim (Tel Aviv, Israel), 1976.

Perakim mi-sefer ha-halom: shirim li-vene ha-ne'urim (children's poems), illustrated by Nahum Kohen, ha-Kibuts ha-me'uhad (Tel Aviv, Israel; Jerusalem, Israel), 1978.

Makom, ha-Kibuts ha-me'uhad (Tel Aviv, Israel), 1978.

Anatomiyah shel geshem (title means "Anatomy of Rain"), ha-Kibuts ha-me'uhad (Tel Aviv, Israel), 1980.

Yalkut li-yedidim, Ya'ir Hurvits (Israel), 1980.

Erets behirah: shirim 1961-1981 (title means "Chosen Land: Poems 1961-1981"), ha-Kibuts ha-me'uhad (Tel Aviv, Israel), 1982.

Yehasim u-de'agah: shirim (title means "Anxious Relations: Poems"), ha-Kibuts ha-me'uhad (Tel Aviv, Israel), 1986.

Tsipor kelu'ah (title means "Atrial Flutter"), ha-Kibuts ha-me'uhad (Tel Aviv, Israel), 1987.

(Translator) *Ha-Shoshan ha-katan Iavan: entologyah Skotitu* (title means "The Little White Rose: An Anthology of Scottish Poetry"), 'Am 'oved (Tel Aviv, Israel), 1988.

Goral ha-gan: kol ha-shirim, ha-Kibuts ha-me'uhad (Tel Aviv, Israel), 1989.

Kol kitve Ya'ir Hurvits, ha-Kibuts ha-me'uhad (Tel Aviv, Israel), 1989.

Authors works included in anthologies of Hebrew poetry, such as *After the First Rain: Israeli Poems on War and Peace,* Syracuse University Press (Syracuse, NY), 1998.

SIDELIGHTS: Yair Hurvitz lived his entire life in Tel Aviv, Israel, and was known as one of the "Tel-Aviv Poets," a group of Israeli poets who emerged in the 1960s. Other poets in this group included Meir Weiseltier, Ahon Shabtai, and Yona Wallach. Writing in Hebrew, Hurvitz and his fellow avant-garde poets believed the poetry of the 1950s to be repressive and experimented with new poetic forms in an effort to make a break from earlier Hebrew poetic forms. The Tel Aviv Poets, as they became known, conducted readings at universities, hotels, and nightclubs and sometimes would mix readings of English and Hebrew poetry and music. They often sold broadsheets of their poetry at these readings, which were usually well attended. The group often published in the Hebrew literary journals *Achsahv* and *Siman Kriah.*

Hurvitz, who made his living as a typesetter and proofreader, became known for his restrained style and the underlying sadness of his poems as he ruminated on mortality. In addition to his several volumes of poetry, Hurvitz's verse can also be found in many Hebrew poetry anthologies. He was also interested in Scottish poetry and in 1988 translated an anthology of poetry from that region. Hurvitz died from heart failure in 1988.

BIOGRAPHICAL AND CRITICAL SOURCES:

PERIODICALS

Siman Kriah, Volume 21, 1990, Oppenheimer Yochai, "Interim-situations in the Poetry of Yair Hurvitz," pp. 280-287.

OTHER

Mifgash 'im mishtatfe Siman keri'ah (sound recording of 1976 radio broadcast), Kol Yisra'el (Jerusalem, Israel), 1995.*

* * *

HUTCHINS, William Maynard 1944-

PERSONAL: Born October 11, 1944, in Berea, KY; son of Francis Stephenson (a college president) and Louise Frances (a physician; maiden name, Gilman) Hutchins; married Sarah Sadler (a graphic artist); children: Franya Elizabeth, Kip Grosvenor. *Ethnicity:* "Anglo." *Education:* Yale University, B.A., 1964; University of Chicago, M.A., 1967, Ph.D., 1971.

ADDRESSES: Home—550 Country Haven Lane, Todd, NC 28684. *Office*—Department of Philosophy and Religion, Appalachian State University, Boone, NC 28608. *E-mail*—hutchwm@appstate.edu.

CAREER: Gerard Institute, Sidon, Lebanon, instructor in English, 1964-65; *Encyclopaedia Britannica,* Chicago, IL, Middle East research editor, 1971-72; Northern Illinois University, DeKalb, instructor in Arabic, 1972-73; University of Chicago, visiting assistant professor of Arabic, 1973-74; University of Ghana, lecturer and head of Arabic studies, 1974-77; Harvard University, Cambridge, MA, postdoctoral researcher at Center for Middle Eastern Studies, 1977-78; Appalachian State University, Boone, NC, assistant professor, 1978-81, associate professor, 1981-86, professor of philosophy and religion, 1986—. Bowdoin College, visiting assistant professor, 1979; Virginia Polytechnic Institute and State University, visiting assistant professor, 1980; New York University, visiting scholar at Center for Near Eastern Studies, 1983; American Research Center in Egypt, fellow, 1984-85; American University in Cairo, professor, 1991-93; University of Angers, exchange professor, 2002-03. ASU Loft Facility, New York, NY, director, 1983.

MEMBER: Middle East Studies Association, American Literary Translators Association.

AWARDS, HONORS: CASA fellow in Egypt, 1968-69; grant for Egypt, National Endowment for the Humanities, 1984-85; first prizes for fiction, *Crucible,* 1987, 1991.

WRITINGS:

Tawfiq al-Hakim: A Reader's Guide, Lynne Rienner Publishers (Boulder, CO), 2003.

Contributor of articles, short stories, and reviews to periodicals, including *Cold Mountain Review, Crucible, Journal of Near Eastern Studies, International Journal of Middle East Studies, Middle East Journal, Paintbrush, Translation Review,* and *Muslim World.*

TRANSLATOR

Plays, Prefaces, and Postscripts of Tawfiq al-Hakim, Three Continents Press (Washington, DC), Volume 1: *Theater of the Mind,* 1981, Volume 2: *Theater of Society,* 1983.

Ibrahim Abd al-Qadir al-Mazini, *Al-Mazini's Egypt,* Three Continents Press (Washington, DC), 1983.

Muhammad Salmawy, *Come Back Tomorrow,* Alef Publishing House (Cairo, Egypt), 1985.

(With others; and editor) *Egyptian Tales and Short Stories of the 1970s and 1980s,* American University in Cairo Press (Cairo, Egypt), 1987.

(And editor) *Nine Essays of al-Jahiz,* Peter Lang Publishing (New York, NY), 1989.

Naguib Mahfouz, *Palace Walk,* Doubleday (New York, NY), 1990.

(And author of introduction) Tawfiq al-Hakim, *Return of the Spirit,* Three Continents Press (Washington, DC), 1990.

Naguib Mahfouz, *Palace of Desire,* Doubleday (New York, NY), 1991.

Naguib Mahfouz, *Sugar Street,* Doubleday (New York, NY), 1992.

(And editor) Tawfiq al-Hakim, *In the Tavern of Life and Other Stories,* Lynne Rienner Publishers (Boulder, CO), 1997.

Naguib Mahfouz, *The Cairo Trilogy,* Everyman's Library (New York, NY), 2001.

WORK IN PROGRESS: Translating *Anubis* by Ibrahim al-Koni, for American University in Cairo Press; translating *Dar al-Basha: The Pasha's Residence* by Hasan Nasr and *A Feminine Ending and Other Stories* by Fatima Yousef al-Ali.

BIOGRAPHICAL AND CRITICAL SOURCES:

PERIODICALS

Research in African Literatures, spring, 2004, Farida Abu-Haidar, review of *Tawfiq al-Hakim: A Reader's Guide,* p. 198.

World Literature Today, summer, 1998, Issa J. Boullata, review of *In the Tavern of Life and Other Stories,* p. 677.

*   *   *

HUTCHINSON, Ron 1947(?)-

PERSONAL: Born c. 1947, in Lisburn, County Antrim, Northern Ireland; married; wife's name Alisa; children: Isabella. *Religion:* Protestant.

ADDRESSES: Home—Los Angeles, CA. *Agent*—c/o Judy Daish Associates, 2 St. Charles Place, London W10 6EG, England.

CAREER: Playwright and screenwriter. Worked at a number of jobs including bookseller, carpet salesman, fish gutter, and scene shifter; Ministry of Defence and Ministry of Labour, clerk; Department of Health and Social Security, Coventry, England, social worker and claims investigator; Royal Shakespeare Company, London, England, resident writer, 1978-79.

AWARDS, HONORS: George Devine Award, 1978; John Whiting Award, 1984; Emmy Award, 1989, for the miniseries *Murderers Among Us: The Simon Wiesenthal Story;* CableAce Award, 1989.

WRITINGS:

PLAYS

Says I, Says He (produced in Sheffield, England, 1977; produced in London, England, 1978; produced in New York, NY, 1979), Proscenium Press (Newark, DE), 1980.
Eejits, produced in London, England, 1978.
Jews/Arabs, produced in London, England, 1978.
Anchorman, produced in London, England, 1979.
(Adapter) *Christmas of a Nobody* (adapted from *Diary of a Nobody*), produced in London, England, 1979.
The Irish Play, produced in London, England, 1980.
Into Europe, produced in London, England, 1981.
Risky City, produced in Coventry, England, 1981.
(Adapter) *The Dillen* (adapted from a work by Angela Hewins), produced in Stratford-on-Avon, England, 1983.
Rat in the Skull (produced in London, England, 1984; produced in New York, NY, 1985), Methuen (London, England), 1984.
(With Angela Hewins) *Mary, after the Queen,* produced in Stratford-on-Avon, England, 1985.
(Adapter) *Curse of the Baskervilles* (adapted from a story by Arthur Conan Doyle), produced in Plymouth, England, 1987.
(Adapter) *Babbit: A Marriage* (adapted from the novel by Sinclair Lewis), produced in Los Angeles, CA, 1987.
Pygmies in the Ruins, produced in Belfast, Northern Ireland, 1991, produced in London, England, 1992.

(Adapter) *Flight* (adapted from the play by Mikhail Bulgakov; produced at Olivier Theatre, London, England, 1998), Nick Hern Books (London, England), 1998.
Burning Issues (two-act; produced in London, England, 2002), Faber and Faber (London, England), 2000.
Beau Brummell, (produced in Brighton, England, 2001), Oberon (London, England, 2001.
Lags, produced in Edinburgh, Scotland, 2002.
Moonlight and Magnolias, produced at Goodman Theater, Chicago, IL, 2004.
Head Case, produced in Stratford-on-Avon, England, 2005.

Also author of radio plays, including *Roaring Boys,* 1977; *Murphy Unchained,* 1978; *There Must Be a Door,* 1979; *Motorcade,* 1980; *Risky City,* 1981; *Troupers,* 1988; and *Larkin,* 1988.

TELEVISION PLAYS

Bull Week (miniseries), British Broadcasting Corporation, 1980.
Bird of Prey, British Broadcasting Corporation, 1982.
Bird of Prey 2, British Broadcasting Corporation, 1984.
Connie (series; also see below), Independent Television, 1985.
"Window, Sir?," *Unnatural Causes,* Independent Television, 1986.
(With others) *Murderers among Us: The Simon Wiesenthal Story,* Citadel Entertainment, 1989.
(With Terry Curtis Fox) *Perfect Witness,* Home Box Office, 1989.
Red King, White Knight, Home Box Office, 1989.
(With Michael Zagor) *The Josephine Baker Story,* Home Box Office, 1991.
Prisoner of Honor, Home Box Office, 1991.
Blue Ice, Home Box Office, 1992.
Against the Wall, Home Box Office, 1994.
(With others) *The Burning Season,* Home Box Office, 1994.
(With Stanley Weiser) *Fatherland,* Home Box Office, 1994.
(With others) *The Tuskegee Airmen,* Home Box Office, 1995.
Slave of Dreams, Showtime Entertainment, 1995.
(And executive producer) *Traffic* (miniseries), USA Network, 2004.

Also author of *Twelve off the Belt,* 1977; *Deasy Desperate,* 1979; *The Last Window Cleaner,* 1979; *The Out of Town Boys,* 1979; *The Winkler,* 1979; *The Marksman* (miniseries), 1987; and *Dead Man Out,* 1989.

OTHER

(With Richard Stanley) *The Island of Dr. Moreau* (screenplay), New Line Cinema, 1996.

Connie (novelization of the television series of the same title), Severn House (London, England), 1985.

WORK IN PROGRESS: Currently working on the script for an unauthorized biography of Oprah Winfrey for the National Broadcasting Company.

SIDELIGHTS: British dramatist Ron Hutchinson has built a diverse writing career that includes work for radio, stage, and screen. Born near Lisburn in Northern Ireland and raised in Coventry, Warwickshire, England, Hutchinson supported himself through a variety of odd jobs during his early years as a writer. In the late 1970s, his plays began to be produced, and in 1978 he was made a resident writer for the Royal Shakespeare Company, then based in London. From there he was able to make the leap to writing for television and film, and he eventually moved to Los Angeles in 1988.

Much of Hutchinson's early writing reflects his Irish background. He addresses the experiences of Irish characters away from their homeland as well as those embroiled in the political turmoil of the country, yet he manages to strike a balance that enables him to connect with audiences regardless of their background, tapping into universal themes. Hutchinson admits to an early awareness of the situation in Ireland, telling *Chicago Sun-Times* contributor Hedy Weiss that "even as a child I was conscious that there was something in the landscape which was brooding. . . . There was a cliff we walked along that had been the scene of a massacre; there was a house . . . which had remained abandoned for forty years because Catholics had once lived in it." He went on to refer to writing plays as an exorcism, noting, "I think theater along with tea and violence are Ireland's three national addictions. . . . I don't really know what led me to this compulsive writing of dialogue; all I know is that I find it difficult to stop doing it."

Hutchinson's play *Rat in the Skull* depicts the interrogation of an Irish Republican Army militant, arrested when a load of explosives is found beneath his bed by a Protestant policeman. During questioning, the policeman slowly begins to understand the futility of the longstanding feud between the groups dividing Northern Ireland as he grows to know the suspect. Don McLeese, in a review for the *Chicago Sun-Times,* noted that "the 'rat in the skull' of Hutchinson's title is the suspicion that whatever one devotes himself to blindly might result in the waste of a life. His play suggests that one cannot escape history . . . but that one needn't be trapped by it." Reviewing the work for the *Irish Voice,* Frank Shouldice wrote that "the writing is tight, forceful, provocative and the message uncompromising. Neither are there any happy endings—if the outlook appears bleak, you can put that down to the play's realism."

Other works that rely heavily on Hutchinson's Irish identity are *Says I, Says He,* the tale of two boys from Ulster who lead very different lives and nearly escape the violence of Northern Ireland before being gunned down; *Risky City,* which depicts through a series of deathbed flashbacks the way in which a Coventry-Irish boy misspent his youth; and *Eejits,* the story of a four-member London-based musical band that cannot escape the divisive nature of their Irish background. *Pygmies in the Ruins* explores the history of Belfast, using time travel to connect nineteenth-century characters involved in an unsolved murder with their twentieth-century counterparts. In a *Chicago Sun-Times* review, Weiss commented, "Hutchinson does not take an entirely hopeful view of the situation in Northern Ireland, but his slightly surreal play at least attempts to get to the roots of the struggle. And the man can write!"

While staging *Rat in the Skull* in Chicago, Hutchinson was given the opportunity to break into writing for Hollywood. Actor Brian Dennehy, who was cast in the role of the policeman, showed Hutchinson's work to his agent, a contact that led to Hutchinson selling a four-page treatment to director and producer Michael Mann. "I earned more money for it than all my plays put together," Hutchinson told Betty Mohr, in an interview with *Script.* He went on to write a number of television scripts, including *The Burning Season,* which recounts the story of Chico Mendes, whose struggle to improve conditions for struggling workers in Brazil ended when he was murdered in 1988;

Against the Wall, a recounting of the 1971 inmate rebellion at Attica Prison; and *The Josephine Baker Story.* He also cowrote the screenplay for the 1996 film remake of *The Island of Dr. Moreau.*

Working in Hollywood has not stopped Hutchinson from continuing to write plays. He explained to Mohr, "I write screenplays because producers want to pay me lots of money to do so, and I write plays because I get inspired by an idea. A lot of budding screenwriters have the mistaken notion that you write a movie because of a passionate desire. That's not really how it is. As a screenwriter, you're really a hired gun."

Hutchinson has also shifted his focus away from Ireland in his more recent works, which include *Flight,* adapted from Mikhail Bulgakov's play, and *Moonlight and Magnolias,* which recounts the behind-the-scenes drama during the filming of *Gone with the Wind.* Weiss, reviewing *Moonlight and Magnolias* for the *Chicago Sun-Times,* called it "a Hollywood dream-factory farce wired to a surprisingly ferocious explosive device," going on to say of Hutchinson, "he has a gift for enveloping you in blackness. And then, with a single line or gesture, he can lift the heavy cloud and get on with the hilarity."

BIOGRAPHICAL AND CRITICAL SOURCES:

BOOKS

Contemporary Dramatists, 6th edition, St. James Press (Detroit, MI), 1999.

PERIODICALS

Chicago Sun-Times, September 8, 1985, Hedy Weiss, "Hutchinson's War of Words: Playwright Reveals the Workings of an Irishman's 'Skull,'" p. 6; September 13, 1985, Don McLeese, "A Revolution of Passion 'Rat in the Skull' Reveals What Happens when Irish Eyes Aren't Smiling," p. 37; March 8, 1992, Weiss, "A Whirlwind Theater Tour: So Many Shows in So Little Time," p. 3; May 20, 2004, Weiss, "Playwright Moolings with Hollywood Scarlett," p. 45; May 27, 2004, Weiss, "Frankly, My Dear, The Real Story of 'GWTW' Was Offstage," p. 49.

Chicago Tribune, May 14, 2004, Chris Jones, "Hollywood Rewrite Guy Pens Shows of His Own," p. 3.

Daily Herald Correspondent (Arlington Heights, IL), May 28, 2004, Jack Helbig, "Behind the Movie: 'Moonlight' Gives Excellent Fictionalized Account of the Making of 'Gone with the Wind,'" p. 28.

Entertainment Weekly, March 25, 1994, review of *Against the Wall,* p. 44; September 16, 1994, Ken Tucker, review of *The Burning Season,* p. 98.

Guardian (Manchester, England), January 8, 1997, Chris Arnot, "Whoring for Hollywood: Ron Hutchinson Is One of the Greats of British Theatre, Yet for the Past Decade He's Been Turning Tricks in Tinsletown," p. T14; October 26, 2001, Michael Billington, "Acting behind Bars in Bristol: *Lags,*" p. 20; June 23, 2004, Michael Billington, "New York's Stages Are in a Slump: Now All America's Liveliest Drama Is in Chicago," p. 12.

Irish Voice, November 5, 1991, Frank Shouldice, "The Scars of History," p. 35.

Nation, May 16, 1994, Lewis Cole, review of *Against the Wall,* p. 678.

New Statesman and Society, March 6, 1992, Andy Lavender, "Aesthetics of Extinction," review of *Pygmies in the Ruins,* pp. 39-40.

People, September 9, 1996, Ralph Novak, review of *The Island of Dr. Moreau,* p. 17.

Spectator, October 21, 1995, Sheridan Morley, "The Agony of Living Apart," review of *Rat in the Skull,* pp. 59-60; April 21, 2001, Morley, review of *Beau Brummell,* p. 50; April 5, 2003, Lloyd Evans, "Sound and Fury," review of *Lags,* p. 49.

Variety, May 15, 2000, Matt Wolf, review of *Burning Issues,* p. 38; June 14, 2004, Chris Jones, "Farce Takes Breezy Look at 'Wind,'" p. 45.

ONLINE

Albemarle-London Web site, http://www.albemarle-london.com/ (September 27, 2004), "Flight."

Doollee.com, http://www.doollee.com/ (September 27, 2004), "Ron Hutchinson."

New York Theatre Guide Online, http://www.newyork theatreguide.com/ (September 27, 2004), "Ron Hutchinson."

Royal Shakespeare Company Web site, http://www.rsc.org.uk/ (September 27, 2004), "Head Case."

Script Online, http://www.scriptmag.com/ (September 27, 2004), Betty Mohr, interview with Hutchinson.*

HUYLER, Frank 1964-

PERSONAL: Born 1964, in Berkeley, CA; married, 2000. *Education:* Williams College, B.A., 1986; University of North Carolina School of Medicine, M.D., M.P.H.

ADDRESSES: Home—Albuquerque, NM. *Office*—c/o University of New Mexico Hospitals, 2211 Lomas Boulevard, N.E., Albuquerque, NM 87106. *Agent*— Christy Fletcher, Fletcher and Parry, The Carriage House, 121 East 17th Street, New York, NY 10003.

CAREER: Emergency medicine physician, educator, and author. University of New Mexico Hospitals, Albuquerque, resident, 1993-96; physician, 1996—; University of New Mexico, Albuquerque, assistant professor of emergency medicine.

WRITINGS:

The Blood of Strangers: Stories from Emergency Medicine, University of California Press (Berkeley, CA), 1999.
The Laws of Invisible Things (novel), Henry Hold (New York, NY), 2004.

Contributor of stories and poetry to periodicals, including *Atlantic Monthly, Georgia Review,* and *Poetry.*

SIDELIGHTS: A practicing physician who works in emergency medicine, Frank Huyler writes about the people and situations he comes in contact with every day on the job. Although he excelled in the humanities over science at school, and majored in English at Williams College in Massachusetts, Huyler felt the natural career paths that followed such an education were less practical than he desired, and so he shifted direction and attended medical school at the University of North Carolina, Chapel Hill. From there he completed his residency at the University of New Mexico Hospitals in Albuquerque, then stayed on after he had qualified as a doctor. Because his love of writing remained he follows in the footsteps of such medical scribes as William Carlos Williams and Ethan Canin, producing both poetry and fiction.

Huyler's first book, *The Blood of Strangers: Stories from Emergency Medicine,* is a collection of short stories based on his emergency room experiences.

Though not strictly true, the situations in his work are grounded in actual events. In an interview with Matt Seaton for the *Guardian Online,* Huyler explained, "the emergency room is a very strange, surreal place at times. . . . You have these very intense moments where you're asking these very personal questions of people who are strangers to you. . . . There's a facelessness on both sides, and yet you're propelled into moments where you discuss issues that you never would in another world. There is a kind of 'distant intimacy.'" Those are the moments, the connections, that drive Huyler's stories. A contributor to *Publishers Weekly* stated that "this haunting, exquisitely observed collection of medical vignettes is much more than a compilation of odd cases from the emergency room. Huyler probes beneath the surface to reveal the marrow." *Hastings Center Report* reviewer Abigail Zuger wrote that "*The Blood of Strangers* is a work of art, an utter pleasure to read and reread, and a good example of how transcendent medical stories can be in the right hands." She went on to say that "the prose is lucid and assured enough, and the view idiosyncratic enough, that the usual clichés are simply not here. . . . Instead, Huyler shows us the startling small poems everywhere." By sharing his experiences, Huyler also helps the reader understand why there is an emotional distance between patient and physician during emergency room care. Julian Keeling, in a review for the *New Statesman,* noted that "Huyler builds a picture of the emergency room and its shifting cast of characters as a lurid, claustrophobic setting, and his infrequent forays out of it. . . allow us welcome breaths of untainted air."

The Laws of Invisible Things recounts the experiences of Michael Grant, a young doctor who has a young girl die in his care. Grant is unsure if he did everything in his power to save the child, so when her father also appears as a patient, Grant does not feel able to turn him away. He discovers an odd pattern on the back of the man's throat and in his eye, but before he can find an explanation, the man dies in a mysterious fire and Grant begins to come down with the same symptoms. A reviewer for *Publishers Weekly* wrote: "Chilling, subdued and scalpel sharp, this debut novel. . . explores the hazy borderlines of sin and disease." Dick Adler, writing for Chicago's *Tribune Books,* commented that, "in lesser hands, the book's ending could easily have turned into just a blast of weird science or heavy-handed symbolism. But Huyler's wisdom and restraint make it something more original." In a review for the *Boston Globe,* Robert Knox remarked that

"Huyler's insider knowledge gives us authoritatively dramatic accounts of the blood-and-gut wrestling of the medical expertise with failing flesh. Combined with his powers of psychological observation and storytelling skill, this privileged perspective gives us the inside story on both sides of the mortal collision in the ER."

BIOGRAPHICAL AND CRITICAL SOURCES:

PERIODICALS

Booklist, September 1, 1999, William Beatty, review of *The Blood of Strangers: Stories from Emergency Medicine,* p. 51; March 15, 2004, Donna Chavez, review of *The Laws of Invisible Things,* p. 1264.

Boston Globe, August 18, 2004, Robert Knox, "Intense Novel Captures a Doctor in Crisis," p. B6.

British Medical Journal, May 19, 2001, Giles Kent, review of *The Blood of Strangers,* p. 1252.

Economist, April 10, 2004, review of *The Laws of Invisible Things,* p. 71.

Entertainment Weekly, April 9, 2004, Thom Geier, review of *The Laws of Invisible Things,* p. 90.

Guardian, January 6, 2001, Matt Seaton, "Distant Intimacy."

Hastings Center Report, May, 2000, Abigail Zuger, review of *The Blood of Strangers,* p. 48.

Journal of the American Medical Association, August 18, 2004, Tony Miksanek, review of *The Laws of Invisible Things,* p. 869.

Kirkus Reviews, January 15, 2004, review of *The Laws of Invisible Things,* p. 54.

Library Journal, April 1, 2004, A. J. Wright, review of *The Laws of Invisible Things,* p. 122.

New Statesman, January 15, 2001, Julian Keeling, "Deathbeds," p. 54.

Publishers Weekly, August 30, 1999, review of *The Blood of Strangers,* p. 65; March 1, 2004, review of *The Laws of Invisible Things,* p. 49.

San Francisco Chronicle, May 25, 2004, David Kipen, "Of Things that Return to Vex Us: Doctor Faces Midlife Crisis," p. E1.

Tribune Books (Chicago, IL), April 4, 2004, Dick Adler, "Domestic Troubles, Foreign Intrigue: Lawyer, Priests, Doctors, and Cops Rule the Roost," p. 3.

ONLINE

FictionWise.com, http://www.fictionwise.com/ (September 27, 2004), "Frank Huyler."

Guardian Online, http://books.guardian.co.uk/ (September 27, 2004), "Frank Huyler."

University of New Mexico Hospitals Web site, http://hsc.unm.edu/ (September 27, 2004), "Frank Huyler."*

*　　*　　*

HYMAN, Trina Schart 1939-2004

OBITUARY NOTICE— See index for *CA* sketch: Born April 8, 1939, in Philadelphia, PA; died of complications from breast cancer November 19, 2004, in Lebanon, NH. Illustrator and author. Hyman was a Caldecott Medal-winning illustrator of children's books. She studied art and illustration at the Philadelphia Museum College of Art and the Boston Museum School of the Arts in the late 1950s, and attended the Konstfackskolan in Sweden from 1960 until 1961. Upon her graduation, she immediately began publishing her work in children's books, with her debut in Hertha Von Gebhardt's *Toffe och den lilla bilen* (1961). Except for working as an artist and then art director for the children's magazine *Cricket* during the 1970s, Hyman spent most of her career as a freelancer. She contributed her illustrations to well over one hundred titles by such children's authors as Virginia Haviland, Donald J. Sobol, Kathryn Lasky, Eleanor Cameron, Myra Cohn Livingston, Betsy Hearne, Eric Kimmel, and Lloyd Alexander. Her illustrations were also published in editions of classics by the Brothers Grimm, Hans Christian Andersen, J. M. Barrie, and Mark Twain. Hyman, who was particularly noted for illustrating classics of folklore and fairy tales, also published seven of her own authored books, including *How Six Found Christmas* (1969), a retelling of *Little Red Riding Hood* (1983), and *The Alphabet Game* (2000). Her numerous awards include three Caldecott medals, the Dorothy Canfield Fisher Award, several *Boston Globe-Horn Book* honors, and many others.

OBITUARIES AND OTHER SOURCES:

PERIODICALS

Chicago Tribune, November 23, 2004, section 3, p. 11.

New York Times, November 24, 2004, p. C15.

I-J

IRVINE, Reed (John) 1922-2004

OBITUARY NOTICE— See index for *CA* sketch: Born September 29, 1922, in Salt Lake City, UT; died of complications following a stroke November 16, 2004, in Rockville, MD. Consumer advocate, economist, and author. Irvine was the founder of the watchdog group Accuracy in Media (AIM). A graduate of the University of Utah, where he earned a B.A. in 1942, Irvine acted as an intelligence officer in the Pacific theater during World War II. After the war, he returned to school, first at the University of Washington and then attending Oxford University on a Fulbright scholarship. He graduated from Oxford in 1951 and was hired as an economist at the Federal Reserve System board of governors. From 1963 until 1977 he was international finance adviser for the Far East section. It was while working for the Federal Reserve that he got his idea to form AIM out of frustration with what he considered to be the slanted liberal perspective of the media. Founded in 1969, AIM often worked to get equal air time on television and space in newspapers for its more conservative views, and Irvine also wrote a syndicated column that was printed in about one hundred newspapers. The organization saw its most influential period during the years Ronald Reagan was president, declining somewhat in the 1990s as Irvine became increasingly preoccupied with investigating conspiracy theories, such as his belief that the crash of TWA Flight 800 was caused by a missile and that White House deputy counsel Vincent W. Foster Jr. might have actually been murdered, not a victim of suicide, in 1993. In 1985, Irvine started a venture similar to AIM, known as Accuracy in Academia, but its conservative agenda and desire to wield influence over academic freedoms found fewer sympathizers. Ir-

vine remained chair of AIM until 2003, when he retired as chairman emeritus. He was the author of *Media Mischief and Misdeeds* (1984).

OBITUARIES AND OTHER SOURCES:

PERIODICALS

New York Times, November 19, 2004, p. A23.
Washington Post, November 18, 2004, p. B8.

* * *

IWASAKI, Chihiro (Matsumoto) 1918-1974

PERSONAL: Born December 15, 1918, in Takefu, Fukui, Japan; died from liver cancer August 8, 1974; married Zenmei Matsumoto, 1950; children: Takeshi. *Education:* Studied sketching and painting under Saburosuke Okada, calligraphy at the Fujiwara Kozei School, oil painting under Tai Nakatani, and art under Toshiko Akamatsu. *Politics:* Communist.

CAREER: Artist and children's book author/illustrator.

MEMBER: Shinfujin ("New Japan Women's Association"; cofounder, 1962).

AWARDS, HONORS: Chihiro Art Museum of Picture Books, founded in Tokyo, Japan, in 1997, in memory of the artist; Fiera di Bologna graphics prize, for *Ko-*

tori no Kuru Hi, 1971; Bronze Medal, Leipzig International Book Fair, 1974, for *Senka no Naka no Kodomo-tachi.*

WRITINGS:

SELF-ILLUSTRATED PICTURE BOOKS

Momoko and the Pretty Bird, [London, England], 1967, Follett (Chicago, IL), 1973.

Momoko's Lovely Day, [London, England], 1968 published as *Staying Home Alone on a Rainy Day,* McGraw-Hill (New York, NY), 1969.

A Brother for Momoko, [London, England], 1970 published as *A New Baby Is Coming to My House,* McGraw-Hill (New York, NY), 1972.

Neighbors, [London, England], 1972 published as *Will You Be My Friend?,* McGraw-Hill (New York, NY), 1973.

Momoko's Birthday, [London, England], 1973, published as *The Birthday Wish,* McGraw-Hill (New York, NY), 1974.

What's Fun without a Friend? McGraw-Hill (New York, NY), 1975.

ILLUSTRATOR

Hirosuke Hamada, *Aiveo nohon,* Orien (Japan), 1963.

Alvin Tresselt (reteller), *The Tears of the Dragon,* Parents' Magazine Press (New York, NY), 1967.

Miyoko Matsutani, *The Crane Maiden,* Parents' Magazine Press (New York, NY), 1968.

Karl Maria van Weber, *K. M. Weber's Invitation to the Dance,* adapted by Keisuke Tsutsui, translated by Ann King Herring, Gakken (Tokyo, Japan), 1969.

Alvin Tresselt (reteller), *The Fisherman under the Sea,* Parents' Magazine Press (New York, NY), 1969.

Hans Christian Andersen, *The Red Shoes,* translated by Anthea Bell, Nugenbauer Press (Boston, MA), 1983.

Hans Christian Andersen, *The Little Mermaid,* adapted by Anthea Bell, Picture Book Studio (Natick, MA), 1984.

Brothers Grimm, *Snow White and the Seven Dwarves,* translated and adapted by Anthea Bell, Picture Book Studio (Natick, MA), 1985.

Anthea Bell (reteller), *Swan Lake: A Traditional Folktale,* Picture Book Studio (Natick, MA), 1986.

Anthea Bell (reteller), *The Wise Queen: A Traditional Folktale,* Picture Book Studio (Natick, MA), 1986.

Tetsuko Kuroyanagi, *Totto-Chan: The Little Girl at the Window,* translated by Dorothy Britton, Kodansha International (Tokyo, Japan), 1996.

Illustrator of more than fifty additional books.

SIDELIGHTS: Japanese-born illustrator and author Chihiro Iwasaki began studying art as a teenager, starting with sketches and oil painting. She mentored under a number of artists, including Saburosuke Okada and Tai Nakatani. During World War II, she saw her family home destroyed in an air raid on Tokyo and was forced to flee to her grandmother's home in Nagano, where she joined the Japanese Communist Party. Once the war was over, she resumed her artistic endeavors, and in 1946 became a writer/illustrator for the *Jimmin Shinbun* (People's Paper).

Iwasaki's career developed further when she began work as an illustrator of children's books and magazines. Her artwork provided the framework for her own original stories as well as works by other authors, and she went on to illustrate more than seventy books, including well-known fairy tales by Hans Christian Andersen and the Brothers Grimm. Iwasaki became noted for her accurate depiction of children, and her ability to portray the small differences between babies of relatively similar age, and attributed her precise vision to the experiences of raising her own child. As her illustrations evolved, Iwasaki created her own unique style, using techniques of Western watercolor painting in combination with traditional Asian styles using India ink and details from her study of calligraphy.

Among Iwasaki's picture books for children are several that focus on the daily activities of a little girl named Momoko (or Allison, in the American versions). Each book takes Momoko through a specific circumstance, from a rainy day at home, to remaining alone while her mother goes out, to getting a new baby brother. Referring to *Staying Home Alone on a Rainy Day,* a contributor to *Kirkus Reviews* wrote that "on pages that simulate the texture of canvas are watercolors that are . . . deft sketches." In *School Library Journal,* Margaret A. Dorsey wrote of Iwasaki that "her vibrant, translucent colors are as eye-catching as ever."

A Brother for Momoko (published in the United States as *A New Baby Is Coming to My House*) continues the child's adventures. Gabrielle Maunder, reviewing the work for *School Librarian,* commented "each page is quite lovely; every turn reveals the same thunder coloring and the story . . . has a perfect simplicity." A reviewer for *Junior Bookshelf* found the sparse text and delicate illustrations insufficient, stating that "this clever, sensitive . . . book fails in one important particular; it cannot communicate fully." However Margery Fisher, writing for *Growing Point,* remarked that the story was told "subtly in words and pictures."

Other "Momoko" volumes include *Momoko and the Pretty Bird* and *Momoko's Birthday* (published in the United States as *The Birthday Wish*). The first story has Momoko wishing for a bird that will sing to sing to her. Margery Fisher wrote in *Growing Point* that the tale "unfolds clearly in the subtle, beautiful pictures." In *Momoko's Birthday,* the little girl learns a lesson about waiting her turn to be the center of attention. Edward Hudson, in *Children's Book Review,* wrote that "the events are all too brief and fleeting," going on to question whether the simple, aesthetic artwork "may have the adverse effect of creating no impression whatsoever." Marcus Crouch, however, reviewing the book for *Junior Bookshelf,* called *Momoko's Birthday* "lovely" and Iwasaki "among the most original artists in this field."

Iwasaki died of liver cancer in 1974. In 1977, her house in Nerima-ku, Tokyo was transformed into the Chihiro Art Museum of Picture Books, and the majority of her work is now housed there. Exhibits change regularly, with approximately one hundred pieces on display at any given time. In an article for *Phaedrus* James Fraser wrotethat "among the post World War Two illustrators of children's books in Japan, Chihiro Iwasaki is certainly one of several who deservedly enjoys an international reputation." He continued by noting that "although her life is over, her books remain as popular, as in her lifetime, if not more so, as reception of her concern for children and peace seems to be increasing." Iwasaki herself was quoted on the *Chihiro Art Museum Web site* as noting: "When I am painting children, I feel as if I am painting my own childhood."

BIOGRAPHICAL AND CRITICAL SOURCES:

BOOKS

Children's Literature Review, Volume 18, Gale (Detroit, MI), 1989.

PERIODICALS

Bulletin of the Center for Children's Books, December, 1975, Zena Sutherland, review of *What's Fun without a Friend?,* p. 64.

Children's Book Review, October, 1972, Edward Hudson, review of *Momoko and the Pretty Bird,* p. 145; December, 1973, Edward Hudson, review of *Momoko's Birthday,* pp. 170-171.

Growing Point, December, 1969, Margery Fisher, review of *Momoko's Lovely Day,* p. 1445; October, 1970, Margery Fisher, review of *A Brother for Momoko,* pp. 1606-1607; July, 1972, Margery Fisher, review of *Momoko and the Pretty Bird,* p. 1967.

Junior Bookshelf, October, 1969, review of *Momoko's Lovely Day,* p. 292; October, 1970, review of *A Brother for Momoko,* p. 285; December, 1973, Marcus Crouch, review of *Momoko's Birthday,* pp. 375-376.

Kirkus Reviews, April 1, 1969, review of *Staying Home Alone on a Rainy Day,* p. 370; October 1, 1972, review of *A New Baby Is Coming to My House,* p. 1140; June 15, 1974, review of *The Birthday Wish,* p. 631.

Phaedrus, Volume 12, 1986-1987, James Fraser, "The Iwasaki Chihiro Art Museum of Picture Books in Tokyo," pp. 63-64.

Publishers Weekly, February 25, 1974, review of *Will You Be My Friend?,* p. 113; June 30, 1975, review of *What's Fun without a Friend?,* p. 709.

School Librarian, December, 1970, Gabrielle Maunder, review of *A Brother for Momoko,* p. 500.

School Library Journal, October, 1969, Margaret A. Dorsey, review of *Staying Home Alone on a Rainy Day,* p. 130; February, 1973, Melinda Schroeder, review of *A New Baby Is Coming to My House,* p. 61; September, 1974, Melinda Schroeder, review of *Will You Be My Friend?,* p. 63.

Washington Post Book World, November 5, 1972, Michael J. Bandler, review of *A New Baby Is Coming to My House,* p. 3.

Wilson Library Bulletin, September, 1974, Barbara Dill, review of *The Birthday Wish,* pp. 84-85.

ONLINE

Chihiro Art Museum Web site, http://www.chihiro.jp/ english/ (September 23, 2004), "Chihiro Iwasaki."*

JACKSON, Sherri L. 1962-

PERSONAL: Born July 7, 1962, in Fort Rucker, AL; daughter of Kenneth (a teacher) and Eleanor (a secretary) Jackson; married Richard Griggs (a professor), July 5, 1991. *Ethnicity:* "Caucasian." *Education:* Attended Houghton College, 1980-82; North Adams State College, B.A. (psychology), 1984; University of Florida, M.S. (psychology), 1986, Ph.D. (psychology), 1988.

ADDRESSES: Home—5128 Northwest 57th Lane, Gainesville, FL 32653. *Office*—Department of Psychology, Jacksonville University, Jacksonville, FL 32211.

CAREER: Jacksonville University, Jacksonville, FL, assistant professor, 1988-93, associate professor, 1993-98, professor of psychology, 1998—, faculty chair, 2002-03. University of Florida, guest speaker, 1990, 1991. Member of scientific review committee for Duval County, 1988-96, and Friends of the Library, Alachua County, FL, 1992—; judge of high-school science fairs.

MEMBER: American Psychological Association, Council of Undergraduate Psychology Programs, Council of Undergraduate Teaching in Psychology, American Association of University Professors (president, 1999-2002), Southeastern Psychological Association, Alpha Chi, Phi Kappa Phi, Omicron Delta Kappa.

WRITINGS:

(With R. A. Griggs) *Study Guide to Accompany Invitation to Psychology by Carole Wade and Carol Tavris,* Addison Wesley Longman (New York, NY), 1998, 2nd edition, Prentice-Hall (Upper Saddle River, NJ), 2002.
Research Methods and Statistics: A Critical-Thinking Approach, Wadsworth Group (Belmont, CA), 2003.

Contributor to periodicals, including *Social Science Perspectives Journal, British Journal of Psychology, Quarterly Journal of Experimental Psychology, Thinking and Reasoning,* and *Teaching of Psychology.*

WORK IN PROGRESS: Statistics Plain and Simple, a textbook, for Wadsworth Group (Belmont, CA).

*   *   *

JAGOSE, Annamarie 1965-

PERSONAL: Born 1965, in Ashburton, New Zealand. *Education:* Victoria University, B.A., Ph.D., 1992.

ADDRESSES: Office—Department of Film, Television, and Media Studies, University of Auckland, Private Bag 92019, Auckland 1020, New Zealand. *E-mail*—a.jagose@auckland.ac.nz.

CAREER: University of Melbourne, Melbourne, Australia, senior lecturer in English, beginning 1992; University of Auckland, Auckland, New Zealand, associate professor of film, television, and media studies, 2003—.

AWARDS, HONORS: Best First Fiction prize, PEN Society of Authors, 1994, and Best First Book Award, New Zealand Society of Authors, both for *In Translation;* Deutz Medal for Fiction, Montana New Zealand Book Awards, and Victorian Premier's Literary Award for Fiction, both 2004, both for *Slow Water.*

WRITINGS:

Lesbian Utopics, Routledge (New York, NY), 1994.
Queer Theory: An Introduction, New York University Press (New York, NY), 1996.
Inconsequence: Lesbian Representation and the Logic of Sexual Sequence, Cornell University Press (Ithaca, NY), 2002.

NOVELS

In Translation, Allen & Unwin (St. Leonards, New South Wales, Australia), 1995.
Lulu: A Romance, Victoria University Press (Wellington, New Zealand), 1998.
Slow Water, Victoria University Press (Wellington, New Zealand), 2003.

OTHER

Also editor, with Chris Berry, of *Australia Queer.* Contributor to *Intimacy,* edited by Lauren Berlant, University of Chicago Press (Chicago, IL), 2000, and *Cross Purposes: Lesbian Studies, Feminist Studies, and the Limits of Alliance,* edited by Dana Heller, Indiana University Press (Bloomington, IN), 1997. Coeditor, *GLQ: A Journal of Lesbian and Gay Studies;* member of editorial board, *Genders.*

SIDELIGHTS: Annamarie Jagose was born in New Zealand and has taught at the university level in that country and in Australia. Her writings include nonfiction work, focusing on gay and lesbian studies, and fiction. In *Queer Theory,* she traces the history of same-sex relations and social movements throughout the twentieth century, including gay liberation, lesbian feminism, and the embrace of the concept of "queer" as a positive identification. Her work, which is informed by the theories of post-structuralism, challenges readers to think in new ways not only about homosexuality, but about basic notions of gender and sexuality.

Jagose's first novel, *In Translation,* was well received; it concerns a love triangle played out between India and New Zealand that is kept alive through air-mail letters concerning the translation of a Japanese novel. In her novel *Lulu: A Romance,* Jagose tells a strange story of two research scientists, Mitch and Kate, whose lives are disrupted by Lulu, a chimpanzee they are using in their study of language development. Kate wants to treat Lulu like the research subject that she is, but Mitch is charmed by the animal; the erotic relationship between the two humans is even derailed by issues related to Lulu. The novel "explores the often fickle relationship between communication and sexuality," noted Wendy Cavenett in a review for *This Swirling Sphere.* "Mixing the chemistry of attraction with the science of psychology and linguistics, Jagose has created a unique take on the tenuous threesome syndrome." Cavenett concluded: "More than just a modern romance, Jagose's *Lulu* is an exceptionally penned tale that explores the complexities of everyday life, the subtleties of language and the ambiguity of gender-based assumptions."

Slow Water is based on historical fact. It depicts a boat journey to New Zealand and Australia during the 1830s. The central character, William Yate, is an ap-

prentice grocer who leaves England to work as a missionary. Eventually, he is disgraced when his homosexual affair with one of the ship's mates is revealed by another missionary. Reviewing the book for the *Sydney Morning Herald,* Michael McGirr remarked that the novel "has a wide emotional range. It is also written in unpragmatically ornate prose. At times, Jagose's prose is exacting; at other times, delightful."

BIOGRAPHICAL AND CRITICAL SOURCES:

ONLINE

New Zealand Book Council Web site, http://www. bookcouncil.org.nz/ (November 10, 2004), "Annamarie Jagose."
Sydney Morning Herald Online, http://www.smh.com. au/ (June 7, 2003), Michael McGirr, review of *Slow Water.*
This Swirling Sphere Web site, http://www.thei.aust. com/ (November 10, 2004), Wendy Cavenett, review of *Lulu: A Romance.* *

*   *   *

JIN, Jian-Ming 1962-

PERSONAL: Name sometimes transliterated Jianming Jin; born February 9, 1962. *Ethnicity:* "Asian." *Education:* University of Michigan, Ph.D., 1989.

ADDRESSES: Office—University of Illinois at Urbana-Champaign, 1406 West Green St., Urbana, IL 61801. *E-mail*—j-jin1@uiuc.edu.

CAREER: University of Illinois at Urbana-Champaign, Urbana, professor, 1993—.

MEMBER: Institute of Electrical and Electronics Engineers (fellow).

WRITINGS:

The Finite Element Method in Electromagnetics, Wiley (New York, NY), 1993, 2nd edition, 2002.

Electromagnetic Analysis and Design in Magnetic Imaging, CRC Press (Boca Raton, FL), 1998.

(With S. Zhang) *Computation of Special Functions,* Wiley (New York, NY), 1996.

(Editor) *Fast and Efficient Algorithms in Computational Electromagnetics,* Artech (Chicago, IL), 2001.

Contributor of more than 130 articles to journals.

*   *   *

JOHNSON, Electa (Search) 1909-2004

OBITUARY NOTICE— See index for *CA* sketch: Born August 17, 1909, in Rochester, NY; died November 19, 2004, in Holyoke, MA. Adventurer and author. Along with her husband, Irving, Johnson made a career of sailing the world and writing about her travels, while also sharing her knowledge with young aspiring sailors. After receiving a B.A. from Smith College in 1929, she attended the University of California at Berkeley for a year. A sailing voyage from France, during which she fell in love with her future husband, resulted in a lifelong love and obsession with sailing. Except for the years of World War II, the Johnsons spent a huge part of their lives exploring their world on various sailing vessels—which they always named *Yankee*—and made a number of discoveries, including three uncharted islands as well as the anchor and other artifacts from the *H.M.S. Bounty.* They also enjoyed sharing their sailing knowledge with young people, such as the Girl Scout Mariners, the at-risk youths charity known as the TopSail program, and, of course, their own children. They published several books about their travels, including *Westward Bound in the Schooner Yankee* (1935), *Yankee's Wander World* (1949), and *Yankee Sails the Nile* (1966). The Johnsons also contributed regularly to *National Geographic* magazine. In 2002 the Los Angeles Maritime Institute named two brigantines after the Johnsons.

OBITUARIES AND OTHER SOURCES:

PERIODICALS

Boston Globe, November 24, 2004.
Seattle Times, December 5, 2004, p. A25.
Washington Post, December 4, 2004, p. B7.

JOHNSTONE, Bob

PERSONAL: Born in Scotland.

ADDRESSES: Home—Melbourne, Australia. *Agent*—c/o Author Mail, Basic Books, 387 Park Avenue South, New York, NY 10016.

CAREER: Journalist, writer, and editor. Japan correspondent for *New Scientist;* technology correspondent for *Far Eastern Economic Review.*

AWARDS, HONORS: Knight Science Journalism fellow, Massachusetts Institute of Technology, 1990-91; Abe Foundation Program grant recipient, 1996.

WRITINGS:

We Were Burning: Japanese Entrepreneurs and the Forging of the Electronic Age, Basic Books (New York, NY), 1999.
Never Mind the Laptops: Kids, Computers, and the Transformation of Learning, iUniverse (New York, NY), 2003.

Contributing editor and writer for *Wired.*

SIDELIGHTS: Bob Johnstone conducted some one hundred interviews while researching his book *We Were Burning: Japanese Entrepreneurs and the Forging of the Electronic Age.* Japanese success in business is often attributed to that country's team management style, but Johnston credits the risk-takers and entrepreneurs who brought Japan to the forefront of the consumer electronics industry during the 1980s. His book "illuminates the differences between U.S. and Japanese company culture," wrote Joseph W. Leonard in *Library Journal.* Johnstone's book relates how the disarmament pacts that followed World War II allowed Japanese engineers and scientists to concentrate on consumer rather than military projects. At that time transistor technology was in its infancy, and antitrust legislation required some major American companies to license patents to Japanese interests. The Japanese Ministry of International Trade is often given credit for the country's rise in the electronics industry, but Johnstone points out that in fact, the government bureaucracy prevented Sony from becoming the first company to get the transistor radio on the market. He also notes that Japanese entrepreneurs did not merely copy American technology, but in many cases adapted and improved technology abandoned by U.S. firms.

Johnstone profiles both well-known and little-known engineers and scientists, such as Seiko's Yamazaki Yoshio; Sony cofounder Morita Akio; Sasaki Tadashi, whose concentration on miniaturization led to the hand-held calculator; and Kuwano Yukinori, whose independent research in amorphous materials resulted in the solar-powered calculator. Johnstone also provides histories of other Japanese companies, including Canon, Yamaha, and Casio, and includes contributions made by U.S. firms. He predicts that the Japanese economy will continue to prosper in the future, inspired by the entrepreneurs who have contributed, often without recognition, to the country's rise as a financial power. A *Publishers Weekly* reviewer concluded: "Comprehensive, smartly written and accessible to the lay reader, this book provides a definitive—virtually encyclopedic—account of how the Japanese consumer electronic industry won the world."

BIOGRAPHICAL AND CRITICAL SOURCES:

PERIODICALS

Booklist, November 15, 1998, David Rouse, review of *We Were Burning: Japanese Entrepreneurs and the Forging of the Electronic Age,* p. 553.
Electronic Engineering Times, November 1, 1999, David Lammers, review of *We Were Burning,* p. 26.
Kirkus Reviews, November 1, 1998.
Library Journal, December, 1998, Joseph W. Leonard, review of *We Were Burning,* p. 124.
Publishers Weekly, November 2, 1998, review of *We Were Burning,* p. 65.*

* * *

JUSSAWALLA, Meheroo 1923-

PERSONAL: Born July 14, 1923, in India; daughter of Sohrab (an attorney) and Pootli (a homemaker; maiden name, Chenoy) Dalal; married Framji Jussawalla (an executive engineer), November, 1945 (deceased); children: Feroza Jussawalla Dasenbrock, Sohrab. *Eth-*

nicity: "Asian." *Education:* Madras University, M.Econ.; Osmania University, Ph.D. *Politics:* Liberal. *Religion:* Zoroastrian/Unity.

ADDRESSES: Home—4300 Waialae Ave., No. 1501A, Honolulu, HI 96816. *Office*—c/o East West Center, 1601 East West Rd., Honolulu, HI 96848. *E-mail*—meherooj@aol.com.

CAREER: Osmania University, Hyderabad, India, professor of economics, 1949-69; University College for Women, Hyderabad, principal, 1969-72; Osmania University, dean of social sciences, 1972-75; St. Mary's College of Maryland, St. Mary's City, professor of economics, 1975-78; East West Center, Honolulu, HI, research fellow in information and communication in economics, beginning 1978, currently research fellow emeritus. International Institute of Communications, London, member of board of directors, 1985-90; Pacific Telecommunications Council, member of board of trustees, 1985-2003; Pacific Telecommunications Foundation, member of board of directors; Pacific and Asian Affairs Council, member.

MEMBER: International Telecommunications Society, American Association of University Women, Hawaii Telecommunications Trade Association, American Association of Retired Persons of East Honolulu, Friends of the East West Center.

AWARDS, HONORS: Lifetime Achievement Award, Pacific Telecommunications Foundation, 2003; Award for Ageless Heroes, Blue Cross/Blue Shield of Hawaii.

WRITINGS:

Dynamics of Economic Development, University Microfilms International (Ann Arbor, MI), 1980.
(With Karen P. Middleton) *The Economics of Communication: A Selected Bibliography,* Pergamon Press (New York, NY), 1981.
(Editor, with Donald M. Lamberton) *Communication Economics and Development,* Pergamon Press (Elmsford, NY), 1982.
(Editor, with Helene Ebenfield) *Communication and Information Economics: New Perspectives,* North Holland (New York, NY), 1984.

(Compiler, with Marcellus S. Snow) *Telecommunication Economics and International Regulatory Policy: An Annotated Bibliography,* Greenwood Press (Westport, CT), 1986.

(Editor, with Dan J. Wedemeyer and Vijay Menon) *The Passing of Remoteness? Information Evolution in the Asia-Pacific,* Asian Mass Communication Research and Information Centre (Singapore), 1986.

(With Chee-Wah Cheah) *The Calculus of International Communications: A Study in the Political Economy of Transborder Data Flows,* Libraries Unlimited (Littleton, CO), 1987.

(Editor, with Donald M. Lamberton and Neil D. Karunaratne) *The Cost of Thinking: Information Economies of Ten Pacific Countries,* Ablex Publishing (Norwood, NJ), 1988.

(Editor, with Tadayuki Okuma and Toshihiro Araki) *Information Technology and Global Interdependence,* Greenwood Press (Westport, CT), 1989.

The Economics of Intellectual Property in a World without Frontiers: A Study of Computer Software, Greenwood Press (Westport, CT), 1992.

(Editor) *Global Telecommunications Policies: The Challenge of Change,* Greenwood Press (Westport, CT), 1993.

(Editor) *United States-Japan Trade in Telecommunications: Conflict and Compromise,* Greenwood Press (Westport, CT), 1993.

(Editor) *Telecommunications: A Bridge to the Twenty-first Century,* Elsevier (New York, NY), 1995.

(With Richard D. Taylor) *Information Technology Parks of the Asia Pacific: Lessons for the Regional Digital Divide,* M. E. Sharpe (Armonk, NY), 2001.

Member of editorial board, *Telecommunications Policy Journal.*

WORK IN PROGRESS: On Eight Dollars to America in Quest of Academic Freedom, a memoir; research on U.S.-China relations in telecommunications market development.

BIOGRAPHICAL AND CRITICAL SOURCES:

BOOKS

Lamberton, Donald M., editor, *Communication and Trade: Essays in Honor of Meheroo Jussawalla,* Hampton Press (Cresskill, NJ), 1998.

K

KABASERVICE, Geoffrey (M.) 1966-

PERSONAL: Male. Born June 21, 1966, in New Haven CT. *Education:* Yale University, B.A., 1988, Ph.D., 1999; Jesus College, Cambridge, M.A. (philosophy), 1988.

ADDRESSES: Home—Washington, DC. *Office*—Advisory Board Company, 2445 M St. NW, Washington, DC 20037; fax: 202-266-5700.

CAREER: Yale University, New Haven, CT, lecturer; Advisory Board Company, Washington, DC, manager.

WRITINGS:

(With William S. Beinecke) *Through Mem'ry's Haze: A Personal Memoir,* Prospect Hill Press (New York, NY), 2000.
The Guardians: Kingman Brewster, His Circle, and the Rise of the Liberal Establishment, Holt (New York, NY), 2004.

SIDELIGHTS: Historian Geoffrey Kabaservice's book *The Guardians: Kingman Brewster, His Circle, and the Rise of the Liberal Establishment* examines the importance of education in modern American politics—not just having an education, but having the right kind of education from the right kind of school. Specifically, Kabaservice's book examines the impact that Kingman Brewster, president of Yale from 1964 to 1977, had on a whole generation of American leaders. Elliot Richardson, who served in four different cabinet positions during Richard Nixon's administration, was a Brewster associate and shared many of the Yale president's goals. Cyrus Vance, another of Brewster's friends, was Jimmy Carter's secretary of state, worked for multilateral solutions to conflict in the late 1970s, and was largely responsible for the SALT II agreements to curb the spread of nuclear weapons. Younger Americans influenced by Brewster's ideology include former president Bill Clinton and Senator Hilary Rodham Clinton, both of whom received their law degrees from Yale in 1973; Senator Joseph Lieberman, who received his undergraduate degree in 1964 and went on to get his law degree from Yale in 1967; and former Vermont Governor Howard Dean, who earned his degree in 1971. Also among the prestigious Yale grads are John Kerry (class of 1966) and George W. Bush (class of 1968), who competed for the presidency in the 2004 election. "By 2008," stated Warren Goldstein in the Chicago *Tribune Books,* "the Oval Office will have been occupied by a graduate of Yale University for at least twenty consecutive years."

Each of these leading political figures, in one way or another, were formed or affected by Brewster's policies at Yale. Unlike other college campuses—such as the University of California at Berkeley, Harvard, and Cornell—which were plagued by student unrest and violence during the 1960s, Yale remained peaceful under Brewster's term. "As a matter of policy and by personal example," Goldstein stated, "Brewster kept his entire administration open and closely connected to the student body." The president opened the university—which had been, up until the early 1960s, a bastion of wealthy white male privilege—to a broader spectrum of both people and ideas. He "accepted and even embraced," commented Alan Brinkley in the *New Republic,* "a series of fundamental changes in the character of Yale that the new, more democratic ethos of the 1960s and 1970s all but required: coeducation, active recruitment of minorities, widening the base from which students at Yale were drawn, diversifying the curriculum and responding to new areas of knowledge that were emerging out of the turbulence of his time." "Is it any wonder," Goldstein asked, "that during Brewster's tenure, an inordinate number of Yalies saw the possibilities in public service within—as opposed to outside—the system?"

Curiously enough, Kabaservice points out, Brewster himself had been a member of the privileged classes who had attended Yale up to that point. A direct descendent of Elder William Brewster, a pilgrim who arrived in America on the *Mayflower,* Brewster was born into a privileged northeastern elite for whom admission to Yale was just one of many social perks to be accepted without question. Brewster, who had been raised in Boston, "was alone among his classmates in choosing to go to Yale rather than to Harvard (in an era when young men at elite schools largely chose the universities that they would attend, rather than the other way around," Brinkley explained. At the same time, however, members of Brewster's social class, were bred for a career of self-sacrificing public service. Brewster designed the new Yale to create a "new elite" that could govern the United States well into the future—a group that would share the old northeastern elite's values of sacrifice and dedication to public service. "What Brewster was seeking," remarked *Los Angeles Times Book Review* contributor Jim Sleeper, "was a leadership whose authority rested in a small 'r' republican civic virtue that is seldom evident now and even less understood."

Men like Brewster saw themselves as patrician guardians of an American liberal tradition that stretched back over a hundred years. "These men," an *Atlantic Monthly* critic commented, "believed it their duty and their right to guide and rule what Kabaservice calls 'the multitude.'" When they made mistakes, however, their arrogance could lead to disaster. McGeorge Bundy, for instance, Kabaservice points out, was one of Brewster's closest associates and served as national security advisor under presidents Kennedy and Johnson. Bundy argued for greater American commitment during the Vietnam War—a policy that cost the lives of thousands of U.S. servicemen and created a public uproar. "One finds oneself," the *Atlantic Monthly* contributor concluded, "agreeing with the young and intemperate (and improbably populist) William F. Buckley Jr., who called this bunch 'haughty totalitarians who refuse to permit the American people to supervise their own destiny.'"

Critics in general celebrated Kabaservice's work. A *Publishers Weekly* writer, referring to Kerry, Bush, Clinton, and Dean, stated that "Kabaservice's history offers valuable insights" into a pedagogy that helped to shape "their political character." Vanessa Bush, writing in *Booklist,* called the work an "absorbing look at the liberal establishment." "Few books," stated *Library Journal* contributor Karl Helicher, "so convincingly portray the spirit and ferment of the times." A *Kirkus Reviews* critic called the book "a capable evocation" of an American landscape, and a "fine cultural history, especially welcome in a time when the L-word is a pejorative."

BIOGRAPHICAL AND CRITICAL SOURCES:

PERIODICALS

Atlantic Monthly, June, 2004, review of *The Guardians: Kingman Brewster, His Circle, and the Rise of the Liberal Establishment,* p. 113.
Booklist, March 15, 2004, Vanessa Bush, review of *The Guardians,* p. 1248.
Kirkus Reviews, December 15, 2003, review of *The Guardians,* p. 1438.
Library Journal, February 15, 2004, Karl Helicher, review of *The Guardians,* p. 140.
Los Angeles Times Book Review, April 4, 2004, Jim Sleeper, review of *The Guardians,* p. 3.
New Republic, June 7, 2004, Alan Brinkley, review of *The Guardians,* p. 36.
Publishers Weekly, February 9, 2004, review of *The Guardians,* p. 65.
Tribune Books (Chicago, IL), July 4, 2004, Warren Goldstein, review of *The Guardians,* p. 7.*

* * *

KAHL, Virginia (Caroline) 1919-2004

OBITUARY NOTICE— See index for *CA* sketch: Born February 18, 1919, in Milwaukee, WI; died November 4, 2004, in Alexandria, VA. Librarian, illustrator, and author. Kahl was an artist and librarian who was best known for her fun-filled picture books such as 1955's *The Duchess Bakes a Cake.* She studied art at Milwaukee-Downer College (now Lawrence University), earning a B.A. in 1940. Her first job, however, was as a library assistant in Milwaukee during the 1940s, and from 1948 until 1955 she served as a librarian for the U.S. Army in Berlin and then Salzburg. She returned to the United States to complete her master's degree in library science at the University of Wisconsin in 1957. From 1958 until 1961, Kahl was the school librarian for the Madison, Wisconsin, Public School system; she was then hired as director of the Menomonee Falls Public Library. In 1971, she moved to Alexandria, Virginia, to be branch librarian for the public library there, becoming coordinator of public services from 1977 until her 1993 retirement. She also taught continuing education at George Washington University during the 1970s. Besides her successful library career, Kahl enjoyed art and writing, publishing over a dozen children's picture books notable for their lighthearted stories with touches of fantasy. Among these are *Away Went Wolfgang* (1954), *Plumb Pudding for Christmas* (1956), *The Perfect Pancake* (1960), *Giants, Indeed!* (1974), and *Whose Cat Is That?* (1979).

OBITUARIES AND OTHER SOURCES:

PERIODICALS

Milwaukee Journal Sentinel, November 13, 2004.
Washington Post, November 23, 2004, p. B7.

* * *

KAPLEAU, Philip 1912-2004

PERSONAL: Born 1912, in New Haven, CT; died from complications of Parkinson's disease May 6, 2004, in Rochester, NY; married; wife's name, deLancey; children; Sudarshana (daughter). *Religion:* Buddhist.

CAREER: Court reporter, serving as chief reporter at International Military Tribunal, Nuremberg, Germany, 1945, and at Tokyo War Crimes Trials, until 1953; ordained zen teacher; Rochester Zen Center, founder.

WRITINGS:

(Compiler, editor, and translator) *The Three Pillars of Zen: Teaching, Practice, and Enlightenment,* Harper and Row (New York, NY), 1966, revised and expanded thirty-fifth-anniversary edition, Anchor Books (Garden City, NY), 2000.

(Compiler, with Paterson Simons) *The Wheel of Death: A Collection of Writings from Zen Buddhist and Other Sources of Death—Rebirth—Dying,* Harper and Row (New York, NY), 1971.

Zen: Dawn in the West, Anchor Press (Garden City, NY), 1979, revised as *Zen: Merging of East and West,* 1989.

To Cherish All Life: A Buddhist View of Animal Slaughter and Meat Eating, Zen Center (Rochester, NY), 1981.

The Wheel of Life and Death: A Practical and Spiritual Guide, Doubleday (New York, NY), 1989, revised edition, Shambhala (Boston, MA), 1998.

Awakening to Zen: The Teachings of Roshi Philip Kapleau, edited by Polly Young-Eisendrath and Rafe Martin, Scribner (New York, NY), 1997.

Straight to the Heart of Zen: Eleven Classic Koans and Their Inner Meanings, Shambhala (Boston, MA), 2001.

Kapleau's works have been translated into several languages.

SIDELIGHTS: Alhough Philip Kapleau studied law and had a successful career as a court reporter, serving in 1945 as the chief reporter at the International Military Tribunal at Nuremberg and the Tokyo War Crimes Trials, he developed an interest in Zen Buddhism that became more important than his chosen profession. Kapleau studied under Dr. D. T. Suzuki and other teachers of Zen Buddhism, before selling his court reporting business in 1953 to join a Zen monastery in Japan. For three years he trained rigorously and was then ordained by Hakuun Yasutani-roshi, who gave Kapleau permission to teach. While teaching under Yasutani-roshi ("roshi" is a title that indicates teacher), Kapleau-roshi got permission to record his teacher's talks (*dokusan*) and interview monks and students. These talks and interviews resulted in *The Three Pillars of Zen: Teaching, Practice, and Enlightenment,* now considered a standard text on Zen in English, that has been revised and expanded three times since its initial publication in 1966, and has been translated into a dozen languages. In 2000 this standard introductory work saw republication in a thirty-fifth anniversary edition.

Throughout his career as founder and teacher at the Zen Center in Rochester, New York, Kapleau published a handful of books on Zen. Late in his life he offered readers *Awakening to Zen: The Teachings of Roshi Philip Kapleau,* an "illuminating collection of Kapleau's lectures, writings, and interviews," according to *Booklist* critic Donna Seaman. In these pieces the author deals with such important issues as sexuality, drugs, death, a human's relationship with animals, and the role of pain and discipline in spiritual enlightenment. David Bourquin stated in *Library Journal* that Kapleau presents difficult concepts "interestingly and clearly" and recommended the work highly. Likewise, a *Publishers Weekly* reviewer concluded, "Kapleau offers readers priceless insights into the core of Zen practices."

BIOGRAPHICAL AND CRITICAL SOURCES:

PERIODICALS

American Libraries, November, 1998, Donna Seaman, review of *Awakening to Zen: The Teachings of Roshi Philip Kapleau,* p. 77.
Booklist, March 1, 1997, Donna Seaman, review of *Awakening to Zen,* p. 1071.
East West, May, 1989, review of *The Wheel of Life and Death: A Practical and Spiritual Guide,* p. 109.
Library Journal, February 15, 1997, David Bourquin, review of *Awakening to Zen,* p. 139.
Publishers Weekly, January 27, 1997, review of *Awakening to Zen,* p. 95.

ONLINE

Rochester Zen Center Web site, http://www.rzc.org/ (November 10, 2004).*

*   *   *

KAPLOW, Louis 1956-

PERSONAL: Born June 17, 1956, in Chicago, IL; married Jody Ellen Forchheimer (an attorney), July 11, 1982; children: Irene Miriam, Leah Rayna. *Ethnicity:* "Jewish." *Education:* Northwestern University, B.A. (with distinction), 1977; Harvard University, A.M. and J.D. (magna cum laude), both 1981, Ph.D., 1987. *Religion:* Jewish.

ADDRESSES: Home—19 Thatcher St., No. 4, Brookline, MA 02446. *Office*—Hauser 322, Harvard Law School, Harvard University, Cambridge, MA 02138.

CAREER: U.S. Court of Appeals, Second Circuit, law clerk, 1981-82; Harvard University Law School, Cambridge, MA, assistant professor, 1982-87, professor, 1987—, associate dean for research, 1989-91, associate director of John M. Olin Center for Law, Economics, and Business. National Bureau of Economic Research, research associate; consultant to Antitrust Division of U.S. Department of Justice, Federal Trade Commission, and State of Israel.

MEMBER: American Economic Association, National Tax Association, American Law and Economics Association (board member, 1995-97, 2002—), American Philosophical Association, Phi Beta Kappa.

WRITINGS:

(With Phillip Areeda) *Antitrust Analysis,* Little, Brown and Co. (Boston, MA), c. 1991, 6th edition, Aspen Publishers (New York, NY), 2004.
(With Steven Shavell) *Fairness versus Welfare: Notes on the Pareto Principle, Preferences, and Distributive Justice,* Harvard University Press (Cambridge, MA), 2003.

Contributor to books, including *Tax Policy in the Real World,* edited by Slemrod, Cambridge University Press (New York, NY), 1999; *Rethinking Estate and Gift Taxation,* edited by Gale, Hines, and Slemrod, Brookings Institution (Washington, DC), 2001; *Inequality and Tax Policy,* edited by Hassett and Hubbard, American Enterprise Institute for Public Policy Research (Washington, DC), 2001; and *Handbook of Public Economics,* edited by Auerbach and Feldstein, Elsevier, 2002. Contributor to academic journals, including *Yale Law Journal, Journal of Political Economy, American Law and Economics Review, Journal of Contemporary Legal Issues, Scandinavian Journal of Economics,* and *Journal of Legal Studies.* Member of editorial board, *International Review of Law and Economics,* 1990-99, *Journal of Public Economics, National Tax Journal, Journal of Law, Economics, and Organization,* and *Legal Theory.* Former managing editor of *Harvard Law Review.*

WORK IN PROGRESS: Income Distribution and the Tax System; Social Welfare and Distributive Justice.

BIOGRAPHICAL AND CRITICAL SOURCES:

PERIODICALS

Yale Law Journal, April, 2003, Jules L. Coleman, review of *Fairness versus Welfare: Notes on the Pareto Principle, Preferences, and Distributive Justice,* p. 1511.

*   *   *

KAUFMAN-OSBORN, Timothy V. 1953-

PERSONAL: Born February 7, 1953, in Camden, NJ; son of Norman and Marjorie (Phipps) Osborn; married, wife's name Sharon; children: Jacob, Tobin. *Education:* Oberlin College, B.A., 1976; University of Wisconsin, Madison, M.A., 1977; Princeton University, M.A., 1980, Ph.D., 1982.

ADDRESSES: Office—Department of Politics, Whitman College, Walla Walla, WA 99362. *E-mail*—kaufmatv@whitman.edu.

CAREER: Whitman College, Walla Walla, WA, assistant professor, 1982-85, associate professor, 1985-92, professor, 1992-96, Baker Ferguson Professor of Politics and Leadership, 1996—; Princeton University, Department of Politics, Princeton, NJ, visiting research fellow, 1985-86; Doshisha University, Kyoto, Japan, visiting scholar, 1990.

MEMBER: American Political Science Association, Society for the Advancement of American Philosophy, Society for Philosophy and Technology, Western Political Science Association, Conference for the Study of Political Thought, American Civil Liberties Union of Washington (president, 2002—), Pacific Northwest Political Science Association, Groupe d'Études Durkheimiennes, Charles S. Peirce Society.

AWARDS, HONORS: Summer stipend, National Endowment for the Humanities, 1983; John Dewey Research Fund grant, 1985; Earhart fellowship

research grant, 1985-86; Paul Farrett fellowship for excellence in undergraduate teaching, 1985-92; Faculty Acheivment Award, Burlington Northern Foundation, 1989; Betty Nesvold Women and Politics Award for best paper on women and politics, 1992; Pi Sigma Alpha Award for best paper, Western Political Science Association, 1995; Robert Fluno Award for distinguished teaching in the social sciences, 1999.

WRITINGS:

Politics/Sense/Experience: A Pragmatic Inquiry into the Promise of Democracy, Cornell University Press (Ithaca, NY), 1991.
Creatures of Prometheus: Gender and the Politics of Technology, Rowman & Littlefield (Lanham, MD), 1997.
From Noose to Needle: Capital Punishment and the Late Liberal State, University of Michigan Press (Ann Arbor, MI), 2002.

Also contributor of essays to collections, including *John Dewey: Critical Assessments,* Volume 2, edited by J. E. Tiles, Routledge (New York, NY), 1992; *Critical Perspectives on Democracy,* edited by Lyman Legters, John Burke, and Arthur DiQuattro, Rowman & Littlefield (Lanham, MD), 1994; *Studies in Law, Politics, and Society,* Volume 20, edited by Austin Sarat and Patricia Weick, JAI Press (Stamford, CT), 2000; and *Studies in Law, Politics, and Society,* Volume 22, edited by Austin Sarat and Patricia Weick, JAI Press (Stamford, CT), 2001.

Contributor to professional journals, including *Yale Law Journal, PS: Political Science and Politics, Liberal Education, Signs, Political Theory, Polity, Theory and Society, Hypatia, Willamette Journal of the Liberal Arts, American Journal of Political Science,* and *Journal of Politics.*

SIDELIGHTS: Political scientist Timothy V. Kaufman-Osborn has published works investigating major issues facing American society today. In *From Noose to Needle: Capital Punishment and the Late Liberal State,* for instance, the author explores the quandary that capital punishment places on modern Western governments. How can a government that claims to respect the natural rights of its citizens—including the rights of life and liberty—also claim the exclusive right to end the lives of certain citizens? In addition, how can a state claim to honor universal human rights by avoiding torture and still execute prisoners using hanging (which was used in the state of Washington as recently as 1993) and the electric chair (which leaves heat scars on the corpses of prisoners)?

Kaufman-Osborn suggests that the relatively recent introduction of execution by lethal injection tries to ameliorate the issue by promoting a "humane" method of execution, but succeeds only in alienating both the proponents of capital punishment (who see executions as a form of vengeance) and the opponents of capital punishment (who see any form of execution as a violation of universal human rights). In the end, the author concludes, capital punishment has at least as much to do with a government's need to feel that it is in control of society as it does with justice and retribution. Jennifer L. Culbert, writing in *Political Theory*, stated that "Kaufman-Osborn's subtle analysis of capital punishment does not fit into any of the traditional categories of death penalty scholarship." As the critic explained, Kaufman-Osborn does not oppose the death penalty because it is immoral, but because "[stripping] the state of its authority to impose and inflict death sentences 'is to move one step closer to a politics we can live with.'"

In *Creatures of Prometheus: Gender and the Politics of Technology*, Kaufman-Osborn examines "the relationships between human identity and the things we make," according to *American Political Science Review* contributor Ruth Abbey. The things that surround us in our everyday life define us and our place in society—including our gender, our language, and our technological tools. "Kaufman-Osborn," declared Abbey, "portrays gender as an artifact, as something produced partly through the different things that men and women typically make and the different tools used in these processes." In his book Kaufman-Osborn states that technology accelerates this process and blurs the distinction between the makers of artifacts and the artifacts themselves. *Hypatia* contributor Jodi Dean noted that "it's crucial to Kaufman-Osborne's argument that artifacts are not simply signs of gender but makers of it." These artifacts are so commonplace to our way of life that we accept them—and the gender roles defined by them—without thinking. Kaufman-Osborn "strives to remind us," stated Abbey, "how influential the things we routinely take for granted are; we usually fail to notice their significance until they break down or confound our expectations in some way."

BIOGRAPHICAL AND CRITICAL SOURCES:

PERIODICALS

American Political Science Review, September, 1998, Ruth Abbey, review of *Creatures of Prometheus: Gender and the Politics of Technology,* p. 684.

Hypatia, summer, 2000, Jodi Dean, review of *Creatures of Prometheus,* p. 187.

Journal of Gender Studies, July, 1999, Hilary Rose, review of *Creatures of Prometheus,* p. 238.

Political Theory, August, 2004, Jennifer L. Culbert, "Why Still Kill?," p. 563.

*   *   *

KENNEDY, James
    See LUSBY, Jim

*   *   *

KENT, Carol 1947-

PERSONAL: Born 1947; married; husband's name, Gene; children: one son. *Education:* Earned a B.A. and an M.A.

ADDRESSES: Home—Port Huron, MI. *Office*—Speak up Speaker Services, 1614 Edison Shores Place, Port Huron, MI 48060-3374 *E-mail*—speakupinc@aol.com.

CAREER: Public speaker and writer. Speak up Speaker Services, Port Huron, MI, founder and president. Formerly radio show co-host; guest on radio and television programs, including *Prime Time America, Family Life Today, 100 Huntley Street,* and *On Main Street.*

MEMBER: National Speakers Association.

WRITINGS:

Speak up with Confidence!: A Step-by-Step Guide to Successful Public Speaking, T. Nelson (Nashville, TN), 1987, published as *Speak up with Confidence: A Step-by-Step Guide for Speakers and Leaders,* 1987.

Secret Passions of the Christian Woman, NavPress (Colorado Springs, CO), 1990.

Tame Your Fears and Transform Them into Faith, Confidence, and Action: Women Reveal What They Fear Most, NavPress (Colorado Springs, CO), 1993.

Tame Your Fears and Transform Them into Faith, Confidence, and Action: A Small Group Discussion Guide, NavPress (Colorado Springs, CO), 1994.

Detours, Tow Trucks, and Angels in Disguise: Finding Humor and Hope in Unexpected Places, NavPress (Colorado Springs, CO), 1996.

Mothers Have Angel Wings: A Tribute to the Tears and Triumphs of Being a Mom, NavPress (Colorado Springs, CO), 1997.

Becoming a Woman of Influence: Making a Lasting Impact on Others, NavPress (Colorado Springs, CO), 2002.

Secret Longings of the Heart: Overcoming Deep Disappointment and Unfulfilled Expectations, NavPress (Colorado Springs, CO), 2003.

When I Lay My Isaac Down: Unshakable Faith in Unthinkable Circumstances, NavPress (Colorado Springs, CO), 2004.

Also author of pamphlet series, *Six Secrets of a Confident Woman, Six Keys to Lasting Friendships, Six Basics of a Balanced Life, Six Essentials of Spiritual Authenticity, Six Steps to Clarify Your Calling,* and *Six Choices That Will Change Your Life*, all NavPress (Colorado Springs, CO). Also author of *Secret Longings of the Heart Discussion Guide, My Soul's Journey,* and *Designed for Influence*. General editor, "Kisses of Sunshine" series, Zondervan. Contributor to periodicals, including *Focus on the Family* and *Today's Christian Woman*.

SIDELIGHTS: Carol Kent's work as a speaker and author is deeply rooted in her Christian faith. In her books and talks, she presents an uplifting message of love and hope. In *Becoming a Woman of Influence: Making a Lasting Impact on Others*, Kent encourages women to choose twelve other women and act as loving mentors to them, as Christ did to his apostles. Inspiring stories of personal transformation illustrate Kent's key points.

Kent draws from a tragic turning point in her own life for her book *When I Lay My Isaac Down: Unshakable Faith in Unthinkable Circumstances*. She tells the hor-

rifying story of learning that her only child, a Navy officer and devout Christian who had previously led an exemplary life, had murdered his wife's ex-husband. Kent and her husband struggled emotionally and financially to support their son, who was eventually sentenced to life in prison without parole. They "lost many of their ideals of what the perfect Christian life would hold," commented Cindy Crosby in *Christianity Today*, "but they discovered the power of Christian community and God's faithfulness."

Using her personal experience as a starting-point, in *When I Lay My Isaac Down* Kent offers guidelines and questions for other people who are trying to find their way after a devastating event. According to a *Publishers Weekly* reviewer, "She shares her story with a transparency and vulnerability that readers will find both disarming and bracing."

In an interview for *Today's Christian Woman*, Kent remarked that what amazes her most about God is that He uses everyday people "to do his extraordinary work. Sometimes we think we have to be the most educated, the most gifted, the most beautiful. But God delights in doing extraordinary things through women who simply say, God, I'm available. When you say that, you truly become a woman of influence."

BIOGRAPHICAL AND CRITICAL SOURCES:

PERIODICALS

Christianity Today, August, 2004, Cindy Crosby, review of *When I Lay My Isaac Down: Unshakable Faith in Unthinkable Circumstances*, p. 58.

Publishers Weekly, October 25, 1999, review of *Becoming a Woman of Influence: Making a Lasting Impact on Others*, p. 71; April 26, 2004, review of *When I Lay My Isaac Down*, p. 59.

Today's Christian Woman, March, 2001, interview with Kent, p. 96; July, 2001, Camerin Courtney and Ginger Kolbaba, review of *Six Secrets of a Confident Woman*, p. 60.

ONLINE

Speaker up Speaker Services Web site, http://speakup speakerservices.com/ (October 6, 1999). "Carol Kent."*

KENTE, Gibson 1932-

PERSONAL: Born 1932, in East London, South Africa. *Education:* Attended Jan Hofmeyer School of Social Work.

ADDRESSES: Agent—c/o Author Mail, Heinemann Educational, Freepost, P.O. Box 381, Oxford OX2 8BR, England.

CAREER: Playwright, composer-arranger, producer, actor, and musician. Former director of Union Artists; G. K. Productions (production company), founder.

WRITINGS:

PLAYS

Manana the Jazz Prophet, produced in South Africa, 1963.
Sikalo, produced in South Africa, 1966.
Life, produced in South Africa, 1968.
Zwi, produced in South Africa, 1970.
How Long, produced in South Africa, 1974.
Our Belief, produced in South Africa, 1974.
Too Late, produced in South Africa, 1974.
Can You Take It?, produced in South Africa, 1977.
La Duma [It Thundered], produced in South Africa, 1980.
Mama and the Load, produced in South Africa, 1980.
The Call, produced in Pretoria, South Africa, at the State Theatre, 2003.

Author's plays have been published in *South African People's Plays: ons phola hi, plays by Gibson Kente, Credo V. Mutwa, Mthuli Sehzi, and Workshop '71,* selected with introduction by Robert Mshengu Kavanagh, Heinemann (London, England), 1981.

SIDELIGHTS: Pioneering South African playwright and producer Gibson Kente, the author of more than twenty plays and several television dramas, is considered the "father" of South African township theater. During his early career, Kente focused on social and community issues that reflected South Africans' daily life. Kente's work turned more and more political, however, as South African apartheid policies crowded more and more native South Africans into urban town-

ships such as Soweto. As a contributor noted on the *National Arts Council of South Africa Web site,* "Kente's plays were among the first to be located in the township reality of crime, hooliganism, alcoholism, love and politics." In addition to helping found "township theatre," Kente also introduced many South Africans to European-style theatre, especially in the forms of musicals, for which he composed and arranged the music. Many of his plays directly attack apartheid, including the musical *How Long,* which was banned by the South African government, as were Kente's anti-apartheid dramas *Our Belief* and *Too Late.*

Kente was arrested in 1976 after he tried to make a film of *How Long.* Following his release from detention in 1977, the playwright returned to his craft. While he wrote some plays strictly for entertainment, such as *Can You Take It?,* a musical love story, he also continued to comment on the political issues of the day, primarily by dramatizing "the conflict between political pressures and family/community solidarity," as a writer noted on the *Contemporary Africa Database.* Plays with political themes include *La Duma [It Thundered]* and *Mama and the Load.*

In 2003, Kente announced publicly that he had contracted HIV, defying the country's strong social stigma regarding AIDS. As reported by Christelle De Jager in *Daily Variety,* he broadcast his condition at a press conference in Johannesburg, noting, "I admire people like [former basketball star] Magic Johnson who disclosed their status. I know I've got a challenge ahead of me because I know I have a duty to the people out there to inspire them." Kente went on to write the play *The Call,* a musical about a man living with HIV/AIDS who brings hope to others with the disease. The main character is a producer, and Kente portrayed himself in the initial 2003 production in Pretoria. The South African government supported the play's production because of its strong message on HIV, which complimented the government's own initiatives to stem the spread of the disease. On the *South African Department of Arts & Culture Web site,* South African Minister Mlambo-Ngcuka was quoted as noting that "Kente was exceptional, because of his stature in the arts community and his contribution to the fight against apartheid. . . . The National Arts Council recently declared Kente a 'Living Treasure'. . . . The process of collecting his works will begin as a source of education and inspiration to up and coming artists."

BIOGRAPHICAL AND CRITICAL SOURCES:

PERIODICALS

Daily Variety, February 27, 2003, Christelle De Jager, "[Kente's] HIV Disclosure Opens Eyes in S.A.," p. 9.

Guardian (Manchester, England), February 22, 2003, Rory Carroll, "Top SA Playwright Says He Has AIDS," p. 17.

ONLINE

Contemporary Africa Database Web site, http://people.africadatabase.org/ (September 9, 2004), "Gibson Kente."

National Arts Council of South Africa Web site, http://www.nac.org.za/ (September 28, 2004), "Showcase, Living Treasure Awards."

South African Department of Arts & Culture Web site, http://www.dac.gov.za/ (March 16, 2004), "Gibson Kente in AIDS Awareness Programme."*

* * *

KER, Ian (Turnbull)

PERSONAL: Male. *Religion:* Roman Catholic.

ADDRESSES: Office—University of Oxford, University Offices, Wellington Square, Oxford, OX1 2JD, England. *E-mail*—ian.ker@theology.ox.ac.uk; ian.ker@campion.ox.ac.uk.

CAREER: Catholic priest, author, and educator. Oxford University, Oxford, England, professor of lecture series on John Henry Newman.

WRITINGS:

John Henry Newman: A Biography, Clarendon (Oxford, England), 1988.

(Author of foreword) John Henry Cardinal Newman, *An Essay on the Development of Christian Doctrine,* Notre Dame Press (Notre Dame, IN), 1989.

The Achievement of John Henry Newman, University of Notre Dame Press (Notre Dame, IN), 1990.

Newman on Being a Christian, University of Notre Dame Press (Notre Dame, IN), 1990.

Healing the Wound of Humanity: The Spirituality of John Henry Newman, Darton, Longman & Todd (London, England), 1993.

The Catholic Revival in English Literature, 1845-1961: Newman, Hopkins, Belloc, Chesterton, Greene, Waugh, University of Notre Dame Press (Notre Dame, IN), 2003.

EDITOR

(And author of introduction and notes) John Henry Newman, *The Idea of a University: Defined and Illustrated,* Clarendon (Oxford, England), 1976.

(And author of introduction and notes) John Henry Newman, *An Essay in Aid of a Grammar of Assent,* Oxford University Press (New York, NY), 1985.

(And author of introduction) *The Genius of John Henry Newman: Selections from His Writings,* Oxford University Press (New York, NY), 1989.

(With Alan G. Hill) *Newman after a Hundred Years,* Oxford University Press (New York, NY), 1990.

Newman the Theologian, University of Notre Dame Press (Notre Dame, IN), 1990.

Apologia pro vita sua, Penguin Books (New York, NY), 1994.

(And author of introduction) *Selected Sermons: John Henry Newman,* preface by Henry Chadwick, Paulist Press (New York, NY), 1994.

Newman and Conversion, University of Notre Dame Press (Notre Dame, IN), 1997.

(With Terrence Merrigan; and contributor) *Newman and the Word,* W. B. Eerdmans (Grand Rapids, MI), 2000.

(With Terrence Merrigan) *Oxford International Newman Conference (3rd: 2001: Keeble College, University of Oxford),* W. B. Eerdmans (Grand Rapids, MI), 2004.

SIDELIGHTS: Roman Catholic priest and Oxford University professor Ian Ker has focused much of his writing and editing career on the life and works of John Henry Newman, one of the most celebrated Catholic priests and theologians of the nineteenth century. Newman gained fame for his authorship of the *Apologia,* considered a masterpiece of religious autobiography. He would go on to write numerous books and sermons and remains one of the most discussed thinkers in the Catholic Church, eliciting strong responses from both his detractors and his admirers. Ker bases his 1989 book *John Henry Newman: A Biography,* almost entirely on Newman's own writings and the works of Father Dessain, who wrote many articles and other works about Newman. *Commonweal* contributor Peter Steinfels wrote that the biography "provides sensitive insights into Newman's personality and helpful analyses of his thinking and writing." In the *Economist,* a reviewer noted, "Ker has . . . written a book that is excellent, timely, comprehensive and fair." Writing in the *Spectator,* Robert Gray called Ker's biography of Newman "a primary authority, in every sense" and "very much an intellectual and literary biography." Gray also commented that "Professor Ker's prose is unobtrusive, clear and easy to read."

Ker has also edited numerous books on Newman, including *Newman the Theologian* and *Selected Sermons: John Henry Newman.* Nicholas Sagovsky, writing in the *Journal of Ecclesiastical History,* noted that Ker's "editorial approach" to *Selected Sermons* "gives to his selection a kind of timeless consistency in which historical and contextual issues sink below the horizon." In *Newman and Conversion,* published in 1997, Ker gathers together eight papers focusing primarily on Newman's conversion to Catholicism. The papers were originally delivered at an international conference celebrating the 150th anniversary of Newman's reception into the Catholic Church.

Ker also served as coeditor of *Newman and the Word.* This collection of papers comes from the proceedings of the second Oxford International Newman Conference held at Oriel College in 1998. *Newman and the Word* includes a paper by Ker on "those who hear and attest the Word, the 'people of God' who read and live the Scripture," according to Gerard Loughlin in a *Journal of Ecclesiastical History* review.

In *The Catholic Revival in English Literature, 1845-1961: Newman, Hopkins, Belloc, Chesterton, Greene, Waugh* Ker discusses not only Newman and his works, but also works of five other writers—Gerard Manley Hopkins, Hilaire Belloc, G.K. Chesterton, Graham Greene, and Evelyn Waugh—whose Catholicism played a central role in their life and writings. According to Francis Phillips in a review on the *Theotokos*

Catholic Books Web page, Ker "ably communicates his love, knowledge and understanding of these distinctive Catholic 'voices' and his carefully selected quotations serve to stimulate a reading or re-reading of the whole text to which he refers." Phillips concluded: "It is Ker's achievement to demonstrate the subtle links between these writers and to illuminate for the reader how Catholicism . . . can be a profound creative stimulus and not the strait-jacket that some would have us believe."

BIOGRAPHICAL AND CRITICAL SOURCES:

PERIODICALS

Commonweal, December 7, 1990, Peter Steinfels, review of *John Henry Newman: A Biography,* p. 727.
Economist, April 1, 1989, review of *John Henry Newman: A Biography,* p. 81.
Journal of Ecclesiastical History, July, 1995, Nicholas Sagovsky, review of *Selected Sermons: John Henry Newman,* p. 537; July, 1998, David Newsome, review of *Newman and Conversion,* p. 585; July, 2003, Gerard Loughlin, review of *Newman and the Word,* p. 600.
Spectator, January 28, 1989, Robert Gray, review of *John Henry Newman: A Biography,* p. 27.

ONLINE

Theotokos Catholic Books Web site, http://www.theotokos.org.uk/ (September 28, 2004), Francis Phillips, review of *The Catholic Revival in English Literature, 1845-1961: Newman, Hopkins, Belloc, Chesterton, Greene, Waugh.**

*   *   *

KERR, Alex 1952-

PERSONAL: Born 1952, in Bethesda, MD. *Education:* Graduated from Yale University and Oxford University; attended Keio University. *Hobbies and other interests:* East Asian art.

ADDRESSES: Home—Bangkok, Thailand. *Agent*—c/o Author Mail, Farrar, Straus, and Giroux, 19 Union Square West, New York, NY 10003.

CAREER: Author, business consultant, art dealer, manager of cultural events, and calligrapher. *Exhibitions:* Pasadena Center, Shumei Hall Gallery, 2002.

MEMBER: Oomoto Foundation.

AWARDS, HONORS: Shincho Gakugei Literature Prize for the best work of nonfiction published in Japan, 1994, for *Lost Japan;* Rhodes scholar.

WRITINGS:

(Translator and editor) Clifton Karhu, *Kyoto Rediscovered: A Portfolio of Woodblock Prints,* Weatherhill/Tankosha (New York, NY), 1980.

Utsukushiki Nihon no Zanzo, Shinchosha (Tokyo, Japan), 1993, translated and adapted as *Lost Japan,* Lonely Planet Publications (Oakland, CA), 1996.

Dogs and Demons: Tales from the Dark Side of Japan, Hill and Wang (New York, NY), 2001.

SIDELIGHTS: Author and business consultant Alex Kerr first experienced Japan as the twelve-year-old son of a naval officer stationed in Yokohama in the mid-1960s. Since then, Kerr has become completely immersed in Japanese landscape and culture. He has lived in Japan since 1977 and speaks and writes the language fluently, producing his books and conducting lectures in Japanese. He participates in a number of Japanese arts, including calligraphy, and is associated with the Oomoto Foundation, a Shinto organization dedicated to teaching and preserving traditional Japanese arts. Kerr is also a collector and dealer in East Asian art. As part of his business, Kerr manages cultural events throughout Asia, including Singapore, Thailand, and Cambodia.

A passionate and knowledgeable advocate for Japanese culture and the country's centuries-old traditions, Kerr laments the gradual loss of these traditions and the inexorable encroachment of modernization in his book, *Lost Japan.* Kerr "makes the case that Japan's modernization has been so rapid and thoughtless that it has come at the price of some of the most valuable features of the national heritage," commented Nicholas D. Kristof in the *New York Times.* Kerr "is scathing, in the book and in conversation, about many aspects of the arts, society, and government in Japan, but nobody accuses him of being a Japan-basher," Kristof observed. "Presumably that was because his book—and his life—are infused with love for Japan and its traditional arts."

Assembled from a series of columns that Kerr wrote for a Japanese newspaper, *Lost Japan* explores a variety of aspects of Japanese art and culture. He delves into the intricacies of Kabuki theater, explores the details of the Japanese tea ceremony, and discusses his interest in Japanese calligraphy. He relates his experiences of the business side of Japan, and also confronts what he sees as the contradiction in Japanese aesthetics that allows his adopted countrymen to ignore the industrial landscape and focus on the remaining greenery. "Sometimes the most perceptive critics are outsiders looking on from the inside," observed a reviewer in *Asiaweek.* A *Time International* critic called *Lost Japan* "an opinionated and thoughtful read."

The original Japanese version of *Lost Japan* won the prestigious Shincho Gakugei Literature Prize for the best work of non-fiction published in Japan; notably, Kerr was the first non-Japanese writer to win the award.

Dogs and Demons: Tales from the Dark Side of Japan presents "a remarkable portrait of modern Japan, virtually no part of which is flattering," remarked Richard J. Samuels in *New York Times Book Review.* "As his subtitle indicates, he goes out of his way to catalog the dysfunctions that dominate an unhappy and declining country." In the book Kerr "confidently cuts a broad swath across the worlds of architecture, education, politics, cinema, business, and the environment to make the case that Japan has fallen victim to its own success," Samuels commented. Form takes precedence over function and purpose in all aspects of Japanese society, Kerr observes. As a result, "what is left is empty: memorization without learning, design without context, building without purpose, information without knowledge, finance without the production of value," Samuels stated.

Kerr offers a variety of relevant observations and facts to support his polemic. Having long ago run out of needed public projects, the Japanese continue to build, expand, and pour concrete over their ever-diminishing open land. Public works spending in Japan exceeds that of the United States by as much as 400 percent in a country with a twentieth of the available land area. Bureaucrats are more interested in creating profits for pet industries and securing their own jobs; officials caught up in demands for accountability have been known to openly and defiantly destroy records and evidence of any wrongdoing. All but three of the country's 113 rivers have been dammed or diverted, and more than sixty percent of the Japanese coastline is drowned in concrete. Public education stresses rote memorization over the learning of critical thinking and analysis skills. The country's bloated construction industry lies at the heart of most of Japan's problems, but it is so inextricably bound to the economy that changes would be financially and economically disastrous—so, the buildings continue to rise and the concrete continues to flow.

"Much of this book is provocative, and deliberately so," noted *Newsweek International* reviewer Andrew Nagorski. Even so, it is "a product of tough love," Nagorski observed. "Instead of simply dismissing the book as a condemnation of their society, as many will, Japanese readers might do well to examine its many valid criticisms and take them as a powerful exhortation to chart a new course." *Dogs and Demons* is "nothing less than a sweeping indictment of a nation gone awry," commented Ann Scott Tyson in the *Christian Science Monitor.* The book "is a must read for anyone with even a cursory interest in the rise and continued fall of postwar Japan," wrote Michael Judge in the *Wall Street Journal.*

BIOGRAPHICAL AND CRITICAL SOURCES:

BOOKS

Kerr, Alex, *Lost Japan,* Lonely Planet Publications (Oakland, CA), 1996.

PERIODICALS

Asiaweek, June 24, 1996, "Narrow View," review of *Lost Japan.*
Booklist, February 15, 2001, David Pitt, review of *Dogs and Demons: Tales from the Dark Side of Japan,* p. 1112.

Christian Science Monitor, May 3, 2001, Ann Scott Tyson, "A Culture of Cheap Industrial Junk—Japan's Economic Woes are Just the Beginning of Its Troubles," p. 20.
Economist, February 10, 2001, "Concretely; Japan Observed; Observing Japan," p. 7.
Ideas on Liberty, March, 2003, Victor A. Matheson, review of *Dogs and Demons,* p. 60.
Kirkus Reviews, January 15, 2001, review of *Dogs and Demons,* p. 94.
Look Japan, November, 2003, Tony McNicol, "Calling Back the Children," p. 38.
Newsweek International, June 25, 2001, Andrew Nagorski, "A 'Misguided' Country," review of *Dogs and Demons,* p. 33.
New York Times, September 5, 1996, Nicholas D. Kristof, "A Fervent Traditionalist in Japan (An American?)."
New York Times Book Review, April 15, 2001, Richard J. Samuels, "Land of the Setting Sun?," review of *Dogs and Demons,* p. 19.
Publishers Weekly, February 12, 2001, review of *Dogs and Demons,* p. 197.
Reason, March, 2002, Charles Oliver, "Tales from the Dark Side: Divining the Causes of Japan's Economic Nightmare," p. 71.
Time International, November 9, 1998, review of *Lost Japan,* p. 8.
Wall Street Journal, May 4, 2001, Michael Judge, review of *Dogs and Demons,* p. W10.

ONLINE

Holtzbrinck Publishers Web site, http://www.holtzbrinckpublishers.com/ (October 4, 2004), "Alex Kerr."
Lonely Planet Web site, http://www.lonelyplanet.com/ (October 4, 2004), "Alex Kerr."
Shumei Arts Web site, http://www.shumeiarts.org/ (October 4, 2004), Patricia McNaughton, "A Finite Brush with Time" (interview).*

*   *   *

KESSELMAN, Wendy (Ann) 1940-

PERSONAL: Born 1940.

ADDRESSES: Home—P.O. Box 680, Wellfleet, MA 02667. *Agent*—George Lane, William Morris Agency, 1325 Avenue of the Americas, New York, NY 10019.

CAREER: Playwright, author, composer, and songwriter. Bryn Mawr College, Bryn Mawr, PA, teaching fellow, 1987.

AWARDS, HONORS: Meet the Composer grants, 1978 and 1982; National Endowment for the Arts fellowship, 1979; Sharman Award, 1980; Susan Smith Blackburn Prize, 1980; Playbill Award, 1980; Guggenheim fellowship, 1982; Ford Foundation grant, 1982; McKnight fellowship, 1985; American Society of Composers, Authors, and Publishers Popular Award, 1992, for musical theatre; Antoinette Perry ("Tony") Award nomination, 1997, for *The Diary of Anne Frank;* New England Theatre Conference Major Award, for outstanding creative achievement in the American theatre.

WRITINGS:

PLAYS

(And author of music and lyrics) *Becca* (for children; produced in New York, 1977), Anchorage Press (New Orleans, LA), 1988.

Maggie Magalita (produced in Washington, DC, 1980; produced in New York, 1986), Samuel French (New York, NY), 1987.

(And author of music) *My Sister in This House* (produced in Louisville, KY, then New York, 1981; revised version produced in London, England, 1987; also see below), Samuel French (New York, NY), 1982.

Merry-Go-Round, produced in Louisville, KY, 1981, and New York, 1983.

I Love You, I Love You Not (one-act version produced in Louisville, KY, 1982, then New York, 1983; full-length version produced St. Paul, MN, 1986, then New York, 1987; also see below), Samuel French (New York, NY), 1988.

(And author of music and lyrics) *The Juniper Tree: A Tragic Household Tale* (produced in Lenox, MA, 1982, then New York, 1983), Samuel French (New York, NY), 1985.

Cinderella in a Mirror, produced in Lenox, MA, 1987.

The Griffin and the Minor Cannon, music by Mary Rodgers, lyrics by Ellen Fitzhugh, produced in Lenox, MA, 1988.

A Tale of Two Cities, (adaptation of the novel by Charles Dickens), produced in Louisville, KY, 1992.

The Butcher's Daughter, produced in Cleveland, OH, 1993.

The Diary of Anne Frank (adapted from the book), produced on Broadway, 1997.

The Last Bridge, produced in New Brunswick, NJ, 2002.

The Notebook, (produced in New York, NY, 2003), Dramatist Play Service (New York, NY), 2004.

Also author of adaptation of *The Black Monk,* by Anton Chekov.

CHILDREN'S FICTION

Franz Tovey and the Rare Animals, photos by Norma Holt, drawings by Eleonore Schmid, Quist (New York, NY), 1968.

Angelita, photos by Norma Holt, Hill and Wang (New York, NY), 1970.

Slash: An Alligator's Story, pictures by Philippe Weisbecker, Quist (New York, NY), 1971.

Joey, photos by Norma Holt, Lawrence Hill (New York, NY), 1972.

Little Salt, pictures by Gerald Dumas, Scholastic Press (New York, NY), 1975.

Time for Jody, pictures by Gerald Dumas, Harper (New York, NY), 1975.

Maine Is a Million Miles Away, Scholastic Press (New York, NY), 1976.

Emma, illustrated by Barbara Cooney, Doubleday, (New York, NY) 1980.

There's a Train Going by My Window, pictures by Tony Chen, Doubleday (New York, NY), 1982.

Flick (novel), Harper (New York, NY), 1983.

Sand in My Shoes, illustrated by Ronald Himler, Hyperion (New York, NY), 1995.

SCREENPLAYS

Sister My Sister (adapted from the play *My Sister in This House*), Image Entertainment, 1995.

I Love You, I Love You Not (based on author's play), Polar Entertainment, 1996.

Mad or In Love, Fox, 2000.

A Separate Peace (teleplay; based on the novel by John Knowles), Showtime, 2004.

Also adapter and author of the screenplay for *Los dos mundos de Angelita,* translated as *The Two Worlds of Angelita,* 1982.

SIDELIGHTS: Wendy Kesselman began her career in the late 1960s writing children's books and also targeted her first play, *Becca,* which was produced in 1977, toward children. Since the late 1980s, Kesselman has focused her career almost entirely on writing plays and screenplays, except for the 1995 children's picture book *Sand in My Shoes.* Although Kesselman had written her previous children's book, *Flick,* more than a decade earlier, she remained in tune with her audience. Writing in *Booklist,* Carolyn Phelan noted that that *Sand in My Shoes* "strikes a chord that will resonate with many children and adults."

Although Kesselman's play *Becca* was largely considered children's theatre, a *Contemporary Dramatists* contributor noted that "older spectators responded to the implicit subtext of parental neglect and a brother's abuse of his sister." In the play, Becca is controlled and tormented by her older brother Jonathan while the siblings' parents never appear on stage but are intimated to be controlling and largely distant figures. The play, however, reaches children through Kesselman's music and lyrics, including songs for Jonathan's pets, which range from a parrot and bullfrog to snakes and spiders. Eventually, Becca stands up to her brother, who learns to treat both his neglected pets and his sister better. The *Contemporary Dramatists* essayist noted that "the most amazing moment in this startling feminist parable occurs when Becca rebels against her tormentor and it finally dawns on us that she is not a doll."

Kesselman's next play, *Maggie Magalita,* tells the story of an adolescent immigrant in New York City who experiences a culture clash with her Spanish-speaking grandmother while she struggles to be accepted by her classmates. In *Merry-Go-Round,* Kesselman continues her focus on childhood by showing how similar children can grow up to be quite different. She does this by having the adult actors reenact the earlier parts of their childhood lives. The *Contemporary Dramatists* contributor called Kesselman's 1981 play, *My Sister in This House,* "Kesselman's early masterpiece." Depicting the separate but parallel lives of maids and the mother and daughter for whom they work, the play is set in France in the early 1930s and depicts women constrained by the existing societal beliefs, which emphasize their domestic duties. As noted by the *Contemporary Dramatists* contributor, Kesselman "constructs the play in a dazzling series of parallels and contrasts, satirizing life in the drawing room and dining room while portraying with compassion life in the kitchen and garret."

In *I Love You, I Love You Not,* Kesselman continues to examine different cultures and generations when adolescent Daisy wants to learn German from her Jewish grandmother Nana, who is from the Old World and survived the Holocaust. But Nana has turned her back on her roots, including the German language of her persecutors, who murdered her parents and sisters. "As in *Becca,* Kesselman keeps Daisy's parents offstage, but she employs them as a formidable hostile presence," wrote the *Contemporary Dramatists* contributor. "Like the playwright's other domestic dramas, this work also compels our attention to the love/hate relationships within a family." Kesselman also wrote the screenplay for the 1996 movie version of her play, which Lael Loewenstein, writing in *Variety,* felt trivialized the Holocaust survivors. Loewenstein asserted, "what might have been a compelling portrait of anti-Semitism instead emerges as a sentimental coming-of-age story."

In 1993, Kesselman's *The Butcher's Daughter* was staged in Cleveland, Ohio, and was inspired by the story of French feminist Olympe de Gouges, perhaps the first woman executed for her beliefs about women's rights. Set during the French revolution, the fictionalized recounting of de Gouges's story tells a tale of two women: a butcher's daughter (de Gouges) and the daughter of an executioner, who beheads the butcher's daughter after his own daughter commits suicide. Throughout the play, Kesselman portrays a world dominated by men who practice capital punishment and incest and who deny women not only their rights but also ultimately often their will to live. The two women barely interact in the play, but their stories are linked by a singing narrator. Writing in *American Theatre,* Chris Jones commented that "much of the stylized dramatic language and action has a strong erotic charge, emphasizing de Gouges's free, cheerfully sexual personality. But sexuality in the play also has a much darker purpose, as Kesselman links physical desire with the lust for blood and power."

Kesselman's adaptation of *The Diary of Anne Frank* was staged on Broadway in 1997. The famous true story is based on the diaries of a young Jewish girl who hid from the Nazis with her family in an attic in Amsterdam during the Holocaust before finally being captured and eventually executed. Earlier versions of the play had been criticized for material deleted by Frank's father, such as Anne's thoughts about sex and her combative relationship with her mother. "Kesselman . . . has done a thorough reworking including material from the expanded edition of the diary published in 1991 (with most of the material restored that Frank had deleted), adding more Jewish references . . . and in general giving the play a less sentimental, more astringent tone," noted Richard Zoglin in *Time*. Writing in *Jewish News*, Donna Ezor commented, "It [the play] has finally realized its Jewish soul. And, as a result, it's a more realistic, more powerful and better play."

In her 2004 play *The Notebook*, Kesselman recounts the story of Warren Stone, a student and voracious reader who keeps his thoughts recorded in a red notebook. When he is invited by Mrs. Thorne to talk at a ninth-grade class, he falls in love with one of the students, Jenny, imagining that she is the character Natasha from *War and Peace*. Mrs. Thorne is also drawn to Jenny but abandons her special interest in her when Jenny's view of the world outgrows Mrs. Thorne's stilted view. At the same time, Warren's love for Jenny helps him to grow and experience life beyond the written word. Writing in the *New York Times*, Anita Gates felt that Kesselman sometimes uses "a little too much subtlety" in her depiction of the characters' relationships but added, "still *The Notebook* is a testament to the giddiness, even magic, of learning, and to the solacing thrill that can be found in poetry." On *CurtainUp.com* Macey Levin called the play "well structured and involving, though at times too episodic." Levin also noted that "Kesselman's dialogue rings true as she captures the nature of adolescents in their speech and sensitivities."

As in *The Butcher's Daughter*, Kesselman was inspired by another historical figure for her play *The Last Bridge*. Based on the story of Holocaust survivor Barbara Ledermann Rodbell, *The Last Bridge* tells the tale of a young Jewish girl who moves with her family to Amsterdam after the rise of anti-Semitism in Germany. When Germany later invades Amsterdam, Barbara ultimately chooses to leave her doomed family, which refuses to recognize the threat to their lives, and pose as a blonde Aryan.

In a review in the *New York Times*, Naomi Siegel stated that *The Last Bridge* "wavers between the thoughtful and the self-consciously theatrical." "The Last Bridge, which Barbara crosses when leaving her family in order to survive, is a metaphor for leaving behind the past, both its good and bad, and embarking on a new life," wrote Bob Rendell on the *Talkin' Broadway* Web site. He added, "Kesselman fully conveys this in a brief coda which can be instantly understood emotionally by all Americans, whatever our family histories."

In addition to the screenplay for her play *I Love You, I Love You Not*, Kesselman has written several other screenplays. Her 1995 screenplay *Sister My Sister*—adapted from her play *My Sister in This House*—is based on the true 1933 story of a pair of French maids who were sisters and who murdered their employers. In real life, the maids, Christine and Lea Papin, posed for photographic portraits just a few months before committing the murder. Kesselman, who had seen one of the portraits, told Justine Elias in the *New York Times*, "I was immersed in it, obsessed. At the time, a psychiatrist called Christine and Lea a psychological couple. That was one of the things that drew me into the story, the complete merging of identities." Kesselman also adapted *A Separate Peace*, John Knowles's well-known novel about a boy's experience at a New England preparatory school in the early 1940s, for *Showtime* television. Although Marilyn Moss, writing on the *Hollywood Reporer Online*, felt that "much of the novel's psychological nuances are lost in the translation," the reviewer also called Kesselman's script "reverent" and noted that *A Separate Peace* "is moving enough to hold onto its family audience."

BIOGRAPHICAL AND CRITICAL SOURCES:

BOOKS

Contemporary Dramatists, sixth edition, St. James Press (Detroit, MI), 1999.

PERIODICALS

American Theatre, April, 1993, Chris Jones, review of *The Butcher's Daughter*, p. 10.
Back Stage, December 19, 1997, David Sheward, review of *The Diary of Anne Frank*, p. 44.
Back Stage West, February 8, 2001, Jesse Dienstag, review of *The Diary of Anne Frank*, p. 17.

Booklist, June 1, 1995, Carolyn Phelan, review of *Sand in My Shoes,* p. 1786.

Daily Variety, September 10, 2004, Laura Fries, review of *A Separate Peace,* p. 17.

Entertainment Weekly, February 13, 1998, William Stevenson, review of *The Diary of Anne Frank,* p. 62.

Jewish News, December 18, 1997, Donna Ezor, review of *The Diary of Anne Frank,* p. 58.

Los Angeles Times, December 5, 1997, Laurie Winer, review of *The Diary of Anne Frank,* p. 1.

Nation, January 26, 1998, Laurie Stone, review of *The Diary of Anne Frank,* p. 34.

New Republic, July 17, 1995, Stanley Kauffmann, review of *Sister My Sister,* p. 34.

Newsweek, December 15, 1997, Jack Kroll, review of *The Diary of Anne Frank,* p. 71.

New York Jewish Week, December 12, 1997, Aaron Mack Schloff, review of *The Diary of Anne Frank,* p. 50.

New York Times, June 18, 1995, Justine Elias, review of *Sister My Sister,* section 2, p. 14; November 30, 1997, Bernard Hammelburg, review of *The Diary of Anne Frank,* section 2, p. 4; October 31, 1999, "Prescriptions for a Troubled Patient: The Theatre" (includes interview), section 2, page 1; June 27, 2002, Anita Gates, review of *The Notebook,* p. E7; April 6, 2003, Naomi Siegel, review of *The Diary of Anne Frank,* section 14NJ, p. 8.

Time, December 15, 1997, Richard Zoglin, review of *The Diary of Anne Frank,* p. 110.

Variety, November 10, 1997, Lael Loewenstein, review of *I Love You, I Love You Not,* p. 41; November 10, 1997, Markland Taylor, review of *The Diary of Anne Frank,* p. 53; December 8, 1997, Greg Evans, review of *The Diary of Anne Frank,* p. 119.

ONLINE

CurtainUp.com, http://curtainup.com/ (September 28, 2004), Macey Levin, review of *The Notebook.*

Hollywood Reporter Online, http://www.hollywood reporter.com/ (September 28, 2004), Marilyn Moss, review of *A Separate Peace.*

Talkin' Broadway Web site, http://www.talkinbroadway. com/ (September 28, 2004), Bob Rendell, review of *The Last Bridge.**

KEYS, Ancel (Benjamin) 1904-2004

OBITUARY NOTICE— See index for *CA* sketch: Born January 26, 1904, in Colorado Springs, CO; died November 20, 2004, in Minneapolis, MN. Physiologist, educator, and author. Keys is best remembered as the developer of the military K-Ration, a high-calorie meal created for soldiers in the field who were without other sources of food, and for his landmark study on the adverse effects of cholesterol on heart disease. He attended the University of California at Berkeley, where he received a B.A. in management and political science in 1925, after which he became a management trainee at Woolworth's department store. Keys went back to school and earned an M.A. in zoology in 1928, followed by a Ph.D. in biology and oceanography in 1930. After studying on a fellowship in Copenhagen, he earned a second Ph.D., in physiology, from King's College, Cambridge. Joining the Harvard University faculty in 1933 as an instructor in biochemical sciences, he traveled to the Andes Mountains to study how altitude affected physiology. A two-year post at the Mayo Clinic in the mid-1930s ended when Keys went to work for the University of Minnesota in 1937. With the onset of war, he was asked by the U.S. military to develop a ration kit for soldiers that would be lightweight but also supply sufficient nutrients. The result was the K-Ration, which became a standard meal for troops during World War II. Also during the war, he studied the physiological and mental effects of starvation on the human body, the results of his research being published in 1950's *Human Starvation.* Keys rose to the position of professor of physiology in 1939 at the University of Minnesota, and then became professor of physiological hygiene and department head from 1943 until 1972, when he retired. One of his other major accomplishments during his career was his research into how diet increases the chances of heart failure in middle-aged men. The extensive project concluded that high cholesterol in the blood— the result of too much saturated fat in the diet— dramatically increased the risk of heart attacks. This was the first major study to demonstrate this fact convincingly to the medical community. As a result of this work, Keys, who also studied the diets of healthier men in Europe in what became known as the Seven Countries Study, advocated a Mediterranean-type diet that included olive oil, pasta, fruits, and vegetables. His ideas on nutrition were published in *Eat Well and Stay Well* (1957; revised edition, 1963), which he wrote with his wife, Margaret. Keys also wrote or cowrote the books *The Benevolent Bean* (1967), *How to Eat Well and Stay Well the Mediterranean Way* (1975), and *Seven Countries: A Multivariate Analysis of Death and Coronary Heart Disease* (1980).

OBITUARIES AND OTHER SOURCES:

PERIODICALS

Chicago Tribune, November 24, 2004, section 3, p. 9.
New York Times, November 23, 2004, p. C17.
Times (London, England), November 26, 2004, p. 71.
Washington Post, November 24, 2004, pp. A1, A6.

*   *   *

KIRK, T(homas) H(obson) 1899-2004
(K. H. Thomas)

OBITUARY NOTICE— See index for *CA* sketch: Born January 13, 1899, in Seaton Carew, County Durham, England; died November 9, 2004, in Woolsington, Tyne and Wear, England. Kirk was a World War I veteran and physician who also published several works of fiction. After attending only two terms of medical school, the eighteen-year-old Kirk found himself thrust into medical practice as a surgeon-probationer for the Royal Navy. Assigned to the *HMS Lydiard,* the inexperienced, unlicensed medical student was put in charge of the health care for not only his ship's crew but also the crews of five other ships. Somehow surviving the experience without killing any of his patients, Kirk returned to school after the war, earning his M.B. and B.S. from the University of Durham in 1921, and his medical degree in 1930. He set up a private medical practice as a general practitioner in Lincolnshire, England, in 1922, where he would remain until 1964. During World War II he commanded his local Home Guard while his partner in the medical practice fought in the war. After his retirement, Kirk published three novels: *Back to the Wall* (1967), *The River Gang* (1968), and *The Ardrey Ambush* (1969). He also tried his hand at writing plays, one of which, *Slack Water,* was written under the pen name K. H. Thomas and produced by the BBC in 1955.

OBITUARIES AND OTHER SOURCES:

PERIODICALS

Daily Post (Liverpool, England), December 3, 2004, p. 13.

Independent (London, England), December 2, 2004, p. 43.
Times (London, England), December 2, 2004, p. 71.

ONLINE

BBC News Online, http://newsvote.bbc.co.uk/ (November 13, 2004).

*   *   *

KISLY, Lorraine

PERSONAL: Female.

ADDRESSES: Office—Parabola, 656 Broadway, New York, NY 10012. *E-mail*—editors@parabola.org.

CAREER: Parabola: Myth, Tradition, and the Search for Meaning (journal), editor-in-chief; co-founder of *Tricycle: The Buddhist Review.*

WRITINGS:

(Editor) *Ordinary Graces: Christian Teachings on the Interior Life,* Bell Tower (New York, NY), 2000.
(Editor) *Watch and Pray: Christian Teachings on the Practice of Prayer,* Bell Tower (New York, NY), 2002.
The Prayer of Fire: Experiencing the Lord's Prayer, Paraclete Press (Brewster, MA), 2004.

SIDELIGHTS: When editor Lorraine Kisly set out to compile *Ordinary Graces: Christian Teachings on the Interior Life,* a collection of texts drawn from several centuries that deal with the Christian experience, it was, as she told Jana Reiss of *Publishers Weekly,* "to reanimate my own connection with Christian teaching." She conducted most of her research at the General and Union Theological seminaries in New York with "no external criteria" about what she would include in the work. "I just went after the teachings that resonated emotionally, spiritually and intellectually." Thus she included selections by ancient fathers of the Christian church, as well as by modern Catholic, Orthodox Catholic, and Protestant writers, teachers, and artists. A *Publishers Weekly* reviewer praised *Ordinary Graces,* describing it as "a book to be savored slowly, marked up thoroughly, and made one's own."

Two years later Kisly published *Watch and Pray: Christian Teachings on the Practice of Prayer.* In this companion volume to *Ordinary Graces* she offers readers sections culled from a wide variety of Christian writings, along with brief introductions. The selections are arranged in ten themed "cycles" that delve into such crucial topics as communion with God, repentance, obedience, the Holy Spirit, the Lord's Prayer, and renunciation. Thematic threads running through these cycles include love, solitude, and community. "Each cycle goes from the most accessible level to the most sublime insight on the topic on that cycle's theme," Kisly explained to a *Beliefnet* interviewer. "The cycles themselves move from what D. H. Lawrence called the 'fundamental religious sense of wonder' through teachings on the neighbor, presence, will, obstacles and so on, through to divine union, which is the ultimate relationship." "As well as the 'old masters' of the development of the interior life," wrote Gordon Barker in *Anglican Journal*, "there are also the writings of those you may never have heard of which may touch you deeply." A *Publishers Weekly* contributor held a similar view: "This gorgeous collection has the potential to inspire, shape and deepen a Christian's life of prayer."

Kisley treats a single prayer in her next title, *The Prayer of Fire: Experiencing the Lord's Prayer.* In this extended mediation, which *Library Journal* reviewer Graham Christian dubbed a "delightful book," Kisly examines line by line the Lord's Prayer, which Christians of all denominations regularly recite. She not only discusses the literary and historical merit of these lines, but also probes the ways in which they help the prayer focus on Christ. A "gentle, probing book" is the way a *Sojourners* reviewer summed up the work.

BIOGRAPHICAL AND CRITICAL SOURCES:

PERIODICALS

Anglican Journal, February, 2002, Gordon Baker, "Lenten Reading Fosters an Intimacy with God."
Library Journal, May 1, 2004, Graham Christian, review of *The Prayer of Fire: Experiencing the Lord's Prayer,* p. 116.

National Catholic Reporter, November 3, 2000, William C. Graham, "Interior Paths," p. 40.
Publishers Weekly, August 28, 2000, review of *Ordinary Graces: Christian Teachings on the Interior Life,* p. 74, Jana Riess, interview with Kisly, p. 75; April 29, 2002, review of *The Next Christendom: The Coming of Global Christianity,* p. 63; March 29, 2004, review of *The Prayer of Fire,* p. 57.
Sojourners, August, 2004, "The Perfect Petition," review of *The Prayer of Fire,* p. 39.
Times-Picayune (New Orleans, LA), December 24, 2000, Susan Larson, "In the Spirit of the Season: Soul Food for Thought at Christmas Time," p. 5.

ONLINE

Beliefnet, http://www.beliefnet.com/ (November 15, 2004), interview with Kisly.*

*   *   *

KOLP, John Gilman 1943-

PERSONAL: Born 1943. *Education:* Iowa State University, B.S., M.A.; University of Iowa, Ph.D.

ADDRESSES: Office—U.S. Naval Academy, 121 Blake Rd., Annapolis, MD 21402-5000. *Agent*—c/o Author Mail, Johns Hopkins University Press, 2715 North Charles St., Baltimore, MD 21218-4363.

CAREER: Historian and writer. U.S. Naval Academy, Annapolis, MD, assistant professor of history.

WRITINGS:

Gentlemen and Freeholders: Electoral Politics in Colonial Virginia, Johns Hopkins University Press (Baltimore, MD), 1998.

SIDELIGHTS: Historian John Gilman Kolp's classes at the U.S. Naval Academy have included studies of colonial and revolutionary America and immigration history. In keeping with his interests, Kolp wrote *Gentlemen and Freeholders: Electoral Politics in Colonial Virginia,* a volume in two parts that studies electoral politics from 1725 to 1776. In the first section, titled "Provincial Patterns," Kolp draws on diaries, newspapers, letters, and other written documents to create a profile of the political culture of the period. He examines the factors that influenced voting by the adult males who were qualified to vote in elections for Virginia's legislative assembly, the House of Burgesses, touching on topics such as nomination processes, campaigning, polling, and socioeconomic and geographical considerations. In discussing voter frequency, he notes that affluent citizens did not turn out in numbers as great as their less wealthy neighbors. A significant finding is that fewer than nine percent of elections were contested by 1775.

Kolp makes comparisons of election processes in four Virginia counties, including Accomack, Lancaster, Fairfax, and Halifax, in the second section of *Gentlemen and Freeholders*. One of the notable prerevolution elections was that of George Washington in 1765, when he was elected to represent Fairfax County in the House of Burgesses. *Times Literary Supplement* reviewer Gwenda Morgan noted that Washington "had done all the right things to get into office. He had become a major landowner, had close social ties to the leading gentry, had won fame as a soldier, and served as a local office-holder." James Homer Williams wrote in *History: Review of New Books* that "with meticulous analysis of pollbooks and tax records, Kolp is able to quantify electoral patterns [in the colony of Virginia] across five decades and in four distinct counties."

BIOGRAPHICAL AND CRITICAL SOURCES:

PERIODICALS

English Historical Review, April, 2001, Peter Thompson, review of *Gentlemen and Freeholders: Electoral Politics in Colonial Virginia,* p. 486.
History: Review of New Books, summer, 1999, James Homer Williams, review of *Gentlemen and Freeholders,* p. 156.
Journal of American History, September, 2000, Rebecca Starr, review of *Gentlemen and Freeholders,* p. 646.
Times Literary Supplement, May 28, 1999, Gwenda Morgan, review of *Gentlemen and Freeholders,* p. 33.*

KRAM, Mark 1932-2002

PERSONAL: Born George Melvin Kram, December 6, 1932, in Baltimore, MD; died of a heart attack June 14, 2002, in Washington, DC; son of Gerard (a factory worker) and Naomi (Arthur) Kram; married Joan Sienkilewski, 1955 (divorced, 1977); married, 1977; second wife's name, René; children: (first marriage) Mark, Tracey, Kerry; (second marriage) Raymond, Robert, Alix. *Religion:* Roman Catholic.

CAREER: Baltimore Sun, Baltimore, MD, 1959-64, began as general assignment sportswriter, became sports columnist; *Sports Illustrated,* New York, NY, 1964-77, began as staff writer, became associate editor and senior writer; freelance writer, 1977-81; *Washington Times,* Washington, DC, sports columnist, 1981-82; contributor to magazines; writer of books and screenplays, 1982-2002. *Military service:* U.S. Army, 1952-53.

WRITINGS:

(With Dean Selmier) *Blow Away: A Killer's Story,* Viking (New York, NY), 1979.
Miles to Go (novel), Morrow (New York, NY), 1982.
Ghosts of Manila: The Fateful Blood Feud between Muhammad Ali and Joe Frazier, HarperCollins (New York, NY), 2001.

Contributor to books, including Irving T. Marsh and Edward Ehre, editors, *Best Sports Stories,* Dutton (New York, NY),1962; *The Wonderful World of Sport,* Time/Life Books (New York, NY), 1967; Gerald Walker, editor, *Best Magazine Articles: 1967,* Crown (New York, NY), 1967; *The Norton Reader,* 4th edition, Norton (New York, NY), 1977; David Fulk and Dan Riley, editors, *The Cubs Reader,* Houghton Mifflin (Boston, MA), 1991; *Sports Illustrated: Baseball,* Oxmoor House (Birmingham, AL), 1993; Frank Deford and Glenn Stout, editors, *The Best American Sports Writing—1993,* Houghton Mifflin,1993; Greg Williams, editor, *The Esquire Book of Sports Writing,* Penguin (New York, NY), 1995; Dan Jenkins and Glenn Stout, editors, *The Best American Sports Writing—1995,* Houghton Mifflin, 1995; Richard Ford, editor and author of introduction, *The Fights,* photographs by Charles Hoff, Chronicle Books (San Francisco, CA), 1996; George Plimpton and Glenn

Stout, editors, *The Best American Sports Writing—1997,* Houghton Mifflin, 1997; Gerald Early, editor, *The Muhammad Ali Reader,* Ecco Press (Hopewell, NJ), 1998; W. C. Heinz and Nathan Ward, editors, *The Book of Boxing,* Bishop Books (New York, NY), 1999; David Halberstam and Glenn Stout, editors, *The Best American Sports Writing of the Century,* Houghton Mifflin, 1999; Mark Collings, editor, *Muhammad Ali: Through the Eyes of the World,* Sanctuary Publishing Ltd. (London, England), 2001; and *The Greatest Boxing Stories Ever Told: Thirty-six Incredible Tales from the Ring,* Lyons Press (Guilford, CT), 2002. Contributor of articles to periodicals, including *Gentleman's Quarterly, Men's Journal, Esquire, Playboy, Regardie's, Health, Men's Health, Special Report, Audience, Wall Street Journal, International Herald Tribune,* and *New York Times.*

SIDELIGHTS: During his career, journalist Mark Kram brought to his work a level of prose style not often seen in traditional coverage of athletic events. In magazines such as *Sports Illustrated* and *Esquire,* and books such as *Ghosts of Manila: The Fateful Blood Feud between Muhammad Ali and Joe Frazier,* Kram elevated sports writing to the literary and examined the mythic underpinnings of professional athletic endeavor. "It seems right to remember Mark Kram as a poet of the dark nights in sports," wrote John Schulian in an obituary for *MSNBC.com.* "He wrote as if he believed that the best stories, like the best songs, are the sad ones, and sometimes he lived sad stories himself. He knew perhaps more than he should have about pain, failure, disgrace, but given time and inspiration, he could transform them all into things of beauty. When you read Mark Kram, even when his subject was a crowd screaming for blood, you could always hear an old jazz band playing." According to Brad Buchholz in the *Austin American-Statesman,* Kram "was one of the quiet writers—subtle, delicate, understated. . . . Kram's narratives were exquisitely crafted, rich with the sort of detail that told us something about a larger humanity. It was all the more impressive that he conveyed this frequently in the world of boxing, the most brutal of sports."

Kram was born and raised in Baltimore and attended the city's Calvert Hall High School, where he excelled in football and baseball. After graduating he signed a contract with the Pittsburgh Pirates organization to play professional baseball. He served in the military during the Korean War and then returned to baseball, but his career as a pro player ended when he was hit by a pitch in a game in Burlington, North Carolina. He returned to Baltimore, embarked on a program of self-education, and joined the staff of the *Baltimore Sun* in 1959.

When Kram became a writer for *Sports Illustrated* in 1964, the magazine was widely recognized for its journalistic excellence. Stories were lengthy and well crafted, and it was not unusual to find within its pages essays on subjects as varied as hunting and ballet. Kram thrived in this environment and became well known primarily, but certainly not exclusively, as a boxing writer. Schulian wrote: "*SI* was where Kram did more than make his name; he established himself as the grandest stylist on a staff embarrassingly rich in talent. Indeed, it can be said that Kram's stablemates—Dan Jenkins, Frank Deford, Bud Shrake and Roy Blount Jr.—have all enjoyed greater long-term success than he did. . . . But for turning journalism into literature, there was no one among them whose dust Kram had to eat." Buchholz observed that Kram's "mission statement was all about the beauty of language."

One of the highlights of Kram's career at *Sports Illustrated* was his coverage of the epic boxing matches between Muhammad Ali and Joe Frazier. His account of the 1975 "Thrilla' in Manila," where the two fighters met for the last time, is frequently anthologized. Buchholz commented: "Kram took us far from the ring, into the rooms of the bruised and battered boxers, not for the sake of revealing something private, but to look into the shadows and share something universal. In the eyes of Frazier, we felt an eternal ache, related to honor and loneliness and pain." *Washington Post* correspondent Jennifer Frey observed that Kram's "article on the 'Thrilla' in Manila' is considered by many to be one of the greatest sports magazine stories of all time."

Kram left *Sports Illustrated* in 1977. Thereafter he contributed articles to magazines such as *Esquire* and *Gentleman's Quarterly,* wrote screenplays, and published books. His novel *Miles to Go* concerns the efforts of three runners who are seeking to break the two-hour barrier for a marathon. He also continued to write about Muhammad Ali, and he took aim at a new generation of boxers, including Mike Tyson. Throughout the remainder of his life he lived in Washington, D.C.

Ghosts of Manila was inspired by what Kram saw as an undue lionization of Muhammad Ali. Writers who had never known the fighter praised Ali as a visionary and revolutionary, holding him in high esteem for his unwillingness to serve in the Vietnam War and for his statements on race relations. Having watched Ali at close range for years, Kram was in a position to challenge the myths that cling to the former boxer. "I grew weary of all the hagiography about Ali," Kram once told an interviewer for the *Washington Post.* "I kept seeing this great social figure, mentioned next to Martin Luther King, and I said, 'This is *wrong*.' So I decided, why not do a book on the person I saw, put some flesh and blood on him."

Ghosts of Manila explores the relationship between Ali and Frazier, beginning with their widely disparate backgrounds and ending with the lasting physical and psychological damage they have inflicted upon one another. The book also examines Ali's position within the Black Muslims and that group's influence on his pronouncements and decisions. Perhaps the most controversial aspect of the work is the way it portrays the darker side of Muhammad Ali: his derogatory remarks about Frazier, his womanizing, and his obsessive courtship of fame. As Richard Sandomir put it in the *New York Times,* "A central theme of Kram's book is that Ali is less than he seems to be, especially as a political and social force, that he was an empty canvas upon which the uninformed painted a world idol."

Not surprisingly, *Ghosts of Manila* earned Kram the enmity of some people who admire Muhammad Ali, including a few of Ali's biographers. Other reviewers, however, appreciated not only the points Kram makes about Ali but also the style in which the book is written. *Pittsburgh Post-Gazette* reviewer Gene Collier declared, "it's evident that Kram's skills have merely swelled and exploded, while Ali's have long since vanished. You need only bathe yourself in any of the hundreds of descriptions of that decline in these pages to appreciate Kram's brilliance." On the *ESPN* Web site, David Halberstam observed that Kram "has produced a quite remarkable book—it is both an exceptional, wonderfully written account of those fights in which he goes back-and-forth in time between then and now, and it is also a screed against many of the journalists who covered the fights, and who, he believes, were taken in by Ali." Halberstam added: "It is very much to Kram's credit—it is one of the things that makes the book so successful—that he manages to give Frazier a dignity and humanity so often denied him by other writers who were so caught up in the mystique of the infinitely more charismatic Ali." *Boston Globe* writer Mark Jurkowitz concluded: "Whether you accept Kram's point of view—and many won't— you have to admire his sparse but rich storytelling technique. He spent considerable time with the principals and their entourages, and it shows."

Ghosts of Manila was published only two years prior to Kram's death. He suffered a fatal heart attack in June of 2002, not long after returning from a Mike Tyson-Lennox Lewis fight in Memphis, Tennessee. Halberstam wrote of Kram: "In the semi-closed world of high-level sportswriting, he was known as a bleeder. No one at *Sports Illustrated,* in the opinion of his peers, agonized over his writing as Kram did, bleeding over every word, and agonizing, as well, over what he was doing, and whether working for *Sports Illustrated* was a worthy enough goal, when perhaps there were more important subjects to write about. . . . At his best . . . no one wrote better about boxing. He did the requisite legwork, he had the requisite connection and trust with the men who formed the inner world of boxing, he knew how to listen, and he brought an inordinate amount of passion to his work."

BIOGRAPHICAL AND CRITICAL SOURCES:

PERIODICALS

Austin American-Statesman, December 29, 2002, Brad Buchholz, "On Narrative, Death, and Four Men Who Loved Words," p. K1.
Boston Globe, July 26, 2001, Mark Jurkowitz, "'Ghosts of Manila' Gets in the Ring with Ali Legend."
Fort Worth Star-Telegram, December 23, 2001, Jeff Guinn, "Weighing in on Ali," p. 1.
New York Times, May 21, 2001, Richard Sandomir, "Book Portrays Ali as Not 'the Greatest,'" p. D10.
Pittsburgh Post-Gazette, June 10, 2001, Gene Collier, "Ali on the Ropes," p. 8.
Wall Street Journal, May 25, 2001, Chris Gay, "A Jab at the Greatest," p. W8.
Washington Post, May 29, 2001, Jennifer Frey, "Mark Kram, Pulling No Punches," pp. C1, C14.

ONLINE

CNN/Sports Illustrated Online, http://www.cnnsi.com/ (May 30, 2001), Frank Deford, "Kram Goes for the Greatest Knockout."

CreativeLoafing.com, http://www.creativeloafing.com/ (April 28, 2001), Sam Shapiro, "Beauty and Beastliness."

ESPN.com, http://sports.espn.go.com/ (August 14, 2001), David Halberstam, "Chasing 'Ghosts of Manila'."

OBITUARIES

PERIODICALS

New York Times, June 15, 2002, p. B18.

ONLINE

MSNBC.com, http://www.msnbc.com/news/ (June 25, 2002), John Schulian, "Unsung Poet of All the Dark Nights."*

*   *   *

KRESSLEY, Carson 1969-

PERSONAL: Born 1969, in Allentown, PA. *Education:* Gettysburg College, B.S., *Hobbies and other interests:* Equestrian, member of U.S. World Cup Equestrian Team.

ADDRESSES: Home—New York, NY. *Agent*—c/o Author Mail, Penguin Group, 375 Hudson St., New York, NY 10014.

CAREER: Fashion stylist for Ralph Lauren; independent stylist; *Queer Eye for the Straight Guy,* fashion expert, 2003—.

AWARDS, HONORS: Phi Beta Kappa.

WRITINGS:

Off the Cuff: The Essential Style Guide for Men and the Women Who Love Them, illustrated by Jason O'Malley, Dutton (New York, NY), 2004.

(With others) *Queer Eye for the Straight Guy: The Fab Five's Guide to Looking Better, Cooking Better, Dressing Better, Behaving Better, and Living Better,* Clarkson Potter (New York, NY), 2004.

Contributor of fashion column for *Us* magazine.

SIDELIGHTS: Known for his role on *Queer Eye for the Straight Guy,* a television reality series, fashion stylist Carson Kressley has written a style column and published two books on fashion. Like his column, both book titles—*Off the Cuff: The Essential Style Guide for Men and the Women Who Love Them* and *Queer Eye for the Straight Guy: The Fab Five's Guide to Looking Better, Cooking Better, Dressing Better, Behaving Better, and Living Better*—demonstrate Kressley's wit as well as his fashion sense.

Kressley grew up in Allentown, Pennsylvania, and graduated with honors from Gettysburg College with degrees in finance and fine art. He had long been interested in fashion and became an independent fashion stylist for such catalog retailers as Saks Fifth Avenue, Bloomingdales, and Neiman Marcus. For a time he worked for the Ralph Lauren fashion label, where he designed men's sportswear. A move into the corporate advertising section of the label allowed Kressley to expand his talents further, working on fashion shows and national retail advertising campaigns. In 2003, he auditioned and became a fashion expert for the *Queer Eye for the Straight Guy,* "the first feel-good primetime reality series," wrote *Daily Variety* reporter Phil Gallo. Kressley's exposure as one of the five hosts of the show has led to a number of other opportunities, including publishing books on fashion.

In an interview with Erica Hill of *America's Intelligence Wire,* Kressley described his *Off the Cuff* as "a lighthearted guide to just get started on the road to . . . looking good and feeling great about it." Viewers who liked what they saw on the television show were the target audience for the book. "I tried to keep it light and entertaining; that's what has worked on our show," Kressley explained to Jayne Haugen Olson in an interview for *MPLS-St. Paul.* A *Publishers Weekly* reviewer thought that Kressley's irreverent television persona "translates nicely to the page," making *Off the Cuff* a "thoroughly entertaining" style guide. More closely tied to the television show is

Queer Eye for the Straight Guy, a culture and style guide, which *Advocate* reviewer Anne Stockwell called a "funny, eye-friendly, and superpractical new book" authored by all of the show's hosts.

BIOGRAPHICAL AND CRITICAL SOURCES:

PERIODICALS

Advocate, March 30, 2004, Anne Stockwell, "Under the Queer Eye," p. 60; June 22, 2004, Adam B. Vary, "Pride, Patriotism, and Queer Eye," p. 120.

America's Intelligence Wire, October 1, 2004, interview with Kressley.

Asia Africa Intelligence Wire, August 8, 2004, review of *Queer Eye for the Straight Guy: The Fab Five's Guide to Looking Better, Cooking Better, Dressing Better, Behaving Better, and Living Better.*

Daily Variety, July 15, 2003, Phil Gallo, review of *Queer Eye for the Straight Guy,* p. 10; August 21, 2003; March 26, 2004, Amy Dawes, "Saving Straight Guys," p. A8.

MPLS-St. Paul, October, 2004, Christine Johnson, "See Carson in Room 101," p. 278; Jayne Haugen Olson, "We Love Carson," pp. 287-289.

Newsweek, August 11, 2003, Marc Peyser, "The Fashion Policeman," p. 51.

ONLINE

BravoTV.com, http://www.bravotv.com/ (August 31, 2003), "*Queer Eye for the Straight Guy* Cast Member Carson Kressley."*

*   *   *

KRONIUK, Lisa
See BERTON, Pierre (Francis Demarigny)

*   *   *

KUH, Patric 1964-

PERSONAL: Born 1964, in France; married; children: one son.

ADDRESSES: Home—Los Angeles, CA. *Agent*—c/o Author Mail, Penguin Group, 375 Hudson St., New York, NY 10014. *E-mail*—letters@lamag.com.

CAREER: Writer and chef, 1990—.

WRITINGS:

An Available Man, Ballantine Books (New York, NY), 1990.
The Last Days of Haute Cuisine: America's Culinary Revolution, Viking (New York, NY), 2001.

Contributor to *Paris in Mind,* edited by Jennifer Lee, Vintage Books (New York, NY), 2003. Contributor of articles and essays to periodicals, including *Gourmet, Esquire,* and *Salon.com.*

SIDELIGHTS: In his book *The Last Days of Haute Cuisine: America's Culinary Revolution,* writer and chef Patric Kuh examines the evolution of restaurants and dining in America, in what a *Publishers Weekly* reviewer called "an excellent, clear-eyed look at the death of old-fashioned American restaurants (exemplified by Le Pavilion) and the advent of a new kind of eating." Kuh seasons the book with large helpings of his own experiences as a chef in a number of high-level restaurants, including such notable eateries as Four Seasons and Chez Panisse. "This moving foray into the world of restaurateuring in modern American proves that cuisine is as crucial to 20th-century history as technology, rock music, and television," wrote a contributor to *Kirkus Reviews.*

Beginning with the impact of the French Pavilion at the New York World's Fair in 1939, Kuh describes how for more than twenty years after the fair, "what passed for culinary distinction in these United States was 'under the shadow of France,'" as reviewer Jonathan Yardley stated in the *Washington Post.* The influence of France and French cooking dominated American fine dining throughout the 1940s and 1950s and into the 1960s, from the layout of restaurants, to the inherent ethnocentrism of being required to know what the French dishes on the menu consisted of, all the way to the calculated snub by a French maitre d'.

With the greater availability of air travel and the advent of credit cards in the mid-1960s, the "gastronomic experience" of fine dining in both American and European restaurants became more available to the middle class. "But the influence of two people about whom Kuh writes with admiration and sympathy would seem to be equally great," Yardley remarked. "Julia Child not merely took much of the mystery out of French cuisine, she moved it into the American kitchens," Yardley observed, "and James Beard legitimized American cooking as itself a cuisine to be appreciated and built upon." Haute cuisine, as exemplified by the highly refined French dining experience, began to give way to what Kuh calls the "modern food sensibility," with a greater emphasis on qualities such as simplicity, authenticity, and earthiness, Yardley wrote. "By developing and respecting our own food, Kuh suggests, we began to take all food more seriously," declared reviewer J. Peder Zane for *NewsObserver.com*. This new attitude eventually allowed Americans to cultivate interest in other types of foods, including Asian, Middle Eastern, Tex-Mex, and even soul food. "The rise of ethnic foods has not only immensely enriched the upmarket end of the food business, it has also enabled more and more Americans to eat good food at reasonable prices," Yardley wrote.

Kuh is also an immigrant to America, a French Jew who came to the United States more than a decade ago. "Although his book addresses the question, 'How has American cuisine changed?', he asks it in the context of a larger yet more personal question, born of the immigrant experience: 'What does it mean to be American?,'" Zane wrote. "Kuh's streamlined history takes on wider significance when we understand that his real aim is to understand his new home the best way he knows: through food." "The great value of this book is that Kuh aligns the history of American cuisine with America itself," Zane remarked, "as a nation ever-struggling to live up to its highest ideals, where the forces of exclusion and inclusion, of privilege and diversity are constantly at battle. That our better angels are triumphing in our kitchens is a hopeful sign." *San Francisco Chronicle*'s Kim Severson also found the work "much more than an academic study of an industry or an emotional ode to the American table." She added that "with an insider's knowledge and a smart sensibility, Kuh understands the social impact a restaurant has, out front and in the back. He knows that restaurants are as much about comfort, celebration and companionship as they are about food." According to William Rice of the *Chicago Tribune,* Kuh "not only writes well—you will find elegant passages throughout the book—he adroitly ties together his themes and his cast of characters."

Kuh is also the author of the novel *An Available Man,* the story of American expatriate Francis Buchanan. Formerly a Wall Street hustler, Francis now hustles rich women as a gigolo in Paris. Yet Francis has one true love, Texas oil heiress Emma Cullington, who has returned to France after a failed attempt to rehabilitate herself from an expensive and destructive drug habit. Emma's father hires Francis to locate and care for Emma. Instead of returning to the safety of a relationship with Francis, Emma flees to a seedy, drug-fueled existence in some of the more dismal locations throughout Texas and France.

An Available Man caught the attention of reviewers. "Patric Kuh has written a new kind of expatriate novel, much closer in spirit to the lost generation, but with the trappings of the lost yuppie generation," commented Sonja Bolle in *Los Angeles Times Book Review.* "Stylish self-absorption and self-loathing aplenty here," wrote a *Kirkus Reviews* contributor.

Kuh's vivid and effective descriptions of the settings in his novel, particular the Parisian scenes, were met with even greater favor, even by those reviewers who found other flaws in the novel. "That Patric Kuh has a gift for conveying a spirit of place, however sordid the atmosphere, is undeniable," wrote Francesca Stanfill in *New York Times Book Review.* "Ultimately, Mr. Kuh's most bewitching and sensual female 'character' is Paris itself—a city the author clearly knows well and whose beauty and unsavory aspects he succeeds equally well in evoking," stated Stanfill. To Peggy Kaganoff, reviewing the book in *Publishers Weekly,* "perhaps the most interesting aspect of the book is its intimate portrayal of Paris." "Kuh's sensuous descriptions of Paris at sunset and at dawn alone set his book apart from run-of-the-mill tales of sex-drugs-etc.," Bolle wrote. But given their excesses, "Kuh's characters do hit bottom, and even though he spares us the awakening at the end," Bolle remarked, "there's a genuine sense of redemption."

BIOGRAPHICAL AND CRITICAL SOURCES:

PERIODICALS

Booklist, March 15, 2001, Mark Knoblauch, review of *The Last Days of Haute Cuisine: America's Culinary Revolution,* p. 1342.

Chicago Tribune, April 29, 2001, William Rice, "The Lows and Highs of American Cuisine," p. 5.

Entertainment Weekly, April 20, 2001, Rebecca Ascher-Walsh, review of *The Last Days of Haute Cuisine,* p. 66.

Forbes, March 5, 2001, Thomas Jackson, review of *The Last Days of Haute Cuisine,* p. 116.

Kirkus Reviews, January 15, 1990, review of *An Available Man,* p. 72; February 1, 2001, review of *The Last Days of Haute Cuisine,* p. 165.

Los Angeles Times Book Review, March 4, 1990, Sonja Bolle, review of *An Available Man,* p. 6.

Nation's Restaurant News, April 23, 2001, "The Times and the Customers, They Are a-Changing'," p. 86.

New York Times, August 16, 2003, Frank J. Prial, "With Writers to Thank, We'll Always Have Paris," pp. A15, A20.

New York Times Book Review, July 29, 1990, Francesca Stanfill, review of *An Available Man,* p. 20.

Publishers Weekly, February 2, 1990, Penny Kaganoff, review of *An Available Man,* p. 80; January 22, 2001, review of *The Last Days of Haute Cuisine,* p. 309.

San Francisco Chronicle, March 18, 2001, Kim Severson, "The Rise and Fall of the Snobby Restaurant," p. 1.

Washington Post, March 1, 2001, Jonathan Yardley, "Getting Off the Sauce," review of *The Last Days of Haute Cuisine,* p. C2.

ONLINE

NewsObserver.com, http://www.newsobserver.com/ (October 23, 2001), J. Peder Zane, "Food and the Meaning of America," review of *The Last Days of Haute Cuisine.**

*　　*　　*

KUITENBROUWER, Kathryn (Ann Frances) 1965-

PERSONAL: Surname is pronounced "*Koo*-ten-brou-wer;" born February 6, 1965, in Ottawa, Ontario, Canada; daughter of Bryan Richard James (a civil engineer) and Beatrice Ann (a homemaker; maiden name, Hudson) Walsh; married Marc Kuitenbrouwer (a film work coordinator), March 15, 1991; children: Linden, Jonas, Christopher. *Ethnicity:* "Irish." *Education:* University of Ottawa, B.A.

ADDRESSES: Agent—Westwood Creative Artists, 94 Harbord St., Toronto, Ontario, Canada M5S 1G6.

CAREER: Freelance writer and reviewer, 1995—.

MEMBER: Writers' Union of Canada.

WRITINGS:

Way Up (short fiction), Goose Lane Editions (Fredericton, New Brunswick, Canada), 2003.
The Nettle Spinner (novel), Goose Lane Editions (Fredericton, New Brunswick, Canada), 2005.

Contributor to periodicals.

WORK IN PROGRESS: Manual for Secret-Keeping, a novel set in Canada and the southern United States.

SIDELIGHTS: Kathryn Kuitenbrouwer told *CA:* "The putting together of words to express ideas has a certain *frisson* that appeals to me. I have been writing stories since I was able to write. I do not have a particular process except that I do not sit to work unless I have some aspects of the story worked out in my mind.

"I am influenced by the symmetry and joy in nature, by the visual arts, by humanity all around me. My work is influenced by early writers like Catherine Parr Traill and Susanna Moodie. It is not, however, anything like their conservatism.

"I am inspired by memory and its falsity. Paradoxically, one could maintain that memory is all one has, yet in its inaccuracy, that amounts to nothing. I am interested in how profoundly meaningful that 'nothing' is to the individual. I am also fascinated with the development of space from wilderness to agriculture, the shift in humanity that has come with that development.

"I am keen to push boundaries in my writing, particularly the thin threshold between the body and its environment. This often leads down some gritty paths.

I write about women working: logging, planting trees, building houses. My characters are often blatantly sexual. Their body functions are entirely earthly so that no act rises to lyricism, but rather it bears the same mundane yet beautiful plateau of being as an animal or, microcosmically, a virus struggling to survive, a weed."

BIOGRAPHICAL AND CRITICAL SOURCES:

ONLINE

Kathryn Kuitenbrouwer Home Page, http://www. kathrynkuitenbrouwer.com (December 4, 2004).

L

LAIRD, Sally

PERSONAL: Born in England. *Education:* Attended Oxford University and Harvard University.

ADDRESSES: Office—Carl Th. Dreyers vej 9, 8400 Ebeltoft, Denmark. *E-mail*—mail@absolute-english.dk.

CAREER: Author, translator, and editor. Absolute English (translating service), owner. Taught at European Film College in Denmark.

WRITINGS:

(Translator) Vladimir Sorokin, *The Queue,* Readers International, 1988.
(Translator) Ludmilla Petrushevskaya, *The Time: Night,* Virago Press (London, England), 1994.
(Translator) Ludmilla Petrushevskaya, *Immortal Love,* Pantheon (New York, NY), 1995.
(Editor) *Voices of Russian Literature: Interviews with Ten Contemporary Writers,* Oxford University Press (New York, NY), 1999.
(Translator) Semen Samuilovich Vilenski, *Till My Tale Is Told: Women's Memoirs of the Gulag,* Indiana University Press (Bloomington, IN), 1999.

Editor of the journal *Index on Censorship.*

SIDELIGHTS: Sally Laird is a writer and editor and has also translated several works from the original Russian. One of her translation projects, *The Queue,* is a novel by author and illustrator Vladimir Sorokin that was described by *Library Journal* reviewer Mary F. Zirin as drawing on "avant-garde experiment and a flair for nonsense." Sorokin's English-language debut revolves around the dialogue and interaction of Soviet citizens waiting in line to buy products. The activities of the crowd include swearing, laughing, lovemaking, drinking, discussions about sports and diets, war and poetry. "People in the queue express themselves idiotically," wrote Zinovy Zinik, a reviewer for the *Times Literary Supplement,* "not because they are all dimwitted, but because those who have joined the crowd are converted into simpletons who despise clever ideas and dignified speech." Zinik noted that works like Sorokin's are seldom printed in the Soviet Union and that Sorokin's devices "pose an enormous problem for a translator." Laird re-sets *The Queue* in suburban London during a time after the war. "This geographical and temporal leap strips the queuers' speech of its tawdry frills and exposes the ingenious logic with which Sorokin constructs his 'movable' dialogues," declared Zinik.

Laird has also translated *The Time: Night* and *Immortal Love,* two novels by Ludmilla Petrushevskaya, a Russian author born in 1938 whose early hardships established the groundwork for her writing. Helena Goscilo wrote in the *Women's Review of Books* that "her fiction and drama illustrate Tennessee Williams's tragic conviction that 'we're all sentenced to solitary confinement inside our own skins.'" Petrushevskaya's writings were excluded from accepted Soviet literature for thirty years even though she received praise worldwide, and their appearance in English translation was well-received by critics.

The story of a woman who attempts to fill all of the roles requires of her and still retain her status as a poet, *The Time* is written in the form of notes. A *Publishers Weekly* reviewer wrote that "while the facts of the story are relentlessly depressing, the author's signature black humor and matter-of-fact prose result in an insightful and sympathetic portrait of a family in crisis." *Booklist* contributor John Shreffler called *The Time* "a bleak portrait of Russian society and of the burdens carried by its women." Lesley Chamberlain, reviewing the book for the *Times Literary Supplement,* noted that the novel's "colloquial language" "is smoothly translated by Sally Laird. The writing is beautifully controlled and the spirit large."

Immortal Love, a collection of twenty-three stories and thirteen monologues, was written over twenty years and reflects the difficult lives of Russian women and girls. "What emerges from these loving, bitter portrayals is a literary experience, and a relationship to literature, that is by turns empty and sublime," wrote Jessica Garrison, reviewing Laird's translation in the *Nation.* Hesba Stretton commented in *New Statesman* that "each piece is cast as urban folk tale, told with the compulsion of gossip. Many end with the bland and unsettling wisdom of 'and that's just the way it is.'"

Voices of Russian Literature: Interviews with Ten Contemporary Writers is a collection of Laird's interviews conducted from 1987 to 1994. The older writers, born during the 1920s and 1930s, include Petrushevskaya, Andrei Bitov, Fazil Iskander, and Vladimir Makanin. The next generation, born from the 1940s to the 1950s, are Sorokin, Tatyana Tolstaya, Yevgeny Popov, Zufar Gareyev, and Igor Pomerantsev. The youngest writer, Viktor Pelevin, was born in 1962. Laird's bibliography lists English translations by these writers. Writing in *Choice,* Goscilo called the collection "splendid," the interviews "engrossing," and commented that Laird's prose "is crisp and lucid, her translations fully idiomatic . . . The interviews brim with unexpected and eloquent insights." *Times Literary Supplement* contributor John Weightman wrote of the authors: "Being Russian intellectuals with the stamina of survivors, they respond with gusto, just as some of them vigorously subvert the canons of Soviet decency in their writings." Weightman advised that "in most of the interviews, the tone is resolutely cheerful. . . . On the one hand, these Russians are very conscious of the amorphousness and backwardness of their huge country and of their non-European characteristics. . . . On the other hand, apart from

the issue of freedom of expression, they display no great keenness to adapt to the more coherent nature of Western society." Karen Rosenberg, a reviewer in *Nation,* commented that "Laird has captured a fascinating era beginning before the breakup of the Soviet Union and continuing today, in which questions of identity are hotly debated. This has been a struggle not only between parties but inside individuals, as revealed by contradictions within the interviews." Rosenberg concluded that *Voices of Russian Literature* "is not just a companion volume to contemporary Russian fiction. Laird . . . has . . . set literature in a philosophical and political context. So although her book concerns Russian authors, it will be intelligible and interesting to those who have only the vaguest acquaintance with them—no mean feat."

BIOGRAPHICAL AND CRITICAL SOURCES:

PERIODICALS

Booklist, August, 1994, John Shreffler, review of *The Time: Night,* p. 2024; March 15, 1996, Donna Seaman, review of *Immortal Love,* p. 1239.

Choice, December, 1999, Helena Goscilo, review of *Voices of Russian Literature: Interviews with Ten Contemporary Writers,* p. 729.

Library Journal, June 15, 1988, Mary F. Zirin, review of *The Queue,* p. 69; July, 1994, M. Anna Falbo, review of *The Time: Night,* p. 129; April 1, 1996, Olivia Opello, review of *Immortal Love,* p. 121.

Nation, June 10, 1996, Jessica Garrison, review of *Immortal Love,* p. 32; October 18, 1999, Karen Rosenberg, "Their Myths and Ours," review of *Voices of Russian Literature,* p. 28.

New Statesman, March 3, 1995, Hesba Stretton, review of *Immortal Love,* p. 39.

New York Times Book Review, March 3, 1983, Steven V. Roberts, "Congress: Slowly, a New Awareness of Women," p. 12; October 2, 1988, Tom Swick, review of *The Queue,* p. 26; September 11, 1994, Ken Kalfus, review of *The Time: Night,* p. 25; June 16, 1996, review of *Immortal Love,* p. 32.

Publishers Weekly, May 13, 1988, Sybil Steinberg, review of *The Queue,* p. 269; July 4, 1994, review of *The Time: Night,* p. 51.

Review of Contemporary Literature, spring, 2001, Michael Pinker, review of *The Time: Night,* p. 199.

Times Literary Supplement, June 24, 1988, Zinovy Zinik, "A Russian Monster," review of *The Queue,* p. 698; February 4, 1994, Lesley Chamberlain,

"Worn out and Worn Down," review of *The Time: Night,* p. 25; August 20, 1999, John Weightman, "You Have to Weep," review of *Voices of Russian Literature,* p. 22.

Women's Review of Books, December, 1994, Helena Goscilo, "The Unbearable Heaviness of Being," p. 19.*

ONLINE

Absolute English Web site, http://www.absolute-english.dk/ (November 20, 2004).*

*   *   *

LANIER, Drew Noble 1962-

PERSONAL: Born December 21, 1962, in Dallas, TX; son of J. E. (a mechanical engineer) and Jeannine (a homemaker) Lanier; married May 5, 2001; wife's name, Allison L. (a homemaker). *Ethnicity:* "White." *Education:* University of North Texas, B.A., 1986, Ph.D., 1997; DePaul University, J.D., 1990.

ADDRESSES: Home—14480 Jamaica Dogwood Dr., Orlando, FL 32828. *Office*—Department of Political Science, University of Central Florida, P.O. Box 161356, Orlando, FL 32816-1356; fax: 407-823-0051. *E-mail*—dlanier@mail.ucf.edu; dlanier6@cfl.rr.com.

CAREER: Hughes, Watters & Askanase, Houston, TX, associate attorney, 1990-92; Law Offices of Drew N. Lanier, Denton, TX, solo practitioner, 1993-97; University of Central Florida, Orlando, assistant professor, 1997-2003, associate professor of political science and director of Lou Frey Institute of Politics and Government, 2003—. Admitted to the Bar of the State of Texas, Supreme Court of Texas, U.S. Court of Appeals for the Fifth Circuit, and U.S. District Courts for Southern and Eastern Districts of Texas. Guest speaker at other institutions, including Washington University, St. Louis, MO, University of Colorado, Boulder, and North Carolina Central University; guest on media programs.

MEMBER: American Political Science Association, Midwest Political Science Association, Southern Political Science Association, Western Political Science Association, Southwestern Political Science Association, Pi Sigma Alpha, Psi Chi, Mortar Board, Order of Barristers Honor Society.

AWARDS, HONORS: American Jurisprudence Award for legal research and writing, 1987; Edward Artinian travel grant, Southern Political Science Association, 2001; award for outstanding teaching in political science, American Political Science Association and Pi Sigma Alpha, 2001; grant from Pew Foundation Trust, 1998.

WRITINGS:

Of Time and Judicial Behavior: Time Series Analyses of United States Supreme Court Agenda-setting and Decision-making, 1888-1997, Susquehanna University Press (Selinsgrove, PA), 2003.

Contributor to books, including *Paths to State Repression: Human Rights Violations and Contentious Politics,* edited by Christian Davenport, Rowman & Littlefield (Lanham, MD), 2000; and *Striking First: The Preemptive Doctrine and the Reshaping of U.S. Foreign Policy after September 11th,* edited by Chris J. Dolan and Betty S. Glad, Palgrave-Macmillan (New York, NY), 2004. Contributor of articles and reviews to periodicals, including *Cardozo Arts and Entertainment Law Journal, Social Science History, American Journal of Political Science, Social Science Quarterly, Judicature, American Review of Politics, Fordham Urban Law Journal, State Politics and Policy Quarterly,* and *Review of Policy Research.*

WORK IN PROGRESS: The State of Judicial Selection, with Mark S. Hurwitz, publication by M. E. Sharpe (Armonk, NY) expected in 2006.

BIOGRAPHICAL AND CRITICAL SOURCES:

ONLINE

University of Central Florida Web site, http://pegasus. cc.ucf.edu/ (December 4, 2004), "Drew Noble Lanier."

LANTZ, Francess L(in) 1952-2004

(Franklin W. Dixon, a house pseudonym, Lance Franklin, Fran Lantz, Jamie Suzanne, a house pseudonym)

OBITUARY NOTICE— See index for *CA* sketch: Born August 27, 1952, in Trenton, NJ; died of ovarian cancer November 22, 2004, in Santa Barbara, CA. Author. Lantz was a frustrated musician who later became a librarian and then popular author of young adult fiction. Graduating from Dickinson College in 1974, she tried to get noticed as a rock musician and song writer without much success. Going back to school, she earned an M.L.S. from Simmons College in 1975 and then found work as a children's librarian in Dedham, Massachusetts. Here she found pleasure reading to children and decided to write her own stories when she began running out of books she felt were suitable for her audience. This led to her first publication success, the young adult novel *Good Rockin' Tonight* (1982). After leaving her post as a librarian to write full-time, Lantz wrote numerous stories for young adult and middle-grade readers under her own name, as well as writing series books pseudonymously for the "Sweet Valley Twins," "Hardy Boys," and "Varsity Coach" series. More recently, in 2003, she had started the "Luna Bay" series for girls. Her books for teens and pre-teens varied from serious novels such as *Fade Far Away* (1998) to more humorous tales such as *Mom, There's a Pig in My Bed!* (1991) and *Stepsister from Planet Weird* (2000), the latter of which was adapted as a film by Disney Studios. A gourmand, Lantz also contributed restaurant reviews to the *Santa Barbara Independent* and coauthored a restaurant guide under the pen name The Three Little Pigs.

OBITUARIES AND OTHER SOURCES:

PERIODICALS

Los Angeles Times, December 9, 2004, p. B14.
Washington Post, December 12, 2004, p. C11.

*   *   *

LANTZ, Fran
See LANTZ, Francess L(in)

LARRICK, Nancy 1910-2004

OBITUARY NOTICE— See index for *CA* sketch: Born December 28, 1910, in Winchester, VA; died of pneumonia November 14, 2004, in Winchester, VA. Educator, editor, and author. The founder of the International Reading Association, Larrick was a champion of literacy who also wrote and edited books that promoted better reading skills for children. After completing her undergraduate work at Goucher College in 1930, she became a public school teacher in Winchester, Virginia, finishing her master's degree at Columbia University in 1937. As an eighth-grade English teacher, Larrick was very involved in her students' home lives, and she learned that the more parents were active in their children's education the better readers their kids became. This discovery influenced her beliefs in education for the rest of her life. During World War II, she worked as an education director for the U.S. Treasury Department, and after the war she became involved in publishing as an editor for *Young America Readers*. Larrick's next job was at the publisher Random House, where she was education director in the children's book department from 1952 until 1959. Having earned her doctorate in education from New York University in 1955, she later joined the faculty at Lehigh University in Bethlehem, Pennsylvania in 1964 as an adjunct professor, retiring in 1979. Much of her time after leaving Random House, however, was spent writing and editing books. Larrick began publishing books with her cowritten *Printing and Promotion Handbook* (1949; third edition, 1966). She was best known, though, for her books that offered guidance to parents and teachers in helping their kids to read. Among these works are *A Parent's Guide to Children's Reading* (1958; fourth edition, 1975), *A Teacher's Guide to Children's Books* (1960), and *A Parent's Guide to Children's Education* (1963). As an editor, Larrick published over a dozen poetry anthologies for children, including *You Come Too: Poetry of Robert Frost* (1959), *Piping down the Valleys Wild* (1967), and *Crazy to Be Alive in Such a Strange World* (1977). Noticing that too much of children's literature being published and promoted was written by white authors, she emphasized that teachers should bring more minority-written stories to the attention of their students. She also founded the International Reading Association, an organization that now has chapters in about one hundred countries. Widely recognized by her colleagues for her success in promoting literacy, Larrick received many honors in her lifetime, including being named to the Reading

Hall of Fame in 1977 and being named to the list of "Seventy Women Who Have Made a Difference in the World of Books" by the Women's National Book Association in 1987.

OBITUARIES AND OTHER SOURCES:

PERIODICALS

Chicago Tribune, November 22, 2004, section 1, p. 12.
New York Times, November 21, 2004, p. A33.
Washington Post, November 27, 2004, p. B4.

*   *   *

LASSITER, Rhiannon 1977-

PERSONAL: Born February 9, 1977, in London, England; daughter of Mary Hoffman (a writer) and Stephen Barber. *Education:* Attended Oxford University.

ADDRESSES: Home—Oxford, England. *Agent*—c/o Author Mail, Simon & Schuster, 1230 Avenue of the Americas, New York, NY 10020. *E-mail*—rhiannon@ rhiannonlassiter.com.

CAREER: Writer and Web designer.

WRITINGS:

FOR YOUNG ADULTS

The Supernatural, Barron's (Hauppage, NY), 1999.
Waking Dream, Macmillan (London, England), 2002.
Super Zeroes, Oxford University Press (London, England), 2005.

"HEX" TRILOGY; FOR YOUNG ADULTS

Hex, Macmillan (London, England), 1998, Simon & Schuster (New York, NY), 2002.
Ghosts, Macmillan (London, England), 2001, Simon & Schuster (New York, NY), 2002.
Shadows, Macmillan (London, England), 2002, Simon & Schuster (New York, NY), 2002.

"RIGHTS OF PASSAGE" SERIES; FOR YOUNG ADULTS

Outland, Oxford University Press (Oxford, England), 2003.
Borderland, Oxford University Press (Oxford, England), 2004.
Shadowland, Oxford University Press (Oxford, England), 2005.

OTHER

(Editor with Mary Hoffman) *Lines in the Sand: New Writing on War and Peace,* Disinformation Company (New York, NY), 2003.

Contributor of book reviews to periodicals, including London *Daily Telegraph.*

SIDELIGHTS: British writer Rhiannon Lassiter became a published author at an early age, perhaps influenced by growing up around her mother, children's author Mary Hoffman, and Hoffman's circle of publishing insiders. Lassiter, an avid reader, and began trying her hand at writing at age fourteen; she submitted work for publication when she was sixteen, and although she did not get published at that time, editors encouraged her to try again. Not surprisingly, Lassiter was thrilled when her first book, the young-adult fantasy novel *Hex,* was published by Macmillan when she was only nineteen years old. The first part of Lassiter's futuristic fantasy trilogy, the novel also marked its author's emergence as a popular YA writer.

The "Hex" trilogy takes place in twenty-fourth-century London. Hexes are people who have been born with the ability to interface directly with computers. As yet, the full force of their powers is unknown, but the European Federation is threatened by them and is determined to destroy them completely. For this reason, most Hexes do not even survive childhood. A group of young Hexes who have evaded capture band together with Raven as their leader. In the first installment in the series, *Hex,* Raven and her brother, Wraith, set about finding their sister who was adopted at an early age. They succeed in locating her and almost abandon their plan to take her back with them when it appears she is happily placed in a loving home. When they discover that she has been kidnapped by the government, however, they know they do not have much time to save her from extermination. Sally Estes, reviewing the novel in *Booklist,* commented that "the action is nonstop" and dubbed *Hex* "a good start for this noir thriller series."

The second book in the trilogy, *Shadows,* finds the group of Hexes in league with another anti-government faction intent upon taking down the arm of the government responsible for destroying Hexes. Although Raven is captured, she escapes and finds her powers even stronger. *School Library Journal* reviewer Ronni Krasnow declared Raven "about as strong a female protagonist as there is," while also noting that the same insecurities and flaws are present within her clique as there are in ordinary teenagers' circles. Krasnow praised the novel as "fast-paced" and "engaging," noting that Lassiter "shows considerable skill in drawing readers into her world of tomorrow."

The final book in the "Hex" trilogy is *Ghosts.* In this book Raven and the others save a pair of siblings whose mother passed on to them a computer file just before she died. The file contains critical information about the Hexes and their future, and reveals that the group now faces dangers from the government and the world's computer system. In *School Library Journal,* Molly S. Kinney remarked that "The strength of the characters, their willingness to fight, their survival instinct, and goodness ring true, even if everything is a little glossed over." Praising the "Hex" trilogy as "tautly plotted and exciting to the max," *Booklist* reviewer Estes concluded that series conclusion *Ghosts.* "will satisfy readers."

In an online interview for *Achuka* Lassiter discussed how she came to write the "Hex" trilogy, noting that she first thought up the story "when I was seventeen and wrote most of it when I was eighteen. It was accepted for publication shortly after my nineteenth birthday." "I wanted to set 'Hex' in London because it's a city I know well but when I started writing . . . I came up with an image of a city with incredibly high buildings where the heights were gleaming and beautiful and the depths hidden from sight. It occurred to me quite soon that the two ideas were complementary and from that was created a London which had swallowed its own history, building on top of the ancient parts of the city in an effort to progress."

In addition to penning fantasy fiction, Lassiter has teamed up with her mother to edit *Lines in the Sand: New Writing on War and Peace,* a book containing writings about war. Intended to shed light on the war in Iraq and its impact on people at a personal level, this book features the work of numerous children's authors, poets, and artists. Topics include the Crusades, the Holocaust, and revolutionary violence occurring in Nigeria, and Kosovo. Hazel Rochman, reviewing *Lines in the Sand* for *Booklist,* wrote that while some of the material is a little heavy-handed, much of it is less propaganda and more storytelling. The critic added that the most effective entries "bring the suffering close to home," and cited the work as a useful springboard for discussion "both in and out of the classroom." All profit from the sale of the book were earmarked for UNICEF.

BIOGRAPHICAL AND CRITICAL SOURCES:

PERIODICALS

Booklist, January 1, 2002, Sally Estes, review of *Hex,* p. 842; April 15, 2002, Sally Estes, review of *Ghosts,* p. 1395; February 1, 2004, Hazel Rochman, review of *Lines in the Sand: New Writing on War and Peace,* p. 968.

Kliatt, March, 2002, Susan Cromby, review of *Hex,* p. 24.

School Library Journal, April, 2002, Ronni Krasnow, review of *Shadows,* p. 152; January, 2003, Molly S. Kinney, review of *Ghosts,* p. 140.

ONLINE

Achuka.co.uk, http://www.achuka.co.uk/ (February 3, 2005), interview with Lassiter.

Rhiannon Lassiter Home Page, http://www.rhiannon lassiter.com (February 3, 2005).*

*   *   *

LEE, Leslie (E.) 1935-

PERSONAL: Born 1935, in Bryn Mawr, PA. *Education:* University of Pennsylvania, B.S. (biology, English); Villanova University, M.A. (theater).

ADDRESSES: Home—250 West 57th St., New York, NY 10019. *Office*—Tisch School of the Arts, New York University, 721 Broadway, 7th Floor, New York, NY. *Agent*—c/o Author Mail, Samuel French, Inc., 45 West 25th St., New York, NY 10010-2751. *E-mail*—LL15@nyu.edu.

CAREER: Writer. Worked as a medical technician at Valley Forge Army Hospital, PA, and as a bacteriologist at the Pennsylvania Department of Health; affiliated with La Mama E.T.C., New York, NY, 1969-70; College of Old Westbury, NY, instructor in play writing, 1975-76; University of Pennsylvania, Philadelphia, playwright-in-residence, beginning 1980; Frederick Douglass Creative Arts Center, New York, instructor in play writing; Tisch School of the Arts, New York University, instructor in dramatic writing. New York State Commission on the Arts, theater panelist, 1982-84; Negro Ensemble Company, coordinator for play writing workshop, 1985.

MEMBER: Writers Guild of America, Dramatists Guild.

AWARDS, HONORS: Rockefeller Foundation grant, 1966-68; Shubert Foundation grants, 1971, 1972; Off-Broadway Award, *Village Voice,* 1975; John Gassner Medallion, Outer Circle Critics Award, and Mississippi ETV Award, all for *The First Breeze of Summer;* Eugene O'Neill fellowship, 1980; National Endowment for the Arts grant, 1982; National Black Film Consortium prize, 1984, for *The Killing Floor;* Isabelle Strickland Award for excellence in the fields of arts and human culture.

WRITINGS:

PLAYS

Elegy to a Down Queen (two-act), produced at La Mama, New York, NY, 1969.
Cops and Robbers (one-act), produced at La Mama, New York, NY, 1970.
As I Lay Dying, a Victim of Spring, produced in New York, NY, 1972.
The Night of the No-Moon, produced in New York, NY, 1973.
The War Party, produced in New York, NY, 1974.
Between Now and Then (two-act; produced in New York, NY, 1975), Samuel French (New York, NY), 1984.
The First Breeze of Summer (two-act; produced in New York, NY, 1975), Samuel French (New York, NY), 1975.
The Book of Lambert, produced in New York, NY, 1977.

Nothin' Comes Easy, produced at Village Gate, New York, NY, 1978.
(With June Carroll and Arthur Siegel) *Life, Love, and Other Minor Matters* (musical review), produced at Village Gate, New York, NY, 1980.
Colored People's Time (two-act; produced in New York, NY, 1982), Samuel French (New York, NY), 1983.
Willie (two-act); produced at National Playwrights' Conference, Waterford, CT, 1983.
(With Charles Strouse and Lee Adams) *Golden Boy* (revision of the 1964 musical), produced in Brooklyn, NY, 1984.
The Wig Lady, produced in New York, NY, 1984.
Phillis (musical), music and lyrics by Micki Grant, produced at the Apollo Theatre, Harlem, New York, NY, 1986.
Hannah Davis, produced in New Brunswick, NJ, 1987.
Martin Luther King, Jr. (musical for children), produced at Brooklyn Center for the Performing Arts, Brooklyn, NY, 1987.
The Rabbit Foot, (produced 1988; revised version produced in New York as *Ground People,* 1990), Samuel French (New York, NY), 1992.
Black Eagles (produced in New Brunswick, NJ), 1989), Samuel French (New York, NY), 1992.
Spirit North (two-act), produced in New Brunswick, NJ, 1998.
Legends, produced in St. Louis, MO, 2001.

OTHER

The Day after Tomorrow (novella), Scholastic (New York, NY), 1974.
"Almos' a Man" (television play; adapted from the story by Richard Wright), *The American Short Story,* Public Broadcasting Service (PBS), 1977.
"Summer Father," *Vegetable Soup,* (television; juvenile), PBS, 1978.
"The Killing Floor" (television play), *American Playhouse,* PBS, 1984.
(With Gus Edwards) *Go Tell It on the Mountain* (screenplay; based on the novel by James Baldwin), Learning in Focus, 1984.
Langston Hughes (television documentary) PBS, 1986.
Voice and Visions (television series), PBS, 1988.
Vernon Johns Story (television movie), USA, 1994.
(With Jill Janows) *Born to Trouble: Adventures of Huckleberry Finn* (television movie), USA, 2000.
(With others) *Ralph Bunche: An American Odyssey* (television movie), USA, 2001.

Also author of novella *Never the Time and Place*, 1985.

ADAPTATIONS: *The First Breeze of Summer* was adapted for the PBS series *Great Performances*, 1976.

SIDELIGHTS: Playwright Leslie Lee's early works for the stage include *The First Breeze of Summer*, in which an elderly woman recalls through flashbacks her affairs with three different men. Lee dramatizes black families in transition and showcases their culture in such plays as *Golden Boy* and *Colored People's Time*. He has also written documentaries that celebrate the lives of such black notables as Richard Wright, Langston Hughes, and Martin Luther King, Jr. Lee's more recent plays include *Spirit North* and *Legends*.

Lee was a fragile child who suffered from osteomyelitis, a bone disease that often required hospitalization. One of nine children, he read and wrote plays for his brothers and sisters. He told Emil Wilbekin of the *New York Times* that his writing "draws on the loneliness and isolation that I experienced in the hospital." Lee said that "the very first person to influence me was Richard Wright, because of the power and passion of his work. I realized, my God we can write as good as whites."

Lee's *Black Eagles* honors the company of World War II black fighter pilots known as the Tuskegee airmen; the unit was established at the Tuskegee Institute in Alabama. These men were more skilled than the white bomber pilots they escorted, but their service did not earn them the right to use the officers' clubs, and they were restricted by the prejudice of the period. Although they never lost a bomber, it was not until the end of the war that they were allowed to fight in combat, achieving an impressive record. The Tuskegee Airmen have ultimately been recognized for their valor, and Lee's powerful story moves in close to view the men as individuals. The story takes place at a reunion during which three members of the squadron remember their adventures and experiences. Writing in the *New Yorker*, Edith Oliver said that *Black Eagles* "is a memory play, impressionistically written; much of it is humorous, but the pressure of emotion underneath gives it strength."

In *The Rabbit Foot* Lee focuses on the performers in black minstrel shows such as the Rabbit Food Minstrels, which toured the South in the 1920s, brighten-ing the lives of black sharecroppers. Featured entertainers included the great Ma Rainey and Bessie Smith. *The Rabbit Foot* was revised and produced as *Ground People*; the stage was divided between the sharecroppers and the minstrels in this production version.

The main character in *Ground People*, Reggie, is a sharecropper. A World War I veteran, he fought in France and had an affair with a white woman, which he now admits to his wife, Berlinda. He tells only his grandmother, Viola, that he and his French lover had a child. The dignity and equality Reggie experienced overseas now embolden him to organize local farmers and demand more equality from their employer. The cast of the minstrel show performed as counterpoint to Reggie's story includes Singin' Willie Ford, the depressed and often drunk lead singer Bertha Mae Primrose, and performer Holly Day.

Mel Gussow noted in the *New York Times* that Lee's idea is "that the nomadic entertainers shared misfortunes similar to those of their rural kinsmen. The farmers and the minstrels were being drawn away from their roots to the opportunities of the industrial North, where they would face inevitable disillusionments." Gussow noted that, at the end of the drama, "the two halves of the play interact, in a touching encounter that makes it evident how valuable the minstrel shows were to those who were land trapped. It offered them illusions as well as entertainment."

Spirit North is set in the present time. Paul, an attorney, and his wife, Leila, an English teacher, plan to move from their suburban home to Harlem. Tension arises when Leila opposes Paul's defense of a black teen who is accused of murdering a white rabbinical student. Paul's own brother is serving a prison sentence in Attica, and Leila's mother is suffering from cancer. As the state of Paul and Leila's marriage becomes fragile, Leila considers aborting the child she is carrying, and the couple is also faced with sending a grandfather to a nursing home. *Variety* writer Robert L. Daniels reviewed the premier, commenting that "the most effective and appealing element is the performance of Ray Aranha as Grandpa, a semi-senile, retired vaudevillian who recalls his glory days on the circuit with vintage jokes. The playwright might have another play in the old comic."

Lee has created a number of productions for the St. Louis Black Repertory, one of which is *Legends*, which is based on true events that occurred not far from Lee's home in New York. The legends of the story are has-beens who now live in a hotel for transients. They include Martha Davenport, a dancer who came to New York from Atlanta with dreams of achieving stardom; Ruben Petit, a former jazz musician; and Othel Henry, who lives through his wartime memories. When the Hell's Angels descend on the hotel, terrorizing the residents and stealing Ruben's saxophone, it is Othel who takes charge and defends them all. Randy Gener wrote in *American Theatre* that "if anything, *Legends* harks back to the crumbling, sad-eyed grandeur of Tennessee Williams's purgatorial rap sessions, or Lanford Wilson's *Hot L Baltimore,* in which a potentially unwieldy ensemble converges into a chorus of lowlife naturalism."

Interviewer Judith Newmark remarked in the *St. Louis Post-Dispatch* that "Lee says that as a playwright, he's in a transitional period—less explicitly political than he has been in the past, more personal, more focused on character than on issues. His latest plays use smaller casts than he's called for in the past and tell more intimate stories." As Lee told Newmark, "I decided to get off my soapbox—well, for a while anyhow. Right now I am asking different questions, questions about why people do what they do, what happened to make them into the people that they are. I think that's usually an interesting question because it gets to the heart of drama. Drama makes ordinary people extraordinary for two hours."

BIOGRAPHICAL AND CRITICAL SOURCES:

PERIODICALS

American Theatre, April, 2001, Randy Gener, review of *Legends,* p. 9.

Back Stage, May 10, 1991, David Sheward, review of *Black Eagles,* p. 30.

Chicago Sun-Times, February 19, 2002, Hedy Weiss, review of *The Rabbit Foot,* p. 39.

New York, May 6, 1991, John Simon, review of *Black Eagles,* pp. 108-110.

New Yorker, May 6, 1991, Edith Oliver, review of *Black Eagles,* p. 81.

New York Times, May 6, 1990, Peter Keepnews, review of *Ground People;* May 7, 1990, Mel Gussow, review of *Ground People;* April 21, 1991, Emil Wilbekin, review of *Black Eagles.*

St. Louis Post-Dispatch, May 3, 2001, Judith Newmark, review of *Legends,* p. D3.

Variety, March 29, 1989, review of *Golden Boy,* p. 60; December 28, 1989, Hari, review of *The Rabbit Foot,* pp. 38, 40; April 22, 1991, Evan Remy, review of *Black Eagles,* p. 58; February 2, 1998, Robert L. Daniels, review of *Spirit North,* p. 47.*

*　　*　　*

LESLIE, Roger (James) 1961-

PERSONAL: Born May 5, 1961, in Lincoln Park, MI; son of Richard Paul (an architect and builder) and Joann Geraldine (a banker) Leslie; married Jerry Lynn Roberts (a singer and counselor), August 4, 1984. *Ethnicity:* "White." *Education:* University of Houston, B.A., 1984, M.L.S., 1997; Antioch University, M.A., 1995. *Hobbies and other interests:* "Spirituality and self-improvement, swimming, weight training and fitness, film studies, popular culture, travel, theater."

ADDRESSES: Agent—c/o Author Mail, Bayou Publishing, 2524 Nottingham, Houston, TX 77005-1412. *E-mail*—roger@rogerleslie.com.

CAREER: Freelance writer, book reviewer, editor, writing coach, and public speaker. Galena Park Intermediate School District, Houston, TX, teacher, 1985-96, librarian, 1996-2000, 2002—. Guest on media programs. School Library Information Science Alumni Board, founding member, 1997—.

MEMBER: Association of Authors and Publishers, Society of Children's Book Writers and Illustrators, Children's and Young Adult Book Writers Cooperative, American Book Cooperative, Texas Library Association.

AWARDS, HONORS: District Teacher of the Year, Galena School District, 1989; Teacher of the Month, North Channel Chamber of Commerce, 1989; Outstanding Teacher in Texas Award, University of Texas, 1992; winner of one-act play writing contest, Scriptwriters Houston, 1993, for *Pardon This Interruption, Teachers;* special citation, City of Galena Park, TX, 1993, for *Galena Park: The Community That Shaped Its Own History;* Outstanding Volunteer Service Award, Project Hope of Houston, 2001-02.

WRITINGS:

(With Sue Elkins Edwards) *Galena Park: The Community That Shaped Its Own History,* privately printed, 1993.

(With Patricia Potter Wilson) *Premiere Events: Library Programs That Inspire Elementary Patrons,* Greenwood Press (Westport, CT), 2001.

(With Patricia Potter Wilson) *Igniting the Spark: Library Programs That Inspire High School Patrons,* Greenwood Press (Westport, CT), 2001.

(With Patricia Potter Wilson) *Center Stage: Library Programs That Inspire Middle School Patrons,* Greenwood Press (Westport, CT), 2002.

Drowning in Secret (a novel), Absey and Co. (Spring, TX), 2002.

Isak Dinesen, Gothic Storyteller, Morgan Reynolds (Greensboro, NC), 2004.

Success Express for Teens: Fifty Activities That Will Change Your Life, Bayou Publishing (Houston, TX), 2004.

Author of *Pardon This Interruption, Teachers,* a one-act play published in the magazine *English in Texas.*

WORK IN PROGRESS: Five Minutes from Home, a novel; a motion-picture history book; other books in the literary genre.

BIOGRAPHICAL AND CRITICAL SOURCES:

PERIODICALS

Booklist, April 1, 2004, Terry Glover, review of *Isak Dinesen, Gothic Storyteller.*

ONLINE

Roger Leslie Home Page, http://www.rogerleslie.com (July 23, 2004).

*   *   *

LI, Guofang 1972-

PERSONAL: Born July 9, 1972, in Hubei, China; immigrated to Canada; daughter of De-Chun Li (a farmer) and Feng-Lan Chen (a farmer). *Ethnicity:* "Chinese." *Education:* Hubei University, B.A. (teaching English as a foreign language), 1993; Wuhan University, M.A. (applied linguistics), 1996; University of Saskatchewan, Ph.D. (family and community literacy, early childhood education), 2000; University of British Columbia, post-doctoral studies (early literacy education and second language education), 2000-01.

ADDRESSES: Home—275 E3 Scamridge Curve, Williamsville, NY 14221. *Office*—Department of Learning and Instruction, Graduate School of Education, State University of New York at Buffalo, 505 Baldy Hall, Buffalo, NY 14260. *Agent*—c/o Author Mail, Peter Lang Publishing Inc., 275 Seventh Ave., 28th Floor, New York, NY 10001. *E-mail*—Guofang_li@yahoo.com, gli2@buffalo.edu.

CAREER: Zhong Shan College, Wuhan, China, lecturer, 1994; Wuhan University, Wuhan, lecturer in English department, 1994; Business Foreign Language Training Center, Wuhan, lecturer, 1995; University of Saskatchewan, Saskatchewan, Canada, faculty of education, research assistant, 1997-99, lecturer, 1998-2000, Second Language Institute, lecturer, 1999-2000, College of Arts and Science, lecturer, 1999-2000; University of British Columbia, Canada, Language and Literacy Education, lecturer, 2000-01; State University of New York at Buffalo, second-language education, assistant professor, 2001—. Instructor in English as a foreign language at numerous schools in China; interpreter and translator in China, 1994-96. Member of board of directors, Chinese Language School, Saskatoon, Saskatchewan, Canada, 1999-2000.

MEMBER: Canadian Society for the Study of Education, Language Arts Researchers of Canada, Teachers of English to Speakers of Other Languages, American Educational Research Association, National Council of Teachers of English.

AWARDS, HONORS: Dr. Kay Whale Memorial Book Prize, 1998; Margaret Gillett Best Article Award, *McGill Journal of Education,* 2001.

WRITINGS:

"East Is East, West Is West?": Home Literacy, Culture, and Schooling, Peter Lang (New York, NY), 2002.

Contributor of numerous scholarly articles to books, including *International Multiculturalism 1998: Preparing Together for the Twenty-first Century,* edited by A.

Richardson, Kanata Learning Company Ltd., 1998; and *Multicultural and Multilingual Literacy and Language Practices,* edited by F. Boyd, C. Brock, and M. Rozendal, Guilford Publications, 2003. Contributor to journals, including *Journal of College English Teaching and Testing, Canadian Children, Canadian Journal of Education, TESL Canada Journal, McGill Journal of Education,* and *Journal of Literacy Research.* Member of review board, *McGill Journal of Education* and *TESL Canada Journal.* Reviewer for *Canadian Journal of Education.*

WORK IN PROGRESS: Battles of Literacy and Culture: Teaching and Learning in a New Social Order, for State University of New York Press.

SIDELIGHTS: An assistant professor at the State University of New York campus at Buffalo, Guofang Li focuses on the study of language acquisition and second language learning. A native of China, Li immigrated to Canada after earning a master's degree on the subject of English education in China. Her doctoral work involved the study of literacy outside of school, and in particular the home practices of immigrant Chinese families in Canada.

Her 2002 title, *"East Is East, West Is West?": Home Literacy, Culture, and Schooling,* builds on Li's doctoral and post-doctoral research. In the book, she challenges the myth of the model Asian-American student who excels in school better than other ethnic groups. Having studied Chinese immigrant families in Canada, Li concluded that it is "a misconception that every Chinese parent can help their children like middle-class parents do," as she told Greg Toppo of *USA Today.* Li found that when parents themselves are unable to help their children with homework because of long work hours or because of their own lack of education, and when the schools fail to come to the aid of the child, then Asian immigrants do just as poorly academically as other minorities. Speaking with Patricia Donovan for the State University of New York at Buffalo *Reporter,* Li noted that "the stereotype of Asian students as model minorities has become a destructive myth for children of all backgrounds whom the school systems are failing—and they are failing many of them."

BIOGRAPHICAL AND CRITICAL SOURCES:

PERIODICALS

Reporter (State University of New York, Buffalo, NY), December 5, 2002, Patricia Donovan, "Dispelling Stereotypes: Researcher Debunks Idea That Asians Make Better Students," p. 5.

USA Today, December 10, 2002, Greg Toppo, "'Model' Asian Student Called a Myth: Middle-Class Status May Be a Better Gauge of Classroom Success," section D, p. 11.

*   *   *

LIEBERMAN, Richard K.

PERSONAL: Male. *Education:* New York University, Ph.D.

ADDRESSES: Office—Department of History, LaGuardia Community College, City University of New York, 31-10 Thomson Ave., Long Island City, NY 11101. *Agent*—c/o Yale University Press, P.O. Box 209040, New Haven, CT 06520-9040. *E-mail*—richardli@lagcc.cuny.edu.

CAREER: LaGuardia Community College, City University of New York, New York, NY, professor and archivist.

WRITINGS:

(With Janet E. Lieberman) *City Limits: A Society History of Queens,* Kendall/Hunt (Dubuque, IA), 1983.
Steinway & Sons, Yale University Press (New Haven, CT), 1995.

SIDELIGHTS: Richard K. Lieberman is an historian who is probably best known as the author of *Steinway & Sons.* Eva Hoffman, writing in the *New York Times Book Review,* described the work as an "institutional chronicle" of the piano-building company that began business in Germany in 1835, then moved to the United States in 1850 and enjoyed a long prominence in the piano-making field. *Steinway & Sons* draws on family and company records preserved in the LaGuardia and Wagner archives of the City University of New York, the institution Lieberman directs. The archives are housed on the campus of LaGuardia Community College in Queens, where the Steinway company has been located since the 1870s.

Lieberman reports on the company's significant prosperity from the 1860s to the 1930s, when other companies finally began to compete with Steinway in the piano market. The book continues with accounts of the company's gradual economic decline due, at least in part, to both the appearance of mass-produced pianos from Japan and a general decline in piano sales. The company's commitment to producing a small number of instruments for elite performers and venues also harmed sales. "The Steinway company actively acquired and nurtured this special position as the instrument upon which the masterworks were to be performed," explained Stuart De Ocampo in *American Music.* "Indeed, this relationship . . . virtually guaranteed Steinway's ascendancy." According to Ocampo, Steinway & Sons lost business when they hesitated to produce "player-pianos and inexpensive upright pianos." Because of this, Lieberman notes, the company has changed ownership at least three times since the 1970s.

In *Steinway & Sons,* Lieberman also describes the original and painstaking piano-making process, which involves drying wood for one year, the protracted application of varnishes, and the hand-fitting of more than two hundred small parts. "Few would argue," commented Richard Ratliff in *Notes,* "that Henry Steinway, Jr. invented the prototype of the modern grand piano." According to Lieberman, one result of the initial sale of the Steinway company in 1972 is that Steinway pianos are now constructed along more modern methods.

In her *New York Times Book Review* assessment of *Steinway & Sons,* Hoffman remarked that "a history of the Steinway is also, implicitly, a history of the pianistic tradition." Hoffman praised Lieberman's book as "a revealing, if not always uplifting, perspective," adding that Lieberman "gives us an often fascinating overview of a musical epoch that may, regrettably, be coming to an end."

BIOGRAPHICAL AND CRITICAL SOURCES:

PERIODICALS

American Music, fall, 1997, Stuart De Ocampo, review of *Steinway & Sons,* p. 407.

Booklist, November 15, 1995, Alan Hirsch, review of *Steinway & Sons,* p. 527.

New York Times Book Review, December 10, 1995, Eva Hoffman, review of *Steinway & Sons,* p. 15.

Notes, September 1996, Richard Ratliff, review of *Steinway & Sons,* p. 81.

Perspectives, March, 1996, Richard Lieberman, David Osborn, "Historical Archives and the Community College Student" history of LaGuardia and Wagner Archives.

Publishers Weekly, October 16, 1995, review of *Steinway & Sons,* p. 53.*

*   *   *

LORIGA, Ray 1967-

PERSONAL: Born 1967, in Madrid, Spain; immigrated to the United States, c. 2000.

ADDRESSES: Agent—c/o Author Mail, St. Martin's Press, 175 Fifth Ave., New York, NY 10010.

CAREER: Author and screenwriter.

AWARDS, HONORS: El Sitio de Bilbao book prize, for *Héroes.*

WRITINGS:

Lo peor de todo, Editorial Debate (Madrid, Spain), 1992.

Héroes, Plaza & Janés (Barcelona, Spain), 1993.

Días extraños, Europeo & La Tripulación (Madrid, Spain), 1994.

Caídos del cielo, Plaza & Janés (Barcelona, Spain), 1995, translation by Kristina Cordero published as *My Brother's Gun,* St. Martin's Press (New York, NY), 1997.

(With Pedro Almodovar) *Carne tremula* (screenplay; based on Ruth Rendell's novel *Live Flesh*), 1997.

La pistola de mi hermano (screenplay; based on *Caídos del cielo*), UIP (Spain), 1997.

Tokio ya no nos quiere, 1999, translation by John King published as *Tokyo Doesn't Love Us Anymore,* Grove Press (New York, NY), 2003.

Trífero, 2000.

El hombre que inventó Manhattan (title means "The Man Who Invented Manhattan"), El Aleph Editores (Barcelona, Spain), 2004.

The Seventh Day (screenplay), Lolafilms (Madrid, Spain), 2004.

Also author of *El canto de la tripulación,* 1992.

WORK IN PROGRESS: A novel and a number of screenplays.

SIDELIGHTS: Ray Loriga is a Spanish-born author and screenwriter who now lives in Manhattan. He began writing at a young age, first for underground publications in Madrid. He told Richard Marshall in an interview for *3 A.M. Online* that "when Franco died, there was suddenly an explosion of artistic activity. After forty years of not being able to do much, everybody was doing something. It was a very fun time to be in Madrid, a good city to be in." Loriga's father was a cartoonist, and books were a part of their household. Loriga chose not to attend college, however, and left home at age seventeen to try a number of different jobs. "I was dreaming of the Kerouac thing and Bukowski: you didn't need to go anywhere to be a writer, you just had to be there and read and live, so that was my plan. Funny enough, it worked out pretty well. I published my first book when I was twenty-three and then I just kept going."

Loriga's best-selling novel, *Caídos del cielo,* was translated into English as *My Brother's Gun* and adapted for film as *La pistola de mi hermano.* An unnamed narrator tells how his handsome brother finds a gun loaded with three bullets and uses it to kill a security guard who is hassling him. The brother steals a car, and its occupant, a beautiful girl, goes along for the ride as he makes his getaway. The point of the story is how the media twists the news, and in this case, speculates that the gunman is a gay, cold-blooded killer. The narrator who, along with his mother, has been forced into the public eye, finds it difficult to overcome the media depiction of his brother.

A *Publishers Weekly* contributor noted that in *My Brother's Gun* Loriga paints "the fine, fragile line that separates functional life—for young people in particular—from the deadly fatalism of this impassive murderer." *Library Journal* reviewer Jim Dwyer commented that "the process of victimization . . . is depicted skillfully and nondidactically." In reviewing the film version of the story, *Variety* critic Jonathan Holland called it a "languid Hispanic reprise of pics such as *Kalifornia* and *Natural Born Killers*" and said that it is "the best Spanish youth movie of its kind to date."

Loriga's *Tokyo Doesn't Love Us Anymore* is narrated by an unnamed man who is a salesman for a drug company. In this futuristic story, the narrator sells the drugs STM and LTM. Because these drugs erase either short-term or long-term memory, users are able to erase the memory of failed love affairs and other sad events; the drugs are also given to child prostitutes in Thailand, so that they will forget their abuse and remain the innocent, virginal victims so desired by sex tourists. As the novel progresses, it becomes apparent that the narrator's own heavy drug use is erasing both his memory and his personality.

"Other authors whose influence this writer clearly feels—Ray Bradbury, William Gibson, Kurt Vonnegut—might have played this twist as action or satire," wrote Andrew Sean Greer in a review of *Tokyo Doesn't Love Us Anymore* for the *Washington Post,* "and that would have made a clever novel, but Loriga bravely ignores cleverness. Instead, the novel reads as desolate and terribly sad." Unexplained dead spaces in the story are the result of the narrator's own memory loss, and eventually the company recalls him when his brain is "a colander, an open net through which all the fish slip." Vanessa Baird wrote in *New Internationalist* that it "is an ambitious and demanding novel which fuses a witty and scathing attack on consumerism with a meditation on the crucial role memory plays in raising us above bestial self-gratification." *Los Angeles Book Review* contributor Susan Salter Reynolds called *Tokyo Doesn't Love Us Anymore* "a nihilist's novel, a portrait of a disintegrating mind."

BIOGRAPHICAL AND CRITICAL SOURCES:

PERIODICALS

Booklist, September 15, 1997, Jim O'Laughlin, review of *My Brother's Gun,* p. 208; July, 2004, Carl Hays, review of *Tokyo Doesn't Love Us Anymore,* p. 1828.
Kirkus Reviews, May 15, 2004, review of *Tokyo Doesn't Love Us Anymore,* p. 463.
Library Journal, August, 1997, Jim Dwyer, review of *My Brother's Gun,* p. 132.
Los Angeles Times Book Review, September 19, 2004, Susan Salter Reynolds, review of *Tokyo Doesn't Love Us Anymore,* p. R11.
New Internationalist, October, 2003, Vanessa Baird, review of *Tokyo Doesn't Love Us Anymore,* p. 31.

Publishers Weekly, July 14, 1997, review of *My Brother's Gun,* p. 63; April 26, 2004, review of *Tokyo Doesn't Love Us Anymore,* p. 37.

Variety, October 13, 1997, Lisa Nesselson, review of *Carne tremula,* p. 84; December 1, 1997, Jonathan Holland, review of *La pistola de mi hermano,* p. 75; May 10, 2004, Jonathan Holland, review of *The Seventh Day,* p. 47.

Washington Post, August 1, 2004, Andrew Sean Greer, review of *Tokyo Doesn't Love Us Anymore,* p. D8.

ONLINE

3 A.M. Online, http://www.3ammagazine.com/ (January, 2004), Richard Marshall, interview with Loriga.*

*   *   *

LUISELLI, James K. 1949-

PERSONAL: Born January 12, 1949, in Malden, MA; son of James L. and Christine A. Luiselli; married Tracy Evans (an educator), May 28, 1990; children: Gabrielle A., Thomas P. *Ethnicity:* "Italian-American." *Education:* Tufts University, B.S., 1971; Goddard College, M.A., 1974; Boston University, Ed.D., 1979.

ADDRESSES: Home—126 Martin St., Carlisle, MA 01741. *Office*—May Institute, Inc., 1 Commerce Way, Norwood, MA 02062; fax: 781-440-0401. *E-mail*—jluiselli@mayinstitute.org.

CAREER: Eunice-Kennedy Shriver Center, Waltham, MA, laboratory research assistant, 1972-73; Walter E. Fernald School, Waltham, developmental day care specialist, 1973-74; LABB Special Education Collaborative, Arlington, MA, codirector of LAB Autistic Unit, 1974-75, director of Behavioral Intervention Project, 1975-77; Perkins School for the Blind, Watertown, MA, staff psychologist, 1979-88; private practice of clinical psychology, Carlisle, MA, 1988-96; May Institute, Inc., Norwood, MA, director of consultation services and peer review, 1996-97, director of applied research and peer review, 1997-2000, vice president for applied research and peer review, 2000-03, senior vice president for applied research, clinical training, and peer review, and director of internship program in clinical psychology, 2003—. Licensed psychologist and certified health service provider in Massachusetts; American Board of Professional Psychology, diplomate in behavior psychology, 1999; Behavior Analyst Certification Board, certification, 2001; private practice of clinical psychology. Lesley College, adjunct instructor, 1980; Harvard University, instructor at Medical School, 1996-2000; Northeastern University, clinical assistant professor, 1997-2002; presenter of workshops and seminars. McLean Hospital, assistant attending child psychologist, 1996-97, clinical affiliate in psychology, 1997-2000; Franciscan Children's Hospital and Rehabilitation Center, staff member, 1997-2002; consultant and advisor to schools and medical institutions.

MEMBER: Massachusetts Psychological Association, Berkshire Association for Behavior Analysis and Therapy.

AWARDS, HONORS: Outstanding journal article award, Pergamon Press, 1986.

WRITINGS:

(Editor and contributor) *Behavioral Medicine and Developmental Disabilities,* Springer-Verlag (New York, NY), 1989.

(Editor, with J. L. Matson and N. N. Singh, and contributor) *Self-Injurious Behavior: Analysis, Assessment, and Treatment,* Springer-Verlag (New York, NY), 1991.

(Editor, with M. J. Cameron, and contributor) *Antecedent Control: Innovative Approaches to Behavior Support,* Paul H. Brooks Publishing (Baltimore, MD), 1998.

(Editor, with C. Diament, and contributor) *Behavior Psychology in the Schools: Innovations in Evaluation, Support, and Consultation,* Haworth Press (West Hazleton, PA), 2002.

(Editor and contributor) *Antecedent Intervention: Recent Developments in Community-focused Behavior Support,* Paul H. Brookes Publishing (Baltimore, MD), 2005.

Author of legal education handbooks. Contributor to books, including *Prader-Willi Syndrome: Recent Advances in Research,* edited by M. L. Caldwell and R. L. Taylor, Springer-Verlag (New York, NY), 1988;

Perspectives on the Use of Nonaversive and Aversive Interventions for Persons with Developmental Disabilities, edited by N. N. Singh and A. C. Repp, Sycamore Publishing (DeKalb, IL), 1990; and *Handbook of Behavior Therapy with Children and Adults: A Developmental and Longitudinal Perspective,* edited by R. T. Ammerman and M. Hersen, Pergamon Press (New York, NY), 1993. Contributor of articles and reviews to professional journals. *Education and Treatment of Children,* associate editor, 1981-84, 2001—, member of board of editors, 1984-86, 1999-2001; contributing editor, *Habilitative Mental HealthCare Newsletter,* 1992-96; member of board of editors, *Journal of Developmental and Physical Disabilities,* 1988—, *Behavior Modification,* 1989—, *Journal of Behavioral Education,* 1990-2001, *Behavioral Interventions,* 1996—, *Mental Health Aspects of Developmental Disabilities,* 1997—, *Handicape Grave: Ritardo Mentale e Pluriminorazioni Sensoriali,* 1999—, *Journal of Positive Behavior Interventions,* 2003—, *International Journal of Behavioral Consultation and Therapy,* 2004—, and *Medical Science Monitor,* 2004—.

SIDELIGHTS: James K. Luiselli told *CA:* "I am a clinical psychologist who has been involved in professional writing for nearly thirty years. As an undergraduate, I intended to major in journalism and got sidetracked into psychology, but I never lost my love of writing. In graduate school and during my postgraduate education, I was fortunate to associate with several professionals who were accomplished researchers and prolific writers. They published regularly in peer-reviewed journals, wrote book chapters, and on occasion published an edited volume. I learned much from these experiences and have continued in that vein.

"My writing has focused on clinical and educational research, primarily through empirical studies, scientific reports, review articles, and commentaries. I've also contributed chapters to books and, to date, edited four books on a variety of topics in psychology, behavioral medicine, and professional practice. I mentor graduate students, psychology interns, and colleagues on research issues and dissemination through publication. I've also presented workshops and seminars on writing for publication in human services and plan to publish a professional guidebook on the topic.

"For me, writing is a wonderfully creative process, and it is something integral to my clinical work. I enjoy conducting a research project, reporting the findings to colleagues, and establishing a publication record that defines my work. Being published has many advantages, allowing a professional to be seen as an expert in a given field, leading to referrals and producing additional writing opportunities. I integrate writing into my weekly schedule and usually have multiple projects going on at the same time.

"For inspiration, I look to the work of colleagues and other researchers. However, I find similar direction from writers who are not psychologists or related professionals. Garrison Keillor, Annie Lamott, David Mamet, and William F. Buckley, Jr. are just a few of the authors I admire. I would add that Lamott's book, *Bird by Bird,* and Stephen King's, *On Writing,* are two of the best sources of writing advice available.

"My desire is to continue writing about the issues that interest me. I have concentrated on professional topics germane to my clinical specialties but would like to tackle other areas. Being a psychologist, I envision writing short fiction pieces, and perhaps books, which blend mystery with dastardly deeds and mayhem (think Jonathan Kellerman). And somewhere in that mix is a memoir, combining life events with, I hope, sage advice. It's the craft of writing that I love, and I expect it will always be so."

* * *

LUNDVALL, Bengt-Åke 1941-
(Bengt-Ake Lundyall)

PERSONAL: Born October 8, 1941, in Karlsborg, Sweden; son of Sven (a sales director) and Aina Lundvall; married Birte Siim (a professor), 1992. *Education:* University of Gothenburg, M.Econ., 1969.

ADDRESSES: Office—University of Ålborg, Fibigersstraede 4, 9000 Aalborg, Denmark. *E-mail*—bal@business.auc.dk.

CAREER: University of Ålborg, Ålborg, Denmark, member of business faculty; OECD-secretariat, Paris, France, deputy director, 1992-95; GLOBELICS, Ålborg, Denmark, coordinator; Tsinghua University, Beijing, China, special term professor.

WRITINGS:

(Editor, with Christopher Freeman) *Small Countries Facing the Technological Revolution,* Pinter (New York, NY), 1988.

(Editor) *National Systems of Innovation: Toward a Theory of Innovation and Interactive Learning,* Pinter Publishers (London, England), 1992.

(Editor, with Daniele Archibugi) *The Globalizing Learning Economy,* Oxford University Press (New York, NY), 2001.

Innovation, Growth, and Social Cohesion: The Danish Model, Edward Elgar Publishing (Northampton, MA), 2002.

(Editor, with Pedro Conceição and Manual V. Heitor) *Innovation, Competence Building, and Social Cohesion in Europe: Towards a Learning Society,* Edward Elgar Publishing (Northampton, MA), 2003.

Contributor to books, including *The New Knowledge Economy in Europe: A Strategy for International Competitiveness and Social Cohesion,* edited by Maria João Rodrigues, Edward Elgar Publishing (Northampton, MA), 2002.

SIDELIGHTS: Bengt-Åke Lundvall told *CA:* "My major motivation is to understand and make understandable socio-economic evolution, with special reference to the role of knowledge and learning. The most important inspiration has come from Christopher Freeman, who is outstanding both in terms of personality and scientific quality. If I have a strong side, it is a capability to cross disciplinary borders and to form syntheses of theoretical elements and empirical observations. My research and writings have been strongly motivated by the fact that standard economics is so weak when it comes to explaining how innovation and learning affect economic development."

*   *   *

LUNDYALL, Bengt-Ake
    See LUNDVALL, Bengt-Åke

*   *   *

LUSBY, Jim
    (James Kennedy)

PERSONAL: Born in Waterford, Ireland.

ADDRESSES: Home—Dublin, Ireland. *Agent*—c/o Author Mail, Orion Books, 5 Upper St. Martin's lane, London WC2H 9EA, England.

CAREER: Short-story writer and novelist.

AWARDS, HONORS: Hennessy Award for short stories.

WRITINGS:

(With Myles Dungan) *Snuff,* Glendale (Dublin, Ireland), 1992.

Making the Cut, Gollancz (London, England), 1995.

Flashback, Gollancz (London, England), 1996.

Kneeling at the Altar, Gollancz (London, England), 1998.

(Under pseudonym James Kennedy) *Silent City,* Heinemann (London, England), 1998.

Serial: A Confession, Orion (London, England), 2003.

A Waste of Shame, Orion (London, England), 2003.

Also author of scripts for the stage and radio.

ADAPTATIONS: Lusby's novels have been adapted for film and produced on Irish television.

SIDELIGHTS: In addition to publishing the novel *Silent City* under the pseudonym James Kennedy, Irish novelist Jim Lusby has written a number of gritty mystery novels featuring Detective Inspector Carl McCadden, whose cases inevitably take him into the dark side of modern Irish life. These mysteries, according to Keith Miles in *Shots Online,* are "quirky, original, devious and chilling."

In *Making the Cut* McCadden must discover who murdered Billy Power, a local factory machinist living Waterford, Ireland, who fancied dog racing and women and whose body has been found in a cargo container down at the docks. As McCadden investigates, the facts about Power's supposedly simple life become murkier and nothing is as it seems to be. The case takes him through the town's run-down housing projects, dog tracks, pubs, and finally to a factory owned by a prominent local businessman. "The sense of atmosphere is created with skill," wrote a reviewer for the *Tangled Web UK Reviews Online,* "and Lusby draws convincingly varied characters."

In *Flashback* Lusby takes McCadden into the world of amateur theatrics as the detective inspector tracks down the brutal killer of a young woman at the Belview Guesthouse, a place popular with actors. The victim's violent beating is similar to that received by a second crime victim found soon after on the other side of town. McCadden begins a search through a sleazy world of nightclubs, home-movie makers, and would-be actors before finding the information he needs from a gravedigger. The *Tangled Web* reviewer praised the character of McCadden: "Unconventional in appearance, with a cool, laid back charm, he observes and comments on aspects of human nature with sensitivity."

Lusby's *Kneeling at the Altar* finds McCadden stumbling upon a case on his own. While waiting in the emergency room at the local hospital, the inspector notices a man who is not waiting to see a patient and yet has flowers and candy with him. He soon discovers that the man is hiding out, trying to avoid a group of people outside who are intent on beating him up for being a pedophile. However, the case is more complex than it first seems when a group of local monks become involved and McCadden finds himself treading increasingly carefully in his investigation. Val McDermid concluded of the novel on the *Tangled Web UK Reviews Online:* "McCadden remains relaxed, perceptive, always himself in the teeth of the extreme frustrations of policing contemporary Ireland."

An elderly woman is found murdered in *A Waste of Shame,* apparently the victim of a botched robbery, but McCadden is not so sure. No money was taken and the body was carefully mutilated. Why a recluse in her nineties should be the target of such a crime is not clear, until McCadden begins to uncover startling details about the victim's early life. Along the way, he must deal with local police corruption and political and religious prejudices. Miles concluded that *A Waste of Shame* "is a fine novel, beautifully-written and highly recommended."

In *Serial: A Confession* Lusby experiments with narrative as he tells his story through three interwoven texts: a serial killer's confession to his crimes,

biographies of the murdered women, and details about the ten-year police investigation to solve the crimes. Detective Kristina Galetti is drawn into the investigation when she finds that a recent homicide is connected to the string of unsolved murders. This latest victim's murder is described in the manuscript of a detective story found in the casket of a dead man; soon there are similar manuscripts found in other graves. Galetti believes the killer may be a writer of detective stories. While a critic for *Kirkus Reviews* described *Serial* as "a self-reflective—but ultimately navel-gazing—look at detective stories," Rex Klett wrote in his *Library Journal* review that "tension builds inexorably to a clever end."

BIOGRAPHICAL AND CRITICAL SOURCES:

PERIODICALS

Globe and Mail (Toronto, Ontario, Canada), February 2, 2002, Margaret Cannon, review of *A Waste of Shame.*

Kirkus Reviews, February 1, 2003, review of *Serial: A Confession,* p. 168.

Library Journal, April 1, 2003, Rex Klett, review of *Serial,* p. 134.

ONLINE

Shots Online, http://www.shotsmag.co.uk/ (October 6, 2003), Keith Miles, review of *A Waste of Shame.*

Tangled Web UK Review Online, http://www.twbooks. co.uk/ (April 9, 1998), Val McDermid, review of *Kneeling at the Altar;* (March 3, 2003) reviews of *Making the Cut* and *Flashback.**

* * *

LUSK, John 1969(?)-

PERSONAL: Born c. 1969, in TX. *Education:* Wharton School, University of Pennsylvania, M.B.A., 1999. *Hobbies and other interests:* Golf.

ADDRESSES: Home—San Francisco, CA. *Agent*—c/o Author Mail, Perseus Books, 387 Park Ave. S., 12th Floor, New York, NY 10016.

CAREER: Ernst & Young Information Technology Group, Senior Consultant; Platinum Concepts, Inc., San Francisco, CA, cofounder, 1999—. Speaker at business schools and conferences on entrepreneurship and start-ups.

WRITINGS:

The MouseDriver Chronicles: The True-Life Adventures of Two First-Time Entrepreneurs, epilogue by Kyle Harrison, Perseus Publishing (Cambridge, MA), 2002.

Also author, with Kyle Harrison, of bimonthly e-mail newsletter *The MouseDriver Insider,* 1999-2002. Contributor of articles to Web sites.

SIDELIGHTS: Even at the height of the dot-com boom of the 1990s, some highly educated young entrepreneurs were willing to take a chance and start old-fashioned consumer-product businesses. John Lusk and Kyle Harrison were the only ones of the 792 1999 M.B.A. graduates of the prestigious Wharton School to take that path, despite lucrative job offers from Internet startups and venture capital firms, and despite their own experience in management consulting. They eventually achieved modest success with their novelty product, the MouseDriver, a computer mouse shaped like the head of a golf club. Blessed with keen insight and communication skills, the two men then parlayed their modest business success into careers as motivational speakers, start-up consultants, and eventually authors.

Faced with the daunting challenges that confront every start-up, and lacking any hands-on experience, Lusk and Harrison started an e-mail newsletter, *The MouseDriver Insider,* to vent their emotions, share their experiences and seek advice and support. Mike Hofman later wrote in *Inc.* that the biweekly newsletter, "filled with observations that are profoundly mundane," quickly attracted a small but elite following among venture capital and investment banking firms, and became assigned reading in a few business schools.

The newsletter attracted enough attention to win its creators a cover story in *Inc.* that, in turn, led to contacts from several literary agents and, eventually, a book offer. The result, *The MouseDriver Chronicles:*

The True-Life Adventures of Two First-Time Entrepreneurs, "takes the reader on an exhilarating ride of the development and debut of an original new product," according to a *Pittsburgh Post-Gazette* writer. A *Strategic Finance* contributor found it "a very good guide for other bright-eyed entrepreneurs with a good idea and little financing."

The book highlights the authors' sometimes unconventional approach. Lusk told *BookPage.com* interviewer Stephanie Swilley that they would "walk into a store, pretend like we were looking for gifts, find MouseDriver on the shelves and then scream and shout about how it was such a cool product." Aiming to appeal with self-deprecating humor, the authors contrast the lessons of business school with such realities as typhoons delaying shipment and distributors defaulting on payment. They describe how they were quickly forced to acquire practical skills in design, financing, manufacturing, marketing, sales, and customer relations. They provide both practical tips and emotional support for budding entrepreneurs. In fact, Lusk told Karin Pekarchik in *Business Week Online* that he would "like to see more emphasis placed on the emotional aspects of entrepreneurship in business school." He explained that the book was designed to help fill that gap, by presenting "a very realistic, honest, and authentic insight into what it's like to go through the entrepreneurial experience—the highs, lows, failures, successes, and emotions associated with it."

Despite inexperience and a series of errors and mishaps, the company eventually managed to break even, earning an annual income of six hundred thousand dollars on sales of fifty thousand units.

BIOGRAPHICAL AND CRITICAL SOURCES:

PERIODICALS

Booklist, December 15, 2001, review of *The MouseDriver Chronicles: The True-Life Adventures of Two First-Time Entrepreneurs,* p. 693.

Boston Globe, February 10, 2002, D. C. Denison, review of *The MouseDriver Chronicles,* p. G2.

Business Week, March 25, 2002, review of *The MouseDriver Chronicles,* p. 14E10.

Inc., February, 2001, Mike Hofman, "An American Start-Up."

Kirkus Reviews, November 1, 2001, review of *The MouseDriver Chronicles,* p. 1536.

Library Journal, February 1, 2002, Norm Hutcherson, review of *The MouseDriver Chronicles,* p. 111.

Pittsburgh Post-Gazette, July 21, 2002, review of *The MouseDriver Chronicles.*

Publishers Weekly, December 3, 2001, review of *The MouseDriver Chronicles,* p. 51.

Strategic Finance, March, 2002, review of *The MouseDriver Chronicles,* p. 21.

Texas Business Weekly, February 6, 2002, Tamara Young, review of *The MouseDriver Chronicles.*

USA Today, January 21, 2002, review of *The MouseDriver Chronicles,* p. B7.

ONLINE

BookPage.com, http://www.bookpage.com/ (February, 2002), Stephanie Swilley, "Driving It Home: Entrepreneurial Advice from the Mouse Men" (interview).

Business Week Online, http://www.businessweek.com/ (July 11, 2002), Karin Pekarchik, "What Drives the MouseDriver Guys?"

MouseDriver Web site, http://www.mousedriver.com/ (November 22, 2004).*

M

MACHOWICZ, Richard J.

PERSONAL: Male.

ADDRESSES: Home—Malibu, CA. *Office*—Bukido Institute, 1223 Wilshire Blvd., Ste. 581, Santa Monica, CA 90403; fax: 310-392-1990. *E-mail*—information@ bukido.com.

CAREER: Personal protection specialist, and martial arts trainer. Bukido Institute, Santa Monica, CA, director, chief instructor, founder of Bukido Training System. *Military service:* U.S. Navy; served ten years with Sea, Air, and Land Capability (SEAL) teams; became certified instructor in special warfare combat fighting.

MEMBER: Screen Actors Guild.

WRITINGS:

Unleashing the Warrior Within: Using the Seven Principles of Combat to Achieve Your Goals, Hyperion (New York, NY), 2000.

SIDELIGHTS: The word "Bukido" translates to "path of the warrior spirit," and it is the principle upon which former Navy SEAL Richard J. Machowicz has built his reputation as an instructor, trainer, and coach. Machowicz has earned multiple belts in the martial arts and applies the focus and discipline necessary to his assignments as a SEAL to help others shape their behavior and master their lives. He created the Bukido Training System and trains clients at his Bukido Institute in Santa Monica, California. He has also served as a combat instructor to other SEALs.

Sumner Jones reviewed Machowicz's workout program for *Joe Weider's Muscle & Fitness.* He noted Machowicz's "telltale cut triceps, biceps, and wide lat spread, and the six-pack abs. . . . His muscles are conditioned for stealth, power, and endurance, which are exactly the kind of attributes the job of Navy SEALs demands. His body has been molded into the tool most appropriate to get the job done, which is the essence of Bukido." Machowicz teaches that in choosing a weapon, or training technique, one must first consider one's target goal. That target might be a bodybuilder's physique, or it may be a goal of general fitness. He teaches through a method he calls the "Training Pyramid," in which skills are learned level upon level, with advancement occurring only when the previous levels are fully learned and developed. He teaches five basics that include fundamentals, concentration, consistency, accuracy, and speed, with the last referring to the time it takes for results to be seen, not how fast one moves.

Machowicz explained his eighty-percent rule to Jones: "People will tell you to give it your all or go 110 percent, but it's impossible to put 110 percent into anything. You only have 100 percent, and the closer you push toward 100 percent, the closer you are to shutting your body down. Similarly, you can run your car at top speed for a few seconds, but after that it starts to shake and ultimately breaks apart. Instead, aim to work at eighty percent of your maximum effort in whatever you do. At eighty percent, you're able to think and your body is able to stay in balance, to flow rather than force."

Machowicz wrote *Unleashing the Warrior Within: Using the Seven Principles of Combat to Achieve Your Goals* to explain the lessons he teaches in his classes to a wider audience. Beth Sonnenburg reviewed the book and interviewed Machowicz for *Muscle & Fitness/Hers,* posing the question of how to translate the term "combat" for people who never have and never will experience actual combat. Machowicz suggested substituting other words for combat. "Call it stress and pressure—you can call it pain, you can call it competition. Rarely, if ever, will most people be in combat, but the principles that make for effectiveness in battle are just as relevant to the daily challenges we face. Basically, this is all about learning to focus." Machowicz teaches focus "through the metaphor of combat. The principles of combat work against an opposing force—a side that does not want you to achieve your goals. Who is the battle against here? The biggest battle on earth is not with somebody else. It's with yourself and who you're capable of being. I think you do more to damage your own capabilities than anybody exterior, whether that's buying into the idea that you're not thin enough, or sexy enough, or smart enough, or that it's this person's world or that person's world. This kind of thinking keeps you from becoming what you're capable of being."

A *Publishers Weekly* contributor reviewed Machowicz's recommendations for taking charge of one's life, saying that those who have unsuccessfully tried to accomplish their goals "may find that his potent prose and no-nonsense approach will motivate them to begin to behave differently."

BIOGRAPHICAL AND CRITICAL SOURCES:

PERIODICALS

Joe Weider's Muscle & Fitness, November, 2000, Sumner Jones, "Direct Hit," p. 134.

Muscle & Fitness/Hers, June, 2002, Beth Sonnenburg, "Finding Your Inner Xena: Here's How to Empower Yourself to Demolish the Barriers Blocking Your Road to Success," p. 105.

Publishers Weekly, January 24, 2000, review of *Unleashing the Warrior Within: Using the Seven Principles of Combat to Achieve Your Goals,* p. 305.

ONLINE

Bukido Institute Web site, http://bukido.com/ (November 17, 2004).*

*   *   *

MACLEOD, Wendy

PERSONAL: Female. *Education:* Kenyon College, B.A.; Yale School of Drama, M.F.A.

ADDRESSES: Office—Kenyon College, Department of Dance and Drama, Gambier, OH 43022. *E-mail*—macleod@kenyon.edu.

CAREER: Playwright. Kenyon College, Gambier, OH, James E. Michael playwright-in-residence, 1990—.

MEMBER: Dramatists Guild, Authors League of America, New Dramatists Alumna.

AWARDS, HONORS: Los Angeles Drama Critics Circle award nomination, for *The Water Children;* Special Jury Award, Sundance Film Festival, for *The House of Yes.*

WRITINGS:

PLAYS

Cinema Verite (one-act), first produced at the Yale Cabaret, New Haven, CT, 1987.
Apocalyptic Butterflies (first produced at Yale Repertory Theater, New Haven, CT, 1987), Dramatists Play Service (New York, NY), 1990.
The House of Yes (first produced at the Magic Theater, San Francisco, CA, 1990), Dramatists Play Service (New York, NY), 1996.

The Lost Colony (one-act; first produced at Ensemble Studio Theater, New York, NY, 1991), Dramatists Play Service (New York, NY), 1993.

The Shallow End (one-act; first produced in New York, NY, 1992), Dramatists Play Service (New York, NY), 1992.

Sin (first produced at the Goodman Theater, Chicago, IL, 1994), Dramatists Play Service (New York, NY), 1998.

Division Three (short play), first produced in San Francisco, CA, 1995.

The Water Children (first produced off-Broadway at Playwrights Horizons, 1997), Dramatists Play Service (New York, NY), 1999.

How to Make an Apple Pie and See the World (children's musical; based on the book by Marjorie Priceman), first produced at Kennedy Center, Washington, DC, 2000.

Schoolgirl Figure, first produced at the Goodman Theater, Chicago, IL, 2000.

Chemistry (short play), first produced at Collaboration, Chicago, IL, 2001.

Things Being What They Are, first produced at Seattle Repertory Theater, Seattle, WA, 2002.

Juvenilia, first produced off-Broadway at Playwrights Horizons, New York, NY, 2003.

Boxes (short play), first produced at Collaboration, Chicago, IL, 2004.

The Water Children was included in *Women Playwrights: The Best Plays of 1998,* edited by Marisa Smith, Smith and Kraus, 1998. Also the author of short play *Shooting Pollock.*

OTHER

Author of CBS pilot, *Ivory Tower,* 2001; author of screenplay adaptation of *Schoolgirl Figure* for HBO, 2002; author of BBC adaptation of *Apocalyptic Butterflies,* 1988. Executive story editor, *Popular,* 1999-2000.

ADAPTATIONS: The House of Yes was adapted for a 1997 film of the same title starring Parker Posey and Genevieve Bujold.

WORK IN PROGRESS: Play called *Phantom Limbs.*

SIDELIGHTS: The author of numerous plays, Wendy MacLeod made a name for herself with the film adaptation of her 1990 play, *The House of Yes.* As a playwright she deals with themes from incest to eating disorders to male bonding. A graduate of the Yale School of Drama, she has been a longtime playwright-in-residence at her undergraduate alma mater, Kenyon College.

MacLeod scored her first success with the 1987 play *Apocalyptic Butterflies,* a drama featuring a young couple having trouble adjusting to parenthood. While the wife feels she has wasted her education by becoming a mother, the father begins to feel trapped in marriage and responsibility. Though the husband strays into the arms of another for a time, the story "ends happily," according to Hedy Weiss, reviewing the play in the *Chicago Sun-Times.* The play was adapted the following year for a BBC production.

The House of Yes was a major critical success. Premiering in San Francisco, the play is "wacky," "funny," "racy," and "definitely twisted," according to Amy Reiter in *Back Stage.* The production features the bizarre Pascal family and touches on themes from incest to alcoholism. For Reiter, MacLeod's play is a "wild ride—so quick and clever that you may find yourself yukking it up at some undeniably sick things." Kristina Mannion, reviewing a 2001 production of the play for *Back Stage West,* thought that "dysfunctional doesn't even begin to describe the family on display in Wendy MacLeod's disturbing black comedy."

MacLeod's play *Sin* premiered in 1994 at Chicago's Goodman Theater. According to Eric Grode in *Back Stage,* "the sum of *Sin*'s parts are considerably greater than the whole." For Grode, this comedy has a "formulaic plot, one-dimensional characters, and a central theme that isn't exactly ground-breaking." However, Grode also commented that "the damn thing works, thanks to MacLeod's perceptive writing." The tale of a female radio traffic reporter, whose god-like viewpoint (aboard a helicopter) begins to take its toll on her personal life as she encounters the biblical seven deadly sins, will be recalled, Grode noted, as an "intriguing, if not flawless early work." Robert Faires, writing in the *Austin Chronicle,* considered *Sin* one of his top theater experiences of the year. "MacLeod's script is clever and funny," Faires lauded, with "each scene sharper and more funny than the last."

In the 1997 play *The Water Children,* MacLeod serves up "controversial issues with wit and candor," according to *Variety* reviewer Robert L. Daniels. In this two-act play, MacLeod tells the story of a pro-choice actress who reluctantly takes part in a pro-life commercial and subsequently becomes romantically involved with the director of an anti-abortion group. Eating disorders are at the center of the 1995 comedy *Schoolgirl Figure,* while in *Juvenilia* "a group of naughty college friends [lure] the Christian fundamentalist down the hall into a three-way," as Gina Bazer described the plot in *Chicago Social* magazine. Alexis Soloski, writing in the *Village Voice,* was not shocked by *Juvenilia,* however, noting that "like its adolescent characters," the play "wants to pretend it's edgier than it is." A reviewer for *CurtainUp.com* credited MacLeod for the content of *Juvenilia,* saying that she managed to "touch on universally interesting issues . . . dealing with youthful uncertainty, insecurity and grief via random sex, alcohol and emotional cover-up."

In her 2003 comedy, *Things Being What They Are,* MacLeod writes about "two men who become unlikely fast pals," as Bazer noted. The same critic went on to observe that "for a playwright who's known for her proclivity to shock, this play is surprisingly normal in a suburban angst kind of way—and MacLeod is OK with that."

Speaking with Caridad Svich in the *Dramatist,* MacLeod explained that she does not think of herself as a "political playwright, although I'd like to. It would make me feel important. Rather, I'm someone who delights in sacred-cow tipping, to use a Midwestern analogy. I delight in contradicting the party line. Call it the Theater of Inversion." In an interview with artistic director Tim Sanford published on the author's Home Page, MacLeod observed, "People have described my work as black comedy, but for me that was not something I was entirely in control of. I think it was the way I saw the world."

MacLeod told *CA:* "I was always interested in writing, both fiction and playwriting. As for influences, like many playwrights, I am a great admirer of Harold Pinter. (Someone once described my work as an unlikely collision between Noel Coward and Harold Pinter.) My writing process is to work on one play at a time. I romp through the first draft, and then build up subsequent drafts the way a painter builds up the surface of a canvas. I often rewrite as I go, going back over a particular section again and again, until I'm impelled forward through the story.

"Occasionally, I can sit back and actually enjoy something I've written, wondering whence it came. I've had the experience with *The House of Yes, Schoolgirl Figure, and Things Being What They Are.* I hope to jolt the imaginations of the audience, to make them look at something familiar in a new way. I want to move them or make them laugh or both. I like to take subjects that have been earnestly explored, like incest or eating disorders, and suggest they're symptomatic of something that's wrong with the larger culture. I want to render them larger, and more surprising."

BIOGRAPHICAL AND CRITICAL SOURCES:

PERIODICALS

American Theatre, January, 1998, Karen Houppert, review of *The Water Children,* p. 46.

Back Stage, February 3, 1995, Amy Reiter, review of *The House of Yes,* p. 44; October 27, 1995, Eric Grode, review of *Sin,* p. 36; November 7, 1997, Victor Gluck, review of *The Water Children,* p. 44.

Back Stage West, April 12, 2001, Kristina Mannion, review of *The House of Yes,* p. 16.

Chicago Social, June, 2003, Gina Bazer, "House of MacLeod."

Chicago Sun-Times, November 29, 1988, Hedy Weiss, review of *Apocalyptic Butterflies,* p. 37.

Chicago Tribune, May 30, 2003, Chris Jones, "The attack of Wendy MacLeod," p. 3.

Denver Post, February 13, 1999, Ed Will, review of *The House of Yes,* p. F5.

Dramatist, May-June, 2003, Caridad Svich, "Wendy MacLeod in Conversation."

Entertainment Weekly, April 17, 1998, Michael Sauter, review of *The House of Yes,* p. 78.

Los Angeles Times, May 1, 1998, Don Shirley, review of *The Water Children,* p. 31; January 14, 2000, F. Kathleen Foley, review of *Sin,* p. 46.

New York Times, October 31, 1999, Alvin Klein, review of *The Water Children,* pg. 14; December 10, 2003, Bruce Weber, review of *Juvenilia,* p. E5.

Time, October 20, 1997, Richard Corliss, review of *The House of Yes,* p. 100.

Variety, November 10, 1997, Robert L. Daniels, review of *The Water Children,* p. 52.

Village Voice, December 17, 2003, Alexis Soloski, review of *Juvenilia,* p. C82.

Washington Post, July 2, 2002, Jane Horowitz, "For Cherry Red, an Appetizing Tale," p. C5.

ONLINE

Austin Chronicle, http://www.austinchronicle.com/ (September 1, 2004), Robert Faires, review of *Sin.*

CurtainUp.com, http://www.curtainup.com/ (September 1, 2004), review of *Juvenilia.*

Official Wendy MacLeod Web site, http://www.ltb.pair.com/ (November, 2003), Tim Sanford, interview with MacLeod.

Wendy MacLeod Home Page, http://www.wendy macleod.com (September 1, 2004).

*   *   *

MacPHERSON, William 1926-

PERSONAL: Born 1926, in Scotland; son of a brigadier; married Sheila Brodie, 1962; children: Annie, Alan, James. *Education:* Attended Oxford University, Wellington College, and Trinity College.

ADDRESSES: Home—Newton Castle, Blairgowrie, Perthshire, Scotland.

CAREER: Barrister, London, England, 1952-83; Queen's Counsel, London, 1971-83; High Court of England and Wales, Queen's Bench Division, London, presiding judge of Northern Circuit, 1983-96. *Military service:* Scots Guard; Twenty-second Territorial Special Air Service, lieutenant colonel (honorary colonel); Royal Company of Archer's (Queen's bodyguard in Scotland).

WRITINGS:

The Stephen Lawrence Inquiry: Report of an Inquiry, Stationery Office (London, England), 1999.

SIDELIGHTS: When William MacPherson, chief of clan MacPherson and a peer of the British realm, was appointed to head an official inquiry into the death of Stephen Lawrence, a black teenager, at the hands of white youths and subsequent bungling of the case by London metropolitan police, there were fears of a whitewash. MacPherson was considered the very epitome of the establishment, with his family pedigree as hereditary chief of an ancient Scottish clan, his service in the elite SAS Territorials and the Queen's official bodyguard in Scotland, and his years as a High Court judge. It also did not help that MacPherson had one of the worst records for allowing judicial review in immigration cases. In light of these facts, the Lawrence family asked the British Home Secretary to reconsider the appointment; their request was denied. However, when MacPherson handed down his report, it was the police who cried foul while Britain's black community praised the integrity and insightfulness of his conclusions.

Instead of putting the blame on a few individuals with racist tendencies, MacPherson produced an unequivocal finding of institutionalized racism throughout the police forces. As Jennie Bourne commented in *Race and Class,* MacPherson "had, with his concept of institutional racism, broken with cultural explanations and remedies, broken with individualised definitions and ethnic identity and thrown the spotlight on the workings of institutions instead. He had listened earnestly and conscientiously to the evidence put before him by individuals, families and community organisations, and had responded accordingly."

MacPherson's most famous case began on April 22, 1993, when a group of white youths surrounded Stephen Lawrence and friend Duwayne Brooks. Lawrence was stabbed while, according to Brooks, at least one of the assailants yelled racial epithets. Unfortunately, when police arrived on the scene, they were told that Lawrence suffered from a head injury, not a stabbing, and so they waited for paramedics rather than rushing him to a hospital. They later claimed not to have seen Lawrence's blood on the sidewalk.

This was the beginning of a series of mistakes that would bedevil the prosecution. As John Upton commented in the *London Review of Books,* "The groundwork for the subsequent case against the Metropolitan Police was most ably laid by the organisation itself, within minutes of the attack. Their shoddy approach to securing the crime scene and their failure to utilise the 'golden 24 hours', vital in any murder investigation, lost them who knows how many opportunities for arresting the murderers or gathering crucial evidence and information." In the end, the flaws in the investigation proved fatal, and the prosecution withdrew its case against the suspects, to the fury of the Lawrence family, Britain's black community, and all those who suspected the police of widespread racism.

In response, the Tony Blair government announced in July of 1997 that it would launch a full-scale investigation into police conduct of this and similar cases. Over the objection of the Lawrence family and his own friends, who feared he was being set up as a scapegoat, MacPherson agreed to come out of retirement and preside over the investigation. In February of 1999 he handed down his conclusions, published as *The Stephen Lawrence Inquiry: Report of an Inquiry.*

MacPherson's report is a devastating condemnation of the racism and racial insensitivity that exists throughout the Metropolitan Police and much of Britain's judicial system, and includes no less than seventy recommendations for major changes. Not surprisingly the report sparked controversy, and in December of 2000, opposition leader William Hague condemned it for fostering the spirit of "political correctness" that he argued has crippled police enforcement against ethnic minority suspects it its wake. In response, Labour Party members accused Hague of playing the race card in a desperate attempt to win the next election.

MacPherson himself remains committed to his report and to the cause of healing the racial divisions within British society.

BIOGRAPHICAL AND CRITICAL SOURCES:

PERIODICALS

Boston Globe, February 25, 1999, Kevin Cullen, "Institutional Racism Marks London Police Report," p. A1.
Financial Times, December 15, 2000, "Hague Sparks Row over Crime Claims," p. 6; February 24, 2001, Jimmy Burns, "The Pioneer-making Changes Fit the Bill," p. 6.
Guardian, February 22, 1999, Nick Hopkins and Ewan MacAskill, "Report Savages Met for Racism," p. 1; February 22, 1999, Nick Hopkins, "Lawrence Inquiry: Report Lays Bare Racism at Met," p. 3.
Hindu, December 17, 2000, "Hague Speech Provokes Anti-Tory Rage."

London Review of Books, July 1, 1999, John Upton, "The Smallest Details Speak the Loudest," pp. 3-9.
New Statesman, February 21, 2000, Mary Ridell, "Sir William MacPherson," p. 18.
New Straits Times, December 29, 2000, "Hard Words for 'Softly' Policy."
New York Times, February 23, 1999, Warren Hoge, "British Report Finds Racism Pervades Police," section A, p. 5.
Race and Class, October-December, 2001, Jenny Bourne, "The Life and Times of Institutional Racism," p. 7.
Spectator, August 2, 2002, Boris Johnson, "Try, Try, and Try Again: Retrials Should Be Possible, Sir William MacPherson Tells Boris Johnson," p. 14.

ONLINE

Clan MacPherson Association, http://www.clan-macpherson.org/ (August 26, 2004), "Chief of Clan Macpherson."
Parsonage Clan Macpherson Association Web site, http://www.parsonage.net/macpherson/news/ (August 26, 2004).*

*   *   *

MADDEN, Chris (Casson) 1948-

PERSONAL: Born June 1, 1948, in Rockville Centre, NY; married Kevin Madden (a publisher), 1974; children: Patrick, Nick. *Education:* Attended Fashion Institute of Technology.

ADDRESSES: Office—Chris Madden, Inc., 181 Westchester Ave., Suite 408, Port Chester, NY 10573.

CAREER: Interior designer and writer. Worked for *Sports Illustrated* and Simon and Schuster, Inc.; Farrar, Straus & Giroux, New York, NY, public relations director; founder of Chris Madden, Inc.; Home and Garden Television (HGTV), host of *Interiors by Design;* designer and spokesperson for Bassett, Mohawk, and J. C. Penney.

WRITINGS:

The Summer House Cookbook, illustrated by Jody Newman, Harcourt (New York, NY), 1979.

(With others) *The Photographed Cat,* Doubleday (New York, NY), 1980.

(With others) *Manhattan,* Harry Abrams (New York, NY), 1981.

Baby's First Helpings: Super-Healthy Meals for Super-Healthy Kids, Mary Ellen Family Books (Garden City, NY), 1983.

Interior Visions: Great American Designers and the Showcase House, Stewart, Tabori & Chang (New York, NY), 1988.

Rooms with a View: Two Decades of Outstanding American Interior Design from Kips Bay Decorator Show Houses, PBC International (Glen Cove, NY), 1992.

Kitchens, photographs by Michael Mundy and John Vaughan, Clarkson Potter (New York, NY), 1993.

Bathrooms, photographs by John Vaughan, Clarkson Potter (New York, NY), 1996.

A Room of Her Own: Women's Personal Spaces, photographs by Jennifer Levy, Clarkson Potter (New York, NY), 1997.

Chris Madden's Guide to Personalizing Your Home: Simple, Beautiful Ideas for Every Room, Clarkson Potter (New York, NY), 1997.

Getaways: Carefree Retreats for All Seasons, photographs by Jennifer Levy and Nancy Hill, Clarkson Potter (New York, NY), 2000.

Bedrooms: Creating the Stylish, Comfortable Room of Your Dreams, photographs by Nancy E. Hill, Clarkson Potter (New York, NY), 2001.

Chris Casson Madden's New American Living Rooms, Clarkson Potter (New York, NY), 2003.

Haven: Finding the Keys to Your Personal Decorating Style, photographs by Nancy E. Hill, Clarkson Potter (New York, NY), 2004.

Author of *The Complete Lemon Cookbook,* 1979; and a column for Scripps Howard News Service.

WORK IN PROGRESS: Chris Madden Haven, a magazine.

SIDELIGHTS: Designer Chris Madden is the host of the television program *Interiors by Design,* the author of a syndicated column carried by 400 newspapers, and the author of a number of books on interior design. She grew up on Long Island, one of eleven children, and showed an early talent for decorating when her mother allowed her to redo her own bedroom. Madden attended the Fashion Institute of Technology but dropped out several credits shy of a degree. She worked in publishing for a time and met her husband, Kevin, when they were on opposing softball teams in Central Park. At the time Kevin was with *New York* magazine. He has been the publisher of *House & Garden, Self,* and *Bon Appetit.* He became her partner and CEO in 1995, concentrating his efforts on running her growing design company.

Madden has served as Oprah Winfrey's design consultant, and her clients have included celebrities Katie Couric and Toni Morrison. She has designed furniture for Bassett, rugs for Mohawk, and soft goods for J. C. Penney and is the host of the popular Home & Garden television program *Interiors by Design.* She began publishing in 1979, first with cookbooks, and produced a number of best sellers that help readers create their own spaces. Madden planned to adapt the title of one of her more recent books, *Haven: Finding the Keys to Your Personal Decorating Style,* as a magazine. Mark Rotella reviewed *Haven* in *Publishers Weekly,* commenting that "the tone throughout is warm and upbeat."

Explaining her role as an interior designer to James Brady in *Parade,* Madden remarked: "I really believe everyone in America deserves a good home. . . . Not a mansion but a good home. That's my message."

BIOGRAPHICAL AND CRITICAL SOURCES:

PERIODICALS

Fortune, October 28, 2002, Julie Rose, "Me Inc.: Is Chris Madden the Next Martha Stewart?" p. F192.

Good Housekeeping, October, 2004, "Haven on Earth," p. 146.

New York Times, March 10, 2004, William L. Hamilton, "Now, the Search for the Next Diva of Domesticity," p. A1.

Parade, July 11, 2004, James Brady, "In Step with Chris Madden."

Publishers Weekly, April 26, 2004, Mark Rotella, review of *Haven: Finding the Keys to Your Personal Decorating Style,* p. 56.

Westchester County Business Journal, March 24, 2003, Elizabeth Hlotyak, "Chris Madden," p. 28.

ONLINE

Chris Madden Home Page, http://www.chrismadden.com (October 26, 2004).*

MAGAS, Branka

PERSONAL: Female.

ADDRESSES: Home—London, England. *Office*—The Bosnian Institute, 14-16 St. Mark's Road, London W11 1RQ, England; fax: +44 20 7243-8874.

CAREER: Historian and journalist. *Bosnia Report,* joint founding editor; Bosnian Institute, London, England, consultant.

MEMBER: Alliance to Save Bosnia.

WRITINGS:

The Destruction of Yugoslavia: Tracing the Break-up, 1980-92, Verso (New York, NY), 1993.

(Editor) *Question of Survival: A Common Education System for Bosnia-Herzegovina,* Bosnian Institute (London, England), 1998.

(Editor, with Ivo Zanic) *Rat u Hrvatskoj i Bosni i Hercegovini, 1991-1995,* translated as *The War in Croatia and Bosnia-Herzegovina, 1991-1995,* Frank Cass (London, England), 2001.

Contributor to periodicals, including the *New Left Review, New Statesman,* and *London Review of Books.*

WORK IN PROGRESS: A history of Croatia.

SIDELIGHTS: Croatian historian and socialist commentator Branka Magas is regarded as a perceptive analyst of Yugoslavia's postwar political development and dissolution. In *The Destruction of Yugoslavia: Tracing the Break-up, 1980-92,* she analyzes the gradual fragmentation of the former socialist Balkan state that occurred in tandem with the decline of the Soviet economy in the late 1980s and early 1990s. An *Economist* reviewer quoted Magas as saying that "Yugoslavia did not die a natural death." Rather, she contends, the nation was deliberately destroyed from within by a cabal of Serbian nationalists intent on creating a racially pure Serbian state and ex-communists and Serb-military officers who were desperate to retain their power. In Magas's view, as quoted in the *Economist,* Yugoslavia was "destroyed

for the cause of Greater Serbia." In this climate, she explains, former communist leader Slobodan Milosevic found a way to exploit the ethnic tensions that had flourished underground in the prewar Yugoslavia and to promote a rabid nationalism.

As Magas notes, Serbian nationalists drew upon ideology that flourished in Yugoslavia during the relatively open period under Marshal Tito. "How many people realize that the concept of 'ethnic purity' (a direct predecessor of 'ethnic cleansing') first surfaced in Serbia as long ago as 1986?" observed Michael Scammell in the *Washington Post Book World.* "How many know that it was the dream of the intelligentsia in the form of two hundred prominent professors, writers, lawyers, journalists, and other intellectuals who introduced it in a petition to the Yugoslav and Serbian national assemblies calling for 'radical measures' to protect the Serbian population in the autonomous province of Kosovo?" Michael Ignatieff, a *New York Review of Books* contributor, took issue with Magas's suggestion that "the entire Yugoslav tragedy can be traced back to Milosevic's program, first set out in the 1986 Serbian Academy of Arts and Science Memorandum, to build a greater Serbia on the ruins of Tito's Yugoslavia." Countering Magas's suggestion that "the Croatian drive for independence was a protective response to Milosevic's expansionism," Ignatieff argued that burgeoning Croatian nationalism was itself an "independent force" that contributed to Yugoslavia's "descent into tragedy."

Despite the fact that Magas's book, based largely upon her left-wing journalism during the period, concludes several years before the initiation of diplomacy to end the Balkan war, critics recognized the work as a significant contribution to the history of Eastern Europe. "Those who traced the crisis of Yugoslavia as it grew during the 1980s have a special claim upon our attention at this point in the unfolding tragedy," wrote Dan Smith in the *Journal of Peace Research.* Smith continued, "in that sense, Magas deserves more than ordinary commendation for her efforts over the years to keep a clear eye on the combination of political opportunism and irresolution which finally exploded into a multi-front war." Writing in *Dissent,* Bogdan Denitch stated that Magas's book "will remain indispensable for those who need to know the details of the internal struggles in the Yugoslav League of Communists that lead to Milosevic's de facto coup against the federal 'Titoist' Constitution of 1974. It is solid in its coverage of the Serbian repression in Kosovo, an autonomous province with an Albanian majority where the disintegrative processes began." However, while praising Magas's "first-rate" knowledge, *Times Literary Supplement* critic Norman Stone found shortcomings in her socialist perspective, noting that "her arguments still follow something of the old Marxist track—that you cannot really explain nationalism without reference to the free market."

Magas has also served as editor, with Ivo Zanic, of *Rat u Hrvatskoj i Bosni i Hercegovini, 1991-1995,* a volume of essays that grew out of a 1998 conference in Budapest sponsored by the Bosnian Institute in London and Central European University. Translated as *The War in Croatia and Bosnia-Herzegovina, 1991-1995,* the collection consists of contributions by academics and military experts on the strategy, combatants, and conduct of the Balkan conflict. In particular, the volume works to demystify the Serbian army's aura of invincibility, a false notion that colored Western commentary on the war. According to Matthew R. Schwonek, a reviewer for *Aerospace Power Journal,* "for the next decade this volume of essays is likely to be the starting point for both academic and military professionals" interested in the subject. A critic for the *Contemporary Review* similarly praised the collection as "one of the crucial studies of a conflict whose end has not yet been seen."

BIOGRAPHICAL AND CRITICAL SOURCES:

PERIODICALS

Aerospace Power Journal, spring, 2002, Matthew R. Schwonek, review of *The War in Croatia and Bosnia-Herzegovina, 1991-1995* p. 123.
Choice, February, 1995, Peter Rutland, review of *The Destruction of Yugoslavia: Tracing the Break-up, 1980-92,* pp. 901-905.
Contemporary Review, December, 2001, review of *The War in Croatia and Bosnia-Herzegovina, 1991-1995* pp. 383-384.
Dissent, fall, 1993, Bogdan Denitch, review of *The Destruction of Yugoslavia,* pp. 569-571.
Economist, May 22, 1993, review of *The Destruction of Yugoslavia,* pp. 96, 101.
Foreign Policy, winter, 1993-94, Ivo Banac, review of *The Destruction of Yugoslavia,* pp. 173-182.

Journal of Peace Research, November, 1993, Dan Smith, review of *The Destruction of Yugoslavia,* pp. 468-469.
London Review of Books, December 16, 1993, Francoise Hampson, review of *The Destruction of Yugoslavia,* p. 10.
New Statesman, June 12, 1994, Branka Magas, "We Have in Our Hands a Piece of Paper . . . ," pp. 15-16.
New York Review of Books, May 13, 1993, Michael Ignatieff, review of *The Destruction of Yugoslavia,* pp. 3-5.
Times Literary Supplement, May 14, 1993, Norman Stone, review of *The Destruction of Yugoslavia,* pp. 10-11.
Washington Post Book World, April 25, 1995, Michael Scammell, review of *The Destruction of Yugoslavia,* p. 6.*

*   *   *

MAHER, Eamon

PERSONAL: Male. *Education:* Earned Ph.D.

ADDRESSES: Office—c/o Institute of Technology Tallaght, Tallaght, Dublin 24, Ireland.

CAREER: Institute of Technology Tallaght, Dublin, Ireland, lecturer in humanities, director of National Centre for Franco-Irish Studies. Writer and translator. Lecturer at scholarly conferences in Ireland and the United Kingdom.

AWARDS, HONORS: Prix de l'Ambassade, French Embassy in Ireland Cultural Services, 1996, for translation of Jean Sulivan's *Anticipate Every Goodbye.*

WRITINGS:

Crosscurrents and Confluences: Echoes of Religion in Twentieth-Century Fiction, Veritas (Dublin, Ireland), 2000.
(Translator) Jean Sulivan, *Anticipate Every Goodbye,* Veritas (Dublin, Ireland), 2000.

(With Nathalie Cazaux) *Faisons Affaires,* Oak Tress Press (Cork, Ireland), 2002.

John McGahern: From the Local to the Universal (part of "Contemporary Irish Writers" series), Liffey Press (Dublin, Ireland), 2003.

(Editor, with Michael Böss; and contributor) *Engaging Modernity: Readings of Irish Politics, Culture, and Literature at the Turn of the Century,* Veritas (Dublin, Ireland), 2003.

(Editor, with Grace Neville) *France-Ireland: Anatomy of a Relationship: Studies in History, Literature and Politics,* Peter Lang (New York, NY), 2004.

Contributor of scholarly articles on Irish and French literature to journals and magazines.

WORK IN PROGRESS: Editor, with Eugene O'Brien, of *La France face à la mondialisation/France in the Struggle against Globalization,* for "Irish Studies" series of Edwin Mellen Press; research on the priest/ writer Jean Sulivan (1913-1980); *The Life and Works of John McGahern.*

SIDELIGHTS: Eamon Maher is a teacher and scholar of French and Anglo-Irish literature who specializes in writers who deal with the interface between religious traditions and the modern world. Maher developed this theme in his first published book, *Crosscurrents and Confluences: Echoes of Religion in Twentieth-Century Fiction,* and has addressed it in several articles. In particular, he has written for literary and religious publications and submitted conference papers on the French priest and writer Jean Sulivan. His translation of Sulivan's memoir written on the death of the priest's mother, *Anticipate Every Goodbye,* received the Prix de l'Ambassade in 1996.

Contemporary religion—specifically the role of the Roman Catholic Church in Ireland—is among the topics dealt with by several contributors to *Engaging Modernity: Readings of Irish Politics, Culture, and Literature at the Turn of the Century,* which Maher edited with Michael Böss. According to Rudiger Imhof in *Irish University Review,* the editors display "a perceptively balanced reading of typical responses to Irish modernization, in order to demonstrate that the conflict between tradition and modernity still informs social debate in Ireland." They also hold that, in Imhof's words, "it is possible to enjoy the benefits of modernity without losing a sense of continuity, his-

tory, and tradition." John McDonagh, in *Studies,* wrote that the book shows "a challenging and fresh approach to the hoary old nut of modernity." The essays include one by Maher himself on the novels of John McGahern, which McDonagh praised as "balanced and sensitive." The book can be seen as part of the "ongoing debate as to the nature of the forces of modernization and modernity in Ireland over the last two hundreds years and more," according to Mary Shine Thompson in the *Irish Literary Supplement.* Thompson noted that several of its essays deal with the issue as it was treated in earlier periods, when "discursive self-consciousness" was also "a key feature of engagement with modernity."

The same year, Maher published his full-length study titled *John McGahern: From the Local to the Universal.* The book, according to William D. Walsh in *Library Journal,* "fills the void of studies on McGahern" because it "thoroughly documents the recurring themes in McGahern's work—namely, failed relationships, family tension, and social commentary." Walsh approvingly quoted Maher's conclusion that McGahern "manages to capture for eternity the rituals and customs of a rural Ireland that may not survive another few decades of globalization."

Maher's continued interest in France led to the publication of *France-Ireland: Anatomy of a Relationship,* a collection of two dozen articles examining the relationship between the two countries and their citizens from literary, political, and historical points of view. He was also coauthor of a French language book, *Faisons Affaires,* designed as a textbook in business French.

BIOGRAPHICAL AND CRITICAL SOURCES:

PERIODICALS

Irish Literary Supplement, fall, 2004, Mary Shine Thompson, review of *Engaging Modernity: Readings of Irish Politics, Culture, and Literature at the Turn of the Century,* p. 20.

Irish University Review; A Journal of Irish Studies, autumn, 2003, Rudiger Imhof, review of *Engaging Modernity,* p. 450.

Library Journal, May 1, 2004, William D. Walsh, review of *John McGahern: From the Local to the Universal,* p. 106.

New Hibernia Review, summer, 2004, Eamonn Wall, review of *John McGahern,* pp. 152-55.
Studies, summer, 2004, John McDonagh, review of *Engaging Modernity.*

*   *   *

MAJOR, John 1936-

PERSONAL: Born 1936.

ADDRESSES: Agent—c/o Author Mail, Cassell, 125 Strand, London WC2R 0BB England.

CAREER: Author, historian, and lecturer. University of Hull, Kingston-upon-Hull, England, lecturer in history.

WRITINGS:

(With Anthony Preston) *Send a Gunboat! A Story of the Gunboat and Its Role in British Policy, 1854-1904,* Longmans (London, England), 1967.
(Editor) *The New Deal,* Barnes & Noble (New York, 1967).
The Contemporary World: A Historical Introduction, Methuen Educational (London, England), 1970.
The Oppenheimer Hearing, Stein and Day (New York, NY), 1971.
Cementing the China Vase: David Hartley and America, 1774-1784, Departments of History, Adult Education/American Studies in the University of Hull (Kingston-upon-Hull, England), 1983.
Prize Possession: The United States and the Panama Canal, 1903-1979, Cambridge University Press (New York, NY), 1993.
(Editor, with Robert Love, Jr.) *The Year of D-Day: The 1944 Diary of Admiral Sir Bertram Ramsay,* University of Hull Press (Hull, England), 1994.
(With M. J. Cohen) *History in Quotations,* Cassell (London, England), 2004.

SIDELIGHTS: Historian John Major started his writing career with two books oriented toward teaching high-school seniors and first-year college students about the twentieth-century world. *The New Deal* presents excerpts from historical documents, including legislative acts, memoirs, periodicals, and monographs—with Major's own introductory comments to place them in their historical context. A *Social Education* reviewer commented that Major "not only introduce[s] the sources but provide[s] a continuous narrative." Major's *The Contemporary World* introduced students to twentieth-century world history and balance between democracies and totalitarian powers.

Major turns to a much more focused subject in *The Oppenheimer Hearing,* which describes atomic scientist J. Robert Oppenheimer's removal from his government post following allegations concerning his loyalty to the U.S. government. Oppenheimer was a leading member of the Manhattan Project, the group of scientists whose mission it was to develop a deployable atomic bomb for the United States during World War II. In 1943, when that work was fully underway, Oppenheimer was warned by friend Haakon Chevalier that Chevalier had been approached by Russian agents and asked about Oppenheimer's secret work (Chevalier himself was not aware that Oppenheimer was working on the atomic bomb). Oppenheimer, recognizing what the Russians were trying to do, wanted to warn the U.S. government of this peril without implicating himself in any way that might lead to his removal from the Manhattan Project. His caution was tempered by the fact that his previous sympathies with the Communist Party had already made him enemies in the U.S. military, and he knew that if he were removed from the Manhattan Project its chances of success were much less secure. Oppenheimer concocted a story that would be taken seriously without raising concerns about himself.

Unfortunately, according to a *Times Literary Supplement* reviewer, in doing so he inadvertently raised "the completely false suggestion that Chevalier himself was a Russian agent." Although Oppenheimer worked to set the story straight and clear Chevalier's name after the war, his task proved impossible. Instead, Chevalier's name came to be used against Oppenheimer himself by his enemies in the military and among his former cohorts in the Manhattan Project, in order to imply that he was a security risk. It was an era of extreme paranoia about Communism, with Senator Joseph McCarthy and others seeking to destroy the careers of any prominent individual who could be implied to have had any connection to the once-popular Communist party. Oppenheimer was railroaded out of his post on the Atomic Energy Commission, where he had the ear of President Eisenhower and other high-level government officials. To avoid a drawn-out investigation and scandal within his administration, Eisenhower revoked Oppenheimer's security clearance, effectively ending the brilliant scientist's public career.

In his book Major concentrates on the hearing before the Atomic Energy Commission's Personnel Security Board, which Oppenheimer requested to attempt to challenge the fairness of Eisenhower's decision. Although the hearing was not a trial, it was treated like one by Oppenheimer's enemies. According to the *Times Literary Supplement* reviewer, "The AEC's legal representative, Roger Robb, cast himself as prosecuting counsel, and was allowed to do so by the Board. Oppenheimer and his counsel were thus thrown on the defensive from the start; yet, because of the procedure laid down, they had none of the protection afforded to a defendant by the common law. . . . Charges were made on the basis of classified documents which the defense were not allowed to see." The hearing was evaluated by a board of three men, none of whom were lawyers able to grasp the legal irregularities of the hearing. The *Times Literary Supplement,* reviewer went on to say that indeed, one board member, Air Force General Nichols, was "one of the chief initiators of the assault on Oppenheimer . . . as it was, Nichols judged a case in which he was also a plaintiff." The board, predictably, upheld Eisenhower's decision, and Oppenheimer retired in disgrace. The obvious unfairness of the hearing was apparent to many observers even at the time, and led to reforms of the hearing process. Although in 1963 Oppenheimer was awarded the Fermi Prize in recognition of his extremely valuable services to his country, his public career was not revived.

Major summarizes the lesson he takes from this episode in American history in his conclusion: "The Oppenheimer case did grave damage to the principles that the United States claims to cherish," he writes in *The Oppenheimer Hearing.* "Above all, perhaps, it indicated that the interests of the state could not be reconciled with the freedom of an individual. It may, of course, be that they are irreconcilable, even in a democracy professing full respect for individual rights."

An *Economist* reviewer noted that while the book contains "not very much that seems new but a great deal that has been well and usefully organized," the

work is designed "for scholars, and only the most devoted Oppenheimer buffs." Conversely, the *Times Literary Supplement* reviewer wrote that "Major's is neither the first nor, we may be sure, the last book on the Oppenheimer affair, though it is likely to remain one of the best." A reviewer in *Choice* called *The Oppenheimer Hearing* "one of the best of the several recent studies of the Oppenheimer case."

In *Prize Possession: The United States and the Panama Canal, 1903-1979,* Major chronicles the sociopolitical history of the great man-made waterworks from the presidency of Theodore Roosevelt to that of Jimmy Carter. A reviewer in *Historian* noted that the early chapters explore the United States' "interest in the isthmus from 1826 through the aftermath of the Panama Revolution of 1903." The book also explores efforts on the parts of Teddy Roosevelt and John Hay to secure treaties with Panama in order to establish U.S. control over the zone in which the canal would be built. The *Historian* reviewer added that "the heart of the book focuses on U.S. administration of the zone and on governmental and economic relations with Panama from 1904 to 1955."

These middle chapters also demonstrate how "blatant racism and discrimination favored white Americans over Panamanians and West Indian contract workers" in the area. Efforts to unionize workers were strongly opposed. The fiscal policies of the United States effectively subsidized U.S. interests and workers in the Canal Zone, cutting off Panamanian merchants and creating what amounted to an independent U.S. commercial center in the zone. While these unfair practices sparked protests that the United States eventually answered by giving up its official power in the canal zone, it maintained an influence that Major calls "pervasive and inescapable." The concluding chapters argue that the United States' 1979 treaty, which allowed for reversion of power in zone back to Panama, in 1999 came as the result of U.S. embarrassment over accusations of its colonizing presence in Panama and its sense of the decreasing military and economic importance of the canal.

Reviewers placed *Prize Possession: The United States and the Panama Canal, 1903-1979,* in the context of other history books about the canal. Thomas H. Appleton, Jr., writing in *Library Journal,* called the book a "considerable achievement." Gustave Anguizole, reviewing the book in *Journal of American History,* found moments of confusion in the text and flaws in the index, but concluded that such "oversights do not diminish the importance of this study" and its conclusions. Anguizole added that Major's book "is a jewel of information," while Joseph A. Fry, reviewing the book in *Historian,* called it a "well-researched, methodical, and informative account," especially in regard to the mid-century events in the zone, as well as a "solid contribution" to the field.

BIOGRAPHICAL AND CRITICAL SOURCES:

BOOKS

Major, John, *The Oppenheimer Hearing,* Stein and Day (New York, NY), 1971.

PERIODICALS

Choice, April, 1972, review of *The Oppenheimer Hearing,* p. 275.
Economist, October 23, 1971, review of *The Oppenheimer Hearing,* p. 67.
Historian, winter, 1995, Joseph A. Fry, review of *Prize Possession: The United States and the Panama Canal, 1903-1979,* pp. 391-392.
Journal of American History, March, 1995, Gustave Anguizola, review of *Prize Possession,* pp. 1778-1779.
Library Journal, September 15, 1993, Thomas H. Appleton, Jr., review of *Prize Possession,* p. 90.
Social Education, January, 1969, review of *The New Deal,* p. 123.
Times Literary Supplement, October 2, 1970, review of *The Contemporary World: A Historical Introduction,* p. 1146; October 19, 1971, "The Hubris of the Clever Man and the Revenge of the Fools," review of *The Oppenheimer Hearing,* p. 1446.*

* * *

MALIA, Martin (Edward) 1924-2004

OBITUARY NOTICE— See index for *CA* sketch: Born March 14, 1924, in Springfield, MA; died of pneumonia November 19, 2004, in Oakland, CA. Historian, educator, and author. An authority on the Soviet Union, Malia foresaw the collapse of the country's communist

government at a time when most of his colleagues believed the Soviet government could simply reform itself to adapt with the times. After serving in the U.S. Navy during World War II, he graduated from Yale University in 1944 with a degree in French; he then attended Harvard University, earning an M.A. in 1947 and a Ph.D. in 1951. Malia spent the early and mid-1950s teaching at Harvard before joining the University of California at Berkeley in 1958. He remained at Berkeley for the rest of his academic career, becoming a full professor of history in 1964 and retiring in 1991 as professor emeritus. Specializing in the history of Russian and Soviet affairs, Malia came to believe that the communist system was inconsistent with European history and sensibilities and therefore could not last. This was a contrary and minority opinion compared to the thinking of many contemporary historians, who especially felt that Mikhail Gorbachev's *perestroika* reforms of the 1980s demonstrated that the Communist Party was capable of adapting itself and, thus, surviving. Malia first gained wide attention for his ideas when he published an article in *Daedulus* in January 1990 under the pen name "Z." In the fall of that year, he admitted that he was the author and had used the pseudonym to protect his sources. Malia continued to explain his theories about Soviet communism in such important works as *The Soviet Tragedy: A History of Socialism in Russia, 1917-1991* (1994) and *Russia under Western Eyes: From the Bronze Horseman to the Lenin Mausoleum* (1999). Vindicated in his belief that communism in Russia would eventually collapse, he explained in his later years that historians needed to rework their thinking about the Soviet age in order to better understand it. At the time of his death, he had just sent his last article, "The Archives of Evil," to the *New Republic.*

OBITUARIES AND OTHER SOURCES:

PERIODICALS

New York Times, November 24, 2004, p. C15.
Washington Post, November 27, 2004, p. B4.

* * *

MANELLA, Raymond L(awrence) 1917-2004

OBITUARY NOTICE— See index for *CA* sketch: Born June 19, 1917; died of cancer November 27, 2004, in Reston, VA. Sociologist, social worker, educator, and author. Manella was a former manager at the Department of Health and Human Services who was an expert on juvenile crime and delinquency. He graduated from the University of Pittsburgh in 1938 and earned his master's degree in social work from Western Reserve University (now Case Western Reserve University) in 1939. After working as a probation and parole officer in Pittsburgh, he was director of juvenile state institutions in Maryland during the 1950s. In 1959 he joined the Department of Health and Human Services as a social worker who specialized in helping runaway youths; during this time he was also an associate professor of sociology at Loyola College and a consultant to the federal government. He retired from social work in 1987. Manella was the author of *Post-Institutional Services for Delinquent Youth* (1967) and *The Hard-Core Juvenile Offender* (1977), as well as the editor of several other books about juvenile delinquency.

OBITUARIES AND OTHER SOURCES:

PERIODICALS

Washington Post, December 4, 2004, p. B6.

*   *   *

MARCUS, James

PERSONAL: Male.

ADDRESSES: Agent—c/o Author Mail, New Press, 38 Greene St., New York, NY 10013.

CAREER: Writer and translator. *Amazon.com,* senior editor, 1996-2001.

WRITINGS:

(Translator) Goffredo Parise *Abecedary,* Marlboro Press (Marlboro, VT), 1990.
Amazonia: Five Years at the Epicenter of the Dot.com Juggernaut, New Press (New York, NY), 2004.
(Translator) Tullio Kezich and Alessandra Levantesi *Dino: The Life and Films of Dino di Laurentiis,* Miramax Books/Hyperion (New York, NY), 2004.

SIDELIGHTS: Writer James Marcus left the world of freelancing in 1996 to become employee number fifty-five of *Amazon.com,* hired by founder and future billionaire Jeff Bezos. His wife quit her job in Portland, Oregon, and they moved with their young son to Seattle, Washington to join the Internet startup, where Marcus remained until 2001. *Amazonia: Five Years at the Epicenter of the Dot.com Juggernaut* is his memoir of that period in his life.

The company was in its infancy, the first of the Internet bookstores, and Marcus churned out thousands of reviews and author interviews. The number of employees swelled to 8,000, and suddenly, everyone was an editor. Marcus was put in charge of the home page, and continued to write his reviews.

Marcus was caught up in the enthusiasm that propelled the young company, worked long hours, packed books in the warehouse during the holidays, and pitched in where needed, as all employees did to get the company off the ground. The company continued to operate at a huge loss, however, and the decision was made to cut back on content. Customer reviews replaced professional reviews, content was generated by data-mining programs, and Amazon became a very different company. In 2001, fifteen percent of the employees, Marcus among them, were laid off. As Catherine Taylor—arts editor at Amazon from 1998 to 2002—commented in the Manchester *Guardian,* Marcus's work "is wry, gently despairing, littered with philosophical musings and passages from Emerson, with a salient if quaint reminder that the earliest Internet pioneers were once part of utopian communities."

Jonathan Yardley noted in his review for the *Washington Post Book World* that "Marcus is right to say that 'as the Internet becomes more and more of a mainstream phenomenon, it's easy to forget just how much utopian baggage it used to carry.' The Internet has a 'transcendental capacity to shrink time and distance' and 'has ushered entire communities into being, and given a literal twist to the notion of kindred spirits,' and it was out of such notions that Amazon was born. Bezos seems to have had imperial designs right from the beginning, but there was also an idealism, even a naivete, to the company's origins."

Like other Amazon employees, Marcus had accepted stock options in lieu of a higher salary, and at the peak of the boom, his were worth $9 million. When the stock tumbled in 2000, it lost much of its value, leaving Marcus to cash out and move back to New York to resume his career as a freelance journalist. Amazon, which rebounded in 2002, acquired *Joyo.com* in 2004. *Joyo.com* is China's largest retailer, with a potential of eighty million customers. Amazon generated $16 million in sales in 1996, and their revenues in 2003 topped $5 billion.

San Francisco Chronicle reviewer David Kipen called Marcus's skills "the book critic's stock in trade: close reading, an ear-plugged trust in the pertinence of one's own responses, plus what he calls, referring to Amazon founder Jeff Bezos's fondness for high SAT scores, 'intellectual candlepower.'" Kipen added that *Amazonia* "brims with fascinating Amazoniana."

Elizabeth Corcoran wrote in the *Boston Globe* that Marcus "is a graceful writer with an eye for detail. This is not a kiss-and-tell story. He liked his colleagues, he liked the company. It is a reflective muse about life inside a tornado."

BIOGRAPHICAL AND CRITICAL SOURCES:

PERIODICALS

Booklist, June 1, 2004, David Siegfried, review of *Amazonia: Five Years at the Epicenter of the Dot. com Juggernaut*, p. 1680.
Boston Globe, June 27, 2004, Elizabeth Corcoran, review of *Amazonia*, p. E2.
Chicago Tribune, July 11, 2004, Henry Alford, review of *Amazonia*, p. 7.
Guardian (Manchester, England), October 2, 2004, Catherine Taylor, review of *Amazonia*, p. 11.
Kirkus Reviews, April 15, 2004, review of *Amazonia*, p. 378.
Library Journal, March 15, 2004, Kim Holston, review of *Dino: The Life and Films of Dino De Laurentiis*, p. 78; May 1, 2004, Carol J. Elsen, review of *Amazonia*, p. 122.
Publishers Weekly, October 26, 1990, Sybil Steinberg, review of *Abecedary*, p. 55; February 16, 2004, review of *Dino*, p. 166; April 5, 2004, Mark Rotella, review of *Amazonia*, p. 49.
San Francisco Chronicle, June 17, 2004, David Kipen, review of *Amazonia*, p. E14.
Washington Post Book World, July 4, 2004, Jonathan Yardley, review of *Amazonia*, p. T2.*

MASSIE, Sonja
(G. A. McKevett)

PERSONAL: Married. *Hobbies and other interests:* Traditional Irish music, Celtic bead needle art.

ADDRESSES: Home—Long Island, NY. *Agent*—c/o Richard Curtis Associates, 171 East 74th St., New York, NY 10021.

CAREER: Writer.

WRITINGS:

Legacy of the Wolf, Harlequin (New York, NY), 1987.
Moon Song, M. Evans (New York, NY), 1990.
Carousel, Pinnacle (New York, NY), 1990.
(With Meg Schneider) *What Every Girl Should Know about Boys,* Newfield Publications (Middletown, CT), 1992.
Far and Away (novelization), Berkeley (New York, NY), 1992.
Betrayal, Zebra (New York, NY), 1996.
The Dark Mirror, Zebra (New York, NY), 1996.
(With Martin H. Greenberg) *The Janet Dailey Companion: A Comprehensive Guide to Her Life and Her Novels,* HarperCollins (New York, NY), 1996.
A Friend in Need, Signal Hill (Syracuse, NY), 1997.
Irish Pride: 101 Reasons to Be Proud You're Irish, Carol Publishing Group (Secaucus, NJ), 1999.
The Complete Idiot's Guide to Irish History and Culture, Alpha Books (New York City), 1999.
Daughter of Ireland, Jove (New York, NY), 2000.

Also author of ebook *Dream Carver,* published by ereads.com.

"SAVANNAH REID MYSTERY" SERIES; UNDER PSEUDONYM G. A. MCKEVETT

Just Desserts, Kensington (New York, NY), 1995.
Bitter Sweets, Kensington (New York, NY), 1996.
Killer Calories, Kensington (New York, NY), 1997.
Cooked Goose, Kensington (New York, NY), 1998.
Sugar and Spite, Kensington (New York, NY), 2000.
Sour Grapes, Kensington (New York, NY), 2001.

Peaches and Screams, Kensington (New York, NY), 2002.

Death by Chocolate, Kensington (New York, NY), 2003.

Cereal Killer, Kensington (New York, NY), 2004.

SIDELIGHTS: Sonja Massie, writing as G. A. McKevett, has carved out a niche for herself in the mystery book market with a series of novels about Savannah Reid, a female detective described by GraceAnne A. DeCandido in a *Booklist* review of *Cooked Goose* as a "fortyist, comfortably sized single southern gal," whose craving for fairness is matched only by her love of fatty foods. Set in southern California, the stories unfold in a spirited spree of mishaps and adventures. Savannah Reid, as her name implies, hails from Georgia, and her sleuthing style belies her southern belle upbringing. "Food-loving, witty and down-to-earth," stated a *Publishers Weekly* contributor in a review of *Sour Grapes,* "Reid is no typical fey Southern belle." She is "armed with a passion for food and oozing steel-magnolia charm," DeCandido declared in a *Booklist* assessment of *Sugar and Spite.*

Just Desserts, the first Savannah Reid novel, tells the story of the murder of Jonathan Winston, the husband of a prominent city councilwoman in San Carmelita, California. What Reid does not realize when she takes the case is that Beverly Winston, the dead man's wife, is having an affair with the police chief. Instead of aiding the investigation, Beverly and her boyfriend try to thwart it by withholding a key piece of evidence. As she moves closer to the truth, Reid is fired from the police force, allegedly for being thirty pounds overweight. Despite the sometimes overly slick characterizations, *Library Journal* reviewer Rex E. Klett felt that the "infectious heroine and self-deprecating humor" rescue the story from boredom. According to *Publishers Weekly* contributor Sybil S. Steinberg, however, *Just Desserts* lacks credibility as the characters simply "careen from one implausible situation to the next." On the other hand, a *Kirkus Reviews* writer praised "McKevett's clean, unpretentious style" and added that "her sweet-toothed heroine could strike a chord among readers."

Bitter Sweets, the second installment of the Savannah Reid series, finds Reid—no longer with the police force—working as a private eye through the Moonlight Magnolia Detective Agency, sometimes with the assistance of her former partner Dirk Coulter. The novel features the hunt for Lisa O'Donnell Mallock, a woman who disappears soon after divorcing her abusive husband, Earl. Separated from his sister since childhood, Brian O'Donnell has been searching for Lisa for several years on his own; he loses her trail in San Carmelita and hires Reid to find her. Lisa soon turns up dead and her daughter Christy goes missing. Just when Earl seems the likely suspect, he becomes the killer's next target. Critics praised *Bitter Sweets* for its lighthearted, fun tone. In contrast to her assessment of *Just Desserts,* Steinberg called this book "a light, satisfying tale." Klett deemed the volume "fun reading" in *Library Journal,* while in *Kirkus Reviews* a critic described it as "a double portion of food, fashion, and full-figured fun."

Likewise, *Killer Calories* presents Savannah eating and sleuthing with great aplomb. Kat Valentina, a disco-era starlet, dies mysteriously at a local health club, and Reid goes undercover to find the killer. To maintain her camouflage, Reid must curb her own appetite as she investigates the characters at the spa. Steinberg, reviewing the book for *Publishers Weekly,* called this contribution to the mystery series a "predictable but entertaining tale." And Klett, reviewing the volume for *Library Journal,* described the story as "a real treat."

In *Cooked Goose,* Reid has to deal with a Yuletide rapist terrorizing a San Carmelita shopping mall. The man, who has disguised himself as Santa using a false white beard, has attacked a number of women in the mall's parking lot. Unfortunately, the first man Reid targets as a potential rapist and "disables with a hard kick to the ornaments," explained a *Publishers Weekly* contributor, turns out to be a legitimate (and innocent) mall Santa. The credibility of Reid's investigation suffers as a result. Eventually she is reduced to the role of babysitter/bodyguard for the daughter of the same police chief who fired her in *Just Desserts,* but in the end she helps bring the criminal to justice.

Peaches and Screams returns Reid to her home state of Georgia to attend her sister's wedding. When a local judge is found shot to death and Reid's youngest brother is fingered for the crime, the private investigator is sucked into still another investigation. "Before standing up with her sister," remarked a *Publishers Weekly* contributor, "Savannah must stand by her brother and clear his name." A *Kirkus Reviews* writer called the volume "a whodunit as old-fashioned and satisfying as one of Granny Reid's bacon-egg-and-grits breakfasts." The author, according to the *Publishers Weekly* reviewer, "delivers a surprise ending with panache."

With *Death by Chocolate* Reid enters into a new contract: to protect chef and grand dame Eleanor Maxwell (the reigning "Queen of Chocolate" of television's Gourmet Network) from someone who has been sending her threatening mail. Lady Eleanor, however, soon collapses after ingesting chocolate during a taping of her own show, leaving her bodyguard to deal with dysfunctional family members and other consequences of her notoriously short temper. "The unexpected arrival of Savannah's sister Cordele . . . tests everyone's patience," noted a *Publishers Weekly* reviewer, "including the reader's." Still, as a *Kirkus Reviews* contributor concluded, while "McKevett's recipe may be tried and true, . . . it still delivers the goods with zest."

Massie has also written numerous works under her own name, including romance novels such as *Betrayal* and *Daughter of Ireland* and nonfiction books including *The Complete Idiot's Guide to Irish History and Culture.*

BIOGRAPHICAL AND CRITICAL SOURCES:

PERIODICALS

Booklist, December 1, 1998, GraceAnne A. DeCandido, review of *Cooked Goose,* p. 654; November 1, 1999, GraceAnne A. DeCandido, review of *Sugar and Spite,* p. 512.

Kirkus Reviews, April 1, 1995, review of *Just Desserts,* p. 429; April 15, 1996, review of *Bitter Sweets,* p. 566; April 1, 1997, review of *Killer Calories,* p. 133; October 15, 2001, review of *Peaches and Screams,* p. 1457; November 15, 2002, review of *Death by Chocolate,* p. 1659.

Library Journal, April 1, 1995, Rex E. Klett, review of *Just Desserts;,* p. 128; May 1, 1996, Rex E. Klett, review of *Bitter Sweets,* p. 136; April 1, 1997, Rex E. Klett, review of *Killer Calories,* p. 133; January, 2000, Rex E. Klett, review of *Sugar and Spite,* p. 167; December, 2001, Rex E.

Klett, review of *Peaches and Screams,* p. 180; January, 2003, Rex E. Klett, review of *Death by Chocolate,* p. 163.

Publishers Weekly, April 3, 1995, Sybil S. Steinberg, review of *Just Desserts,* p. 49; April 22, 1996, Sybil S. Steinberg, review of *Bitter Sweets,* p. 62; February 24, 1997, Sybil S. Steinberg, review of *Killer Calories,* p. 66; November 2, 1998, review of *Cooked Goose,* p. 74; December 11, 2000, review of *Sour Grapes,* p. 66; December 17, 2001, review of *Peaches and Screams,* p. 66; December 9, 2002, review of *Death by Chocolate,* p. 65; December 8, 2003, review of *Cereal Killer,* p. 50.

ONLINE

Romantic Times Online, http://www.romantictimes.com/data/books/ (August 12, 2004), reviews of *Betrayal, Daughter of Ireland, Cereal Killer, Death by Chocolate, Peaches and Screams,* and *Sour Grapes.**

* * *

MAUER, Marc

PERSONAL: Male. *Education:* State University of New York, Stony Brook, B.A.; University of Michigan, M.S. (social work).

ADDRESSES: Office—The Sentencing Project, 514 Tenth St. NW, Suite 1000, Washington, DC 20004. *E-mail*—mauer@sentencingproject.org

CAREER: Author and activist. Sentencing Project, Washington, DC, assistant director, 1987—. Consultant to Bureau of Justice Assistance, National Institute of Corrections, and American Bar Association.

AWARDS, HONORS: Helen L. Buttenweiser award, Fortune Society, 1991; Donald Cressey award, National Council on Crime and Delinquency, 1996.

WRITINGS:

(With Arthur Boyd) *Bail Out: The Community Bail Fund Organizing Manual,* American Friends Service Committee (Ann Arbor, MI), 1980.

(With others) *The Race to Incarcerate,* New Press (New York, NY), 1999.

(Editor, with Meda Chesney-Lind) *Invisible Punishment: The Collateral Consequences of Mass-Imprisonment,* New Press (New York, NY), 2002.

Author of reports for Sentencing Project, including (with Jenni Gainsborough) *Diminishing Returns: Crime and Incarceration in the 1990s,* 1990; *Young Black Men and the Criminal Justice System: A Growing National Problem,* 1990; *Americans behind Bars: A Comparison of International Rates of Incarceration,* 1991; (with Cathy Shine) *Does the Punishment Fit the Crime? Drug Users and Drunk Drivers: Questions of Race and Class,* 1993; *Americans behind Bars: The International Use of Incarceration, 1992-1993,* 1994; (with Tracy Huling) *Young Black Men and the Criminal Justice System: Five Years Later,* 1995; and (with Cathy Potler and Richard Wolf) *Gender and Justice: Women, Drugs, and Sentencing Policy,* 1999. Contributor to *Behind the Razor Wire: Portrait of a Contemporary American Prison System,* edited by Michael Jacobson-Hardy, New York University Press (New York, NY), 1999.

SIDELIGHTS: Described by a *Publishers Weekly* contributor as among the "few voices in the media decrying the explosive increase in the U.S. prison population," long-time activist Marc Mauer is the assistant director of the Washington, D.C.-based Sentencing Project, an organization founded in 1986 that promotes reforms in the U.S. criminal justice system and works to find alternatives to incarceration. In addition to authoring reports for the Sentencing Project and appearing as an advocate for judicial reform at hearings, Mauer has authored a number of books designed to alert the general public about the racial, economic, and other inequities inherent in sentencing guidelines in the U.S. criminal justice system.

His 1999 work *The Race to Incarcerate* cites a series of statistics, among them that U.S. courts imprison people up to ten times more than other industrialized nations, that in 1995 half of U.S. prison inmates were black, and that at the time of the book's publication it cost U.S. taxpayers 109 million dollars per day to run the nation's prisons. In his concluding chapter, Mauer argues for a change in the "prison as a deterrent" approach to crime, noting: "Most of us refrain from committing crimes each day not out of fear of a prison

sentence but because we have better things to do with our lives." Marshaling "three decades worth of statistical evidence, program evaluations and governmental research," as Colman McCarthy explained in his review of *The Race to Incarcerate* for the *Washington Post Book World,* Mauer "presents evidence that reformers who were once dismissed as being 'soft on crime' turn out to have been sensible on crime." Praising the book as "meticulously researched," a *Kirkus* reviewer added that Mauer presents readers with a "sobering, crucial voice amid the obfuscatory, insensate 'tough-on-crime' din."

In *Invisible Punishment: The Collateral Consequences of Mass Imprisonment* Mauer and coeditor Meda Chesney-Lind collect sixteen essays by noted sociologists, criminologists, scholars, and journalists from throughout the United States. The editors preface the collection—which includes the essays "Black Economic Progress in the Ear of Mass Imprisonment" and "Entrepreneurial Corrections: Incarceration as a Business"—by noting that almost one fourth of the adult population of the United States can boast a criminal record, a surprising number of them members of racial or ethnic minorities. Looking back over the "get tough on crime" policies established by local, state, and federal authorities during the mid-1970s and into the 1990s as the United States waged its war on drugs, contributors examine the consequences of such policies in essays that *Counterpunch* contributor Elaine Cassel termed "thoughtful." *Invisible Punishment* "exposes the hidden, repugnant retribution policies of the American criminal justice . . . system," added Cassel. "It leaves the reader to judge whether the policies were well-intentioned . . . efforts to deal with crime, or deliberate acts of a vengeful society."

BIOGRAPHICAL AND CRITICAL SOURCES:

BOOKS

Mauer, Marc, and others, *The Race to Incarcerate,* New Press (New York, NY), 1999.

PERIODICALS

Contemporary Sociology, May, 2001, Jill McCorkel, review of *The Race to Incarcerate,* pp. 294-295.

Kirkus Reviews, July 15, 1999, review of *The Race to Incarcerate,* p. 1109.

Publishers Weekly, July 12, 1999, review of *The Race to Incarcerate,* p. 87; October 28, 2002, review of *Invisible Punishment: The Collateral Consequences of Mass Imprisonment,* p. 64.

Washington Post Book World, January 16, 2000, Colman McCarthy, review of *The Race to Incarcerate,* p. 13.

ONLINE

Counterpunch Web site, http://www.counterpunch.org/ (January 13, 2003), Elaine Cassel, review of *Invisible Punishment.*

*   *   *

MCKEVETT, G. A.
See MASSIE, Sonja

*   *   *

McLAUGHLIN, Martin L.

PERSONAL: Male.

ADDRESSES: Office—Magdalen College, Oxford University, Oxford OX1 4AU, England. *E-mail*—martin.mclaughlin@magd.ox.ac.uk.

CAREER: Madgalen College, Oxford, Oxford, England, Fiat-Serena Professor of Italian Studies.

WRITINGS:

(Editor, with R. D. S. Jack and C. Whyte) *Leopardi: A Scottis Quair,* University of Edinburgh Press (Edinburgh, Scotland), 1987.

Literary Imitation in the Italian Renaissance: The Theory and Practice of Literary Imitation in Italy from Dante to Bembo, Oxford University Press (New York, NY), 1995.

Italo Calvino (biography), Edinburgh University Press (Edinburgh, Scotland), 1998.

(Editor) Italo Calvino, *The Path to the Spiders' Nests,* revised edition, translated by Archibald Colquhoun, Ecco Press (Hopewell, NJ), 1998.

(Translator) Italo Calvino, *Why Read the Classics?,* Pantheon Books (New York, NY), 1999.

(Editor) *Britain and Italy From Romanticism to Modernism: A Festschrift for Peter Brand,* Modern Humanities Research Association (Oxford, England), 2000.

(Translator) Italo Calvino, *Hermit in Paris: Autobiographical Writings,* Pantheon Books (New York, NY), 2003.

(Translator) Sergio Ghione, *Turtle Island: A Journey to Britain's Oddest Colony,* St. Martin's Press (New York, NY), 2003.

(Translator) Umberto Eco, *On Literature,* Harcourt (New York, NY), 2004.

Contributor to books, including *Mapping Lives: The Uses of Biography,* British Academy, 2002.

SIDELIGHTS: British educator, author, and translator Martin McLaughlin specializes in the Italian language, the literature of the Italian Renaissance from Petrarch to Tasso; Dante; contemporary Italian fiction, especially the work of Italo Calvino; and translation studies. He has translated a number of volumes from Italian into English, particularly the writings of Calvino, as well as serving as author or editor of several other books.

With *Literary Imitation in the Italian Renaissance: The Theory and Practice of Literary Imitation in Italy from Dante to Bembo* McLaughlin presents a comprehensive survey of the role of imitation in the literature of the Italian Renaissance, examining both its theory and its practice and including both works written in Latin and those in the vernacular. The book covers numerous authors, including an overview of scholarly opinions, as well as McLaughlin's own critical analysis. Brian Vickers, writing for the *Modern Language Review,* found the book too abbreviated, and called for a sequel in order that some of the presented theories could be expanded into a later time period In general, the critic felt, "McLaughlin's analyses are mostly convincing, he has mastered a wide literature, primary and secondary, and has made exemplary use of manuscript sources. . . . No one interested in Renaissance literature and its involvement with the past should ignore this scholarly and critically alert study." In a review for *Renaissance Quarterly,* G. W. Pigman III wrote, "McLaughlin has produced a masterful synthesis, judicious, light of touch, and deft at selecting cogent examples from an extraordinary amount of material. . . . He is particularly good at sketching an author's stylistic development." Pigman went on to comment that "McLaughlin has written an extraordinary book, and it should become the standard work on its subject."

McLaughlin's interest in the works of Italo Calvino has led to his serving as translator for a number of books by the author, including *Hermit in Paris: Autobiographical Writings,* for which McLaughlin was the first English translator. The book covers three decades of Calvino's personal work, and is made up of twelve pieces, including a series of letters the Italian novelist wrote to his publisher while touring the United States at the end of the 1950s. The result, according to Pedro Ponce in the *Review of Contemporary Fiction,* is that "Calvino is revealed in a less whimsical light . . . an ambivalent man, struggling to engage with the world." A contributor to *Contemporary Review* commented that the writings "give us a unique insight into the Italian novelist and . . . to Italian history of the twentieth century."

Another translation of the works of Calvino, *Why Read the Classics?,* examines a series of respected books from the author's viewpoint and includes a number of his essays on theory. *American Scholar* critic Rachel Hadas quoted McLaughlin as saying that *Why Read the Classics?* "as a whole . . . offers a . . . view into the everyday workshop of a great creative writer: what Calvino read was often metamorphosed creatively, intertextually into what Calvino wrote." Hadas praised McLaughlin's choices for the volume, noting that "the recovery of such work from the twilight of out-of-printdom or the anarchy of cyberspace is an exemplary act of recycling." *Times Literary Supplement* reviewer Anna Laura Leschy, commenting on both *Why Read the Classics?* and *Italo Calvino,* averred that "McLaughlin is to be commended for putting these critical riches at the disposal of English readers."

In addition to his writings and translations, McLaughlin edited *Britain and Italy from Romanticism to Modernism: A Festschrift for Peter Brand,* and authored the book's introduction. The volume serves as a sort of continuation to Brand's *Italy and the English*

Romantics, picking up where the writer left off in the mid-nineteenth century and continuing into the early twentieth century. Carmine G. Di Biase, in a review for *Italica,* called the work a "rich and varied collection of essays." Nine pieces follow McLaughlin's introduction, and they cover such topics as art, literature, politics, and history. Contributions include "Performance of Italian Opera in Early Victorian England" by David Kimbell, and "Ruskin, Italy, and the Past" by Hilary Fraser, along with essays on Dante, Italian nationalism versus Welsh liberalism, and the British support of Italian unification.

BIOGRAPHICAL AND CRITICAL SOURCES:

PERIODICALS

American Scholar, autumn, 1999, Rachel Hadas, review of *Why Read the Classics?,* p. 137.
Biography, summer, 2003, Michael Meshaw, review of *Hermit in Paris: Autobiographical Writings,* p. 519.
Choice, December, 1996, C. Fantazzi, review of *Literary Imitation in the Italian Renaissance: The Theory and Practice of Literary Imitation in Italy from Dante to Bembo,* p. 620.
Contemporary Review, April, 2003, review of *Hermit in Paris,* p. 256.
Italica, winter, 2002, Carmine G. Di Biase, review of *Britain and Italy from Romanticism to Modernism: A Festschrift for Peter Brand,* pp. 568-572.
Modern Language Review, July, 1998, Brian Vickers, review of *Literary Imitation in the Italian Renaissance,* pp. 850-852.
Publishers Weekly, November 3, 2003, review of *Turtle Island: A Journey to the World's Oddest Colony,* p. 68.
Renaissance Quarterly, winter, 1998, G. W. Pigman III, review of *Literary Imitation in the Italian Renaissance,* pp. 1354-1355.
Review of Contemporary Fiction, summer, 2003, Pedro Ponce, review of *Hermit in Paris,* p. 155.
Times Literary Supplement, October 15, 1999, Anna Laura Lepschy, "Brief Intimacies."
Washington Post Book World, September 26, 1999, Michael Dirda, review of *Why Read the Classics?,* p. 15.

ONLINE

Oxford University Faculty of Medieval and Modern Languages Web site, http://faculty.mml.ox.ac.uk/ (November 11, 2004), "Martin McLaughlin."

McNALL, Bruce 1950-

PERSONAL: Born 1950; married Jane Cody; children: Katie, Bruce. *Education:* University of California— Los Angeles, bachelor's degree and doctoral program studies.

ADDRESSES: Home—Malibu Beach, CA. *Agent*—c/o Author Mail, Hyperion Books, 77 West 66th St., 11th Floor, New York, NY 10023.

CAREER: Movie financier, former sports team owner and dealer in antique coins. Numismatic Fine Arts Inc., Los Angeles, CA, founder and chair of board; Summa Stable, Inc., owner and chair of board; Dallas Mavericks (National Basketball Association team), Dallas, TX, former partner; Los Angeles Kings (National Hockey League team), Inglewood, CA, co-owner, 1986-87 and 1994—, sole owner, 1988-94; Toronto Argonauts (Canadian Football League team), Toronto, Ontario, Canada, owner, 1991—; former chair of board of governors of National Hockey League.

AWARDS, HONORS: Regents fellowship, University of California, c. 1971; named Owner of the Year, National Hockey League, 1987.

WRITINGS:

(With Michael D'Antonio) *Fun While It Lasted: My Rise and Fall in the Land of Fame and Fortune,* Hyperion (New York, NY), 2003.

SIDELIGHTS: Bruce McNall first became famous as a dealer in antique coins, a career he began as a high school student. At the University of California, Los Angeles, McNall studied Roman history but continued to deal in coins. Through his professors he met media moguls who wanted him to help them deal in coins themselves, and McNall made a small fortune giving them advice. He used this money first to open his own rare coin store, Numismatic Fine Arts, and then to buy racehorses and sports teams. He made headlines across North America when he lured hockey superstar Wayne Gretzky away from the Edmonton Oilers to his own Los Angeles Kings. In 1994 it was revealed that much of McNall's sports empire had been paid for through fraud, and in 1997 he was sentenced to seventy months in prison.

Fun While It Lasted: My Rise and Fall in the Land of Fame and Fortune chronicles these events, as well as McNall's prison term and his life immediately after he was released in 2001. The book "offers lots of name-dropping of sports and entertainment figures and a very breezy writing style," Patrick J. Brunet wrote in *Library Journal,* "which make it a very good read." *Booklist* reviewer Vanessa Bush particularly recommended the book "for readers who enjoy insider tales of financial skullduggery."

BIOGRAPHICAL AND CRITICAL SOURCES:

PERIODICALS

Booklist, July, 2003, Vanessa Bush, review of *Fun While It Lasted: My Rise and Fall in the Land of Fame and Fortune,* p. 1852.

Business Week, August 29, 1988, Patrick E. Cole, "The Man Who Paid a Kings' Ransom for Gretsky," p. 80.

Daily News (Los Angeles, CA), January 10, 1997, Bill Schlotter and Janet Gilmore, "Ex-Kings Owner Gets Seventy Months," p. N3.

Dallas Morning News, October 5, 2003, Anuradha Raghunathan, review of *Fun While It Lasted,* p. D5.

Globe and Mail (Toronto, Ontario, Canada), July 26, 2003, Charles Foran, review of *Fun While It Lasted,* p. D4.

Hockey News, December, 2000, Helene Elliott, "McNall Seeks Halfway House in 2001 in Bid for Freedom," p. 13; August 26, 2003, Rudy Mezzetta, review of *Fun While It Lasted,* p. 7.

Kirkus Reviews, May 1, 2003, review of *Fun While It Lasted,* p. 661.

Library Journal, June 15, 2003, Patrick J. Brunet, review of *Fun While It Lasted,* p. 81.

Maclean's, May 6, 1991, Brenda Dalglish, "Antiques and Athletes: Bruce McNall Has Always Taken Big Risks," p. 45.

New York Times, July 8, 2003, Rick Lyman, "The Rise, the Fall, and Now a New Day" (interview), p. E1.

Publishers Weekly, May 19, 2003, review of *Fun While It Lasted,* p. 61.

Sports Illustrated, May 13, 1991, Richard Hoffer, "The Collector: Bruce McNall Is an Acquisitive Owner Whose Tastes Run from Antiquities to the Priciest Athletes," pp. 82-90.

U.S. News and World Report, May 6, 1991, Tom Callahan, "A Savvy Collector of Passions," p. 67.

Vanity Fair, April, 1994, Bryan Burrough, interview with McNall, p. 72.

ONLINE

CNN.com, http://www.cnn.com/ (June 6, 2003), transcript of interview with McNall.

ESPN.com, http://www.espn.com/ (March 7, 2001), Greg Garber, "Four Years of Club Fed Anything but Relaxing for McNall."

Slam! Sports, http://www.canoe.ca/ (June 15, 2004), Al Strachan, "The Last Word: Former Los Angeles Kings Owner Bruce McNall Knew Who His True Friends Were during His Stay in Prison, and He Had to Look No Further than Wayne Gretzky", Mike Ulmer, "The Last Word: Former Los Angeles Kings and Toronto Argonauts Owner Bruce Mc-Nall Struggles with Reality. But His Legacy in the NHL Continues to Live On."

TSN Online, http://tsn.tsnmax.ca/ (June 15, 2004), Reed Holmes, "He's out of Jail, but He Can't Take a Phone Call."*

* * *

McNAUGHTON, Deborah (L.) 1950-

PERSONAL: Born November 17, 1950, in Hollywood, CA; daughter of Victor (owner of a grocery store) and Pauline Patricia (a homemaker; maiden name, Lincoln) Damus; married Hal McNaughton (a financial advisor), September 19, 1970; children: Tiffany McNaughton Milby, Christy McNaughton Ferguson, Mindy McNaughton Weinstein. *Ethnicity:* "Caucasian." *Education:* Attended Pasadena College. *Politics:* Republican. *Religion:* Protestant.

ADDRESSES: Office—Professional Credit Counselors, Inc., 417 Associated Rd., Suite A102, Brea, CA 92821. *Agent*—Chip MacGregor, Alive Communications, 7680 Goddard St., Suite 200, Colorado Springs, CO 80920. *E-mail*—tcmdeb@aol.com.

CAREER: Professional Credit Counselors, Inc., Brea, CA, owner and president, 1984—.

WRITINGS:

(With John F. Avanzini) *Christian Credit Repair,* Volume 4: *Have a Good Report,* H I S Publishing, 1991.

Everything You Need to Know about Credit, Thomas Nelson Publishing (Nashville, TN), 1993.

The Insider's Guide to Managing Your Credit: How to Establish, Maintain, Repair, and Protect Your Credit, Dearborn Financial Publishing (Chicago, IL), 1998.

All about Credit: Questions (and Answers) about the Most Common Credit Problems, Dearborn Financial Publishing (Chicago, IL), 1999.

Financially Secure: An Easy-to-Follow Money Program for Women, Thomas Nelson Publishing (Nashville, TN), 2001.

Destroy Your Debt! Your Guide to Total Financial Freedom: Strategies for Personal and Entrepreneurial Debt Elimination, Archer-Ellison Publishing (College Station, TX), 2001.

Yes You Can!, Archer-Ellison, (Winter Park, FL) 2001.

The Get out of Debt Kit: Your Roadmap to Total Financial Freedom, Dearborn Financial Publishing (Chicago, IL), 2002.

WORK IN PROGRESS: Ms. Entrepreneur.

SIDELIGHTS: Deborah McNaughton told *CA:* "My desire is to educate and encourage individuals to better themselves financially. I began writing books on credit and finances after personally experiencing and overcoming a financial crisis. Helping people develop a financial plan through challenging times is my goal. My motto is faith, hope, and a plan!"

BIOGRAPHICAL AND CRITICAL SOURCES:

ONLINE

FinancialVictory.com, http://www.financialvictory.com/ (August 29, 2004).

* * *

MEAD, Walter Russell 1952-

PERSONAL: Born June 12, 1952, in Columbia, SC. *Education:* Yale University, B.A., 1976.

ADDRESSES: Office—Council on Foreign Relations, Harold Pratt House, 58 East 68th St., New York, NY 10021.

CAREER: Author, editor, and foreign policy fellow. Worked various jobs, including editing a labor union newspaper; Cumomo Commission on Competitiveness and Trade, New York, NY, chief writer, 1987-88; *Harper's,* New York, NY, contributing editor, 1986-91; *Los Angeles Times,* Los Angeles, CA, contributing editor, 1991; *Worth,* New York, NY, contributing editor, 1993-96, senior contributing editor, 1996; World Policy Institute, New School University, New York, NY, president's fellow, 1994-97; senior fellow in U.S. foreign policy for the Council on Foreign Relations; 1997—.

MEMBER: New American Foundation (member of board of directors).

AWARDS, HONORS: Lionel Gelber Prize, 2002, for *Special Providence: American Foreign Policy and How It Changed the World;* New York University Olive Branch award, 1993.

WRITINGS:

Mortal Splendor: The American Empire in Transition, Houghton Mifflin (Boston, MA), 1987.
Special Providence: American Foreign Policy and How It Changed the World, Knopf (New York, NY), 2001.
(Editor, with Sherle R. Schwenninger) *The Bridge to a Global Middle Class: Development, Trade, and International Finance,* Kluwer Academic Publishers (Boston, MA), 2003.
Power, Terror, Peace, and War: America's Grand Strategy in a World at Risk, Knopf (New York, NY), 2004.

Contributor to periodicals, including *Esquire, Worth, New York Times, International Herald Tribune, Wall Street Journal,* and *New Yorker.*

SIDELIGHTS: Walter Russell Mead, a senior fellow for the Council on Foreign Relations, is an expert on U.S. foreign policy. He was born in South Carolina, but due to his father's position as an Episcopal minister, he moved frequently throughout the South as he was growing up. At age thirteen, he won a scholarship to attend a college preparatory school in Massachusetts and later attended Yale University, where he

studied literature. His early interests in foreign policy stemmed from growing up during the Vietnam era, but that same exposure caused him to turn away from the subject during his youth. Only after several years of working temporary jobs and in low-end positions did he return to politics and policy. Mead has since become an expert on foreign relations and international political economy.

In *Mortal Splendor: The American Empire in Transition,* Mead examines contemporary American political and economic mythologies, addressing the development of society and the nation's psyche. *Washington Monthly* contributor Michael D. Mosettig called the book "maddeningly uneven," and noted that it is "far longer on analysis than prescription." However, Ronald Steel, in a review for *New Republic,* called the book "an inquiry of considerable originality and daring that cuts across the usual categories. For [Mead] empire is both a condition and a metaphor, and the way in which he plays one against the other is what gives this book its special strength." Steel went on to call the book "sometimes exasperating, usually irreverent, and almost continually thought-provoking," and concluded that "even if one cannot quite share Mead's indignation about the evils of our empire, his intensity of feeling gives this book a special thrust . . . a study of culture and history as well as of economics, *Mortal Splendor* is that rarest of things, a work of political imagination."

Special Providence: American Foreign Policy and How It Changed the World is based on Mead's belief that in order to understand current foreign policy one must understand its foundations. The book addresses four ways of examining foreign policy that, he states, date back to the nation's founding fathers. *American Prospect* contributor David M. Kennedy observed that "Mead makes a heroic effort to comprehend the entirety of Americans diplomatic past in a complex structure composed of four 'schools' of foreign policy. The interplay among these schools, he claims, is what makes American foreign policy both distinctive and successful." Kennedy went on to note that the author "never clearly explains the precise dynamics of the relationships among his schools that supposedly have generated that 'unique style.' He relies instead on the metaphor of a kaleidoscope, in which his various schools perpetually reassemble themselves in random patterns." However, James P. Rubin, in *New Republic,* commented that "Mead's framework for the analysis of foreign policy strikes me as at least conceptually adequate. The schools that he portrays do represent the competing currents that a policy-maker in Washington faces today. His framework is certainly more precise than the old categories of hawk and dove, left and right, internationalist and isolationist, unilateralist and multilateralist." *National Review* critic Arnold Beichman called Mead's book a "highly readable history and analysis of American foreign policy" that "offers an answer to a question that was never more pertinent: How has the United States, 'with a notoriously erratic and undisciplined foreign policy process, [implemented] foreign policies that have consistently advanced the country toward greater power and wealth than any other power in the history of the world'?" He pointed out, however, that because the volume was printed shortly after the events of September 11, 2001,it became obsolete almost instantly, something a reader should take into account. A contributor to the *Economist* found the book to be "a highly intelligent analysis of America's foreign policy, which is full of common sense and learning, and is clear and readable to boot."

Power, Terror, Peace, and War: America's Grand Strategy in a World at Risk looks at American foreign policy in the light of the many changes occurring during the last decades of the twentieth century, from the loss of the Soviet Union as a rival superpower to the war in Iraq. Mead examines how familiar policy strategies have become less effective due to an altered world economy and proposes what steps might be taken to improve policy in the future. A contributor to *Publishers Weekly* remarked that the work "demonstrates the value and difficult of analyzing the 'architecture of America's world policy' from such heights of abstraction before hindsight has clarified what is historically determined and what is contingent." Harvey Sicherman, reviewing *Power, Terror, Peace, and War* for *National Interest*, stated that "Mead writes brilliantly about the French pratfalls on the eve of the Iraq War, and Franco-German relations," and went on to conclude that, "overall, Mead's book is an interesting try."

BIOGRAPHICAL AND CRITICAL SOURCES:

PERIODICALS

American Prospect, March 25, 2002, David M. Kennedy, review of *Special Providence: American Foreign Policy and How It Changed the World,* pp. 34-36.

Atlantic Monthly, January, 2002, James Fallows, "Councils of War: Every American War Has Changed Our Society in Ways That Were Not Anticipated," p. 23.

Booklist, November 15, 2001, Mary Carroll, review of *Special Providence,* p. 528; May 15, 2004, Brendan Driscoll, review of *Power, Terror, Peace, and War: America's Grand Strategy in a World at Risk,* p. 1583.

Economist, November 17, 2001, "Four Threads, One Mighty Rope," review of *Special Providence.*

Journal of American History, June, 1988, James Oliver Robertson, review of *Mortal Splendor: The American Empire in Transition,* p. 322.

Kirkus Reviews, September 15, 2001, review of *Special Providence,* p. 1341; March 1, 2004, review of *Power Terror, Peace, and War,* p. 212.

Library Journal, November 1, 2001, James R. Holmes, review of *Special Providence,* p. 110.

National Interest, winter, 2001, H. W. Brands, "The Four Schoolmasters," review of *Special Providence,* p. 143; summer, 2004, Harvey Sicherman, "Where Have All the Cowboys Gone?," review of *Power, Terror, Peace, and War,* p. 163.

National Review, January 28, 2002, Arnold Beichman, "Providence Abroad," p. 56.

New Republic, January 4, 1998, Ronald Steel, review of *Mortal Splendor,* p. 32; March 18, 2002, James P. Rubin, "Santayana Syndrome," review of *Special Providence,* p. 29.

Publishers Weekly, October 22, 2001, review of *Special Providence,* p. 63; April 5, 2004, review of *Power, Terror, Peace, and War,* p. 57.

Washington Monthly, June, 1987, Michael D. Mosettig, review of *Mortal Splendor,* p. 60.

Wilson Quarterly, winter, 2002, Jonathan Rosenberg, review of *Special Providence,* p. 122.

ONLINE

Council on Foreign Relations Web site, http://www.cfr.org/ (November 12, 2004), "Walter Russell Mead."

Foreign Affairs Online, http://www.foreignaffairs.org/ (November 12, 2004), "Walter Russell Mead."

Globalist Web site, http://www.theglobalist.com/ (November 12, 2004), "Walter Russell Mead."

University of California—Berkeley Web site, http://globetrotter.berkeley.edu/ (November 12, 2004), "Walter Russell Mead."

U.S. Embassy Distinguished American Speakers Web site, http://www.usembassy-israel.org/ (November 12, 2004), "Walter Russell Mead."*

MEBUS, Scott 1974-

PERSONAL: Born November 28, 1974. *Education:* Attended Wesleyan University.

ADDRESSES: Home—New York, NY. *Agent*—David Dunton, Harvey Klinger Inc., 301 West 53rd St., New York, NY 10019.

CAREER: Television producer, music producer, editor, novelist, playwright, and composer. Producer for Music Television (MTV) and Video Hits One (VH1), New York, NY. Has also performed as a stand-up comedian. Member of BAD SAM sketch comedy performance group.

WRITINGS:

Booty Nomad (novel), Miramax Books (New York, NY), 2003.

Author and producer of rock musical *Tarnish,* performed at International Fringe Festival. Author of plays and writer for television commercials. Composer of musical scores for television programs.

SIDELIGHTS: Scott Mebus is a writer, television producer, music producer, and stand-up comedian who lives in New York. Mebus published his debut novel, *Booty Nomad,* in 2003. He also wrote and produced the rock musical *Tarnish* in the late 1990s that was staged at the International Fringe Festival. As a producer for MTV and VH1, Mebus has worked on projects such as *The Tom Green Show* and *The Real World.* He has also composed musical scores for MTV, VH1, and the Discovery Channel.

Mebus's interest in the arts began when he was a teenager; he first published his writing in the school newspaper. At age sixteen, he co-composed a theme song for a local theater, earning his first commission as a songwriter. As he grew older, Mebus continued to develop as an entertainer and writer, crafting plays and performing comedy.

Booty Nomad is the fictional account of a twenty-something television producer who breaks up with his girlfriend and begins to navigate the New York dating scene. This romantic comedy, narrated from a man's perspective, joins the growing number of novels that combine comedy, romance, and fiction to appeal to a predominantly male audience. The book received mixed reviews from critics. While a *Publishers Weekly* contributor wrote that the book contains "flashes of sharp urban observation." *Booklist* contributor John Green felt that the novel is lacking in some respects but appealing in others. He commented, "Though the novel is marred by awkward plot devices and gags that fall flat, it proves to have a surprisingly big heart (and the slapstick is often very funny)."

BIOGRAPHICAL AND CRITICAL SOURCES:

PERIODICALS

Booklist, November 15, 2003, John Green, review of *Booty Nomad,* p. 576.
Kirkus Reviews, December 15, 2003, review of *Booty Nomad,* p. 1417.
New York Times, February 22, 2004, Kate Zernike, "Oh, to Write a 'Bridget Jones' for Men: A Guy Can Dream," p. 9.
Publishers Weekly, February 2, 2004, review of *Booty Nomad,* p. 61.

ONLINE

Scott Mebus Home Page, http://www.scottmebus.com (August 25, 2004).*

*   *   *

MEDDEB, Abdelwahab 1946-

PERSONAL: Born 1946, in Tunis, Tunisia; married; children: one. *Education:* University of Paris IV, B.A., 1969, M.A., 1970; University Aix-Marseilles, Ph.D. (writing and double genealogy), 1991.

ADDRESSES: Home—Paris, France. *Office*—c/o University of Paris X at Nanterre, 100, av de la République, 92001 Nanterre Cedex, France.

CAREER: Author, editor, and educator. Sinbad Editions, Paris, France, literary director and advisor, 1974-88; University of Geneva, Geneva, Switzerland, visiting professor, 1989-90; European University Institute of Florence, Florence, Italy, visiting researcher, 1991; Transcultura Foundation, Milan, Italy, director of research, 1991; SUPELEC, Orsay, France, associated professor, 1991-93; UNESCO, consultant, 1993; Yale University, New Haven, CT, visiting professor, 1993; University of Paris V Rene Descartes, temporary research professor, 1993-94; University of Paris X at Nanterre, Nanterre, France, professor of comparative literature.

AWARDS, HONORS: Prix Max Jacob for poetry, 2002; Prix François Mauriac, 2002, for *La maladie de l'Islam.*

WRITINGS:

Talismano (novel), Christian Bourgois (Paris, France), 1979.

Phantasia (novel), Sindbad Editions (Paris, France), 1986.

Tombeau d'Ibn Arabi (poetry), Sillages (Paris, France), 1987.

Les dits de Bistami (poetry), Fayard (Paris, France), 1989.

La gazelle et l'enfant (play), Actes-Sud/Papiers (Arles, France), 1992.

(With Jean Arrouye and Predrag Matvejevitch) *Méditerranées, portraits de Lieux avec mémoire,* photographs by Fabienne Barre, Contrejour (Paris, France), 1995.

(Editor and contributor, with Manfred Metzner and Hans Thrill) *Tunesien 1936-1940: Fotografien,* photographs by Ré Soupault, Wunderhorn (Heidelberg, Germany), 1996.

Aya dans les villes, illustrated by Alexandre Hollan, Fata Morgana (Saint-Clément-la-Rivière, France), 1999.

La maladie de l'Islam (essays), Seuil (Paris, France), 2002, translation by Pierre Joris and Ann Reid published as *The Malady of Islam,* Basic Books (New York, NY), 2003.

Face á l'Islam (essays), Textuel (Paris, France), 2004.

(Translator and commentator, with Hiromi Tsukui) *Saigyô, vers le vide* (poetry), by Saigyô, Albin-Michel (Paris, France), 2004.

Author of poems, essays, and translations, including *99 Yale Stations* and *Matière des Oiseaux* (poetry); *Blanches traverses de passé* (essays); *Récit de l'exil*

occidental de Sohrawardi; and *La Mu'allaqa d'Imru'al-Qays* (translations with commentaries). Also coauthor, with Albert Memmi, of *En Tunisie,* photographs by Jellel Gastelli, Eric Koehler (Paris, France). Editor of periodicals, including *Intersignes,* 1991-94, and *Dédale,* 1995—.

SIDELIGHTS: Born in Tunis in 1946, writer and educator Abdelwahab Meddeb attended French schools and studied Arab theology. His writings include poetry, novels, essays, scholarly papers, and translations on topics ranging from Islamic mysticism to North African politics, with a particular interest in the relationship between East and West. Meddeb moved to Paris, where he became a professor of comparative literature at the University of Paris X at Nanterre, and has served as editor of the magazine *Dédale.*

The theme of exile is a major focus in Meddeb's novel *Phantasia.* In the book, Meddeb examines identity and ideology in relation to the narrator who, like the author, is a Tunisian who has relocated to France. Meddeb uses architecture, language, and structure to highlight the blending of French and Arabic, while showing both sides struggling to maintain their unique identity. Suzanne Gauch, in a review for *Mosaic,* wrote that "*Phantasia* formulates an ethics of exile whose aim is to expose the politics of representation found not only in discourses of the nation, but also in art, architecture and language itself." Meddeb's story addresses cultural relations at a time when the Arabs are standing on their own, no longer subject to French colonial rule. Yet the French influences on the Arabic world are firmly entrenched. Gauch wrote that "while the narrator makes frequent reference to Islamic philosophy, theology, and history, the text itself is written in French. . . . Reflecting this linguistic exile in its 'plot,' *Phantasia* chronicles the solitary peregrinations of its narrator/exile through Paris and Tunisia."

The Malady of Islam, a series of essays on the condition of modern Islam, is a very different type of book, yet it still reflects Meddeb's position as a Tunisian living in France and regarding his former home from an outsider's viewpoint. Douglas McCready, writing for *Military Review,* observed that "the book's strength is also its weakness: it is written by a Muslim scholar deeply involved in the debate about Islam's direction in the modern world." McCready added that the book "is the product of one conversant in Islamic history and thought but it is also the work of a Muslim whose thought fits better in Paris . . . than in the cities and villages of the Middle East." Meddeb attempts to address what he views as the problems with the Middle East, citing Islamic fundamentalism as a reaction to the world's increasing Americanization. *Middle East Quarterly* reviewer Daniel Pipes commented that, "on the subject of Islam, Meddeb presents a brave and insightful Muslim voice; on the subject of politics, he is just another group-think French intellectual. Fortunately his thoughts on the first topic have real importance."

Meddeb told *CA:* "I always read ancient poets and thinkers; I write under the influence of two of them: the Arabic sufi Ibn Arabi (1165-1240), and the Tuscan poet Dante (1265-1319). I try to invent a very new form with consideration of the very antiques.

"At the beginning, the text is composed in my mind, when I am moving, walking in the cities or in countries. For me, travel is the mover of writing, it's why I promulgate transcultural and trans-linguistic aesthetics and poetics, it's the best way to compose the novel or the poem to thought in this time of globalization.

"Of my published books, my favorite is *Talismano* because it's my first book. When I read it again, I'm surprising by it's audacious freedom."

BIOGRAPHICAL AND CRITICAL SOURCES:

PERIODICALS

Kirkus Reviews, June 15, 2003, review of *The Malady of Islam,* p. 848.

Middle East Quarterly, winter, 2004, Daniel Pipes, review of *The Malady of Islam,* p. 85.

Military Review, May-June, 2004, Douglas McCready, review of *The Malady of Islam,* p. 77.

Mosaic, June, 1998, Suzanne Gauch, "Phantasmatic Artifacts: Postcolonial Meditations by a Tunisian Exile," review of *Phantasia,* p. 123.

Public Culture, winter, 2001, Dina Al-Kassim, "Calligraphesis and Kinship in Abdelwahab Meddeb's *Talismano.*"

Sites, fall, 1998, Abdellatif el Alami, review of *Talismano, Phantasia,* and *Tombeau d'Ibn Arabi,* pp. 377-387.

ONLINE

Littératures dux Maghreb Online, http://www.limag. refer.org/ (September 12, 2004), "Abdelwahab Meddeb."

Masthead Online, http://www.masthead.net.au/ (August 30, 2004), "Abdelwahab Meddeb."

Random House UK Web site, http://www.randomhouse. co.uk/ (August 30, 2004), "Abdelwahab Meddeb."

*   *   *

MELOY, Ellen (Ditzler) 1946-2004

OBITUARY NOTICE— See index for *CA* sketch: Born June 21, 1946, in Pasadena, CA; died November 4, 2004, in Bluff, UT. Naturalist, illustrator, and author. Meloy was best known for her essay collections about the natural beauty of the American Southwest. A graduate of Goucher College, where she earned a degree in art, she worked as an art gallery curator and illustrator but left these pursuits to earn an M.S. in environmental science from the University of Montana. After moving to Utah, she fell in love with the area while traveling with her husband, a U.S. Bureau of Land Management ranger. Her desert excursions inspired her to write her first book, *Raven's Exile: A Season on the Green River* (1994), which won the Spur Award from the Western Writers of America and the Whiting Foundation Writer's Award. Two more collections followed, *The Last Cheater's Waltz: Beauty and Violence in the Desert Southwest* (1999) and the Pulitzer Prize-nominated *The Anthropology of Turquoise: Meditations on Landscape, Art, and Spirit* (2002). The latter also won the Utah Book Award and the *Los Angeles Times* Book of the Year Award. In addition to writing, Meloy taught at writers' workshops, contributed to Utah Public Radio, and was a riverboat guide. Because she led such an active lifestyle, her early death from either an aneurism or heart attack was shocking to friends and family. At the time, she had just completed her fourth book, *Eating Stone.*

OBITUARIES AND OTHER SOURCES:

PERIODICALS

Los Angeles Times, November 12, 2004, p. B10.
Salt Lake City Tribune, November 9, 2004.
Washington Post, November 13, 2004, p. B6.

MEREDITH, Martin

PERSONAL: Male.

ADDRESSES: Office—c/o Author Mail, Public Affairs, 250 West Fifty-seventh St., Suite 1321, New York, NY 10107.

CAREER: Independent scholar, biographer, and journalist. Foreign correspondent for London *Observer* and *Sunday Times;* research fellow at St. Antony's College, Oxford.

WRITINGS:

The Past Is Another Country: Rhodesia, 1890-1979, A. Deutsch (London, England), 1979, revised and expanded edition published as *The Past Is Another Country: Rhodesia, UDI to Zimbabwe,* Pan (London, England), 1980.

The First Dance of Freedom: Black Africa in the Postwar Era, Harper & Row (New York, NY), 1984.

In the Name of Apartheid: South Africa in the Postwar Period, Harper & Row (New York, NY), 1988.

A Guide to South Africa's 1994 Election, Mandarin (London, England), 1994.

Nelson Mandela: A Biography, St. Martin's Press (New York, NY), 1998.

Coming to Terms: South Africa's Search for Truth, Public Affairs (New York, NY), 1999.

Africa's Elephant: A Biography, Hodder & Stoughton (London, England), 2001, published as *Elephant Destiny: Biography of an Endangered Species in Africa,* Public Affairs (New York, NY), 2003.

Fischer's Choice: A Life of Bram Fischer, Jonathan Hall (Johannesburg, South Africa), 2002.

Our Votes, Our Guns: Robert Mugabe and the Tragedy of Zimbabwe, Public Affairs (New York, NY), 2002, published as *Mugabe: Power and Plunder in Zimbabwe,* Public Affairs (Oxford, England), 2002.

SIDELIGHTS: An expert on South African history and politics, Martin Meredith has authored numerous works on the postcolonial development of African nations, notably South Africa and Zimbabwe. He has also published biographies of anti-apartheid activists

Nelson Mandela and Bram Fischer, as well as a study of the African elephant's plight as an endangered species. Meredith has spent much of his life in Africa, beginning as a foreign correspondent for the London *Observer* and the London *Sunday Times,* then as an Oxford University research fellow and independent scholar.

In *The Past Is Another Country: Rhodesia, 1890-1979* Meredith recounts the history of Rhodesia from its late-nineteenth-century occupation by British speculators through its break from the commonwealth in 1965 and eventual liberation in 1979; Rhodesia was renamed Zimbabwe in 1980. "Although the title suggests that we are to be guided through the whole history of colonial Rhodesia," *New Statesman* contributor Roger Riddell noted, "only 24 pages out of 370 cover the first 70 years of colonial rule." Indeed, Meredith places special emphasis on the political career of Ian Smith, the white-supremacist prime minister of colonial Rhodesia who led the nation's independence movement during the 1960s and 1970s. Though Riddell found shortcomings in Meredith's lack of analysis and narrow historical focus, *Spectator* critic Robert Blake wrote that "Meredith traces this sorry story with clarity and detachment." *Times Literary Supplement* contributor J. E. Spence commended Meredith's "detailed account" of Smith's feud with the British government, adding that the author "deploys his journalistic skills to good effect" in describing key figures associated with the African National Congress. As Blake remarked, "The very recent past is always the part of history on which there is least information. Mr. Meredith . . . has admirably filled this gap as far as Zimbabwe-Rhodesia is concerned."

In *The First Dance of Freedom: Black Africa in the Postwar Era* Meredith presents the history of postcolonial independence in sub-Sahara Africa, focusing on major events and key figures behind the liberation of each nation. "The value of Martin Meredith's *The First Dance of Freedom* is its scrupulous fair-mindedness as it places Africa's failings in context," wrote Blaine Harden in the *Washington Post Book World.* However, Edward A. Alpers noted in the *Los Angeles Times Book Review* that the author's emphasis on isolated events and individual leaders prevents "a more critical examination of the deeper historical dynamics and wider economic and political forces" that shaped postcolonial Africa. While commending Meredith's competent "encyclopedia-like chapters" on individual

African nations, Harden cited similar shortcomings in the book's lack of analytical depth, remarking that *The First Dance of Freedom* reads like "a dry nation-by-nation recitation of post-colonial history in black Africa."

In the Name of Apartheid: South Africa in the Postwar Period documents the history of official racial segregation in South Africa from the rise of the Afrikaner Nationalist party in 1948 through the 1980s. Meredith describes how the Afrikaner Nationalist party institutionalized apartheid, and how black South Africans resisted white domination. Commenting on the work in the *New York Review of Books,* George M. Fredrickson approved of Meredith's objectivity and described *In the Name of Apartheid* as "a perceptive and readable popular history of South Africa since 1948." *Los Angeles Times* commentator Martin Rubin similarly appreciated Meredith's even-handed perspective as "a dispassionate observer" and commended his account as "clear, cogent, and accurate." According to *New York Times* reviewer Christopher S. Wren, "anyone who wants to understand how South Africans, white as well as black, have been scarred by apartheid will find reasons persuasively presented in [this] compelling, if disturbing, book."

Nelson Mandela: A Biography is an in-depth account of the anti-apartheid activist and celebrated South African statesman. *Times Literary Supplement* contributor Tom Lodge commended Meredith's judicious portrait of Mandela, which includes balanced coverage of the black activist's extraordinary career as well as his personal failings. According to Lodge, "Meredith's book is the first biography which seriously attempts to separate the man from the myth." *America* reviewer Sean Redding praised the work as an "extremely well-researched and readable biography," adding that "Meredith does an excellent job of depicting the life story of this remarkable person." However, Lodge noted that Mandela's disciplined public persona and Meredith's failure to move beyond public sources prevented the biography from offering new insight into Mandela's personality. Despite such criticism, *Library Journal* reviewer Edward G. McCormack called the work "an invaluable resource."

In *Coming to Terms: South African's Search for Truth* Meredith provides an account of the shameful human rights violations perpetrated against black South Africans under apartheid. Based largely upon the find-

ings of the Truth and Reconciliation Commission (TRC), the investigatory body charged with documenting such apartheid-era crimes, Meredith describes this dark and exceptionally violent chapter in that nation's history, including official police torture, assassinations, and anti-apartheid terrorism. Under the direction of Archbishop Desmond Tutu, the TRC granted amnesty to self-confessed torturers and murderers in exchange for their testimony, a decision Meredith questions on moral grounds. However, such testimony, along with that of victims, average citizens, and former presidents Botha and de Klerk, permits the author to construct a well-rounded account of suffering and atrocity under apartheid. Commenting on *Coming to Terms* in the *New York Times,* critic Mary Ellen Sullivan commended Meredith's "thorough and impeccably reported account of South Africa's Truth and Reconciliation Commission."

Our Votes, Our Guns: Robert Mugabe and the Tragedy of Zimbabwe, published in England as *Mugabe: Power and Plunder in Zimbabwe,* focuses on Mugabe's heavy-headed leadership of Zimbabwe. During the early 1960s, Mugabe, a Marxist nationalist, helped found the Zimbabwe African National Union (ZANU) and spent a decade in jail as a political prisoner. He was released in 1975 and in 1980 became Zimbabwe's first prime minister. During the mid-1980s he moved to convert the nation's democratic government into a single-party socialist system with himself as its head. Phil England noted in the *New Internationalist* that Meredith's "highly readable" book "paints the now-familiar portrait of Mugabe as a power-crazy despot whose cronies have embezzled at the country's expense." However, as *African Affairs* reviewer Stephen Chan observed, "despite the fluent, almost racey prose, Meredith's work seems very one-dimensional." While England faulted the work for its omissions, Chan wrote, "The book is a 'good read', but a frustrating one for those wanting greater explanatory power, or to use it as a starting point for their own investigations."

Africa's Elephant: A Biography, published in the United States as *Elephant Destiny: Biography of an Endangered Species in Africa,* represents a departure from Meredith's political histories. In this work he presents an account of the African elephant, including its history, biology, behavior, and, most significantly, its potential extinction as a result of ivory-trading poachers. *Booklist* reviewer Nancy Bent commended

Meredith's "succinct account" of the elephant's tragic relationship with humans and the author's "obvious affection for his subject." A *Publishers Weekly* critic called the book "a solid introduction to the world of elephants."

BIOGRAPHICAL AND CRITICAL SOURCES:

PERIODICALS

African Affairs, April 1, 2003, Stephen Chan, review of *Mugabe: Power and Plunder in Zimbabwe,* pp. 343-347.
America, January 2, 1999, Sean Redding, review of *Nelson Mandela: A Biography,* p. 596.
Booklist, January 1, 1998, Hazel Rochman, review of *Nelson Mandela,* pp. 741-742; January 1, 2000, Rochman, review of *Coming to Terms: South Africa's Search for Truth,* p. 867; April 1, 2003, Nancy Bent, review of *Elephant Destiny: Biography of an Endangered Species in Africa,* p. 1362.
Library Journal, February 1, 1998, Edward G. McCormack, review of *Nelson Mandela,* p. 96; February 1, 2000, McCormack, review of *Coming to Terms,* p. 105.
Los Angeles Times Book Review, July 28, 1985, Edward A. Alpers, review of *The First Dance of Freedom: Black Africa in the Postwar Era,* p. 11; October 30, 1988, Martin Rubin, review of *In the Name of Apartheid: South Africa in the Postwar Period,* p. 2.
New Internationalist, May, 2002, Phil England, review of *Mugabe,* pp. 31-32.
New Republic, March 18, 1985, Conor Cruise O'Brien, review of *The First Dance of Freedom,* pp. 31-35.
New Statesman, November 9, 1979, Roger Riddell, review of *The Past Is Another Country: Rhodesia, 1890-1979,* p. 724.
New York Review of Books, October 26, 1989, George M. Fredrickson, review of *In the Name of Apartheid,* pp. 48-55.
New York Times Book Review, December 18, 1988, Christopher S. Wren, review of *In the Name of Apartheid,* p. 9; February 13, 2000, Mary Ellen Sullivan, review of *Coming to Terms,* p. 20.
Publishers Weekly, January 12, 1998, review of *Nelson Mandela,* p. 54; November 29, 1989, review of *Coming to Terms,* p. 58; March 31, 2003, review of *Elephant Destiny,* pp. 53-54.
Spectator, November 3, 1979, Robert Blake, review of *The Past Is Another Country,* p. 20.
Times Literary Supplement, February 8, 1980, J. E. Spence, review of *The Past Is Another Country,* p. 151; December 26, 1997, Tom Lodge, review of *Nelson Mandela,* p. 11.
Washington Post Book World, March 3, 1985, Blaine Harden, review of *The First Dance of Freedom,* p. 11.*

*   *   *

MESSERLI, Jonathan C(arl) 1926-2004

OBITUARY NOTICE— See index for *CA* sketch: Born February 14, 1926, in Albany, OR; died of a heart attack November 28, 2004, in Berks County, PA. College president, educator, and author. Messerli was a former president of Muhlenberg College and Susquehanna University. A 1947 graduate of Concordia Teachers College, he earned his M.A. from Washington University in St. Louis in 1952 and his doctorate in the history of American education from Harvard University in 1963. Messerli's teaching career began at the high school level, teaching biology and sciences at a St. Louis, Missouri, school from 1947 until 1957. During the early 1960s, he worked at Harvard University and the University of Washington in Seattle. He then joined the Columbia University faculty in 1964, staying there for four years before being hired as dean of the School of Education at Hofstra University in 1968. From 1972 until 1977 he was dean at Fordham University. Selected to be president of Susquehanna University, he led that university until 1984, then became president of Muhlenberg College in Allentown, Pennsylvania, until 1992. Messerli was the author of *Horace Mann, a Biography* (1973).

OBITUARIES AND OTHER SOURCES:

ONLINE

Evangelical Lutheran Church in America Web site, http://www.elca.org/ (December 3, 2004).
WKOK News Online, http://www.wkok.com/ (January 26, 2005).

*   *   *

METCALF, Allan (Albert) 1940-

PERSONAL: Born April 18, 1940, in Clayton, MO; married, 1994; children: four. *Education:* Cornell University, B.A., 1961; University of California, Berkeley, M.A., 1964, Ph.D. (English), 1966.

ADDRESSES: Office—Department of English, Mac-Murray College, 477 East College Ave., Jacksonville, IL 62650-2510. *E-mail*—aallan@aol.com.

CAREER: University of California, Riverside, assistant professor, 1966-73, associate professor of English, 1973-81; MacMurray College, Jacksonville, IL, professor of English and department chair, 1981—.

MEMBER: Modern Language Association, National Council of Teachers of English, Linguistic Society of America, Mediaeval Academy of America, American Dialect Society (executive secretary, 1981—).

WRITINGS:

(With Thomas E. Armbruster, Edgar C. Howell, IV, and Sandre Prasad) *Riverside English: The Spoken Language of a Southern California Community,* University of California, Riverside (Riverside, CA), 1971.

Poetic Diction in the Old English Meters of Boethius, Mouton (The Hague, Netherlands), 1973.

Chicano English, Center for Applied Linguistics (Arlington, VA), 1979.

(With William J. Kerrigan) *Writing to the Point,* Harcourt Brace Jovanovich (San Diego, CA), 1987, published as *Essentials of Writing to the Point* (adapted from *Writing to the Point*), Harcourt Brace College Publishers (Fort Worth, TX), 1995.

Research to the Point, Harcourt Brace Jovanovich (San Diego, CA), 1991.

(With David K. Barnhart) *America in So Many Words: Words That Have Shaped America,* Houghton Mifflin (Boston, MA), 1997.

The World in So Many Words: A Country-by-Country Tour of the Words That Have Shaped Our Language, Houghton Mifflin (Boston, MA), 1999.

How We Talk: American Regional English Today, Houghton Mifflin (Boston, MA), 2000.

Predicting New Words: The Secrets of Their Success, Houghton Mifflin (Boston, MA), 2002.

Presidential Voices: Speaking Styles from George Washington to George W. Bush, Houghton Mifflin (Boston, MA), 2004.

Contributor of numerous articles to academic journals, including *Chaucer Review* and *Dictionaries.*

SIDELIGHTS: Allan Metcalf has been a scholar of American English for many years. He has written several books for an academic audience, but he may be best known to nonlinguists for two books that examine the history of American speech for a popular audience. In the first of these books, *America in So Many Words: Words That Have Shaped America,* Metcalf and coauthor David K. Barnhart look at the history of the United States, year by year, through one new word that was added to the language in each year. For example, "Yankee" first came into common usage in 1765, "flapper" in 1915, and "software" in 1959. The roughly page-long discussions of the words are "written with punch and verve," Thomas E. Nunnally wrote in a review for *American Speech.* The book "should appeal to both browsers and reference personnel in high-school, public, and academic libraries," reviewer Mary Ellen Quinn commented in *Booklist.*

The World in So Many Words: A Country-by-Country Tour of the Words That Have Shaped Our Language takes a similar approach to American English, this time dividing up new words by the country that "gave" them to the United States. In roughly two hundred "brief yet discursive essays," as Jeffrey E. Long described them in *American Reference Books Annual,* Metcalf covers some eight hundred words, including "boondocks" (from Tagalog), "bizarre" (from Basque), and "chocolate" (Native American). *The World in So Many Words* is not a book for professional linguists as it avoids diving too deeply into the original etymologies, or origins and historical developments, of these borrowed words. Instead, "it's for the word lover who deserves a good frolic with the language," concluded *Booklist*'s Philip Herbst.

How We Talk: American Regional English Today is a more scholarly work than *America in So Many Words* and *The World in So Many Words.* In *How We Talk,* Metcalf examines the numerous differences in speech among the regions of the United States, as well as among various American ethnic groups. Southern accents and dialects are discussed at length, as are those of New York and Boston. In the section on ethnic speech, attention is given to African-, Hispanic-, and Native Americans, as well as Jewish speakers of Yiddish. "For fiction writers hoping to create authentic-sounding dialogue, this book could function as an indispensable guide," commented *Booklist* reviewer David Pitt.

Metcalf makes a serious linguistic argument in *Predicting New Words: The Secrets of Their Success,* but he does so in the context of a "brisk, scholarly romp that will appeal beyond the usual word mavens," according to *Christian Science Monitor* reviewer Todd Nelson. The book sprang from Metcalf's work with the American Dialect Society. At Metcalf's urging, the society began recognizing a "Word of the Year" in 1990. As described on the *American Dialect Society Web site,* "Words of the Year are those that reflect the concerns and preoccupations of the year gone by. They need not be new, but they usually are newly prominent." Some words of the year remained in common usage, but others quickly faded, and Metcalf began to wonder what determined which words succeeded and which failed. His research found five characteristics that make a word likely to endure. As he explains in *Predicting New Words,* these characteristics form the FUDGE scale: frequency, unobtrusiveness, diversity of users, generation of forms and meanings, and endurance of concept. "Metcalf's style suits his subject well: he is humorous and often plays with words himself," Katherine Poltorak commented in the *Yale Review of Books.* "But his entertaining writing doesn't diminish his serious insights into language."

BIOGRAPHICAL AND CRITICAL SOURCES:

PERIODICALS

American Reference Books Annual, 2000, Jeffrey E. Long, review of *The World in So Many Words: A Country-by-Country Tour of the Words That Have Shaped Our Language,* p. 413; 2001, Shannon Graff Hysell, review of *How We Talk: American Regional English Today,* p. 463.

American Speech, summer, 2001, Thomas E. Nunnally, review of *America in So Many Words: Words That Have Shaped America,* pp. 158-176.

Booklist, April, 1998, Mary Ellen Quinn, review of *America in So Many Words,* p. 1340; August, 1999, Philip Herbst, review of *The World in So Many Words,* p. 2003; December 1, 1999, Bill Ott, review of *America in So Many Words,* p. 736; October 15, 2000, David Pitt, review of *How We Talk,* p. 397; September 1, 2002, David Pitt, review of *Predicting New Words: The Secrets of Their Success,* p. 32; June 1, 2004, Gilbert Taylor, review of *Presidential Voices: Speaking Styles from George Washington to George W. Bush,* p. 1679.

Choice, February, 2003, R. B. Shuman, review of *Predicting New Words,* pp. 977-978.

Christian Science Monitor, November 27, 2002, Todd Nelson, review of *Predicting New Words,* p. 21.

Insight on the News, June 25, 2001, Stephen Goode, review of *America in So Many Words,* p. 4; October 1, 2001, Stephen Goode, review of *The World in So Many Words,* p. 4; February 18, 2003, review of *America in So Many Words,* p. 8.

Kirkus Reviews, July 15, 1999, review of *The World in So Many Words,* p. 1110; August 15, 2002, review of *Predicting New Words,* p. 1201.

Library Journal, December, 1997, Ilse Heidmann, review of *America in So Many Words,* p. 105; August, 1999, Neal Wyatt, review of *The World in So Many Words,* p. 89.

New York Times Magazine, August 12, 2001, William Safire, review of *How We Talk,* p. 20.

Publishers Weekly, August 16, 1999, review of *The World in So Many Words,* p. 74.

Speculum, July, 1977, Fred C. Robinson, review of *Poetic Diction in the Old English Meters of Boethius,* pp. 714-715.

Yale Review of Books, spring, 2004, Katherine Poltorak, review of *Predicting New Words.*

ONLINE

American Dialect Society Web site, http://www.americandialect.org/ (June 24, 2004), "Words of the Year."

Houghton Mifflin Books Web site, http://www.houghtonmifflinbooks.com/ (June 9, 2004), "Allan Metcalf."*

*   *   *

MICKLEM, Sarah 1955-

PERSONAL: Born 1955, in VA; married Cornelius Eady (a poet and playwright). *Education:* Graduate of Princeton University.

ADDRESSES: Home—Washington, DC. *Agent*—c/o Author Mail, Simon & Schuster, 1230 Avenue of the Americas, New York, NY 10020. *E-mail*—firethorn@firethorn.info.

CAREER: Graphic designer and author. Worked for a nonprofit in New York, NY, and as a teacher in VA; Time Warner, New York, NY, graphic designer. Cofounder of Cave Canem, New York, NY, 1996.

WRITINGS:

Firethorn: A Novel, Scribner (New York, NY), 2004.

WORK IN PROGRESS: The second book in the "Firethorn" trilogy.

SIDELIGHTS: Sarah Micklem was born in Virginia and spent much of her childhood in Rochester, New York, where her father was a teacher and naturalist and both of her parents were activists. Micklem married poet Cornelius Eady, a friend from high school, and moved to New York, where she helped settle refugees for a nonprofit organization. When the couple moved to Virginia, Micklem worked as a teacher before taking a job as a graphic designer that turned into a career. Upon returning to New York, she spent fourteen years with Time Warner, designing children's magazines. Beginning in 1996, Micklem worked as a volunteer for Cave Canem, a nonprofit she helped form to support black poets.

Micklem's first novel, *Firethorn,* was years in the writing and is the first book in a planned trilogy. She put it down in 1998 to take writing classes, then went back to it and completed the fantasy. The heroine is the red-haired Luck, an orphan born of the mudfolk people, who changes her name to Firethorn in honor of berries she eats after being raped by the warrior for whom she had worked. Firethorn has gifts, including night vision, which intensify, as does her resolve to escape. And she does, with high-born Sir Galan, agreeing to act as his sheath and bedmate in the camps of the warriors, where she also practices her healing skills. When Galan makes a bet that has dire consequences, she uses her powers to change the course of fate.

Booklist contributor Paula Leudtke called *Firethorn* "a great piece of gritty, feminist fiction, distinguished by a heroine whose vulnerabilities and fresh voice as narrator make her easy to love." A *Publishers Weekly* contributor called the novel "majestic and powerful," and concluded that "this hypnotic tale of passion and survival will resonate with sophisticated readers of both sexes."

BIOGRAPHICAL AND CRITICAL SOURCES:

PERIODICALS

Booklist, June 1, 2004, Paula Leudtke, review of *Firethorn,* p. 1713.

Kirkus Reviews, March 1, 2004, review of *Firethorn,* p. 206.
Library Journal, June 1, 2004, Deborah Shippy, review of *Firethorn,* p. 128.
Publishers Weekly, April 5, 2004, review of *Firethorn,* p. 46.

ONLINE

Sarah Micklem Home Page, http://www.firethorn.info (October 31, 2004).*

*　　*　　*

MILLER, N(ewton) Edd 1920-2004

OBITUARY NOTICE— See index for *CA* sketch: Born March 13, 1920, in Houston, TX; died November 13, 2004, in Reno, NV. College president, educator, and author. Miller was best remembered for his calm leadership as president of the University of Nevada, Reno, during the dramatic student protests of the Vietnam War era. A graduate of the University of Texas, where he earned an M.A. in 1940, he completed his Ph.D. at the University of Michigan in 1951. From 1941 until 1947, he taught speech at the University of Texas at Austin. He then joined the University of Michigan faculty as an assistant professor in 1950 where he became a full professor of speech in 1959 and was assistant to the vice president of academic affairs in the mid-1960s. Miller was hired by the University of Nevada in 1965 to be its chancellor, and was named president three years later. Unlike many other university professors around the country during the student protests of the late 1960s and early 1970s, Miller was loved and admired by students for his willingness to listen to their concerns and for his calm leadership. His model leadership during a 1969 student protest made national news. Miller left the university in 1973 to accept the position as president of the University of Main at Portland-Gorham, moving on to Northern Kentucky University in 1978, where he was chair of the communications department until 1987. He was also interim general manager of university station WNKU from 1985 until 1986. After retiring, he moved back to Reno. Miller was the author of several books on speech, including *First Course in Speech* (1945), *Discussion and Debate* (1953), and the coauthored *Public Speaking: A Practical Handbook* (1985; second edition, 1989).

OBITUARIES AND OTHER SOURCES:

PERIODICALS

Chronicle of Higher Education, December 3, 2004, p. A42.
Reno Gazette-Journal, November 21, 2004.

ONLINE

University of Nevada, Reno, News Online, http://www.unr.edu/nevadanews/ (November 15, 2004).

*   *   *

MONSOUR, Theresa

PERSONAL: Married; children: two sons.

ADDRESSES: Home—MN. *Office*—Pioneer Press, 345 Cedar St., St. Paul, MN 55101.

CAREER: Journalist. *Pioneer Press,* St. Paul, MN, reporter and staff writer, 1980s—.

WRITINGS:

"PARIS MURPHY" SERIES

Clean Cut, G. P. Putnam's Sons (New York, NY), 2003.
Cold Blood, G. P. Putnam's Sons (New York, NY), 2004.
Dark House, G. P. Putnam's Sons (New York, NY), 2005.

SIDELIGHTS: Journalist Theresa Monsour created her character Paris Murphy, a homicide detective with the St. Paul, Minnesota police force for her mystery *Clean Cut.* A *Publishers Weekly* contributor wrote that "sex, violence, Catholic guilt, and sloppy police work mark Monsour's debut thriller." Paris, who lives on a houseboat on the Mississippi River, is estranged from her husband, Jack, but she continues to sleep with him, as well as her lover, Erik. Her partner, Gabriel

Nash, is an older cop who grows fatter on liverwurst and mayo sandwiches. They solve the case early on, but it takes the rest of the book to understand the killer's motives.

A. Romann Michaels is a handsome doctor who was psychologically damaged as a teen when his mother tried to seduce him just hours before she committed suicide. Now obsessed with killing women who have beautiful hair like his mother's he kills his victim, then cuts her hair and adds it to the collection he keeps in a Victorian hat box. Paris takes the case when a prostitute she knew and liked is murdered. Because the killer has strong ties with politicians, the dots are not connected, so Paris, with her beautiful raven hair and violet eyes, sets herself up as bait.

Library Journal reviewer Jane Jorgenson felt that Monsour's writing sometimes resembles newspaper reporting. "The storytelling is straightforward and rarely delves into the characters or plot," she wrote. *Booklist* reviewer Connie Fletcher called Monsour's pacing "truly chilling" and noted that the writer's background "shows in her realistic depictions of cops, the press, and prostitutes" to produce a "stunning" novel. *Washington Book World* critic Patrick Anderson called *Clean Cut* "a solid piece of work" "because of the precision and toughmindedness of [Monsour's] writing."

A third love interest enters Paris's life in the sequel, *Cold Blood,* when Axel Duncan becomes head of the homicide squad. Fletcher felt that this outing "is almost excessively creepy crawly." Paris is on the hunt for a serial killer, who she suspects to be Justice Trip, nicknamed "Sweet" by their classmates in high school. Social outcast Justice committed his first crime when he ran down and killed four of Paris's friends after they beat him for asking her to Homecoming. Now he acts the part of hero, first killing drunken bridesmaid Bunny Pederson and burying her in a shallow grave, then planting a finger he has severed from her hand and "finding" it during a search for clues. Soon Paris realizes she is also a target.

A *Publishers Weekly* contributor felt that "the harrowing relationship Trip has with his father contrasts neatly with Murphy's organized work and more normal personal life, despite its romantic confusions." Thea Davis, who reviewed *Cold Blood* for *MysteryReader.*

com, wrote that "the plot structure is tight, and the story rushes to a quixotic ending. It is clear that Theresa Monsour has joined today's ranks of leading authors in the crime thriller genre."

BIOGRAPHICAL AND CRITICAL SOURCES:

PERIODICALS

Booklist, January 1, 2003, Connie Fletcher, review of *Clean Cut,* p. 856; April 1, 2004, Connie Fletcher, review of *Cold Blood,* p. 1353.
Kirkus Reviews, January 15, 2003, review of *Clean Cut,* p. 109; March 15, 2004, review of *Cold Blood,* p. 252.
Library Journal, February 1, 2003, Jane Jorgenson, review of *Clean Cut,* p. 122.
Publishers Weekly, January 27, 2003, review of *Clean Cut,* p. 238; April 19, 2004, review of *Cold Blood,* p. 41.
Washington Post Book World, March 16, 2003, Patrick Anderson, review of *Clean Cut,* p. T5.

ONLINE

BookPage.com, http://www.bookpage.com/ (October 31, 2004), Bruce Tierney, review of *Clean Cut.*
MysteryReader.com, http://www.themysteryreader.com/ (October 31, 2004), Thea Davis, review of *Cold Blood.**

*   *   *

MONTOYA, Peter

PERSONAL: Born in CA; married; wife's name, Lynn. *Education:* University of California—Irvine, graduated.

ADDRESSES: Agent—c/o Author Mail, Personal Branding Press, 1540 South Lyon St., Santa Ana, CA 92705. *E-mail*—petermontoya@petermontoya.com.

CAREER: Worked as a professional trainer for five years; worked for an advertising agency in southern California; Peter Montoya, Inc., founder, president, and publisher of magazine *Personal Branding,* 1997—.

WRITINGS:

(With Tim Vandehey) *The Brand Called You: The Ultimate Brand-building and Business Development Handbook to Transform Anyone into an Indispensable Personal Brand,* Personal Branding Press (Santa Ana, CA), 1999.
(With Tim Vandehey) *The Personal Branding Phenomenon: Apply the Personal Branding Techniques of Oprah, Michael, and Martha to Build Your Enduring Brand,* Personal Branding Press (Santa Ana, CA), 2002.

BIOGRAPHICAL AND CRITICAL SOURCES:

PERIODICALS

America's Intelligence Wire, June 4, 2003, interview by David Asman, Molly de Ramel, and Andrew Napolitano.
PR Newswire, June 20, 2002, "Publisher of Personal Branding Magazine, Peter Montoya, Offers a Survival Guide for Martha Stewart" July 10, 2002, "Personal Branding Magazine Launched by Peter Montoya Inc.; Stedman Graham Becomes Senior Editor, Regular Contributor."

ONLINE

Peter Montoya Inc. Web site, http://petermontoya.com/ (August 1, 2003).

*   *   *

MOORE, Glover 1911-2004

OBITUARY NOTICE— See index for *CA* sketch: Born September 22, 1911, in Birmingham, AL; died November 9, 2004, in Birmingham, AL. Moore was professor emeritus at Mississippi State University. He completed undergraduate work at Birmingham-Southern College in 1932, earning an M.A. in 1933 and Ph.D. in 1936, both from Vanderbilt University. He joined the Mississippi State University faculty after completing his doctorate, becoming a full professor of history in 1953 and retiring in 1977. Moore was the author of *The Missouri Controversy, 1819-1821* (1953) and *William Jemison Mims: Soldier and Squire* (1966), and edited *A Calhoun County, Alabama, Boy in the 1860s* (1978).

OBITUARIES AND OTHER SOURCES:

PERIODICALS

Chronicle of Higher Education, December 10, 2004, p. A32.

*   *   *

MOORE, Tim 1964-

PERSONAL: Born 1964; married; children: three.

ADDRESSES: Home—West London, England. *Agent*—c/o Author Mail, St. Martin's Press, 175 Fifth Ave., New York, NY 10010.

CAREER: Writer.

WRITINGS:

Frost on My Moustache: The Arctic Exploits of a Lord and a Loafer, Abacus (London, England), 1999, St. Martin's Press (New York, NY), 2000.

The Grand Tour: The European Adventure of a Continental Drifter, St. Martin's Press (New York, NY), 2001, published as *Continental Drifter: Taking the Low Road with the First Grand Tourist,* Abacus (London, England), 2001.

French Revolutions, Yellow Jersey (London, England), 2001, published as *French Revolutions: Cycling the Tour de France,* St. Martin's Press (New York, NY), 2002.

Do Not Pass "Go": From the Old Kent Road to Mayfair, Yellow Jersey (London, England), 2002.

Spanish Steps: One Man and His Ass on the Pilgrimage Way to Santiago, Jonathan Cape (London, England), 2004, published as *Travels with My Donkey: One Man and His Ass on the Pilgrimage Way to Santiago,* St. Martin's Press (New York, NY), 2005.

Contributor to periodicals, including London *Daily Telegraph, Observer,* and *Sunday Times.*

SIDELIGHTS: British travel writer Tim Moore has created unique strategies for approaching his journeys before writing down accounts of his experiences in his books. His first book, *Frost on My Moustache: The Arctic Exploits of a Lord and a Loafer,* relates how Moore tried to follow the same course traveled by Victorian aristocrat Lord Dufferin in 1856. Dufferin, along with his wife and crew, set out on his yacht toward the Arctic archipelago of Spitzbergen, visiting Iceland and Norway as they went, before returning home to Scotland. He recorded his adventures in his autobiographical *Letters from High Latitudes,* a copy of which fell into Moore's hands.

Moore made the trip some 140 years later, but without benefit of Dufferin's fancy yacht. Instead, Moore traveled by cargo ship and plane, bike, bus, motor boat, cruise ship, and rubber dinghy. He began in Ireland after meeting the current Lady Dufferin. Dufferin had crossed part of Iceland on horseback; Moore rode a bike.

In his book Moore pokes mild fun at those he meets, as well as at himself. He recalls his three days in the Shetlands that they "marked the lowest point of my short career as an adventurer. I was going south when I should have been going north, back in Britain drinking Tartan in breezeblock pubs when I should have been standing, proud and alone, at the foot of Jan Mayen's volcano." Moore writes of his misery, brought about by seasickness, encounters with whales and polar bears, both dead and alive, frigid weather, and homemade alcohol.

Booklist critic David Pitt compared Moore's travelogue to the work of Bill Bryson and Tim Cahill, calling it "literary travel writing with a heavy dose of wit." A *Publishers Weekly* contributor made the comparison to Cahill, too, and also to Dave Barry, noting that Moore "presents himself as the ever-complaining curmudgeon." And *Geographical* writer Melanie Train felt that "despite Moore's incompetence compared to the almost almighty Dufferin, this book provides an excellent overview of the countries and places the two adventurers visit." Train declared *Frost on My Moustache* "a laugh-a-minute, unputdownable book."

Moore documents his retracing of the trip of another traveler in *The Grand Tour: The European Adventure of a Continental Drifter.* Thomas Coryate established the "Grand Tour" when centuries earlier he traveled from London to Venice and back, visiting forty-five cities along the way. Although the tour came to be an adventure enjoyed by the monied classes, Coryate had no income and a limited budget. In making his way across Europe, he begged, borrowed, and stole, and he documented his adventures in *Coryate's Crudities.* Moore did not fare much better. He started out wearing an old velvet suit and driving a pink Rolls-Royce. He took with him a smelly nylon tent. He feasted on fast food and endlessly sought out public toilets, usually finding them in a McDonald's restaurant. Chris Martin, writing in another *Geographical* article, noted that "Coryate meets a tragic end. Moore simply grows weary of what turns out to be hard and lonely traveling. Nonetheless, there are some genuine and hilarious adventures along the way."

French Revolutions: Cycling the Tour de France is a chronicle of the inexperienced and unprepared Moore's attempt to cycle the 2000 Tour de France course. *Booklist* reviewer David Pitt called the book "not so much a travelogue as a travel situation comedy. Like the protagonist of a sitcom, things just keep happening to Moore." Moore writes of his and others' use of performance-enhancing drugs and of a history of doping in cycling, including the use of cocaine flakes that are dropped onto the tongues of cyclists as they ride by. Moore cheated by beginning six weeks before the official start, then eliminated the first four hundred miles of the 2,256-mile circuit. He bypassed steep climbs and walked others. But his endurance increased, and he successfully ascended the Cols de Galibier and Izoard in the Alps. Moore completed 1,863 miles by the time he reached Paris. A *Kirkus Reviews* critic said that the narrative is carried by Moore's history of the Tour, writing that "from Paul Kimmage's race laundry tips to Bernard Hinault's champagne-filled water bottles, interesting detail abounds."

Do Not Pass "Go": From the Old Kent Road to May-fair is Moore's travelogue based on the real estate found on the game board of the British version of Monopoly. The game was created in 1936 by a company manager from Leeds who knew very little about London. At the time, London was the most populated city on Earth, with nine million people, and Moore questions the reasoning behind choosing some of the sites for the game. Other sites are good choices, according to the author, including the Café de Paris, a nightclub located on Coventry Street purported to be

the meeting place of the Prince of Wales and Wallis Simpson. "But frankly," he says, "it's as good a way as any to explore London, and there are fascinating stories for every single street."

BIOGRAPHICAL AND CRITICAL SOURCES:

BOOKS

Moore, Tim, *Frost on My Moustache: The Arctic Exploits of a Lord and a Loafer,* St. Martin's Press (New York, NY), 2000.
Moore, Tim, *Do Not Pass "Go": From the Old Kent Road to Mayfair,* Yellow Jersey (London, England), 2002.

PERIODICALS

Booklist, December 1, 1999, David Pitt, review of *Frost on My Moustache: The Arctic Exploits of a Lord and a Loafer,* p. 682; May 1, 2002, David Pitt, review of *French Revolutions: Cycling the Tour de France,* p. 1499.
Bookseller, August 2, 2002, review of *Do Not Pass "Go": From the Old Kent Road to Mayfair,* p. 31.
Geographical, April, 1999, Melanie Train, review of *Frost on My Moustache,* p. 67; March, 2001, Chris Martin, review of *Continental Drifter: Taking the Low Road with the First Grand Tourist,* p. 92.
Kirkus Reviews, April 15, 2002, review of *French Revolutions,* p. 549.
Library Journal, February 1, 2000, John Kenny, review of *Frost on My Moustache,* p. 108; August, 2001, Stephanie Papa, review of *The Grand Tour: The European Adventure of a Continental Drifter,* p. 144.
New Statesman, July 16, 2001, Henry Sheen, review of *French Revolutions,* p. 57.
Publishers Weekly, December 20, 1999, review of *Frost on My Moustache,* p. 68; June 18, 2001, review of *The Grand Tour,* p. 76.
Times Literary Supplement, May 7, 1999, John Spurling, review of *Frost on My Moustache,* p. 27.

ONLINE

Shetland Times Ltd. Online, http://www.shetlandtoday.co.uk/ (April, 1999), review of *Frost on My Moustache.**

MORGAN, Elizabeth Seydel 1939-

PERSONAL: Born 1939, in Atlanta, GA. *Education:* Hollis College, B.A., 1960; Virginia Commonwealth University, M.F.A., 1986.

ADDRESSES: Agent—c/o Author Mail, Louisiana State University Press, P.O. Box 25053, Baton Rouge, LA 70894-5053.

CAREER: Poet and writer. Founder of creative writing program at St. Catherine's School, Richmond, VA.

AWARDS, HONORS: Virginia Film Festival's Governor's Screenwriting Competition Award winner, 1993, for *Queen Esther;* National Endowment for the Humanities fellowship; Emily Clark Balch Award, *Virginia Quarterly Review,* for fiction; Algernon Sydney Sullivan Award, Hollins College.

WRITINGS:

Parties (poems), Louisiana State University Press (Baton Rouge, LA), 1988.
The Governor of Desire (poems), Louisiana State University Press (Baton Rouge, LA), 1993.
Queen Esther (screenplay), 1993.
On Long Mountain: Poems (poems), Louisiana State University (Baton Rouge, LA), 1998.

Contributor of fiction to anthologies and collections, including *New Stories from the South: The Year's Best 2004,* edited by Shannon Ravenel, Algonquin Books (Chapel Hill, NC), 2004; *Downhome,* edited by Susie Mee, Harcourt Brace (Orlando, FL), 1995; and *New Stories from the South: 1993,* edited by Shannon Ravenel, Algonquin Books (Chapel Hill, NC), 1993.

Contributor of poetry to anthologies and collections, including *Poetry 180,* edited by Billy Collins, Random House (New York, NY), 2003; *Poetry Daily,* edited by Diane Boller, and others, Sourcebooks (Naperville, IL), 2003; *Common Wealth: Contemporary Poets of Virginia,* edited by R. T. Smith, University Press of Virginia (Charlottesville, VA), 2003; *Buck and Wing: Southern Poetry at 2000,* edited by R. T. Smith, *Shenandoah,* 2000; *The Yellowshoe Poets,* edited by George Garrett, Louisiana State University Press

(Baton Rouge, LA), 1999; and *Claiming the Spirit Within,* edited by Marilyn Sewell, Beacon Press (Boston, MA), 1996.

Also author of limited-edition poetry collection *Language,* illustrations by Laura Pharis; translator, with Christopher Pelling, of "Electra" in *Euripides 2,* edited by David R. Slavitt and Palmer Bovie, University of Pennsylvania Press (Philadelphia, PA), 1997. Contributor of poems to periodicals, including *Southern Review, Five Points, Shenandoah, New Virginia Review, Poetry,* and *Cortland Review,* and to Library of Congress's Poetry Web site, *Poetry180.*

WORK IN PROGRESS: Without a Philosophy (poems), for Louisiana State University Press.

SIDELIGHTS: Poet Elizabeth Seydel Morgan's verses are inclusive, encouraging the reader to share a moment captured on paper, yet they also illustrate how isolated people can be. Her second collection, *The Governor of Desire,* is titled after Shakespeare's one-hundred-thirteenth sonnet, from which two lines are used as an epigraph for the book: "And that which governs me to go about / Doth part his function and is partly blind." The volume is uneven, according to some reviewers, who also felt that some fine poems can be found here, especially those that address family and relationships. Morgan examines the commonplace, highlighting minute details to enhance her imagery. A contributor to the *Virginia Quarterly Review* noted that the strongest works included in the book "display an emotional honesty, an overriding sense of desire, and a playful tone that keeps one off-balance." In *Publishers Weekly,* a reviewer expressed disappointment that the focus of the book seems to be a weak sequence of poems, but added that "Morgan's voices explicitly evoke sound and smell. They . . . explore the ways nature resembles humanity."

With *On Long Mountain* Morgan demonstrates the breadth of her talent, according to several critics. David Yezzi, reviewing the book for *Poetry,* called the poems in this volume "modest," going on to remark that "such modesty's a virtue. With levity and formal aplomb, Morgan deftly records the reflections of, as she puts it, a 'city girl' in deep Appalachia." Poems of rural life are matched by a section reflecting Morgan's more cosmopolitan side, and then complemented by works that focus on family. Yezzi concluded that

"Morgan's means are consistently up to her subjects, and her eye—always with its companionable glint—rarely misses the mark: the poems are well turned and tuneful."

BIOGRAPHICAL AND CRITICAL SOURCES:

PERIODICALS

Georgia Review, spring, 1990, review of *Parties,* pp. 161-163.
Hudson Review, spring, 1989, review of *Parties,* pp. 155-156; autumn, 1992, review of *The Governor of Desire,* pp. 474-475.
New England Review, fall, 1994, review of *The Governor of Desire,* p. 185.
Poetry, June, 1999, David Yezzi, review of *On Long Mountain,* p. 174.
Publishers Weekly, September 13, 1993, review of *The Governor of Desire,* p. 122.
Virginia Quarterly Review, summer, 1994, review of *The Governor of Desire,* p. 98.

ONLINE

Blackbird, http://www.blackbird.vcu.edu/ (January 27, 2005), "Elizabeth Seydel Morgan."
James River Writers Festival, http://www.jrwf.org/ (November 12, 2004), "Elizabeth Seydel Morgan."

*   *   *

MORING, John (R.) 1946-2002

PERSONAL: Born 1946; died 2002. *Education:* Humboldt State University, B.S., 1968, M.S., 1970; University of Washington, Ph.D., 1973.

CAREER: Nyanza Fish Company, Vancouver, British Columbia, and Seattle, WA, biological consultant and fish culture manager, 1973-74; Oregon Department of Fish and Wildlife, Corvallis, fisheries research biologist and project leader, 1974-79; University of Maine, Orono, assistant leader, 1979-83, acting leader of Maine Cooperative Fishery Research Unit, 1983-85; University of Maine, Orono, assistant professor of zoology, 1979-91, Main Cooperative Fish & Wildlife Research Unit, assistant leader for fisheries, 1985-2002, cooperating professor of marine studies, 1987-96; professor of zoology, 1991-2002.

AWARDS, HONORS: Quality Performance Award for Research Productivity, U.S. Fish & Wildlife Service, 1991; fellow, American Institute of Fishery Research Biologists, 1995; Dwight Webster Award of Excellence, Northeastern Division, American Fisheries Society, 1997.

WRITINGS:

Men with Sand: Great Explorers of the North American West, TwoDot (Helena, MT), 1998.
Early American Naturalists: Exploring the American West, 1804-1900, Cooper Square Press (New York, NY), 2002.
(With others) *Life between the Tides: Marine Plants and Animals of the Northeast,* Tilbury House (Gardiner, ME), 2003.

Contributor to *North American Journal of Fisheries Management, Bulletin of Marine Science, Hydrobiologia,* and *American Fisheries Society Symposium.*

SIDELIGHTS: John Moring was a professor of zoology, whose research interests included fish population ecology, Atlantic salmon, and fisheries management.

In *Early American Naturalists: Exploring the American West, 1804-1900* Moring examines the lives and expeditions of naturalists in the United States during the nineteenth century. These naturalists, who included Lewis and Clark, John Muir, Florence Merriam Bailey, and John Audubon, were sent across the land to find and document plants and animals. Their work was not easy. Most had limited tools, and many of their specimens were either ruined by the weather, eaten by animals, or lost. They had to live in the wild where the insects, animals, and weather could be harsh. Often those exploring the western territories ran into Indians and were occasionally killed by them. *Seattle Times* contributor David B. Williams wrote that "Moring's work is an engaging, enjoyable study that conveys the sense of passion and wonder that these early naturalists felt." A *Publishers Weekly* contributor concluded "These biographical sketches make for an absorbing and accessible—if somewhat narrowly focused—survey that should please those with a bent for natural history."

BIOGRAPHICAL AND CRITICAL SOURCES:

PERIODICALS

Choice, January, 2003, K. B. Sterling, review of *Early American Naturalists: Exploring the American West, 1804-1900,* p. 846.

Library Journal, October 15, 2002, Patricia Ann Owens, review of *Early American Naturalists,* p. 92.

Publishers Weekly, August 12, 2002, review of *Early American Naturalists,* p. 291.

Seattle Times, September 29, 2002, David B. Williams, "Perils, Petals Awaited Early Naturalists."*

*   *   *

MOSETTIG, Michael David 1942-

PERSONAL: Born July, 21, 1942, in Washington, DC; son of Erich (a chemist) and Ann (a writer; maiden name, Nelson) Mosettig; married Ruth L. Leon, September 23, 1970. *Education:* Attended Indiana University, 1960-61; George Washington University, B.A. (political science), 1964; Georgetown University, M.A. (European history), 1968.

ADDRESSES: Home—155 West 68th St., New York, NY 10023. *Office*—356 West 58th St., New York, NY 10019. *Agent*—Andrew Wylie, 250 West 57th St. New York, NY 10019.

CAREER: Journalist. Carpenter News Bureau, Washington, DC, reporter, 1961-65; Newhouse National News Service, 1965-69; United Press International, London, England, reporter, 1969-70; NBC News, Washington, DC, and New York, NY, producer, 1971-79; *MacNeil-Lehrer News Hour,* New York, NY, producer, 1983-85, senior producer, 1985—. Columbia University, New York, NY, associate professor, 1972-83, adjunct professor, 1983—. *Military service:* U.S. Coast Guard Reserve, 1966-67; U.S. Naval Reserve, 1968-78.

MEMBER: International Institute for Strategic Studies, Mid-Atlantic Club, Overseas Writers, American Historical Association.

WRITINGS:

(With Ronald E. Müller) *Revitalizing America: Politics for Prosperity,* Simon & Schuster (New York, NY), 1980.

Contributor to journals and magazines, including *Washington Star, Economist, Boston Globe, New Republic, Europe,* and *Los Angeles Times.*

SIDELIGHTS: Michael David Mosettig has had a very successful career in the field of political journalism. He began as a reporter and eventually made his way up the ranks to become a senior producer of the Public Television broadcast, *MacNeil-Lehrer News Hour.* About twenty years into his profession he and coauthor Robert E. Müller wrote *Revitalizing America: Politics for Prosperity.*

Mosettig's first work focuses on arguing why the American government needs to act more forcefully in economic matters, especially concerning Third World nations. Mosettig and Müller contend that in order for the United States to remain one of the strongest economies it must fund growth in underdeveloped nations and recognize the economic prosperity these countries promise; at the time of the writing there were thirty-four of the world's five hundred largest multinational companies headquartered in a Third World country. David Vogel, writing in the *New York Review of Books,* found that the authors "convincingly demonstrate" their point, while James Traub, writing in the *New York Times Book Review,* observed that Mosettig and Müller "refuse to foretell the end of the world and in fact [end] with a flourish of plausible alternatives to doom." *Washington Post Book World* contributor Richard E. Feinberg praised *Revitalizing America* as "coherent and refreshing" and noted that it "is a timely compilation of ideas currently in the air but not yet in the mainstream."

BIOGRAPHICAL AND CRITICAL SOURCES:

PERIODICALS

New York Review of Books, June 11, 1981, David Vogel, "How to Put Humpty Together Again," pp. 29-32.

New York Times Book Review, January 4, 1981, James Traub, review of *Revitalizing America: Politics for Prosperity,* p. 10.

Washington Post Book World, January 4, 1981, Richard E. Feinberg, "Tuning up the Economic Engine," p. 3.*

*   *   *

MOSKIN, Julia

PERSONAL: Female.

ADDRESSES: Agent—c/o Author Mail, Hyperion Books, 77 West 66th St., New York, NY 10023.

CAREER: Food writer. *New York Times,* New York, NY, staff writer.

WRITINGS:

(With Gale Gand and Rick Tramonto) *American Brasserie: 180 Simple, Robust Recipes Inspired by the Rustic Foods of France, Italy, and America,* wine notes by Marty Tiersky, photographs by Tim Turner, Macmillan (New York, NY), 1997.

(With Rafael Palomino) *Bistro Latino: Home Cooking Fired up with the Flavors of Latin America,* William Morrow (New York, NY), 1998.

(With Gale Gand and Rick Tramonto) *Butter, Sugar, Flour, Eggs,* photographs by Kelly Budgen, Clarkson Potter (New York, NY), 1999.

(With Gale Gand) *Gale Gand's Just a Bite: 125 Luscious, Little Desserts,* photographs by Tim Turner, Clarkson Potter (New York, NY), 2001.

(With Bobby Flay) *Bobby Flay Cooks American: Great Regional Recipes with Sizzling New Flavors,* Hyperion (New York, NY), 2001.

(With Patricia Yeo) *Patricia Yeo: Cooking from A to Z,* foreword by Bobby Flay, St. Martin's Press (New York, NY), 2002.

(With Gale Gand) *Gale Gand's Short and Sweet: Quick Desserts with Eight Ingredients or Less,* photographs by Tim Turner, Clarkson Potter (New York, NY), 2004.

(With Bobby Flay) *Bobby Flay's Boy Gets Grill: 125 Reasons to Light Your Fire!,* photographs by Gentl & Hyers and John Dolan, Scribner (New York, NY), 2004.

Contributor to periodicals, including *Saveur, New York,* and *Metropolitan Home.*

SIDELIGHTS: Food writer Julia Moskin contributes to the "Dining In/Dining Out" section of the *New York Times,* as well as to a number of food and wine publications. In addition, she has coauthored a number of popular cookbooks with well-known chefs and restaurateurs. She brings Latin cuisine to the page with Rafael Palomino in *Bistro Latino: Home Cooking Fired up with the Flavors of Latin America.* Palomino, who was born in Colombia and trained in classic French cuisine, calls his style "Nueva Mundo" or New World. His recipes are cross-cultural and reflect his love of Mediterranean dishes.

Moskin his written a number of books with Gale Gand, pastry chef at Chicago's Tru and host of the Food Network's *Sweet Dreams.* With Gand and Rick Tramonto, she creates *American Brasserie: 180 Simple, Robust Recipes Inspired by the Rustic Foods of France, Italy, and America,* and *Butter, Sugar, Flour, Eggs,* a collection of sweet recipes that include chocolate chip pancakes, taffy apples, and a traditional pound cake. The chapters are organized by ingredients, and the authors include tips on each.

Moskin and Gand also wrote *Gale Gand's Just a Bite: 125 Luscious, Little Desserts* and *Gale Gand's Short and Sweet: Quick Desserts with Eight Ingredients or Less.* The former offers recipes for exquisite little desserts, while the recipes in the latter are more quickly concocted with a limited number of ingredients. *Library Journal* reviewer Judith C. Sutton wrote that "although the recipes are generally simple, they are still sophisticated and imaginative." Included is a chapter of recipes for child cooks, which contains recipes such as peanut butter worms.

Moskin also paired up with Patricia Yeo, executive chef and owner of the three-star AZ in New York City in writing *Patricia Yeo: Cooking from A to Z.* Yeo is Malaysian and was trained on both coasts, including by Bobby Flay, and her dishes combine the best of East and West in a style that can be best described as fusion cuisine. Sutton wrote that the book "has an engaging, approachable style."

Moskin and Food Network icon Flay produced the popular chef's fourth cookbook, *Bobby Flay Cooks American: Great Regional Recipes with Sizzling New*

Flavors. Flay departs from his traditional Southwestern style to explore regional delicacies that range from New England clam chowder to Southern gumbo. They also wrote *Bobby Flay's Boy Gets Grill: 125 Reasons to Light Your Fire!,* a book named for his show. Flay adds extra and unexpected touches to favorites like quesadillas, potato salad, and even the bacon, lettuce, and tomato sandwich, as well as new ideas like grilled squid. A *Publishers Weekly* reviewer commented that the book reflects the "sensitive, more elegant side of grilling," and concluded by saying that the dishes "are uncomplicated and draw on fresh ingredients, and novices should have no trouble following [Flay's] easygoing instructions."

BIOGRAPHICAL AND CRITICAL SOURCES:

PERIODICALS

Booklist, July, 1998, Mark Knoblauch, review of *Bistro Latino: Home Cooking Fire Up with the Flavors of Latin America,* p. 1846; October 15, 2001, Mark Knoblauch, review of *Gale Gand's Just a Bite: 125 Luscious, Little Desserts,* p. 370; May 1, 2004, Mark Knoblauch, review of *Bobby Flay's Boy Gets Grill: 125 Reasons to Light Your Fire!,* p. 1523.

Library Journal, September 15, 1998, Judith C. Sutton, review of *Bistro Latino,* p. 108; October 15, 2001, Judith C. Sutton, review of *Gale Gand's Just a Bite,* p. 103; November 15, 2002, Judith C. Sutton, review of *Patricia Yeo: Cooking from A to Z,* p. 95; December, 2003, Judith C. Sutton, review of *Gale Gand's Short and Sweet: Quick Desserts with Eight Ingredients or Less,* p. 154.

People, November 19, 2001, Max Alexander, review of *Bobby Flay Cooks American: Great Regional Recipes with Sizzling New Flavors,* p. 57.

Publishers Weekly, July 20, 1998, review of *Bistro Latino,* p. 213; July 19, 1999, review of *Butter, Sugar, Flour, Eggs,* p. 189; September 9, 2002, review of *Patricia Yeo,* p. 59; April 26, 2004, review of *Bobby Flay's Boy Gets Grill,* p. 55.*

*   *   *

MUNE, Ian 1941-

PERSONAL: Born 1941, in Auckland, New Zealand.

CAREER: Actor, director, producer, art director, and writer. Actor in films, including (as Bullen) *Sleeping Dogs,* Satori, 1977; (as U-boat commodore) *Nutcase,*

1980; (as Barry Gordon) *Shaker Run,* 1985; (as Hanna) *Dangerous Orphans,* 1985; (as Mangin) *Backstage,* 1988; *The Piano,* Miramax, 1993; (as judge) *Once Were Warriors,* Fine Line, 1994; *Topless Women Talk about Their Lives,* 1997; (as Gary) *Savage Honeymoon,* 2000; (interviewee), *Numero Bruno,* 2000; and (as Bounder) *The Lord of the Rings: The Fellowship of the Ring,* New Line Cinema, 2001. Also appeared in short film *COW.* Director of films, including *Came a Hot Friday,* Orion Classics, 1985; *Bridge to Nowhere,* 1986; *The Grasscutter,* 1990; (and producer) *The End of the Golden Weather,* 1991; *The Whole of the Moon,* 1996; *What Becomes of the Broken Hearted?,* 1999; and *The Sweet Singers* (short film), 2000; also directed health-education short films. Additional second unit director of film *Lord of the Rings: The Fellowship of the Ring,* New Line Cinema, 2001. Art director of film *Sleeping Dogs,* 1977; script advisor for film *Once Were Warriors,* Fine Line, 1994. Actor in television series, including (as Wilbur Skeggins) *Shortland Street,* TVNZ, 1992; (as Michael Weston) *Marlin Bay,* Television New Zealand (TVNZ), 1992; and (as Colin) *Letter to Blanchy,* 1994. Actor in television movies, including (as Henry Bolte) *The Last of the Ryans,* 9 Network, 1997; and (as Buster Keaton) *Lucy,* 2003. Guest star in television series, including (as Gardiner Adams) "Thou Shalt Not Want," *Homicide,* 7 Network, 1975; (as Garrett/Pikes) "Usher II," *The Ray Bradbury Theatre* (also known as *The Bradbury Trilogy* and *Mystery Theatre*), USA Network, 1990; (as Menus Maxius) "Gladiator," *Hercules: The Legendary Journeys,* syndicated, 1995; (as King Sidon) "The Apple," *Hercules: The Legendary Journeys,* 1996; and (as detective) "The Heirloom," *Mataku,* 2002; also appeared as Wilbur Skeggins in an episode of *Shortland Street,* TVNZ. Director of episodes of television series, including *The Ray Bradbury Theatre,* USA Network, 1992; and *Letter to Blanchy.* Has worked as a mask-maker for the Welsh Theatre Company.

WRITINGS:

SCREENPLAYS

(With Arthur Baysting) *Sleeping Dogs* (based on the novel *Smith's Dream* by Christian K. Stead), Satori, 1977.

(With Keith Aberdein) *Nutcase,* 1980.

(With Geoff Murphy) *Goodbye Pork Pie,* 1981.

The Silent One, New Zealand Film Commission, 1984.

(With Dean Parker) *Came on a Hot Friday* (based on a novel by Ronald Hugh Morrieson), Orion Classics, 1985.

(With Bill Baer) *Bridge to Nowhere*, 1986.

(With Bruce Mason) *The End of the Golden Weather*, 1991.

(With Richard Lymposs) *The Whole of the Moon*, 1996.

Also author of episodes of television series *Buck House*, 1974-75, and children's television series *The Mad Dog Gang Meets Rotten Fred and Ratsguts*.

BIOGRAPHICAL AND CRITICAL SOURCES:

PERIODICALS

Booklist, June 1, 1993, Nancy McCray, review of *The Lonely One*, p. 1872.

Los Angeles Times, April 27, 1983, Kevin Thomas, review of *Sleeping Dogs*, p. 4.

Nation, March 6, 1982, Robert Hatch, review of *Sleeping Dogs*, p. 283.

New Statesman, December 13, 1985, John Coleman, review of *Came on a Hot Friday*, p. 30.

New York Times, October 4, 1985, Richard F. Shepard, review of *Came on a Hot Friday*, pp. 16, C15.

Sight and Sound, February, 1993, Philip Kemp, review of *The End of the Golden Weather*, p. 45.

Time International, August 16, 1999, Michael Fitzgerald, "Another Bash: Maori Warriors Return for Perfunctory Punches," p. 63.

Variety, February 20, 1985, review of *Came on a Hot Friday*, p. 23.

ONLINE

Internet Movie Database, http://www.imdb.com/ (July 8, 2003), "Ian Mune."

OneRing.net, http://www.theonering.net/ (July 16, 2003), "Cast: Ian Mune as Bounder."*

*　　*　　*

MYERS, Eric

PERSONAL: Male.

ADDRESSES: Agent—c/o Author Mail, St. Martin's Press, 175 Fifth Ave., New York, NY 10010.

CAREER: Film publicist, writer.

WRITINGS:

(With Howard Mandelbaum) *Screen Deco: A Celebration of High Style in Hollywood* ("Architecture and Film" series), St. Martin's Press (New York, NY), 1985.

(With Howard Mandelbaum) *Forties Screen Style: A Celebration of High Pastiche in Hollywood* ("Architecture and Film" series), St. Martin's Press (New York, NY), 1989.

Uncle Mame: The Life of Patrick Dennis, St. Martin's Press (New York, NY), 2000.

Contributor to periodicals, including the *New York Times, Quest, Variety*, and *Opera News*.

SIDELIGHTS: Eric Myers's broad understanding of the world of film is evident in his first book, *Screen Deco: A Celebration of High Style in Hollywood*, which he wrote with Howard Mandelbaum. This volume documents the use of Art Deco in 1920s to 1940s film design, not only for the musicals with which it is most commonly associated, but also in comedies and dramas. Kevin Jack Hagopian wrote in *Quarterly Review of Film and Video* that "oddly, the most interesting segments deal with the most seemingly prosaic of Art Deco motifs: the decoration of home, office, and the ubiquitous nightclub. The variety of ornamentation, the construction of profilmic space, and the evolution of these styles over time are richly demonstrated in Mandelbaum and Myers's stills presentation, and *Screen Deco* does demonstrate the extent to which Art Deco was absorbed into filmmaking." *Film Comment* contributor Russell Merritt wrote that "the portfolio of stills brings together for the first time that extraordinary, ultra-manufactured world of lush boudoirs, make-believe ballrooms, and smart supper clubs that defined classic Hollywood glamour."

Myers and Mandelbaum followed their debut with *Forties Screen Style: A Celebration of High Pastiche in Hollywood*, which studies trends in the making of post-war Hollywood films.

Uncle Mame: The Life of Patrick Dennis, is the biography of one of the most interesting gay men in Hollywood, Patrick Dennis, author of the book *Auntie Mame*, which was adapted for the film that starred Rosalind Russell and later appeared on Broadway. Dennis, born Edward Everett Tanner III, also published under the name of Virginia Rowans, and in the 1950s he wrote a number of stories featuring the outlandish Mame, all of which were rejected. Then a visionary editor at Vanguard Press suggested that he turn them into a novel. The book made Dennis a millionaire, and he was the first author to have three books on the *New York Times* bestseller list at once. The others were *Guestward Ho!* and *The Loving Couple.* His career peaked in 1962, when his play *Little Me* opened on Broadway.

Lambda Book Report critic Andrew Holleran wrote that "for those gay readers who always thought little Patrick's aunt was somehow a big queen in disguise, or wondered if Dennis was gay, Myers's biography has some astonishing answers. Yes Dennis was homosexual (as if *Little Me* left any doubt), but he was also an upper middle class, Midwestern American Protestant." His life until that point had been conventional. Dennis served in World War II, married a New York debutante, had two children, and worked for the Council on Foreign Relations. But after *Little Me* opened, Dennis left—but never divorced—his wife for a man he met at the Luxor Baths. Another novel, *Tony,* is purportedly about that man, a social climber who then left Dennis for a woman who may or may not have been the owner of a diamond mine. Holleran noted that it is fortunate that some of the people in Dennis's life were still alive to contribute to Myers's biography. His wife said that although a shy man, Dennis was prone to undressing in public after having had a few drinks.

As Myers writes in *Uncle Mame,* even with all of his literary triumphs, the handsome and fashionable Dennis never felt successful. He drank to excess, attempted suicide, and underwent shock therapy at a sanatorium before he came to the realization that he had to follow his heart. He hit bottom in the 1970s, finally drying out to take jobs that included being a butler to MacDonald's founder Ray Kroc and his wife, Joan. He also ran a Houston art gallery, a Mexico City public relations firm, and produced and hosted Mexican television shows. Dennis was working in his third job as a butler when he developed pancreatic cancer. In 1976 he returned to live with his wife and died in that

same year. When she died more than two decades later, she was buried with the urn that contained his ashes in her arms.

Holleran called *Uncle Mame* a "hilarious, sad, and touching story." Mark Griffin wrote in *Gay & Lesbian Review Worldwide* that Dennis and Myers "remind us that gay life once pulsated with acerbic wit and sparkling showmanship, qualities not found in, say, the average Calvin Klein underwear ad." *Advocate* writer Robert Plunket noted that *Uncle Mame* "is exciting news, not only because it rescues from oblivion one of the great comic writers of the century . . . , but also because it has an amazing story to tell."

BIOGRAPHICAL AND CRITICAL SOURCES:

PERIODICALS

Advocate, November 21, 2000, Robert Plunket, review of *Uncle Mame: The Life of Patrick Dennis,* p 112.

Film Comment, May, 1986, Russell Merritt, review of *Screen Deco: A Celebration of High Style in Hollywood,* pp. 72-74.

Gay & Lesbian Review Worldwide, July, 2001, Mark Griffin, review of *Uncle Mame,* p. 40.

Lambda Book Report, December, 2000, Andrew Holleran, review of *Uncle Mame,* p. 14.

New York Times Book Review, December 17, 2000, Ted Loos, review of *Uncle Mame,* p. 22.

Publishers Weekly, November 1, 1985, review of *Screen Deco,* pp. 60-61; October 16, 2000, review of *Uncle Mame,* p. 63.

Quarterly Review of Film and Video, October, 1989, Kevin Jack Hagopian, review of *Screen Deco,* pp. 93-97.

Times-Picayune, February 6, 2001, review of *Uncle Mame,* Living section, p. 4.

Variety, January 17, 1990, review of *Forties Screen Style: A Celebration of High Pastiche in Hollywood,* p. 66.

ONLINE

PlanetOut.com, http://www.planetout.com/ (November 9, 2004), review of *Uncle Mame.**

N-O

NORDAN, Robert W(arren) 1934-2004

OBITUARY NOTICE— See index for *CA* sketch: Born June 20, 1934, in Raleigh, NC; died of pneumonia and complications from Parkinson's disease, November 8, 2004, in Ft. Lauderdale, FL. Psychologist and author. Nordan was a children's advocate and director of children's services for the Illinois Masonic Medical Center, as well as the author of several mystery novels. An only child growing up in the American South, he often found himself taunted by people who discovered he was a homosexual. This experience would later influence his decision to help children as a career. Graduating from Duke University in 1956 with an English degree, he traveled to New York City and became a copywriter for *Life* magazine. While in New York, however, he decided he wanted to do more to help others, so he went back to school at the University of Chicago and earned a Ph.D. in psychology in 1968. Nordan was hired by Illinois Masonic in 1973 as a child psychologist and became director of children's services at the Katherine Wright Center. He worked at the center until 1998, helping children who often had nowhere else to turn. Nordan had other interests, too, he was an accomplished chef and he wrote several detective novels featuring the character Mavis Lashley. Among these are *All Dressed up to Die* (1989), *Death on Wheels* (1991), and *Dead and Breakfast* (2001). He also wrote a novel for young readers, *The Secret Road* (2001).

OBITUARIES AND OTHER SOURCES:

PERIODICALS

Chicago Sun-Times, November 24, 2004.
Chicago Tribune, November 26, 2004, section 3, p. 9.

O'MALLEY, Penelope Grenoble

PERSONAL: Female.

ADDRESSES: Home—Agoura, CA. *Agent*—c/o Author Mail, University of Nebraska Press, Mail Stop 166, Reno, NV 89557.

CAREER: Journalist and editor. Santa Catalina Island Conservancy, former director of communications; research associate at Santa Barbara Museum of Natural History.

AWARDS, HONORS: Recipient of three Los Angeles Press Club awards.

WRITINGS:

Takeoffs Are Optional, Landings Are Mandatory: Airline Pilots Talk about Deregulation, Safety, and the Future of Commercial Aviation, Iowa State University Press (Ames, IA), 1993.
Malibu Diary: Notes from an Urban Refugee, University of Nevada Press (Reno, NV), 2004.

Contributor to numerous magazines and newspapers, including *Malibu Times, Orion, Northern Lights,* and *American Nature Writing.*

SIDELIGHTS: Journalist and author Penelope Grenoble O'Malley has covered stories involving the greater Los Angeles area since the late 1970s. As a writer for both newspapers and magazines, she specializes in subject matter involving conservation, urban planning, and land use.

Moving to the coastal community of Malibu, California, in 1986, O'Malley hoped to find a peaceful community in tune with nature—a change from the urban sprawl of Los Angeles. Instead, through her experiences as a homeowner and as a reporter for the *Malibu Times,* O'Malley discovered the struggle Malibu residents faced involving natural disasters, local politics, land development, and the town's encroachment upon nature. Published in 2004, *Malibu Diary: Notes from an Urban Refugee* is O'Malley's story of Malibu's attempt to balance the rights of property owners and environmental protection. Part history and part memoir, the book tells Malibu's story while also making insights into other communities around the country that struggle with a similar situation.

Critics have praised O'Malley for her multifaceted approach in writing *Malibu Diary. Acorn* contributor Stephanie Bertholdo wrote that O'Malley shares her story with "a reporter's eye for objectivity, an environmentalist's heart and a pragmatist's intellect." Others have pointed out O'Malley's ability to write about both a specific situation and its implications on the bigger picture. "She initiates us into the frustrations of municipal politics while offering valuable insights on how to live within our chosen place," commented Maureen Delaney-Lehman, in a review for *Library Journal.*

BIOGRAPHICAL AND CRITICAL SOURCES:

BOOKS

O'Malley, Penelope Grenoble, *Malibu Diary: Notes from an Urban Refugee,* University of Nevada Press (Reno, NV), 2004.

PERIODICALS

Acorn (Agoura Hills, CA), June 24, 2004, Stephanie Bertholdo, "Agoura Hills Author Writes Book on Malibu."
Booklist, March 1, 2004, David Pitt, review of *Malibu Diary: Notes from an Urban Refugee,* p. 1121.

Library Journal, February 1, 2004, Maureen Delaney-Lehman, review of *Malibu Diary,* p. 110.
Palisadian-Post (Pacific Palisades, CA), June 17, 2004, Nancy Smith, "'Malibu Diary' Focuses on People, Politics, and Land."

ONLINE

University of Nevada Press Web site, http://www.nvbooks.nevada.edu/ (September 29, 2004), "Penelope Grenoble O'Malley."*

*　　*　　*

OAKES, Andy 1952-

PERSONAL: Born 1952; married; children: two. *Education:* Certificate in engineering; degree in psychology.

ADDRESSES: Home—London, England. *Agent*—c/o Author Mail, Overlook Press, 141 Wooster St., New York, NY 10012.

CAREER: Author and youth counselor specializing in alcohol and substance abuse. Has also worked as an engineer and photographer.

WRITINGS:

Dragon's Eye: A Novel, Overlook Press (Woodstock, NY), 2004.

SIDELIGHTS: Andy Oakes's novel *Dragon's Eye* offers readers meticulous details of life in modern Shanghai. In the book, eight mutilated bodies, all chained together, are found in the Huangpu River. Senior police investigator Sun Piao and his assistant Yaobang ignore warnings that the killings are connected to powerful political figures. When his own supervisors and the medical investigator hinder his inquiry, Piao solicits help from Yaobang's brother, a young medical student, and discovers that the corpses are likely victims of the illegal organ transplant trade. Among the victims is an American archeology student; his mother arrives on the scene and becomes involved in both the case and Piao's personal life. The danger of pursuing the case increases when two men involved in storing and examining the bodies are killed and Piao is framed as a murderer.

Though reviewers felt that the book is a bit too long, they applauded Piao's character and the description of his surroundings. Fred Gervat remarked in *Library Journal* that Oakes has crafted "a rich, palpable ambiance" in a book that includes "several almost poetic passages." A *Kirkus Reviews* writer credited the author with a "a masterly depiction of modern Shanghai" and called Piao "an admirable hero." *Dragon's Eye* is a "melancholy, evocative" thriller, according to a *Publishers Weekly* critic.

BIOGRAPHICAL AND CRITICAL SOURCES:

PERIODICALS

Kirkus Reviews, January 1, 2004, review of *Dragon's Eye,* p. 11.

Library Journal, March 1, 2004, Fred Gervat, review of *Dragon's Eye,* p. 108.

Publishers Weekly, November 17, 2003, review of *Dragon's Eye,* p. 38.

ONLINE

Triangle.com, http://www.triangle.com/ (August 26, 2004), Rod Cockshutt, review of *Dragon's Eye.**

*   *   *

OPPENHEIMER, Todd

PERSONAL: Married; wife's name Anh; children: A.J., Moss. *Education:* University of California at Berkeley, B.A., 1981; Portland State University, graduate study, 1991. *Hobbies and other interests:* "Woodworking, portrait sculpture, calligraphy, and various sports."

ADDRESSES: Home—San Francisco, CA. *Agent*—c/o Author Mail, Random House, 1745 Broadway, New York, NY 10019.

CAREER: Freelance journalist and investigative reporter. Has worked as a calligrapher, portrait sculptor, professional actor, and mime. Has appeared as a guest on radio and television programs, including American Broadcasting Company's (ABC) *Nightline.*

MEMBER: Writer's Grotto Collective.

AWARDS, HONORS: Investigative Reporters & Editors' Award for small newspapers, 1986, for "Durham's Hidden Tax Breaks," and *Washington Monthly* monthly journalism award for excellence in government reporting, 1987, for "Solutions to Sprawl," both published in North Carolina *Independent;* Chairman's Award for environmental journalism, 1996, for "The Rancher Subsidy," National Magazine Award for public interest reporting, 1997, for "The Computer Delusion," and Education Writer's Association Award for national magazines, 1999, for "Schooling the Imagination," all published in *Atlantic Monthly.*

WRITINGS:

The Flickering Mind: The False Promise of Technology in the Classroom, and How Learning Can Be Saved, Random House (New York, NY), 2003.

Contributor to periodicals, including *Newsweek, Washington Post, Atlantic Monthly, National Journal, Washington Post, Utne Reader, Mother Jones, Sacramento Bee,* and London *Observer.*

SIDELIGHTS: A veteran journalist and youth mentor, Todd Oppenheimer spent seven years researching the dramatic and growing impact of computers on today's classrooms. The result is *The Flickering Mind: The False Promise of Technology in the Classroom, and How Learning Can Be Saved.* Despite the book's premise, Oppenheimer is not opposed to technology. Indeed, he was one of the first journalists to embrace the new technology, eagerly delving into the world of personal computers and the Internet. And like many, Oppenheimer had high hopes for the use of new technology in the classroom. But as he began visiting those classrooms, he "observed many students noodling about on the Web, clicking aimlessly from site to site," as *School Library Journal* contributor Walter Minkel explained. More and more, Oppenheimer began to question the money being spent to make classrooms Internet-accessible, and the underlying philosophy that equated glitzy new technology with progress in learning. As Timothy A. Hacsi explained in the *New York Times Book Review,* "His descriptions of excellent schools using computers in a limited way, if at all, gets at the heart of what good classrooms look like: teachers who know how to teach . . . and students who believe they can and should learn from those teachers." According to *Seattle Times* reviewer Steve Weinberg, "Anybody who cares about the successes and failures of kindergarten through grade-twelve education should read *The Flickering Mind,* a painstakingly reported, passionately argued book."

BIOGRAPHICAL AND CRITICAL SOURCES:

PERIODICALS

Booklist, September 1, 2003, Vanessa Bush, review of *The Flickering Mind: The False Promise of Technology in the Classroom, and How Learning Can Be Saved,* p. 30.

Boulder Daily Camera, January 4, 2004, Geof Wollerman, review of *The Flickering Mind.*

Christian Science Monitor, October 14, 2003, review of *The Flickering Mind.*

Contra Costa Times, December 21, 2003, Suzanne Pardington, "'Flickering' Plugs into Tech/Learning Disconnect."

Dallas Morning News, January 18, 2004, Joshua Benton, review of *The Flickering Mind.*

Denver Post, December 7, 2003, Steve Weinberg, review of *The Flickering Mind,* section F, p. 15.

Education Next, summer, 2004, Brian Nelson, "Quality Curricula: The Timeless Technology," p. 79.

Kirkus Reviews, August 1, 2003, review of *The Flickering Mind,* p. 1007.

Library Journal, September 15, 2003, Jean Caspers, review of *The Flickering Mind,* p. 67.

New Criterion, April, 2004, Mark Bauerlein, "As Seen on TV," p. 84.

New Leader, September-October, 2003, Paul Gray, "Conflicting Visions of Education," p. 18.

New York Times Book Review, January 4, 2004, Timothy A. Hacsi, "Tales out of School," p. 19.

Publishers Weekly, August 11, 2003, review of *The Flickering Mind,* p. 266.

School Library Journal, November 1, 2003, Walter Minkel, "Rage against the Machine," p. 34.

Seattle Times, October 26, 2003, Steve Weinberg, "The Short-circuiting of U.S. Education."

ONLINE

Booknoise.net, http://www.booknoise.net/ (September 29, 2004), author profile.

Newsweek Online, http://www.newsweek.com/ (October 14, 2003), "Are Computers Wrecking Schools?"

*   *   *

OPPERSDORFF, Mathias T. 1935-

PERSONAL: Born September 11, 1935, in Boston, MA; son of Mathias and Katherine (Thomas) Oppersdorff. *Ethnicity:* "Caucasian." *Education:* Fairfield University, B.A., 1959; American University, M.A., 1965.

ADDRESSES: Home—P.O. Box 737, Wakefield, RI 02880.

CAREER: Photographer.

WRITINGS:

PHOTOJOURNALISM

Adirondack Faces (photographs), text by Alice Wolf Gilborn, foreword by Adam Hochschild, Syracuse University Press (Syracuse, NY), 1991.

People of the Road: The Irish Travellers, (photographs), Syracuse University Press (Syracuse, NY), 1997.

Under the Spell of Arabia (photographs), Syracuse University Press (Syracuse, NY), 2001.

BIOGRAPHICAL AND CRITICAL SOURCES:

PERIODICALS

Middle East Journal, autumn, 2002, Michelle d'Amico, review of *Under the Spell of Arabia,* p. 741.

ORBANES, Philip E. 1947-

PERSONAL: Born June 1, 1947, in Somers Point, NJ; son of Philip (a mechanical and electronic technician) and Antta (a bookkeeper; maiden name, Gihorski) Orbanes; married May 31, 1969; wifes name, Anna Rozsa (a registered nurse); children: Philip C., Julian E. *Education:* Case Institute of Technology (now Case Western Reserve University), B.S. *Hobbies and other interests:* Inventing games, musical composition.

ADDRESSES: Home—56 Bartletts Reach, Amesbury, MA 01913. *Office*—Winning Moves, Inc., 100 Conifer Hill, Suite 102, Danvers, MA 01923. *E-mail*—philorb@aol.com.

CAREER: Parker Brothers, Salem, MA, senior vice president of research and development, 1979-90; Pop! Inc., Topsfield, MA, president, 1990—; Winning Moves, Inc., Danvers, MA, president, 1995—; vice chair, 1997—. Peabody Essex Museum, member.

MEMBER: National Railroad Historical Society, Phi Kappa Tau.

WRITINGS:

The Monopoly Companion, by Rich Uncle Pennybags, as Told to Philip Orbanes, B. Adams (Boston, MA), 1988, 2nd edition published as *The Monopoly Companion: The Players Guide; The Game from A to Z, Winning Tips, Trivia, by Mr. Monopoly as Told to Philip Orbanes,* Adams Media (Holbrook, MA), 1999.
Rook in a Book, Winning Moves Press (Danvers, MA), 1998.

The Game Makers: The Story of Parker Brothers from Tiddledy Winks to Trivial Pursuit, Harvard Business School Publishing (Boston, MA), 2004.

SIDELIGHTS: Philip E. Orbanes told *CA:* "My primary motivation is to set forth my love and knowledge of the games industry, 'Monopoly' in particular, and make this accessible via my books—be they nonfiction or historical fiction.

"I've always had a desire to share what I learn. My career has required a balance between creating and business management. From the latter, I've learned the value of clarity and precision. When I write, my goal is to provide knowledge enjoyably and clearly.

"Discovery of fascinating facts or powerful concepts influences my work. I write like a sculptor works: rapidly finishing a rough 'whole,' then taking time to perfect and tune every word. My most pleasant surprise is the connection readers have to my works, and the good memories my writing had triggered.

"*The Game Makers: The Story of Parker Brothers from Tiddledy Winks to Trivial Pursuit* is my favorite work to date because it spans more than 100 years of American history and connects the principles of success at playing games to success in real life.

"I hope my books will help people see the connection between the forces of history that have influenced how we live, and play to win."

BIOGRAPHICAL AND CRITICAL SOURCES:

PERIODICALS

Booklist, November 15, 2003, David Pitt, review of *The Game Makers: The Story of Parker Brothers from Tiddledy Winks to Trivial Pursuit,* p. 555.
Economist, November 22, 2003, review of *The Game Makers,* p. 82.

P

PARKER, Barbara Keevil 1938-

PERSONAL: Born May 17, 1938, in Tacoma, WA; daughter of William H. and Jean (Durkee) Keevil; married Duane F. Parker (a minister), June 11, 1960; children: Stacy, Pamela, Jon. *Education:* University of Puget Sound, B.A., 1960; Kansas State University, M.S., 1973, Ph.D., 1976. *Hobbies and other interests:* Travel, toy trains, collecting German nutcrackers.

ADDRESSES: Home—Everett WA. *Agent*—c/o Author Mail, Lerner Publications, 241 First Ave. North, Minneapolis, MN 55401. *E-mail*—bkeevil5@aol.com.

CAREER: Therapist, educator, and writer. Rhode Island College Department of Economics and Management, Center for Economic Education, coordinator, 1976-78; curriculum consultant, 1978-79; Salve Regina College, Newport, RI, graduate instructor in health services administration, 1981-82; Rhode Island Hospital, Providence, manager of employee education and training staff, 1979-84; Wesley Homes, Atlanta, GA, director of education, 1985-91, coordinator of employee assistance program, 1987-91; Covenant Counseling Institute, Snellville, GA, therapist and director of education, 1991-94; Interfaith Counseling Center, therapist, 1995-98. Freelance writer, beginning 1986; Institute of Children's Literature, West Redding, CT, writing instructor, beginning 2000.

MEMBER: Society of Children's Book Writers and Illustrators, American Association of Marriage and Family Therapists.

AWARDS, HONORS: Parchment and Quill Award, Georgia Society of Healthcare and Training, 1986,

1992; Distinguished Achievement Award, American Society of Healthcare Education and Training 1991.

WRITINGS:

FOR CHILDREN

Christian Celebrations, Pockets of Learning, 1998.
The Lord Is My Shepherd, Pockets of Learning, 1998.
The Good Samaritan, Pockets of Learning, 1998.
North American Wolves, Carolrhoda Books (Minneapolis, MN), 1998.
Susan B. Anthony: Daring to Vote, Millbrook Press (Brookfield, CT), 1998.
(With Duane F. Parker) *Miguel de Cervantes,* Chelsea House Publishers (Philadelphia, PA), 2003.
Giraffes, Carolrhoda Books (Minneapolis, MN), 2004.
Cheetahs, Lerner Publication Co. (Minneapolis, MN), 2005.
(With Dwayne F. Parker) *Canada Lynx,* Lerner Publication Co. (Minneapolis, MN), 2005.

OTHER

Healthcare Education: A Guide to Staff Development, 1986.

Contributor to periodicals, including *Grit, Your Big Backyard, Cogniz, Boys' Quest, Collector Editions, Aim,* and various professional journals.

SIDELIGHTS: Barbara Keevil Parker is the author of several children's books, including *North American Wolves* and *Susan B. Anthony: Daring to Vote.* Inspired by Parker's interest in wildlife and the outdoors, *North American Wolves* introduces elementary-grade readers to the everyday world of wild wolves, including their physiology, their habits, and their unique behavior, which includes instinctive territoriality, hunting strategies, and communication techniques. Clear photos depicting the sometimes maligned and controversial animals accompany the text so young researchers can more clearly visualize the topics under discussion. Characterizing the book's introduction as "dramatic," Stephanie Zvirin added in a review of the book for *Booklist* that the author quickly "gets down to business, clearly and informatively."

Parker once commented: "I live in the Pacific Northwest and grew up a country girl. We lived on a small lake, and I spend many hours on the lake swimming, fishing, and canoeing, and an equal number of hours hiking in the woods, building secret camps, and learning to appreciate nature.

"In high school, I was deeply involved in journalism—editing the yearbook and writing for the school paper. I changed direction in college and majored in speech and drama with the goal of teaching in that area. Fortunately, I minored in English and American literature, because that's where I found my first teaching job.

"Marriage right after college took me to Evanston, Illinois, where my husband was attending school at Garrett Theological Seminary. During his graduate school years I taught school, and delivered our first child. From Evanston, we moved to Kansas, where two more children were born. Here, when our children were young, I took my first stab at writing children's books. The publishers rejected them. Then I got busy teaching preschool, middle school, and high school. I put aside my writing.

"When all the children were in school, I needed something new for me. I decided to go to graduate school. As a graduate assistant in adult education, I discovered I could write and publish articles about my work. I also studied marriage and family therapy and spent a year at the Menninger Foundation doing an internship in counseling.

"After another move I started my Rhode Island career in a fascinating job at a college. As coordinator of the Center for Economic Education, I collaborated with a local puppeteer to write a play called *Dollars and Sense*. Armed with puppets and a portable stage, I traveled to schools throughout the state presenting a puppet show to elementary children to get them thinking about basic economic concepts. Later I moved away from children to become director of education at a hospital. Here I wrote my first book, published in 1986, about developing courses for use in a hospital setting. In the meantime, we moved to Atlanta, Georgia. Emory University offered a class called Writing for Children, and I enrolled.

"I love animals so one of my early stories was about a wolf. I mailed it to a publisher. They wrote back that they didn't take fiction. Would I be interested in writing a nonfiction book on wolves? Of course I said yes! However, when I sent the manuscript to them, they rejected it. Brokenhearted, I paced around the house and finally mustered up enough courage to call them to ask what was wrong. 'Boring presentation,' they said. 'Well if I can rewrite it and make it more exciting, would you still be interested?' I asked. They agreed. A few months later I had my first children' book contract.

"After ten years in Georgia, we moved back to New England to be near children and grandchildren. New England was home for eight years. In addition to my writing career, I was a marriage and family therapist.

"My husband and I enjoy several hobbies, travel being one of them. We also love toy trains and German nutcrackers. Scattered throughout our houses we have two hundred nutcracker eyes staring at us year-round.

"From my window, I can watch the wind and sun play games on the nearby water. Mt. Baker towers above the hills and water, wearing its gleaming white snow cover year-round. Seeing nature in action right outside my window provides inspiration and an abundance of story ideas. I write every weekday, usually in the morning, however, when I get deep into a manuscript, time stops and I get lost in my writing."

BIOGRAPHICAL AND CRITICAL SOURCES:

PERIODICALS

Booklist, June 1, 1998, Ilene Cooper, review of *Susan B. Anthony: Daring to Vote,* p. 1758; December 1, 1998, Stephanie Zvirin, review of *North American Wolves,* p. 681.

PASSARELLA, J. G.
See GANGEMI, Joseph

*   *   *

PEARLMAN, Jeff

PERSONAL: Married; wife's name Catherine; children: Casey (daughter).

ADDRESSES: Office—Newsday, 235 Pinelawn Rd., Melville, NY 11747-4250. *Agent*—c/o Author Mail, HarperCollins, 10 East 53rd St., New York, NY 10022.

CAREER: Journalist. *Tennessean,* Nashville, TN, features writer; *Sports Illustrated,* New York, NY, baseball writer; *Newsday,* Melville, NY, features writer.

WRITINGS:

The Bad Guys Won: A Season of Brawling, Boozing, Bimbo-chasing, and Championship Baseball with Straw, Doc, Mookie, Nails, the Kid, and the Rest of the 1986 Mets, the Rowdiest Team to Put on a New York Uniform, and Maybe the Best, Harper-Collins (New York, NY), 2004.

SIDELIGHTS: Jeff Pearlman spent six years as a baseball writer for *Sports Illustrated,* during which time he conducted well-publicized interview with Atlanta Braves dynamo pitcher John Rocker, a player whose attitude and behavior cut short a promising career. In his interview with Pearlman, Rocker stated that he would never play for a New York team because he didn't want to ride a train "next to some kid with purple hair, next to some queer with AIDS, right next to some dude who just got out of jail for the fourth time, right next to some twenty-year-old mom with four kids." Rocker, a Georgia native who pulled no punches in taunting Mets fans, was fined for his conduct. After Pearlman's article appeared, Rocker threatened the journalist and was again fined and demoted to the minor leagues.

Five years after that inflammatory interview, Pearlman's first full-length book was published. *The Bad Guys Won: A Season of Brawling, Boozing,*

Bimbo-chasing, and Championship Baseball with Straw, Doc, Mookie, Nails, the Kid, and the Rest of the 1986 Mets, the Rowdiest Team to Put on a New York Uniform, and Maybe the Best is a tribute to his favorite team during an outstanding year. In 1986 the Mets had 108 wins, beat the Houston Astros in the playoffs, and went on to defeat the Boston Red Sox in the world series. Pearlman writes of general manager Frank Cashen, manager Davey Johnson, and the events of the entire season. But the book is more of a tell-all of the bad behavior of various players. "There is no boozing, drug use, or bimbo eruption that he does not describe," commented *Booklist* contributor GraceAnne A. DeCandido. However, as long as the players performed well, most of this behavior was tolerated by management. Among the players profiled by Pearlman are Darryl Strawberry and Doc Gooden. *Library Journal* reviewer Robert C. Cottrell called "particularly sad" the accounts of their "falls from baseball grace," but added, "All this makes for a fascinating read." *Publishers Weekly* contributor Mark Rotella wrote that "baseball aficionados, especially Mets fans, will enjoy this affectionate but critical look at this exciting season."

Pearlman told *CA:* "I liked stirring up trouble at my high school, and the best way to do that was to write for the school paper and agitate people. The writer I am most influenced by is Greg Orlando, an editor for *XBox Nation* magazine, and a truly gifted wordsmith.

"I write by waiting until the last hour, guzzling twelve cans of Coke, and going. The most surprising thing I've learned as a writer is that I can make a living doing it. I, like many writers, hate most everything I do."

BIOGRAPHICAL AND CRITICAL SOURCES:

PERIODICALS

Booklist, May 1, 2004, GraceAnne A. DeCandido, review of *The Bad Guys Won: A Season of Brawling, Boozing, Bimbo-chasing, and Championship Baseball with Straw, Doc, Mookie, Nails, the Kid, and the Rest of the 1986 Mets, the Rowdiest Team to Put on a New York Uniform, and Maybe the Best,* p. 1536.
Library Journal, May 1, 2004, Robert C. Cottrell, review of *The Bad Guys Won,* p. 118.
Publishers Weekly, April 26, 2004, Mark Rotella, review of *The Bad Guys Won,* p. 53.

PELL, Ed(ward) 1950-
(Bob Boudelang)

PERSONAL: Born April 5, 1950, in Baltimore, MD.

ADDRESSES: Home—NJ. *Agent*—c/o Author Mail, Capstone Press, 151 Good Counsel Dr., P.O. Box 669, Mankato, MN 56002. *E-mail*—espvent@bellatlantic.net.

CAREER: Writer, journalist, and marketing consultant. ESP Ventures (marketing consultant firm), Morristown, NJ, president.

AWARDS, HONORS: Jesse H. Neal Business Journalism Competition award, 1989; American Society of Business Press Editors award, 1995.

WRITINGS:

Maryland ("Land of Liberty" series), Capstone Press (Mankato, MN), 2003.
Connecticut ("Land of Liberty" series), Capstone Press (Mankato, MN), 2003.
Indiana ("Land of Liberty" series), Capstone Press (Mankato, MN), 2003.
John Winthrop: Governor of the Massachusetts Bay Colony, Capstone Press (Mankato, MN), 2004.

Author of online column "Equal Time with Bob Boudelang, Angry American Patriot," for *DemocraticUnderground.com.* Contributor to periodicals, including *Simply the Best, Internet Publishing, NJ Savvy Living,* and *Prehistoric Times.*

BIOGRAPHICAL AND CRITICAL SOURCES:

PERIODICALS

School Library Journal, August, 2004, Kathleen Simonetta, review of *The Salem Witch Trials,* p. 133.

ONLINE

DemocraticUnderground.com, http://www.democraticunderground.com/bob/ (August 12, 2004).

PERRIN, (Edwin) Noel 1927-2004

OBITUARY NOTICE— See index for *CA* sketch: Born September 18, 1927, in New York, NY; died of Shy-Drager syndrome November 21, 2004, in Thetford Center, VT. Educator and author. Perrin was professor emeritus at Dartmouth College and an author best known for his essay collections about rural life in Vermont. An English major, he earned a B.A. from Williams College in 1949 and an M.A. from Duke University in 1950. A brief post at the New York City *Daily News* as a copy boy ended when he enlisted in the U.S. Army. During the Korean War he earned a Bronze Star. After the war, he worked from 1953 until 1956 as an associate editor for the periodical *Medical Economics.* Perrin was then hired to teach at the Women's College of the University of North Carolina (now the University of North Carolina at Greensboro), while completing an M.Litt. at Trinity Hall, Cambridge, in 1958. In 1959 he joined the Dartmouth College faculty, where he became a full professor of English in 1964 and chaired the department from 1972 until 1975. His interest in environmental conservation also led to an appointment as adjunct professor of environmental studies in 1991, a year after he retired from teaching English. Also known as a book critic who wrote reviews for the *New Yorker* and a column for the *Washington Post Book World,* Perrin had a great love of reading and writing. He is best known for his essay collections about Vermont, including *First Person Rural: Essays of a Sometime Farmer* (1978), *Second Person Rural: More Essays of a Sometime Farmer* (1980), *Third Person Rural: Further Essays of a Sometime Farmer* (1983), and, finally, *Last Person Rural* (1991). His other, more recent, books include *Solo: Life with an Electric Car* (1992) and *A Child's Delight* (1997).

OBITUARIES AND OTHER SOURCES:

PERIODICALS

New York Times, November 25, 2004, p. C10.
Washington Post, November 26, 2004, p. B6.

*   *   *

PETRINO, Elizabeth (Anne) 1962-

PERSONAL: Born July 18, 1962. *Education:* State University of New York at Buffalo, B.A. (summa cum laude); Cornell University, M.A., Ph.D., 1991.

ADDRESSES: Office—Dept. of English, DMH 109, Fairfield University, 1073 North Benson Rd., Fairfield, CT 06824. *E-mail*—epetrino@mail.fairfield.edu.

CAREER: Louisiana Tech University, Ruston, assistant professor of English; Wake Forest University, Winston-Salem, NC, assistant professor of English; Fairfield University, Fairfield, CT, assistant professor of English.

MEMBER: Phi Beta Kappa.

WRITINGS:

Emily Dickinson and Her Contemporaries: Women's Verses in America, 1820-1885, University Press of New England (Hanover, NH), 1998.

Contributor to *The Cambridge Companion to Nineteenth-Century American Women's Writing,* Cambridge University Press (Cambridge, England), 2001.

SIDELIGHTS: With her debut work *Emily Dickinson and Her Contemporaries: Women's Verses in America, 1820-1885,* Elizabeth Petrino examines the state of women's writing in nineteenth-century America. Based on over ten years of research, *Emily Dickinson and Her Contemporaries* builds on topics originally presented in Petrino's doctoral dissertation, such as how Dickinson's works compare to those of her contemporaries, including Louisa May Alcott, Helen Hunt Jackson, Lydia Sigourney, and Frances Osgood. Petrino also addresses such issues as why Dickinson refrained from publishing her poems, and why many of her writings center on death. Citing examples such as nineteenth-century reviews by male editors of other women's poems, Petrino describes Dickinson's motive for not publishing her poems as an unwillingness to let her writings be limited by convention.

Kim Woodbridge, writing for *Library Journal,* commented that "Petrino discusses how Dickinson, rather than being separate from her contemporaries, actually used the same poetic themes deemed acceptable to women writers but differed in creating 'a new powerful means of expression within the prescribed limits.'" Marianne Noble, a reviewer for *Legacy* stated that the

book "reveals Dickinson as a poet who both observed conventional boundaries of Victorian female expression and transformed them to create her own startling, brilliant poetic voice."

BIOGRAPHICAL AND CRITICAL SOURCES:

PERIODICALS

Legacy, June, 2000, Marianne Noble, review of *Emily Dickinson and Her Contemporaries: Women's Verses in America, 1820-1885,* p. 232.
Library Journal, April 15, 1998, Kim Woodbridge, review of *Emily Dickinson and Her Contemporaries: Women's Verses in America, 1820-1885,* p. 81.
Times Literary Supplement, September 17, 1999, Mark Ford, "But, Oh, I Love the Danger!," pp. 6-7.
Virginia Quarterly Review, winter, 1999, review of *Emily Dickinson and Her Contemporaries,* pp. 29-30.

ONLINE

Fairfield University Web site, http://www.fairfield.edu/ (November 8, 2004), "Elizabeth Petrino."
University Press of New England, http://www.upne.com/ (July 14, 2004), Martha Nell Smith, review of *Emily Dickinson and Her Contemporaries.**

*   *   *

PILARDI, Jo-Ann 1941-

PERSONAL: Born 1941. *Education:* Duquesne University, B.A.; Pennsylvania State University, M.Phil.; Johns Hopkins University, Ph.D.

ADDRESSES: Office—Department of Philosophy and Religious Studies, Towson University, 8000 York Rd., Towson, MD 21252-0001; fax: 410-830-4398 and 410-830-3753.

CAREER: Author and educator. Towson University, Towson, MD, professor of philosophy and women's studies and director of women's studies program.

WRITINGS:

Simon de Beauvoir Writing the Self: Philosophy Becomes Autobiography, Greenwood Press (Westport, CT), 1999.

SIDELIGHTS: Author and educator Jo-Ann Pilardi serves as Professor of philosophy and women's studies at Towson University in Maryland. Her varied research interests include feminist philosophy; existentialism; postmodernism and deconstruction; social and political philosophy; race, class, and gender studies; and the life and work of French feminist Simone de Beauvoir, the last on whom she focuses her book, *Simone de Beauvoir Writing the Self: Philosophy Becomes Autobiography.*

Pilardi's goal in *Simone de Beauvoir Writing the Self* is not to provide a biography or simple critique of the author's writing. Instead, she attempts to examine Beauvoir's theory of self as she presented it in her works, analyzing essays, Beauvoir's influential work *The Second Self,* and subsequent autobiographical writings. Ursula Tidd, in a review for *Hypatia,* called Pilardi's book "a welcome contribution to Simone de Beauvoir studies and, more particularly, to critical studies of Beauvoir's autobiographical project." The critic went on to label *Simone de Beauvoir Writing the Self* "an ambitions project for it seeks to interrelate two substantial areas of Beauvoir's corpus and invites us to see how she developed her philosophical thinking through the representation of her singular life." *Biography* contributor Barbara Klaw remarked that Pilardi's book will be "of appeal to those with little background in philosophy or in Beauvoir studies, as well as to a seasoned scholar," and concluded that it "stands out as a worthy text which could easily be used in philosophy or literature courses . . . It is a very understandable and valuable addition to current Beauvoirian scholarship."

BIOGRAPHICAL AND CRITICAL SOURCES:

PERIODICALS

Biography, spring, 2000, Barbara Klaw, review of *Simone de Beauvoir Writing the Self: Philosophy Becomes Autobiography,* p. 379.

Choice, January, 2000, S. S. Merrill, review of *Simone de Beauvoir Writing the Self,* p. 950.
Hypatia, fall, 1999, Ursula Tidd, review of *Simone de Beauvoir Writing the Self,* p. 182.
Reference and Research Book News, May, 1999, review of *Simone de Beauvoir Writing the Self,* p. 3.

ONLINE

Towson University Web site, http://www.towson.edu/ (November 12, 2004), "Jo-Ann Pilardi."*

*   *   *

PILLEMER, David B. 1950-

PERSONAL: Born 1950. *Education:* Graduated from University of Chicago; Harvard Graduate School of Education, Ph.D.

ADDRESSES: Office—Wellesley College, 106 Central St., Wellesley, MA 02481.

CAREER: Psychologist and educator. Wellesley College, Wellesley, MA, 1978—, professor of psychology, faculty director of Learning and Teaching Center, psychological director of Child Study Center, and William R. Kenan, Jr. Professor Chair, 1999-2001.

WRITINGS:

(With Richard J. Light) *Summing Up: The Science of Reviewing Research,* Harvard University Press (Cambridge, MA), 1984.
Momentous Events, Vivid Memories: How Unforgettable Moments Help Us Understand the Meaning of Our Lives, Harvard University Press (Cambridge, MA), 1998.
(Editor, with Sheldon H. White) *Developmental Psychology and Social Change: Research, History, and Policy* ("Cambridge Studies in Social and Emotional Development" series), Cambridge University Press (New York, NY), 2005.

SIDELIGHTS: David B. Pillemer is a psychologist whose research specialty is autobiographical memory, and he has studied memory development in children, including memory of trauma. His first book, *Summing Up: The Science of Reviewing Research,* approaches the subject of research in the social sciences. *Science* writer Donald W. Fiske commented that "for a problem in social science, the pertinent research literature is usually more diverse than that for one in natural science." Fiske felt that Pillemer and coauthor Richard J. Light "not only provide an excellent introduction to the new systematic methods for summing up and analyzing bodies of research but also examine the standard qualitative type of review, assessing the strengths and weaknesses of each approach." The authors suggest how results can be synthesized and provide guidelines to those who depend on such research, particularly educators.

Pillemer writes in *Momentous Events, Vivid Memories: How Unforgettable Moments Help Us Understand the Meaning of Our Lives* that "it is permissible and often valuable to view personal event memory as a belief system rather than a mechanistic entity filled with traces that are objectively true or false." Pillemer defines personal event memories as those that recall a single event and details of the rememberer's personal circumstances, and which are filled with sensory information that enables the remember to have a sense of reexperiencing the event. Pillemer studies how these memories teach us and help us in experiencing life.

He notes different types of recollections, including what he calls "flashbulb" memories. An example would be recalling exactly what you were doing when you heard that President Kennedy was shot. He calls memories of traumatic events, such as Hiroshima, "flashbacks." An example of an "insight" memory would be recalling arriving on a college campus for the first time. He writes that personal event memories can be either of two kinds of representation, image or narrative.

Biography reviewers Kathryn A. Becker and Jennifer J. Freyd noted that the focus of this book "differs from the focus of memory research traditionally performed by cognitive psychologists. Unlike laboratory memory research that asks college students to memorize lists of words or numbers, Pillemer's work, while still primarily empirical in nature, is more concerned with the personal significance of emotionally laden events than with the absolute accuracy or processing of details of memory for the mundane." Becker and Freyd concluded by saying that this volume "is remarkable

in the comprehensive way the concept of personal event memories spans a great number of personally significant memories. The wide coverage is even more impressive in the context of insightful discussion on basic memory systems and child development."

Oral History Review contributor Valerie Raleigh Yow noted that Pillemer "summarizes many recent studies and shows their relationship to other studies." Yow felt that *Momentous Events, Vivid Memories* "is an outstanding text which presents research in a coherent way and is readable for people outside psychology."

BIOGRAPHICAL AND CRITICAL SOURCES:

PERIODICALS

Biography, spring, 2000, Kathryn A. Becker, Jennifer J. Freyd, review of *Momentous Events, Vivid Memories: How Unforgettable Moments Help Us Understand the Meaning of Our Lives,* p. 372.

Education Digest, March, 1985, review of *Summing Up: The Science of Reviewing Research,* pp. 70-71.

Oral History Review, summer-fall, 2001, Valerie Raleigh Yow, review of *Momentous Events, Vivid Memories,* p. 151.

Science, January 25, 1985, Donald W. Fiske, review of *Summing Up,* p. 407.

Times Literary Supplement, October 30, 1998, Janet Feigenbaum, review of *Momentous Events, Vivid Memories,* pp. 14-15.*

*   *   *

PINCUS, Fred L. 1942-

PERSONAL: Born September 6, 1942, in New York, NY; son of Sam (a slipcover cutter) and Leah (an administrative assistant; maiden name, Kugler) Pincus; married Natalie J. Sokoloff (a university professor), March 12, 1982; children: Joshua M. Pincus-Sokoloff. *Ethnicity:* "Jewish." *Education:* University of California, Los Angeles, B.A., 1964, M.A., 1967, Ph.D., 1969. *Politics:* "Left." *Religion:* "Atheist."

ADDRESSES: Home—2417 Briarwood Rd., Baltimore, MD 21209. *Office*—Department of Sociology and Anthropology, University of Maryland—Baltimore County, 1000 Hilltop Cir., Baltimore, MD 21250. *E-mail*—pincus@umbc.edu.

CAREER: University of Maryland—Baltimore County, Baltimore, professor of sociology, 1968—.

WRITINGS:

(With Elayne Archer) *Bridges to Opportunity: Are Community Colleges Meeting the Needs of Minority Students?,* Academy for Educational Development (New York, NY), 1989.

(Editor, with Howard J. Ehrlich) *Race and Ethnic Conflict: Contending Views on Prejudice, Discrimination, and Ethnoviolence,* Westview Press (Boulder, CO), 1994, 2nd edition, 1999.

Reverse Discrimination: Dismantling the Myth, Lynne Rienner Publishers (Boulder, CO), 2003.

Understanding Diversity, Lynne Rienner Publishers (Boulder, CO), 2005.

Contributor to books, including *Risk-taking Behavior,* edited by R. E. Carnoy, Charles E. Thomas (New York, NY), 1971; *Cracks in the Classroom Wall,* edited by T. G. Robischon and others, Goodyear Publishing (Pacific Palisades, CA), 1975; *The Great School Debate,* edited by Beatrice Gross and Ronald Gross, Simon & Schuster (New York, NY), 1985; *A Handbook on the Community College in America: Its History, Mission, and Management,* edited by George A. Baker III, Greenwood Press (Westport, CT), 1994; and *Education Is Politics, Post Secondary,* edited by Ira Shor and Caroline Pari, Heinemann (Portsmouth, NH), 2000. Contributor of articles and reviews to periodicals, including *Journal of Intergroup Relations, Race and Society, Critical Sociology, American Behavioral Scientist, Radical Teacher, Review of Education, Review of Radical Political Economics, Educational Forum, Harvard Educational Review, Insurgent Sociologist,* and *Current World Leaders.*

BIOGRAPHICAL AND CRITICAL SOURCES:

PERIODICALS

Journal of American Ethnic History, fall, 1995, James Jennings, review of *Race and Ethnic Conflict: Contending Views on Prejudice, Discrimination, and Ethnoviolence,* p. 56.

PINKSTON, Tristi 1976-

PERSONAL: Born March 8, 1976, in Ogden, UT; daughter of Joel W. (an office machine field technician) and Ruthe (in sales; maiden name, Clark) Norton; married Matthew Pinkston (a customer service representative and iridologist); children: Caryn Camille, Ammon Josiah, Joseph Erin. *Education:* Attended Brigham Young University. *Politics:* Republican. *Religion:* Church of Jesus Christ of Latter-day Saints (Mormon).

ADDRESSES: Agent—c/o Author Mail, Granite Publishing and Distribution, 868 North 1430 W., Orem, UT 84057. *E-mail*—mattandtristipinkston@ juno.com.

CAREER: Homemaker for eight years; writer. Worked as demonstrator for Stampin' Up! and as a florist. Past trustee of local Friends of the Library.

WRITINGS:

Nothing to Regret (Lhistorical novel), Granite Publishing and Distribution (Orem, UT), 2002.

Strength to Endure (historical novel), Granite Publishing and Distribution (Orem, UT), 2004.

WORK IN PROGRESS: Faith beyond Fear, a contemporary romantic suspense; *Test of Time,* historical fiction; *Forgive, Not Forget,* an historical novel, a sequel to *Nothing to Regret; Season of Sacrifice,* an historical novel, all with Mormon themes.

SIDELIGHTS: Tristi Pinkston told *CA:* "My main goals in writing are to entertain, enlighten, and uplift the reader. If someone walks away from one of my books saying 'I learned so much' or 'I feel like a better person for having read that book,' that's my ultimate payoff. I'm a stay-at-home mom with three small children, so most of my writing takes place really late at night.

"I've been influenced in my life by so many great authors; I'm reading something almost constantly. Some of my favorites are Catherine Marshall, L. M. Montgomery, Ann Rinaldi, and Robin McKinley. As far as authors who have influenced my writing are concerned, I feel that my style is my own. I don't believe I've emulated my favorite authors except in regard to their love of the written word."

BIOGRAPHICAL AND CRITICAL SOURCES:

ONLINE

Tristi Pinkston Home Page, http://www.tristipinkston. com (November 1, 2004).

*   *   *

POOLE, Elizabeth (Anne) 1969-

PERSONAL: Born March 1, 1969, in Crewe, Cheshire, England; daughter of Gordon (a manager in insurance business) and Pamela Anne (a primary school teacher) Poole; married Richard Metz (a carpenter), June 29, 2001; children: Jude. *Ethnicity:* "White." *Education:* University of Lancaster, B.Ed. (with honors), 1991; University of Warwick, M.A. (British cultural studies), 1993; University of Leicester, Ph.D. (mass communications), 2000.

ADDRESSES: Office—Department of Media, Journalism, and Cultural Studies, Staffordshire University, College Rd., Stoke-on-Trent, Staffordshire ST4 2DE, England. *E-mail*—e.poole@staffs.ac.uk.

CAREER: Began career as primary school teacher; social studies teacher at a secondary school in Essex, England, 1993-96; Staffordshire University, Stoke-on-Trent, England, senior lecturer in media studies, 2000—. Guest speaker at other institutions, including University of Hull and University of Westminster.

MEMBER: Media, Communication, and Cultural Studies Association, Institute of Learning and Teaching.

WRITINGS:

Reporting Islam: Media Representations of British Muslims, I. B. Tauris and Co. (New York, NY), 2002.

Contributor to books, including *Islam and the West in the Mass Media: Fragmented Images in a Globalising World,* edited by K. Hafez, Hampton Press, 1999; and *Black Marks: Minority Ethnic Audiences and Media,* edited by K. Ross and P. Playdon, Ashgate Publishing (Burlington, VT), 2001. Contributor to periodicals, including *Inter/sections,* and *Sociological Review.*

WORK IN PROGRESS: Research on ethnicity, news, minority media, globalization, new technologies, diaspora, and research methods.

SIDELIGHTS: Elizabeth Poole told *CA:* "My motivations for my current career are based on enjoyment of reading, research, and teaching. I began with a career in teaching, which I found rewarding, developing rapport with students and generating debate. My interest in social issues and sociology in general were stimulated in post-sixteen education where, having been brought up in a monocultural, conservative environment, I studied Islam in religious studies at 'A level.'

"Although I began my career in primary education, I missed the learning involved in teaching at a higher level, so I returned to university to study cultural studies. Here I began to study the media, politics, and society, and I was excited by knowledge not previously encountered, which allowed me to look at life in a different way. In one course we discussed the Rushdie Affair, which stimulated my interest further in the relationship between religion, politics, and society, and which heightened my awareness of Muslims in Britain. I was able to pursue my interest in the role of the media in our perceptions of others in a further teaching position in post-sixteen education, teaching social sciences. I developed this interest fully when, for my doctorate, I was able to examine the theory that the media has a role in our perception of others but that this is mediated by other factors. Events since then have further heightened awareness of Muslims in the public sphere. It is vital in today's society that we have an awareness of the media's role in reporting events to us.

"My family have been hugely motivational and the bedrock of my life—unequivocally supportive. Without them, my writing would not have been possible.

"Through my work I am able to challenge some perceptions and encourage people to think critically about information that is presented to them. My work is currently research-led and therefore well grounded with evidence, rather than speculative or solely theoretical. It is this aspect of the work I particularly enjoy.

"An academic career allows one to stand back and have the chance to reflect on society. Education should be valued for education's sake, as it encourages people to be critical and reflective, and hopefully more considerate human beings. Being a student allows people to experience a different kind of life. Being a student, for me, opened up my eyes to new experiences and knowledge and allowed me to travel, move around, and therefore be introduced to new experiences."

*   *   *

POPOV, Linda Kavelin

PERSONAL: Married Dan Popov (a psychologist); children: two.

ADDRESSES: Office—The Virtues Project, 192, Sun Eagle Dr., Salt Spring Island, British Columbia, Canada V8K 1E5. *E-mail*—BookSpeakears@virtuesproject.com.

CAREER: Psychotherapist, consultant, and public speaker. The Virtues Project, Salt Spring Island, British Columbia, Canada, cofounder, 1991; Virtues Project International, Salt Spring Island, president and chief executive officer. Coproducer of television series *Virtues: A Family Affair.*

MEMBER: Boys and Girls Clubs of America (charter member of think tank on character).

AWARDS, HONORS: Woman of Distinction award, YW/YMCA, 2001.

WRITINGS:

(With husband, Dan Popov, and brother, John Kavelin) *The Family Virtues Guide: Simple Ways to Bring out the Best in Our Children and Ourselves,* Plume (New York, NY), 1997.

Sacred Moments: Daily Meditations on the Virtues, Plume (New York, NY), 1997.
A Pace of Grace: The Virtues of a Sustainable Life, Plume (New York, NY), 2004.

Member of advisory editorial board of the spirituality and ethics segment of CTV National News, Canada.

SIDELIGHTS: Linda Kavelin Popov is a trained psychotherapist who has been a consultant to corporations and governmental agencies in the United States and abroad. With her husband and brother, she founded The Virtues Project, which became the basis for a thirteen-part television series. The principles of the project were also the basis of the book *The Family Virtues Guide: Simple Ways to Bring out the Best in Our Children and Ourselves.* When the authors began their program, they studied the great books of several religions for the virtues they would promote. They adopted fifty-two virtues, one for each week of the year.

Alberta Report writer Terry O'Neill, who spoke with Popov, noted that "at the heart of The Virtues Project is a simple yet profound thesis: that children have within them the innate ability to recognize virtue and to act virtuously, but that modern culture has transformed them into moral illiterates." Popov told O'Neill, "We're so lost. We are lost to ourselves. We are out of our minds, because we've become so distracted by materialism. We've become so overurbanized and so overstressed that, really, we live a lifestyle that disconnects ourselves from our own spirit. And this is one of the main purposes of The Virtues Project, to help people honor their own spirit, to get back to some routine of reverence." Popov was raised in the Baha'i faith, which places great value on service, a calling she felt as a child and which grew stronger as she became an adult.

Popov is the author of *Sacred Moments: Daily Meditations on the Virtues* and *A Pace of Grace: The Virtues of a Sustainable Life.* In the latter she calls up the virtues upon which her project focuses and offers advice on how to simplify one's life. She recommends yoga, deep breathing, slowing down, eating well, adequate exercise, play, and prayer. She recommends that we accept and show appreciation for those close to us, be thankful for what we have, and bring more joy into our lives. *Publishers Weekly* contributor Mark Rotella said that "there's very little to argue with here."

BIOGRAPHICAL AND CRITICAL SOURCES:

PERIODICALS

Alberta Report, February 7, 2000, Terry O'Neill, "Virtues for Young and Old," p. 52.
Library Journal, July, 2004, Douglas C. Lord, review of *A Pace of Grace: The Virtues of a Sustainable Life,* p. 107.
Publishers Weekly, April 26, 2004, Mark Rotella, review of *A Pace of Grace,* p. 49.

ONLINE

Virtues Project, http://www.virtuesproject.com/ (November 6, 2004).*

*   *   *

PRENDERGAST, Mark J(oseph Anthony) 1959-

PERSONAL: Born September 30, 1959, in Dublin, Ireland; son of William D. (a gardener) and Elizabeth Prendergast; married Genie A. Cosmas (a musician and teacher), July, 1989; children: Natasha. *Ethnicity:* "Irish/Black" *Education:* Trinity College, Dublin, B.A., 1982, and M.A., 1998. *Politics:* "Individualist, free spirit." *Religion:* "Formerly Roman Catholic, now a mystery!"

ADDRESSES: Home and office—2 Liphook Crescent, Forest Hill, London SE2 33BW, England; fax: 0208-693-0349. *E-mail*—markp@cdboxset.co.uk.

CAREER: Writer, music critic, and journalist. *Irish Times,* Dublin, journalist, 1981-83; *Irish Rock,* journalist, 1983-85; *Hi-Fi Choice* reviewer, writer, and interviewer 2002—. Launched *Altair5* (Web 'zine), 1997. Lecturer at universities, including Edinburgh College.

MEMBER: Authors Licensing and Collection Society.

WRITINGS:

Irish Rock: Roots, Personalities, Directions, O'Brien Press (Dublin, Ireland), 1987.
The Isle of Noises, St. Martin's Press (New York, NY), 1990.

Classical Music, Rough Guides, 1994.
Tangerine Dream Tangents, Virgin, 1994.
Jimi Hendrix Companion, Schirminger Books, 1996.
The Ambient Century: From Mahler to Trance: The Evolution of Sound in the Electronic Age, Bloomsbury (London, England), 2000, Bloomsbury (New York, NY), 2001, updated edition published as *The Ambient Century: From Mahler to Moby: The Evolution of Sound in the Electronic Age,* Bloomsbury (New York, NY), 2003.

Contributor to journals and newspapers, including *Sound on Sound, New Statesman, Independent, Observer, Record Collector, Keyboard Player, UNCUT,* and *Moto.*

WORK IN PROGRESS: Researching the history of film music and books on progressive rock and English new wave music.

SIDELIGHTS: Irish music critic and journalist Mark Prendergast has written on music-related topics ranging from classical music to rock, and has published both books and reviews for the *Irish Times* and several music magazines. His particular interest is in new music and electronic forms, and according to a contributor to the *Ambient Century* Web site, Prendergast has written more than a million words on these topics. His book-length work *The Ambient Century: From Mahler to Moby: The Evolution of Sound in the Electronic Age* tackles the history and development of ambient music since the early 1900s. The book "covers a huge amount of territory, and serves as an easy introduction to many of the significant composers and musicians of the twentieth century," commented a reviewer on the *Synthtopia* Web site.

Beginning with composers such as Mahler, Debussy, and Satie, Prendergast examines dozens of individual musicians, musical groups, and collaborations that delineate the evolution of electronic music. "He credits Mahler with first evoking the hypnotic 'ambient experience of landscape and emotion,' kicking off the century of 'repetitive conceptual music,'" noted a *Publishers Weekly* reviewer. As music became less dependent upon live performance for transmission to listeners and more commonly available through recordings, it also became an integral part of listeners' self-constructed landscapes, a part of their commute to work, their evening hours, their everyday lives. In this context, music evolved to take advantage of the "widening of sonic possibilities with advancements in recording, amplification, and electronic instruments," stated the *Publishers Weekly* reviewer. Prendergast examines the effects of these advances in technology on music, including the development of musical instruments, the introduction of synthesizers and sampling machines, and the enhancements made possible by rapidly evolving recording technology.

In *The Ambient Century* Prendergast covers dozens of popular musical styles, including minimalism, house, techno, and straightforward rock. He looks at the works of influential artists such as Pink Floyd, Mike Oldfield, Brian Eno, John Cage, and Jimi Hendrix. Sections of the book cover the work of artists such as Enya, Peter Gabriel, Kraftwerk, Tangerine Dream, Emerson, Lake, and Palmer, Laurie Anderson, who were greatly influenced by synthesizers and electronic experimentation. Prendergast also includes recommended listening lists and a compilation of what he considers the "Essential 100 Recordings" that best representing ambient music. "Prendergast has an astonishing grasp of the global scene in popular music and writes with authority and conviction," commented *Library Journal* reviewer Larry Lipkis in his review of *The Ambient Century,* while Michael Chamy remarked for the *Austin Chronicle Online* that "it's hard to imagine a better entry point into a world of musical exploration," and praise the book as "brain food for the musically adventurous."

Prendergast once told *CA:* "My primary motivation for writing is to illuminate to myself and others the occluded means of culture, primarily music. I write out of necessity, letting the message dictate form and content. If its done to death I tend to ignore it." He characterized his writing process as "long and very slow," and noted that writing *The Ambient Century* took five years. "I allow my research and other work to filter through my consciousness for a long time before touching my processor," the author explained. "I edit it only once by reading it aloud and then leave it until proof stage."

Prendergast's inspiration for writing about music comes "from the musicians themselves." "Since I was twelve years old I've written many things," he once explained, "essays on Freud, essays on art, essays on bowls." "I got into music writing via a job in a Dublin record shop," he added, noting that he became a reviewer for the *Irish Times.* He was assigned to do interviews, and "before I knew it I was writing my first book. . . . After a couple of false starts I got into technology magazines. Ten years of that led to *The Ambient Century.*"

BIOGRAPHICAL AND CRITICAL SOURCES:

PERIODICALS

Entertainment Weekly, February 16, 2001, Evan Serpick, review of *The Ambient Century: From Mahler to Trance: The Evolution of Sound in the Electronic Age,* p. 92.
Library Journal, February 1, 2001, Larry Lipkis, review of *The Ambient Century,* p. 98.
Publishers Weekly, January 1, 2001, review of *The Ambient Century,* p. 85.

ONLINE

Ambient Century Web site, http://www.ambientcentury. co.uk/ (November 18, 2004).
Austin Chronicle Online, December 5, 2003, Michael Chamy, review of *The Ambient Century.*
Bloomsbury Web site, http://www.bloomsbury.com/ (November 18, 2004), "Mark Prendergast."
Synthtopia.com, http://www.synthtopia.com/ (November 18, 2004), review of *The Ambient Century.*

*   *   *

Prud'HOMME, Alex

PERSONAL: Male. *Education:* Graduated from Middlebury College, 1984.

ADDRESSES: Home—Brooklyn, NY. *Agent*—c/o Author Mail, HarperCollins Publishers, 10 East 53rd Street, Seventh Floor, New York, NY 10022.

CAREER: Freelance journalist and investigative reporter. *Talk* magazine, staff writer. Has appeared as a guest on Central News Network (CNN).

WRITINGS:

Rosie O'Donnell: A Biography, Time (New York, NY), 1999.

(With Michael Chernasky) *Forewarned: Why the Government Is Failing to Protect Us, and What We Must Do to Protect Ourselves,* Ballantine Books (New York, NY), 2003.

The Cell Game: Sam Waksal's Fast Money and False Promises—And the Fate of ImClone's Cancer Drug, HarperBusiness (New York, NY), 2004.

Contributor to periodicals, including *Vanity Fair, New Yorker,* and *Time.*

SIDELIGHTS: In 2001 veteran business journalist Alex Prud'homme began to take an interest in the interplay between Wall Street and the biotechnology revolution. Eventually Prud'homme researched Sam Waksal, head of ImClone Systems, and his efforts to earn fame and fortune with Erbitux, a very promising new cancer drug. Waksal's drive and enthusiasm was winning over investors (most notoriously, domestic lifestyle guru, Martha Stewart), but as Prud'homme began to dig into the story, he discovered that Waksal had a history of involvement in elaborate deceptions and exaggerations that had caused him to be fired from a number of scientific laboratories. Eventually, Waksal did achieve fame, but as the man who brought down Martha Stewart in an insider trading scandal that ultimately sent Stewart and Waksal to jail after Erbitux failed to win FDA approval. Prud'homme tells the whole story in *The Cell Game: Sam Waksal's Fast Money and False Promises—And the Fate of ImClone's Cancer Drug.*

Prud'homme's book is "an intriguing look into a fascinating world," according to *Salon.com* reviewer Andrew Leonard. While Leonard faulted the book for "a lengthy rehashing of the already well-told tale of Martha Stewart," as Prud'homme explained to *Publishers Weekly* contributor Ron Hogan, "I resisted the Martha angle for a long time. . . . But then her celebrity took over the story; it's how most people know about ImClone, and I had to embrace that." A *Publishers Weekly* reviewer concluded that "it's well worth reading the book now to appreciate what's really at stake in ImClone's downfall." Oddly enough, noted *Booklist* reviewer Ray Olson, Erbitux "remains very promising as a specific against tumors." The real tragedy,

Prud'homme notes *The Cell Game,* is the fact that Waksal's and ImClone's unsavory business practices have delayed the release of a potentially lifesaving drug.

BIOGRAPHICAL AND CRITICAL SOURCES:

PERIODICALS

Booklist, February 1, 2004, Ray Olson, review of *The Cell Game: Sam Waksal's Fast Money and False Promises—And the Fate of ImClone's Cancer Drug,* p. 930.

Library Journal, February 15, 2004, Lucy Heckman, review of *The Cell Game,* p. 137.

Publishers Weekly, January 26, 2004, review of *The Cell Game,* p. 137; Ron Hogan, interview with Prud'homme, p. 246.

U.S. News & World Report, January 26, 2004, Megan Barnett, "How the Mighty Fall," p. 16.

ONLINE

CNN Student News Online, http://cnnstudentnews.cnn.com/ (September 29, 2004), Bill Hemmer, transcript of CNN interview with Alex Prud'homme.

Middlebury Campus Web site, http://www.middleburycampus.com/ (April 15, 2004), Lynn Gray, "Author Spins Tale of Corporate Greed."

Salon.com, http://archive.salon.com/ (January 29, 2004), Andrew Leonard, "Drug Money."*

*   *   *

PRUETT, Candace (J.) 1968-

PERSONAL: Born March 31, 1968, in Denver, CO; daughter of Corwin Alexander (a realtor, broker, and appraiser) and Carol J. (a city manager) Brown; married Bart W. Pruett (a sales manager), June 4, 1994; children: Morgan, Benjamin. *Ethnicity:* "Caucasian." *Education:* University of Colorado, B.A.. *Politics:* Republican. *Religion:* Lutheran.

ADDRESSES: Home—Nunn, CO. *Office*—Poudre Valley Health System, 1024 South Lemay Ave., Fort Collins, CO 80524. *E-mail*—cjp2@pvhs.org.

CAREER: Writer, registered nurse, and consultant. Poudre Valley Health System, Fort Collins, CO, human resources consultant and nurse recruiter, 1993—. Project Self-Sufficiency, counselor; mentor for International Telementor program.

MEMBER: American Nurses Association, Colorado Nurses Association (vice president of District 9), Northern Colorado Nurses Coalition.

WRITINGS:

A Visit with My Uncle Ted, Elderberry Press (Oakland, OR), 2003.

WORK IN PROGRESS: Two other children's books focused on increasing interest in nursing: *My Mommy Is Special* and *I Made a New Friend Today.*

R

RAKE, Jody 1961-
(Jody Sullivan)

PERSONAL: Born November 21, 1961, in Hollywood, CA; daughter of J. Gordon and Jacqueline (a homemaker, maiden name Dente) Brown; married Scott Byrum, June 19, 1989 (divorced, March, 1998); married Andrew Rake (a computer graphics animator), February 16, 2002; children: Jeffrey Byrum, Justine Byrum. *Ethnicity:* "Caucasian." *Education:* College of San Mateo, A.A., 1981; San Francisco State University, B.A. (zoology), 1987; Mesa College, certificate in technical writing, 1994. *Politics:* Republican. *Religion:* Christian. *Hobbies and other interests:* Antique collecting, hiking, traveling, trivia, movies.

ADDRESSES: Home—7813-60 Tommy Dr., San Diego, CA 92119. *E-mail*—raked@sbcglobal.net.

CAREER: Freelance writer and proofreader, 1999—; Capstone Press, Mankato, MN, consultant, beginning 1999.

MEMBER: Southwest Marine Educators Association.

WRITINGS:

UNDER NAME JODY SULLIVAN

Cheetahs: Spotted Speedster, Bridgestone Books (Mankato, MN), 2003.
Beavers: Big-toothed Builders, Bridgestone Books (Mankato, MN), 2003.

Deer: Graceful Grazers, Capstone Press (Mankato, MN), 2003.
Georgia, Capstone Press (Mankato, MN), 2003.
Hawaii, Capstone Press (Mankato, MN), 2003.
Parrotfish, Capstone Press (Mankato, MN), 2006.
Crabs, Capstone Press (Mankato, MN), 2006.
Sea Anemones, Capstone Press (Mankato, MN), 2006.
Sea Stars, Capstone Press (Mankato, MN), 2006.

Also author of informational booklets, teacher's guides, and other educational materials for SeaWorld. Contributor of articles to periodicals, including *Satlink,* and *Christian Classroom.* Editor of newsletter for Southwest Marine Educators Association, 1998-2002.

WORK IN PROGRESS: Beagles, Dalmatians, Pugs, and *St. Bernards,* for Capstone Press.

SIDELIGHTS: Writing under the pen name Jody Sullivan, Jody Rake is the author of several nonfiction children's books, including *Beavers: Big-toothed Builders* and *Cheetahs: Spotted Speedsters,* both part of the "Wild World of Animals" series. *Booklist* reviewer Stephanie Zvirin enjoyed the clear and colorful photographs in *Cheetahs* and also noted that the "'fast facts' scattered through the book" provide a lively format for readers. In addition to continuing to write nonfiction titles that draw on her interest and training in the sciences, Rake produced many educational materials for SeaWorld and has also been a scientific consultant to Capstone Press's "Ocean Life" series.

Rake once commented: "I took the scenic route toward becoming an author. It wasn't the first job that came to mind. Never in my life have I demonstrated any talent for creative writing. I came to San Diego in 1989 with a degree in zoology and a desire to work with animals. I got a job at SeaWorld, but because my practical experience was in child care and education, I was hired by the education department. I was confident that I would eventually work my way into the mammal department. In the course of my job, I was given some writing assignments, and discovered the art of nonfiction writing. I discovered that the education department had a science writer. I thought that sounded very cool, and then and there I did some serious re-evaluation.

"I went back to school and earned a certificate in technical writing. I landed an internship with the aforementioned science writer, and within six months attained a permanent position as a science writer. For ten years I wrote numerous nonfiction publication for SeaWorld, mostly about marine animals. I eventually began doing some freelance projects at home, and gradually, the urge to quit my job and stay home with my children grew into an overwhelming pull. My last day at SeaWorld was September 5, 2003, and I've been a freelance writer and editor ever since.

"As a mother of an elementary student, I often help gather research materials for reports and projects. While the Internet is amazing and useful, it is no substitute for quality books. Sometimes I find that resources are limited, outdated, too high-level, or otherwise unable to support the state and national teaching standards. It is a goal of mine to help contribute to the body of resources that help teachers fulfill these standards.

"My advice for aspiring writers? Read! Read much and often. There is no better way to learn how to write. I also recommend identifying what type of writer you are: fiction or nonfiction? Do you have a story to tell? Are the words just bursting out of you? Or are you better suited at expressing information? Try writing both ways—which one comes more naturally? In either case, pick a topic you are passionate about, otherwise you'll struggle. Always develop the gifts you are given—don't waste your time trying to be something you're not."

BIOGRAPHICAL AND CRITICAL SOURCES:

PERIODICALS

Booklist, January 1, 2003, Stephanie Zvirin, review of *Groundhogs: Woodchuck, Marmots, and Whistle Pigs,* p. 900.

School Library Journal, April, 2003, Susan Oliver, review of *Woodchucks, Marmots, and Whistle Pigs,* p. 154.

*   *   *

RANDELL, Nigel

PERSONAL: Male.

ADDRESSES: Agent—Author Mail, c/o Carroll & Graf, 245 West 17th St., 11th Fl., New York, NY 10011.

CAREER: Documentary filmmaker and author.

WRITINGS:

The White Headhunter: The Story of a Nineteenth-Century Sailor Who Survived a Heart of Darkness, Carroll & Graf Publishers (New York, NY), 2003.

SIDELIGHTS: A documentary filmmaker, Nigel Randell turned his storytelling talents to writing *The White Headhunter: The Story of a Nineteenth-Century Sailor Who Survived a Heart of Darkness,* "a fascinating look at Jack Renton's experience as a castaway in the Solomon Islands during the 19th century," in the words of *Academia* reviewer Colleen Duggan. Shanghaied in San Francisco in 1868, Renton soon found himself on a guano ship in the South Seas. Managing to jump overboard one night with several companions, he washed up on the island of Malaita. Unfortunately Renton's shipmates were killed by a tribe of headhunters, while Renton himself was taken in by the chief and gradually found a place in the tribe. First treated as a slave, he eventually grew to be a valued member of society, prized for his skills as both a boatmaker and a soldier.

In addition to Renton's own memoir, Randell draws on native oral traditions to recapture the events Renton left out, such as his relationship with a native woman that was omitted because it would have offended Victorian readers and his own participation in head-hunting raids. Eventually returned to the company of white men, Renton became a government agent and helped kidnap natives for use on European plantations. He was eventually killed by his victims' relatives, a fact Randell uses as a springboard to describe the brutal European incursion into the South Seas. In praise of *The White Headhunter,* a *Kirkus Reviews* contributor praised Randell's work as "a fabulous ethnographic tale inside a larger tragedy of cultural genocide and retaliatory murders."

BIOGRAPHICAL AND CRITICAL SOURCES:

PERIODICALS

Geographical, August, 2003, review of *The White Headhunter: The Story of a Nineteenth-Century Sailor Who Survived a Heart of Darkness,* p. 64.
Kirkus Reviews, July 15, 2003, review of *The White Headhunter: The Story of a Nineteenth-Century Sailor Who Survived a Heart of Darkness,* p. 956.
Publishers Weekly, August 4, 2003, review of *The White Headhunter,* p. 69.

ONLINE

Academia Online, http://www.ybp.com/acad/ (September 29, 2004), Colleen Duggan, review of *The White Headhunter.**

* * *

RAYMOND, Jonathan

PERSONAL: Born in CA. *Education:* Attended Swarthmore College; New School University, M.F.A.

ADDRESSES: Home—New York, NY. *Agent*—c/o Author Mail, Bloomsbury Publishing Place, 38 Soho Sq., London W1D 3HB, England.

CAREER: Author. Formerly an editor at *Plazm* magazine.

WRITINGS:

The Half-Life (novel), Bloomsbury (New York, NY), 2004.

SIDELIGHTS: Jonathan Raymond made a strong debut with his first novel, *The Half-Life.* In the book, the geography of Portland, Oregon, links two storylines, one from the early nineteenth century and one from the 1980s. The earlier story involves two men who become friends under strange circumstances. Cookie works for a fur trapping party that is running out of food. While foraging, he discovers Henry, naked and hiding from Russians who have killed his Indian friends. Henry convinces Cookie that they can make a fortune by extracting and selling castoreum, a beaver musk valued by the Chinese. The pair makes it to China, but Cookie winds up in prison. Chapters of this story alternate with that of Tina and Trixie, teens who meet on a hippie commune in the same area. Trixie arrives at the commune after getting in legal trouble in Los Angeles. Tina also hails from Los Angeles, and has reluctantly left because her mother lost her job. The girls decide to fill their time by making a film together, but need the funds to do so. They decide to grow marijuana as a way of making money. The themes of friendship, entrepreneurship, and relocation already link these two tales; yet when the commune's owner discovers a pair of skeletons in a swamp, the friends' stories are further bound together.

Reviewers described the novel as ambitious and, often, exceptional. Writing in *Artforum,* Nina Mehta remarked that "the author's regard for the natural world is one of this novel's chief delights." On the other hand, Mehta commented that "the friendships never quite jell." *Los Angeles Times* critic Mark Rozzo noted that, "as entertaining and audacious as *The Half-Life* is, there's an alarming lack of focus as the book moves forward." Rozzo concluded, however, that Raymond's novel "is a potent fairy tale of who we are, how we got here and the unknowable history under our feet."

Other critics also applauded *The Half-Life.* According to *Booklist* contributor Jay Freeman, Raymond draws "a seductively beautiful landscape" and "seamlessly links the two narratives with elegant and often haunting prose." A *Kirkus Reviews* writer stated that *The Half-Life* is an "impressive debut" and that the story is "unglamorous and sad, but compelling." Jeff Zaleski called the book "ambitious and assured" in *Publishers Weekly,* concluding, "The synchronicity of the two stories is subtly engineered and never belabored."

BIOGRAPHICAL AND CRITICAL SOURCES:

PERIODICALS

Artforum, summer, 2004, Nina Mehta, review of *The Half-Life,* p. 53.

Booklist, May 15, 2004, Jay Freeman, review of *The Half-Life,* p. 1611.

Denver Post, May 9, 2004, Sybil Downing, review of *The Half-Life,* p. F12.

Kirkus Reviews, March 1, 2004, review of *The Half-Life,* p. 199.

Los Angeles Times, June 13, 2004, Mark Rozzo, review of *The Half-Life,* p. R10.

Publishers Weekly, March 8, 2004, Jeff Zaleski, review of *The Half-Life,* p. 45.

ONLINE

Bookbrowse.com, http://www.bookbrowse.com/ (August 26, 2004), "Jonathan Raymond."*

*   *   *

REINES, Alvin J. 1926-2004

OBITUARY NOTICE— See index for *CA* sketch: Born October 12, 1926, in Paterson, NJ; died November 14, 2004, in Clifton, OH. Reines was a Jewish philosophy professor at Hebrew Union College. After receiving his M.A.H.L. at Hebrew Union College in 1952, he completed a Ph.D. at Harvard University in 1958. He joined Hebrew Union in 1959 as an assistant professor and later became a full professor. An authority on Maimonides, he was the author of *Maimonides and Abrabanel on Prophecy* (1970). A liberal philosopher, he advocated for the ordination of female rabbis and the importance of keeping an open mind about other theological and philosophical beliefs. Among his other publications are *Elements in Philosophy of Reform Judaism* (1972) and *Polydoxy: Explorations in a Philosophy of Liberal Religion* (1987).

OBITUARIES AND OTHER SOURCES:

PERIODICALS

Chronicle of Higher Education, December 17, 2004, p. A50.

ONLINE

Jewish Ledger Online, http://www.jewishledger.com/ (January 19, 2005).

REUSS, Frederick 1960-

PERSONAL: Born 1960, in Addis Ababa, Ethiopia.

ADDRESSES: *Home*—Washington, DC. *Agent*—c/o Author Mail, Pantheon Books, 1540 Broadway, New York, NY 10036.

CAREER: Writer.

WRITINGS:

Horace Afoot, MacMurray and Beck (Denver, CO), 1997.

Henry of Atlantic City, MacMurray and Beck (Denver, CO), 1999.

The Wasties, Pantheon Books (New York, NY), 2002.

SIDELIGHTS: Frederick Reuss has emerged as a writer of unusual, off-kilter novels that place odd characters in ordinary settings that seem incapable of comprehending them. In *Horace Afoot,* a middle-aged loner with a modest, independent income decides to settle in the small Midwestern town of Oblivion. Horace, who has taken his name from the ancient Roman poet, is given to making random phone calls to the residents, challenging them to explain the nature of beauty or true happiness. Naturally, the loner soon gains a reputation as a weirdo, and at first his desire to live without attachments is fulfilled. But gradually he develops a friendship with the town librarian, and gets caught up with a rape victim named Sylvia, whose messy life of hoodlums and drug deals draws him into Oblivion's buried secrets and puts his own life in danger.

For *Washington Post* reviewer Michael Dirda, "The narrative voice is particularly congenial—cool and unflappable, often humorous without being laugh-out-loud funny, particularly when Horace reacts to and tries to interpret the events around him." Similarly, *Booklist* reviewer Nancy Pearl found *Horace Afoot* a "quietly humorous, engaging novel." Although he described the central character as "a bit wearing," a *Kirkus Reviews* contributor concluded that Horace's "voice lingers, as do many scenes in this terse, moving explanation of modern anomie and the longing for—and fear of—intimacy."

In *Henry of Atlantic City,* Reuss presents a six-year-old oddity who has memorized the Gnostic Gospels and believes himself to be a saint living in fifth-century Byzantium. More prosaically, Henry is the son of a Caesar's Palace security officer who has skipped out after embezzling millions of dollars from his employer, leaving the boy to make his way in a world of abusive, hostile, or simply confounded adults. For Henry, the two worlds join together, so that a local mobster becomes the Emperor Justinian, cars turn into chariots, and the casino becomes the actual Caesar's Palace. As Henry travels around, he encounters priests and prostitutes, thieves and police officers, none of whom seem to accept his sainthood—or to shake his certainty that he is nonetheless indeed a saint, as an invisible angel assures him. "Along the way, Reuss shows us . . . the dark philosophical and psychological labyrinths in which we search for glimmers of ourselves," according to *Booklist* reviewer Veronica Scrol. A *Publishers Weekly* reviewer wrote, "Reuss achieves a brilliant pathos, reminding us that at any age, 'loneliness is the most meaningless treasure in existence.'" For a *Kirkus Reviews* contributor, "this ambitious fiction—blending a child's search for love and certainty with a restless examination of the nature of faith—is often profoundly moving. It is also further evidence that Reuss is one of our most unpredictable and original novelists."

Reuss published *The Wasties* in 2002. This time, instead of a precocious child making his way in an adult world, the protagonist is a middle-aged man slipping into an infantile state. English professor Michael "Caruso" Taylor is suffering from what he calls "the wasties," an undefined ailment that removes his power of speech, allows him to see deceased literary figures such as Walt Whitman and Ralph Ellison, and gradually leaves him utterly dependent on others. While those around him struggle to find a cure, Taylor himself sees his disease as a soul weariness, incapable of cure or solution. "But while we feel compassion for Michael, his failure to resist . . . is ultimately exasperating," according to *Library Journal* reviewer Joshua Cohen. A *Kirkus Reviews* contributor noted that although this "elegant, sometimes amusing" story has its clever moments, Reuss "burdens his reader with a dreariness of situation that continues—and continues." According to *Booklist* reviewer Joanne Wilkinson, the novel "should appeal to sophisticated readers who like darkly humorous, cerebral fiction."

BIOGRAPHICAL AND CRITICAL SOURCES:

PERIODICALS

Booklist, October 15, 1997, Nancy Pearl, review of *Horace Afoot,* p. 389; July, 1999, Veronica Scrol, review of *Henry of Atlantic City,* p. 1924; July, 2002, Joanne Wilkinson, review of *The Wasties,* p. 1823.

Kirkus Reviews, September 15, 1997, review of *Horace Afoot,* p. 1412; July 1, 1999, review of *Henry of Atlantic City,* p. 994; June 15, 2002, review of *The Wasties,* p. 835.

Library Journal, October 1, 1997, Patrick Sullivan, review of *Horace Afoot,* p 125; July, 1999, Harold Augenbraum, review of *Henry of Atlantic City,* p. 135; August, 2002, Joshua Cohen, review of *The Wasties,* p. 145.

New York Times Book Review, December 28, 1997, David Sacks, review of *Horace Afoot,* p. 5; November 28, 1999, Megan Harlan, review of *Henry of Atlantic City,* p. 20; August 26, 2001, Scott Veale, review of *Henry of Atlantic City,* p. 24.

Publishers Weekly, September 15, 1997, review of *Horace Afoot,* p. 46; June 28, 1999, review of *Henry of Atlantic City,* p. 52; July 29, 2002, review of *The Wasties,* p. 53.

Washington Post Book World, October 12, 1997, Michael Dirda, "On the Edge of Oblivion," p. 5.*

ONLINE

Baltimore City Paper Online, http://www.citypaper. com/ (December 10, 2002), Heather Joslyn, review of *The Wasties.*

MacAdam Cage Publishing Web site, http://www. macadamcage.com/ (December 10, 2002), "Frederick Reuss."

Washingtonian Online, http://www.washingtonian.com/ (December 10, 2002), Laura Stickney, review of *The Wasties.**

* * *

REVELL, J(ohn) R(obert) S(tephen) 1920-2004

OBITUARY NOTICE— See index for *CA* sketch: Born April 15, 1920, in Tunbridge Wells, Kent, England; died November 4, 2004, in Cambridge, England. Economist, educator, and author. Revell was an innovative economist with socialist leanings who advocated more egalitarian banking practices and more governmental supervision of financial institutions in England. Graduating from the London School of Economics in 1950 and earning his master's degree from Cambridge University ten years later, his first professional job was working for the Soviet news agency Tass as a researcher. His early belief in communism was shattered by the Soviet Communist Party's dictatorial methods, and he finally left the party in 1956 after the USSR invaded Hungary. He next became a senior research officer in the department of applied economics at Cambridge from 1957 until 1968. At the same time, he was director of studies in economics at Selwyn College, Cambridge, from 1960 until 1965, and director of studies in economics for Fitzwilliam College, Cambridge, from 1964 to 1967. He was a tutor at Fitzwilliam from 1965 to 1967, senior tutor from 1967 to 1968, and a fellow from 1965 to 1968. Leaving Cambridge, he became professor of economics at the University of Wales, Bangor, where he remained until his 1983 retirement. Although he left the classroom behind, he remained active for many more years as a prolific author of economics books. Many of his colleagues now consider Revell to have been decades ahead of his time when it came to such ideas as bank regulation and the importance of measuring the capital adequacy of financial institutions to ensure their stability. He also believed that a country's economy is better served when it does not practice "financial exclusion"; that is, limiting the lower classes' access to financial products. Many of his concerns are only now being addressed in the "Basel 2" standards of banking supervision that are to be enforced in Britain beginning in 2007. Revell published dozens of books in his lifetime, including *Changes in British Banking: The Growth of a Secondary Banking System* (1968), *Solvency and Regulation of Banks* (1975), *Mergers and the Role of Large Banks* (1987), and *Changes in West European Public Banks* (1991).

OBITUARIES AND OTHER SOURCES:

PERIODICALS

Independent (London, England), November 26, 2004, p. 43.

RICHARDS, Denis (George) 1910-2004

OBITUARY NOTICE— See index for *CA* sketch: Born September 10, 1910, in London, England; died November 25, 2004, in London, England. Historian, civil servant, and author. Richards was well known as the author of British history books, especially those concerning the Royal Air Force. A graduate of Trinity Hall, Cambridge, where he earned a B.A. in 1931 and an M.A. in 1935, he was assistant master at Manchester Grammar School during the 1930s and senior history and English master at Bradfield College from 1939 to 1941. When Great Britain entered the war, he enlisted in the Royal Air Force. Assigned to the Air Ministry, he was senior narrator there for the duration of World War II. As such, he worked in the RAF's historical branch and recorded the air force's operations. This led to his publications on the RAF, beginning with the three-volume *Royal Air Force, 1939-1945* (1953-54). He would later write more books about the RAF, including *Portal of Hungerford* (1978), *The Battle of Britain* (1989), which he wrote with Richard Hough, *The Few and the Many* (1990), and *The Hardest Victory* (1994). After the war, Richards was hired as a principal for the Air Ministry, a job he left in 1950 to become head of Morley College. In this role, Richards was instrumental in the difficult challenge of rebuilding the war-decimated campus. In 1965, he went to work for the University of Sussex, where he was Longmans fellow from 1965 until he retired in 1968. He worked as a full-time freelance writer after that, producing many respected history texts. Among his history publications are *An Illustrated History of Modern Europe, 1789-1938* (1938; fifth edition, 1950), which was published in Canada as *The Modern Age* (1955), *Britain under the Tudors and Stuarts* (1958), *Medieval Britain* (1971), written with A. Ellis, and the memoirs *Just to Recall the Flavour* (1999) and *It Might Have Been Worse* (1999). Named to the Order of the British Empire in 1990, Richards kept active in later life (despite suffering from Parkinson's disease), by serving as vice president of the Purcell School for Young Musicians and chairing the Women's League of Health and Beauty.

OBITUARIES AND OTHER SOURCES:

PERIODICALS

Guardian (London, England), December 13, 2004, p. 19.

Independent (London, England), December 6, 2004, p. 34.

Times (London, England), December 16, 2004, p. 59.

*   *   *

RINGLER, Richard Newman 1934-
(Dick Ringler)

PERSONAL: Born January 21, 1934, in Milwaukee, WI; son of H. Paul (a journalist) and Frieda (a musician; maiden name, Newman) Ringler; married Karin Louise Erickson (a psychologist), December 18, 1959; children: Thor Stephen, Thomasin Louise. *Ethnicity:* "White." *Education:* Harvard University, A.B., 1955, Ph.D., 1961; University of Wisconsin—Madison, M.A., 1956.

ADDRESSES: Home—1240 Dartmouth Rd., Madison, WI 53705. *Office*—c/o Department of Scandinavian Studies, 1306 Van Hise Hall, University of Wisconsin—Madison, Madison, WI 53706. *E-mail*—rringler@wisc.edu.

CAREER: University of Wisconsin—Madison, began as instructor, became professor of English and Scandinavian studies, 1961-2002, professor emeritus, 2002—, Scandinavian department chair, 1968-71, 1980-83, 1999-2000, member of executive committee of Humanities Division, 1969-72, director of Center for International Cooperation and Security Studies, 1985-88, founding executive director of Wisconsin Institute: Consortium for the Study of War, Peace, and Global Cooperation, 1985-89, professor in study abroad program, London, England, 1999. University of Gießen, visiting professor, 1989; guest lecturer at other institutions, including University of Durham, and Alderson-Broaddus College; public speaker on a wide variety of topics, from Scandinavian studies to Zen Buddhism and war and peace; presenter of radio programs for *University of the Air,* Wisconsin Public Radio, 1995-2002; Wisconsin Humanities Council, member of Speakers Bureau, 2002-03; conference and seminar leader; gives poetry readings.

MEMBER: National Educators for Social Responsibility (member of board of directors, 1983-87; board chair, 1985), Peace Studies Association (member of board of directors, 1988-89), Wisconsin Educators for Social Responsibility (founding president, 1983-88).

AWARDS, HONORS: Woodrow Wilson fellow, 1955-56; fellow of American Council of Learned Societies at University of Iceland, 1965-66, and British Museum, 1971-72; Lithgow Osborne Lecturer, American Scandinavian Foundation, 1971; Broad Street Pump Award, Physicians for Social Responsibility, 1986; Ohio State Award for Excellence in Broadcasting, 1993, for radio series *Dilemmas of War and Peace: Gulf War Specials,* and 1994, for audiotape series *Dilemmas of War and Peace;* Distinguished Course Award, Division of Independent Study, National University Continuing Education Association, 1994, for *Dilemmas of War and Peace;* grant from Fund for the Promotion of Icelandic Literature, Icelandic Ministry of Education, 1994; commendation, Icelandic Ministry of Science, 2000; Knight's Cross of the Order of the Falcon (Iceland), 2004; honorary Ph.D., University of Iceland, 2004; AMOCO teaching award.

WRITINGS:

(Editor, with Frederic G. Cassidy) *Bright's Old English Grammar and Reader,* 3rd edition, Holt, Rinehart & Winston (New York, NY), 1971, corrected edition, 1975.

(Editor, with Joan H. Hall and Nick Doane) *Old English and New: Studies in Language and Linguistics in Honor of Frederic G. Cassidy,* Garland Publishing (New York, NY), 1992.

(And narrator) *Dilemmas of War and Peace: Gulf War Specials* (radio series), Wisconsin Public Radio, c. 1993.

Dilemmas of War and Peace: A Companion to Studies, 1993.

Indra's Net (prose and poetry), privately printed, 1994.

(Under name Dick Ringler) *Bard of Iceland: Jónas Hallgrímsson, Poet and Scientist,* University of Wisconsin Press (Madison, WI), 2002.

Contributor to books, including *Saga og Språk: Studies in Language and Literature,* edited by John M. Weinstock, University of Texas Press (Austin, TX), 1972; and *Essential Articles for the Study of Edmund Spenser,* edited by A. C. Hamilton, [Hamden, CT], 1972. Contributor of articles, poetry, and reviews to periodicals, including *Beloit Poetry Journal, Quarry, Scandinavian Review, Bulletin of the Atomic Scientists, Messenger, Academe, Modern Language Review, Philological Quarterly,* and *Studies in Philology.* Coeditor, *Literary Monographs,* 1969. General editor of *Dilemmas of War and Peace: A Sourcebook,* 1993.

WORK IN PROGRESS: A new translation of *Beowulf;* developing (with others) a free-access Internet Web-based course of instruction in modern Icelandic.

BIOGRAPHICAL AND CRITICAL SOURCES:

PERIODICALS

Times Literary Supplement, September 5, 2003, Carolyne Larrington review of *Bard of Iceland: Jónas Hallgrímsson, Poet and Scientist,* p. 10.

*　　*　　*

RINGLER, Dick
　　See RINGLER, Richard Newman

*　　*　　*

ROBERTSON, C(harles) K(evin) 1964-

PERSONAL: Born March 19, 1964, in El Paso, TX; son of Francis E. (an army officer) and Virginia M. (a homemaker; maiden name, Dunman) Robertson; married Ann Vinson (a homemaker); children: David F., Jonathan W. G., Abigail V. *Ethnicity:* "Caucasian." *Education:* Virginia Polytechnic Institute and State University, B.A., 1985; Virginia Theological Seminary, M.Div., 1993; University of Durham, Ph.D., 1999. *Religion:* Episcopalian. *Hobbies and other interests:* Reading, travel, movies.

ADDRESSES: Office—St. Stephen's Episcopal Church, P.O. Box 309, Milledgeville, GA 31059-0309. *E-mail*—rector@alltel.net.

CAREER: Priest in charge of Episcopal church in Melbourne, FL, 1993-96; priest-in-residence at Church of England in Durham, England, 1996-99; St. Stephen's Episcopal Church, Milledgeville, GA, pastor, 1999—. Georgia State University, professor of communications, 1999—; Virginia Theological Seminary, adjunct professor, 2003—. Oconee Regional Christian Ministers Alliance, member, 2001—. TENS, member of board of directors, 2001—; Film Clips, Inc., member

of advisory board, 2002—; Center for Film-enhanced Education, director, 2003—. Faith and Values Network, panel member for weekly television series *Day 1,* broadcast by Hallmark Channel, 2002—.

MEMBER: Society of Biblical Literature, Popular Culture Association, Fellows Forum.

AWARDS, HONORS: Bell-Woolfal fellow, Virginia Theological Seminary, 1996; Muntz fellow, Episcopal Church Foundation, 1998; named honors professor, Phi Kappa Phi, 2000.

WRITINGS:

The Kerygma of Billy Graham, Worldwide Press, 1987.
Conflict in Corinth: Redefining the System, Peter Lang Publishing (New York, NY), 2001.
Religion as Entertainment, Peter Lang Publishing (New York, NY), 2002.
(Editor) *Religion and Alcohol: Sobering Thoughts,* Peter Lang Publishing (New York, NY), 2004.
(Editor) *Religion and Sexuality: Compromising Positions,* Peter Lang Publishing (New York, NY), 2004.

Author of booklet, "Barnabas: A Model for Holistic Stewardship," TENS Publishing, 2003. Contributor to books, including *Religion and Science Fiction,* edited by J. McGrath, 2004. Contributor to periodicals, including *Anglican Theological Review, Networking,* and *Living Church.*

SIDELIGHTS: C. K. Robertson told *CA:* "As a priest and communications professor/consultant, I find great pleasure in bridging these two worlds, exploring how religious belief interacts with popular culture, both in present-day culture and in the ancient world. I find great energy in moving between a work entirely of my own as author and an edited work, where I can benefit from the wisdom and experience of others. I also love to bridge the worlds of writing and speaking/consulting, as my research gives foundational support to my work with people, which, I hope, in turn energizes me and infuses my writing with a sense of relevance."

ROSE, Alison (C.) 1944(?)-

PERSONAL: Born c. 1944, in Palo Alto, CA.

ADDRESSES: Home—New York, NY. *Agent*—c/o Author Mail, Random House, Inc., 1745 Broadway, New York, NY 10019.

CAREER: Model, actress, and author. *New Yorker,* New York, NY, receptionist 1987—.

WRITINGS:

Better than Sane: Tales from a Dangling Girl, Alfred A. Knopf (New York, NY), 2004.

Contributor to the column, "Talk of the Town," in the *New Yorker.* Also frequent contributor to *Vogue.*

SIDELIGHTS: Occasional model and sometime actress Alison Rose finally found a niche for herself when she took a job as a receptionist at the *New Yorker* in 1987. Attractive, witty, and engaging, Rose managed to draw the attention of the magazine's glitterati, including Harold Brodkey and George W. S. Trow, and began collaborating on its popular "Talk of the Town" feature. Rose's years at the *New Yorker* are the heart of her memoir, *Better than Sane: Tales from a Dangling Girl.*

In a book that is "deadpan, smart, hypersensitive, and mordantly funny," in the words of *Booklist* reviewer Donna Seaman, Rose recounts her California childhood and her escape to New York, where she experiences intermittent periods of intense ambition and apathetic lethargy before finding a place with other "unemployables" at the magazine. She soon exchanged *bon mots* with the writers (at least the males) and recorded her favorite conversations on scraps of paper—and later in her memoir.

According to a *Kirkus Reviews* contributor, the result "is a compendious, enervating catalogue of snappy responses and witticisms between her and the men" on the *New Yorker* staff. Stacy Schiff, writing in the *New York Times Book Review,* concluded: "There is something regal about the gleaming, brittle, unhinged

Rose, and if you want to hear two distinguished writers debating whether she was the princess or the duchess of the 20th century, you can do so here."

BIOGRAPHICAL AND CRITICAL SOURCES:

PERIODICALS

Booklist, April 15, 2004, Donna Seaman, review of *Better than Sane: Tales from a Dangling Girl,* p. 1406.

Boston Globe, May 23, 2004, Kate Bolick, "Loneliness, Little Examined or Loudly Expressed," p. L6.

Entertainment Weekly, May 7, 2004, Nicholas Fonseca, review of *Better than Sane,* p. 91.

Kirkus Reviews, March 15, 2004, review of *Better than Sane,* p. 263.

New York Times Book Review, May 9, 2004, Stacy Schiff, review of *Better than Sane,* p. 5.

Publishers Weekly, April 19, 2004, review of *Better than Sane,* p. 52.*

* * *

ROSOWSKI, Susan J(ean) 1942-2004

OBITUARY NOTICE— See index for *CA* sketch: Born January 2, 1942, in Topeka, KS; died of cancer November 2, 2004, in Garland, NE. Educator and author. Rosowski was an English professor best known as an authority on American author Willa Cather. A 1964 graduate of Whittier College, she did her graduate work at the University of Arizona, where she earned an M.A. in 1967 and a Ph.D. in 1974. Hired as an instructor at the University of Nebraska—Lincoln in 1971, she became a full professor in 1986 and was named the Adele Hall Distinguished Professor of English in 1991. With the exception of the years 1976 through 1982, when she taught at the University of Nebraska at Omaha, Rosowski spent her entire career at Lincoln. It was there that she worked tirelessly on researching Cather, the author of the novel *My Antonia.* Rosowski is often credited with helping Cather's work gain the recognition it deserves in American literature. The scholar was the founding director of the Plains Humanities Alliance, editor-in-chief of *Cather Studies,* and general editor of the "Cather Edition" at the

University of Nebraska Press. She edited or coedited a number of studies about Cather, including *The Voyage Perilous: Willa Cather's Romanticism* (1986) and *Approaches to Teaching Cather's "My Antonia"* (1989), as well as editing Cather's *O Pioneers!: Willa Cather Scholarly Edition* (1992). Rosowski was also interested in the literature of the American West in general, and was the author of *Birthing a Nation: Gender, Creativity, and the West in American Literature* (1999). Internationally recognized for her scholarship, Rosowski was honored several times; she received the Mildred R. Bennett Nebraska Literature Award in 1994 and earned the Outstanding Research and Creative Activity Award from the University of Nebraska in 2004.

OBITUARIES AND OTHER SOURCES:

ONLINE

University of Nebraska—Lincoln Web site, http://ascweb.unl.edu/ (January 27, 2005).

OTHER

UNL English Department Newsletter & Calendar, November 5, 2004.

* * *

RUFUS, Anneli S. 1959-

PERSONAL: Female; given name is pronounced "ANna-lee." Born June 24, 1959, in Los Angeles, CA.

ADDRESSES: Agent—c/o Author Mail, Marlowe & Co., 161 William St., 16th Fl., New York, NY 10038. *E-mail*—anneli@annelirufus.com.

CAREER: Author, editor, and journalist.

AWARDS, HONORS: Southwest Press Association Award, 1975; Women in Communications Journalism Award, 1977; Joan Lee Yang Poetry Prize, University of California, Berkeley, 1981.

WRITINGS:

The World Holiday Book: Celebrations for Every Day of the Year, HarperSanFrancisco (San Francisco, CA), 1994.
Magnificent Corpses: Searching through Europe for St. Peter's Head, St. Chiara's Heart, St. Stephen's Hand, and Other Saints' Relics, Marlowe (New York, NY), 1999.
Party of One: The Loners' Manifesto, Marlowe & Co. (New York, NY), 2003.

WITH KRISTAN LAWSON

Europe Off the Wall: A Guide to Unusual Sights, Wiley (New York, NY), 1988.
America Off the Wall: The West Coast: A Guide to Unusual Sights, Wiley (New York, NY), 1989.
Goddess Sites, Europe: Discover Places Where the Goddess Has Been Celebrated and Worshipped throughout Time, HarperSanFrancisco (San Francisco, CA), 1991.
Weird Europe: A Guide to Bizarre, Macabre, and Just Plain Weird Sights, St. Martin's Griffin (New York, NY), 1999.
California Babylon: A Guide to Sites of Scandal, Mayhem, and Celluloid in the Golden State, St. Martin's Griffin (New York, NY), 2000.

Contributor to publications such as *San Francisco Chronicle, Fate, Salon.com, ArtNews, Tropical Fish Hobbyist,* and *Boston Globe.*

SIDELIGHTS: Journalist and editor Anneli S. Rufus is the author of several travel guides, five of which are coauthored with Kristan Lawson. In her books, she explores a variety of quirky, unusual destinations throughout Europe and the United States. *Goddess Sites, Europe: Discover Places Where the Goddess Has Been Celebrated and Worshipped throughout Time,* written with Lawson, describes a number of European sites where female deities have been revered. Italy boasts of the sacred grove of Hecate; the Sheila-na-gig exposes herself to otherwise staid visitors to Oxford; and Isis/Mary, Star of the Sea, dwells in the Netherlands. The book is "full of wry anecdotes" and "makes discovering the goddess more like family fun than heavy study," commented Robin Bishop in *Whole Earth Review.*

Magnificent Corpses: Searching through Europe for St. Peter's Head, St. Chiara's Heart, St. Stephen's Hand, and Other Saints' Relics also touches on religion and religious history, but this time with more tangible results. Rufus relates her personal story of visits to some two dozen sites in Europe housing portions of the mortal remains of saints. Rufus admits that as a teenager, she was fascinated by the stories of the pious individuals who maintained their faith even through the agonies of their often gruesome ends. Tongues, hearts, heads, fingernails, hair, blood, even entire bodies—all make up the relics that draw from the miracle of individual saints' lives, and that inspire pilgrims from far-off destinations who gather for a chance to see or touch such vestiges. Rufus relates how relics brought economic benefits to the towns that house them, and how even this sphere of religion succumbed sometimes to trickery and forgery—at least one set of bones attributed to a saint has been positively identified as being the bones of a goat.

Rufus's reactions to the relics are informed by her Jewish upbringing, and her writing helps her come to terms with the veneration that contradicted her own religious education. "*Magnificent Corpses* is a uniquely exotic 'armchair adventure' that invites the reader to visit unheard-of places and see remarkable sights through the eyes of a hip and hardy writer with an edgy but engaging sense of humor," wrote Jonathan Kirsch in the *Los Angeles Times*. "Rufus's splendid storytelling takes readers on a European tour not soon forgotten, one that explores religion's fascination with death," commented a reviewer in *Publishers Weekly*. Kirsch concluded that "both as a travel book and as a meditation on what prompts us to regard a life and the relics of life as holy, *Magnificent Corpses* is a magnificent if eccentric success."

In *Party of One: The Loners' Manifesto,* Rufus sets out the notion that people who prefer to be alone are perfectly well-adjusted psychologically, capable of fulfilling relationships with others and productive work in society—they just prefer to spend most of their time in their own company. Rufus draws a definite distinction between being alone and being lonely; loners are happy to spend their time by themselves and to seek out contact with others on their own terms. Far from being friendless and unloved, loners maintain healthy friendships and intimate relationships. Rufus suggests that loners' friendships, while perhaps fewer than their more gregarious colleagues, are stronger

than most, and relationships with spouses are more faithful and intense. Rufus also addresses the stereotype of the criminal loner, whose existence taints the enjoyment that true loners derive from their solitude. She "argues persuasively that some of the most notorious criminals—from Ted Kaczynski to Timothy McVeigh—were, in fact, pseudoloners who didn't shun other people's approval but acted out after they were rejected," observed Rhonda Stewart in *Boston Globe*.

Rufus's "important, at times strident, but wholly unprecedented new book . . . regularly implores 'the mob' not to stigmatize loners—those, like her, who prefer to leave the phone off the hook and let the machine answer," remarked David Kipen in *San Francisco Chronicle*. "Whenever she isn't blistering society like some one-woman anti-loner-defamation league, she's exhorting loners themselves to quit apologizing and embrace their solitary ways. Whichever category a reader falls into," Kipen stated, "it's a fresh, persuasive argument, riddled with some off-putting tics but never undermined by them." A *Kirkus Reviews* critic found the book to be "a clever and spirited defense, perhaps more energetic than the actual amount of prejudice requires."

Rufus told *CA:* "I am inspired to write the sort of books that I would want to read—that offer information and insights I would have found useful, if I could have found them anywhere, written by anyone else. In other words, I write because I have to—because there are readers out there who want this information and these insights, and someone needs to give it to them. That someone might as well be me—and the heartfelt letters and emails I receive regularly from grateful readers indicate that yes, these books needed to be written.

"My books tend to address the independent thinker, the loner (which was itself the subject of my latest book)—the person who lives somehow outside the mainstream but whom I want to encourage to feel self-confident. The purpose of my offbeat travel books (authored with my husband, Kristan Lawson), and my loner book and the rest has been to tell the world, 'Hey, there are a million ways of looking at the world. Call them weird ways if you will—irreverent or untested or whatever. But they're valid, and no one should have to feel ashamed or afraid to follow his or her own star.' If readers need permission to feel okay about being 'weird,' and if I can give them that permission, then I've done my job, and the world will be a much more interesting place as a result."

BIOGRAPHICAL AND CRITICAL SOURCES:

PERIODICALS

Booklist, August, 1999, Michael Spinella, review of *Magnificent Corpses: Searching through Europe for St. Peter's Head, St. Chiara's Heart, St. Stephen's Hand, and Other Saints' Relics,* p. 1994.

Boston Globe, May 20, 2003, Rhonda Stewart, "'Party of One' Reassures Loners That They Are in Smart, Creative Company," p. C2.

Kirkus Reviews, January 1, 2003, review of *Party of One: The Loners' Manifesto,* p. 46.

Library Journal, July, 1999, Carolyn M. Craft, review of *Magnificent Corpses,* p. 98; October 15, 2000, John McCormick, review of *California Babylon: A Guide to Sites of Scandal, Mayhem, and Celluloid in the Golden State,* p. 91.

Los Angeles Times, September 4, 1999, Jonathan Kirsch, "An Eccentric Odyssey to See Relics of Faith," review of *Magnificent Corpses,* p. 2; November 29, 2000, Jonathan Kirsch, "West Words; Guide Tracks Notorious Sites and Names—From Manson to Monroe," p. E1.

Los Angeles Times Book Review, July 20, 2003, D. J. Waldie, "At Peace with One Self," p. R2.

Publishers Weekly, June 28, 1999, review of *Magnificent Corpses,* p. 70; January 27, 2003, review of *Party of One,* p. 248.

San Francisco Chronicle, March 16, 2003, David Kipen, "O Solo Mio: 'Party' Casts Loners as a Misunderstood Class," p. M1.

Whole Earth Review, spring, 1992, Robin Bishop, review of *Goddess Sites, Europe: Discover Places Where the Goddess Has Been Celebrated and Worshiped throughout Time,* p. 63.

ONLINE

Anneli Rufus Home Page, http://www.annelirufus.com (October 3, 2004).

*   *   *

RUGELEY, Terry 1956-

PERSONAL: Born September 3, 1956, in Wharton, TX; son of Frank (a doctor) and Theresa (a nurse; maiden name, Matocha) Rugeley; married Margarita Peraza Sauri (an instructor). *Ethnicity:* "Caucasian."

Education: University of Texas, B.A., 1977; Rice University, M.A., 1982; University of Houston, Ph.D., 1992.

ADDRESSES: Office—Department of History, University of Oklahoma, 455 West Lindsey, Norman, OK 73019-0535. *E-mail*—trugeley@ou.edu.

CAREER: University of Oklahoma, Norman, professor of history, 1992—.

WRITINGS:

Yucatán's Maya Peasantry and the Origins of the Caste War, University of Texas Press (Austin, TX), 1996.
Of Wonders and Wise Men: Religion and Popular Cultures in Southeast Mexico, 1800-1876, University of Texas Press (Austin, TX), 2001.
(Editor) *Maya Wars: Ethnographic Accounts from Nineteenth-Century Yucatán,* University of Oklahoma (Norman, OK), 2001.

WORK IN PROGRESS: Rebellion Now and Forever: Mayas, Hispanics, and the Yucatecan Civil Wars, 1800-1880.

SIDELIGHTS: Terry Rugeley told *CA:* "I am interested in many features of Mexican history: its geographic panorama, its pre-Columbian past, the Hispanic tradition that took root in Mexico, the language that came and the languages that refused to die, the struggle to transcend ancient ills and create a better life. Historical research is unsolicited detective work, and I find myself particularly drawn to the case of themes and individuals that are unknown or forgotten, often people living tiny lives in the remotest corners of nowhere, but who tell us something about the dramas we create and the absurdities we endure. Above all, the words and scenes of the tropical southeast have provided my inspiration. There is a sultry glow to a Tabascan river, or a pelican-lined coast, or a Yucatecan pueblo on a late Saturday afternoon which awakens the sense of an immense past lost these many years but waiting to return.

"The historian enables that return. Yet to do so the historian also becomes the writer. Fact must be present as the precondition, but those forgotten people and their scenes of bloodshed and reconciliation no longer exist apart from the words which we use to reanimate them, and for that reason the act of historical expression carries its peculiar weight. The world of all boils down to the words of one. And since things lost demand of each person a manner of statement that no other person would use, history must always emerge from what happens among ourselves, the artifacts of the past, and the blank page."

*   *   *

RUSSELL, Jan Jarboe 1951-

PERSONAL: Born 1951; married (husband is a doctor); children: Maury, Tyler.

ADDRESSES: Home—San Antonio, TX. *Office*—San Antonio Express-News, 400 Third St., San Antonio, TX 78287-2171. *E-mail*—jjarboe@express-news.net.

CAREER: Journalist, author, and educator. *San Antonio Express-News* (formerly *San Antonio Express*), San Antonio, TX, columnist, 1981-85 and 2000—; *Texas Monthly,* Austin, TX, was contributing editor, became writer at large; King Features, nationally syndicated columnist, 2001—. American Society of Newspaper Editors High School Journalism Institute, University of Texas at Austin, visiting and professional lecturer.

AWARDS, HONORS: Nieman fellow, Harvard University, 1984.

WRITINGS:

(With Kemper Diehl) *Cisneros: Portrait of a New American,* Corona Publishing (San Antonio, TX), 1984.
(With Mark Langford and Cathy Smith) *San Antonio: A Cultural Tapestry,* captions by Patti Larsen, Towery Publishing (Memphis, TN), 1998.
Lady Bird: A Biography of Mrs. Johnson, Scribner (New York, NY), 1999.
(With others) *Dreaming Red: Creating ArtPace,* Distributed Art Publishers (New York, NY), 2003.

Contributor to numerous publications, including *Good Housekeeping, New York Times,* and *Slate.*

SIDELIGHTS: Texas-based journalist Jan Jarboe Russell is best known for her syndicated columns, her writing for both the *San Antonio Express-News* and *Texas Monthly* magazine, and for her biography of former First Lady Claudia "Lady Bird" Johnson. The biography began when Russell wrote a cover story about the former first lady for *Texas Monthly* in 1994. Inspired by the topic, she went on to interview nearly two hundred people, including Johnson herself, in order to write *Lady Bird: A Biography of Mrs. Johnson.*

Johnson's husband, Lyndon Baines Johnson—or LBJ as he was often called—was a career politician who was elected John F. Kennedy's vice president in 1960. When Kennedy was assassinated three years later, Johnson ascended to the presidency. Until Johnson retired from political life in 1968, Lady Bird was constantly by his side, supporting him both politically and personally. Even after Johnson's death in 1973, Lady Bird defended her husband in the face of extramarital affairs he was rumored to have had.

After sixty hours of interviews with Lady Bird, Russell broached the subject of President Johnson's affairs, and the former first lady abruptly ceased cooperating with her. "Your conclusion about me may well come at Lyndon's expense," Johnson wrote in a letter to Russell formally breaking off the interviews. "There is no way to separate us and our roles in each other's lives." Besides, Johnson wrote, "The public should weigh what public servants are doing, not their private, innermost feelings." "I was terrified," Russell told *Austin American-Statesman* interviewer Anne Morris about receiving that letter. "I thought: how can I recover from this? I've really blown it." But Russell did recover. Russell integrated her interviews with Lady Bird and interviews she "conducted with everyone who was anyone in the Johnson administration," asRob Stout noted in the *Milwaukee Journal Sentinel.* Despite the termination of the former first lady's cooperation, *Lady Bird* "should stand as the definitive biography [of Johnson] for years to come," Rick Tamble wrote in the *Tennessean.*

Russell remained highly respectful of her subject despite their estrangement, most reviewers noticed. *Austin American-Statesman* critic Dick Holland went even further, declaring that "this portrait is more than sympathetic: it dramatically portrays Mrs. Johnson not only as the crucial support to the often-impossible LBJ, but also as a major player who herself shaped and influenced events." Yvonne Crittenden of the *Toronto Sun* reached a similar conclusion, noting that Johnson "comes off as a gutsy, intelligent and accomplished woman" in *Lady Bird.*

BIOGRAPHICAL AND CRITICAL SOURCES:

PERIODICALS

Atlanta Journal-Constitution, September 26, 1999, Caroline Heldman, review of *Lady Bird: A Biography of Mrs. Johnson,* p. L13.

Austin American-Statesman, July 13, 1999, Dick Holland, review of *Lady Bird,* p. E1; July 13, 1999, Anne Morris, interview with Russell, p. E1; January 23, 2000, Anne Morris, review of *Lady Bird,* p. K6.

Booklist, August, 1999, Mary Carroll, review of *Lady Bird,* p. 2016.

Clarion-Ledger (Jackson, MS), September 5, 1999, Joe White, review of *Lady Bird,* p. G4.

Florida Times Union, September 24, 1999, Jules Wagman, review of *Lady Bird,* p. 3.

Fresno Bee, September 26, 1999, Carolyn Barta, review of *Lady Bird,* p. E3.

Green Bay Press-Gazette, August 29, 1999, Jean Peerenboom, review of *Lady Bird,* p. D5.

Houston Chronicle, July 18, 1999, Shelby Hodge, review of *Lady Bird,* p. 2; July 23, 1999, Maxine Mesinger, review of *Lady Bird,* p. 1; August 29, 1999, Elizabeth Bennett, review of *Lady Bird,* p. 23.

Kirkus Reviews, June 15, 1999, review of *Lady Bird,* p. 947.

Knight Ridder/Tribune News Service, October 13, 1999, Art Chapman, review of *Lady Bird,* p. K0964.

Library Journal, April 1, 1985, Mark K. Jones, review of *Cisneros: Portrait of a New American,* p. 133.

Milwaukee Journal Sentinel, August 8, 1999, Rob Stout, review of *Lady Bird,* p. E13.

New York Times Book Review, October 31, 1999, Julia Douglas, review of *Lady Bird,* p. 24.

People, September 20, 1999, Rob Stout, review of *Lady Bird,* p. 57.

Publishers Weekly, February 15, 1985, review of *Cisneros,* p. 90.

San Antonio Business Journal, September 28, 2001, Michele Krier, "Local Columnist Jan Jarboe Russell to be Syndicated Nationally," p. 15.

Tennessean, August 22, 1999, Rick Tamble, review of *Lady Bird,* p. K5.

Toronto Sun, October 24, 1999, Yvonne Crittenden, review of *Lady Bird.*

Virginian Pilot, October 17, 1999, Jonathan Yardley, review of *Lady Bird,* p. E4.

ONLINE

iVillage.com, http://www.ivillage.com/ (October 24, 2003), interview with Russell.

San Antonio Express-News Web site http://www.mysanantonio.com/ (December 9, 2003), "Jan Jarboe Russell."

Texas Monthly Online, http://www.texasmonthly.com/ (November 3, 2003), "Jan Jarboe Russell."*

*   *   *

RUTLAND, Suzanne D. 1946-

PERSONAL: Born July 3, 1946, in Sydney, New South Wales, Australia; daughter of Naftali Benjamin (a jeweler) and Perla (Freilich) Perlman; married Jonathan Rutland, 1966 (divorced, 1994); children: Benjamin Naftali, Ronit Yaffa. *Education:* University of Sydney, B.A. (with honors), 1969, diploma of education, 1970, M.A. (with honors), 1978, Ph.D., 1991. *Religion:* Jewish. *Hobbies and other interests:* Walking, swimming.

ADDRESSES: Office—Department of Hebrew, Biblical, and Jewish Studies, University of Sydney, Sydney, New South Wales 2006, Australia. *E-mail*—suzanne.rutland@arts.usyd.edu.au.

CAREER: High school teacher, 1970-74, 1976-78; University of Sydney, Sydney, New South Wales, Australia, lecturer in Jewish education, 1990-96, senior lecturer in Jewish civilization, 1997-2004, associate professor, 2004—, chair of fepartment of Hebrew, biblical, and Jewish studies, 1999—. International School for Holocaust Studies, Yad Vashem, Jerusalem, Israel, Australian academic representative to seminar for educators from abroad, 1998—. Jewish Educators' Network, committee member, 1990-97, honorary secretary, 1995-97; New South Wales Board of Studies, member of advisory committee, 1995—; Joint

Authority for Jewish/Zionist Education in the Diaspora, cochair of national advisory council for Australia, 1995-98; Joint Committee for Jewish Higher Education, honorary secretary, 1997—. B'nei Akiva Youth Movement, leader, 1965-67; Australian Zionist Youth Council, member, 1965-67; Moriah War Memorial College, member of school board, 1985-91; Mandelbaum Trust, member of board of trustees, 2000—; Melton Adult Education Program, academic chair of Shalom Institute, 2001, member of academic board, 2002—.

MEMBER: Australian and New Zealand History of Education Association, Royal Australian Historical Society, Australian Association for Jewish Studies (president, 1993-95, 1997-99, 2002-04), Australian Jewish Historical Society (vice president, 1990-96; president, 1997-2004), Australian Society of Authors, Oral History Association of Australia, Association of Jewish Community Professionals, Local History Association, Professional Historians Association.

AWARDS, HONORS: Linkage grant, Australian Research Council.

WRITINGS:

Seventy-five Years: The History of a Jewish Newspaper, Australian Jewish Historical Society (Sydney, New South Wales, Australia), 1970.

Edge of the Diaspora: Two Centuries of Jewish Settlements in Australia, Collins (Sydney, New South Wales, Australia), 1988, 2nd edition published as *Edge of the Diaspora: Two Centuries of Jewish Settlement in Australia,* Holmes & Meier Publishers (New York, NY), 2001.

Pages of History: A Century of the Australian Jewish Press, Australian Jewish Press (Darlinghurst, New South Wales, Australia), 1995.

(With Sophie Caplan) *With One Voice: A History of the New South Wales Jewish Board of Deputies,* Australian Jewish Historical Society (Sydney, New South Wales, Australia), 1998.

"If You Will It, It Is No Dream": The Moriah Story, Playwright Publishing (Sydney, New South Wales, Australia), 2003.

Contributor to books, including *The New South Wales Jewish Community: A Survey,* by S. Encel and B. Buckley, 2nd edition, New South Wales University Press (Kensington, New South Wales, Australia), 1978. Sydney editor, *AJHS Journal,* 1991—; journal editor, Jewish Educators' Network, 1990-97; newsletter editor, Australian Association for Jewish Studies, 1995-97, 1999-2001.

WORK IN PROGRESS: A concise history of the Jews in Australia to be published by Cambridge University Press; a book on the political sociology of Australian Jewry.

S

SAMMAN, Ghada
    See AL-SAMMAN, Ghadah

*   *   *

SANDER, Heather L. 1947-

PERSONAL: Born December 4, 1947, in Saskatoon, Saskatchewan, Canada; daughter of William and Audrey Walker; married Eugene Sander (a college teacher), June 28, 1969; children: Ian, Ronald. *Ethnicity:* "Scottish." *Education:* University of Saskatchewan, B.A., 1967, Dip.Ed., 1969; University of Victoria, M.A., 1985.

ADDRESSES: Agent—c/o Author Mail, Orca Book Publishers Ltd., P.O. Box 5626, Station B, Victoria, British Columbia, Canada V8R 6S4. *E-mail*—gandh. sander@shaw.ca.

CAREER: Writer and school councillor. Victoria School District, Victoria, British Columbia, Canada, elementary school councillor, 1987—.

MEMBER: British Columbia School Counsellors' Association; Victoria Writers' Association.

WRITINGS:

Robbie Packford: Alien Monster, Orca Book Publishers (Victoria, British Columbia, Canada), 2003.

Make Mine with Everything ("Robbie Packford" series), Orca Book Publishers (Custer, WA), 2004.
Whatever Happened to My Dog Cuddles? ("Robbie Packford" series), Orca Book Publishers (Custer, WA), 2004.

SIDELIGHTS: A native of western Canada, Heather L. Sander is the author of a series of humorous children's books that includes *Robbie Packford: Alien Monster* and its sequels, *Make Mine with Everything* and *Whatever Happened to My Dog Cuddles?* In the series opener, sixth grader Robbie does not want to believe that his new friend is really an alien from the planet Kerbosky, but the fantastic chain of events that unfolds in *Robbie Packford: Alien Monster* forces him to face the unearthly reality. Robbie is transformed into an reptilian-looking creature with amazing powers after being exposed to a secret formula belonging to this now-questionable "friend," and soon finds himself aboard a space shop and enlisted in a crusade to save planet Kerbosky from nasty killer robots. Noting that the "killer-robots-conquer-the-world plot has been used countless times," *School Library Journal* reviewer Elaine E. Knight nonetheless credited Sander for adding "a touch of wry humor as Robbie continually tries to balance his human and monster nature." Teresa Hughes, reviewing *Robbie Packford: Alien Monster* for *Resource Links,* stated that although Sander's novel "is short enough for the reluctant reader who is intimidated by larger novels," the humorous space adventure is"still interesting and funny."

Sander once commented: "I've researched my career as a kid's writer for a long time. First I was a kid. Then I had them. When they grew up and were more or less unavailable for research, they produced grandchildren. (Hooray!) In the meantime, by a clever scheme, I managed to get paid by the public school system to continue my research as a teacher and elementary school counselor where I could invite children into my office or wander through classes at silent reading time and quiz kids at will as to what they were reading. In a recent values exercise, a lot of grade-six boys rated good books at the bottom of their list, so I'm still working on that one.

"I've always been a fantasy and science-fiction fan since you don't have to be bound by the laws of physics and if you get tired of one planet you can try another. My science-fiction reading passion fell neatly between two other reading periods in my childhood; horses, where I wished I could have my own and keep it in the backyard, and archaeology, where I dreamed of sailing across the Pacific in a papyrus boat like Thor Heyerdahl. I started with Tom Swift and graduated to Isaac Asimov. As an adult, reading *HitchHiker's Guide to the Galaxy* in one go while sick at home with a high fever was a mind-altering experience. I've never been the same since.

"*Robbie Packford: Alien Monster,* for kids aged eight through twelve, considers the following important question: What would happen if that new kid in your class was actually telling the truth when he said he was an alien?"

BIOGRAPHICAL AND CRITICAL SOURCES:

PERIODICALS

Canadian Review of Materials, October 1, 2004, Mary Thomas, review of *Make Mine with Everything.*
Resource Links, December, 2003, Teresa Hughes, review of *Robbie Packford: Alien Monster,* p. 20.
School Library Journal, September, 2004, Elaine E. Knight, review of *Robbie Packford: Alien Monster,* p. 217.

*   *   *

SCHEIBERG, Susan L. 1962-

PERSONAL: Born December 19, 1962, in Chicago, IL; daughter of Steven and Margo Scheiberg. *Education:* Indiana University—Bloomington, B.A. (cum laude), 1984; University of California, Los Angeles, M.A., 1986; University of Kentucky, M.S.L.I.S., 1997.

ADDRESSES: Office—RAND Corp., 1776 Main St., P.O. Box 2138, Santa Monica, CA 90407-2138. *E-mail*—susanls@rand.org.

CAREER: University of California, Los Angeles, instructor in folklore and mythology, 1984-87; Morehead State University, Morehead, KY, coordinator of folk art marketing program at Folk Art Center, 1992-94; University of Louisville, Louisville, KY, public services supervisor at Kersey Library of Engineering, Sciences, and Technology, 1994-95, collection management program assistant, 1995-97, chair of technology work design group, 1996-97; University of Southern California, Los Angeles, research and collection development librarian, 1997-98, team leader for serials acquisitions, 1998-2001, member of library faculty executive council, 1998-2001; RAND Corp., Santa Monica, CA, head of serials and acquisitions, 2001-02, coordinator of library outreach services, 2002, assistant director of library, 2002—. University of California, San Diego, visiting lecturer, 1991; guest on media programs, including *Human Nature,* Canadian Broadcasting Corp., 1991. Statewide California Electronic Library Consortium, member of product review advisory committee, 2003-06. Association for Library Collections and Technical Services, member of acquisitions organization and management committee, 2001-03, serials acquisitions committee, 2000-03, collection development issues for the practitioner committee, 2001-04, and quantitative measures for collection development committee, 2004—. Also member of editorial board, *Owl Newsletter,* 1995-97.

MEMBER: North American Serials Interest Group, American Library Association, Association for Library Collections and Technical Services, Library Administration and Management Association, Reference and User Services Association, Association of College and Research Libraries, Special Libraries Association, Phi Beta Kappa, Beta Phi Mu.

AWARDS, HONORS: Research grants, Bardin Endowment, 1998, 1999, 2000.

WRITINGS:

(Editor, with Shelley Neville) *NASIG 2001: A Serials Odyssey,* Haworth Press (New York, NY), 2002.
(Editor, with Shelley Neville) *Transforming Serials: The Revolution Continues,* Haworth Press (New York, NY), 2003.

Contributor to books, including *From Carnegie to Internet 2: Forging the Serials Future,* edited by Michelle Fiander, Joe Harmon, and Jonathan Makepeace, Haworth Press (New York, NY), 2000. Contributor of articles and reviews to periodicals, including *Western Folklore, American Behavioral Scientist, Folklore and Mythology Studies,* and *Library Collections, Acquisitions, and Technical Services.* Editor, *Books, Bytes, and Beyond: RAND Library Newsletter,* 2002—.

WORK IN PROGRESS: Research on client services in special libraries.

*   *   *

SCHLEIN, Miriam 1926-2004

OBITUARY NOTICE— See index for *CA* sketch: Born June 6, 1926, in New York, NY; died of vasculitis November 23, 2004, in New York, NY. Author. Schlein was a prolific author of children's books who was best known for her ability to teach young readers about animals, science, and other topics in an entertaining way. She earned a B.A. in psychology from Brooklyn College in 1947 before embarking on a variety of jobs in the fields of publishing and advertising. While working for the publisher Simon & Schuster in the children's department, she was inspired to write her own books for children. Beginning with 1951's *A Day at the Playground,* she would go on to write nearly one hundred books over five decades. Although she wrote a number of fiction stories, such as *Oomi, the New Hunter* (1955), *The Snake in the Carpool* (1963), and *I Sailed with Columbus* (1991), she was often considered to be at her best when writing about the natural sciences. Among her award-winning efforts in this genre are *Fast Is Not a Ladybug: A Book about Fast and Slow Things* (1953), *Elephant Herd* (1954), *What's Wrong with Being a Skunk?* (1974), *Giraffe, the Silent Giant* (1976), *The Dangerous Life of the Sea Horse* (1986), and *Discovering Dinosaur Babies* (1991).

OBITUARIES AND OTHER SOURCES:

PERIODICALS

New York Times, December 2, 2004, p. C10.

SCHNEIDER, Wayne (Joseph) 1950-

PERSONAL: Born 1950; married Paula Olsen (a librarian). *Education:* Cornell University, Ph.D.

ADDRESSES: Office—Music Department, University of Vermont, Burlington, VT 05405. *Agent*—c/o Author Mail, Oxford University Press, 198 Madison Ave., New York, NY 10016. *E-mail*—wschneid@zoo.uvm. edu.

CAREER: Musician, music scholar, educator, and editor. University of Vermont, Burlington, associate professor of music and university organist. Editor of musical scores, including compositions by Ruth Crawford Seeger.

WRITINGS:

(Editor) *The Gershwin Style: New Looks at the Music of George Gershwin,* Oxford University Press (New York, NY), 1999.

Contributor of entries to *Harvard Dictionary of Music, Grove Dictionary of American Music, Grove Dictionary of Jazz,* and *New Grove Dictionary of Music and Musicians,* and to periodicals, including *Notes, American Music, Humanities,* and *Institute for Studies in American Music Newsletter.*

SIDELIGHTS: A musician and scholar who has aided in the first publication of orchestral works by twentieth-century American composer Ruth Crawford Seeger, Wayne Schneider has also written widely on musical matters and has served as editor of *The Gershwin Style: New Looks at the Music of George Gershwin,* a 1999 collection of essays on the music of the American composer. Contributors include Gershwin biographer Edward Jablonski, music scholar Charles Hamm, and Steven Gilbert, author of *Music of Gershwin.* Various works are studied, as is Gershwin's place in the development of the player piano, the film *Rhapsody in Blue* (the title of which comes from one of his most-enjoyed works), and his later influence on popular music. *Library Journal*'s Barry Zaslow felt that in order to fully enjoy this volume, readers should have a musical background. Zaslow called the collection "an eclectic mix of essays."

BIOGRAPHICAL AND CRITICAL SOURCES:

PERIODICALS

Library Journal, February 1, 1999, Barry Zaslow, review of *The Gershwin Style: New Looks at the Music of George Gershwin,* p. 88.
Music & Letters, February, 1998, p. 156.
Notes, December, 1996, p. 626.

*　　*　　*

SCHWARZ, Robin

PERSONAL: Female. *Education:* Hampshire College, graduated, 1976; Columbia University, M.F.A., 1979.

ADDRESSES: Home—New York, NY. *Agent*—c/o Author Mail, Warner Books, 1271 Avenue of the Americas, New York, NY 10020.

CAREER: Author, environmentalist, and advertising executive. J. Walter Thompson, New York, NY, former advertising executive and copywriter; Kaplan Thaler Group, New York, NY, creative director/writer; also worked as a musician and songwriter.

AWARDS, HONORS: John Lennon Song-Writing Contest winner, Gospel Category; International TV and Radio Award, best writer world-wide award.

WRITINGS:

Night Swimming (novel), Warner Books (New York, NY), 2004.

Contributor of poems to periodicals. Author of poetic notes (with James Patterson) in Paterson's novel *Jack and Jill.* Also author of children's books, including *The Book of Natural Magic* and *An Orchestra of Crickets.*

WORK IN PROGRESS: A second novel.

SIDELIGHTS: Robin Schwarz has spent a major portion of her career working for New York City-based advertising agencies. With J. Walter Thompson, one of America's premier agencies, for fifteen years, she handled projects for clients that included Kodak, Pepsi, Nestle, Bell Atlantic, Motts, and others, and she has more recently divided her time between working on a second novel and serving as creative director and writer for the city's Kaplan Thaler Group.

In Schwarz's debut novel, *Night Swimming,* 253-pound, thirty-four-year-old Charlotte Clapp is in all ways miserable. She has sacrificed much of her own life to care for her ailing mother, and has become alienated from her lifelong best friend, Mary Ann. Her only solace lies in food. During a routine medical check-up, however, Charlotte receives devastating news from her doctor: she has advanced cancer, and only a year left to live. Faced with this finite mortality, she decides to ditch her drab and dull existence in Gorham, New Hampshire and attempt to experience a full and exciting life in her final year.

At the start of *Night Swimming* Charlotte quits her job at the local bank, and on her last night there, robs the institution of two million dollars. Heading east, she adopts the name Blossom McBeal from an elderly woman who has recently died. Purchasing a luxurious condominium in Los Angeles for cash, Charlotte then sets about to experience what she has missed. Much of her new life centers around the pool at her condominium and Skip, the strikingly good-looking pool boy that comes with it. Smitten by Skip, who harbors a few secrets of his own, Charlotte begins swimming laps in the night, shedding pounds and hoping to become more physically attractive to him. Ultimately, however, her plan begins to unravel, leading to complications in her budding relationship with Skip and the necessity of reconciling with her past, particularly her short stint as a bank robber.

"Schwarz arouses genuine sympathy from her readers," noted Judy Gigstad in a review of *Night Swimming* for *BookReporter.com.* The novelist has "a sharp eye and a wicked sense of humor," added Kelly Hartog in the *California Literary Review Online. Booklist* critic Kaite Mediatore observed that in the novel "characters may behave outlandishly but they're realistic. Comic situations are preposterous yet believable." "Overall, *Night Swimming* is a lighthearted look at one woman's desperate need to reinvent herself,"

Hartog stated, while *Library Journal* reviewer Rebecca Kelm predicted that readers "will love Blossom's fantasy year and cheer as newcomer Schwarz wraps this one up."

While her advertising projects have garnered her many awards, Schwarz commented on the *Time Warner Web site* that she has found most of her satisfaction in volunteer work for organizations such as Red Cross, the Dolphin Research Lab, and the *Adventurer,* the last a Gloucester, Massachusetts-based schooner being refurbished as a hands-on teaching site.

BIOGRAPHICAL AND CRITICAL SOURCES:

PERIODICALS

Booklist, May 15, 2004, Kaite Mediatore, review of *Night Swimming,* p. 1599.
Kirkus Reviews, June 1, 2004, review of *Night Swimming,* p. 515.
Library Journal, May 1, 2004, Rebecca Kelm, review of *Night Swimming,* p. 141.
Publishers Weekly, June 28, 2004, review of *Night Swimming,* p. 32.

ONLINE

BookReporter.com, http://www.bookreporter.com/ (November 18, 2004), Judy Gigstad, review of *Night Swimming.*
California Literary Review Online, Kelly Hartog, review of *Night Swimming.*
Time Warner Bookmark Web site, http://www.twbookmark.com/ (November 18, 2004), "Robin Schwarz."

*   *   *

SEARLS, David 1947-
(Doc Searls)

PERSONAL: Born July 29, 1947, in Ft. Lee, NJ; son of Allen Henry and Eleanor (Oman) Searls; children: Colette, Peter. *Education:* Guilford College, B.A., 1969.

ADDRESSES: Office—Linux Journal, P.O. Box 55549, Seattle, WA 98155-0549.

CAREER: Matzner Newspapers, Wayne, NJ, editor, 1970-71; Community Action Council, Hewitt, NJ, social worker, 1971-72; broadcaster for various radio stations in Durham, NC, 1972-75; consultant in Chapel Hill, NC, 1975-76; Hodskins, Simone & Searls, Inc. (public relations and advertising company), Palo Alto, CA, partner and vice president, 1976-98; founder of The Searls Group (marketing consulting firm), beginning 1978; *Linux Journal,* Seattle, WA, senior editor, 1999—. Cofounder of political action committee GeekPAC. Has appeared on many media programs, including for CNBC, CNET Radio, and TechTV, and on Web radio programs *The Linux Show* and *The Gillmor Gang;* director of Web journal *Reality 2.0.* Member of advisory boards, Ping Identity Corp., Technorati, and Jabber, Inc.

WRITINGS:

(With Rick Levine, Christopher Lock, and David Weinberger) *The Cluetrain Manifesto: The End of Business as Usual,* Perseus (Cambridge, MA), 2000.

Contributor to periodicals, including *PC, Omni, Upside, Wired,* and the Toronto *Globe & Mail.* Sometimes writes as Doc Searls for *Linux Journal* and other periodicals.

SIDELIGHTS: Journalist and public relations/marketing consultant David Searls has been interested in the marketing potential of the Internet for decades. Having worked with many companies—from corporate giants such as Motorola, Hitachi, and Nortel to new start-ups endeavors—Searls quickly came under the impression that the majority of these businesses did not have a good understanding of how the Web affected their marketing efforts. When creating Web sites or advertising for the Internet, these companies were still stuck in the mind-set that they needed to force-fully persuade customers into buying their products, and they had no clue as to how to take advantage of the potential of customer service on the Internet. Instead, Searls believes that the Internet is much more effective as a type of interactive forum between businesses and customers, where the two sides should participate on a much more even playing field. To get this message across, in 1999 Searls and collaborators Rick Levine, Christopher Lock, and David Weinberger began the Web site *Cluetrain.com,* where they outlined their manifesto for the new Web era of marketing. The next year, they expanded this concept into the book *The Cluetrain Manifesto: The End of Business as Usual.*

The Cluetrain Manifesto includes chapters from each of the authors, all technology journalists, arguing that companies need to look at e-commerce as a series of communications, rather than focusing on only the actual transactions. As Giles Turnbull put it in a Manchester *Guardian* article, "Fundamental to the Manifesto was the idea that online communication is between real people—individuals with humour, sarcasm and an ability to spot insincerity a mile away. A person with a human voice speaking from within a company would have far more impact on that company's reputation than a multimillion dollar public relations campaign, the Manifesto said."

But while the Web site idea for the manifesto was often lauded by reviewers, some felt tha ttransforming *Cluetrain.com* as a book worked less well. For instance, *Washington Post* contributor T. R. Reid wrote, "Frankly, it was better on the Web. As an attention grabber, a conversation starter, the seven-page document on the Web is great. The basic idea, that businesses need to adapt to the Net, is clearly right, and the warning that customers know more than the boardroom thinks they do is valuable. But the authors haven't done enough—haven't done much of anything, really—to turn these two insights into a book." Richard Blackburn similarly noted in *Personnel Psychology* that the authors have not really organized their thoughts well in the book version, commenting that they evidently "did not spend a great deal of time talking with each other, or with their editor(s). We read the same things over and over again in succeeding chapters." Blackburn was also bothered by the fact that "the authors seem to assume that all who are carrying on these Web conversations by which we make the market smarter are honest and trustworthy. Given the recent scams in the penny stock markets, in stock chat rooms, and at auction sites, this seems rather naive."

However, many reviewers still appreciated the book as containing themes that needed to be said. For instance, *New York Times Book Review* contributor Rob Walker,

felt that "while this [manifesto] . . . often strains credulity in the particulars, the general thrust is on the mark." *Marketing* reviewer Abby Hardoon asserted, "This book is for anyone interested in the internet and e-commerce," and Terry O'Keefe concluded in *Long Island Business News* that "you owe it to yourself to check out the world from Cluetrain's point of view."

BIOGRAPHICAL AND CRITICAL SOURCES:

PERIODICALS

Business Communication Quarterly, December, 2000, Melinda L. Kreth, review of *The Cluetrain Manifesto: The End of Business as Usual,* p. 106.
Denver Post, April 30, 2000, Stephen Keating, "Business Gets Dot.comeuppance High-Tech 4 Sniff at Top-down Types," p. F5.
Guardian (Manchester, England), May 27, 2004, Giles Turnbull, "Life: Online: The Long Conversation: How Have Business and the Media Adapted to the Arrival of the Internet? Giles Turnbull Spoke to the Authors of the Seminal *Cluetrain Manifesto,* Five Years after It First Appeared Online," p. 19.
Latin Trade, June, 2000, Andres Hernandez Alende, review of *The Cluetrain Manifesto,* p. 100.
Long Island Business News, June 2, 2000, Terry O'Keefe, review of *The Cluetrain Manifesto,* p. A47.
Marketing, August 3, 2000, Abby Hardoon, review of *The Cluetrain Manifesto,* p. 64.
Newsbytes, April 10, 2002, Brian Krebs, "GeekPac Takes on Microsoft, Hollywood, Tauzin-Dingell," p. NWSB02107004.
New York Times Book Review, March 26, 2000, Rob Walker, "Biz.com," p. 17.
Personnel Psychology, summer, 2001, Richard Blackburn, review of *The Cluetrain Manifesto,* p. 541.
Sales & Marketing Management, February, 2000, Andy Cohen, review of *The Cluetrain Manifesto,* p. 22.
USA Today, April 17, 2000, Bruce Rosenstein, "Climb Aboard 'Cluetrain' for Net Lesson," p. B13.
Washington Post Book World, May 14, 2000, T. R. Reid, "Net Profits," p. 4.

ONLINE

Linux Journal Online, http://www2.linuxjournal.com/ (January 6, 2000), "David Searls."
Searls Group Web site, http://www.searls.com/ (November 9, 2004).*

SEARLS, Doc
    See SEARLS, David

*   *   *

SEGHERS, Jan
    See ALTENBURG, Matthias

*   *   *

SELIGMAN, Craig

PERSONAL: Born in LA. *Education:* Attended Stanford University and Oxford University.

ADDRESSES: Home—Brooklyn, NY. *Agent*—c/o Author Mail, Counterpoint Press, 387 Park Avenue South, New York, NY 10016.

CAREER: Author, critic, and editor. Former editor, *New Yorker* and *Salon.com;* former executive editor, *Food & Wine* (magazine); former arts critic, *San Francisco Examiner,* San Francisco, CA.

WRITINGS:

Sontag and Kael: Opposites Attract Me, Counterpoint Press (New York, NY), 2004.

SIDELIGHTS: Craig Seligman is a New York-based author, critic, and editor who has been an editor for the *New Yorker* magazine as well as a critic for *Salon.com.* In his book *Sontag and Kael: Opposites Attract Me,* he examines in depth the lives and careers of Pauline Kael and Susan Sontag, two of the most prominent voices in American cultural criticism in the second half of the twentieth century. Seligman seeks to put Kael's and Sontag's works into perspective, both in contrast with each other and within the larger context of arts and culture in the United States. At its base, the book is "a dense, meta-level work of criticism by one critic about two other critics," commented *Washington Post Book World* reviewer Philip Kennicott. The "strength of this delightful little book is that it is about much more than its title suggests," Kennicott continued. "It is about the way people

experience and understand art and culture; it is about criticism not just as practiced by professional critics, but as lived by all of us who try to make sense of art; and it delves deeply into the ever-tortuous way in which the rhetoric of populism threads through American culture."

Kael, who died in 2001, and Sontag are considered to be on roughly equal footing among their generation's heavyweights of cultural criticism and intellectual discourse. Kael's arena was the movies, while Sontag worked on a broader canvas that encompassed the arts and intellectual culture. While Seligman was a close friend of Kael's, this friendship did not impede his critical appreciation of her work, in the opinion of critics such as *Variety*'s Allison Burnett, who wrote: "His love for Kael is so powerful that it is never diminished by his clear-eyed understanding of her foibles as a human being and a writer." "Seligman's very good book isn't flawed by its prejudice for Kael; rather, it's rendered more human," Kennicott added. In contrast, while he had not met Sontag when he wrote his book, Seligman still attempted to defend her importance, "and he pretty much succeeds." This task was all the more challenging, in the opinion of a *Kirkus* reviewer, because Seligman "isn't the only person in America who thinks the author of *Against Interpretation* and other groundbreaking works of criticism is arrogant, humorless, and charmless." "Seligman's respect for Sontag as a thinker is vast, but it is his misgivings about her as a human being that make for good reading," Burnett added. His "admiration for Sontag's writing is genuine, and his close reading of her work imparts a rich understanding of her intentions in a manner that would compliment any writer," agreed Chris Navratil in his review of *Sontag and Kael* for the *Boston Globe.*

John Newlin, writing in the New Orleans *Times-Picayune,* called *Sontag and Kael* "an elegant and adroit performance," while *Harper's* reviewer John Leonard dubbed the book "lucid and affectionate." In *Booklist,* reviewer Donna Seaman declared the work to comprise a "bravura inquiry into [the] ethos and influence" of the two cultural critics. "Seligman's style is so engaging . . . that he's a pleasure to read for his own sake," David Kipen remarked in the *San Francisco Chronicle.*

Even though reviewers such as *Atlantic Monthly* critic David Thompson had some misgivings about *Sontag and Kael*—Thompson called it "a magazine essay stretched out to book length"—praise for Seligman himself has remained high. He is "smart, gracious, and so good a writer that you know he needs to get a first book out of the way so that he can turn to something more compelling or grounded," Thompson commented. Seligman's "openness and fluency, his willingness to roll out his doubts and changes his mind, take us to a place we couldn't have reached without him," observed Michael Wood in the *New York Times Book Review.*

BIOGRAPHICAL AND CRITICAL SOURCES:

PERIODICALS

Atlantic Monthly, July-August, 2004, David Thompson, review of *Sontag and Kael: Opposites Attract Me,* p. 159.

Booklist, March 1, 2004, Donna Seaman, review of *Sontag and Kael,* p. 1130.

Boston Globe, June 6, 2004, Chris Navratil, review of *Sontag and Kael,* p. L7.

Entertainment Weekly, May 21, 2004, Ken Tucker, review of *Sontag and Kael,* p. 85.

Harper's, May, 2004, John Leonard, review of *Sontag and Kael,* p. 85.

Kirkus Reviews, March 1, 2004, review of *Sontag and Kael,* p. 214.

Library Journal, May 1, 2004, Maria Kochis, review of *Sontag and Kael,* p. 108.

New York Times Book Review, May 30, 2004, Michael Wood, "The Perils of Pauline and Susan," p. 7.

San Francisco Chronicle, June 1, 2004, David Kipen, "Critical Look at Critics Sontag, Kael," p. E1.

Times-Picayune (New Orleans, LA), September 5, 2004, John Newlin, "The Perils of Pauline Worship," p. 8.

Variety, August 9, 2004, Allison Burnett, review of *Sontag and Kael,* p. 36.

Washington Post Book World, June 13, 2004, Philip Kennicott, "Poles Apart: A Passionate Look at Two Influential Writers," p. T8.*

*   *   *

SESSIONS, William A(lfred) 1938-
  (W. A. Sessions)

PERSONAL: Born August 4, 1938, in Conway, SC; married, 1961; children: two. *Education:* University of North Carolina at Chapel Hill, B.A., 1957; Columbia University, M.A., 1959, Ph.D., 1966.

ADDRESSES: Office—Department of English, Georgia State University, 33 Gilmer St., Atlanta, GA 30303-3080. *E-mail*—wsessions@gsu.edu.

CAREER: State University of West Georgia, Carrollton, assistant professor of English, 1959-60; Spring Hill College, Mobile, AL, assistant professor, 1960-62; St. John's University, Jamaica, NY, assistant professor, 1962-66; Georgia State University, Atlanta, associate professor, 1966-72, professor, 1972-93, Regents' Professor of English, 1993—, director of English department graduate school, 1969-75. Member of Medieval Institute and Institute for Historical Research.

MEMBER: Modern Language Association, Renaissance Society of America, American Literature Association, Southeastern Renaissance Society.

WRITINGS:

Shakespeare's Romeo and Juliet, Barrister Publishing (New York, NY), 1966.

(With Bert C. Bach and William Walling) *The Liberating Form: A Handbook-Anthology of English and American Poetry,* Dodd, Mead (New York, NY), 1972.

Henry Howard, Earl of Surrey, Twayne Publishers (New York, NY), 1986.

(Editor) *Francis Bacon's Legacy of Texts: "The Art of Discovery Grows with Discovery,"* AMS Press (New York, NY), 1990.

(As W. A. Sessions) *Francis Bacon Revisited,* Twayne Publishers (New York, NY), 1996.

(As W. A. Sessions) *Henry Howard, the Poet Earl of Surrey: A Life* (biography), Oxford University Press (New York, NY), 1999.

Contributor to books, including *Milton and the Fine Arts,* Pennsylvania State University Press, 1989; and *Rethinking the Henrician Age,* University of Illinois Press, 1994. Contributor to journals, including *Profession, Southern Review,* and *Literature and Belief.*

SIDELIGHTS: Literature professor William A. Sessions is well known for his scholarship of sixteenth-century English poet Henry Howard, earl of Surrey, who is often credited as the inventor of the English sonnet—a poem of fourteen lines—and heroic quatrain forms, as well as of blank verse—unrhymed verse consisting of alternating stressed and unstressed syllables. The rest of Surrey's fame lies with his frequent conflicts with King Henry VIII and British royalty; he was imprisoned several times as a result, and finally executed for treason in 1547. In his widely praised cultural biography *Henry Howard, the Poet Earl of Surrey: A Life,* Sessions attempts to bring together the two sides of Surrey: the innovative poet, and the nobleman some historians consider to have been tragically out of touch with the changing political climate of Renaissance England. Surrey, who was a cousin of one of Henry VIII's wives, Anne Boleyn, was upset by the advancement of certain associates of the royal family to aristocratic positions; in particular, he was upset by the advancement of his rival Edward Seymour. Surrey felt that England should have a nobility modeled more closely on the system employed by the Roman Empire, and even though his political maneuverings did not include aspirations to the throne itself, Surrey was seen as a threat by the king because of these beliefs.

Surrey's ideas about literature and poetry were influenced by his concepts concerning aristocracy. As Michael Ullyot observed in an *Early Modern Literary Studies* review, it was through art that "Surrey sought to reinforce a new sense of nobility based on Roman models: the lyrics and translations, the architecture and landscape of Surrey House." While under house arrest Surrey created the English sonnet, and his inspiration to write heroic verse echoed his sadness over what he felt was the decline of the aristocracy, as Sessions observes. But the poet's position on the royalty eventually proved his undoing. Already suffering the disfavor of the king because of his military defeat at St. Etienne in 1546, the poet provoked further controversy when he displayed a coat of arms boasting his lineage; this his enemies interpreted as a direct challenge to the prince of Wales. Though he protested that his intent was innocent, Surrey was imprisoned and then executed for treason.

Although Sessions portrays Surrey as a noble figure in history and literature, Katherine Duncan-Jones argued in her *Times Literary Supplement* review of *Henry Howard, the Poet Earl of Surrey* that Surrey was actually an upstart undeserving of Sessions' willingness to forgive certain flaws. Duncan-Jones cited Surrey as an elitist who had the "conviction that his noble birth entitled him to harass commoners," and she noted that

in Sessions' book "many of the documented events of Surrey's short life almost vanish—or, when they are visible, are puzzlingly difficult to connect with the grand claims made for Surrey's high seriousness." On the other hand, Robert C. Braddock maintained in *Renaissance Quarterly* that the biography is a "carefully documented" work that "reveals a Surrey far more complex than previously depicted." Ullyot had high praise for the book, as well, calling it "an exhaustive and densely-footnoted biography, as remarkable for its ambition as for its resounding success." Ullyot concluded, "Sessions' book succeeds where most biographies fail, dispensing with the standard hyperbole only to justify it in the end."

BIOGRAPHICAL AND CRITICAL SOURCES:

PERIODICALS

Early Modern Literary Studies, September, 2000, Michael Ullyot, review of *Henry Howard, the Poet Earl of Surrey: A Life.*
Journal of English and Germanic Philology, January, 1999, Charles Whitney, review of *Francis Bacon Revisited,* p. 93.
Renaissance Quarterly, spring, 2001, Robert C. Braddock, review of *Henry Howard, the Poet Earl of Surrey,* p. 306.
Times Literary Supplement, June 25, 1999, Katherine Duncan-Jones, "The Sound of Broken Glass" (review of *Henry Howard, the Poet Earl of Surrey,* pp. 26-27.*

*   *   *

SESSIONS, W. A.
  See SESSIONS, William A(lfred)

*   *   *

SINGLETON, Janet Elyse
  (Elyse Singleton)

PERSONAL: Born August 30, in Chicago, IL; daughter of John (a bus driver) and Jacqueline (a hair stylist) Singleton. *Ethnicity:* African American. *Education:* Attended University of Wisconsin; attended Bennington College summer writing workshops, 1991-93, 1995. *Politics:* Democrat. *Hobbies and other interests:* Sewing and refurbishing vintage clothing, photography, traveling, movies made in the '30s, '40s, '50s, and early '60s.

ADDRESSES: Agent—Sally Wofford-Girand, 80 Fifth Avenue, Suite 1101-03, New York, NY 10010. *E-mail*—thissideofthesky@aol.com.

CAREER: Freelance journalist and travel writer.

AWARDS, HONORS: Bread Loaf writers conference scholarship, 1988; selected literary associate, Rocky Mountain Women's Institute, 1989-90; first place, National Writers Association Short-Story Contest, 1991; first place, Society of Professional Journalist Excellence in Journalism Award for commentary, 1993; Recognition Award in Literature, Colorado Council on the Arts, 1994; projects award, Colorado Council on the Arts, 1995; Barnes & Noble Discover Great New Writers selection, and Colorado Book Award for Fiction, both 2002, both for *This Side of the Sky;* Best of the Best Award, *Rawsistaz Review,* for Best Newcomer, 2003.

WRITINGS:

(As Elyse Singleton) *This Side of the Sky,* BlueHen Books (Denver, CO), 2002.

Contributor to periodicals, including *USA Today, Chicago Tribune, Miami Herald, Ladies' Home Journal, Essence, Woman's World, Atlanta Journal-Constitution, Dallas Morning News, Denver Post, Cleveland Plain Dealer, Bella, New Zealand Women's Weekly,* and *New Zealand Herald.*

ADAPTATIONS: This Side of the Sky was adapted to audio by Recorded Books.

WORK IN PROGRESS: A Thousand Horsemen, a novel, for Penguin Putnam.

SIDELIGHTS: Janet Elyse Singleton is a Chicago-born transplant to Denver, Colorado, where she began a career as a freelance journalist. Singleton published

the book *This Side of the Sky* under her middle name, Elyse, and wrote the novel in her Denver apartment, where she told *Blackflix.com* contributor Tara Casanova she lives like a recluse. Casanova noted that "the only lifestyle differences between Singleton and the Unabomber, who hibernated in a remote Montana shack [is that] Singleton says the bomber mailed more packages, but she had better furniture." On her book's Web site, Singleton says she has enjoyed solitude since she was a child. "I read a lot, wrote spy stories, sewed original fashions for my Barbie dolls, and consumed the standard American-kid dosage of four hours of television daily."

As a student, Singleton envisioned being a psychotherapist, volunteered at local women's counseling centers, and took part in a summer internship program in Denver that treated substance abusers and psychotics. She monitored the behavior of rhesus monkeys at the university's research lab and "watched them run around in circles, not knowing they were giving me a metaphorical demonstration of what my life as an adult would be like. . . . Sadly, I never became a clinician. But I hope to eventually continue my study of psychology. I'd hate to think I tortured all those monkeys for nothing."

Singleton's life took a different turn, however, and as a journalist, she was able to feed her passion for travel and the freedom to pursue another career—as a novelist. In reviewing her debut for *Rawsistaz Review* online, Tee C. Royal commented that Singleton "has written a story that isn't easily labeled because it is so much more than simply a historical fiction novel." Singleton drew from the experiences of relatives who had grown up in the segregated South and books of history and videos about World War II. Her settings include a German submarine, the Dresden firestorm, a meat-packing plant, and a sugar cane field.

The story traces the friendship of two black women from 1917 until 2000. Lilian Mayfield and Myraleen Chadham are children in Nadir, Mississippi, their families so poor that the Great Depression has no effect on their lives. They have been friends since they shared the same babysitter as infants. Shy, dark-skinned Lilian is the daughter of a woman who shucks oysters and performs abortions on the side. Myraleen, who is light enough to pass for white, is forced by her mother to marry at thirteen and is banished to a sugar cane field when she rebels. When the young women graduate from high school, they become domestics, and Lilian develops a friendship with Kellner Strauss, an Oxford-educated psychiatrist and the son of a Nazi, who was captured by U.S. forces when the U-boat on which he was serving as a medic was destroyed. Now a detainee, he works nearby as a laborer on a work farm. Their attraction results in just a kiss before the two women flee to Philadelphia where they join the Women's Army Corp and begin an adventure that takes them to Glasgow, Scotland, London, England, and Paris, France.

After the war, Lilian moves to Paris and Myraleen stays in Philadelphia. Their loves and lives play out but are never overshadowed by their friendship, which remains the most powerful element of the story.

Christine Wald-Hopkins reviewed the novel for the *Denver Post Online,* saying that it "doesn't read like a first novel. Singleton . . . knows audience, voice, and how to build a tight, multilayered text. She's produced buff, funny, smart, well-paced writing, with broad appeal. Themes of hate, race, independence, the nature of relationship and 'enemy' appear but don't outmuscle the narrative. Singleton set out to write a book that would be 'both literary and enjoyable.' She's succeeded."

Booklist contributor Elsa Gaztambide wrote that Singleton takes her characters into "a spiraling mix of love, heartbreak, and humor with a novel that is a compassionate and compelling work of fiction written from the heart."

When asked what she has learned as a writer, Singleton told *CA:* "I have learned that there is no greater form of secular, practical redemption. Writing allows you to use every part of your thoughts, experience, and self as material for your craft. Novel writing, particularly, is existential ecology. It is not that every discouraging or hurtful moment I experienced was worth it— definitely not. But at least, possibly, nothing will have been in vain."

BIOGRAPHICAL AND CRITICAL SOURCES:

PERIODICALS

Black Issues Book Review, November-December, 2002, Katia A. Nelson, review of *This Side of the Sky,* p. 30.

Booklist, September 15, 2002, Elsa Gaztambide, review of *This Side of the Sky,* p. 209.
Library Journal, September 15, 2002, David A. Berona, review of *This Side of the Sky,* p. 94.
Publishers Weekly, September 30, 2002, review of *This Side of the Sky,* p. 48.
Washington Post, October 29, 2002, Jabari Asim, review of *This Side of the Sky.*

ONLINE

Blackflix.com, http://www.blackflix.com/ (August 26, 2003), Tara Casanova, "A Lyrical Novelist: Elyse Singleton" (interview).
Denver Post Online, http://www.denverpost.com/ (October 27, 2002), Christine Wald-Hopkins, review of *This Side of the Sky.*
Rawsistaz Review Online, http://www.therawreviewers. com/ (October 14, 2002), Tee C. Royal, review of *This Side of the Sky.*
Rocky Mountain News Online, http://www. rockymountainnews.com/ (September 21, 2002), Patti Thorn, review of *This Side of the Sky.*
Star-Telegram Online (Dallas-Fort Worth, TX), http:// www.dfw.com/mld/startelegram/ (December 1, 2002), Claude Crowley, review of *This Side of the Sky.*
This Side of the Sky Web site, http://www.thisside ofthesky.com (August 26, 2003).

*   *   *

SINGLETON, Elyse
   See SINGLETON, Janet Elyse

*   *   *

SIVERLING, Mike

PERSONAL: Male.

ADDRESSES: Home—Sacramento, CA. *Agent*—c/o Author Mail, St. Martin's Press, 175 Fifth Ave., New York, NY 10010.

CAREER: Author and public servant. Member of child abduction and kidnapped child recovery team, Office of the District Attorney, Sacramento County, CA.

AWARDS, HONORS: Best First Private-Eye Mystery Contest winner, St. Martin's Press/Private Eye Writers of America, 2002, for *The Sterling Inheritance.*

WRITINGS:

The Sterling Inheritance, Thomas Dunne Books (New York, NY), 2004.

SIDELIGHTS: Mike Siverling's debut novel, *The Sterling Inheritance,* introduces the unlikely mother-son private investigator duo of Jason and Victoria Wilder. The confident and self-assured Victoria, a former police detective, runs the Midnight Detective Agency, where she keeps a busy slate of investigations going while providing work for her retiree buddies from the police force. Jason, a hopeful rock guitarist, works for his mom part time. Though he would rather be playing onstage somewhere, he is quite good at gumshoe work—and is, in some ways, carrying on the family tradition, since his father was also a police officer. The affectionately intrusive Victoria and the reluctant but brilliant Jason enjoy a genuinely loving, if sometimes high-strung, relationship.

When an unidentified man is found brutally murdered outside an old movie theater, police suspect the theater's co-owner, Anthony Sterling, of the deed. Sterling, however, is missing, and his beautiful Russian wife Katerina engages the Midnight Agency to find him. Jason finds him easily enough, even disarms him when he pulls a gun, but ends up in custody when the police arrive. Victoria's contacts on the force help clear up the problem. The nervous Sterling insisted he engaged in gunplay because someone was out to kill him—justifiable paranoia, it seems, as he is later found murdered. Jason takes on the investigation.

At first, Jason eyes a number of Sterling's Russian business associates as possible suspects, but other members of the Sterling clan think the murderer lies elsewhere. Anthony's father, Malcolm, insists that his rebellious daughter, Janice—Anthony's sister—is the culprit. As his investigation progresses, Jason finds himself more and more attracted to Janice and her daughter Angelique. He also becomes more and more willing to believe her version of events and her interpretation of the way things work in the Sterling family empire. That is, until Victoria steps in to keep the investigation—and her wayward son—on track.

Library Journal reviewer Rex E. Klett remarked that Siverling "uses the standard PI setup, dialog, and characterization with alacrity and panache" in the novel. "The tart narrative . . . has an appealing retro feel and clever solution," noted a *Kirkus Reviews* critic. Harriet Klausner, in a review *The Sterling Inheritance* for *AllReaders.com,* commented that "readers will enjoy this urban Noir with a host of delightful characters." A *Publishers Weekly* reviewer detected overtones of Raymond Chandler in the novel, but observed that Siverling "adds enough clever modern touches, especially in the relationship between Victoria and Jason, to make this look like the start of a promising series."

BIOGRAPHICAL AND CRITICAL SOURCES:

PERIODICALS

Kirkus Reviews, May 1, 2004, review of *The Sterling Inheritance,* p. 425.
Library Journal, June 1, 2004, Rex E. Klett, review of *The Sterling Inheritance,* p. 106.
Publishers Weekly, May 17, 2004, review of *The Sterling Inheritance,* p. 36.

ONLINE

AllReaders.com, http://www.allreaders.com/ (November 18, 2004), Harriet Klausner, review of *The Sterling Inheritance.**

* * *

SLATTERY, Dennis Patrick 1944-

PERSONAL: Born 1944. *Education:* Attended Cuyahoga Community College, 1963-65, and Cleveland State University, 1965-67; Kent State University, B.A., 1968, M.A. (comparative literature), 1972; University of Dallas, M.A. (literature and phenomenology), M.A., 1976, Ph.D.

ADDRESSES: Home—7849 Langlo Ranch Rd., Goleta, CA 93117. *Office*—Pacifica Graduate Institute, 249 Lambert Rd., Carpinteria, CA 93013. *E-mail*—dslattery@pacifica.edu.

CAREER: Palmyra Elementary School, Ravenna, OH, instructor in special education, 1968-70; Lorain Catholic High School, Lorain, OH, instructor in English and psychology, 1970-72; Mountain View College, Dallas, TX, instructor of English and composition, 1976-80; University of Dallas, Irving, TX, assistant professor of English, 1978-79; Texas Christian University, Fort Worth, instructor of freshman composition, 1980-81; Southern Methodist University, Dallas, TX, instructor of rhetoric, 1981-87; Incarnate Word College, director of summer study abroad program in Italy, 1989-95, chairman of department of English and chairman of curriculum committee, 1989-91; Pacifica Graduate Institute, Carpinteria, CA, mythological studies and depth psychology program, visiting lecturer, 1993-95, member of core faculty, 1995—, interdisciplinary coordinator, master's in counseling psychology program, 1995-98. Instructor of English, University of Dallas in Rome, 1976-78; faculty member, Summer Institute in Literature, Dallas, 1984-86; graduate faculty member, Fairhope Institute of Humanities and Culture, Fairhope, AL, 1992, 1993; graduate faculty member, University of Mobile, 1995; visiting lecturer and seminar leader, Dallas Institute Summer Classics Programs for Teachers, 1999—. Initiator, Dennis P. and Sandra L. Slattery Writing Achievement Award, Villa Angela/St. Joseph High School, Cleveland, OH. Member of advisory board, *Salt Journal*, 1999—, and *Spring: A Journal of Archetype and Culture*, 2000—.

MEMBER: International Dostoevsky Society, International Society for the Comparative Study of Civilizations, North American Dostoevsky Society, Association of Russian-American Scholars in the U.S.A., National Council of Teachers of English, American Literature Association, Conference of College Teachers of English, Association of Cultural Mythologists, Academy of American Poets, South Central Modern Language Association.

AWARDS, HONORS: National Education grant to Kent State University, 1966-68; Andrew Mellon grant, 1982; National Endowment for the Humanities summer grant to Harvard University, 1991; Homer Institute summer grant program, University of Arizona, 1994.

WRITINGS:

The Idiot: Dostoevsky's Fantastic Prince, a Phenomenonological Approach, Peter Lang (New York, NY), 1984.

The Wounded Body: Remembering the Markings of Flesh, State University of New York Press (Albany, NY), 2000.

(Co-editor with Lionel Corbett) *Depth Psychology: Meditations in the Field,* Daimon-Verlag (Einsiedeln, Switzerland), 2001.

Casting the Shadows: Selected Poetry, Winchester Canyon Press, 2002.

Psychology at the Threshold, Pacifica Graduate Institute Press (Carpinteria, CA), 2002.

Grace in the Desert: Awakening to the Gifts of Monastic Life, Jossey-Bass (San Francisco, CA), 2004.

Just below the Water Line: Selected Poems, Winchester Canyon Press (Goleta, CA), 2004.

Contributor of numerous articles to professional journals, including *Renascence, South Central Bulletin, Missouri Philological Journal, International Dostoevsky Society Bulletin, South Central Review, Dostoevsky Studies, Legal Studies Forum, New Orleans Review, Flannery O'Connor Bulletin,* and *Palo Alto Review.* Also contributor to newspapers and magazines, including *Zion's Herald, Newsweek, Dallas Morning News, San Antonio Express News, Santa Barbara News Press, Santa Barbara Independent,* and *Los Angeles Times.*

WORK IN PROGRESS: Simon's Crossing, a novel co-written with Charles Asher.

SIDELIGHTS: Poet, psychologist, and critic Dennis Patrick Slattery has written on subjects ranging from classic nineteenth-century Russian literature to cultural events from a poetic and mythic perspective. In his position at Pacifica Graduate Institute, Slattery teaches courses not only in mythological studies, but also in depth psychology and clinical psychology, as well as courses in the master's-in-counseling program.

In *The Wounded Body: Remembering the Markings of Flesh* Slattery investigates the ways in which literary figures ranging from Captain Ahab in *Moby Dick* to Odysseus in the *Odyssey* experience psychological injury as bodily injury, or wounds. By doing so, the characters communicate their internal problems through concrete external symbols. "Typically," declared Armando R. Favazza in the *American Journal of Psychiatry,* "we believe that the mind-brain gives meaning to the body, but the relationship is reciprocal.

In fact, the body must endure the insults of twisted thoughts, chaotic emotions, and demonic spirituality when the mind-brain sputters and goes awry." In the process, said Favazza, "the body may invoke an entire cosmology; it is cosmic in its symbolic nature." Even the great Romantic thinker Jean-Jacques Rousseau, Favazza stated, expressed his mental illness using the language and imagery of wounds.

That form of analysis—mixing literary criticism, religious symbolism, and an understanding of the relationship between mind and body—typifies Slattery's approach to criticism. The themes recur in his *Grace in the Desert: Awakening to the Gifts of Monastic Life.* On one level, *Grace in the Desert* is an account of the author's personal spiritual journey through a dozen different religious institutions (most of them Catholic) over the course of three months. Slattery made the journey in order to come to terms with the recent death of his alcoholic father and his own troubled relations with his wife and children. The book also tells how the author confronts questions about his own identity, his role as a teacher, and his understanding of his faith. "Slattery describes the flavor of each retreat center," explained a *Publishers Weekly* reviewer, "but spends the bulk of each chapter recounting the spiritual musings prompted by each place he visited." In the process, according to *Booklist* contributor June Sawyers, he transformed a personal, spiritual journey into an understanding of how different spiritual traditions affect the growth of the mind. "Each was different," Sawyers said, "and each bestowed its own individual lessons and rewards." "And through the wounds of Christ," she concluded, "he found . . . a new way of seeing and understanding the suffering of others." "Many will be moved," declared Graham Christian in his review of the book for *Library Journal*, by Slattery's story of his own journey and the effects it had on his life.

Slattery told *CA:* "Years ago as an undergraduate I was very shy about speaking up in class. I was one of those students content to let the more extroverted folks carry the discussion. So when I wrote papers, I would pour out all the ideas I did not have the courage to address orally. Writing was my most conspicuous and rewarding form of communicating ideas.

"The most surprising thing I have learned about writing is that it is a form of meditation, of contemplation. When I do not know something, I begin to write about it; then mind, body, heart, soul connect in the physical act of writing. When I read books, I write out my notes and ideas long hand, then later transcribe to print via the computer. But handwriting slows all the processes down and let things steep like a good stew or soup; the aromas are marvelous.

"In terms of which book of mine is my favorite, you might as well ask a parent which is his favorite child. Each book I have written bubbled up at a particular time in my own development, so the book I just finished is always my favorite—until the next one comes along, seeking birth.

"I hope that what I write makes the readers aware that they are individual and unique, paradoxically, to the extent that they see their own sufferings, wounds, joys and satisfactions are indeed shared by all others. If what I write makes that tension felt, then the effort was worth the doing."

BIOGRAPHICAL AND CRITICAL SOURCES:

PERIODICALS

American Journal of Psychiatry, September, 2000, Armando R. Favazza, review of *The Wounded Body: Remembering the Markings of Flesh,* p. 1536.

Booklist, April 15, 2004, June Sawyers, review of *Grace in the Desert: Awakening to the Gifts of Monastic Life,* p. 1407.

Library Journal, May 1, 2004, Graham Christian, review of *Grace in the Desert,* p. 118.

Publishers Weekly, March 8, 2004, review of *Grace in the Desert,* p. 71.

ONLINE

Dennis Patrick Slattery's Author Page, http://www.mythicartist.org/artists/profiles/dennisslattery.html (November 19, 2004).

*   *   *

SLOTTEN, Ross A. 1954-

PERSONAL: Born May 30, 1954, in Chicago, IL; son of Richard (a grocer) and Lillian (a homemaker) Slotten; partner of Kevin Murphy (a physician), since 1983. *Education:* Stanford University, B.A. (classics) and B.S. (biology), 1976; Northwestern University, M.D., 1981; University of Illinois, Chicago, M.P.H., 1994.

ADDRESSES: Office—Klein, Slotten & French Medical Associates, 711 West North Ave., Suite 209, Chicago, IL 60610. *E-mail*—RSlotten@aol.com.

CAREER: Physician in private practice, Chicago, IL, 1984—; Northwestern University School of Medicine, Evanston, IL, member of faculty; St. Joseph Hospital, Chicago, associate attending physician, beginning 1984, cofounder of Acquired Immune Deficiency Syndrome (AIDS) unit, adviser for Human Immune Deficiency Virus (HIV) and aging study, and member of ad hoc AIDS task force. Served on the boards of organizations, including Bonaventure House (homeless shelter for AIDS patients); Horizon Hospice, Chicago, adviser.

MEMBER: International AIDS Society, American Medical Association, American Academy of Family Physicians.

WRITINGS:

The Heretic in Darwin's Court: The Life of Alfred Russel Wallace (biography), Columbia University Press (New York, NY), 2004.

SIDELIGHTS: Ross A. Slotten is a Chicago, Illinois, physician who specializes in the treatment and study of Human Immune Deficiency Virus (HIV). Slotten has been involved in the clinical trials of many HIV medications and served on the Acquired Immune Deficiency Syndrome (AIDS) task force at Chicago's St. Joseph Hospital, where he cofounded the AIDS unit. For nine years he served on the board of directors of Bonaventure House, a refuge for homeless AIDS patients. Within Slotten's family medicine practice, he has taken responsibility for more than one thousand patients with HIV.

Slotten has written a biography of the British naturalist whose work threatened to scoop nineteenth-century English naturalist Charles Darwin's own, and which prompted Darwin to publish his now-classic *On the Origin of the Species.* In *The Heretic in Darwin's Court: The Life of Alfred Russel Wallace,* Slotten notes that the little-known Wallace (1823-1913) was a self-educated scientist, born of the working class, who in 1858 sent Darwin a manuscript outlining his own concept of natural selection and its importance in the creation of new species. Darwin, who had been working on his theory for more than twenty years, had yet to publish on the topic. Oren Solomon Harman noted in *American Scientist* that "through a 'gentlemanly arrangement' brokered by Darwin's powerful scientific friends Charles Lyell and Joseph Hooker, Wallace's offering to Darwin was presented at, and published by, the Linnean Society in July 1858, along with an abstract of an unpublished paper Darwin had written in 1844 and an abstract of an 1857 letter from Darwin to Asa Gray, an American botanist. By presenting this material chronologically, Lyell and Hooker implied that Wallace was merely supporting Darwin's earlier discoveries, and Darwin's priority was secured." Although the two men shared ideas for decades, it was Darwin who received credit for their mutual theories on evolution.

Wallace later changed his thinking, contending that the origins of morality and man's intellectual nature are based in spirituality, but his theories were given no weight in comparison with those of Darwin, whose upper-class background gave him more validity in scientific circles. Wallace's new beliefs also led him to participate in seances and contact with the dead through mediums, all of which greatly embarrassed Darwin and other scientific naturalists. But Wallace was a great contributor to many disciplines. By his return in 1862 from an eight-year tropical expedition, he had collected 125,660 specimens of mammals, reptiles, birds, shells, butterflies and moths, and beetles and other insects.

Slotten provides a broad analysis of Wallace's life, noting the naturalist's passion for social justice and land reform and his opposition to the smallpox vaccine. A *Publishers Weekly* contributor felt that "Slotten's enjoyable exposition provides insight into the scientific process and the role of class structure in Victorian England."

Harman wrote that Slotten "has an amateur's enthusiasm for his subject, which lends his account a kind of intimacy." Slotten told *Library Journal* contributor Andrew Richard Albanese that he discovered Wallace's work while preparing for a trip to Indonesia. A guidebook recommended Wallace's *Malay Archipelago* as a travel-literature classic. Upon returning to the United States, Slotten began his own research of the man who had lived in Darwin's shadow.

Harman concluded by saying that Slotten has given Wallace "his most complete and colorful viewing, as a leading evolutionary theorist, social philosopher, hopeless dreamer, anthropologist and spiritualist, friend, explorer, and tireless seeker of justice and of truth. This is a good, old-fashioned, beautifully written biography, devoid of pretension and with both a wonderful eye for detail and an impressive command of history and fact. Those unfamiliar with Wallace's life will greatly enjoy Slotten's fine book. When all is said and done, there's no substitute for a well-told story."

BIOGRAPHICAL AND CRITICAL SOURCES:

PERIODICALS

American Scientist, September-October, 2004, Oren Solomon Harman, review of *The Heretic in Darwin's Court: The Life of Alfred Russel Wallace,* p. 470.
Booklist, July, 2004, Bryce Christensen, review of *The Heretic in Darwin's Court,* p. 1807.
Library Journal, June 15, 2004, Gloria Maxwell, review of *The Heretic in Darwin's Court,* p. 94; June 15, 2004, Andrew Richard Albanese, interview with Slotten.
Natural History, September, 2004, Menno Schilthuizen, review of *The Heretic in Darwin's Court,* p. 58.
New Scientist, July 31, 2004, Douglas Palmer, review of *The Heretic in Darwin's Court,* p. 53.
Publishers Weekly, April 26, 2004, review of *The Heretic in Darwin's Court,* p. 48.

*   *   *

SOLOMITA, Stephen
(David Cray)

PERSONAL: Male.

ADDRESSES: Office—c/o Author Mail, Carroll and Graf Publishers, 161 William St., 16th Fl., New York, NY 10038.

CAREER: Writer. Drove a taxi cab in New York, NY.

WRITINGS:

MYSTERY NOVELS

A Twist of the Knife, Putnam (New York, NY), 1988.
Force of Nature, Putnam (New York, NY), 1989.
Forced Entry, Putnam (New York, NY), 1990.
Bad to the Bone, Putnam (New York, NY), 1991.
A Piece of the Action, Putnam (New York, NY), 1992.
A Good Day to Die, Otto Penzler Books (New York, NY), 1993.
Last Chance for Glory, Otto Penzler Books (New York, NY), 1994.
Damaged Goods, Scribner (New York, NY), 1996.
Trick Me Twice, Bantam (New York, NY), 1998.
No Control, Bantam (New York, NY), 1999.

UNDER PSEUDONYM DAVID CRAY; MYSTERY NOVELS

Keeplock, Simon and Schuster/Otto Penzler Books (New York, NY), 1995.
Bad Lawyer, Carroll and Graf/Otto Penzler Books (New York, NY), 2001.
Little Girl Blue, Carroll and Graf/Otto Penzler Books (New York, NY), 2002.
What You Wish For, Carroll and Graf/Otto Penzler Books (New York, NY), 2002.

Work represented in anthologies, including *Crimes of Passion* and *Criminal Records.*

SIDELIGHTS: Stephen Solomita, who also publishes under the pen name David Cray, usually sets his mystery novels in New York City, portraying the steamier side of urban life in an unflinching fashion. The author's best work has a "gritty sensibility,"according to a *Publishers Weekly* contributor in a review of *Damaged Goods.* Several of the novels written under Solomita's own name have as their central character Stanley Moodrow, originally a New York police detective and later a private investigator. In his work as Cray, he has created another recurring protagonist, Julia Brennan, introduced as a New York police officer in *Little Girl Blue* and promoted to the district attorney's sex crimes unit in *What You Wish For.*

Moodrow made his debut in *A Twist of the Knife,* in which he is on the trail of terrorist bombers. His interest becomes personal after his fiancé dies in one of their blasts, set in front of a Macy's department store. Moodrow is portrayed as a man of integrity who does things his own way, and his pursuit of the terrorists takes him through "several twists" and culminates in "a terrific confrontation," commented Charles Champlin in the *Los Angeles Book Review.* Champlin praised Solomita's detailed depictions of New York City life, as did Marilyn Stasio of the *New York Times Book Review,* who said the descriptions have "a certain raw truth."

The second "Moodrow" book, *Force of Nature,* pairs him with a new, inexperienced partner, former prizefighter Jim Tilley. Their assignment is to catch a crack addict who is on a killing spree. *Washington Post Book World* contributor Daniel Woodrell thought the plot sometimes "cartoonish" and the characters ill-defined, but allowed that the book has "an occasional fine moment, a good aside or snap of dialogue." Stasio, while advising readers not to "expect any subtleties," had positive things to say about the development of Moodrow's character and about Solomita's portraits of poor city neighborhoods, which "certainly seems authentic."

Forced Entry finds Moodrow retired but unable to leave crime-solving behind. The new woman in his life, a legal aid lawyer named Betty Haluka, asks him to look into the changing character of the occupants of a rent-controlled apartment building, where prostitutes and drug dealers are moving in among the elderly. The moves turn out to be part of a plot by the building's owners to chase away the longtime tenants and turn it into a cooperative. Solomita tells this story in a fashion that is "pure prole poetry," remarked Amy Pagnozzi in the *New York Times Book Review,* adding that his "writing is so natural, you don't know you're reading." Pagnozzi thought he moves the action a bit slowly, but added that the novel "is still a worthwhile trip." She praised Solomita's depiction of "things gritty and garish," and observed, "At his best, he has Elmore Leonard's flair for letting you view the world through his character's eyes." A *Publishers Weekly* critic, meanwhile, called *Forced Entry* "a straightforward and realistic slice of city life."

In *Bad to the Bone,* Moodrow, working as a private investigator, is on the case of a cult leader who has partnered with a drug dealer to create a highly addictive new drug. Solomita "balances the familiar . . . with the unexpected" in this tale, related a *Publishers*

Weekly reviewer. As usual, Solomita "gives you the best ride in town," commented Stasio in the *New York Times Book Review,* praising the setting's local color, the dialogue's naturalism, and the plot's "exciting moments."

A Piece of the Action is set in 1957 and portrays Moodrow as a young man who has just graduated from beat cop to detective. Trying to solve a murder, he uncovers police corruption involving his mentor, who also happens to be the father of the woman Moodrow loves. Dick Adler, writing in Chicago *Tribune Books,* found Solomita spins a "compelling story" with interesting characters and an excellent depiction of the era. A *Publishers Weekly* reviewer also had good words for the book's setting and storytelling, summing it up as "hard-boiled police fiction at its best."

After featuring other protagonists in *A Good Day to Die* and *Last Chance for Glory,* Solomita returns to Moodrow—and to a present-day setting—in *Damaged Goods.* In this novel, aging private eye Moodrow and a young partner, Guinevere "Ginny" Gadd, go after murderous Mafioso Jilly Sappone, who resumes his criminal ways after being released from prison. The *New York Times Book Review*'s Stasio thought the story "overburdened with cute devices," although "the pace is energetic." A *Publishers Weekly* critic was glad to see Moodrow back, deeming Solomita's work without the character "weaker." The critic praised *Damaged Goods* for its fast movement and "piercing urban melancholy."

The first of the non-Moodrow books, *A Good Day to Die* has as its main character another maverick New York police detective, Roland Means. Fellow officer Vanessa Bouton dislikes Means but nevertheless enlists his help in solving a string of murders of male prostitutes. In the *New York Times Book Review,* Stasio commented that Solomita seems more removed from his characters and settings than in the "Moodrow" stories, and that "Means is more talk than action." A *Publishers Weekly* reviewer also found the book "relentlessly talky" and "predictable" as well. *Last Chance for Glory* features another veteran cop, Bela Kosinski, now retired but helping technology-savvy private eye Marty Blake with his first case, joining a lawyer in efforts to free a man wrongly convicted of murder. In the view of a *Publishers Weekly* contributor, this book is "more successful" than *A Good Day to Die,* "but not by much." To Champlin, however, again critiquing for the *Los Angeles Times Book Review, Last Chance for Glory* is "good and notably readable," with "engrossing" character portraits and a "heart-chilling" story.

Solomita's first book as David Cray, *Keeplock,* deals with a recently paroled career criminal, Peter Frangello, who is trying to lead a law-abiding life in the face of pressure from crooked friends and dishonest cops. "Cray . . . gives plenty of insider dope on the crime world and creates, in Frangello, an unexpectedly sympathetic unheroic hero," remarked a *Publishers Weekly* critic. Similarly, *New York Times Book Review* contributor Stasio called the characterization of Frangello "the big score" of "this gripping crime novel," and Chicago *Tribune Books* reviewer Adler observed that the narrative has a "burning honesty" that "makes us wish for [Frangello's] success." George Needham, writing in *Booklist,* gave *Keeplock* the status of highly recommended and found its ending reminiscent of "the classic finale of the 1930s movie *I Am a Fugitive from a Chain Gang.*" A *Kirkus Reviews* commentator compared the book to another film (and novel), dubbing it "grimly exciting as *The Asphalt Jungle.*"

Bad Laywer, the next Cray effort, features another protagonist seeking redemption: lawyer Sid Kaplan, who is trying to rebuild a once-brilliant career ruined by drugs and alcohol. In his comeback case, Kaplan represents a woman who admits she killed her husband but says she did so in self-defense. Both were involved with drugs, but the husband, the wife says, was abusive; Kaplan also thinks he can play to racial bigotry, as the wife is white and the late husband black. But Kaplan soon finds that the case is more complicated than he thought. The novel shows Cray to be "a master manipulator," reported Stasio in the *New York Times Book Review,* while a *Kirkus Revews* critic deemed it "a refreshingly unsentimental reply to all those fairy tales about lawyers whose ideals rise miraculously from the ashes." A *Publishers Weekly* reviewer added that the story is "clever, gritty, sordid and surprising."

Little Girl Blue features Julia Brennan, a New York homicide detective and single mother, investigating a young girl's murder. Brennan eventually finds herself going after a child prostitution and pornography ring whose members are threatening her teenage daughter. A *Publishers Weekly* reviewer described the novel as "riveting," adding, "If a writer can produce a readable book about this odious subject, Cray has done it." Along the same lines, Stasio wrote that *Little Girl Blue* is "a credible business report on a vile cottage industry." Connie Fletcher, critiquing for *Booklist,* called the author "deft with procedure" and "a cunning plotter." *What You Wish For* finds Brennan working for the distric attorney's sex crimes unit and looking into the murder of a rich widow who has disinherited the children of her husband's previous marriage. Brennan's love interest, Peter Foley, introduced in *Little Girl Blue* as an investigator for the sex crimes unit, is on a case of his own, trying to free his daughter from the hands of a child pornography outfit that has kidnapped her. A *Kirkus Reviews* contributor thought the novel "has more a police procedural flavor—and, sadly, less flavor altogether" than its predecessor. A *Publishers Weekly* critic, however, deemed *What You Wish For* a "well-oiled crime novel" that "doesn't disappoint." Meanwhile, Mary Frances Wilken, writing in *Booklist,* characterized the book as "thoroughly engaging."

BIOGRAPHICAL AND CRITICAL SOURCES:

PERIODICALS

Booklist, January 15, 1995, George Needham, review of *Keeplock,* p. 898; November 1, 2001, Connie Fletcher, review of *Little Girl Blue,* p. 461; December 15, 2002, Mary Frances Wilkens, review of *What You Wish For,* p. 737.

Kirkus Reviews, February 1, 1995, review of *Keeplock,* pp. 86-87; December 1, 2000, review of *Bad Lawyer,* p. 1631; October 1, 2002, review of *What You Wish For,* p. 1428.

Los Angeles Times Book Review, October 9, 1988, Charles Champlin, "Bloody Sunday," p. 12; August 14, 1994, Charles Champlin, "Criminal Pursuits," p. 7.

New York Times Book Review, December 11, 1988, Marilyn Stasio, review of *A Twist of the Knife,* p. 34; October 8, 1989, Stasio, review of *Force of Nature,* p. 20; October 14, 1990, Amy Pagnozzi, "Too Obnoxious to Live," p. 47; June 16, 1991, Marilyn Stasio, review of *Bad to the Bone,* p. 21; October 24, 1993, Marilyn Stasio, review of *A Good Day to Die,* p. 28; March 19, 1995, Marilyn Stasio, review of *Damaged Goods,* p. 23; April 15, 2001, Marilyn Stasio, review of *Bad Lawyer,* p. 20; January 2, 2002, Marilyn Stasio, review of *Little Girl Blue,* p. 19.

Publishers Weekly, August 30, 1990, review of *Forced Entry,* p. 63; March 15, 1991, review of *Bad to the Bone,* p. 48; June 1, 1992, review of *A Piece of the Action,* p. 51; September 27, 1993, review of *A Good Day to Die,* p. 48; July 4, 1994, review of *Last Chance for Glory,* p. 54; January 30, 1995, review of *Keeplock,* p. 88; November 20, 1995, review of *Damaged Goods,* p. 68; June 15, 1998, review of *Trick Me Twice,* p. 57; December 4, 2000, review of *Bad Lawyer,* p. 56; October 29, 2001, review of *Little Girl Blue,* p. 38; October 14, 2002, review of *What You Wish For,* p. 63.

Tribune Books (Chicago, IL), July 5, 1992, Dick Adler, "Crime Thrives on the Bayou, at Cambridge and in Cairo," p. 6; March 5, 1995, Adler, "The Case of the Torn Lawyer," p. 7.

Washington Post Book World, December 17, 1989, Daniel Woodrell, "Rounding up the Usual Suspects," p. 9.*

*   *   *

SOTERIOU, Alexandra

PERSONAL: Female. *Hobbies and other interests:* Papermaking.

ADDRESSES: Home—NJ. *Agent*—Mapin Publishing, c/o Grantha Corporation, 31 Somnath Rd., Usmanpura, Ahmedabad 380 013, India.

CAREER: Anthropologist, researcher, exhibit curator, lecturer, and writer. World Paper, Inc., Bergenfield, NJ, founder. Former consultant to U.S. Aid for International Development and United Nations Industrial Development Organization.

AWARDS, HONORS: Indo-American Fellowship Award.

WRITINGS:

Gift of the Conquerors: Hand Paper-making in India, Grantha Corporation (Middletown, NJ), 1997.

SIDELIGHTS: Anthropologist Alexandra Soteriou has had a continuing interest in the art of papermaking in India since 1985. Researching this subject intensely by traveling throughout India and meeting with the artisans who still practiced hand papermaking, she decided she would do what she could to keep the craft from fading into obscurity. Practicing the art of papermaking herself, she also founded World Paper, Inc., which works to promote the craft, and she published an illustrated book on the subject, *Gift of the Conquerors: Hand Paper-making in India,* in 1997.

Gift of the Conquerors is used to help others learn papermaking, while offering an extensive history of the process and discussing its cultural links with the political and religious tides of India. The book also includes passages on the lives of papermakers, a map that illustrates where the country's important papermaking regions are, recipes and methods of papermaking, a variety of paintings and drawings, and a thorough bibliography. Papermaking in India, where it was introduced by Muslims centuries ago, had fallen out of practice at the time the author was visiting that country. But with the help of Soteriou's and other's efforts, it experienced a revival. At the beginning of the twenty-first century, India was one of the leading countries continuing the art.

BIOGRAPHICAL AND CRITICAL SOURCES:

PERIODICALS

India in New York, July 30, 1999, p. 14.
Library Journal, June 15, 1999, p. 76.*

*   *   *

SPANGLER, Catherine

PERSONAL: Born in Oak Ridge, TN; married James A. Spangler, Sr. (an antiques dealer); children: James A., Jr., Deborah Marie. *Education:* Attended University of Alabama, 1973. *Hobbies and other interests:* Reading, spiritual studies.

ADDRESSES: Agent—Roberta M. Brown, Brown Literary Agency, 410 Seventh N.W., Naples, FL 34120. *E-mail*—romance@catherinespangler.com.

CAREER: Romance novelist.

MEMBER: Romance Writers of America, North Texas Romance Writers of America, Dallas Area Romance Authors.

AWARDS, HONORS: Laurel Wreath, Volusa County Romance Writers, and Aspen Gold Award, Heart of Denver Romance Writers, both 2000, both for *Shielder.*

WRITINGS:

SCIENCE FICTION ROMANCE NOVELS

Shielder, Dorchester Publishing (New York, NY), 1999.
Shadower, Dorchester Publishing (New York, NY), 2000.
Shamara, Dorchester Publishing (New York, NY), 2001.
Shadow Crossing, Dorchester Publishing (New York, NY), 2003.
Shadow Fires, Dorchester Publishing (New York, NY), 2004.

WORK IN PROGRESS: Romance comedies; paranormal fiction.

SIDELIGHTS: Catherine Spangler told *CA:* "I think my love of books inspired me to write. My parents read to me from a very early age, then when I could read on my own, I devoured books. I've been writing ever since I was a young girl.

"I think my preference to write science-fiction romances came from living in Huntsville, Alabama, where a lot of the space program was developed through the National Aeronautics and Space Administration on Redstone Arsenal. My father worked for some years on the space program, and it was very important to me.

"My writing process is very erratic. I write in spurts and might go months without writing at all. I'm also what I call an 'unconscious writer,' depending very heavily on my subconscious to work out story details. I'm not strong on external methods of plotting or character charts. I also find that having a contracted deadline forces me to finish books that might otherwise take forever.

"I have published five futuristic/science fiction romance novels. Now I'd like to try my hand at something different. I believe I will always write romance, but I'm working on some romantic comedies, and some paranormal series involving immortals and aliens."

BIOGRAPHICAL AND CRITICAL SOURCES:

PERIODICALS

Booklist, January 1, 2004, Nina C. Davis, review of *Shadow Fires,* p. 838.

*   *   *

SPINRAD, Norman (Richard) 1940-

PERSONAL: Born September 15, 1940, in New York, NY; son of Morris and Ray (Greenhut) Spinrad. *Education:* City College of the City University of New York, B.S., 1961. *Politics:* "Independent Conservative Radical."

ADDRESSES: Agent—Russel Galen, Scoville Chichak Galen, 381 Park Aveue South, New York, NY 10016.

CAREER: Writer, 1963—. Worked as a sandalmaker, welfare investigator, and radio talk show host; Scott Meredith Literary Agency, New York, NY, literary agent, 1965-66. Performed as guest singer on albums inspired by his works with group Heldon.

MEMBER: Writers Guild of America, Science Fiction Writers of America (vice president, 1972-74; president, 1980-81, 2001; western regional director).

AWARDS, HONORS: Hugo Award nominations, World Science Fiction Society, 1968, for teleplay "The Doomsday Machine," 1970, for *Bug Jack Barron,* and 1975, for "Riding the Torch"; Nebula Award nominations, Science Fiction Writers of America, 1969, for "The Big Flash" and *Bug Jack Barron,* 1972, for *The Iron Dream,* and 1984, for *The Void Captain's Tale;* Association of American Publishers, National Book Award nomination, 1973, for *The Iron Dream,* and American Book Award nomination, 1980, for *The Star*

Norman Spinrad

Spangled Future; Prix Apollo, 1974, for *The Iron Dream;* Jupiter Award for best science fiction novella, 1975, for "Riding the Torch"; Career Achievement Award, Utopia Congress, 2003.

WRITINGS:

SCIENCE FICTION NOVELS

The Solarians, Paperback Library (New York, NY), 1966.
Agent of Chaos, Belmont Books (New York, NY), 1967, introduction by Barry Malzberg, F. Watts (New York, NY), 1988, e-book edition, Pulpless. com (Mill Valley, CA), 1999.
The Men in the Jungle, Doubleday (New York, NY), 1967.
Bug Jack Barron, Walker Co. (New York, NY), 1969.
The Iron Dream, Avon (New York, NY), 1972, published with a new introduction by Theodore Sturgeon, Gregg Press (Boston, MA), 1977.
Riding the Torch (short novel), bound with *Destiny Times Three,* by Fritz Leiber, Dell (New York, NY), 1978, published separately, Bluejay (New York, NY), 1984.

A World Between, Pocket Books (New York, NY), 1979.
Songs from the Stars, Simon Schuster (New York, NY), 1980.
The Void Captain's Tale, Timescape Books (New York, NY), 1983, reprinted, Orb (New York, NY), 2001.
Child of Fortune, Bantam (New York, NY), 1986.
Little Heroes, Bantam (New York, NY), 1987.
Russian Spring, Bantam (New York, NY), 1991.
Deus (short novel; also see below), Bantam (New York, NY), 1993.
Vampire Junkies (short novel), Gryphon (Brooklyn, NY), 1994.
Pictures at Eleven, Bantam (New York, NY), 1994.
Journals of the Plague Years (short novel), Bantam (New York, NY), 1995.
Greenhouse Summer, Tor (New York, NY), 1999.
He Walked among Us, Heyne Verlag (Germany), 2002, e-book version, eReads.com, 2003.

SHORT STORY COLLECTIONS

The Last Hurrah of the Golden Horde (short stories), Doubleday (New York, NY), 1970.
No Direction Home: An Anthology of Science-Fiction Stories (includes *"The Big Flash"*), Pocket Books (New York, NY), 1975.
The Star Spangled Future (short stories), Ace (New York, NY), 1979.
Other Americas (four novellas), Bantam (New York, NY), 1988.

SCREEN WRITING

"The Doomsday Machine" (teleplay; episode of *Star Trek* series), National Broadcasting Co. (NBC-TV)/Paramount, 1967.
"Tag Team" (teleplay; episode of *Land of the Lost*), NBC-TV, 1974.
(With others) *Vercingètorix* (screenplay; also see below; released as *Druids* in Canada), [France], 2001.
(With others) *La sirène rouge* (screenplay; released as *The Red Siren*), [France] 2002.

NONFICTION

Fragments of America (commentary), Now Library Press, 1970.

(Editor, author of introduction, and contributor) *The New Tomorrows,* Belmont Books (New York, NY), 1971.

(Editor, author of introduction, and contributor) *Modern Science Fiction,* Anchor Press, 1974.

Staying Alive: A Writer's Guide, Donning (Norfolk, VA), 1983.

Science Fiction in the Real World, Southern Illinois University Press (Carbondale, IL), 1990.

OTHER

Passing through the Flame: The Last Hollywood Novel, Berkley (New York, NY), 1975.

The Mind Game, Bantam (New York, NY), 1985.

The Children of Hamlin, Tafford, 1991.

Deus X and Other Stories, Fivestar (Waterville, ME), 2003.

The Druid King (loosely based on the screenplay for *Vercingètorix*), Knopf (New York, NY), 2003.

Mexica, Little, Brown (UK), 2005.

Author of weekly column on politics for Los Angeles *Free Press,* 1970-71; author of monthly column on writing and publishing for *Locus,* 1979-85. Author of review column for *Asimov's Science Fiction Magazine.* Contributor to numerous science fiction anthologies and books about science fiction, including *SF: The Other Side of Realism,* edited by Thomas D. Clareson, Bowling Green University Popular Press, 1971; *Threads of Time: Three Original Novellas of Science Fiction,* edited by Robert Silverberg, Thomas Nelson, 1974; *Experiment Perilous: Three Essays on Science Fiction,* edited by Andrew Porter, Algol Press, 1976; and *The Craft of Science Fiction,* edited by Reginald Bretnor, Harper, 1976. Contributor of political and social essays to *Knight* magazine, of film criticism to Los Angeles *Free Press, Cinema,* and *Staff,* and of fiction to *Playboy, New Worlds, Analog Science Fiction/ Science Fact,* and other periodicals. Author of lyrics and performer, with others, of songs for Heldon album *Only Chaos Is Real,* 2000.

Spinrad's books have been translated into several languages, including French, Italian, and German.

ADAPTATIONS: The film rights to *Bug Jack Barron* were purchased by Universal.

SIDELIGHTS: As a member of the science fiction new wave of the 1960s and more recently as president of the Science Fiction Writers of America, Norman Spinrad has campaigned for a new acceptance of the genre and its writers. He once suggested in a *CA* interview that the emergence of science fiction in pulp magazines and its subsequent categorization as popular culture has proven a barrier to its consideration as serious literature. Critics and innovators have emerged to broaden the scope of the genre, but as Spinrad explained to Robert Dahlin in a *Publishers Weekly* interview, categorization persists because it serves the interests of publishers. "These categories are a publisher's trip," he said. "What I'd like to do, but can't in this country, is just have my books published as books."

Added to the struggle for acceptance, Spinrad noted in his contribution to *SF: The Other Side of Realism,* the science fiction writer faces creative challenges. The science fiction novelist "must not only create characters, theme, forces of destiny and plot but (unlike the mainstream novelist) must create from scratch a universe entire in which character, plot and destiny interact with each other and with the postulated environment." This, in turn, presents technical obstacles, he points out. "While one is in the process of creating in detail the sf context, the characters and plot hang in limbo; while one is advancing plot and characterization, one's grip on one's created universe tends to loosen." Yet, as the author indicated in *Modern Science Fiction,* science fiction is "the only fiction that deals with modern reality in the only way that it can be comprehended—as the interface between a rapidly evolving and fissioning environment and the resultant continuously mutating human consciousness."

"Science fiction, for me, is relating the total external environment to the inner psyche, something I find missing in many contemporary books," he told Dahlin. "The media, technology, politics—all these are part of us, and what I care about is the way people are changed by external means." Spinrad's first three novels, *The Solarians, Agent of Chaos,* and *The Men in the Jungle,* as well as his short fiction of this period, show a progression away from traditional science-fiction forms and concerns toward the external/internal approach and an awareness of contemporary issues. According to *Dictionary of Literary Biography* contributor Ina Rae Hark, a recurring theme in much of this early fiction is one in which "a home world that seems a source of security and power must by willingly or unwillingly sacrificed in order to liberate human potential, thus enabling men to rise from its ashes and conquer the stars."

With his fourth novel, *Bug Jack Barron,* Spinrad separated himself from pulp science fiction forever. The host of a popular weekly phone-in television show set in the near future, Jack Barron has made his reputation by placing viewers, who call in their complaints on videophones, face to face with their alleged offender for a nationally televised debate of the issue. One phoned-in tip puts the television muckraker on the trail of a millionaire scheming to control cryogenic operations and research into immortality. In order to expose the hideous side of the millionaire's obsession, Barron must first free himself from the seduction of the immortality offered him as a bribe. In this book, Spinrad scrutinizes the powerful, noted a *Times Literary Supplement* contributor, especially those outside politics; he "writes about two of the most potentially dangerous elites: the super-television inquisitors and the men with the scientific power to control and extend human life for ever." Locating the book along the science-fiction spectrum, Hark wrote in her *Dictionary of Literary Biography* article that "besides its lack of traditional pulp accessories, *Bug Jack Barron* leans toward the New Wave by including elements traditionally foreign to the science-fiction genre: an experimental, stream-of-consciousness style . . . abundant obscenity, and explicitly detailed sexual encounters." In the larger framework of contemporary fiction, "*Bug Jack Barron* remains a novel of considerable strengths and considerable flaws," commented Hark. "Most of its faults stem from the 'wicked mad businessman' plot, most of the strengths from the sociological observations for whose expression the plot provides a framework." The *Times Literary Supplement* contributor concluded, "Spinrad writes with verve and has a lively ear for current idiom. His 'political science fiction' has a deadly plausibility."

Spinrad's *The Iron Dream,* an alternate history, presents itself as the second edition of the book, *Lord of the Swastika,* complete with an informative introduction and a scholarly afterword. This fictitious science-fiction classic from the 1950s was written by the illustrator and Hugo award-winning science-fiction writer Adolf Hitler, who immigrated to the United States from Germany in 1919. "Spinrad's craft is sure and imaginative," observed Albert I. Berger in the *Sci-*

ence Fiction and Fantasy Book Review. "He makes astonishingly good and thoroughly logical and consistent use of an old science fiction device, the parallel time-track, to examine the individual and mass psychology of fascism." Hark commented, "*Lord of the Swastika* is a very badly written sword-and-sorcery opus, full of nauseating battles and grotesque and obsessive phallic and scatological imagery," She continued, "The book mythopoeticizes Hitler's actual rise to power, with the military victory he would have desired substituting for the actual course of World War II." Hall added that *The Iron Dream* "is, despite being a rather unpleasant reading experience, far and away Spinrad's best novel because its format emphasizes his virtues as an ironist and social moralist and minimizes—even uses to advantage—his weaknesses as a stylist and plot constructor."

H. Bruce Franklin, in his review for the *Washington Post Book World,* proclaimed that, "at the very least, *The Iron Dream* must be admired as a remarkable tour de force, a dazzling display of ingenuity and originality. . . . But it is much more than that, for it forces us to confront elements of fascism within our own culture, low and high." As Berger noted, "The forword . . . nicely ties Spinrad's examination of Nazism to contemporary popular culture." Franklin agreed, writing that "we recognize the similarities between [the protagonist's] brutal omnipotent maleness and the diseased fantasies of both fascism and the latest sword-and-sorcery epics." As Berger noted, "the afterword similarly skewers the easy academic acceptance of fundamentally barbaric principles if they can be made to fit preconceived notions or anti-communist cant," and concluded: "as a thoughtful, incisive satire on the roots of fascism and an example of the thoroughgoing fashion in which Spinrad maintains the internal logic of his parallel time-track to serve his ends, *The Iron Dream* belongs in any serious science fiction collection."

Two of Spinrad's novels from the 1980s, *The Void Captain's Tale* and *Child of Fortune*—both set in a far-future universe filled with exotic and distant worlds made closer by an erotic form of space travel—received considerable attention. "Spinrad's ingenious space-drive," explained Theodore Sturgeon in the *Los Angeles Times Book Review,* "has the ship's machine create a field . . . which at peak and at captain's command melds with the pilot's psyche, causing the ship to cease to exist in one spatial locus and reappear in another." The captain of the first book tells the story of his forbidden relationship with his ship's Void Pilot, the woman whose special training facilitates the hyperspace jumps—jumps during which she experiences transcendent orgasm, unity with the cosmos. Drawn by her desire to remain in this higher state, the Void Pilot proposes to her captain that he commit her to the hyperspace jump forever. To do so, however, he must sacrifice himself, his crew, and passengers. As Sturgeon pointed out, the captain comes to a "slow realization, and ultimate conviction, that there may be a value in the release of a single human being into a higher consciousness far greater than the worth of any number of . . . people." The reviewer, himself a well-known science-fiction writer, wrote that "what makes this book important . . . is its demand that our most deeply conditioned ethics be examined as freely—as meticulously and courageously—as anything else." In *The Void Captain's Tale,* wrote Howard Waldrop in the *Washington Post Book World,* "Spinrad has written a . . . book, dark and somber in tone, subject matter and method." Waldrop continued, "he has come up with an idea, a style and a narrative that perfectly fits his talent." The book generated some controversy because of its eroticism and some criticism of Spinrad's future language. Yet, as Gerald Jonas concluded in the *New York Times Book Review,* "Spinrad, like his characters, takes great risks; the rewards for readers willing to meet him halfway are commensurate."

Child of Fortune is the story of a flower child of the future who sets out on a journey of self-discovery that takes her to many of the exotic worlds of Spinrad's future universe; one is a garden of pleasures from which no one has ever returned. "How the heroine regains her freedom—and discovers her true calling—by wielding the peculiarly human weapon of speech—is the core of the story," observed Jonas in another *New York Times Book Review* article. Though he faulted Spinrad's future language, Toronto *Globe and Mail* contributor H. J. Kirchhoff found this novel "complex, colorful, zesty and bawdy. The characters are drawn in such depth that it is hard not to empathize with them, and the settings are flamboyant, even sensational." Gary K. Wolfe in *Fantasy Review* wrote, "Despite echoes of Cordwainer Smith—as well as Henry Miller, Baudelaire, and perhaps even Octave Mirbeau—*Child of Fortune* is a highly original work and one of considerable merit. . . . I hope the book achieves the audience it deserves."

In the 1990s Spinrad continued to publish novels at an undiminished rate. *Russian Spring,* set in the twenty-first century, relates the story of two generations of a family over a thirty-year period. The book opens on a world in which the United States has remained a military power but has incurred a heavy national debt while becoming increasingly isolationist and hostile in its foreign policy. Would-be astronaut Jerry Reed must travel to Common Europe, the only place where space exploration is being planned, in an attempt to fulfill his ambitions. In Paris he meets and falls in love with Soviet career bureaucrat Sonya Gagarin.

Once the couple are married, Spinrad's narrative leaps twenty years into the future. While Jerry's plans for a career in space have been foiled by a pervasive anti-Americanism, Sonya's career has steadily progressed. The couple now have two children, daughter Franja, who has inherited her father's space wanderlust, and son Bob, who is enamored by a vision of America as it once existed in the twentieth century. After Franja enrolls in a Russian space academy and Bob takes off to discover the current state of the United States, the story takes another ten-year jump into the future.

Commenting on the resolution of the novel, a *Publishers Weekly* reviewer observed: "A series of odd, occasionally tragic events brings the family (and the world) together. . . . Spinrad gives us a wild, exhilarating ride into the next century."

In *The Children of Hamlin,* also published in 1991, Spinrad presents a loosely autobiographical novel set in the 1960s counterculture of New York City. The action revolves around Tom Hollander, ex-junkie and a reader for a literary agency. Tom's best friends, a couple named Ted and Doris, are obsessed with therapy and consciousness expansion. He is torn between two lovers, the free-spirited drug-dealer Robin, and Arlene, a woman who is as obsessed with therapy as are Tom's friends. A *Publishers Weekly* reviewer noted: "If this . . . novel . . . had been published . . . during the era that it reflects, it would have achieved cult status by now." The reviewer added: "The stumbling block here is the determined use of slang; overindulgence in such words as 'bummers' and 'groovies' quickly becomes tiresome."

Spinrad's *Pictures at Eleven* presents a thriller revolving around ecoterrorism. Radical environmental activists seize a television station in Los Angeles and negotiate with their hostages about program changes, including a show for terrorists. Spinrad puts a Hollywood agent in charge of the team of outside negotiators who are trying to gain the hostages' freedom. D. A. Ball, writing in *Entertainment Weekly,* found the idea for the book to be "brilliant . . . unbelievably interesting," but also felt that Spinrad's execution fails to realize the promise in that idea. "Spinrad writes with an outsider's notion of police procedure, the news media, and hostage behavior," Ball stated. In direct contrast, Dennis Winters of *Booklist* found the novelist's plot "tired and hackneyed," but concluded: "Along the way, Spinrad gets beyond the cliched faces of his characters and even beyond the conventionally unconventional faces behind them. The characters turn into real people, able to carry the action where it's going. Spinrad has shown his mastery of this genre as well as his preferred haunts along its edges yet again."

Pictures at Eleven did not do as well in sales as Spinrad's publisher, Bantam, hoped, and they consequently dropped what was to have been Spinrad's next book from their publishing schedule. After a battle to win the rights back, Spinrad took the novel, *He Walked among Us* to a German publisher, but only after making news for an offer he put on his Web site: he proclaimed he would sell the U.S. rights to publish the book for only one dollar. "The offer is his way of saying that the publishing industry, dominated as it is by conglomorates, is doing bad business by putting the bottom-line value of books above their literary value," explained Brad Spurgeon in his article for the *International Herald Tribune.*

Spinrad received letters from many authors who felt their novels had been treated unfairly by their publishers, and he began to feel as though he had become their spokesperson. The book was eventually released in the U.S. as an e-book from eReads.com, and is also available as a print-on-demand title from the publisher.

Spinrad, who had written for television shows such as *Star Trek* and *Land of the Lost,* began working in the movie industry with his work on the screenplay for the French movie *Vercingètorix,* a tale of the Gaul rebellion against the Roman Empire. The movie did poorly at the box office, and Spinrad was unhappy with the final version of the script. Over the next few years he reworked the tale, this time in novel form. The result is *The Druid King,* a novel of ancient Rome and the heroic leader who united the Gauls in a nearly successful bid to keep their own nation. In the novel,

Vercingetorix is only a boy when his father is murdered for trying to unite all of Gaul. Raised in secret by druids and taught weaponry by an Amazon warrior, Vercingetorix is determined to avenge his father's death. When he returns home, he attracts the attention of Julius Caesar, who becomes his teacher—until Vercingetorix realizes Caesar's Rome was responsible for the plot to murder his father. He turns against Rome and begins to unite the people of Gaul to make a final stand against the empire. "Spinrad knows his way round Caesar's histories and rightly positions them as brilliant spin doctoring," complimented Roz Kaveney, writing for London's *Independent,* though the reviewer also found that the novel lacked a passion that would have given the story more depth. A reviewer for *Publishers Weekly* found the novel to be "sweeping but unremarkable," acknowledging that "it's a solid, intelligent effort." A contributor for *Kirkus Reviews,* however, found it "intriguing to see the anti-Roman side of things," and Margaret Flanagan in *Booklist* proclaimed that "Spinrad breathes new life into a mythical figure."

AUTOBIOGRAPHICAL ESSAY: Norman Spinrad contributed the following autobiographical essay to *CA:*

Although it presents certain technical difficulties, maybe you shouldn't write an autobiography until you are dead.

The story of a life, even if your own, published for the benefit of readers, becomes, well, a *story.* And true or not a good story requires, if not necessarily a traditional beginning, middle, and end, then at least certainly *some* sort of structure leading to a sense of satisfying resolution at the end of the reading experience.

But since I'm fifty-three years old as I write this, not exactly on the brink of retirement, I can hardly be expected to bring *this* story to a successful thematic closure in any of the usual manners.

Then too, while "write what you know about" may be the hoariest of literary maxims and autobiography seemingly the ideal exemplar thereof, upon a moment's uncomfortable reflection, maybe not.

Sure, you know the sequence of events better than you know anything else, but it's no easy task to negotiate the treacherous literary waters between the Scylla of the extended brag and the Charybdis of a deadly dull recitation of the complete bibliography and nothing more.

So what I've opted for here is a rather experimental form, itself perhaps a bit of autobiographical characterization, since fairly early on in my career I came to the realization that form should be chosen by the requirements of content. And *this* particular content certainly seems to call for something rather schizoid—a montage of split points of view, *persons* that is, in more than the usual technical sense.

So this autobiography is divided into three clearly labeled tracks.

"Continuity" is, as Sergeant Friday would have it, just the facts, Ma'am, written in third person as if "Norman Spinrad" were someone other than the author thereof.

"Flashbacks" are little novelistic bits and pieces designed to illumine some of the events of "Continuity" with some more intimate visions of what the character in question was thinking and feeling at the time.

"Frame" is what you are reading now—the author and the subject, the novelist and the literary critic, speaking to you and maybe myself as directly as I can manage under the circumstances, and trying to extract some overall meaning from it all.

CONTINUITY

Norman Spinrad was born in New York City, on September 15, 1940, the son of Morris and Ray Spinrad. Except for a brief period in Kingston, New York, he spent his entire childhood and adolescence residing with his parents and his sister Helene in various locations in the Bronx, where he attended Public School 87, Junior High Schools 113 and 22, and the Bronx High School of Science.

In 1957, he entered the College of the City of New York, from which he graduated in 1961 with a bachelor of science degree as a pre-law major.

FLASHBACK

I was a subway commuter as a college student, living in the family apartment in the Bronx, hanging out in Greenwich Village on the weekends.

My father, eldest son of a family of five, had never finished high school, having left to earn family bread, and only after serving as a medical corpsman in the navy during World War II did he realize that medicine would have been his calling, and by then it was much too late. Like many such children of the Great Depression, he wanted nothing more or less for *his* son than a secure professional career, ideally the one he wished *he* had been able to have.

So I was always under pressure, not just to perform academically, but to follow a path toward the bankable sciences. I passed the stiff entrance test for the Bronx High School of Science, graduated in 1957 at the age of sixteen, and, at the behest of my father, seeing as how medicine obviously actively turned me off, entered City College as an engineering major.

This lasted about a term and a half, terminated by my confrontation with the horrors of preelectronic-calculator calculus. Okay, said my dad, what about chemistry? You don't need so much math for that. So I became a chemistry major long enough to convince me that I had no genius for the subject and less interest in it as a life's work.

Okay, said my dad, with less enthusiasm, what about, uh, psychology? He seemed to view the vector from medicine to hard engineering through stinky liquids into the murk of the social sciences as a kind of intellectual slippery slope.

What did *I* want to do with my life at this point?

Hey, come on, I was about nineteen years old! Although it's common enough for one's parents and guidance counselors to demand that one get serious and make a commitment, it's both cruel and naive to suppose that a nineteen-year-old kid is intellectually or emotionally equipped to decide what he's going to do with the rest of his life. What did I want at this point?

I didn't really want to be in college at all. I didn't want to be living *en famille* in the Bronx until I graduated. What I wanted was *la vie boheme* in the Village.

FRAME

What is included here and what is left out: Unless you've lived an extraordinarily dull and uneventful life under a bell jar with your typewriter, and I haven't, you will have broken hearts, had your own broken, and engaged in any number of acts sexual and otherwise that were politically incorrect at the time or, in hindsight, illegal, or even the sort of thing your older and wiser self may now find immoral.

Then too, my life has intersected, in various degrees of intimacy, the lives of many people of more than passing literary interests—Philip K. Dick, Timothy Leary, Theodore Sturgeon, Harlan Ellison, J. G. Ballard, William Burroughs, Frank Herbert, Michael Moorcock, to name a random sample of a long, long list.

Some of these luminaries were or are real friends, others acquaintances of one degree or another. I've written about many of them extensively in various places already, and so you must take my word for it that it's length limitations rather than ego that limits mention of them in this compass to the effect they may have had on *my* life or career.

I have been commissioned to write a short literary autobiography, and as I interpret that commission, this is supposed to be the story of Norman Spinrad the writer, not a juicy exposé of my private life, nor of the private lives of people who may have been involved with it.

However. . . .

However, there are times when such matters *do* impinge on what gets written, and I *am* trying to tell the true story to the best of my ability, so when they do, I guess I'm going to have to try to bite the bullet. . . .

FLASHBACK

The Village, circa 1959, pre-Beatles, the Beat Era. Coffee houses. Craft shops. Folk music. I remember seeing a fat-faced kid from Minnesota performing for free at a Monday amateur night at Gerde's Folk City. Name of Bob Dylan. A hot act was the Holy Modal Rounders, a bluegrass group which later metamorphosed into the Fugs. One of its members was Peter Stampfel, who is now a science-fiction editor at Daw Books. Another was Ed Sanders, who was to cover the Manson family trial in Los Angeles for the *Free Press* while I was writing for the same paper.

But in 1959 I never knew Sanders, and Stampfel, whom I did party with upon occasion, would not remember the me of that era. They were culture heroes, and I was just another day-tripping college kid.

Another culture hero of sorts in this space-time was Bruce Britton, proprietor of the Britton Leather Shop. Bruce was a famous sandalmaker. Bruce Britton was a charismatic party animal, and the Britton Leather Shop was a major party scene. When work was done (and sometimes when it wasn't), it became an open house, and also a place where you found out where the *other* parties were.

The Britton Leather Shop became my central weekend hangout, and Bruce became my friend, an older role model of sorts, and later one of the earliest patrons of my writing career.

But I didn't aspire to a writing career at that point. Truth be told, and my father not, I didn't aspire to a career at all. From his point of view, what I aspired to was quite appalling, namely, to spend all my time the way I spent my weekends—as, well, a beatnik in Greenwich Village.

FRAME

Beatniks, even teenage wannabee beatniks living with their parents in the Bronx, did drugs. Mostly pot, which was readily available, but I was introduced to consciousness-altering chemicals with rather stronger stuff, namely peyote, which I experienced before I so much as puffed on a joint.

Ah yes, we've all committed our youthful indiscretions. Why, even President Clinton has copped to tasting the Devil's Weed, though since he didn't inhale, he didn't enjoy it. I, however, did inhale, and therefore did get off. Often. And to my creative advantage. Nor do I regret it.

Norman, about two years old

If there's one gaping void in the story of American literary history in the second half of the twentieth century as currently promulgated, it's the influence of grass and psychedelic drugs, not only on the lives of writers, but on the content of what's been written, and on the form and style too. It's hard to be critically or biographically courageous when so much creative work was done under the influences of jailable offenses.

In the Beat Era, however, the literary culture heroes of bohemia—William Burroughs, Jack Kerouac, Allen Ginsberg, and company—were not only entirely up front about it, but openly advocated the chemical enhancement of consciousness as a literary, spiritual, and cultural *virtue*. And wrote much stylistically mighty work under the influence to prove it.

Even a mainstream literary lion like Norman Mailer wrote a famous essay called "The White Negro" extolling the "Hip" world of sex, dope, and transcendence over the "Square" workaday world of the Lonely Crowd, though elsewhere he was to correctly opine that writing *final draft* stoned was maybe not such a terrific idea.

I raise this issue now because I would be lying shamelessly if I denied that I was a devotee of this tradition or renounced herein my belief that on the whole a bit of grass and a more significant trip now and again is beneficial to the creative juices. Nor could the story of the sort of writer I became make much sense in the absence of its consideration.

Most writers of science fiction, at least prior to the New Wave of the 1960s, emerged as writers from a formative adolescence immersed in the hermetic subculture of "science fiction fandom," reading science fiction obsessively, attending science fiction conventions, as well as writing letters and articles in science fiction fanzines. SF fans even have an acronym for it, FIAWOL—Fandom Is A Way Of Life.

Not my teenage planet, Monkey Boy. I didn't even know that this subculture existed until after I had published about a dozen stories and a novel. Yes, I read a lot of sf—Sturgeon, Bester, Dick, Bradbury being early obsessions—but I was just as deeply into Mailer, Kerouac, William Burroughs, and their precursor, Henry Miller.

And *theirs* was the subculture I wanted to grow up to live in before I even had any serious thoughts about a writing career; the hip world of free love, pot, psychedelics, literary and personal transcendence—all that which, with the addition and via the medium of rock and roll, was to call into being the Counterculture half a decade later.

FLASHBACK

This was something I could hardly admit to my parents, the guidance counselor, or even quite to myself at the time. And at least being a psych major was something I found far more congenial than my previous provisional career choices.

However, two unpleasant academic satoris were to convince me that this was not to be my planet either.

I was fortunate enough to be assigned to a section in motivational psychology taught by Dr. Kenneth B. Clark, who, among other things, had written part of the brief in *Brown versus Board of Education*. There were no tests. You discussed texts that had been assigned for consideration in class and you wrote three papers, and Clark marked you on that.

At the beginning of the term you were handed a list of the books and papers that would be discussed. In addition to the expected scientific treatises, there was a

About four years of age during World War II

five-foot shelf of novels, plays, and assorted literary works. How could anyone be expected to read through all that in a term? They couldn't. Clark believed that any college upper classman who hadn't already read most of this stuff didn't belong in a class on this level in the first place.

I loved this class. It was worth the price of admission. Clark was brilliant and witty and brought out the best in his students. The class was educational, but it was also a kind of high intellectual entertainment.

All during the term Clark complained of the conventionality of the papers students were turning in. Can't you give me something *original?*

I admired Clark greatly and for my final paper I determined to write something that would pay him back intellectually and knock him out of his socks in the bargain.

I had read my way through all Kerouac, Ginsberg and on into Herman Hesse, Alan Watts, and D. T. Suzuki, a common intellectual vector in my Village extracurricular circles, and so I knew quite a bit about Buddhism.

So I wrote a paper comparing Buddhism and Freudian theory as systems of psychology.

This is brilliant, fascinating, Dr. Clark told me after he had read it. I glowed.

"But I can only give you an A-."

"Huh? Why?"

He shrugged. "Because I don't know enough about Buddhism to judge whether you really know what you're talking about," he admitted.

And had not been willing to make the intellectual effort to acquire the necessary background.

Another required course that I had to do a term paper for was abnormal psychology. I suggested to the professor that I do it on the mental states induced by consumption of peyote. He seemed quite interested.

"But as far as I know, there's not much source material in the literature," he added dubiously.

"Don't need it," I assured him. "Not only do I have plenty of primary experimental subjects to interview, I have firsthand experience myself."

Did he gape at me as if I was some kind of crazed dope fiend?

Nope.

That wasn't what made him refuse to consider the subject appropriate for a term paper in his course. If I could have rehashed secondary sources and studded the paper with appropriate footnotes, no problem. But original research in the form of direct reportage of the mental states in question was not academically acceptable.

CONTINUITY

In his senior year at CCNY, he took two courses in short story writing and made his first submissions to magazines. Having secured entry to Fordham University law school, he spent the summer of 1961 traveling in Mexico with friends.

FLASHBACK

By my senior year, all I really wanted was out—out of college, out of my parents' apartment, out from under their pressures and influences, out of the square world and into the hip.

But I still had it in my head that I had to get a degree to please my parents. By this time, I had changed my major so many times that the only way to graduate was to lump together what I had already taken with a few more random courses, call it a "pre-law major," and bullshit it past the guidance counselors by being admitted to law school.

One course I took in short story writing was formative. It was taught by a writer named Irwin Stark who had sold fiction to magazines and had not lost the habit of submitting. Stark, like Clark, bitched about the conventionality of what the students were writing, and I took another shot at taking a teacher at his word.

I wrote a story called "Not with a Bang," in which a couple finds true love screwing in a bathtub full of chocolate syrup during a nuclear apocalypse, good enough to eventually sell to a low-grade men's magazine about a decade later.

The look that Stark gave me when he handed back that week's assignment was choice.

"I can't have you read a thing like that in class," he told me in his office later.

Uh-oh.

"Why don't you submit it to *Playboy?*"

"Playboy. . . . "

"Yeah, it's a long shot, but they're the top market, and if you start at the top and work down, you can take the first offer you get for a story and know it's the best you can do."

And he told me how to submit stories to magazines: stick them in an envelope with a cover letter and a self-addressed, stamped return envelope, and drop 'em in a mailbox. If you get a check, cash it before it bounces. If you get a rejection, submit it to the next best market.

I submitted "Not with a Bang" to *Playboy.* They didn't buy it, so I sent it elsewhere. And elsewhere. And wrote some more stories. And started submitting *them.*

And that's how I became a writer. Not yet a published writer, that was about three years in the future, but by the time I graduated from CCNY, I knew what I wanted to do with my life, and how one went about doing it. You write 'em, you drop 'em in the mail, you wait.

Best advice I ever had. Best advice any would-be writer can ever get. It's ultimately all you need to know. The Big Secret is that there is no Big Secret. It drives me crazy how many wannabee writers just won't believe it.

CONTINUITY

Upon returning to New York, he decided not to attend law school but to pursue a writing career instead. He rented a cheap apartment in the East Village, secured part-time employment in a friend's leather shop, wrote a first novel which has never been published and about a dozen short stories, finally making his first sale to *Analog* in 1962. The story, "The Last of the Romany," was published in 1963.

FLASHBACK

Actually, the thought of entering law school in the fall of 1961 was filling me with nauseous dread before I even graduated. By this time I knew I wanted to be a writer, but what I lacked was any notion of how to support myself while doing it, plus the courage to make such a beatnik move sure to outrage my parents. The road trip to Mexico in a rotten old car (*never* buy a car from a relative!) with two college friends, Marty Mach and Bob Denberg, was part temporary escape from this dilemma, part personal vision quest, part hopeful emulation of Huck Finn and Kerouac.

When we finally managed to coax the wretched clunker back to New York after an exhaustive education in automotive Spanish, the Greenwich Village outdoor Arts and Craft Show was in full swing. One weekend afternoon, I took over the Britton Leather Shop's table as relief for an hour and moved two hundred dollars worth of goods, about what they had done all week.

Bingo! I had a part-time job. Bruce Britton, and later his partner and successor at the leather shop, Ken Martin, supported my writing ambition and more or less let me make my own hours. And my own wage, since what they were paying me was a commission on sales.

I found a foul little apartment in the East Village that I could rent for $36 a month, meaning, what with food and utilities, I could survive on about $120 a month, and in a good week I could make $40 at the leather-shop working twenty hours.

I could survive, more or less, as a would-be writer.

FRAME

My naivete was total. I knew no other writers, I hadn't published a thing, and my brilliant notion was that I would support myself writing short stories while work-ing on my first novel. I wrote an unpublishable novel, which, years later, I was to some extent cannibalize in the writing of *Bug Jack Barron*. I wrote stories and sent them off to magazines, mostly science-fiction magazines.

When I finished the novel, I knew nothing better to do with it than pay my thirty-five dollars to have it "evaluated for the market" by the Scott Meredith Literary Agency, who advertised this service in various magazines. They rejected it, as they did 99 percent of such fee submissions, as I was soon to learn in another incarnation, but the "agent" who wrote the rejection letter over Scott Meredith's signature met me in secret, praised my talent, and wised me up to the SMLA fee-reading scam, strongly suggesting that I not waste my money on it again.

Nor had I sold anything. And the final turn of the screw was that *Analog* had been sitting on "The Last of the Romany" for an unconscionable six months.

What I didn't know was that the reason for the delay was that John W. Campbell, Jr., the legendary editor thereof, had discovered the lion's share of the major science-fiction writers of the last quarter century or so by the tedious and time-consuming process of reading his entire slush pile himself.

Needless to say, when his acceptance letter arrived in the mail, all was forgiven.

CONTINUITY

He sold several more short stories during the next year or so, on the strength of which he secured a professional agent, the Scott Meredith Literary Agency.

FRAME

I had been dead broke before I sold a novelette to Campbell for the princely sum of $450, so broke that I had taken a job as a welfare investigator in Bedford-Stuyvesant for a month to keep me going.

When I made my third magazine sale, I wrote a letter to Scott Meredith, the only agent I knew, and was accepted as a client on a professional basis.

Meanwhile, an ulcer I had developed under the pressure of adolescent angst, and no doubt exacerbated by eating all that cheap hot stuff in Mexico, landed me in a hospital for an operation. The operation was successful, but the patient should have died. They screwed up bad and infected me with something called toxic hepatitis, supposedly universally fatal. I ran a fever of about 106 degrees for days. I lost about twenty-five pounds. I survived. Still running a fever and looking like death warmed over but not by much, I took a cab directly to the draft board and got myself reclassified 4-F so it wouldn't be a total loss.

FLASHBACK

A prolonged ultra-high fever, aside from usually being fatal, makes a 1,000-mile acid trip seem like a warm glass of 3.2 beer. I was not only hallucinating, I had . . . Powers.

Laboring under the hallucinatory delusion that I was being tortured for secret rocket fuel information by spies, I had the hysterical strength to snap the bandages tying me to my deathbed, yank out the IV's, and hold off a squad of interns while I used another Power on the bedside telephone.

It was the wee hours of the morning. The hospital staff must've thought I was raving into a dead phone; understandable, considering what they were hearing on my end.

Somehow I had fixated on the name of what turned out to be a real air force general. I got an outside line. I got a long distance operator. I made a collect long distance call to said general at the Pentagon. He had long since gone home to bed. I did . . . a thing. I ordered the Pentagon switchboard to patch me through to his home phone, validating it with a blather of letters and numbers that was my top secret command override code. They did it. A bleary general's voice came on the line.

I started babbling about spies, rocket fuels, send a rescue squad to—

"Huh—? What the—?"

At which point, the interns jumped me from behind and hung up the phone on the sucker.

By the next morning, my fever had broken.

And the hospital had some tall explaining to do when the Pentagon traced the call back.

FRAME

Qué pasa? I've contemplated that question ever since, my best take being the story "Carcinoma Angeles," a literary breakthrough for me that I wrote about three years later, and which, long after that, seems to have been picked up by a doctor in Texas as a treatment for cancer.

As on an acid trip, only more so, I think the fever warped me into a metaphorical reality in which the disease ravaging my body was transmogrified into a paranoid image system overlaid on actual real-world events. By giving *that* story the ending I wanted, by actually waking up the general, I somehow was able to triumph over the infection for which the whole thing was metaphor.

Unless you've got a better explanation.

The facts are that I survived a fatal disease, that this experience, whatever it was, later was the impetus for the story that was the real take-off point for the writer that I was to become, and I don't think I was the same person afterward.

CONTINUITY

SMLA made no sales for him during the six months, and he was economically constrained to seek full-time employment.

He answered an ad in the *New York Times* offering an entry-level position as an editor. When he took the test for the job at the employment agency, he realized that the prospective employer was his own literary agent, Scott Meredith. Armed with this knowledge, he did very well on the test and was tentatively offered the position by the employment agency.

FLASHBACK

As a client, I had never even met Scott Meredith. When I showed up in the office as a job applicant, he was nonplussed. Many writers who later became clients had worked for him, but Scott had never hired one of his own writers through the employment agency cattle call and didn't want to do it.

"What do you mean, you won't hire me?" I demanded. "The only reason I need this damn job in the first place is because you haven't sold a thing for me in six months!"

Having never confronted this argument either, Scott relented. Voila, the twenty-four-year-old kid whose own stuff wasn't selling had a job anonymously representing a list of something like a hundred established writers, some of them, like Philip K. Dick, Philip Jose Farmer, Frank Herbert, John Brunner, and Jack Vance, among others, literary idols of mine at the time, and people who were later to become my friends.

FRAME

The pro desk at SMLA was an excruciating experience. Scott Meredith was a genius at squeezing work out of his peons by force of paranoid pressure, and after a full day's work writing letters under his name to authors, sometimes typing them over and over again until he was satisfied, you had to read manuscripts on your own time at home. It was like being back in *school.* It was nearly impossible to get anything of my own written. And there I was, agenting stories and novels anonymously for the very writers whose illustrious company I longed to join myself!

On the other hand, it was a crash course in the realities of publishing from the inside out, and the bottom up. By the time I was twenty-five, I had more publishing street smarts than venerable greats twice my age,

The author signing autographs in the Ambiance Bookstore in Paris, about 1989

and before I was thirty found myself playing the strange role of career advisor, father-figure even, to my own literary idols, like Theodore Sturgeon and Philip K. Dick.

CONTINUITY.

While working at SMLA in various capacities from 1964 to 1966, he continued to write stories, some of which sold, and completed *The Solarians,* his first published novel, which appeared in 1966.

FRAME

I have always been a lousy typist, and, in the end, I simply couldn't keep up with the workload on an SMLA pro desk. Scott fired me. He then rehired me for a part-time job supervising the fee-reading operation, where piece-work editors wrote letters of criticism on submissions from amateurs for a fee.

Somewhat morally ambiguous maybe, but I had time and energy to write my own stuff again. Stories sold, including one to *Playboy:* "Deathwatch." I wrote a space opera, *The Solarians,* which SMLA sold to Paperback Library for $1,250.

After I left the Meredith agency for good, I never held another job and, for better or worse, sometimes much worse, have survived on my writing ever since.

And though I seriously suspect that years later Scott Meredith was responsible for the non-publication of *The Children of Hamelin,* I doubt whether I would be saying that now, if it wasn't for the education I got in his rough school of hard publishing knocks.

CONTINUITY

In 1966, he decided to move to San Francisco. He gave up his East Village apartment and his by-then part-time work at the Meredith agency, bought a $300 Rambler, loaded his worldly goods in it, and set out for California.

FRAME

Bruce Britton and his wife, Marilyn, had moved to San Francisco in the train of their psychotherapy guru (a story that was to be an inspiration for a part of *The Children of Hamelin*), somehow bringing a curtain down on part of my life. But it also meant I now had friends in California.

And California, San Francisco in particular, for me like so many others, was the mythical Golden West toward which Young Men were supposed to go, the land with no winter, North Beach, the Sunset end of the Road, the object of a thousand and one vision quests, the Future itself, somehow, the glorious leap into the Great Unknown.

Appropriately enough, Frank Herbert and about three hundred milligrams of mescaline sent me on my way.

FLASHBACK

Walking west through the Village night on Fourth Street, peaking on mescaline after reading the final installment of the magazine serialization of *Dune*—a

powerful meditation on space-time, precognition, and destiny soon to launch a hundred thousand trips—I had a flash-forward of my own.

I would be a famous science-fiction writer; I would publish many stories and novels, and many of the people who were my literary idols, inspirations, and role models, and former clients, people I had never met, would come to accept me as their equal, as their ally, as their friend.

And my life's mission would be to take this commercial science-fiction genre and turn it into something else somehow, write works that transcended its commercial parameters, works that could aspire to the literary company of Burroughs and Mailer and Kerouac, that would help to open a new Way. . . .

This is what you're here for. This is why you passed through the fever's fire and didn't die in that hospital bed. This is what you must do. You must go West to meet your future.

The mescaline talking? An overdose of twenty-five-year-old ego? A stoned-out ego-tripping wish-fulfillment fantasy?

Call it what you will.

Everything I saw in that timeless Einsteinian moment would come to pass.

CONTINUITY

On the way to San Francisco, he attended the Milford Science-Fiction Writers' Conference in Milford, Pennsylvania, to which he had been invited by the organizer, Damon Knight.

FLASHBACK

Damon Knight had invited me on the basis of "The Equalizer," a story I published in *Analog*. The only other science fiction writers I had met before had been Terry Carr and Barry Malzberg, fellow SMLA wage-slaves, and suddenly there I was in Damon's huge crumbling Victorian manse for ten days of workshop-ping and socializing with a couple dozen of them, a few whom *I had actually agented anonymously,* though considering what had habitually come down, I wasn't about to mention *that.*

Damon's motto was "No Chiefs, no Indians." This was a professional workshop and everyone invited was by definition a professional, hence an equal, whether they were Damon, Gordon Dickson, James Blish, Judith Merril, or one of the selected new guys like me.

What's more, I was indeed accepted as an equal colleague on a certain level, and the sense of awed isolation I felt when I first stepped into the house's big kitchen and met all these people who were names on book jackets lasted maybe an hour and a half.

You can say a lot of critical things about the community of science fiction writers, and down through the years I certainly have, but it really is a community that not only tends to protect and nurture its own but actually *welcomes* newcomers into the fold. Like all gatherings of writers, the sf community engages in bragging, backbiting, vicious gossip, and cruel games, but nowhere else in my experience are established writers so genuinely openhearted to the new kids on the block.

CONTINUITY

He became fast friends with Harlan Ellison, who was at Milford, and was strongly attracted to Dona Sadock, with whom he was to live many years later, who was there with Ellison.

FLASHBACK

Harlan arrived in Milford in a flash of Hollywood street punk ectoplasm with the tiny elfin Dona in tow. It was just one of those weird chemical things. He hadn't been in Damon's kitchen for twenty minutes before we were talking as if we were already old buddies picking up a conversation that had been going on for years.

Harlan at that time was about thirty, dressing and bullshitting like the Hollywood star writer. Dona was this tiny little twenty-year-old groupie, or so it seemed until she opened her mouth and out came this preternaturally powerful voice redolent of fifty-year-old sophistication and speaking for someone who seemed about a thousand years older than that.

Instant fascination. Unrequited love that would go on for years.

The beginning of the two longest friendships of my life.

CONTINUITY

Instead of driving directly to San Francisco after Milford, he passed through Los Angeles and looked up Ellison, who put him up at his house for a week or so, persuaded him to try Los Angeles instead, and found him an affordable studio apartment.

F R A M E

I hadn't intended to stay more than a few days in Los Angeles. I took a random exit on the Hollywood Freeway and called Harlan, the only person I knew in LA. He invited me to crash in his little house up in Beverly Glen. Before I quite knew what was happening, he was persuading me to give LA a try and finding me an apartment. All in a week.

It couldn't have been a week after that when he asked to borrow two thousand dollars, about half my net worth, this from a guy who was knocking down a thousand a week on contract to Paramount. Just for ten days, he assured me. How could I say no to a guy who had been so generous to me?

Thus began a weird pecuniary relationship that went on for years. Harlan would borrow large sums from me for a week or two, pay them back, then borrow the bread again a week later. The same few grand got recycled over and over. No matter how much money he made, Harlan had the creative need to ride the edge of insolvency. No matter how much he borrowed, he always paid it back.

CONTINUITY

He stayed in Los Angeles for about six months, where he wrote, among other stories, the now-much-reprinted "Carcinoma Angels," the very first story purchased for Harlan Ellison's landmark anthology *Dangerous Visions*. A previous attempt at a story for *Dangerous Visions* turned into an outline for the novel *The Men in the Jungle*. Doubleday gave him a contract and a modest advance, and he moved to San Francisco to write it.

FRAME

Why did I leave Los Angeles after six months?

Why did I stay that long?

The Summer of Love, the Counterculture, might be two years in the future on a mass level, but the tension between the hip and the square from which it was to emerge was a very real identity crisis for a young writer from Bohemia.

I had made one lifelong friend in Los Angeles, I had made the stylistic breakthrough of "Carcinoma Angels" there, and the attempt to write *The Men in the Jungle,* my take on Vietnam and professional revolutionaries, as a novelette for *Dangerous Visions* had led to my first hardcover contract, so I can't say the atmosphere wasn't creative, but there didn't seem to be any *there* there. No street life. No scene like the Village.

San Francisco, on the other hand, the chosen object of my odyssey in the first place, was still mythical country, Kerouac's North Beach, the Village West, the California capital of hip. Harlan's and Los Angeles' distant disdain for the misty metropolis to the contrary, I had to at least check it out myself, now didn't I?

FLASHBACK

When I hit San Francisco, the first place I went to was Bruce Britton's apartment, since I knew no one else in town. Bruce being Bruce, and as luck would have it, he and his wife were going to what would be one of the historic parties of the decade that very night.

Yes, I spent my first night in San Francisco at Ken Kesey's very first Acid Test blowout in Seaman's Hall, an event often considered the birth of the Counterculture. Thousands of stoned people, loud music, acid in the punch, general frenzy, the whole tie-dyed ball of wax.

What a homecoming to the hipster community!

And yet. . . .

FRAME

Fabulous North Beach proved to be an expensive bummer. The Beat scene having turned it into a primo tourist attraction, the authorities in their infinite wisdom figured all they had to do to make it *perfect* was to get rid of the dirty beatniks who had made it famous in the first place.

The result was a depressing mixture of high rent apartments, plastic coffeehouses and topless bars, and a hip scene that had followed the low rents elsewhere.

Namely to the Haight.

CONTINUITY

In San Francisco, Spinrad lived on a street close by Buena Vista park, bordering on the Haight-Ashbury. There he wrote both *The Men in the Jungle* and *Agent of Chaos* in the space of less than a year.

FRAME

The bohemian communities of Greenwich Village and North Beach had had economic bases in the arts, the crafts, the tourist industry, but Haight-Ashbury in 1966, the year before the Summer of Love, had no such legitimate economic base at all. People like me, actually making a living in an artistic endeavor, were rare; people with straight nine-to-fivers even rarer.

The unfortunate result being that the economy of the hippie community there (so named by *Time* in 1967) could only be based on the drug trade. At street level, indigent connections collected money for nickel bags of grass or crystal meth or individual tabs of LSD from high school kids or day-trippers, and scored ounces or lids from the lowest true dealers, their cut amounting to ten dollars or so or a nickel for their own stash. The low-level dealers bought from wholesalers in maybe kilo quantities, and so on up the food chain, which in those days did not extend to drug lords, narco terrorists, or the Maf.

Not my planet either, not what *On the Road* had advertised as the hip scene in San Francisco at all, though there seemed to be no other. In the process of cleaning up North Beach, the powers that be had created Dope City in the Haight.

Call it street smarts, or call it luck, I found myself a nice little garden apartment on a hill just above this scene, where I could write *The Men in the Jungle* and later *Agent of Chaos* during the day, and boogie in the Haight at night and weekends.

No doubt some of the nastiness in *The Men in the Jungle* owed as much to the environment of the Haight as to the Vietnam War, which was beginning at the time. For sure, the three-sided conflict between Establishment, Revolution, and Forces of Chaos in *Agent of Chaos* owed even more to my identity crisis at the time.

I was a hipster, right? A Beat, a bohemian; these were my people, weren't they? *Weren't they?* The square world sucked, didn't it? Official reality was boring and oppressive, for sure, and, hey, it was the Establishment itself that created the Haight by driving the Beats out of North Beach. Surely I didn't want to be part of *that.*

But I saw things in the Haight. . . .

I saw people smoking coffee grounds because they had nothing better. I saw people smoking *match heads* to get off on the sulfur fumes. I saw needle freaks shooting up with *hot water* just for "the Surge." A guy said to me, "I'd eat *shit* if I thought it'd get me high," and he wasn't joking.

And there were people who regarded me as a square because I wouldn't get involved in dealing.

I spent a long time looking for a third way. So did the country. And maybe we're all searching for it still.

CONTINUITY

A certain deterioration in the cultural milieu in the Haight persuaded Spinrad to return to Los Angeles.

FLASHBACK

One day two Texan girls I knew pleaded with me to come over to their apartment and rescue them from a couple of dealers for whom their kid brother was a connection, and who were refusing to leave.

I put on my White Knight suit and drove over.

Given the level of paranoia in the Haight, ejecting them was easier than it might seem. All I had to do was glower at them enigmatically until they started giving *me* paranoid looks.

"Whatsa matter, you guys think I'm a *narc* or something?" I snarled defensively.

"Oh, no, man, nothing like—"

"Yeah, I think you *do!* Whatsa matter, I look like a cop to you?"

"Oh, no, man—"

"You think I'm a f——' *narc,* don't you?"

Sinister these schmucks were, but they *were* schmucks, and after about a half an hour of this, they slithered out the door. But not before telling a story that they found highly amusing.

They were big-time acid dealers, or so they claimed. Peace, Love, Higher Consciousness in hundred tab lots.

"An' two out of every hundred hits are cyanide, some people are in for a really heavy trip, haw! haw! haw!"

I left the Haight for LA the next week.

FRAME

I spent about a month living in Harlan Ellison's large new house with Harlan and one of my main literary heroes, Theodore Sturgeon. Both Sturgeon and I were chasing unsuccessfully after Dona Sadock, who had arrived in LA, and it got kind of weird.

I was still trying to digest the results of what I had seen in the Haight. The Counterculture hadn't even been born yet, but I was already thinking twenty years ahead to what would emerge out the other side. Ted and Harlan were both working on TV scripts, and I was thinking about what immortality would mean as an item of commerce too. *Bug Jack Barron* was somehow coming together in my mind.

CONTINUITY

Spinrad drove to New York, where he secured a contract from Doubleday to write *Bug Jack Barron,* and then to Cleveland, where he attended his first science fiction convention.

FRAME

The elusive Dona had fled from Sturgeon and myself back to New York, and I did another transcontinental run, in pursuit of her and a book contract from Doubleday. Didn't catch her, but I did cadge the contract for *Bug Jack Barron,* at a rather wet lunch with Larry Ashmead, who had been my editor on *The Men in the Jungle,* then about to be published.

Ashmead grandly assured me that there were no taboos, that I was free to follow my literary star in writing this novel of immortality, television, and American Presidential politics.

FLASHBACK

Harlan was also in New York, on his way to be Guest of Honor at the World Science Fiction Convention in Cleveland. "You gotta go to the Worldcon," he told me.

"Worldcon? What's that?"

"Two thousand fans of writers like us, half of them women. Need I say more?"

I had failed to connect up with Dona once more, so enough said, he didn't.

I pictured a thousand literary groupies of the sort one might in one's dreams encounter in a Village coffeehouse, avid for intellectual discourse and fornication with science fiction writers.

Instead, I had my first encounter with the subculture of science fiction fandom—dominantly male, adolescent, overweight, and literarily jejune to say the least. An unsettling experience for writers who come to science fiction from elsewhere for strictly literary reasons. J. G. Ballard didn't write for a year after his first and last convention. When I encountered Keith Laumer after his first convention, he was in a state of gibbering shock.

Not my planet either, but being the venue of much publishing wheeling and dealing—as well as places to meet your friends and colleagues—sf conventions, I was to find, are rather seductive to science fiction writers; bad for the head, but hard to avoid.

CONTINUITY

Upon returning to Los Angeles, Spinrad rented an apartment in Laurel Canyon, where, in 1967–68, he wrote *Bug Jack Barron,* as well as short stories, journalism, and two television scripts for *Star Trek,* one of which was produced as "The Doomsday Machine."

With Yeremy Parnov of the Soviet Writers' Union and his wife Elena Parnov of Novosti Press Service, at the Peking Hotel, Moscow, 1989

FRAME

Los Angeles seemed a lot more like home the second time around, or rather Laurel Canyon did—wild overgrown hills five minutes off the Sunset Strip, inhabited by wild overgrown people—and I've never lived anywhere else in LA ever since.

Harlan introduced me to Jared Rutter, editor of *Knight* magazine, and I wrote a piece about science fiction fandom for him which led to a monthly column chronicling the times as we passed through them, collected in 1970 in *Fragments of America.*

This was to be published by something called Now Library Press, another line of a large porn publisher, who at *this* time was doing the Essex House line of literary porn novels under the aegis of Brian Kirby. The writers who wrote the novels—and there were

some formidable ones like Theodore Sturgeon, Philip Jose Farmer, David Meltzer, Michael Perkins—got $1,500. I got $300 to read them and write six pages afterwards justifying their redeeming social significance.

Thanks to another Harlan Ellison connection, I wrote a piece for *Cinema* magazine, and thanks to a favorable mention of his pilot for the show therein, I was invited to write a script for *Star Trek* by Gene Roddenberry, and then a second.

Thanks to all of the above, I managed to survive economically for the eight months or so it took me to write *Bug Jack Barron* on the first half of a $1,500 advance from Doubleday.

This was, in retrospect, the apogee of the countercultural revolution, when everything seemed possible, when the world was being made anew, when even *Time* could do a naively positive cover story on the Summer of Love.

I was writing commentary on it all every month. I had been invited to write for *Star Trek.* My first hardcover had come out. I was riding as high as the times.

So I took Ashmead at his word, sat down with my copy of *Understanding Media,* a lid or two of grass, and the blithe assumption that science fiction could also be made anew, that is, that all the commercial, political, stylistic, and linguistic strictures no longer applied, and I let the muse, the evolutionary imperative of the time, take me where it would.

Where it took me was into a highly political tale of love, sex, immortality, suicide, drugs, idealism lost and ultimately regained, informed by a sexual explicitness the science fiction genre had never seen before, though, in 1990s retrospect, relentlessly heterosexual, and almost naively free of anything that would today be called "perverse."

The style that seemed to move through me in a great Kerouacian gush was curiously similar in spirit to that of Norman Mailer's *Why Are We in Vietnam?,* Brian Aldiss's *Barefoot in the Head,* and even Robert A. Heinlein's *The Moon Is a Harsh Mistress,* all of which had to have been written at roughly the same time, and none of which could have influenced any of the others. None of the four of us had written anything like that sort of thing before, and none of us really ever did again.

It may sound arch in 1993 to suggest that the spirit of the times must have been speaking through us. But not in Psychedelic Sixty-seven.

CONTINUITY

Doubleday rejected the finished manuscript of *Bug Jack Barron.* Spinrad spent the next year or so trying to sell it to major hardcover houses without success.

FLASHBACK

On the other hand, the years 1968–1969 were, as I called them in the title of one of my *Knight* pieces, "Year of Lightning, Year of Dread."

Martin Luther King, Jr., and Bobby Kennedy were assassinated, Russian tanks crushed the Prague Spring, Richard Nixon emerged as president after Lyndon Johnson was driven from office, and Doubleday bounced *Bug Jack Barron.*

Not to suggest that these were events of similar magnitude, but the nature of the clashing forces were the same in the microcosm as in the macrocosm.

"Take out all the sex, drugs, and politics, and we'll publish the book," Doubleday told me.

"All that would be left would be a novelette," I pointed out.

Multiply this by ten million such incidents, small and large, and you have the transformation of the cultural awakening of 1967 into the cultural war of 1968–72. Hip versus square. Counterculture versus Power Structure. Revolution versus Establishment. Sex, Drugs, and Rock and Roll versus the Judeo-Christian Tradition. Me versus You. Us versus Them.

Bug Jack Barron bounced around New York from publisher to publisher, rejection to rejection. The mainstream publishers rejected it because it was too much like science fiction. And I resisted the easy out of publishing it as a genre book.

As in the macrocosm, so in the microcosm.

CONTINUITY

During this period, he took the manuscript with him to Milford, where he met Michael Moorcock, British fiction writer, literary theoretician, and editor of the experimental magazine *New Worlds.*

FRAME

In the microcosm of science fiction, the countercultural literary trend was called the "New Wave."

So dubbed by critic Judith Merril to describe a recondite *stylistic* revolution within the genre taking place primarily in Britain under the theoretical aegis of Mike Moorcock. But by 1968, the term had come to include *anything* that its proponents considered taboo-breaking or that conservatives believed polluted the vital bodily fluids of the science fiction genre, as exemplified by the stories in Harlan Ellison's landmark *Dangerous Visions* anthology.

And of course by *Bug Jack Barron,* "New Wave" by all three definitions and a novel that had become notorious before it even found a publisher.

It was already notorious in part because I had already gone public on the subject in articles in science fiction fanzines, in appearances at science fiction conventions, even on the radio. I definitely did not want *Bug Jack Barron* published as just another genre sf paperback, but things being what they were, I used my voice wherever I could make it heard.

And took the manuscript with me to the Milford Conference.

CONTINUITY

Moorcock was very enthusiastic about *Bug Jack Barron,* and serialized it in *New Worlds* in six monthly installments. The magazine had a grant from the British Arts Council, and when the W. H. Smith bookstore chain refused to stock it because of their objections to *Bug Jack Barron* and the Arts Council successfully pressured them to rescind the ban, questions were raised in Parliament, where Spinrad was called a "degenerate."

Meanwhile, Spinrad was finally persuaded to sell the American book rights to *Bug Jack Barron* to Avon Books as a science fiction paperback original.

F R A M E

Mike Moorcock was not the only one at Milford who was enthusiastic about the notorious *Bug Jack Barron* when they got to read a piece of it. The encouraging reception it got from writers on both sides of the so-called New Wave controversy pulled me out of a personal pit and dropped me in the middle of a paradox with which I have wrestled ever since.

Ever since *Bug Jack Barron,* it has always seemed to me that what I was writing, like much else that got published as "sf," did not belong in the sf marketing category, genre sf being commercially targeted at an audience of literarily and politically unsophisticated male adolescents, while what I wrote, judging from reader response, was appealing to a demographic slice that was older, more female, more interested in literary and political matters than in the "action adventure" formula dominant in the sf genre.

A more general audience, conditioned by decades of sf genre packaging *not* to seek out such fiction within such covers, where in fact, paradoxically, much of the best of it is in fact to be found, precisely because the writers thereof have been ghettoized therein by the mainstream publishing apparatus, itself conditioned by the very prejudices its own sf lines have done so much to promulgate.

Like other science fiction writers of my generation and our older soul mates of similar literary ambition— Ellison, Moorcock, Thomas M. Disch, Barry Malzberg, Robert Silverberg, Samuel R. Delaney, Philip K. Dick, Brian Aldiss, Fritz Leiber, Alfred Bester, Theodore Sturgeon, to name a few—I have fought to break my work out of this literary ghetto.

The paradox being that there has always been more comprehension for this desire to break the bounds of the genre, more emotional and intellectual support for literarily adventurous speculative fiction, *within* the walls of the very ghetto from which it seeks to escape than from without.

This being the short form of the long analyses in my teaching anthology *Modern Science Fiction* and my critical overview of the literature and its place in society, *Science Fiction in the Real World,* both published quite later.

FLASHBACK

A year or so of trying to sell *Bug Jack Barron* as a major mainstream novel finally convinced me that I was banging my brains out against a stone wall. And indeed, as soon as I gave up and unhappily agreed to let Scott Meredith try the sf publishers, the book was involved in a kind of half-assed auction. And after I reluctantly sold the novel to Avon as a paperback original, I managed to secure a simultaneous hardcover edition from Walker Books.

Still, I wanted out. Or rather, in. To larger literary realms. And the only way to do it seemed to be to write a novel that was not science fiction, and to do it without a contract.

This, after having had a *contracted* novel rejected and bounce around for a year without selling, was scary. Though, upon reflection, maybe not. After all, the three thousand dollars I had finally gotten for *Bug Jack Barron* via competitive bidding was still less than what I had made in two weeks writing a *Star Trek* script. And my *Knight* column covered the rent.

And I had a story to tell, or rather several of them that fit together thematically. I would write *The Children of Hamelin,* relating the karmic connections between the roots of the Counterculture in the old Village bohemia, drug dealing, psychotherapy cults, and the fee-reading operation at a literary agency not entirely unlike Scott Meredith's.

CONTINUITY

About this time, he met Terry Champagne, with whom he was to live for the next year or so.

After he finished *The Children of Hamelin* and persuaded Meredith to agent it, he and Terry Champagne moved to London in 1969.

FLASHBACK

Yes, Theresa Louisa Champagne was her real name, and in retrospect it was a relationship that was not so much doomed as destined to be a limited run for a certain season.

Terry was still married to a friend of mine while she was chasing after me, and I was too square to let her catch me until she had resolved her situation. Terry was not into monogamy except perhaps of the short-term serial variety. Terry was not looking for a permanent relationship, and I was.

Or was I?

For by the time she moved into my Laurel Canyon apartment, I was committed to moving out. All the way to London.

The American publication of *Bug Jack Barron* was set, and I was in the process of finishing *The Children of Hamelin.* I had become something of a minor countercultural hero in "swinging" London in absentia. Who could resist? Why should I?

Hooking up with Terry didn't change my plans. Terry was an archetypal child of the sixties, a stone willing to roll wherever. An artist, a topless dancer, a jeweler, a dealer, and when, through me, she got to take a shot at writing stories and doing journalism, she succeeded at that too, albeit, on her usual terms. "It's all the same shit," she used to say to me, to my consternation.

If I had ever thought of *myself* as a hippie, living with Terry Champagne disabused me of any such notion.

Still, for a time, it worked. I finished *The Children of Hamelin,* somehow managed to bullshit the Scott Meredith Literary Agency into marketing it despite, uh, certain aspects, and off we went, in March of 1969, via a flood in LA, a blizzard in New York, and a five-day, barfing seasick crossing on the SS *United States* to London, to a Europe that neither of us had ever seen.

FRAME

Neither Terry nor I had been outside of North America before, and now here we were in London. At first it was all an adventure: the scene around *New Worlds,* the fringes of the countercultural underground, Midsummer's Eve at Stonehenge. It was all new, even the *smell* of everything was subtly different.

But after we had sublet an apartment in Bayswater and started actually *living* in London, it all settled into a sort of normal routine, something like living in New York for me, but more alien for a California girl like Terry.

Which is to say that London in the end was more interesting to me than to her. She was writing about as much as I was, and good stuff too, but she was never as *serious* about the literary scene as I was, or for that matter, about much of anything else.

Nor was I getting much writing done, waiting for *Bug Jack Barron* to be published, waiting for *The Children of Hamelin* to sell as it bounced from publisher to publisher, talking literary theory with Mike Moorcock and colleagues, playing the minor underground literary celebrity. . . .

FLASHBACK

After J. G. Ballard and Mike Moorcock backed out, Christopher Priest and I were invited as the token science-fiction writers to the Harrogate Festival of Literature and Science by the noted publisher and literary figure John Calder. Off we went by train, Chris and his wife, Terry and I; Chris nervous about mingling with all the awesome literary luminaries.

Calder, quite frantic, met the train with his humongous Jaguar saloon, the four of us and two Indian professors stuffed ourselves into it, and Calder started to drive out of the parking lot. . . .

"Oh no, man!" I shouted. "You're gonna—"

Too late. Calder had already driven the Jag halfway down a flight of stone steps, where it hung quivering on its belly-pan.

Calder, freaking, had no idea what to do next. Somehow, this grand entrance into the literary high life ended any trepidation I might have felt about being a twenty-eight-year-old sf punk amidst my intellectual betters.

"You stay behind the wheel and gun the engine when I tell you to," I told him, "and the rest of us get out and lift the rear end."

And that's how we did it, bouncing the car down the steps in stages. It managed to get us to the hotel before all the oil leaked out, but the repair bill was enormous.

So it goes, as Kurt Vonnegut would say. So it went.

The theme of the conference was the interface between science and technology and literature, but they had one microphone to be passed among twenty panelists, like an exaggeration of a typical science fiction convention. My experience therewith served me well, and I sort of began to ooze front and center.

Then, Erich Fried, a German Marxist writer, and his attendant groupies decided to organize a revolution. This was 1969, I was the author of the notorious *Bug Jack Barron,* and thought my heart was surely in the right revolutionary place, so I attended his evening strategy session in the auditorium as invited.

Fried's thesis was that the relationship between the speakers up on the platform and the audience down here in rows of seats facing them was hierarchical, therefore fascist. He would demand that the seats be rearranged in a circle with the audience surrounding the speakers on the same equal level. Much more democratic.

Okay. . . .

But when I looked down, I observed that the chair I was sitting on, like every other seat in the auditorium, was quite thoroughly nailed to the floor. It would take a team of carpenters days to move them all.

When I pointed this out to Fried, he scowled at me with bemused contempt. "Hardly the point!" he sniffed.

Uh-huh.

The next day, Fried stood up in the audience and made his demand, backed up by many shouts of "Right On!" from his supporters. There then ensued half an hour of tedious argument about seating arrangements to the discomfort of the paying customers and the total befuddlement of the chairman, science writer Nigel Calder (no relation to John), who had completely lost control.

After a half hour of listening to this totally pointless argument, I had finally had enough. I snatched the one free microphone and gave Fried what he wanted.

I observed none too gently that, the seats being nailed to the floor, the argument was moot, the audience was bored with it, and it was time to get on with the program.

"You, sir," Fried shouted righteously on cue, "are a fascist swine and a bastard!" And stormed out of the audience at the head of his troops, as he had obviously planned to do all along.

It was the major media event of the conference. It made all the papers. That's how I got called a fascist swine and a bastard in every major newspaper in Britain.

Well, not precisely. Because John Calder had spelled my name wrong in the press kit, the fascist bastard was "Norman Spinard."

FRAME

Bug Jack Barron had been published, *The Children of Hamelin* hadn't sold, I was still writing my monthly column for *Knight* but had no other significant source of income, Terry was getting homesick for California, the sublet on the London apartment was up, so, somewhat reluctantly on my part, perhaps, after a month staggering about the continent after the car we had borrowed from Mike Moorcock expired in Germany, we returned to Richard Nixon's America in the fall of 1969 and rented a house in Laurel Canyon.

FLASHBACK

Coda to Harrogate:

We took the train back to London in the company of, among others, William Burroughs. We had to change at York. Burroughs went to a newsstand after reading matter for the trip and returned with a handful of sleazy British tabloids.

"Look at this stuff!" he chortled. "Juicy!"

They were all full of this lurid Hollywood murder story. Pregnant actress Sharon Tate, wife of Roman Polanski, famous hair stylist to the stars Jay Sebring and several others had been gorily murdered by a tribe of drug-crazed hippies in thrall to some weirdo named Charles Manson.

I never paid attention to crap like that and marveled at how someone like Burroughs could.

Little did I know how close I was to get to the Manson Family.

Too close for comfort. And soon.

CONTINUITY

There Spinrad, in 1970–71, wrote *The Iron Dream,* his satire of science fiction, Nazism, and Adolf Hitler, which had emerged as a concept from a conversation in London with Moorcock, during the writing of which his relationship with Terry Champagne ended.

During this period, he was also writing political journalism, film criticism, and the occasional book review for the *Los Angeles Free Press,* America's best-selling weekly underground newspaper.

FRAME

A crazy time.

My relationship with Terry was breaking up. I was writing a novel that amounted to channeling the consciousness of Hitler in order to exorcise the demon of Nazism. And I had become a main man of the Underground Press on the side.

Arthur Kunkin, founder of the *Free Press,* had hired Brian Kirby as managing editor, and I was one of the writers he brought in. The money was next to nothing, but as a film critic I was on all the freebie review lists, as a political columnist I developed a certain following, and I loved the instant feedback of weekly journalism, a welcome relief from getting inside the head of Hitler while my relationship was falling apart.

But what I, and everyone else at the paper, could have done without was the Mansonoids.

Kirby had brought in Ed Sanders, poet and former Fug, from New York to cover the murder trial of Charlie Manson. As soon as he hit the tarmac at LAX, Ed was writing stuff about how the Establishment was railroading this innocent hippie tribe in order to crush the Counterculture.

Charlie and his Family *loved* the coverage. They *loved* the paper. They *loved* Ed. There were more of them on the loose than anybody not at the *Freep* realized. And as the trial progressed, every stoned-out nut in California seemed to want to join the Manson Family too. . . .

The Mansonoids *trusted* Ed. They trusted him so much that they told him about *all these other neat snuffs* they had done that only their good buddies at the *Free Press* now knew about, hee, hee, hee. . . .

So early on we all knew that Manson and company were indeed the crazed killers the wicked Establishment claimed they were, but Kirby had to keep on their good side, such as it was; the *Freep* had to hew to the Mansonoid line, print Charlie's poems and manifestos, or the murderous creeps hanging around the paper *might not like us any more.* . . . .

Years later, I met Ed Sanders in New York.

He told me that even there, even then, he still slept with the lights on.

One good thing did come of it, though: one of the best front page headlines ever.

Remember when Richard Nixon butted into the trial? "MANSON GUILTY, NIXON DECLARES," screamed the headlines in the Establishment papers.

The next issue of the *Free Press* carried a piece by Charlie himself about the then-unfolding Watergate scandal.

With English novelist Doris Lessing outside a conference center in Valbonne, France

"NIXON GUILTY, MANSON DECLARES," said Brian Kirby's headline.

How right they both were!

CONTINUITY

The Children of Hamelin still hadn't found a book publisher, and Brian Kirby, editor of the *Free Press,* began an unprecedented weekly serialization of the novel in the paper.

FLASHBACK

Speaking of Watergate and the Underground Press, if George McGovern hadn't won the Wisconsin Democratic primary in 1972, I would probably have made him president.

A couple of weeks before the primary, I got a call from a guy who was an admirer of the political analysis I'd been publishing in the *Free Press* and who'd been offered the job of press secretary for the McGovern campaign in California.

He wanted my advice. Should he take the job? McGovern seemed like such a loser, but what other instrument of change *was* there? We kicked it around a bit.

"Look," he said, "McGovern's probably gonna lose in Wisconsin, and then he's gonna be receptive to some changes in his campaign. Would you be willing to fly there with me to talk to him?"

"Well, sure." How could I resist?

"Well, what would you tell him? What would be *the* winning campaign issue?"

"Watergate," said I.

"*Watergate?*"

This was before the real story broke, before the hearings, before the tapes, back when the whole thing seemed to be just a bunch of isolated dirty tricks and a bungled amateur burglary and was being covered as such in the Establishment papers. McGovern had hardly mentioned it.

The paranoiacs of the Underground Press, though, were convinced that Nixon had planned a coup against the Constitution. Concentration camps set up for dissidents. Enemies lists and use of the IRS against those on them. Illegal bugging. Financing of Nixon's campaign by the Mafia through the Teamster Pension Fund and Bebe Rebozo's bank.

Crazy, right? Only drug-crazed hippies would believe such stuff. Only those Underground rags would print it.

Art Kunkin, however, had his mitts on something hot enough to blow the whole lid off if someone like McGovern chose to push it. . . .

An airliner had crashed killing all aboard, including the wife of one of the then-key Watergate figures, upon whose person was found a large bag of cash. That much had been covered in the Establishment papers.

The FAA report had found cyanide in the lungs of the victims.

The White House had suppressed it.

Kunkin had somehow gotten hold of a copy and printed it in the *Freep*. But the *Free Press* was only an Underground paper. . . .

"Watergate is a complex conspiracy by the Nixon administration against the Constitution, is what I would tell George McGovern," I declared. "Half the dirty tricks are the Nixonoids' efforts to keep the lid on till after the election. But if you make it the centerpiece of your campaign, George, I'd say, hit it hard, hit it often; you can make the story break early enough to count. Yeah, this sounds like science fiction, but I kid you not; there's enough dirt under this rug not only to defeat Tricky Dick in an election, but, who knows, even get him *impeached*. . . .

George McGovern, alas, *won* the Wisconsin primary.

The rest, alas, was not history.

CONTINUITY

About two-thirds of the way through its serialization of *The Children of Hamelin*, the *Free Press* was taken over by a pornographer to whom Arthur Kunkin had become indebted, and the staff and writers of the paper left en masse to found the *Staff*, which published the rest of what was to be twenty-eight installments.

FLASHBACK

A crazy time.

How crazy?

I had been in the same room with Philip K. Dick only once, and I had been too much in awe of this literary idol of mine to actually *talk* to him.

Then, late one night in 1972, I got a phone call from Vancouver. It was Phil Dick, and the conversation started like this: "My girlfriend just left me, and I think I'm going to kill myself, but I read your story "Carcinoma Angels" in *Dangerous Visions,* and I thought I should talk to you first."

And that was how my friendship with Phil began, in midstream, as if it were a pre-existing condition. All at once it seemed natural to be deep in a long intimate conversation with this old friend who had been a total stranger before my phone rang.

"On the other hand," Phil finally said, "I've got this offer from Willis McNelly at Cal State Fullerton to come down there to Orange County to live. What's your honest opinion? Now don't bullshit me. Would I be better off moving to Orange County, or killing myself?"

"Well, Phil, personally, I can't *stand* Orange County," I found myself saying, "but you might as well give it a try. If you don't like it, you can always kill yourself later."

"Yeah, that makes sense," Phil said reasonably, and moved to southern California.

CONTINUITY

Even though *The Children of Hamelin* appeared every week for six months in papers with a circulation of about 100,000, the Scott Meredith Literary Agency still didn't find a book publisher for it, and in 1973, Spinrad finally fired them and secured the services of Lurton Blassingame.

F R A M E

Was the Meredith Agency actually trying to keep *The Children of Hamelin* from being published in the guise of ineptly agenting it? Were they submitting it to publishers out of one side of their mouths while making it known that its publication would vex Scott out of the other?

Quien sabe?

What I *did* find out for sure was that it was no longer being submitted. Months previously, they had talked me out of my carbon copy on some pretext, and on a trip to New York, I discovered that the top copy had been either lost or destroyed, and they were paying peon wages to a professional book editor to (badly) retype a new one from my carbon *very* slowly.

Without ever telling me what was happening.

CONTINUITY

In 1973, Spinrad secured a contract from Putnam Berkley to write *Passing through the Flame,* a long novel about, among other things, filmmaking in Hollywood, the rock music industry, the death of the Counterculture, and the takeover of an underground paper by the porn mafia.

FLASHBACK

Stone-broke, the IRS having cleaned out my bank account, I flew to New York on a credit card to try to sell a novel version of what was later to become my oft-printed novella, *Riding the Torch,* maybe my own choice as my best piece of short fiction.

George Ernsberger, who had been my editor at Avon on *Bug Jack Barron* and *The Iron Dream,* was now editor-in-chief at Berkley Books, a position of much more power.

Blassingame and I had lunch with him at a Moroccan restaurant to pitch the science fiction novel proposal.

"Naw," said George, "I think you should write me some kind of big mainstream novel instead. . . . "

"Well, George, I dunno. . . . "

"Give me an eight-page outline I like, and I'll give you an advance of ten thousand dollars."

I think I played it cool. I think I managed to avoid choking on my couscous.

Ten thousand dollars seemed a princely sum at the time, more than twice what I'd gotten for anything before.

"Well . . . I'll think it over, George. . . . "

I went straight back to the friend's apartment where I was staying and banged out the outline in five days on my portable typewriter.

FRAME

Around this same time, one person I met and one I failed to meet were to have serious career consequences. The person I met before I got the contract to write *Passing through the Flame* was Larry Schiller, later to collaborate successfully with Norman Mailer on *The Executioner's Song,* but then as broke as I was and my unsuccessful collaborator in any number of Scams of the Week.

The person I failed to meet was L. Ron Hubbard, once and future science fiction writer and founder of the Church of Scientology. Hubbard had never granted a major interview. I knew A. E. Van Vogt, who had been quite close to him in the old days, and through Van I got in touch with the upper levels of the Scientology hierarchy in Los Angeles.

This was one Scam of the Week that went on for months, as I pursued the journalistic coup of the Hubbard interview while they strung me along, playing with my head, suggesting that if I played my cards right, I might get to write the authorized biography, and so forth. I found out much more about Scientology than I wanted to, maybe more than it was entirely healthy to know.

Of course, I never got the interview with Hubbard.

But several years later the experience was to be the inspiration for the novel I was to write after *Passing through the Flame: The Mind Game.*

FLASHBACK

When I finished writing *Passing through the Flame,* I flew back to New York to deliver it and to do some final work on *Modern Science Fiction,* the teaching anthology I was doing for Anchor Books.

There I chanced to meet Dona Sadock, whom I had pursued futilely for so long way back when, at the tag end of a bad marriage. Now, somehow, the time was right for us. She came back with me to Laurel Canyon, the beginning of a series of transcoastal staggers which were finally to end with us moving back to New York about the time of the first publication of *Passing through the Flame.*

Before that, though, we were visited in Los Angeles by Richard Pinhas and his significant other, Agnetta Nielsen.

Richard had been described to me as a French rock musician so deep into *The Iron Dream* that he had named his group after the mythical country in the book, Heldon, and we nervously awaited the arrival of Nazi skinheads in jackboots.

Instead, Richard proved to be the most intellectual of musicians, a pioneer synthesist who was also to write a thesis in philosophy, and Agnetta a Swedish model rather than Eva Braun in black leather. Both of them were about as right wing as the Paris student movement of 1968, of which they were veterans. We hit it off right away, and today they are two of my oldest friends.

More to the point here, their visit was the beginning of my relationship with France, and *Little Heroes* is dedicated to Richard, who was to be instrumental in its conception years later.

CONTINUITY

After *Passing through the Flame* was accepted by George Ernsberger, Walter Minton, owner of Putnam at the time, arbitrarily decided to publish it as a paperback original, despite Ernsberger's previous assurances to the contrary.

Spinrad got on a plane to New York to object strenuously, and after much argument, Minton agreed to do the book in hardcover.

FLASHBACK

I had George's assurance that *Passing through the Flame* would be a hardcover, but nothing in the contract. I was quite cross when he told me Minton's plans. I called my agent, Lurton Blassingame. Minton, it turned out, had discussed the matter with him, and it was Lurton's considered opinion that, Walter Minton being one of the most powerful executives in publishing, it would not be wise for either of us to take him on.

We'd see about that.

I called George back and told him to tell Minton that I would be in his office next Monday, and that if things were not settled to my satisfaction, I would "pull him across the desk and beat the living shit out of him, or worse. Maybe *much* worse."

I then called Larry Schiller, who just happened to be in New York at the time, trying to sell some scam with Mario Puzo to none other than Minton himself. I asked him to impress Mr. Minton with the idea that I was a dangerous hothead with unsavory connections who just might be pissed off enough to have him offed.

Minton was ever so polite when I arrived in his office. Not a harsh word was spoken between us. *Passing through the Flame* was done as a hardcover.

With, however, no support.

CONTINUITY

Ernsberger was later fired by Minton, and when the paperback of *Passing through the Flame* was published, the dedication to Ernsberger, which had appeared in the hardcover, was removed. During this period, MCA bought Putnam and eased out Walter Minton, and Spinrad changed agents again, signing on with the Jane Rotrosen Agency.

FLASHBACK

By the time the paperback came out, Dona and I had moved back to New York, and I saw the first copy in the Putnam office. In the absence of Minton, I raved on about how I was going to talk to certain people in Hollywood who would see to it that he would be gone ere the year was out.

It was admittedly a cheap thrill. Putnam had already been bought by MCA, and from the experience of my friends Betty and Ian Ballantine, I knew all too well what happened to owners who sold their companies to such conglomerates believing they could cash the fat check and still retain effective control.

Then too, Minton was not exactly a hero to his troops. He once fired a couple dozen people at the office Christmas party, to give you an idea.

I was at a big publishing party when it came down. A whole bunch of people from the Putnam office arrived, drunk as skunks, and lugging champagne, which they proceeded to pour for me.

MCA just axed Walter Minton, they told me. How did you do it?

I just smiled enigmatically over the rim of my glass and toasted his demise.

CONTINUITY

In another attempt to secure major mainstream hardcover publication, Spinrad wrote *The Mind Game* without a contract. Though the completed book seemed on the verge of being accepted by major hardcover houses several times, something always seemed to happen between the editorial and legal ends.

FLASHBACK

Was Scientology or the fear thereof responsible? They had certainly complained when their street-solicitor minions appeared in my comic short story in *Playboy,* "Holy War on 34th Street," and had tried unsuccessfully to get Anchor Books to edit my comments on Hubbard out of *Modern Science Fiction.*

And while *The Mind Game* was bouncing around, we did have this rather peculiar burglary. The apartment was ransacked, but nothing was taken. Not the stereo, not the TV, not Dona's mink coat which was hanging in plain view, not even cash.

A search for a manuscript?

A not-so-friendly warning?

The cops said it was probably crazed dopers.

I could hardly tell them that the burglars hadn't taken my grass either.

FRAME

Whatever the cause, *The Mind Game* wasn't selling, so I decided it was time to write another science fiction novel, and wrote an outline for *A World Between,* my meditation on sex roles, feminism, media, and electronic democracy.

My friend David Hartwell wanted to buy it, and I had been instrumental in securing him his position, but unfortunately that position was sf editor at Putnam Berkley. I had recommended him to Ernsberger, but at this time George was already gone and Walter Minton was still in power.

So Jane Rotrosen auctioned the outline, and the winner was Jove Books, the hot new paperback line just started by Harcourt Brace Jovanovich. And they made a deal to do new editions of *The Iron Dream* and *Bug Jack Barron.* And bought *The Mind Game* too.

For the first time in my career, I had some significant capital.

CONTINUITY

Jove published *The Iron Dream,* but before any of Spinrad's other books there could be published, corporate upheavals at Harcourt Brace Jovanovich

intervened. The Jove science fiction program expired, and Jove itself was sold to Putnam Berkley, under which corporate aegis it finally published *The Mind Game* in 1980.

Spinrad, meanwhile, had moved *A World Between* to Simon and Schuster/Pocketbooks, where David Hartwell had started a new line of books, Timescape. Hartwell published *A World Between* as a paperback original, but published Spinrad's next two novels, *Songs from the Stars* and *The Void Captain's Tale,* in hardcover.

FRAME

Songs from the Stars was a post-apocalypse alien-contact story, among other things, and I wanted the "narration" of the alien data-packets to be, well, songs . . . poetry, that is. Could I pull this off? Fortunately, David Hartwell was an experienced poetry editor whom I could count on to tell me if I was making a fool of myself.

David thought the verse worked, with some tinkering, but felt that the forty pages or so of description around it should be in metric prose.

"Metric prose? What's that?"

David proceeded to teach me, as we went over forty pages of manuscript, syllable by syllable, phoneme by phoneme.

Somehow, this learning experience, combined with a scene that had been kicking around in my head for years without leading anywhere, synergized into *The Void Captain's Tale,* a (non-)love story of the far future written in a kind of "world-speak" called Lingo, my first piece of book-length fiction in experimental prose since *Bug Jack Barron,* although in a style light-years apart.

I had written three novels since the publication of *Passing through the Flame* in 1975, but owing to all these publishing upheavals, none of them were published until 1979–1980, when all three of them

The wedding of Norman Spinrad and N. Lee Wood, Fort Myers Beach, Florida, April 28, 1990, with Morris Spinrad, Norman's father, and Christine Goddard, Lee's grandmother, looking on

were published in a space of eighteen months. First it looked as if I had had a four-year writing block, then as if I had. written three major novels in less than two years!

CONTINUITY

In 1976, soon after the writing of *A World Between,* Spinrad's relationship with Dona Sadock ended, though the two remained good friends. Between 1980 and 1982, Spinrad was twice elected president of the Science Fiction Writers of America. During this period he also began a quarterly column of criticism for *Isaac Asimov's Science Fiction Magazine,* which, at this writing, still continues. In 1982, Universal Pictures, which had previously had the book *Bug Jack Barron*

under option, bought the film rights for $75,000, the film to be written by Harlan Ellison and directed by Costa-Gavras.

FLASHBACK

Universal was trying to get me to sell them another cheap option. I knew that I could force them to pay me the pick-up money only because Costa-Gavras wanted Harlan to write it. It was a high-stakes game of chicken.

Finally, I got my long awaited $75,000 phone call. I had about two hours to enjoy it. Then I got another phone call telling me that Phil Dick had had a massive stroke and had lapsed into a terminal coma.

Universal still owns the film rights to *Bug Jack Barron.* To this date, they have pissed away maybe $2 million on the project, and the film has not been made.

CONTINUITY

During this period, he began visiting France, the first time as guest of honor at the Metz Science Fiction Festival. On this trip, in Paris, he recorded two tracks on Richard Pinhas's album *East-West* as a cyborged vocalist.

FLASHBACK

"*Me* sing on a record album, Richard? Are you nuts? I can't even carry a tune with a forklift!"

"Not to worry," he told me, "just write some words to this music, chant them into the microphone, and I, the vocoder, and the computer will do the rest."

So we went into the studio, and I put on the earphones, and started just chanting these simple lyrics. We did some takes like this, and then. . . .

And then Richard tried something. He let me hear my own voice being processed through the vocoder circuitry in real time and something happened. . . .

I was supplying analog input to the electronic augmentation circuitry, in a positive feedback loop with the vocoder, collaborating with it, with whatever Richard was doing, manipulating it as it was augmenting me; and out the other end *something* was singing . . . me, maybe, but not quite not me either, and then. . . .

And then, unbeknownst to me, Richard cut the vocoder out of the circuit like Daddy surreptitiously removing the training wheels from a kid's bicycle.

And played the result back to me.

"That's you," he told me, "au nature!" And so it was. And so it is. For better or worse, you can hear it on the album, re-released on CD in 1992.

I wrote a piece on the experience for a magazine. And started playing with the first little electronic keyboards. And got to thinking. . . .

Electronic circuitry can replace human drummers, even do whole rhythm tracks untouched by human hands.

And if electronic circuitry can make a singer out of *me,* it can make a rock star out of *anyone.* . . .

And if out of anyone, why not out of *no one,* why not *virtual* rock stars who aren't there to not show up for concerts, or get busted for drugs, or command all that money . . . ?

If the music industry *could* do this, they sure would, now wouldn't they?

And that was to be the genesis of *Little Heroes.*

F R A M E

But *Little Heroes* was one book in the future. I had never done a sequel to anything before, or since, but I wanted to do a sequel to *The Void Captain's Tale.* Sort of.

The Void Captain's Tale, narrated in his own "sprach of Lingo," that is, his private melange of human languages, by the Captain in question, takes place entirely on a single spaceship, and is written in a rather hermetic Germanic sprach.

I didn't want to keep the characters, or the setting, or even the style. I wanted to write a wider-screen, more up-beat, joyous bildungsroman from a female point of view, and in a more Latinate, baroque, wise-cracking sprach of Lingo. . . .

CONTINUITY

After the hardcover publication of *The Void Captain's Tale* by Timescape in 1983, David Hartwell made a deal for a new thematically and stylistically related novel, *Child of Fortune,* and Spinrad once more returned to Los Angeles and rented yet another house in Laurel Canyon in which to write it.

The breakup with Dona left me emotionally devastated. New York was filled with memories, bad karma, high rents; I was getting homesick for California, and *Child of Fortune,* with its long sequence in an alien forest of flowers, seemed like a California book. . . .

But I had friends in New York, I had plenty of money from various books and the movie deal. So I decided to give New York one more try. I'd make a fresh start, I'd move into a nice new apartment. After all, I could now afford *twice* the rent I was presently paying for my crappy little three-room railroad flat on Perry Street.

I looked, and looked, and was finally about to give up when I saw an ad for an apartment that seemed perfect. Double my current rent, but I was prepared to pay it.

"Large beautiful four room apt. on tree-lined Village street, eat-in kitchen, sunny garden view. . . . "

Only wasn't there something familiar about the phone number . . . ?

Indeed there was, as it turned out when I called it.

It was the number of my current landlord.

The wonderful apartment I could move into for twice the rent I was paying was a clone of my own in the same building two floors down.

CONTINUITY

Before contracts for *Child of Fortune* could be drawn up, the Timescape line got caught up in a power struggle between Richard Snyder, head of Simon and Schuster, and Ron Busch, head of its Pocket Books subsidiary. Snyder canceled the Timescape line and caused Busch to fire Hartwell, simultaneously making a deal with Scott Meredith for his literary agency to package a new line of science fiction for the company.

FLASHBACK

David Hartwell used to throw Friday afternoon parties in his office. Dick Snyder's office had a private dining room and attached kitchen. One Friday, after Snyder had left, Dave snuck up to his office to cop some ice from the machine in his private kitchen.

He returned with a bucket of ice cubes and a dazed expression.

Snyder's ice machine had embossed the cubes with his monogram.

FRAME

Which will give you some idea of the egos involved. But it was corporate hardball too. Busch, not Snyder, had hired Hartwell to start the Timescape line, and now Timescape was doing Pocket Books *hardcovers,* which Snyder chose to see as infringement by Busch on his turf. So canceling Busch's sf line, and making a deal with his good buddy and my ex-agent Scott Meredith to package a replacement, was a ploy in a larger power struggle.

Making *Busch* take the public heat for a move that was directed against *himself* was pure Dick Snyder.

CONTINUITY

The Science Fiction Writers of America, under President Marta Randall, strenuously objected to this obvious conflict of interest. Randall had been Spinrad's vice president and his choice to succeed him, a task she had accepted only on condition that Spinrad make himself available if called upon by her in an emergency. During the period when this crisis broke,

The author on the French Mediterranean, 1990

Marta Randall found herself teaching a writers' workshop on an isolated island with only a pay phone as her contact to the outside world.

FLASHBACK

So I found myself representing the SFWA in a loud, national, four-cornered media battle against my former agent and employer, and two competing powers within the publisher of my own last three novels!

They never had a chance.

For an agency to package a line of books featuring work by its own writers was a blatant conflict of interest that stank like a codfish in the media moonlight. And to make my job even easier, when Busch canceled Timescape and fired Hartwell, he had told the press that he had done it because the *literary quality of Hartwell's product was too high.* Meredith would do a *much* better job of providing cynical schlock.

Guess whose side *Publishers Weekly* was on? Guess how it looked in the *New York Times* and the *Washington Post?* Guess how happy Gulf and Western, who owned Simon and Schuster, was with Snyder and Busch as they devoured their own feet in public print?

For about ten days, I found myself dribbling Busch, Snyder, and Meredith in the press like a basketball, not that you had to be a media Magic Johnson to do it.

When they finally capitulated, Busch actually complained to the *New York Times* that the SFWA had thrown its weight around unfairly, that we had *bullied* poor Pocket Books, Simon and Schuster, and Gulf and Western, that I was guilty of practicing "gunboat diplomacy."

CONTINUITY

The winners, paradoxically enough, were the SFWA and Dick Snyder. For the first time in American publishing history, a writers' organization used the public press to overturn a high-level corporate decision at a major publisher. On the other hand, while Snyder was unable to consummate his deal with Scott Meredith, he won the power struggle with Busch, eventually forcing him out of the company.

Timescape, however, was still canceled, Hartwell was still fired, and Spinrad was understandably less than confident in his future at Simon and Schuster/Pocket Books.

He moved *Child of Fortune* to Bantam, which published it in 1985.

From 1984 to 1986, while writing *Little Heroes,* under contract to Bantam, Spinrad taught the novel at the Clarion West Science Fiction Writer's Workshop in Seattle, where, in 1985, he met Nancy Lee Wood, who writes under the name N. Lee Wood and was there as a student. In 1986, she moved into his house in Laurel Canyon.

F R A M E

Science fiction writing workshops had proliferated, and I had often expressed my dubious opinion thereof, much preferring Damon Knight's old "No Chiefs, No Indians" formula to the hierarchical structure of teachers and students, established writers and wannabes.

"Don't knock it till you try it," I was told, particularly by Harlan Ellison. So finally, when I was invited to teach a week at the six-week Clarion West Conference, I accepted on condition that I teach the novel, which no one else had tried to do, the idea being to teach novelistic *structure* by having the students turn an idea into an outline.

Somewhat to my own surprise, it worked well enough to persuade me to teach it three years in a row, which had never been my intention.

Lee, a resident of Portland at the time, was one of my students in the middle year and showed up in Los Angeles a few months later.

We met at various events and venues in between Portland and Los Angeles. During the next year, I went to visit her in Portland, and she finally moved into my house in Los Angeles.

Terry Champagne had written and published while living with me, but this was the first time I had lived with someone who had been a writer *before* I had met her, and who was as serious about it as I was.

And we've actually been able to work consistently while living together. I've written two long major novels, 100,000 or so words of short fiction, and much else as of 1993. And Lee has written two complete novels and parts of three others and quite a bit of short fiction during the same period.

If you don't think this is rare, you don't know that many writing couples. Which is exactly the point—a writer has a hard enough time living with *anyone* and working at the same time. For *two* of them to do it sharing the same space-time ain't smooth and easy!

CONTINUITY

In 1987, Spinrad and Wood traveled together to Europe for the first time, to England, and then to Paris. The conjunction of their mutual love for the city and the political changes occurring in Europe caused Spinrad to conceive *Russian Spring* in New York on the way back to Los Angeles, and secure a contract to write it from Bantam.

FLASHBACK

By this time, I had been to Paris by myself several times; most of my books had been published there, I was popular in France, I had a circle of friends in Paris. I had always fantasized living there at some time, but had never gotten up the nerve to do it alone.

What I *had* done, years earlier, while still living in New York, was write the beginning of something I called "La vie continue" in which my future self was living as a political refugee in Paris, in which the Soviet Union had undergone a "Russian Spring" analogous to the "Prague Spring" of 1968. . . . About twelve pages into it, I realized I had the beginning of a *much* longer work than I had bargained for, and set it aside.

Now, years later, in Los Angeles, I owed Bantam a long novella for *Other Americas,* a collection they were going to publish, which seemed just the right length for "La vie continue," so I sat down and wrote the first draft in L.A.

That's right, I wrote "La vie continue" *before* I moved to Paris. Call it prescience. Call it a flash-forward. Call it a self-fulfilling prophecy.

FRAME

One anglophone writer living alone in a francophone culture had always been a scary creative prospect to me, but Lee fell in love with Paris on this first visit, and together I felt we could live in France successfully for a protracted period, even though she spoke no French at the time and my French was what I had learned on my previous visits.

Then too, I was between drafts on "La vie continue," scouting locations for the rewrite, going around Paris contemplating the life of this American exile who was myself, living in the very same city, while at the same time, thanks to Gorbachev, the future I had envisioned for Europe years earlier in New York was beginning to unfold here in real time. . . .

The setting of *Russian Spring,* the characters, the context, all began to come together, and so too the adventure of writing it. This would be a novel dealing

Spinrad holding the very first copy of the Russian edition of Russian Spring to come off the presses, in the office of Literature Gazette in Moscow, 1992. Lenin still on the wall. From left to right: the editor of the magazine; Volodya, Marketing Director of TexT; Spinrad; Vitaly Babenko, president of TexT; another editor of the magazine

with the future of Europe, the Soviet Union, and the United States, and would be primarily set in Paris, so we had an excellent excuse to live there for a year or so while I wrote it.

CONTINUITY

In the summer of 1988, Spinrad and Wood moved to Paris, and soon thereafter Spinrad was elected president of World SF at a meeting in Budapest, an international organization of which N. Lee Wood was later to be elected general secretary.

Shortly thereafter, Spinrad began writing *Russian Spring,* and after finishing the first draft, he and N. Lee Wood traveled to Moscow in the winter of 1989 as guests of the Soviet Writer's Union to do further

research for the book, which was not finally finished until about three months before the August 1991 coup attempt, and which was published in the United States the month afterward.

FLASHBACK

At the World SF meeting in Budapest in 1988, we had met Vitaly Babenko, then a depressed Russian writer having a hard time getting anything published. When we visited Moscow in 1989, he felt he had to sneak into the Peking Hotel where we were staying courtesy of the Writer's Union, and I felt I had to be circumspect about seeing him.

By 1992, he was the president of TexT, the second biggest private publisher in Russia, and he had brought us there for the publication of the Russian edition of *Russian Spring.* Mad, mad Moscow!

He paid me my advance in the form of a huge bag of rubles. "Spend it all before it disappears!" we were told by one and all.

It wasn't easy, but we did. Like everyone else in Moscow, we became obsessive shoppers. It was a crash course in the psychology of inflation, believe me!

And how right they were. When I was handed the money, the ruble was 135 to the dollar. Less than a year later it was to be about 1,000 to the dollar.

Moscow is a tough, crazy town, but one of the most exciting places I've ever been at this mad moment in history, and as we stood atop the Lenin Hills with some Russian friends the day of our departure, one of them gave me a strange look.

"You *like* it here, don't you?" she said in some bemusement. "You could *live* here. . . . "

Maybe she was right. Maybe I could.

CONTINUITY

Spinrad and Wood decided not to return to the United States as residents, though they returned for visits, and were married on one of them in Florida in 1990.

Norman Spinrad's latest novel, *Pictures at 11,* though set in Los Angeles, was written in Paris where he still resides, and deals partially with the strains of German reunification. Completed in the middle of 1993 under contract to Bantam, it will be published in the fall of 1994.

F R A M E

CONTINUITY

FLASHBACK

FLASH-FORWARD

This close to the real time of me sitting in my Paris apartment writing this attempt at the closure of a story that is not yet finished, they all finally merge.

The story of how two American writers came to Paris for a year or so and ended up staying is certainly material for a whole novel, several of which have probably already been written.

The historical context in which it took place is a novel I have already written, namely *Russian Spring,* conceived on a one-month visit to Paris, developed in New York, treatment written in Los Angeles, first draft written in Paris before Wall came down, before our first trip to Moscow at the time of the death of Sakharov, and finally published in Russia itself in 1992, in a society not that much unlike what is described in the book, but which didn't exist before it was written.

So why is Norman Spinrad still living in Paris?

The answer is *not* to be found in "La vie continue." The Norman Spinrad in that novella is ten years older than the present writer, and the present writer does not consider himself an American exile, political or otherwise.

I'm not living in Paris because I can't bear to live in the United States.

I'm living in Paris because I want to live in Europe.

We've been here five years now. We've braved the Russian winter. We've walked *through* the Berlin Wall in the very process of its demolition. We've both been officers in an international writer's organization. We've made friends in France, Russia, the (former) two Germanies, (former) Yugoslavia, (former) Czechoslovakia, Italy, Holland, points between. We've been part of our friends' lives and they've been part of ours, at a time of rapid-fire evolution that is transforming this supposedly tired old continent into the cutting edge of the twenty-first century.

And I'm doing another cut on one of Richard's albums via the very instrumentalities I predicted in *Little Heroes.*

Why would an American writer of speculative fiction choose to live in Europe?

Why not?

Or, as I usually say when asked this question, hey, to an American science fiction writer, Europe isn't merely another planet, it's a whole other *solar system!*

Planet France, Planet Germany, Planet Russia, Planet Italy, and other major bodies, plus untold scores of ethnic asteroids! And each of them a world entire!

I'm fifty-three now, improbable as it seems to me. I've lived by my words for thirty years. I've witnessed three decades of history in many places, and been part of some of it. I've been rich and poor. I've been flush and broke. I've fought the good fights, and I've won and lost. I've achieved a certain amount of literary recognition, but not, of course, what I consider my just share. I've had my ups and downs. I have my good moments and my bad.

And when I'm really feeling down, I remember a twenty-five-year-old kid stoned on mescaline, walking across Fourth Street to the Village, high on *Dune,* and dreaming those crazy prescient dreams. . . .

He was going to be a famous science fiction writer, he would publish many stories and novels, and many of the people who were his literary idols, inspirations, and role models would accept him as their equal, would become his allies, his friends.

And his life's mission would be to take this commercial science fiction genre and turn it into something else somehow, write works that transcended its commercial parameters, works that could aspire to the literary company of Burroughs and Mailer and Kerouac, that would open a new Way. . . .

This is what you're here for.

And so I was. And so I am.

When I look into the mirror and am appalled to see this middle-aged guy looking back, when my latest novel fails to make the best-seller lists, when the bills start coming in faster than the checks, and I bemoan all that I haven't done, all the just desserts that haven't been piled up on my plate, all I long to be and haven't achieved. . . .

Then that twenty-five-year-old kid grins back at me and gives my fifty-three-year-old self a swift kick in the psychic ass. At my age now, maybe I know much too much to feel the same, but *he's* certainly got cause to feel entirely satisfied with the story so far.

Everything he saw in that timeless Einsteinian moment has come to pass.

Everything he wanted to be, I have become.

I look out my window onto my Paris garden. And when I finish this, I will walk out into the summer streets of Paris, a minor princeling of the City of Light.

Beyond the wild dreams of that twenty-five-year-old kid!

I've become what he wanted to grow up to be and so much more.

I should be satisfied, right?

Sure.

I've spent my whole life looking forward, not back. Sure, this fifty-three-year-old has got what that twenty-five-year-old wanted.

But I'm not him, and it's not enough, and I'm old and wise enough now to know that it never will be.

If I live to be a hundred with a Nobel on the mantelpiece, I'll probably say the same thing.

I'll probably even believe it.

This story doesn't end here.

It begins tomorrow.

Norman Spinrad contributed the following update to *CA* in 2005:

FLASHBACK

Russian Spring was first published in the Soviet Union, and in the United States the same month as the failed coup that was to turn it into an alternate history novel. For days, there was fear that the reactionary junta would take over, but it took me only hours of watching it on television in Paris to know it would fail. Why?

Because I *was* watching it on CNN! These fools hadn't even captured the TV broadcast facilities in Moscow! And I knew it was all over when they themselves were on television dead drunk!

CONTINUITY

By the time *Russian Spring* had been published in the United States, Spinrad had signed a two-book contract with its American publisher, Bantam Books.

Farewell to Moscow, atop the (former) Lenin Hills: (from left) Babenko, Vanya (our grand prix driver and puppetmaker for the Moscow Puppet Theater), Luda (friend and translator), and Spinrad

FRAME

I had never agreed to a multi-book contract before because I never thought more than one novel ahead, but Lou Aronica, who had been my editor there on three novels, offered a deal for my ecoterrorism novel *Pictures at 11,* which I wanted to write next, and a second novel which he convinced me I wanted to do after that.

I had written a proposal for a nonfiction book called *The Transformation Crisis* about a concept that had informed much of my fiction for years.

Any intelligent species must confront a transformational crisis when it develops atomic weapons, genetic engineering, a greenhouse warming technology. It will either evolve into a transformational civilization capable of enduring for millions of years, or destroy itself. Our planet had entered this crisis with Hiroshima and the outcome hung very much in the balance.

Lou had turned it down as a nonfiction proposal, but now he wanted me to write it as the second *novel!*

"Only if I can do it as a comedy," I blurted.

A future Earth that has failed its transformation crisis sends back a time traveler to change history. Not a politician or a scientists who no one would believe, but a comedian who no one would believe either, but who would get to spiel his story on television.

Voila, the genesis of *He Walked among Us.*

CONTINUITY

Spinrad's contract called for *Pictures at 11* to be published as a hardcover, but Aronica wanted to publish it as a major trade paperback, verbally guaranteeing a much large printing and a major marketing effort, and Spinrad agreed. U.S. publishing rhythms being slow, he had already written *He Walked among Us* by the time Bantam published *Pictures at 11,* and Bantam had already accepted it for publication.

FRAME

Before Bantam could publish *Pictures at 11,* Lou was gone. I hadn't signed any amendment to the existing contract, but more verbal promises of a massive print run and a major promotion effort if I went along gulled me into agreeing to it again.

But Bantam published *Pictures at 11* with a schlocko cover, no advertising, and a minimal printing. The reviews ranged from excellent to rave and a film option was taken, but by the time the novel made the *New York Times Book Review*'s Recommended Summer Reading list, it was out of print.

FLASHBACK

While this publishing monkey business was going on, writing *He Walked among Us* was an intense, passionate, writing experience, which produced what I believe is still probably my best novel. A novel about science fiction as a literature, as a calling, as a cultural necessity, as a subculture; a novel about the so-called New Age; show business; the life of the street.

A novel which, dealing as it did with *the* critical cultural question, had transliterary importance, and a novel I therefore believed was in that sense more important than its literary value or my career.

I knew that if I allowed Bantam to publish *He Walked among Us,* they would trash the publication the way they had *Pictures at 11*. To test the waters, I submitted

a treatment for a new novel, *Greenhouse Summer,* dealing with some of the same matters, to Bantam, as the option clause of my two-book contract required.

As I expected, they rejected it.

FRAME

By the 1990s, the major bookstore chains, not the book publishers, ruled the publishing roost. Their computer programs tracked how many copies they had sold of the author's previous book, which determined how many they ordered of the next one, which determined the print run, which determined the level of promotion, which determined the fate of the book.

The way Bantam had published *Pictures at 11* had so devalued my recent track record that only a major publicity campaign of the sort that they hadn't delivered on *that* novel could break *He Walked among Us* out of the commercial trap they had put it in. And when they turned down the option book, I knew they would not spend the money to do it.

FLASHBACK

I had allowed Bantam to breach the contract on *Pictures at 11* by publishing it in trade paperback, but I had never signed anything, so I *did* have the legal means to take *He Walked among Us* away from Bantam, where, as an "orphan novel," it would sink without a trace.

I *could* do it. But *should* I?

What had happened to *Pictures at 11* had damaged the commercial viability of whatever my next novel would to be. But I felt I would be betraying something larger than myself if I didn't fight to have *He Walked among Us* read by an audience of significant size.

So I did it. I convinced myself that literary and cultural worth would trump the numbers, allowing such a novel to find major publication elsewhere.

I believed it, Lee believed it, my agent believed it.

It didn't.

CONTINUITY

He Walked among Us bounced from publisher to publisher with none willing to publish it; the list of possible major houses became exhausted and even the science fiction editors turned it down, while Spinrad's marriage to N. Lee Wood devolved into a separation that left him in Paris and her in England.

F R A M E

Had *Pictures at 11* been a best seller, some major "mainstream" publisher would have gobbled up *He Walked among Us* for top dollar, "sci-fi" or not, but coming after a numbers flop, they wouldn't touch the novel because they regarded it as "science fiction" and the "science fiction" publishers were terrified to publish it because it dealt with the subculture of science fiction in a manner they feared would alienate their "fan base." David Hartwell turned it down as "too ambitious" for his publisher, even though he would later buy my next novel, *Greenhouse Summer,* for the same publisher. It appeared my career, at least as a major mainstream writer, like my marriage, was over.

But at least I was still in show business.

CONTINUITY

Spinrad's friend, sound designer Richard Shorr, had worked with French producer-director Jacques Dorfmann on a previous film, and now Dorfmann wanted to make a film about Vercingetorix, the Gallic hero who had opposed Julius Caesar's conquest of Gaul, and he was looking for a screenwriter. Shorr and Dorfmann called Spinrad to ask his advice.

F R A M E

Of course I wanted the assignment for myself, but I wasn't in the running because I had no feature film credits, and why Richie and Jacques thought I would

have a better idea than they did I never quite understood, but I did have one. My friend Rospo Pallenberg, whose feature credits included *The Emerald Forest,* had written the historical-mythical screenplay for *Excalibur,* which led me to recommend him for *Vercingètorix,* or, as the film was to be titled outside of France, *Druids,* and I put together the deal between Rospo and Dorfmann.

Perhaps as a thank you, I was hired to do a back-up treatment.

CONTINUITY

While Pallenberg was writing three drafts of his script, Dorfmann was putting together his project. He had the financing, he had a shoot date, he had an internationally recognizable name in Gerard Depardieu to play Vercingetorix's father, and Gerard's son, Guillaime, a bankable name in France, to play the lead.

But what he didn't have was a script that satisfied him.

FLASHBACK

As president of the Science Fiction Writers of America, I was once asked by Dentsu, the Japanese PR giant, to get them Isaac Asimov for a plush junket to speak at a major space conference in Tokyo. When Isaac turned them down, as I knew he would because he refused to fly, they asked me get them Ray Bradbury, who wouldn't fly either. When Ray turned them down, they asked for Robert Heinlein, who I knew was ill at the time, and after he turned them down, they finally asked *me* if I would do it. Three strikes and I was in.

Likewise I had gotten Jacques Rospo Pallenberg, knowing it would have been futile to put myself forward, and now my knowledge of Japanese protocol stood me in good stead again, as Jacques called me in a tizzy to ask me to please rewrite Rospo's script to his order.

The catch was that while Rospo had had many months to bomb, the shooting date was fixed, and I had only five weeks to fix it.

CONTINUITY

Spinrad finished his rewrite of the screenplay on time, but Guillaime Depardieu broke his leg in a motorcycle accident, and the shooting date for *Druids* was postponed.

FRAME

Then cancelled. Revived. Postponed. Cancelled. This went on for *years,* during which I learned that for a film to start shooting, the script, the casting, and the financing must all come together at the same time, and that the magic moment is narrow and fleeting.

But Jacques persisted, as the *Druids* project fell apart through the lack of one element or another and then was put back together, only to have it happen again and again. This gave him far too much time to drive me crazy with far too many rewrites for the film's eventual good.

Long enough for me to be put through the same process on *another* film at the same time, *La Sirene Rouge,* which I adapted from a French novel. By the time Jacques had replaced Guillaime Depardieu with Christophe Lambert and was about to shoot *Druids* in Bulgaria, I was on about on draft seven of *La Sirene Rouge,* another film project that would also fall apart and be put together any number of times, and wouldn't be shot until *Druids* had been finished, had been released, and had bombed.

FLASHBACK

About ten days before the first day's shoot of *Druids,* Jacques invited me to spend a long weekend at his "villa" outside Sophia to "thank me" for all the work I had done. Uh, there *were* two or three little scenes that he had rewritten in French (the film would be shot in both French and English versions) that he'd like me to put into proper English. . . .

He talked me into it. I didn't see the script until I was on the plane to Bulgaria, when a horrible mess was literally dumped in my lap, half in French and half in

English (the film was to be shot in French and English versions), the whole thing heavily rewritten by Jacques. I had four days to produce a coherent English version, which would then be translated back into French.

To make matters worse, all Jacques wanted me to do was translate his bad French dialog into bad English dialog, while the overqualified Bulgarian thespians he had hired for secondary roles were rightly and professionally imploring me to fix it.

Jacques refused to even discuss this with me, so in the end I went ahead and did it on my own, and Jacques didn't see what I had done until the night before my escape flight on the heels of what was going to be a total eclipse of the sun. He was pissed off at my lèse-majesté. I was pissed off at him for being pissed off at me. I suggested that the assistant director read it and give a neutral opinion.

"I don't care what anyone else thinks!" Jacques shouted. "It's *my* movie!"

When the producer and director who also fancies himself a writer tells you that, it's over, right?

Well not quite. On the way to the airport the next day, I was handed one last scene that he'd rewritten to please, pretty please, put into English, and found myself in the production office in Sophia actually doing it as the eclipse started, after which I was rushed to the airport, experienced the totality outside the terminal, and escaped with what was left of my sanity.

FRAME

Druids was a French national epic, so when it tanked in France, it tanked big time, though it mercifully disappeared in the rest of the world without a stench-ful trace. *La sirene rouge* bombed too, but it simply disappeared.

From these writing experiences, I learned that there is a point beyond which any further rewriting of anything is only going to make it worse. The director of *La sirene rouge* never got this, but a few years later, Jacques 'fessed up, which is why we are still friends, and why I've even worked with him after the *Druids* fiasco. He had a powerful vision, but he screwed up, and he and his film paid dearly for it.

I also learned that no one person should be producer, director, and co-writer on the same film. If Jacques as the director had had a producer to rein in Jacques the writer, or Jacques the producer had not had total power over what was shot, Jacques Dorfmann the film-maker would have ended up much happier.

FLASHBACK

By utter coincidence, *La sirene Rouge* was based on a novel by my musical collaborator, Maurice Dantec. While my career as a novelist was reeling, not only was I up to my ears in the movie end of show biz, I was dabbling in what might loosely be called rock and roll. I had done this with Richard Pinhas before in a studio, but this time around I would end up as a live performer.

Richard had revived his old group, Heldon, and in the middle of all this film work, I was writing about half the lyrics for the album *Only Chaos Is Real* with Maurice writing most of the rest, then spending time in the studio with the recording and mixing. I also did one cut as a vocalist, which ended up on a different album under a different band name, and so. . . .

Only Chaos Is Real was finished and Maurice was gone to Montreal when Richard was asked to play at a major club called Elysée Montmartre. A popular journalist had died and left money in his will for a farewell bash for about a thousand people at the club directly after his burial.

Richard hates performing alone, there was no one else to do it, and so he persuaded me to go on with him. We were the opening act as the audience filed in directly from the cemetery.

It sounds like a joke or a musician's worst nightmare.

My debut as a live vocalist was as opening act at a wake.

Not as bad as it sounds. We went down as well as could be expected.

And after that, I feared nothing as a live performer.

CONTINUITY

Spinrad went on to perform with Richard Pinhas, and various configurations of the group variously called Heldon, Schizotrope, or Psychtrope around France in Nevers, Bordeaux, Paris, and the Transmusical Festival in Rennes, among other venues.

FLASHBACK

Schizotrope indeed! With a film shot and another in the works, high ego high times as a performer, but *He Walked among Us* still without a publisher, and my main career as a novelist still thwarted, I went to the World Fantasy Convention in London.

This was a gathering of SF editors, fans, and writers, and yes, I was one of the luminaries, but none of my books were available in the book dealers' room. I hadn't written a novel since *He Walked among Us*, hadn't had one published in an even longer span, had nothing in the works, and didn't have a publisher.

F R A M E

I was reading a newspaper piece about how the greenhouse warming was going to be a world-wide disaster on a cold gray winter day in Paris. I looked out the window at the gray sky.

"Can't happen too soon enough here! Bring on Tropical Paris!"

There were going to be winners as well as losers.

That was the genesis of *Greenhouse Summer.*

When Bantam had rejected a treatment for this novel, I had submitted it to my old friend and editor David Hartwell at Tor, who sheepishly came up with an insulting low-ball offer he knew would not be acceptable.

After which I got involved in writing two feature films at once, and songs and journalism on the side, and performing on the side of that.

But now. . . .

FLASHBACK

Walking around the convention hotel like a ghost of myself, I decided that I had to write *Greenhouse Summer* and see it published. Show biz success or not, I had to get back to writing novels, even if it meant swallowing my pride and taking a low-ball offer, however little economic sense it might make when I could pursue a more lucrative career writing movies—even without the belief that the novel would be published in anything other than a minimalist manner.

David Hartwell was there in London. Over a few drinks I accepted more or less the same offer for *Greenhouse Summer* that I had previously rejected. Now it really had become an offer I could not refuse.

CONTINUITY

Tor published *Greenhouse Summer* in the expected unexceptional manner. *Vercingètorix* opened in France to terrible reviews that hardly mentioned Spinrad, flopped at the box office, and went straight to DVD as *Druids* in the United States.

F R A M E

Richie Shorr had read my third-draft screenplay, and when he saw the film, told me that whereas what had been shot was drek, *it* was a masterpiece and should not be lost. "You've got to turn it into a novel!" he insisted.

I had never novelized a screenplay, mine or anyone else's, and never wanted any part of any such thing.

"Read it and tell me that!" Richie demanded.

Richie was right. I was proud of what I had written, whereas I had been grateful for the mercy of the French press in keeping my name out of their slaughter of the film.

But novelize a screenplay, even if it was my own. . . ?

Shrugging, I sent it to my book agent in New York, Russell Galen, who effused to the point where he compared it to Shakespeare, but said, how am I supposed to market a novel on the basis of a screenplay for an already-released flop? And asked me if there was anyone high enough up in publishing who might know my work well enough to make this possible.

FLASHBACK

Well, I said in all innocence, there's a guy who was editor at Pan, a secondary science fiction paperback line back in London in the 1960s when my novel *Bug Jack Barron* was getting me denounced in Parliament, a fringie of the New Wave scene, who I think now has some kind of job in New York, and would know who I was and be familiar with my work. Sonny Mehta.

Russ did a take.

Sonny Mehta?!

You really don't know that Sonny Mehta is the honcho of Knopf and probably the most powerful and highly regarded publishing executive in New York?

Uh, no.

But it was nice to see that Sonny had found a job in New York. Mike Moorcock admitted that Sonny was an okay guy back in his Pan days, "but of course not to be trusted."

FRAME

As agent for the estate of Philip K. Dick, Russ had a relationship with Vintage, a subsidiary of Knopf, and its publisher Marty Asher, and so the submission went through him and he did the negotiating.

I was in New York doing a gig at a venue called the Knitting Factory with Richard and Maurice when Knopf decided to buy *The Druid King,* the negotiations started while we were rehearsing, and I was staying at the apartment of Dona Sadock, still my close friend, when the deal was concluded.

CONTINUITY

Spinrad returned to Paris to write the first draft of *The Druid King* and Time Warner UK made a major deal to publish the unwritten novel in Britain on the basis of the screenplay and some conversations with the editor, Tim Holman.

FRAME

Ah yes, the literary high life! Or so I thought.

But Asher had insisted on a contract clause paying out a portion of the advance upon my showing him 200 pages, like a Hollywood producer cracking the whip over a screenwriter, and an even bigger insult to an author of twenty published novels.

Worse, I had always felt that going back to rewrite before completing a draft was a creative mistake, and showing raw partial first draft was both dangerous and unprofessional.

But Asher was a lord of the New York Literary Literary Jungle, in which ecology I was a lowly "sci-fi guy," a species of literary snobbery with which I was all too familiar. I had no choice, but I would put the novel itself first. Thanks to my British publisher, I could afford to write a complete first draft before showing anything to Asher, who would be pleased at seeing something much more than the contract called for, something that could then benefit from meaningful editorial input.

But while arrogance was something I expected at this level, I was not prepared for professional incompetence. Asher was not pleased with the first draft I had turned in. He thought it was sloppy. It was not easy getting through to him that what he had read *was* first draft. He never seemed to even quite get the concept, for when I asked for his editorial input, I was told that he didn't want to comment until he had seen a rewrite.

Like a Hollywood producer, he had just wanted pages to prove I wasn't goofing off.

In like West Coastal manner, it was made clear that Knopf/Vintage would cut me off and reject the book on the basis of what I really hadn't wanted to show them in the first place, unless I convinced Edward Kastenmeier, Asher's right-hand man, that I would and could take his direction.

I was back in show biz pitching a rewrite to another species of producer/director who fancied himself a writer. At least this was a game in which I was well-schooled, and I had little trouble convincing Kastenmeier to pick up the option or convincing myself that while he wasn't working on a level that would be very useful in making the transition to my first historical novel, at least he wasn't any mogul's nephew.

We had our story conferences and I took the rewrite notes and I went to work.

FLASHBACK

Meanwhile my friend, French director Diane Kurys, had met the French ambassador to Mexico, Bruno Delaye, who was an admirer of my work. I had done events for cultural programs of the French government in France and New Caledonia. Bruno wanted to meet me, and so he arranged for me to do likewise for his embassy in Mexico.

One of these events was a press conference, and when a writer does a press conference, he's asked what he's working on now, and what he's planning to do next. . . .

FRAME

Three decades previously, after I had finished writing *The Iron Dream,* I'd gotten to wondering if there had been any other instances of civilizations falling prey to a national psychosis in the manner of Nazi Germany. The closest thing I'd found was the Aztecs, with their massive rites of human sacrifice.

It had started as idle intellectual curiosity, but I was living with Dona Sadock then, who had an avid interest in mystical and psychological theology. We'd delved deeper, and what had emerged was the fascinating story of how Hernando Cortez had *really* conquered Mexico by a sixteenth-century version of theological media manipulation.

This had progressed to the notion of writing a stage play called *The Feathered Serpent,* a small-scale confrontation between Cortez and Montezuma that would tell the story compressed into surreal haiku terms. But I had never written a play, wouldn't have known what to do with one, and nothing had ever come of it. . . .

FLASHBACK

Now, in a press conference in Mexico City, this popped into my mind and out of my mouth as a notion for a novel, and I was surprised to see it all over the newspapers the next day.

Well, why not?

It ended up becoming a self-fulfilling prophecy. The idea for a little surreal play became a full-scale historical novel and the title became *Mexica* because *The Feathered Serpent* had been used on two previous novels.

CONTINUITY

Spinrad finished the second draft of *The Druid King* and sent it to Edward Kastenmeier two months before a planned trip to New York in connection with the World Science Fiction Convention being held in Philadelphia on Labor Day weekend, 2001.

Spinrad arrived in New York a week before the convention, staying with Dona Sadock in her apartment on Ninth Street in Manhattan. They went to Philadelphia together, then returned to New York, where Spinrad made an appointment to go over the rewritten manuscript with Kastenmeier on September 12, 2001.

He then flew to Florida to see his mother, returning to Dona Sadock's apartment late at night on September 10, 2001.

FLASHBACK

I awoke about 9:30 A.M. on September 11, and looked out the window of Dona's apartment on the corner of Ninth Street and Sixth Avenue. From that angle the Twin Towers would not have been visible, but what *was* visible was a crowd on Sixth Avenue looking south. I showed this to Dona, expressing my curiosity at what they could all be looking at.

"Oh," she said diffidently, "they shoot movies here all the time."

I called my agent but I was told by his receptionist that he wouldn't be coming into work today because of what had happened.

And she told me.

And I dashed down in the street, into the buzzing, milling crowd, looked south, and saw—nothing.

The familiar giant monoliths simply were not there. There was an immense roiling rising cloud of dense black smoke where they had been. And from these few miles away, I could smell it, that and the pheremonal odor of the shock and anger of the dazed onlookers.

FRAME

Dona and I were in the process of rekindling our old relationship before September 11, but being thrust together into the Ground Zero of history added the sheer charge of love during wartime, life at the center of destiny, at the heart of the whirlwind.

No non-emergency vehicles were permitted south of 14th Street, but the subway was running, and crazy as it sounds, on September 12, I took it uptown out of the blockaded zone to my editorial meeting with Edward Kastenmeier.

FLASHBACK

Midtown was functioning as if everything were normal. Nothing could have seen crazier than that. Or so I thought.

But Kastenmeier had marked up the manuscript sentence by sentence as if he were a college teacher and I were a student. He had run paragraphs together, rewritten sentences attempting to bend the prose of an historical novel closer to his style-deaf concept of standard modern English. Yet despite the amazing arrogance on display, he had so little confidence in his own editorial judgment that he had had his assistant reading ahead of him and marking up this mess in a different handwriting.

It was an editorial process that made rewriting a bilingual script in Bulgaria for Jacques Dorfmann during an eclipse seem like a session with Maxwell Perkins in the Algonquin. I was constrained to debate virtually every sentence with Kastenmeier. Buildings on either side us were evacuated because of bomb threats and then reoccupied. It went on all day and into the evening, for I could not let Kastenmeier leave until the nightmare task he had inflicted on me was done and I could escape with what was left of my sanity.

F R A M E

I returned to Paris and put together a clean final draft of *The Druid King*. But I was put through literally endless picayune rewrites that accomplished nothing but the loss of almost a year of my life in agonizing wheel-spinning.

Dona had come to Paris to live with me, but still had her apartment in New York, and we began ping-ponging back and forth. On one of these sojourns in New York, I had given Kastenmeier six weeks advance notice that I would be there for a month, and would therefore be available to go over the final manuscript with him in person. But he couldn't even get his reading of it done before we returned to Paris.

Time Warner UK, long satisfied with the novel, scheduled it for February 2003, while Knopf was wasting my time, while I and my agent, thoroughly exasperated, were on the verge of pulling the book and taking it elsewhere. But I prevailed on Sonny to bring the process to an end, and *The Druid King* was finally scheduled for May 2003.

FLASHBACK

But when I got the catalog, I discovered that *The Druid King* had been dumped into August, a dead month for sales, promotion, and reviews. And a cheaper British edition would be out a half year before the Knopf edition. I knew in my gut that the novel had been torpedoed. I called to vent my ire at Kastenmeier, only to learn that he too learned of the change only when he saw the catalog.

Further inquiry revealed that Sonny Mehta had done it unilaterally.

F R A M E

What act of lèse-majesté had I committed against Sonny Mehta? Why would he torpedo a novel he himself had rescued from purgatory?

This is the "SF writer" speculating now, entirely appropriate, for I can only surmise that this had everything to do with it.

When the New Wave had made science fiction a Fave Wave with the trendie set in London, Sonny had been a paperback science fiction editor. Now he was a New York literary lion, in which circles he would not want such a past clinging to his Gucci bootheels. Especially when he had been looked down on as *nikulturni* by the snob element at Knopf when he had taken over from the sainted Robert Gottlieb.

Please don't let on that you knew me when.

Time Warner had already published *The Druid King* in Britain, and bought the treatment for *Mexica,* and I was well into writing the novel. The plan had been to submit the *Mexica* treatment to Knopf as the option novel when the catalog came out, but when *The Druid King* was moved to August, I decided to wait for a complete first draft to be in the strongest possible position.

When the finished first draft of *Mexica* was submitted to Knopf, they had sixty days to exercise their option. The option period expired without a word, but we decided not to press them, since by then *The Druid King* was going to be published in a month or two.

FRAME

I had allowed myself to be put through an amateurish and demeaning editorial experience chasing the marketing might of Knopf as the pot of gold at the end of the rainbow. Now I knew it would not be used to my novel's benefit—no book tour, no ad money, nada.

But I went to New York in August for the publication on my own nickel, for I was experienced on radio and TV and had an 800-pound gorilla of a demo tape, what has generally been regarded as the best interview with Woody Allen ever by those who have heard it. I sent it to the Knopf publicity department well in advance—use *this* to get me the bookings!

The end result: one local New York radio show that I booked myself.

CONTINUITY

In October, months after the option period on *Mexica* had expired, Spinrad's agent pressed Knopf for a decision and was told "we are not prepared to make an offer at this time." There was no formal rejection nor was the manuscript returned.

FLASHBACK

Phone calls and e-mails to Sonny by my agent were never even answered. Meanwhile I found out that *Mexica* had not even been read by anyone but Kastenmeier's lowly assistant.

So I sent an e-mail to Sonny apprising him of the situation.

The only reply was the return of the manuscript.

FRAME

At the time, I took it all personally, and maybe some of it did involve personal factors, but now I understand that what happened to me was not all that atypical of what has happened to many writers as a result of what has happened to American publishing.

American publishing is now dominated by a very few conglomerates that have gobbled up the hallowed imprints of yore and turned them into little more than brands. Knopf is owned by Random House, along with a bouquet of other brands like Doubleday, Bantam, Dell, among many others, and Random House is owned by the German giant Bertelsmann AG. And that one combine is about 40 percent of U.S. book publishing.

Even so, two bookstore chains control the market to the point where they even dictate the cover prices of books to the publishers. If they don't order a sufficient number of copies or don't order at all, a book is not commercially viable. And the publishers know when this will happen before they even read a manuscript because the chains base most of their distribution on "order to net."

If the chains ordered 10,000 copies of your last book and sold 8,000, they order 8,000 of the next one, and if they sell 6,000, they order 6,000 of the one after that, and if that sells 4,000. . . .

Where the math leads is of course to the tar pits for writers without previous best-seller numbers, which I didn't have when Knopf published *The Druid King.* Only by telling the chains in advance of their buy that there would be an author tour and a significant promotion budget could Knopf or anyone else break any writer out of this trap. When they didn't, that novel, like thousands of others, was chewed up by the gears of the machine.

When it was, Knopf rejected *Mexica* unread since the iron diktat of the numbers now renders literary judgement of such a submission redundant. And threatens to render my career as a novelist, along with those of many other, redundant with it.

The end of the line for me as a novelist?

Or not. I have been here before.

And *Mexica* is shortly to be published in a serious manner in Britain. And when I arrived in New York to confront the terminal phase of the Knopf mess, I had just received a Lifetime Achievement award at a major literary event in Nantes from the hands of the mayor.

So let's just call it the end of this chapter of my autobiography.

And rather than leave it and myself with an unresolved cliff-hanger, I'll expiate the necessary egotism of this experiment in autobiography by closing it with a summary version of a little story written not by me, but by Ray Bradbury.

FLASH FORWARD

The United States has been nuked and gringo tourists are pouring north past a roadside gas station as two Mexican attendants watch in bemusement. When one stops to gas up, one of the Mexicans asks the American tourist what's happened.

"Haven't you heard?" says the American. "It's the end of the world!"

And dashes frantically back up the road.

One Mexican looks at the other and shrugs.

"What do they mean by *the world?*"

BIOGRAPHICAL AND CRITICAL SOURCES:

BOOKS

Bretnor, Reginald, editor, *The Craft of Science Fiction,* Harper (New York, NY), 1976.

Clareson, Thomas D., editor, *SF: The Other Side of Realism,* Bowling Green University, 1971.

Dictionary of Literary Biography, Volume VIII: *Twentieth-Century Science-Fiction Writers,* Gale (Detroit, MI), 1981.

Platt, Charles, *Dream Makers: The Uncommon People Who Write Science Fiction,* Berkley Publishing (New York, NY), 1980.

Spinrad, Norman, editor, *The New Tomorrows,* Belmont Books, 1971.

Spinrad, Norman, editor, *Modern Science Fiction,* Anchor Books (New York, NY), 1974.

PERIODICALS

Analog Science Fiction/Science Fact, April, 1983.

Best Sellers, March, 1983.

Booklist, November 1, 1994, Dennis Winters, review of *Pictures at Eleven,* p. 482; November 1, 1999, John Mort, review of *Greenhouse Summer,* p. 513; June 1, 2003, Margaret Flanagan, review of *The Druid King,* p. 1746.

Entertainment Weekly, December 2, 1994, D. A. Ball, review of *Pictures at Eleven,* p. 66.

Extrapolation, winter, 1995, Wendy E. Erisman, "Inverting the Ideal World: Carnival and the Carnivalesque in Contemporary Utopian Science Fiction," pp. 333-344; spring, 1995, Jennifer Lynn Browning, "Science Fiction in the Real World," pp. 70-74.

Fantasy Review, July, 1985; August, 1985, Gary K. Wolfe, review of *Child of Fortune.*

Globe and Mail (Toronto, Ontario, Canada), August 24, 1985, H. J. Kirchhoff, review of *Child of Fortune.*

History Today, May, 2003, Richard Cavendish, review of *The Druid King,* p. 88.

Independent (London, England), February 1, 2003, Roz Kaveney, "No More Neros," p. 23.

International Herald Tribune, November 12, 1997, Brad Spurgeon, "Author's Protest: U.S. Book Rights Go on Sale for One Dollar," p. 13.

Kirkus Reviews, May 15, 2003, review of *The Druid King,* p. 712.

Kliatt, January, 2005, Donna Scanlon, review of *The Druid King,* p. 22.

Library Journal, November 15, 1999, Jackie Cassada, review of *Greenhouse Summer,* p. 101; June 1, 2003, Harold Augenbraum, review of *The Druid King,* p. 170.

Los Angeles Times Book Review, April 3, 1983, Theodore Sturgeon, review of *The Void Captain's Tale;* October 27, 1985.

New York Times Book Review, May 22, 1983, Gerald
   Jonas, review of *The Void Captain's Tale;* September 8, 1985, Gerard Jonas, review of *Child of
   Fortune.*
Publishers Weekly, January 2, 1981; August 16, 1991,
   review of *Russian Spring,* p. 46; September 13,
   1991, p. 62; October 18, 1999, review of *Greenhouse Summer,* p. 75; June 16, 2003, review of
   The Druid King, p. 48.
Science Fiction and Fantasy Book Review, October,
   1982.
Science Fiction Chronicle, December, 1985.
Science Fiction Studies, spring, 1973.
Times Literary Supplement, March 26, 1970, review of
   Bug Jack Barron.
Variety, January 29, 2001, Lisa Nesselson, review of
   Vercingètorix, p. 44.
Washington Post Book World, July 27, 1980, H. Bruce
   Franklin, review of *The Iron Dream;* July 25,
   1982; February 27, 1983, Howard Waldrop, review
   of *The Void Captain's Tale.*

ONLINE

Norman Spinrad's Home Page, http://ourworld.compu
   serve.com/homepages/normanspinrad (April 11,
   2004).
Templeton Gate Web site, http://members.tripod.com/
   templetongate/ (April 11, 2004), "Norman Spinrad."

*   *   *

STANISH, Charles 1956-

PERSONAL: Born 1956. *Education:* Pennsylvania
State University, B.A., 1979; University of Chicago,
A.M., 1983, Ph.D., 1985.

ADDRESSES: Office—Cotsen Institute of Archaeology,
University of California—Los Angeles, A210 Fowler
Building/Box 951510, Los Angeles, CA 90095-1510.
E-mail—stanish@anthro.ucla.edu.

CAREER: University of Illinois, Chicago, adjunct associate professor, 1988-97; University of Chicago,
research associate, 1990-97; Field Museum of Natural
History, Chicago, assistant curator, 1988-92, associate
curator and vice-chair, department of anthropology,
1992-95, associate curator and chair, department of
anthropology, 1995-97; University of California—Los
Angeles, associate professor, 1998-2000, professor of
anthropology, 2000—, director, Cotsen Institute of
Archaeology; Los Angeles County Museum of Natural
History, Department of Anthropology, Los Angeles,
research associate, 2001—. Participant on WGN Radio
"Extension 720" panel discussion; academic tour
leader for Peru/Machu Picchu archaeology tours;
academic tour leader for Mexico/Belize archaeology/
natural history tour; consultant for U.S. Customs
Service; expert witness in Federal Courts.

MEMBER: American Association for the Ethical Treatment of Burials (founding board member), Chicago
Archaeological Society (vice president 1993-94).

WRITINGS:

(Editor with Don S. Rice and Phillip R. Scarr) *Ecology, Settlement, and History in the Osmore Drainage, Peru,* B.A.R. (Oxford, England), 1989.
Ancient Andean Political Economy, University of
   Texas Press (Austin, TX), 1992.
(With Brian S. Bauer) *Ritual and Pilgrimage in the
   Ancient Andes: The Islands of the Sun and the
   Moon,* University of Texas Press (Austin, TX),
   2001.
*Ancient Titicaca: The Evolution of Complex Society in
   Southern Peru and Northern Bolivia,* University
   of California Press (Berkeley, CA), 2003.
(Editor with Brian S. Bauer) *Archaeological Research
   on the Islands of the Sun and Moon, Lake Titicaca, Bolivia: Final Results of the Proyecto Takai
   Kjarka,* Cotsen Institute of Archaeology at the
   University of California—Los Angeles (Los
   Angeles, CA), 2004.

Latin American Antiquity, book review editor, 1992-
93. Member of editorial board, Prehistory Press and
Latin American Antiquity, 1998—.

SIDELIGHTS: Anthropologist Charles Stanish has
specialized in the study of ancient South American
civilizations. His area of search is along the shores of
Lake Titicaca, the high-altitude lake deep in the Andes
mountains bordering both Peru and Bolivia. Stanish
believes that one of the primary evidences for the
existence of these high-level ancient civilizations—

perhaps as old as ancient Sumer, the first civilization in what is now Iraq and thought by most historians to be the first civilization in the world—is the existence of long-distance trade between the Lake Titicaca residents and dwellers in the Amazon basin to the east. "We think that inter-regional trade is one of the key factors in the development of civilization, as we know it," Stanish told National Public Radio interviewer Alex Chadwick, as posted on the radio's Web site. "The more he searches," Chadwick explained, "the more he finds the ancient cultures of the lake to be more complex than previously believed—highly advanced architecture, sophisticated trade and even canal systems that reversed the flow of rivers."

Ritual and Pilgrimage in the Ancient Andes: The Islands of the Sun and the Moon looks at the surviving evidence of religious celebrations before the Inca came to power in the Andes, about a hundred years before the Spanish conquest. "Late prehistoric Andean shrines and oracles continued to be revered into the Colonial era and were documented as centers of paganism by Catholic extirpators of idolatry," wrote Jerry D. Moore in *American Anthropologist*. The shrines which Stanish and his co-author Brian Bauer concentrate on were "two islands in Lake Titicaca, from which [in Inca cosmology] the Creator Viracocha had caused the sun and moon to emerge after a period of universal night," Moor explained. "Along with Pachacamac and the Qoricancha, the islands of the Sun and Moon were sacred pilgrimage centers in the Inca empire." But, according to Stanish and Bauer, the sacred landscape of the shrines predates the rise of the Inca by many centuries. They may have become important under the Tiwanaku culture, which flourished between about 500 BCE and about 1000 CE—in other words, about four hundred years before the rise of the Inca.

Later Andean rulers took over the sites and transformed them into places for celebrating imperial myth. "The vestiges of empire and state-level involvement cover the shrines," stated Moore. "The Inca controlled access to the islands, covered the sacred rock from which the sun emerged with gold sheet, built storehouses, temples, and quarters for the shrines' attendants." "Sacred sites and symbols are a vital part of the battleground between dominating and dominated cultures," declared Astvaldur Astvaldsson in the *Journal of Latin American Studies*, "and it is because of the culture-specific meanings inscribed and preserved

in them that they become such pivoral spaces to be conquered and transformed so that subordination can be complete." In other words, stated Penelope Dransart in the *Journal of the Royal Anthropological Society,* "Bauer and Stanish argue that the Incas manipulated the pilgrimage within a hegemonic ideology."

Stanish examines the evidence for these ancient pre-Incan cultures and looks at their significance in his 2003 study *Ancient Titicaca: The Evolution of Complex Society in Southern Peru and Northern Bolivia.* The book takes an intense look at the history of the Titicaca area, ranging back to around 2000 BCE. There were two primary cultures on the shores of the late before the rise of the Inca: the Tiwanaku and Pucara. Both civilizations thrived along the shores of the lake and created cultures that rivaled the Inca in wealth and sophistication. By looking at the rise and decline of pre-Incan empires, Stanish makes scholars questions their assumptions about the nature of empires in particular and civilizations in general.

BIOGRAPHICAL AND CRITICAL SOURCES:

PERIODICALS

American Anthropologist, March, 2003, Jerry D. Moore, review of *Ritual and Pilgrimage in the Ancient Andes: The Islands of the Sun and the Moon,* p. 180.
American Antiquity, January, 1994, Timothy K. Earle, review of *Ancient Andean Political Economy,* p. 174.
Antiquity, June, 1995, Jose Oliver, review of *Ancient Andean Political Economy,* p. 398.
Journal of Latin American Studies, May, 1993, Penny Dransart, review of *Ancient Andean Political Economy,* p. 391; November, 2003, Astvaldur Astvaldsson, revew of *Ritual and Pilgrimage in the Ancient Andes,* p. 897.
Journal of the Royal Anthropological Institute, September, 2003, Penelope Dransart, review of *Ritual and Pilgrimage in the Ancient Andes,* p. 593.
Latin American Research Review, spring, 1994, David L. Browman, review of *Ancient Andean Political Economy,* p. 236.

ONLINE

Charles Stanish Web site, http://www.sscnet.ucla.edu/ioa/stanish.htm (November 19, 2004).

National Public Radio Web site, http://www.npr.org/ (November 19, 2004), Alex Chadwick, transcript of interview with Stanish.*

*   *   *

STILLER, Jerry 1927-

PERSONAL: Born Gerard Stiller, June 8, 1927, in Brooklyn, NY; son of William (a bus driver) and Bella Stiller; married Anne Meara (an actress), September 14, 1954; children: Amy (an actress), Benjamin (an actor and director). *Education:* Syracuse University, B.A., 1950. *Religion:* Jewish.

ADDRESSES: Home—New York, NY. *Agent*—Michael Hartig Agency, 156 Fifth Ave., Suite 820, New York, NY 10010.

CAREER: Actor and comedian; with wife, Anne Meara, formed comedy duo Stiller and Meara. Actor in television series, including (as Barney Dickerson) *The Paul Lynde Show,* American Broadcasting Companies (ABC), 1972-73; (as Gus Duzik) *Joe and Sons,* Columbia Broadcasting System (CBS), 1975-76; *Take Five with Stiller and Meara,* syndicated, 1977; (as co-host) *HBO Sneak Preview,* Home Box Office (HBO), 1979-82; (as Carmine) *Archie Bunker's Place,* CBS, 1980-82; (as Jerry Bender) *The Stiller and Meara Show,* National Broadcasting Company (NBC), 1986; (as Sid Wilbur) *Tattinger's* (also known as *Nick and Hillary*), NBC, 1988-9; (as voice) *Good and Evil,* ABC, 1991; (as Frank Costanza) *Seinfeld,* NBC, 1993-98; (as Arthur Spooner) *The King of Queens,* CBS, 1998—; and (as voice of Pretty Boy) *Teacher's Pet* (animated; also known as *Disney's Teacher's Pet*), ABC, 2000. Actor in television movies, including (as Burt Orland) *Madame X,* NBC, 1981; (as Mel Binns) *The Other Woman,* CBS, 1983; (as Marty de Rezke) *The McGuffin,* British Broadcasting Company (BBC), 1985; (as Slicko McDee) *The Hustler of Money,* 1988; (as old man) "The 5:24," *Subway Stories: Tales from the Underground,* HBO, 1997; (uncredited; in archive footage; as Arthur Spooner) *The Victoria's Secret Fashion Show,* and (as Old Jingle) *Legend of the Lost Tribe,* 2002. Actor in television pilots, including (as Harold) *Acres and Pains,* CBS, 1965; (as Brahms) *The Equalizer,* CBS, 1985; and (as Jerry Bender) *The Stiller and Meara Show,* CBS, 1986. Appeared in

episodes of television series, including *The Ed Sullivan Show* (also known as *Toast of the Town*), CBS, c. 1960-64; "Acres and Pains," *G.E. Theater,* CBS, 1962; "Occupancy, August First," *Car 54, Where Are You?,* NBC, 1962; "The Plain Truth," *Brenner,* CBS, 1964; *That's Life,* ABC, 1969; *Love, American Style,* ABC, 1969, 1973; "A Memory of Two Mondays," *N.E.T. Playhouse,* Public Broadcasting System (PBS), 1971; (as Paul) "Thy Neighbor Loves Thee," *The Courtship of Eddie's Father,* ABC, 1972; *Phyllis,* CBS, 1976; (as Lloyd Zimmer) "A Touch of Classy," *Rhoda,* CBS, 1976; "The Garbage Man," *Time Express,* CBS, 1979; (as Bud Hanrahan) "Super Mom/I'll See You Again/April's Return," *The Love Boat,* ABC, 1979; (as Myron Finkle) "Murder Takes a Bow," *Hart to Hart,* ABC, 1981; "Orphans, Waifs, and Wards," *CBS Library,* CBS, 1981; (as Tony Vitelli) "Love, Honor, and Obey/Gladys and Agnes/Radioactive Isaac," *The Love Boat,* ABC, 1981; *Private Benjamin,* CBS, 1981; (as Harold Traxler) "The Uncivil Servant," *Simon and Simon,* CBS, 1982; "The Squealer," *No Soap, Radio,* ABC, 1982; (as Gordy) "Do You Take This Waitress?," *Alice,* CBS, 1982; (as voice of dinosaur comic) "Digging up Dinosaurs," *Reading Rainbow,* 1983; "We the Jury," *The Love Boat,* ABC, 1983; "Where There's a Will," *Trapper John, M.D.,* CBS, 1984; (as Mandrake) "Devil's Advocate," *Tales from the Darkside,* syndicated, 1985; (as Dr. Tamkin) "Seize the Day," *Great Performances,* PBS, 1987; (as himself) "Jerry Seinfeld: Master of His Domain," *Biography,* Arts and Entertainment, 1987; (as Lieutenant Birnbaum) "When the Fat Lady Sings," *Murder, She Wrote,* CBS, 1989; (as Milt Waterman) "Sweet 15," *WonderWorks,* PBS, 1990; (as Sam Rosenbloom) "The Hollow Boy," *American Playhouse,* PBS, 1991; (as Seymour Shapiro) "The Sunset Gang," *American Playhouse,* PBS, 1991; (as Michael Tobis) "The Fertile Fields," *Law & Order,* NBC, 1992; (as Nat Pincus) "Rhyme and Punishment," *L.A. Law,* 1993; (as Rabbi Feldman) "The Rabbi," *In the Heat of the Night,* 1994; (as McGonnigal) "In Search of Crimes Past," *Homicide: Life on the Street,* NBC, 1995; (as Phil Cullen) "Dr. Kramer," *Deadly Games,* UPN, 1996; (as Sam Pokras) "Deadbeat," *Law & Order,* NBC, 1996; (as Maury Salt) "Cry and You Cry Alone," *Touched by an Angel,* CBS, 1998; (as himself) "I Buried Sid," *The Larry Sanders Show,* HBO, 1998; (as voice of Eagle) "Prometheus Affair," *Hercules* (animated; also known as *Disney's Hercules*), ABC and syndicated, 1998; (as himself) "Ben Stiller," *Biography,* Arts and Entertainment, 2001; (as himself) *"I Love the '70s,"* 2003; (as hot dog vendor) "Distance, Time and Speed: Hot Dog Heaven," and (as Gus) "Statistics: The Lucky Batting

Glove," *The Eddie Files;* (as Mr. Landon) "We Love Annie," *The Courtship of Eddie's Father,* ABC; and in an episode of *Joe and Mabel.* Appeared in television specials, including *55th Annual King Orange Jamboree Parade,* NBC, 1988; (as pizzeria owner) *Colin Quinn Back in Brooklyn* (also known as *Colin Back to Brooklyn*), syndicated, 1989; (as Irving) *Women and Men 2: In Love There Are No Rules,* 1991; *Tracey Takes on New York,* HBO, 1993; *Tom Arnold: The Naked Truth 3,* HBO, 1993; *Going, Going, Almost Gone! Animals in Danger,* 1994; and (as himself) *CBS at 75,* CBS, 2003. Appeared (as voice) in miniseries *Baseball,* 1994. Appeared (as Eddie Condon) in radio program *Riverwalk, Live from the Landing,* 1999; also appeared on *Selected Shorts,* public radio. With Meara, host of video *So You Want to Be an Actor?,* Home Video, 1993. Actor in films, including (uncredited; as Jim, Carol's father) *Lovers and Other Strangers,* 1970; (as Lieutenant Rico Patrone) *The Taking of Pelham One, Two, Three,* United Artists, 1974; (as Sam) *Airport 1975,* Universal, 1974; (as Carmine Vespucci) *The Ritz,* Warner Bros., 1976; (as P. R. Priest) *Nasty Habits* (also known as *The Abbess*), Brut, 1976; (as Mr. Shoemaker) *Those Lips, Those Eyes,* United Artists, 1980; *In Our Hands,* 1984; (as Raymond Escobar) *Nadine,* TriStar, 1987; (as Victor Honeywell) *Hot Pursuit,* Paramount, 1987; *Shoeshine,* 1987; (as Wilbur Turnblad) *Hairspray,* New Line Cinema, 1988; (as Sid Lane) *That's Adequate,* 1989; (uncredited) *Beyond "JFK": The Question of Conspiracy,* 1992; (as the desk cop) *Highway to Hell,* Hemdale Releasing, 1992; (as Sam) *Little Vegas,* IRS Releasing, 1992; (as Phil Hirsch) *The Pickle,* Columbia, 1993; (as Harvey Bushkin) *Heavyweights,* Buena Vista, 1995; (as Professor Plumpingham) *Die Story von Monty Spinnerratz* (also known as *A Rat's Tale*), Legacy Releasing, 1997; (as Schlomo) *Camp Stories,* Artistic License, 1997; (as Ted) *Stag,* New City Releasing, 1997; (as Petey) *The Deli,* Golden Monkey Pictures, 1997; (as Speedo Silverberg) *The Suburbans,* TriStar, 1999; (as Sam) *A Fish in the Bathtub,* Northern Arts Entertainment, 1999; (as Morty Fineman) *The Independent,* Arrow Releasing, 2000; (as Don Giovanni) *My Five Wives,* Artisan Entertainment, 2000; (as himself) *Amy Stiller's Breast,* 2000; (as Maury Ballstein) *Zoolander,* Paramount, 2001; (as Nathan) *On the Line,* Miramax, 2001; (as Milton) *Serving Sara,* Paramount, 2002; (as voice of Pretty Boy) *Teacher's Pet: The Movie,* Disney, 2003; (as the colonel) *Chump Change,* 2004; and (as Timon's Uncle Max) *The Lion King 1 1/2* (video; also known as *Lion King 3: Hakuna Matata*), Disney, 2004. Actor in stage productions, including (as Billy Barnes) *Showboat,* Chicago, IL, 1950; (as Mayor Juniper) *The*

Golden Apple, Alvin Theatre, New York, NY, 1954; *Boubouroche,* New York, 1971; (as Carmine Vespucci) *The Ritz,* Longacre Theatre, New York, 1975-76; (as Harry Mullin) *Unexpected Guests,* Little Theatre, New York, 1977; (as Berto) *Passione,* Morosco Theatre, New York, 1980; (as Artie) *Hurlyburly,* Promenade Theatre, then Ethel Barrymore Theatre, New York, 1984-85; (as Dogberry) *Much Ado about Nothing,* New York Shakespeare Festival, 1988; (as Charlie) *Three Men on a Horse,* Lyceum Theatre, New York, 1993; *Beau Jest,* 1994; (as Sid) *What's Wrong with This Picture?,* Brooks Atkinson Theatre, New York, 1994; *After-Play,* off-Broadway, 1995; and (as Chebutykin) *Three Sisters,* Criterion Theatre, New York, 1997; also appeared in *Coriolanus, The Power and the Glory, Measure for Measure, Taming of the Shrew, Carefree Tree, Diary of a Scoundrel, Romeo and Juliet, As You Like It, Two Gentlemen of Verona,* and *Prairie/Shawl.* Performed in various summer stock companies, 1951-53, and at Henry Street Settlement and Cherry Lane Theatre, New York; Erie Playhouse, PA; Memphis Arena Theatre, TN; Phoenix, NY; Shakespeare Festival Theatre, Stratford, CT; and with the New York Shakespeare Festival. Actor in the touring production *Peter Pan,* U.S. cities, 1951. *Military service:* Served in U.S. Army during World War II.

AWARDS, HONORS: Ellis Island Medal of Honor; Emmy nomination for best supporting actor, for *Seinfeld.*

WRITINGS:

(With wife, Anne Meara) *Laugh When You Like* (comedy album), Atlantic, 1972.
(With others) *The Stiller and Meara Show,* National Broadcasting Company (NBC), 1986.
Married to Laughter: A Love Story Featuring Anne Meara (autobiography), Simon & Schuster (New York, NY), 2000.

Also narrator of the audiobook version of *Married to Laughter,* Random House (New York, NY), 2000.

SIDELIGHTS: Jerry Stiller and his long-time wife Anne Meara have been entertaining Americans for over half a century, first through acting on stage, then doing a stand-up comedy routine together, and later in separate paths, with Stiller continuing to act and Meara turning more to playwriting. Stiller relates their lives, private and on stage, in his memoirs, *Married to Laughter: A Love Story Featuring Anne Meara.*

Stiller grew up in a Brooklyn family that was hit hard by the Great Depression. As a teenager he served in the army during the waning days of World War II, then returned to the United States and got a degree in theater. He acted in various stage productions around the country for several years, during which time he met and months later married Meara. Meara, a tall, red-headed Irish Catholic from an affluent Long Island family, was a most unlikely match for Stiller, but the two put their contrasting looks (Stiller is short, only 5 feet 6 inches tall), backgrounds, and personalities to good use in their long-running comedy routine. At first they performed in clubs and coffeehouses, but the duo rose to national prominence when they became frequent guests on *The Ed Sullivan Show,* one of the most popular variety shows of the 1950s and 1960s. The two gained further fame for their commercials for Blue Nun wines; these spots, written by Meara, were some of the first funny advertisements to be successful in selling their product.

Stiller's biggest roles came at an age when most actors look toward retirement. He brought to life Frank Costanza, the perennially angry but always hilarious father of George Costanza, one of the four stars of the hit sitcom *Seinfeld,* in the mid-1990s. When *Seinfeld* ceased production in 1998, Stiller reprised the loud-mouthed father role on another sitcom, *The King of Queens.* Stiller speaks little of these roles in *Married to Laughter,* instead focusing on his childhood and early years in the business.

Surprisingly to some reviewers who know him only for his comedy, Stiller wrote his autobiography in a voice more tender and reflective than comedic. This is especially true when he is speaking of Meara or of his mentor, Syracuse University professor Sawyer Falk. The book is a "heartfelt, sometimes painful, mostly sweet memoir," Ilene Cooper wrote in *Booklist;* it is "the real stuff about his real life," another critic explained in *Publishers Weekly.* "I always found that I could attract people by telling stories about what went on in my life," Stiller told a *People* interviewer. "I'd tell these stories and people would say, 'If this were a book, I'd buy it!'." Stiller mulled over the idea of writing the stories down for fifteen years, until the cancellation of *Seinfeld* finally gave him the time and motivation to do so.

"Stiller . . . sees a world that rewards hard work and patience," Michael Lazan wrote in a review of *Married to Laughter* for *Back Stage.* "It is an old-fashioned vision, bereft of cynicism and irony," that "works to create an uplifting affect." *Los Angeles Times* contributor Tony Peyser concluded that "*Married to Laughter* is a testament to love and perseverance and a reminder that behind every successful Hollywood story is a lot of rejection, family woes and tough luck."

BIOGRAPHICAL AND CRITICAL SOURCES:

PERIODICALS

Back Stage, November 17, 2000, Michael Lazan, review of *Married to Laughter: A Love Story Featuring Anne Meara,* p. 44.

Booklist, August, 2000, Ilene Cooper, review of *Married to Laughter,* p. 2096; March 1, 2001, Mary McCay, review of *Married to Laughter* (audiobook), p. 1296.

Boston Herald, March 3, 1999, Paul Sherman, interview with Stiller and Meara, p. 41; June 3, 2002, Stephen Schaefer, interview with Stiller, p. 35.

Buffalo News, November 5, 2000, Kathleen Rizzo Young, review of *Married to Laughter,* p. F6.

Courier-Mail (Brisbane, Queensland, Australia), September 2, 1999, Vicki Englund, interview with Stiller, p. 2.

Daily News (Los Angeles, CA), December 30, 1997, Keith Marder, interview with Stiller, p. L8.

Esquire, June, 1999, Cal Fussman, interview with Stiller, p. 112.

Library Journal, August, 2000, Rosellen Brewer, review of *Married to Laughter,* p. 108; February 15, 2001, Nann Blaine Hilyard, review of *Married to Laughter* (audiobook), p. 219.

Los Angeles Times, September 21, 2000, Tony Peyser, review of *Married to Laughter,* p. E3.

Palm Beach Post, April 1, 2002, Hap Erstein, interview with Stiller, p. E1.

People, October 16, 2000, interview with Stiller, p. 113.

Publishers Weekly, July 24, 2000, review of *Married to Laughter,* p. 77; November 6, 2000, review of *Married to Laughter* (audiobook), p. 50.

St. Louis Post-Dispatch, October 31, 1997, Ellen Futterman, interview with Stiller, p. 1E.

Seattle Times, December 15, 1998, Frazier Moore, interview with Stiller, p. F3.

Star-Ledger (Newark, NJ), August 6, 2002, "La-La Land's Nice, but Stiller Still Loves N.Y. People," p. 36.

Star Tribune (Minneapolis, MN), February 1, 2002, Colin Covert, "After Five Decades, Jerry Stiller Hits Stride," p. E11.

ONLINE

Internet Movie Database, http://www.imdb.com/ (May 24, 2004), "Jerry Stiller."

Jerry Stiller Home Page, http://www.arlo.net/jerry (September 4, 2003).*

*   *   *

STINNETT, Robert B.

PERSONAL: Born in Oakland, CA; son of Curtis and Margaret Stinnett; married Peggy McBride (associate editor and newspaper columnist); children: Colleen, James.

ADDRESSES: Home—Oakland, CA, and HI. *Agent*—c/o Author Mail, Simon & Schuster, 1230 Avenue of the Americas, New York, NY 10020.

CAREER: Photojournalist and author. Worked for *Oakland Tribune* until retirement in 1986; consultant for Brtish Broadcastin Service, Asahi, and NHK Television. *Military service:* Served in U.S. Navy during World War II.

AWARDS, HONORS: Ten battle citations, U.S. Navy; Presidential Unit citation.

WRITINGS:

George Bush: His World War II Years, Brassey's (Washington, DC), 1992.

Day of Deceit: The Truth about FDR and Pearl Harbor, Free Press (New York, NY), 2000.

Day of Deceit has also been published in the United Kingdom, Japan, and Italy; editions are also planned in Germany, France, and Norway.

SIDELIGHTS: As a teenager, photojournalist Robert B. Stinnett was fascinated by radio newscasts from Europe and sold photographs to the *Oakland Tribune* prior to U.S. involvement in World War II. He enlisted in the U.S. Navy after graduating from high school in 1942 and was assigned to aerial photo school, where he met future president George H. W. Bush. Stinnett served under Bush for four years and earned ten Navy battle citations. These experiences preceded two books, *George Bush: His World War II Years* and *Day of Deceit: The Truth about FDR and Pearl Harbor.*

Eighteen years of research went into *Day of Deceit,* including work done after Stinnett resigned from the *Oakland Tribune* in 1986 to write full time. He sought to prove that President Roosevelt not only knew Pearl Harbor was going to be attacked by the Japanese, but that he wanted to use the event to persuade Americans to go to war. Others have also questioned this possibility, proof of which hinges on whether American intelligence broke the Japanese naval code, if the Japanese fleet did in fact maintain radio silence as it crossed the Pacific, and the honesty of U.S. officers who were interviewed on the subject.

The difficulty of Stinnett's task was highlighted by reviewers. Writing for *Foreign Affairs,* Philip Zelikow maintained that Stinnett's "old argument" is based on the erroneous idea that American intelligence had broken the Japanese naval code. *Library Journal* reviewer William D. Pederson suggested that acceptance of the author's ideas would largely be based on preconceived ideas: "contemporary and classic Roosevelt haters . . . will cherish this book," he said, while "academic historians and FDR supporters will be far less convinced." In a review for *Booklist,* Gilbert Taylor noted that that "accusatory light doesn't definitively fall on FDR," but added that "Pearl Harbor holds fewer secrets because of Stinnctt's research." Reviewers who fully supported Stinnett's conclusions include a writer for *Publishers Weekly* who saw "overwhelming evidence that FDR . . . knew that Japanese warships were heading toward Hawaii" and judged that the book "establishes almost beyond question that the U.S. Navy could have at least anticipated the attack." A *Kirkus Reviews* critic called *Day of Deceit* "explosive, well-written" and believed that it "should rewrite the historical record of WWII."

BIOGRAPHICAL AND CRITICAL SOURCES:

PERIODICALS

Booklist, November 1, 1999, Gilbert Taylor, review of *Day of Deceit: The Truth about FDR and Pearl Harbor,* p. 507.

Journal of American History, June, 2002, Justus D. Doenecke, review of *Day of Deceit,* p. 281.

Journal of Military History, April, 2000, Edward J. Drea, review of *Day of Deceit,* p. 582.

Kirkus Reviews, October 15, 1999, review of *Day of Deceit,* p. 1627.

Library Journal, November 15, 1999, William D. Pederson, review of *Day of Deceit,* p. 82.

Military Review, March-April, 2003, Richard L. Milligan, review of *Day of Deceit,* p. 94.

New York Review of Books, November 2, 2000, David Kahn, review of *Day of Deceit,* p. 59.

New York Times, December 15, 1999, Richard Bernstein, review of *Day of Deceit,* p. B10.

Publishers Weekly, November 29, 1999, review of *Day of Deceit,* p. 59.

Spectator, February 26, 2000, John Charmley, review of *Day of Deceit,* p. 38.

Wall Street Journal, December 7, 1999, Bruce Bartlett, review of *Day of Deceit,* p. A24.

ONLINE

Foreign Affairs Online, http://www.foreignaffairs.org/ (March-April, 2000), Philip Zelikow, review of *Day of Deceit.**

* * *

STOUT, Maureen

PERSONAL: Born in British Columbia, Canada. *Education:* University of British Columbia, B.A. (English), 1985; London School of Economics, postgraduate diploma, in international and compariative politics, 1986; University of London, M.A. (European language and literature), 1987; University of California, Los Angeles, Ph.D. (education), 1994.

ADDRESSES: Home—Vancouver, British Columbia, Canada. *Office*—Imaginative Education Research Group, Simon Fraser University, 8888 University Dr., Burnaby, British Columbia V5A 1S6, Canada. *E-mail*—drmaureenstout@telus.net.

CAREER: California State University, Northridge, assistant professor of education, c. 1994-2000; Imaginative Education Research Group, Burnaby, British Columbia, Canada, post-doctoral fellow; has also taught at University of British Columbia and University of Victoria.

MEMBER: Authors Guild, American Educational Research Association, Philosophy of Education Society, Comparative and International Education Society.

AWARDS, HONORS: Social Sciences and Humanities Research Council of Canada fellowship.

WRITINGS:

The Feel-Good Curriculum: The Dumbing Down of America's Kids in the Name of Self-Esteem, Perseus Books (Cambridge, MA), 1999.

Contributor to books, including *Parent School: Simple Lessons from the Leading Experts on Being a Mom and Dad,* edited by Jerry and Lorin Biederman, M. Evans, 2002.

WORK IN PROGRESS: Guide book for parents to help their children become successful learners.

SIDELIGHTS: Educational theorist Maureen Stout's first book, *The Feel-Good Curriculum: The Dumbing Down of America's Kids in the Name of Self-Esteem,* is a "passionately argued and fluidly written attack on contemporary education philosophy and practice," Jack Forman explained in *Library Journal.* As the title suggests, in *The Feel-Good Curriculum* Stout shows how the modern emphasis on instilling self-esteem in schoolchildren has led to evolving methods of instruction, like cooperative learning, whole-language reading, discovery math, and creative spelling, that do little to instruct children in the basic skills of reading, writing, and arithmetic. Praising her book, a *Publishers Weekly* contributor wrote that *The Feel-Good Curriculum* "couldn't be more timely."

BIOGRAPHICAL AND CRITICAL SOURCES:

BOOKS

Stout, Maureen, *The Feel-Good Curriculum: The Dumbing Down of America's Kids in the Name of Self-Esteem,* Perseus Books (Cambridge, MA), 1999.

PERIODICALS

Alberta Report, May 8, 2000, Nathan Greenfield, review of *The Feel-Good Curriculum: The Dumbing Down of America's Kids in the Name of Self-Esteem,* p. 57.
Choice, July-August, 2000, J. A. Beckwith, review of *The Feel-Good Curriculum,* p. 2028.
Library Journal, February 1, 2000, Jack Forman, review of *The Feel-Good Curriculum,* p. 98.
Publishers Weekly, January 10, 2000, review of *The Feel-Good Curriculum,* p. 52.
Report Newsmagazine (British Columbia, Canada), May 8, 2000, review of *The Feel-Good Curriculum.*

ONLINE

Imaginative Education Research Group Web site, http://www.ierg.net/ (November 14, 2003), "Maureen Stout."
Maureen Stout Web site, http://www.drmaureenstout.com (May 23, 2005).

*   *   *

SULLIVAN, Jody
See RAKE, Jody

*   *   *

SUTHERLAND, Luke 1971(?)-

PERSONAL: Born c. 1971. *Education:* Attended University of Glasgow.

ADDRESSES: Home—London, England. *Agent*—Merric Davidson, Marsh Agency, 11 Dover St., London W1S 4LJ England.

CAREER: Songwriter, musician, and writer. Vocalist with bands Long Fin Killie, c. 1990s, and Mogwai; founder of concept band, Bows; recordings include (with Long Fin Killie) *Houdini, Valentino,* and *Amelia;* and (with Bows) *Blush* and *Cassidy,* 2001.

AWARDS, HONORS: Whitbread First Novel Award nomination, 1998, for *Jelly Roll.*

WRITINGS:

Jelly Roll, Anchor (London, England), 1998.
Sweetmeat, Doubleday (London, England), 2002.
Venus as a Boy, Bloomsbury (London, England), 2004.

also author of lyrics for songs performed by bands Bows and Long Fin Killie.

ADAPTATIONS: Jelly Roll was filmed by Fraser Macdonald.

SIDELIGHTS: As a black man raised on the Orkney Islands off the northeastern coast of Scotland, Luke Sutherland has developed a unique perspective on the nature of life that is reflected in his fiction. A musician and songwriter as well as an author, he has earned success in both fields. His fiction, however, taps into his experience of racism in the far north of Scotland and the magical, mystical, evocative landscape of the islands in which he was raised. "Being black, adopted by white parents, and having black, white and mixed-race siblings would have raised a few eyebrows pretty much anywhere in the mid-1970s," explained Sean Merrigan on the *Spoiled Ink* Web site, "however, the insular Orcadian community into which his family moved in 1976 turned out to be particularly hostile." "My family was a miniature league of nations I guess you could say," the author told *Bookmunch* online interviewer Jerome de Groot, "white parents, white older sister, there is me, my little sister is black and my younger brother's mix-race white Asian, so wherever we went we were going to attract attention." As the oldest of the family's adopted children, Sutherland "came in for a lot of hassle," he told an interviewer for *Dr.Drew.com.* "I'm a fast runner. I also have the gift of the gab, so I'm able to talk myself out of trouble most of the time. I got bullied a bit up until I started getting bigger. Then people started leaving me alone and chatted to me from a distance."

Sutherland's experiences growing up in the Orkneys play a major role in his celebrated 2004 novel *Venus as a Boy.* The protagonist of the story, Desiree, is, at the time the tale begins, a prostitute living in London.

But twenty years before, Desiree had been one of those young men who bullied Sutherland with racist taunts. "Siding with the bigots," explained Michael Arditti, reviewing the book for the *Independent,* "takes the pressure off him as an oddball and suspected 'pouf.'" Desiree, now dying, wants to make amends with Sutherland. By the time Sutherland is ready to forgive, however, Desiree—confined to a flat in Soho—has already succumbed to a rare affliction that has caused his body to turn to gold. He sends Sutherland a small legacy, consisting mainly of records and the bits and pieces of an autobiography—which turn out to be his own story of torment and passion that form the basis of *Venus as a Boy.*

The thing that makes Desiree special is that he has the gift to evoke passion in any partner of either sex. "Should he lay hands on you, or rather, should he lay you," explained Alice Ferrebe in her review of the novel for *Scotland on Sunday,* "you would tremble, wracked by visions of angels, orchards, trumpets and stars. He can floor a violent homophobe, make him helpless with love and lust." Desiree first comes into his power with a local girl named Tracy, who allows him to see what his gift makes her see, angels, orchards, and all. "When she leaves him for university," Ferrebe explained, "he goes to London and starts to sell himself in a complex transaction of masochism and redemption." Eventually Desiree ends up living in a cheap flat, victimized by a rough pimp who forces him to take hormones and other drugs that begin his dual transformation into both a woman and a golden corpse, wracked by hepatitis.

Many reviewers celebrated Sutherland's accomplishments in *Venus as a Boy,* particularly his evocation of the magical landscapes of the island of South Ronaldsay, where he grew up. "Again and again in this novel we come upon lines that have a kind of throw-away beauty," wrote Thomas Hodgkinson in the *Independent,* "as if Sutherland had so many of them he didn't feel the need to make a big deal out of any particular one." "We get an incredibly vivid portrait of the island: its treeless fields, its blinding stars," stated a *Guardian* contributor. "The strong emotions of Sutherland's difficult childhood suffuse every word." "A confident stylist with the chops to back up his gambles, Sutherland doesn't need to be flashy," declared Damien Weaver in a *Bookslut.com* review. "He is a graceful, effective storyteller, and he paints the Orkneys in particular with such fierce wonder that, after reading his descriptions, actually visiting the islands could only be a let-down."

BIOGRAPHICAL AND CRITICAL SOURCES:

PERIODICALS

Guardian (Manchester, England), January 12, 1999, Emily Moore, interview with Sutherland, p. 4; March 27, 2004, "Heaven on Earth."

Independent, March 26, 2004, Thomas Hodgkinson, review of *Venus as a Boy;* April 21, 2004, Michael Arditti, review of *Venus as a Boy.*

Kirkus Reviews, December 15, 2003, review of *Venus as a Boy,* p. 1421.

Lambda Book Report, May, 2004, Michael Graves, "Fast Love," p. 31.

Newsweek International, April 12, 2004, G. Brownell, review of *Venus as a Boy,* p. 57.

Northern Echo, May 11, 2004, Peta King, "The Power of Love," p. 12.

Publishers Weekly, February 9, 2004, review of *Venus as a Boy,* p. 56.

San Francisco Chronicle, March 7, 2004, June Sawyers, review of *Venus as a Boy.*

Scotland on Sunday, March 14, 2004, Alice Ferrebe, "Venus with the Midas Touch."

Sunday Herald, March 7, 2004, Alan Taylor, "The Life and Death of Bleak Venus."

ONLINE

Allmusic.com, http://www.allmusic.com/ (May 20. 2005), "Luke Sunderland."

Bookmunch Web site, http://www.bookmunch.co.uk/ (October 28, 2004), Jerome de Groot, interview with Sunderland.

Bookslut.com, http://www.bookslut.com/ (October 28, 2004), Damien Weaver, review of *Venus as a Boy.*

Dr.Drew.com, http://www.drdrew.com/ (October 28, 2004), "Bows and Whistles: An Interview with Luke Sutherland."

Re:mote Induction Web site, http://www.remote induction.co.uk/ (October 28, 2004), interview with Sunderland.

Spoiled Ink.com, http://www.spoiledink.com/ (October 28, 2004), Sean Merrigan, interview with Sunderland.

Strathmore and the Glens Web site, http://www.strathmoreglens.org/ (September 13, 2004), Luke Sutherland visit.*

*   *   *

SUZANNE, Jamie
    See LANTZ, Francess L(in)

*   *   *

SYRETT, David 1939-2004

OBITUARY NOTICE— See index for *CA* sketch: Born January 8, 1939, in White Plains, NY; died October 18, 2004, in Leonia, NJ. Historian, educator, and author. Syrett was a military historian and professor at Queens College of the University of New York. Struggling successfully to overcome dyslexia, he graduated from Columbia University with a master's degree in 1964, then completed his doctorate at University College London in 1966. That year, he joined the faculty at Queens College as an assistant professor, rising to the post of full professor of history in 1980 and Distinguished Professor in 2000. As a researcher, Syrett was a well-known expert on eighteenth-century naval history, with an additional expertise on World War II's Battle of the Atlantic and the intelligence efforts at code breaking during this period. Among his publications are *The Siege and Capture of Havana, 1762* (1970), *The Royal Nave in American Waters, 1775-1783* (1989), and *The Defeat of the German U-Boats: The Battle of the Atlantic* (1994).

OBITUARIES AND OTHER SOURCES:

PERIODICALS

Independent (London, England), January 19, 2005, p. 35.
New York Times, October 23, 2004, p. A18.

T

TAKÁCS, Tibor 1954-

PERSONAL: Born September 11, 1954, in Budapest, Hungary.

ADDRESSES: Agent—Agency for the Performing Arts, 9200 West Sunset Blvd., Suite 900, Los Angeles, CA 90069-3604; (commercials and music videos) Boyington Studios, Inc., 17 Galleon St., Marina del Rey, CA 90232.

CAREER: Director, producer, editor, and screenwriter. Director of films, including (and editor) *Metal Messiah,* MM Productions, 1978; *The Gate,* New Century Vista, 1987; *I, Madman* (also known as *Hardcover*), TransWorld Entertainment, 1989; *The Gate II: Trespassers* (also known as *Gate II—Return to the Nightmare*), Triumph Releasing, 1992; (and executive producer) *Viper* (also known as *Bad Blood*), MDP Worldwide/Third Coast Entertainment, 1994; *Deadly Past,* Atlantic Group Films/Curb Entertainment International, 1995; *Sabotage,* Imperial Entertainment/ New City Releasing, 1996; *Deathline* (also known as *Armageddon* and *Redline*), Nu Image, 1997; *Sanctuary,* New City Releasing, 1997; *Nostradamus,* Regent Entertainment, 2000; *Once upon a Christmas,* 2000; *Rats* (also known as *Killer Rats*) Nu Image, 2003; and *Earthquake,* 2004. Other film work includes production manager, *Screwballs,* 1983; producer, *Snow* (short film), 1983; and assistant director, *Bloody Wednesday,* 1987. Director of television movies, including *Sabrina Goes to Rome,* American Broadcasting Companies (ABC), 1998; *Once upon a Christmas,* PAX, 2000; *Twice upon a Christmas,* PAX, 2001; and *Tornado Warning,* 2002. Director of episodes of television series, including "Sex, Lies, and Lullabies" and "Tara, Tara, Tara," *Sweating Bullets* (also known as *Tropical Heat*), Columbia Broadcasting System (CBS), 1992; "Blood Brothers," "White Light Fever," "The Voyage Home," "I, Robot," and "If These Walls Could Talk," *The Outer Limits,* Showtime and syndicated, 1995; "Pandora's Box" and "If You Could Read My Mind," *Earth: Final Conflict* (also known as *Gene Roddenberry's Battleground Earth*), syndicated, 1998; "Quiz Show," *Sabrina, the Teenage Witch* (also known as *Sabrina Goes to College*), American Broadcasting Companies (ABC), 1999; "Through a Dark Circle" and "The People vs. Eric Draven," *The Crow: Stairway to Heaven,* syndicated, 1999; "Cul-de-sac," *First Wave,* Sci-Fi Channel, 1999; "Double Dare," *Red Shoe Diaries,* Showtime; and an episode of *Lonesome Dove.* Director and editor of television program *984: Prisoner of the Future* (also known as *The Tomorrow Man*), 1982. Director of pilot *Sabrina, the Teenage Witch,* Showtime, 1996.

WRITINGS:

(With Brian Irving) *Deathline* (screenplay; also known as *Armageddon* and *Redline*), Nu Image, 1997.

SIDELIGHTS: Canadian-based director Tibor Takács is best known for his low-budget science-fiction and action films, although he has also directed for such television series as *Sabrina, the Teenage Witch* and *The Outer Limits.* Takács also wrote the script for one of his films, *Deathline.* The film is set in an anarchic Russia of the future that is dominated by the Mafia;

the film's protagonist is a smuggler who is double-crossed by his partner and seeks revenge. Among the film's more notable features are a scene which parodies the famous "Odessa Steps" section of the 1925 Soviet film *Battleship Potemkin,* and another inspired by the junkyard full of old statues of Soviet-era leaders from the 1995 James Bond film *GoldenEye.* Through such devices, "Takács creates an abundance of atmosphere," Richard Scheib commented on the *Science-Fiction, Horror, and Fantasy Film Review* Web site.

BIOGRAPHICAL AND CRITICAL SOURCES:

PERIODICALS

Cinema Canada, July-August, 1987, Andrew Dowler, review of *The Gate,* pp. 25-26.
New York Times, April 10, 1996, John J. O'Connor, review of *Sabrina the Teenage Witch,* p. C18.
People, June 8, 1987, Tom Cunneff, review of *The Gate,* p. 10.
Variety, April 12, 1989, review of *I, Madman,* p. 26.

ONLINE

Science-Fiction, Horror, and Fantasy Film Review, http://www.roogulator.esmartweb.com/ (July 10, 2003), Richard Scheib, review of *Redline.*
Sci-Fi Movie Page, http://members.tripod.com/scifimoviepage/ (July 10, 2003), James O'Ehley, review of *Redline.**

*   *   *

TAKEMAE, Eiji 1930-

PERSONAL: Born August 4, 1930, in Japan; son of Kikutaro and Tokuno Takemae (farmers); married Atsuko; children: Kenichi. *Education:* Tokyo Kyoiku University, B.A., 1955; Tokyo Metropolitan University, M.A., 1963, Ph.D., 1971; attended graduate school at University of Hawaii and University of California, Berkeley. *Religion:* Buddhist.

ADDRESSES: Home—1129-52 Kiso-machi, Machida-shi, Tokyo 194-0033, Japan. *E-mail*—est@tihic.com.

CAREER: Tokyo Keizai University, professor, 1974-2004, professor emeritus, 2004—; Chuo University, lecturer, 1968-2001, Fulbright visiting professor, 1977-78.

AWARDS, HONORS: Most Distinguished Publication in the Field of Labor and Industrial Relations Award, Japan Institute of Labor and Yomiuri Shimbun-sha, 1983.

WRITINGS:

Amerika Tainichi Rodo Seisaku no Kenkyu (title means "Study of U.S. Labor Policy for Japan"), Ninon Hyoron-sha (Tokyo, Japan), 1970.
Senryo Sengoshi (title means "The Occupation and Japanese Postwar History"), Soshisya (Tokyo, Japan), 1980, revised edition, Iwanami Shoten (Tokyo, Japan), 1992.
Sengo Rodo Kaikaku: GHQ Rodo Seisakushi (title means "Postwar Labor Reform: History of GHQ Labor Policy"), Tokyo University Press (Tokyo, Japan), 1982.
Shogen Nihon Senryoshi: GHQ Rodoka no Gunzo (annotated interviews, title means "The History of Occupied Japan: Labor Crows in GHQ/SCAP"), Iwanami Shoten (Tokyo, Japan), 1983.
GHQ, Iwanami Shoten (Tokyo, Japan), 1983.
DDT Kakumei: Senryoki no Iryo Fukushi Seisaku o Kaisosuru (title means "The DDT Revolution: Looking Back at the Reform of Medicine and Social Welfare during the Occupation"), Iwanami Shoten (Tokyo, Japan), 1986.
Nihon Senryo: GHQ Kokan no Shogen (title means "Occupation of Japan: Interview with GHQ High Officers"), Chuo Koronsha (Tokyo, Japan), 1988.
GHQ Rodoka no Hito to Seisaku (title means "Reformers and Policies of Labor Division, GHQ/SCAP"), MT Shuppan (Tokyo, Japan), 1991.
Nihon no Rodo-roudoukaikaku, roudouhou, roudouundou (annotated documents, title means "Labor in Japan: Labor Reforms, Labor Laws and Labor Movements"), Yushisha (Tokyo, Japan), 1992.
Sengo Nihon no Genten (title means "Starting Points of Postwar Japan"), Yushisha (Tokyo, Japan), 1992.
Kenpo Seiteishi (title means "The History of Remaking the Japanese Constitution"), Shogakkan (Tokyo, Japan), 2000.

Inside GHQ: The Allied Occupation of Japan and Its Legacy, translated and adapted from the Japanese by Robert Ricketts and Sebastian Swann, Continuum (New York, NY), 2002, also published as *The Allied Occupation of Japan,* Continuum (2003).

Shogaisha Seisaku no Kokusai Hikaku (title means "Comparative Studies of Policies on Persons with Disabilities"), Akashi Shoten (Tokyo, Japan), 2002.

Kenpo Bunken Daijiten: 1945 (Showa 20) nen-2002 (Heisei 14) nen (annotated bibliography of Japanese Constitution), Nihon Tosho Senta (Tokyo, Japan), 2004.

SIDELIGHTS: Professor, political scientist, and historian Eiji Takemae is an expert in what is known as "occupation history," or *senryoshi,* "which has become an important subfield of Japanese historical studies," according to reviewer Yoichi Nakano in *Public Affairs.* A groundbreaker in the field, Takemae researches and writes on the post-World War II occupation of Japan by the victorious American forces, particularly the reforms and influence of the American General Headquarters (GHQ) from 1945 to 1952. A translation of Takemae's work, *Inside GHQ: The Allied Occupation of Japan and Its Legacy* "presents a very detailed and comprehensive analysis of the structure of GHQ and its reform programs while incorporating a number of episodes from the political as well as social and cultural history of occupied Japan," Nakano remarked. The book is "exemplary in its clarity and in its concern for factual accuracy," noted Richard Sims in *History Today.*

In the years following World War II, General Douglas MacArthur and the GHQ imposed significant changes on Japan. The constitution was revised, land was redistributed, politics were liberalized, economic change was implemented, and the overall treatment of minorities was improved. Hirohito, the emperor of Japan, was left in a position of symbolic power, "a symbol of national unity in a democratic society," instead of being tried as a war criminal, remarked William K. Tabb in *Monthly Review.* "This particular crucial choice [made by MacArthur] was based on the judgment that leaving the Emperor in place while redefining his role would make the job of the Occupation easier," Tabb noted.

Takemae provides detailed profiles of both American and Japanese personnel who were charged with implementing the new policies and reforms. "Indeed, a major strength of this study is the densely woven fabric of the many elements of the story, the civil servants, both Japanese and American, the academics and movement activists, the politicians and military figures, who shaped the Occupation's effects," Tabb commented. As the reforms were developed, conflicts occurred between liberals who wanted to reshape Japan in ways resembling the New Deal in the United States and conservative military personnel and bureaucrats who feared that liberal reform would provide communism with a perfect opportunity to surge throughout Japan. In particular, Takemae emphasizes "the role of Japanese people who embraced the progressive reforms" and created the atmosphere in which the GHQ's changes could be implemented successfully, noted Nakano. Cold war anticommunist sentiment led to reversal of some of the liberal political changes in the late 1940s and early 1950s, but in the end, the American occupation created "the foundation for a modern, democratic Japan," noted a *Publishers Weekly* reviewer.

"*Inside GHQ* provides both specialists and general readers with a masterful account of the Occupation, focusing on the origin, structure, personnel, and policies of General MacArthur's headquarters and those men and women—Japanese and American—who shaped its decisions," commented Michael Schaller in *Journal of Asian Studies.* "Few books about contemporary Japan are as detailed, penetrating, and compellingly objective as this overview of the postwar half-century," stated the *Publishers Weekly* critic. Takemae's work "takes its place as one of the most important studies of the post-1945 years," asserted Sims. "The summation of a lifetime of study, this is the definitive English-language work on its subject," concluded *Library Journal* reviewer Steven I. Levine.

Takemae told *CA:* "The motivation of my writing of *The Allied Occupation of Japan* derives from, first, my high school experience of learning English conversation from American soldiers and their families. I was very interested in American democracy. Secondly, as an East West Center grantee at the graduate schools of the University of Hawaii and the University of California, Berkeley, I wrote my Ph.D. dissertation in 1970 on U.S. Labor Policy for Japan. I explored the impact of U.S. labor policy, including GHQ SCAP policies, on Japanese postwar labor policy, union movements, and labor relations systems. Subsequently,

I expanded my research field to all aspects of the U.S. occupation of Japan. I discussed the impact American democracy had on the democratization of Japanese postwar political, economical, social, and cultural systems and how Japanese received and absorbed it.

"My recent interest is how we should promote the rights and dignity of persons with disabilities and their right to access public facilities and public transportation. I had a small experience to contribute to the legislation promoting the rights of persons with disabilities, accompanied by a service dog, to full access to public facilities and public transportation."

BIOGRAPHICAL AND CRITICAL SOURCES:

PERIODICALS

History Today, November, 2002, Richard Sims, review of *Inside GHQ: The Allied Occupation of Japan and Its Legacy,* p. 83.
Journal of Asian Studies, February, 2003, Michael Schaller, review of *Inside GHQ,* p. 291.
Library Journal, August, 2002, Steven I. Levine, review of *Inside GHQ,* p. 118.
Monthly Review, January, 2003, William K. Tabb, "Occupation's Mixed Legacy," review of *Inside GHQ.*
Pacific Affairs, fall, 2003, Yoichi Nakano, review of *Inside GHQ,* p. 475.
Publishers Weekly, May 13, 2002, review of *Inside GHQ,* p. 61.

*   *   *

TAN, Kok-Chor 1964-

PERSONAL: Born December 3, 1964, in Singapore; son of K. L. and K. L. Tan; married K. E. Detlefsen (a professor). *Ethnicity:* "Singaporean." *Education:* University of Toronto, Ph.D., 1998.

ADDRESSES: Home—310 South 36th St., No. 4, Philadelphia, PA 19104. *Office*—Department of Philosophy, 433 Logan Hall, University of Pennsylvania, Philadelphia, PA 19104. *E-mail*—kctan@sas.upenn.edu.

CAREER: University of Pennsylvania, Philadelphia, assistant professor of philosophy, 2002—.

WRITINGS:

Toleration, Diversity, and Global Justice, Pennsylvania State University Press (University Park, PA), 2000.
Justice without Borders, Cambridge University Press (New York, NY), 2004.

BIOGRAPHICAL AND CRITICAL SOURCES:

PERIODICALS

Ethics, October, 2002, Jeffrey R. Flynn, review of *Toleration, Diversity, and Global Justice,* p. 196.
Perspectives on Political Science, fall, 2001, Paul Kriese, review of *Toleration, Diversity, and Global Justice,* p. 247.

*   *   *

TARLTON, John S. 1950-

PERSONAL: Born 1950.

ADDRESSES: Agent—c/o Author Mail, Bridge Works Publishing, P.O. Box 1798 Bridge Lane, Bridgehampton, NY 11932.

CAREER: Author. Has worked as an oil company lease negotiator.

WRITINGS:

A Window Facing West (novel), Bridge Works Publishing (Bridgehampton, NJ), 1999.
The Cost of Doing Business (novel), Bridge Works Publishing (Bridgehampton, NJ), 2001.

Also author of short stories.

SIDELIGHTS: John S. Tarlton is the author of novels dealing with middle-aged characters facing tough challenges in their lives. In his debut book, *A Window*

Facing West, the author tells of forty-seven-year-old Gatlin, who tries to ride out his midlife crisis; he reflects on his life and wonders whether he did not sew enough of his wild oats when he had the chance. Comfortably married to Sarah for two dozen years, Gatlin is the same age his father was when his father committed suicide, and he is suddenly overcome by a "masculine meltdown," as one *Publishers Weekly* writer put it. He consequently begins to believe he should imitate the ways of his cheating and philandering friends. Exploring Gatlin's psychological state through several sometimes humorous episodes, Tarlton reveals his character's personal crisis as he frets about his sex life and his mortality, problems that can only be faced head-on if he comes to terms with his father's death. The *Publishers Weekly* critic called *A Window Facing West* a "witty, though sometimes labored debut," while Joanna M. Burkhardt asserted in *Library Journal* that it is "well crafted and provocative."

In the follow-up novel, *The Cost of Doing Business,* Tarlton creates a complex Southern tale featuring a thirty-something woman named Diane Morris, who works as an oil company's lease negotiator trying to persuade Louisiana residents to sell their land for the drilling rights. The book relates not only her difficulties in dealing with the property owners, all of whom have various reasons for not cooperating with her, but also her family problems, including an ex-husband who is an ex-convict in trouble. In addition, Morris is living with her widowed father and taking care of her own son, Tim. Events become even trickier for Morris when A. E. Baughman—the wealthy landowner who is trying to grab the land rights of his neighbors so that he can profit from the oil deal—starts receiving threatening messages. This leads to the involvement of the local law enforcement and a new romantic interest for Morris: the sheriff.

A number of reviewers received *The Cost of Doing Business* warmly, with one *Kirkus Reviews* contributor describing it as a "fine, funny potboiler, with only an unlikely twist at the end to give the reader pause." *Booklist* writer Brendan Dowling especially enjoyed the story's quirky characters who still "remain multifaceted and true to life," and a *Publishers Weekly* critic concluded that "the novel is worth reading for its insight into the truths that motivate people of all regions."

BIOGRAPHICAL AND CRITICAL SOURCES:

PERIODICALS

Booklist, August, 2001, Brendan Dowling, review of *The Cost of Doing Business,* p. 2092.
Kirkus Reviews, August 15, 2001, review of *The Cost of Doing Business,* p. 1161.
Library Journal, October 15, 1999, Joanna M. Burkhardt, review of *A Window Facing West,* p. 108.
New York Times Book Review, January 2, 2000, Erik Burns, review of *A Window Facing West,* p. 14.
Publishers Weekly, August 23, 1999, review of *A Window Facing West,* p. 46; September 24, 2001, review of *The Cost of Doing Business,* p. 66.

ONLINE

January Online, http://www.januarymagazine.com/ (October 27, 2003), Linda Richards, "A Terrible Beauty," review of *The Cost of Doing Business.*

*   *   *

TAYLOR, Mary F.

PERSONAL: Married; children: one son. *Education:* Earned psychology degree; received training in Gestalt therapy; attended Le Cordon Bleu (Paris, France); Ecôle des Trois Gourmandes, grand diploma. *Hobbies and other interests:* Yoga, meditation.

ADDRESSES: Home—3020 Jefferson St., Boulder, CO 80304. *Agent*—Jane Dystel, Dystel and Goderich Literary Management, 1 Union Square West, Suite 904, New York, NY, 10003. *E-mail*—authors@ whatareyouhungryfor.net.

CAREER: Author and counselor. Instructor and counselor on diet and nutrition.; Appeared in video *Low Fat Cooking Techniques* with Graham Kerr.

WRITINGS:

New Vegetarian Classics: Soups, photographs by Diane Farris, Crossing Press (Freedom, CA), 1994.

New Vegetarian Classics: Entrées, photographs by Diane Farris, Crossing Press (Freedom, CA), 1995.

Lunch Crunch: Beating the Lunchbox Blues, The Yoga Workshop (Boulder, CO), 1997.

(With Lynn Ginsberg) *What Are You Hungry For?: Women, Food, and Spirituality,* illustrations by Josef Pusedu, St. Martin's Press (New York, NY), 2002.

Coauthor with Lynn Ginsberg of *Better Living through Balance,* published by Natural Foods Merchandiser. *Yoga Journal* author of articles and column "Eating Wisely", beginning 1999.

SIDELIGHTS: After winning a personal battle with anorexia, Mary F. Taylor studied the relationship between food and happiness. She wondered why women equated thinness with happiness when a woman who is starving is certainly not happy. Taylor concluded that women use food to fill a spiritual void. As long as this void exists, diets will never work. With coauthor Lynn Ginsberg, Taylor published her discoveries in the book, *What Are You Hungry For?: Women, Food, and Spirituality.* Taylor and Ginsberg contend that the body issues women suffer stem from their disconnection with their personal selves. *What Are You Hungry For?* demonstrates how mind and body practices such as yoga can help women overcome body/food issues.

Unlike other "diet" books, *What Are You Hungry For?* focuses not on the right foods to eat, but on how to think about food. The authors want readers to consider how much time they have spent fantasizing about food and obsessing about their bodies. Jane Dystel of *Publishers Weekly* concluded that readers "will learn to savor the 'rasa' (essence) of food and to eat what feels right for them."

Taylor and Ginsberg travel throughout the country conducting workshops on women, food, and spirituality.

BIOGRAPHICAL AND CRITICAL SOURCES:

PERIODICALS

Publishers Weekly, December 17, 2001, Jane Dystal, review of *What Are You Hungry For?: Women, Food, and Spirituality.*

ONLINE

Mary Taylor Web site, http://www.whatareyouhungryfor.net (May 28, 2003).

St. Martin's Press Web site, http://www.holtzbrinckpublishers.com/stmartins/ (May 28, 2003), review of *What Are You Hungry For?.*

Yoga Chicago Web site, http://www.yogachicago.com (May 28, 2003), review of *What Are You Hungry For?.**

*   *   *

THALMANN, William G. 1947-

PERSONAL: Born 1947. *Education:* Amherst College, B.A., 1969; Yale University, Ph.D., 1975.

ADDRESSES: Office—Department of Classics and Comparative Literature, University of Southern California College of Letters, Arts, and Sciences, Los Angeles, CA 90089. *E-mail*—thalmann@usc.edu.

CAREER: Yale University, New Haven, CT, 1975-84, began as assistant professor of classics, became associate professor of classics; Hobart and William Smith Colleges, Geneva, NY, associate professor of classics, 1984-87; University of Southern California, Los Angeles, professor of classics, 1987-2001, professor of classics and comparative literature, 2001—.

MEMBER: American Philological Association, Classical Association of the Midwest and South, California Classical Association.

AWARDS, HONORS: General Education Teaching Award, University of Southern California, 1997-98; Raubenheimer Outstanding Senior Faculty Award, University of Southern California, 1998.

WRITINGS:

Dramatic Art in Aeschylus's "Seven against Thebes," Yale University Press (New Haven, CT), 1978.

Conventions of Form and Thought in Early Greek Epic Poetry, Johns Hopkins University Press (Baltimore, MD), 1984.

"The Odyssey": An Epic of Return, Twayne (Boston, MA), 1992.

The Swineherd and the Bow: Representations of Class in "The Odyssey," Cornell University Press (Ithaca, NY), 1998.

Editor of ancient world titles, *Norton Anthology of World Masterpieces,* 1998—; member of editorial board, *Classical Antiquity,* 1994—. Contributor of scholarly articles to periodicals.

SIDELIGHTS: William G. Thalmann analyzes classical Greek epic poetry and drama, searching the texts for clues on the culture and societal structure of the ancient Greek world. To quote William C. Scott in the *Classical Journal,* Thalmann "has a firm and unified conception of a song culture in the early poetic world which would allow both poet and audience to be educated within the same conventions of poetry." The critic continued that Thalmann demonstrates how ancient poets knew "what their audiences would have expected and thereby had an area of creative potential to play upon." Thalmann's research ranges widely through the available ancient texts, but he particularly focuses on Homer's *Odyssey* and the ways in which it reveals the accepted religious, social, and political tenets of its time.

Thalmann's *Conventions of Form and Thought in Early Greek Epic Poetry* uses several texts and fragments to analyze the song culture and the expectations of its audience. Scott called the work "a major book on early Greek hexameter poetry . . . firm, persuasive, and compelling." In *Classical World,* Walter Donlan likewise praised the book as "sound, careful, and thoughtful structural criticism." In the *Times Literary Supplement,* Peter Walcot praised Thalmann's scholarship but also noted the text's accessibility to non-technical readers. "His book is characterized by a welcome lack of jargon and the arcane," the critic commented. Walcot concluded that *Conventions of Form and Thought in Early Greek Epic Poetry* is "a splendid assessment of early Greek verse."

The Swineherd and the Bow: Representations of Class in "The Odyssey" concentrates on the Homeric epic and explores how it reflects ancient Greek attitudes toward class, slavery, and domestic relationships. Thalmann challenges those who would see *The Odyssey* as subversive of its society, writing instead that the poem "belongs to, and justifies, a world that is strongly hierarchical," according to Robin Osborne in the *Times Literary Supplement.* Indeed, P. Nieto in *Choice* cited Thalmann's book for its "many good observations about slaves and other underprivileged social groups." In his *Classical Philology* review of *The Swineherd and the Bow,* Ryan Balot characterized the work as "rigorous in its attention to philological detail, eclectic in its use of modern theory, and laudable in its attempt to unify the often separate discourses of literary interpretation, history, and political thought." Balot further contended that the book is "admirably interdisciplinary" and that it "usefully introduces the reader to work done in this area, and which provocatively applies modern theory to ancient texts."

BIOGRAPHICAL AND CRITICAL SOURCES:

PERIODICALS

Antiquity, December, 1999, N. James, review of *The Swineherd and the Bow: Representations of Class in "The Odyssey,"* p. 929.

Choice, February, 1979, review of *Dramatic Art in Aeschylus's "Seven against Thebes,"* p. 1660; February, 1999, P. Nieto, review of *The Swineherd and the Bow,* p. 1061.

Classical Journal, February-March, 1986, William C. Scott, review of *Conventions of Form and Thought in Early Greek Epic Poetry,* pp. 258-260.

Classical Philology, January, 2001, Ryan Balot, review of *The Swineherd and the Bow,* p. 82.

Classical World, May-June, 1986, Walter Donlan, review of *Conventions of Form and Thought in Early Greek Epic Poetry,* p. 341.

Times Literary Supplement, February 22, 1985, Peter Walcot, "A Shared Enterprise," p. 209; June 18, 1999, Robin Osborne, "Going Back to Sea," p. 35.

Yale Review, summer, 1979, review of *Dramatic Art in Aeschylus's "Seven against Thebes,"* pp. 12-13.*

*   *   *

THOMAS, Will 1958-

PERSONAL: Born 1958; married: wife's name, Julia; children: two. *Hobbies and other interests:* Martial arts, railway modeling.

ADDRESSES: Home—Metropolitan Tulsa, OK. *Agent*—c/o Author Mail, Simon & Schuster, 1230 Avenue of the Americas, New York, NY 10020.

CAREER: Novelist, librarian, and Internet instructor.

WRITINGS:

Some Danger Involved, Simon & Schuster (New York, NY), 2004.

Contributor of short fiction to periodicals, including *Ellery Queen's Mystery Magazine.*

SIDELIGHTS: A professional librarian, Will Thomas applied his Internet research skills and writing talent to produce *Some Danger Involved,* a mystery set in his favorite historical era, Victorian England. The story concerns a young Welshman named Thomas Llewelyn who answers an ad for an assistant from an enquiry agent, or private investigator, named Cyrus Barker. After surviving a job interview that includes dodging a knife Barker throws at his chest, Llewelyn is taken on and becomes the chronicler of Barker's cases. While comparisons to famous fictional sleuths Sherlock Holmes and Dr. Watson are inevitable, "this team is clearly different, and their journey into the London ghettoes is fast-paced, vividly alive, and filled with action," noted Harriet Klausner in a review of *Some Danger Involved* for *AllReaders.com.*

In "the first of what will hopefully be a long-running series," according to *Bookreporter.com* contributor Joe Hartlaub, Barker is called in by London's Jewish community when a rabbinical student is found crucified. Anti-Semitism is rife throughout London, and the leaders of the Jewish community, mainly refugees from Eastern Europe, are fearful that a pogrom is starting in their new homeland. As Barker and Llewelyn chase clues and suspects through synagogues and churches, they discover an underworld of virulent hate groups hiding under the mantel of Christianity. "The exploration of the chasm between Christians and Jews, the details of Jewish customs, and the vivid period ambience lend philosophical depth" to the novel, according to *Booklist* reviewer Jennifer Baker. In addition to the Jewish ghetto, the sleuths find themselves in other exotic neighborhoods, and "the author's lively, learned tour of the various foreign enclaves of 19th-century London is notably contemporary," commented a *Publishers Weekly* reviewer.

In addition to an intriguing setting, Thomas provides interesting characters, including his two protagonists. Llewelyn is an Oxford student, but he is also an alumnus of Oxford Prison, where he was once wrongly incarcerated. Barker is an eccentric who combines the knowledge of a Biblical scholar with the skills of a martial artist. While now a wealthy gentleman, he actually endured a difficult, hardscrabble childhood and worked at various positions that included a stint as a clipper-ship captain. Indeed, noted Tim Hoke in the *Green Man Review Online,* "the real interest here is neither the rough and tumble . . . or the search for a murderer, but rather Llewelyn's quest to learn about his employer." Thomas also provides some interesting minor characters, including Barker's sarcastic butler, who is a mean shot, and a French chef who also cultivates a taste for sabotage. The victim also turns out to be a bit of a puzzle. An intelligent and attractive young man, he seems to have consciously sought to marginalize himself even within London's embattled Jewish community. The result is "an auspicious start for Thomas's planned series and should find a ready audience among fans of historical mystery," concluded *TheMysteryReader.com* contributor Jessica Plonka.

Thomas told *CA:* "Of course, I was influenced by Doyle, but I also studied Hardy, George Gissing, and George MacDonald while writing *Some Danger Involved.* Since my novels often feature real characters, I study their writings and history.

"Though I use a computer quite often, I write in longhand, frequently outside on my porch, with a pipe between my teeth. Staring into the clouds helps transport me back to 1884.

"I first became interested in writing when my wife, Julia, was pregnant with our first child. I was an actor, and was frequently gone most nights at performances and rehearsals. I needed to find a creative outlet that didn't take me away from home so often. Writing became that outlet."

BIOGRAPHICAL AND CRITICAL SOURCES:

PERIODICALS

Booklist, May 1, 2004, Jennifer Baker, review of *Some Danger Involved,* p. 1524.

Kirkus Reviews, February 15, 2004, review of *Some Danger Involved,* p. 159.

Library Journal, May 1, 2004, Michele Leber, review of *Some Danger Involved,* p. 145.

Publishers Weekly, March 22, 2004, review of *Some Danger Involved,* p. 65.

ONLINE

AllReaders.com, http://www.allreaders.com/ (November 22, 2004), Harriet Klausner, review of *Some Danger Involved.*

Bookreporter.com, http://www.bookreporter.com/ (November 22, 2004), Joe Hartlaub, review of *Some Danger Involved.*

Green Man Review Online, http://www.greenman review.com/ (November 22, 2004), Tim Hoke, review of *Some Danger Involved.*

Roundtable Reviews Online, http://www.roundtable reviews.com/ (June, 2004), Tracy Farnsworth, interview with Thomas.

TheMysteryReader.com, http://www.themysteryreader. com/ (November 22, 2004), Jessica Plonka, review of *Some Danger Involved.*

*   *   *

THOMAS, K. H.
See KIRK, T(homas) H(obson)

*   *   *

TODES, Samuel (Judah) 1927-1994

PERSONAL: Born June 27, 1927, in Stamford, CT; died 1994. *Education:* Swarthmore College, B.A., 1949; Harvard University, M.A., 1952, Ph.D., 1963.

CAREER: Massachusetts Institute of Technology, began as instructor, became assistant professor of philosophy, 1959-66; Northwestern University, associate professor of philosophy, 1968-94. Yale University, visiting lecturer, 1967; University of California—Berkeley, visiting associate professor of philosophy, 1977. *Military service:* U.S. Army, 1953-55, clinical psychologist.

AWARDS, HONORS: Danforth Foundation fellowships, 1966-67; Everett Baker Moore Teaching Award, Massachusetts Institute of Technology, 1966.

WRITINGS:

The Human Body as Material Subject of the World, Garland (New York, NY), 1990, revised as *Body and World,* introductions by Hubert L. Dreyfus and Piotr Hoffman, MIT Press (Cambridge, MA), 2001.

Contributor to scholarly journals, including *Journal of Existentialism;* contributor to anthologies, including *Kant: A Collection of Critical Essays,* Doubleday (New York, NY), 1967; *New Essays in Phenomenology,* Quadrangle, 1969; *Patterns of the Life-World* Northwestern University Press (Evanston, IL), 1970; and *Dialogues with Phenomenology,* Nihoff (The Hague, Netherlands), 1975.

SIDELIGHTS: American philosopher Samuel Todes wrote *The Human Body as Material Subject of the World* as his dissertation at Harvard University in 1963. It was first published in book form in 1990 and then republished in 2001 as *Body and World,* bringing new readership and acclaim to the work.

Todes studied gestalt psychology with Wolfgang Köhler at Swarthmore College. While a student at Harvard University in the mid-1950s, Todes met regularly with German philosopher Aron Gurwitsch, who in turn had studied with Edmund Husserl in Germany and had influenced French existentialist philosopher Maurice Merleau-Ponty. Out of Todes's interaction with Gurwitsch grew the inspiration for his dissertation, which, according to Shaun Gallagher of the *Times Literary Supplement,* "continues and extends Gurwitsch's phenomenological analysis of the perceptual field and Merleau-Ponty's phenomenology of embodied perception."

Yet the work of these philosophers was only a starting point for Todes's theories. He lightly touches on the work of Merleau-Ponty, Jean-Paul Sartre, Martin Heidegger, and Husserl and then moves on to his original analysis that the body is essential to cognitive experience. The theories of seventeenth-and eighteenth-century philosophers Descartes, Hume, Kant, and Leibniz come most often into the discussion, as Todes shows how they erred in underestimating the importance of the body in perception. According to Gallagher, *Body and World* is "a fresh account of embodied, environmentally situated cognition" that "aims to show how objects come into our experience, how that experience is the body's experience, and how that is shaped by the body's capacity for movement through the physical environment," using examples from simple motor activities to playing sports and dancing. Gallagher found that the work has two shortfalls—it does not account for the way humans perceive other humans, and it does not offer ways in which the analysis of movement might be used to advance developmental psychology and neuro-psychology. However, these do not detract from Todes's work, Gallagher observed. He called it "a rich phenomenological resource" that others could use as a basis for further research.

Robert Pepperell, in a review of the book for *Leonardo Digital Reviews Online,* commented that "for Todes it is the awkwardnesses and imbalances, frictions and contraints characterising our real existence . . . that are a precondition of our subjective experience." Todes, wrote Pepperell, "mounts the claim that we can distinguish between imaginary figments and veridical knowledge by the feedback gained from physical intervention." Pepperell questioned this theory, asking whether an inactive state or even hyperactivity might produce hallucinations. He was dissatisfied with Todes's logical counter to such a question. However, in conclusion, Pepperell noted, "Todes' style is clear and consistent, while the book has obviously been expertly edited. So with determination and patience there is much to be drawn from it."

BIOGRAPHICAL AND CRITICAL SOURCES:

PERIODICALS

Times Literary Supplement, October 18, 2002, Shaun Gallagher, "Realism in Mind," review of *Body and World,* p. 13.

ONLINE

Leonardo Digital Reviews Online, http://mitpress2.mit.edu/e-journals/Leonardo/ (November 2, 2002), Robert Pepperell, review of *Body and World.*
Thymos.com, http://www.thymos.com/ (May 5, 2003), Piero Scaruffi, review of *Body and World.**

V

VANE, John R(obert) 1927-2004

OBITUARY NOTICE— See index for *CA* sketch: Born March 29, 1927, in Tardebigge, Worcestershire, England; died of complications from bone fractures November 19, 2004, in Farnborough, England. Pharmacologist, educator, and author. Vane was a Nobel Prize-winning pharmacologist most noted for his discovery of how aspirin works, which in turn led to more uses for the popular drug, as well as to the development of other medications. As a child, Vane fell in love with experimentation, spending many hours playing with a chemistry set his parents had given him. However, when he started attending the University of Birmingham, he found he did not like chemistry, just experimentation. After graduating with a B.S. in 1946, a professor suggested he take up pharmacology. At the time, Vane was not sure what that was, but he accepted the proposal and enrolled at Oxford University, where, discovering his aptitude for pharmacology, he received a B.S. in 1949 and a Ph.D. in 1953. He then taught for two years at Yale University and for six years at the Institute of Basic Medical Science at the Royal College of Surgeons. During the early 1960s, he was a reader at London University, and from 1966 to 1973 he was a professor of experimental pharmacology there. Despite advice against it from his friends, Vane left academia for a job in private industry with the Wellcome Foundation in 1973. It was during this period that he made his discovery of prostacyclin, a type of prostaglandin that is responsible for generating fever and pain when a body is sick or in trauma. Vane also learned that aspirin works by blocking cyclooxygenase, which in turn stops the production of prostaglandins, thus reducing fever, swelling, and pain. This work led to his being the co-recipient of the No-

bel Prize for Medicine in 1982. Vane's discovery also led to the creation of a variety of pain-relief medicines categorized as COX-2 drugs, such as Vioxx, and angiotensin-converting enzyme (ACE) inhibitors, which are used to treat circulatory and heart problems. Vane was the author or editor of numerous books on pharmacology, including *Anti-Inflammatory Drugs* (1979), *Perspectives in Prostaglandin Research* (1983), and *Selective COX-2 Inhibitors: Pharmacology, Clinical Effects, and Therapeutic Potential* (1998).

OBITUARIES AND OTHER SOURCES:

PERIODICALS

Chicago Tribune, November 23, 2004, section 3, p. 12.
New York Times, November 23, 2004, p. C17.
Times, November 25, 2004, p. 71.
Washington Post, November 24, 2004, p. B7.

*   *   *

VELARDE, Giles 1935-

PERSONAL: Surname is pronounced "Ve-LAR-de"; born December 2, 1935, in Liverpool, England; son of F. X. (an architect) and M. E. Velarde; married 1967; wife's name Celia Mary; children: Felix, Camilla, one other child. *Ethnicity:* "Mongrel." *Education:* Attended Chelsea School of Art. *Politics:* "Left of center." *Hobbies and other interests:* Cooking, painting, the English countryside.

ADDRESSES: Home and office—Fir Trees Studio, Cliff End Lane, Pett Level, East Sussex TN35 4EF, England; fax: 01424-813266. *E-mail*—gilesvelarde@gva-fts.freeserve.co.uk.

CAREER: Designer of museum exhibitions, 1959-2001; part-time designer and consultant, 2001—. Geological Museum (now Natural History Museum), designer and head of design, 1977-88; designer of more than 100 other commercial and government exhibitions in England and Europe. Lecturer in English and French, including lectures at Kingston Polytechnic, University of Humberside, Institute of Archaeology, London, University of Essex, University of Salford, and University of Southampton. *Military service:* Royal Navy, 1953-55; became sub-lieutenant.

MEMBER: Royal Society of Arts (fellow), Museums Association (fellow).

WRITINGS:

Designing Exhibitions, Design Council (London, England), 1988, Whitney Library of Design (New York, NY), 1989, 2nd edition, Ashgate Publishing (Brookfield, VT), 2001.

Contributor to books, including *Manual of Curatorship,* Museums Association (London, England), 1984; *Did Britain Make It?,* Design Council (London, England), 1986; and *Manual of Touring Exhibitions,* Touring Exhibition Group (London, England), 1995, 2nd edition, 2000. Contributor to periodicals, including *Museum and Exhibition Design, Design,* and *Museums Journal.*

*   *   *

Von FALKENSTEIN, Waldeen 1913-1993

PERSONAL: Born February 1, 1913, in Dallas, TX; died, August 19, 1993, in Cuernavaca, Morelios, Mexico; married Rudolfo de Valencia; children: one son. *Education:* Attended Kosloff's School of Imperial Russian Ballet, 1918-28.

CAREER: Los Angeles Opera, soloist dancer, beginning 1926; Kosloff's Ballet, soloist dancer, beginning 1926; Michio Ito company, dancer, 1931; performed as dance soloist, Mexico, 1934; School of Modern Dance, founder, 1939; Ballet of the National Fine Arts Institute, Mexico City, Mexico, director, 1940, 1958; Theatre of the Arts, dancer, 1940-60; Fine Arts Academy, dancer, 1941; Ballet Waldeen, director, created first mass ballet *Siembra,* 1942-45; Sir Thomas Beecham's Mozart Festival, Mexico City, Mexico, choreographer, 1944; Hunter College Choreographers Workshop, choreographer, 1946; New School for Social Research, choreographer, 1946; Nicholas Roerich Museum, choreographer, 1946; 100th Anniversary Celebration of the Communist Party, choreographer, 1946; Ballet Moderno, Mexico, founder, 1948; Ballet Waldeen, Mexico, founder, 1960; National School of Modern Dance, Cuba, director, 1962; Cuban School of Dance for Art Instructors, Cuba, director, 1962; Mexican Contemporary Dance Company, director and choreographer, 1976-81; National Institute of Art, Mexico, created Ometeotl workshop, 1980.

AWARDS, HONORS: Mexican Music and Theatre Critics' Award, 1969, for best choreographer.

WRITINGS:

(Translator) Pablo Neruda, *Canto general,* 1950.
La danza: imagen de creación Serdan, (title means "The Dance: An Image of Creació Serdan"), [Mexico], 1982.

Contributor to anthology *The Dance Has Many Faces,* edited by Walter Sorrell, 1951. Contributor to *Magazine of the National University of Mexico, Boletin CID DANZA,* and *Revista: Plural.*

SIDELIGHTS: Waldeen Von Falkenstein, professionally known as Waldeen, began studying classical ballet as a young child, and began performing classical ballet solos at the age of thirteen for the Kosloff Ballet and the Los Angeles Opera. At the age of fifteen she gave up classical ballet to develop her own form of expressive dance.

Waldeen had great influence and popularity in Mexico, a country she loved. In 1938 she was invited to perform and set up a school of dance by the Mexican secretary general of education, an invitation she gladly accepted. She also performed solo concerts in Mexico, which received positive reviews. Waldeen taught, choreographed, and wrote up until her death, on August 19, 1993.

BIOGRAPHICAL AND CRITICAL SOURCES:

BOOKS

International Dictionary of Modern Dance, St James Press (Detroit, MI), 1998.

OTHER

Stony Brook University Hospital Web site, http://www.hsc.stonybrook.edu/ (April 16, 2002), "Waldeen and the Americas: The Dance Has Many Faces."*

*   *   *

VRKLJAN, Irena 1930-

PERSONAL: Born August 21, 1930, in Belgrade, Yugoslavia (now Serbia and Montenegro); married. *Education:* Attended schools in Zagreb, Croatia, and Berlin, Germany.

ADDRESSES: Home—Zagreb, Croatia, and Berlin, Germany. *Agent*—c/o Author Mail, Northwestern University Press, 629 Noyes Street, Evanston, IL 60208-4210.

CAREER: Writer. Poet, novelist, and television screenwriter.

WRITINGS:

Krik je samo tisina, Nolit (Belgrade, Yugoslavia), 1954.
Paralele, Lykos (Zagreb, Croatia), 1957.
Stvari vec daleke, Zora (Zagreb, Croatia), 1962.
Doba prijateljstva, Mladost (Zagreb, Croatia), 1966.
Soba, taj strasni vrt, Prosveta (Belgrade, Yugoslavia), 1966.
(With Benno Meyer-Wehlack) *Modderkrebse,* Wagenbach (Berlin, Germany), 1971.

Ihre Paulina Golis, Reclam (Stuttgart, West Germany), 1980.
U kozi moje sestre, Naprijed (Zagreb, Croatia), 1982.
Tochter wischen und West, Rogners (Berlin, West Germany), 1982.
Svila, škare, Grafiĉki zavod Hrvatske (Zagreb, Croatia), 1984, translation by Sibelan Forrester and Celia Hawkesworth published with *Marina, ili o biografiji* as *The Silk, the Shears; and Marina, or, About Biography,* Northwestern University Press (Evanston, IL), 1999.
Marina, ili o biografiji, Grafiĉki zavod Hrvatske (Zagreb, Croatia), 1986, translation by Sibelan Forrester and Celia Hawkesworth published with *Svila, škare* as *The Silk, the Shears; and Marina, or, About Biography,* Northwestern University Press (Evanston, IL), 1999.
Vece poezije, CDK (Zagreb, Croatia), 1987.
Berlinski rukopis, Grafiĉki zavod Hrvatske (Zagreb, Croatia), 1988.
Dora, ove jeseni, Grafiĉki zavod Hrvatske (Zagreb, Croatia), 1991.
Pred crvenim zidom, Durieux (Zagreb, Croatia), 1994.
Posljednje putovanje u Bec (title means "The Last Journey to Vienna"), Znanje (Zagreb, Croatia), 2000.
Smrt dolazi sa suncem, SysPrint (Zagreb, Croatia), 2002.

SIDELIGHTS: Croatian writer Irena Vrkljan is a poet, a television screenwriter, and the author of the critically acclaimed two-part memoir *The Silk, the Shears; and Marina, or, About Biography.* Born in Belgrade, Yugoslavia, Vrkljan's family moved to Zagreb, Croatia, in 1941, after the Nazis occupied Belgrade. During the 1950s and 1960s she published several works of highly regarded poetry, and in 1969 she moved to Berlin, West Germany, to attend a film academy. After establishing a successful career in television, Vrkljan began to divide her time between Berlin and Zagreb.

The two parts of *The Silk, the Shears; and Marina, or, About Biography,* were originally published separately as *Svila, škare* and *Marina, ili o biografiji.* According to *Women's Review of Books* critic Alison Anderson, "the first part is a typical memoir, intimate and subjective; the second is more of a literary work, an intellectual reflection on both Vrkljan's own life and that of Marina Tsvetayeva, one of Russia's greatest twentieth-century poets." In *The Silk, the Shears; and Marina, or, About Biography* Vrkljan "vividly captures a sense of the chaos on both the historical and the personal level that continues to sweep southeastern Europe," remarked Aida Vidan in *World Literature Today.* Vidan added that the "autobiographical works do not have an explicit political dimension, but they nevertheless depict the profound effect that historical changes can have on an individual and on the way that individual understands these changes at different points in her life."

In *Svila, škare* Vrkljan recounts her childhood in Yugoslavia, her adolescence in Croatia, and her formative years as a writer in Zagreb and Berlin. *World Literature Today* critic Ivo Vidan, reviewing the original publication of *Svila, škare,* described the work as a "mosaic" of Vrkljan's life. The narrative is not chronological, Vidan observed; instead, the author's "life story is created through a sequence of selective details representative of people, environment, and personal contacts, functioning as allusions to social circumstances, historical changes, and human behavior rather than as self-standing and comprehensive symbols." A critic in *Kirkus Reviews* praised the work, stating that "Vrkljan writes with honesty and tenderness about her family and friends, about her development as a poet, her own and her mother's unsatisfactory role as wife, her oppressive father, and the troubles of women in society."

In the second part of the work, the fictionalized biography of Tsvetayeva, Vrkljan "turns to both recorded fact and imagination to provide the elements of another woman's life, and in so doing to illuminate her own," wrote Anderson in *Women's Review of Books.* Like Vrkljan, Tsvetayeva left her homeland because of political turmoil; she lived much of her life in poverty and eventually committed suicide in 1941. "Clearly, the theme of exile, and the strong effect it can have on the life of the artist, is shared by the two women," Anderson noted. The separate memoirs in *The Silk, the Shears; and Marina, or, About Biography* "complement each other in a way no ordinary memoir or series of memoirs can do," Anderson continued. "This may well have been Vrkljan's intention, to start out by telling her own life in a simple and evocative way, then to re-examine both her life and her first memoir through the study of the life of a much-admired predecessor."

BIOGRAPHICAL AND CRITICAL SOURCES:

PERIODICALS

Booklist, May 15, 2003, review of *Smrt dolazi sa suncem,* p. 1653.

Kirkus Reviews, January 1, 1999, review of *The Silk, the Shears; and Marina, or, About Biography,* p. 55.

Women's Review of Books, September, 1999, Alison Anderson, review of *The Silk, the Shears; and Marina, or, About Biography,* p. 11.

World Literature Today, winter, 1986, Ivo Vidan, review of *Svila, škare,* p. 142; winter, 2000, Aida Vidan, review of *The Silk, the Shears; and Marina, or, About Biography,* p. 191; spring, 2001, Aida Vidan, review of *Posljednje putovanje u Bec,* p. 387.*

W

WAGAR, W(alter) Warren 1932-2004

OBITUARY NOTICE— See index for *CA* sketch: Born June 5, 1932, in Baltimore, MD; died November 16, 2004, in Vestal, NY. Historian, educator, and author. Wagar was a history professor whose interest in science fiction also led to books about H. G. Wells and several of his own published sci-fi stories. His undergraduate work was completed at Franklin and Marshall College in 1953, followed by a master's degree at Indiana University the next year and a Ph.D. from Yale University in 1959. During the early 1960s, Wagar taught at Wellesley College, then moved in the late 1960s to the University of New Mexico. He then joined the faculty at the State University of New York at Binghamton, where he was a history professor from 1970 until his 2002 retirement. Among his courses were classes that speculated on future events; these were extremely popular at Binghamton and led to his being named a Distinguished Teaching Professor by the university. As a scholar, Wagar specialized in the intellectual history of modern-day Europe, editing the book *European Intellectual History since Darwin and Marx* (1967) and authoring *Good Tidings: The Belief in Progress from Darwin to Marcuse* (1972). An expert on the literature of H. G. Wells, he served as vice president of the H. G. Well Society in 1988 and was a member of the World Future Society. Beginning in the 1980s, Wagar wrote a number of science-fiction stories that were published in genre magazines and anthologies. On the subject of Wells, he was the author of *H. G. Wells and the World State* (1961) and *H. G. Wells: Traversing Time* (2004), and editor of *H. G. Wells: Journalism and Prophecy* (1964; revised edition, 1966), among other titles. Many of Wagar's more recent titles were on futurism and include *A Short His-*tory of the Future* (1989; revised edition, 1999) and *Memoirs of the Future* (2001).

OBITUARIES AND OTHER SOURCES:

PERIODICALS

Chronicle of Higher Education, December 3, 2004, p. 42.

ONLINE

H. G. Wells Society Web site, http://www.hgwellsusa.50megs.com/ (January 27, 2005).
History Department at Binghamton University Web site, http://history.binghamton.edu/ (January 27, 2005).
Pipe Dream on the Web, http://www.bupipedream.com/ (December 3, 2004).
World Network of Religious Futurists Web site, http://www.wnrf.org/ (December 1, 2004).

*   *   *

WAGNER, Michele R. 1975-

PERSONAL: Born September 8, 1975, in San Diego, CA; daughter of Richard Henry and Barbara (an escrow officer; maiden name, Wilson) Cecelski; married Mark S. Wagner (an engineering lab supervisor) August 2, 1997; children: Gwendolyn. *Ethnicity:*

"Caucasian." *Education:* California State University, San Marcas, B.A. (English), 1997. *Politics:* Republican Conservative. *Religion:* Reformed Presbyterian.

ADDRESSES: Agent—c/o Author Mail, Gareth Stevens, Inc., 330 West Olive St., No. 100, Milwaukee, WI 53212-1068.

CAREER: Writer and editor. Greehaven Press, San Diego, CA, editor and proofreader, 1998-2001.

WRITINGS:

At Issue: How Should Prisons Treat Their Inmates?, Greenhaven Press (San Diego, CA), 2000.
Sweden, Gareth Stevens (Milwaukee, WI), 2001, expanded with text by Vimala Alexander as *Welcome to Sweden,* 2002.
Haiti, Gareth Stevens (Milwaukee, WI), 2002, expanded with text by Katharine Brown as *Welcome to Haiti,* 2003.

SIDELIGHTS: Michele R. Wagner once commented: "I have always been more comfortable reading rather than writing. While studying for my English degree, I chose a literature emphasis over writing. Writing books to educate children has been a step towards finally crossing that line and trying something different. I have enjoyed my forays into the world of writing and hope that as my confidence in my writing grows, so will my collection of work."

BIOGRAPHICAL AND CRITICAL SOURCES:

PERIODICALS

School Library Journal, February, 2002, Blair Christolon, review of *Sweden,* p. 151; February, 2003, Be Astengo, review of *Sri Lanka,* p. 160.

*   *   *

WAKLING, Christopher 1970-

PERSONAL: Born 1970; married a physician. *Education:* Studied English at Oxford University.

ADDRESSES: Agent—c/o Author Mail, Pan Macmillan-Picador, 20 New Wharf Rd., London N1 9RR, England. *E-mail*—responses@christopher wakling.com.

CAREER: Has worked as a teacher and as an barrister in London, England.

WRITINGS:

The Immortal Part (novel), Riverhead Books (New York, NY), 2003, published as *On Cape Three Points,* Picador (London, England), 2003.

WORK IN PROGRESS: A novel, set in Kashmir, about a kidnapping.

SIDELIGHTS: Christopher Wakling is a former corporate lawyer who drew on his professional background to write his first novel, a thriller titled *The Immortal Part.* The author was working for a law firm in London, England, when, as *Bookseller* writer Benedicte Page reported, he and a colleague "were faced with an opportunity to cover up something that had gone wrong. 'For a lawyer, that's absolutely prohibited, and obviously we didn't,' explains Wakling. 'But there was a sense of "Well, what if . . . ?"'" In *The Immortal Part* young attorney Lewis Penn accidentally loses an important file belonging to UKI, a Ukrainian company that is a big client for his firm. Retracing his steps, he believes he has located the file and sends it to an office in Washington, D.C. He soon finds out his horrible mistake: not only has he lost the first file, which contained sensitive financial information, but the second file contains information regarding UKI's illegal accounting practices. Penn consequently becomes a target for UKI's security chief. He flees to Washington to retrieve the file in a desperate attempt to save both his skin and his career.

While reviewers appreciated the moral dilemma Wakling creates for his humanly flawed character, several reviewers felt this debut to be notably lacking in suspense. *Daily Mirror* writer Andrea Henry enjoyed Wakling's main character, "a normal bloke who finds himself in a bit of a spot," but she complained of a plot with too much talk and not enough action: "Wakling even manages to make the car chases and fights boring." A *Kirkus Reviews* contributor similarly faulted the novel for too many "flashbacks, side trips, maundering, and dire hints whose import is never quite clear." On the other hand, a *Publishers Weekly* reviewer declared *The Immortal Part* a "taut debut [that] is a study of human foibles, with a vivid and all too fallible hero."

BIOGRAPHICAL AND CRITICAL SOURCES:

PERIODICALS

Booklist, February 15, 2003, Joanne Wilkinson, review of *The Immortal Part*, p. 1051.
Bookseller, February 14, 2003, Benedicte Page, "A Moment of Weakness: In Christopher Wakling's Debut Thriller, One Bad Decision Leads His Protagonist into a Nightmare," p. 29.
Daily Mirror (London, England), May 17, 2003, Andrea Henry, "Legally Grinding: Andrea Henry Passes Judgment on a Brit Thriller Lacking in Thrills," p. 56.
Kirkus Reviews, February 1, 2003, review of *The Immortal Part*, p. 178.
Publishers Weekly, March 24, 2003, review of *The Immortal Part*, p. 57.*

*   *   *

WALDMAN, Mark Robert

PERSONAL: Children: one son. *Hobbies and other interests:* Gardening.

ADDRESSES: Office—Mark Waldman Counseling and Ministerial Services, 21900 Marylee St., 274, Woodland Hills, CA 91367. *E-mail*—markwaldman@cyberhotline.com.

CAREER: Mark Waldman Counseling and Ministerial Services, Woodland Hills, CA, director and therapist; Penguin Putnam Group, New York, NY, acquisitions editor; writer.

WRITINGS:

(Editor) *The Art of Staying Together: Embracing Love, Intimacy, and Spirit in Relationships,* Tarcher/Putnam (New York, NY), 1998.

(Editor with Stanley Krippner) *Dreamscaping: New and Creative Ways to Work with Your Dreams,* Roxbury Park/Lowell House (Los Angeles, CA), 1999.
(Editor) *Love Games: How to Deepen Communication, Resolve Conflict, and Discover Who Your Partner Really Is,* Tarcher/Putnam (New York, NY), 2000.
(Editor) *The Spirit of Writing: Classic and Contemporary Essays Celebrating the Writing Life,* Tarcher/Putnam (New York, NY), 2001.
(With Toni Gilbert) *Messages from the Archetypes: Using Tarot for Healing and Spiritual Growth: A Guidebook for Personal and Professional Use,* White Cloud Press (Ashland, OR), 2003.
(Editor) *Archetypes of the Collective Unconscious: Reflecting American Culture through Literature and Art,* Volume 1: *Shadow: Searching for the Hidden Self,* Volume 2: *Healer: Dancing with the Healing Spirit,* Volume 3: *Seeker: Traveling the Path to Enlightenment,* Volume 4: *Lover: Embracing the Passionate Heart,* Tarcher/Putnam (New York, NY), 2003.

Founding editor, *Transpersonal Review.*

SIDELIGHTS: Mark Robert Waldman draws upon his experiences as a therapist to write and edit books about personal and interpersonal fulfillment. Both *The Art of Staying Together: Embracing Love, Intimacy, and Spirit in Relationships* and *Love Games: How to Deepen Communication, Resolve Conflict, and Discover Who Your Partner Really Is* present strategies for couples who seek more depth to their relationships. *Love Games* offers a series of relationship exercises that can be "played" to extend mutual understanding and physical intimacy. A *Publishers Weekly* reviewer described the book as a "gentle primer for couples on improving communication." Waldman told the *Seattle Times* that his love games "make extensive use of the powers of your imagination and creativity, and they challenge you to take emotional risks."

Waldman has made a collection of writings *about* writing and the pleasures and pains of the creative life. In 2001 he released *The Spirit of Writing: Classic and Contemporary Essays Celebrating the Writing Life.* This project began as a collection of essays on the writing process by such luminaries as Mark Twain, Henry Miller, Anaïs Nin, and Joseph Conrad. Then

Waldman decided to query a group of modern writers from a variety of genres and solicit their essays on creativity as well. To his delight, some thirty contemporary authors responded, and their essays are included in the volume. More than sixty writers are represented in *The Spirit of Writing.*

According to Nancy Mehl on *Myshelf.com, The Spirit of Writing* is "a book that will stay close by the side of anyone who writes, who wants to write, or who knows a writer." In her *Writer's Block* online review, Lorie Boucher noted that the book presents "a more balanced view of the work of writing than is usual to collections of this type." Boucher concluded that the work "offers a buffet of opinions, insights, and perspectives."

In an interview with Susan McBride for *Myshelf.com,* Waldman said that publication of *The Spirit of Writing* fulfilled a dream he had "harbored for years." He added: "Being an editor . . . is as enriching as being a therapist. Both require a profoundly intimate dialogue with some of the most interesting people I've ever met. . . . Be it publishing, editing, writing or being a therapist-it's all about people for me. Writing and conversation, sitting in nature with your friends, what more does a person need?"

BIOGRAPHICAL AND CRITICAL SOURCES:

PERIODICALS

Library Journal, December, 1999, Pamela A. Matthews, review of *Love Games: How to Deepen Communication, Resolve Conflict, and Discover Who Your Partner Really Is,* p. 163.
Publishers Weekly, November 15, 1999, review of *Love Games,* p. 48.
Seattle Times, January 27, 2000, Stephanie Dunnewind, "Games Can Reinforce Couple's Relationship," p. C2.
Tennessean, February 10, 2000, Tasneem Ansariyah-Grace, "Love Games More than Just Play," p. D6.

ONLINE

Disinfotainment Today, http://www.disinfotainment today.com/darenet/ (October 23, 2003), Michael Dare, "How I Ended up in *The Spirit of Writing: Classic and Contemporary Essays Celebrating the Writing Life.*"

Myshelf.com, http://www.myshelf.com/ (October 23, 2003), Nancy Mehl, review of *The Spirit of Writing;* Susan McBride, interview with Waldman.
Spirituality & Health Web site, http://www.spirituality health.com/ (October 23, 2003), Frederic and Mary Ann Brussat, review of *Lover: Embracing the Passionate Heart.*
Writer's Block Web site, http://www.writersblock.ca/ (winter, 2001), Lorie Boucher, review of *The Spirit of Writing.**

*   *   *

WEIR, Molly 1920-2004

OBITUARY NOTICE— See index for *CA* sketch: Born March 17, 1920, in Glasgow, Scotland; died November 28, 2004, in Middlesex, England. Actress and author. Weir was an actress best known for her roles as Aggie MacDonald in the radio—and later television—series *Life with the Lyons* and as Hazel the McWitch in the children's TV program *Rentaghost;* she also wrote popular memoirs. She originally trained to be a secretary and was notable for her amazing speed as a typist and in shorthand. An interest in theater led her to start acting in amateur productions, where she also developed a talent for impersonations. While doing some of these impersonations, she was noticed by a talent scout and soon hired to play the part of Ivy McTweed in the radio series *The McFlannels* in 1939. During World War II, she acted in films produced by the British Ministry of Information, and after the war she appeared in a number of feature films, such as *Floodtide* (1949) and *Flesh and Blood* (1951). Weir gained fame in the 1940s, when she played two parts for the radio comedy series *It's That Man Again,* as Tattie Mackintosh and as Tattie's mother. National acclaim came with her next big part as Aggie in *Life with the Lyons,* which was broadcast on radio from 1950 until 1961. Two movies, *Life with the Lyons* (1954) and *The Lyons in Paris* (1951), were also made before the series was produced on British television, beginning in 1957. After the series ended, Weir acted in a number of films, such as *Carry on Regardless* (1961) and *Scrooge* (1970), but she returned to television with a hugely popular children's show called *Rentaghost,* which ran from 1977 until 1984. Weir, who was a familiar face in Britain as the woman who promoted Flash cleaning products for television commercials, also wrote a number of well-received memoirs, including *Shoes Were for Sunday* (1970), *Toe on the Ladder* (1973), *Stepping into the Spotlight* (1977), and *Spinning Like a Peerie* (1983). Her memoirs of her younger days were more recently collected and reprinted in *Molly Weir's Trilogy of Scottish Childhood* (1988).

OBITUARIES AND OTHER SOURCES:

PERIODICALS

Daily Mail (London, England), November 30, 2004, p. 25.

Daily Post (Liverpool, England), December 2, 2004, p. 13.

Daily Record (Glasgow, Scotland), November 30, 2004, p. 22.

Daily Telegraph (London, England), December 2, 2004.

Guardian (Manchester, England), December 1, 2004, p. 27.

Herald (Glasgow, Scotland), November 30, 2004, p. 7.

Independent (London, England), December 1, 2004, p. 35.

Sun (London, England), November 30, 2004, p. 31.

*   *   *

WIESNER, Karen Sue 1969-
(K. S. Wiesner, Karen Wiesner, Karen S. Wiesner)

PERSONAL: Born July 5, 1969; married; husband an artist.

ADDRESSES: Agent—c/o Author Mail, Hard Shell Word Factory, P.O. Box 161,8946 Loberg Rd., Amherst Junction, WI 54407. *E-mail*—kwiesner@cuttingedge.net.

CAREER: Writer.

MEMBER: Electronically Published Internet Connection, Electronic Publishers Coalition, Romance Writers of America (From the Heart chapter), Sisters in Crime, Divas of Romance, Wisconsin Romance Writers of America, Electronically Published Professionals, AERPA.

AWARDS, HONORS: Reviewer's choice award, *Romantic Times,* c. 1999, for *Falling Star;* reviewer's choice award, *Scribes World,* c. 2000, for *Vows and the Vagabond;* Eppie Award, nonfiction category, Electronically Published Internet Connection, 2001, and eBooks n' Bytes Award of Excellence, 2002, both for *Electronic Publishing: The Definitive Guide;* Year 200 for eXcellence in E-publishing Award; two E-Pub Ambassador Awards; two Inscriptions Engraver Award for best online column; Simply Charming Award, for outstanding promotion of e-books.

WRITINGS:

UNDER NAME KAREN WIESNER

Leather and Lace (Book 1 in "Gypsy Road" series; also see below), Hard Shell Word Factory (Amherst Junction, WI), 1999.

Fire and Ice (Book 3 in "Gypsy Road" series), Hard Shell Word Factory (Amherst Junction, WI), Volume 1, 1999, Volume 2, 2002, Volume 3, 2002.

Falling Star (Book 1 in "Angelfire Trilogy"), Hard Shell Word Factory (Amherst Junction, WI), 1999.

Vows and the Vagabond (Book 4 in "Gypsy Road" series), Hard Shell Word Factory (Amherst Junction, WI), 2000.

Sweet Dreams (paranormal romance), Avid Press (England), 2001, Hard Shell Word Factory (Amherst Junction, WI), 2003.

Leather and Lace/Flesh and Blood (Books 1 and 2 in "Gypsy Road" series), Hard Shell Word Factory (Amherst Junction, WI), 2001.

Reluctant Hearts (romance novel; Book 1 in "Wounded Warrior Series"), Hard Shell Word Factory (Amherst Junction, WI), 2002.

Restless as Rain (romantic suspense novel), Hard Shell Word Factory (Amherst Junction, WI), 2002.

First Love (Book 2 in "Angelfire Trilogy"), Hard Shell Word Factory (Amherst Junction, WI), Volume 2, 2002.

Waiting for an Eclipse (romance novel; Book 2 in "Wounded Warriors Series"), Hard Shell Word Factory (Amherst Junction, WI), 2003.

(With Chris Spindler) *Degrees of Separation* (mystery novel; Book 1 in "Falcon's Bend" series), Quiet Storm Publishing (Martinsburg, WV), 2004.

(With Chris Spindler) *Tears on Stone* (Book 2 in "Falcon's Bend" series), Quiet Storm Publishing (Martinsburg, WV), 2005.

Mirror Mirror, Hard Shell Word Factory (Amherst Junction, WI), 2005.

Also author of *Forever Man* (Book 3 in "Angelfire Trilogy"), Hard Shell Word Factory (Amherst Junction, WI). Work represented in anthologies, including *Mistletoe Marriages,* DiskUs Publishing, 1999.

UNDER NAME KAREN S. WIESNER

Electronic Publishing: The Definitive Guide, Petals of Life Publishing, 1999, published as *Electronic Publishing, the Definitive Guide; 2003 Edition: The Most Complete Reference to Non-Subsidy E-Publishing,* Hard Shell Word Factory (Amherst Junction, WI), 2003.

Weave Your Web: The Promotional Companion to Electronic Publishing, the Definitive Guide, 2003 Edition, Hard Shell Word Factory (Amherst Junction, WI), 2003.

Also author of *Electronic Publishing Q&A,* Hard Shell Word Factory (Amherst Junction, WI). Author of "Inkspot," an online column published by Hard Shell Word Factory (Amherst Junction, WI).

UNDER NAME KAREN SUE WIESNER

Taking Responsibility Builds Trust (children's interactive picture book; Book 1 in "Making Good Choices" series), illustrated by Robert Beers, Writer's Exchange E-Publishing (Atherton, Queensland, Australia), 2003.

(With Linda Derkez) *Cody Knows* (children's picture book), illustrated by Candace Hardy, Writer's Exchange E-Publishing (Atherton, Queensland, Australia), 2003.

(With Linda Derkez) *Cody Knows II,* illustrated by Candace Hardy, Writer's Exchange E-Publishing (Atherton, Queensland, Australia), in press.

Taking Care of Your Things (children's interactive picture book; Book 2 in "Making Good Choices" series), illustrated by Robert Lee Beers, Writer's Exchange E-Publishing (Atherton, Queensland, Australia), in press.

OTHER

(Under name K. S. Wiesner) *Soul Bleeds: The Dark Poetry and Other Wanderings of K. S. Wiesner,* Atlantic Bridge Publishing (Indianapolis, IN), 2001.

WORK IN PROGRESS: Wayward Angels, a romance novel, Hard Shell Word Factory (Amherst Junction, WI), 2006; *The Fifteenth Letter,* a mystery novel (Book 3 in "Falcon's Bend" series), under name Karen Wiesner, with Chris Spindler, Quiet Storm Publishing (Martinsburg, WV), 2006; *Until It's Gone,* a romance novel, Hard Shell Word Factory (Amherst Junction, WI), 2007; *White Rainbow,* a romance novel, Hard Shell Word Factory (Amherst Junction, WI), 2008; *Learning to Play Alone, Being Nice,* and *Eating a Balanced Diet,* all children's interactive picture books, under name Karen Sue Wiesner, illustrated by Robert Lee Beers, for Writer's Exchange E-Publishing (Atherton, Queensland, Australia); *The Tree of Life,* a children's book in the "Hard Christian Questions" series, Writer's Exchange E-Publishing (Atherton, Queensland, Australia); research for *No Ordinary Love,* the first book of a projected series titled "Incognito."

BIOGRAPHICAL AND CRITICAL SOURCES:

ONLINE

Karen Wiesner Web site, http://www.karenwiesner.com (March 5, 2004).

*   *   *

WIESNER, K. S.
  See WIESNER, Karen Sue

*   *   *

WIESNER, Karen
  See WIESNER, Karen Sue

*   *   *

WIESNER, Karen S.
  See WIESNER, Karen Sue

WILLIAMS, Paul K. 1966-

PERSONAL: Born June 10, 1966, in Midland, MI; son of Charles and Nancy (Kelsey) Williams. *Ethnicity:* "Caucasian." *Education:* Roger Williams University, B.S., 1989; attended Cornell University, 1989-91. *Politics:* Democrat. *Hobbies and other interests:* Historic preservation.

ADDRESSES: Office—Kelsey and Associates, Inc., 1929 13th St. N.W., Washington, DC 20009. *E-mail*—paul@washingtonhistory.com.

CAREER: U.S. Air Force Pentagon Headquarters, Washington, DC, Legacy Resource Management program director, 1992-97; Kelsey and Associates, Inc. (consulting firm), Washington, DC, owner and operator, 1995—.

MEMBER: World Congress on Art Deco, National Trust for Historic Preservation.

WRITINGS:

Dupont Circle, Arcadia Publishing (Mount Pleasant, SC), 2000.

The Neighborhoods of Logan, Scott, and Thomas Circles, Arcadia Publishing (Mount Pleasant, SC), 2001.

Greater U Street, Arcadia Publishing (Mount Pleasant, SC), 2002.

(With T. Luke Young) *Washington, DC, Then and Now,* Arcadia Publishing (Mount Pleasant, SC), 2002.

(With Charles Williams) *Skaneateles Lake,* Arcadia Publishing (Mount Pleasant, SC), 2002.

Owasco Lake, Arcadia Publishing (Mount Pleasant, SC), 2002.

(With Gregory Alexander) *Woodley Park,* Arcadia Publishing (Mount Pleasant, SC), 2003.

(With Kelton Higgins) *Cleveland Park,* Arcadia Publishing (Mount Pleasant, SC), 2003.

(With Paul R. O'Neill) *Georgetown University,* Arcadia Publishing (Mount Pleasant, SC), 2003.

(With Gregory Alexander) *Capitol Hill,* Arcadia Publishing (Mount Pleasant, SC), 2004.

Washington, DC: The World War II Years, Arcadia Publishing (Mount Pleasant, SC), 2004.

Contributor to periodicals, including *Old House Journal* and *InTowner* newspaper.

WORK IN PROGRESS: How to Research Your House History.

SIDELIGHTS: Paul K. Williams told *CA:* "I own and operate a 'house history' consulting firm that specializes in research on individual buildings or dwellings primarily in Washington, DC, and Baltimore, MD, and all across the United States. I also write for journals on a regular basis on history, historic preservation, and 'how-to' topics."

*   *   *

WILSON, Rob
See GORE, Patrick Wilson

*   *   *

WISEMAN, Richard 1966-

PERSONAL: Born 1966. *Education:* University College, London, England, received degree (with first class honors; psychology); University of Edinburgh, Ph.D. (psychology).

ADDRESSES: Office—Psychology Department, University of Hertfordshire, College Lane, Hatfield, Herts AL10 9AB, England. *E-mail*—R.Wiseman@herts.ac.uk.

CAREER: University of Hertfordshire, England, director of Perrot-Warrick Research Unit, 1994—, professor of psychology, 2003—. Has appeared on such British radio and television programs as *Tomorrow's World* and *The Today Programme.*

MEMBER: Magic Circle.

AWARDS, HONORS: Public Education in Science Award, CSICOP, 2000; Joseph Lister Award, British Association for the Advancement of Science, 2002.

WRITINGS:

(With Richard Morris) *Guidelines for Testing Psychic Claimants,* Prometheus Books (Amherst, NY), 1995.

Deception and Self-Deception: Investigating Psychics, Prometheus Books (Amherst, NY), 1997.

(With Julie Milton) *Guidelines for Extrasensory Perception Research,* University of Hertfordshire Press (Hertfordshire, England), 1997.

(With Peter Lamont) *Magic in Theory,* University of Hertfordshire Press (Hertfordshire, England), 1999.

The Luck Factor: Changing Your Luck, Changing Your Life, the Four Essential Principles, Miramax/ Hyperion (New York, NY), 2003, published as *The Luck Factor: Change Your Luck—And Change Your Life,* Century (London, England), 2003, published as *The Luck Factor: The Scientific Study of the Lucky Mind,* Arrow (London, England), 2004, abridged version published as *The Little Book of Luck,* Arrow, 2004.

Did You Spot the Gorilla?: How to Recognize Hidden Opportunities, Arrow, 2004.

Contributor to *Magic in Theory,* University of Hertfordshire Press, 1999, and to periodicals.

SIDELIGHTS: One of the youngest members ever to be accepted into the Magic Circle, the prestigious organization of magicians and illusionists, Richard Wiseman has also had a highly successful career as a psychologist, an author, and a frequent guest on BBC television and England's Radio 4. His humor and range of interests have enhanced his psychological insights, and, according to one survey, made him the most frequently quoted psychologist in the British media. He has often combined showmanship with serious research to explore unusual psychological phenomena. He brought the world of Victorian spiritualists alive in an exhibit called "Séance," currently housed in London's Science Museum. To study national differences in humor, he launched a worldwide search for the funniest joke, which attracted 100,000 visitors from seventy countries to his Web site. More recently, Wiseman has begun to look into the psychology of luck, offering workshops for those seeking to change this feature of life, long seen as completely out of our control.

One of Wiseman's strongest interests has been in the area of extrasensory perception (ESP) and psychic phenomena, and he has written a number of books on the testing of psychic claims. There is a long history of professional magicians (such as James Randi) using their skills to debunk the claims of false psychics, but Wiseman has sought a more evenhanded approach, looking for ways science can test the elusive claims of psychics in a mutually acceptable way. In *Guidelines for Testing Psychic Claimants,* he and Richard Morris outline various principles designed both to combat fraud and to allow for honest testing of sincere psychics. The authors cover ethical issues, mutually acceptable procedures, and the differences between proof-oriented and process-oriented research.

At only fifty pages, the book is brief, and some critics questioned how useful it might be for novice investigators. "On the other hand, I believe that experienced and skillful investigators can be helped by these guidelines," wrote Ray Hyman in the *Journal of Parapsychology.* He continued, "Although . . . the suggestions are too succinct to instruct an investigator in the specifics of procedures, the total set of guidelines serves as a very useful checklist or reminder of the many considerations that need to be addressed if the test is to have a chance to succeed." In a review of *Guidelines for Extrasensory Perception Research* in the same journal, Nancy Zingrone and Carlos Alvarado also faulted the book for its brevity, but commended it as "a useful little volume that is sure to find its place among the design tools of veteran and student parapsychologist alike."

While ESP and clairvoyance have a long history of claims and counterclaims, tests and experiments, few people have ever looked at luck in such a skeptical manner. For most people luck is viewed as an intangible factor that comes and goes; one either has it or one does not. Wiseman was not satisfied with this attitude, however, and through a series of workshops and experiments decided to test the possibility of consciously changing one's luck. He published his findings in *The Luck Factor: Changing Your Luck, Changing Your Life, the Four Essential Principles,* "a self-help book for people on whom pianos tend to fall out of the sky," in the words of a contributor to *O.* What Wiseman found was that in many ways "people are not born lucky. Rather they create their own luck through their mental attitudes and behavior," as reviewer Clare Hughes explained in *Student BMJ.* The person who "lucks" into a great job is the same one who habitually talks to strangers and so maximizes their opportunities of hearing about opportunities. Others find their luck through a relaxed attitude. In one interesting experiment, Wiseman scattered money on the ground. The "lucky" participants took the time to scan the sidewalk for loose change. Those who thought themselves unlucky habitually stepped over the money, assuming there was nothing there. The four principles of creating luck are maximizing opportunities, accepting "gut feelings," optimism, and the ability to see possibilities in apparent setbacks, and according to a *Publishers Weekly* reviewer, his "upbeat, charismatic tone might persuade even skeptical readers of the transformative effect luck can have in their personal and professional lives."

BIOGRAPHICAL AND CRITICAL SOURCES:

PERIODICALS

Book, March-April, 2003, Steve Wilson, "Something for Nothing: Luck in America," p. 81.

Journal of Parapsychology, December, 1995, Ray Hyman, review of *Guidelines for Testing Psychic Claimants,* p. 381; September, 1999, Nancy Zingrone and Carlos Alvarado, review of *Guidelines for Extrasensory Perception Research;* June, 2000, Rex G. Stanford, review of *Deception and Self-Deception: Investigating Psychics,* p. 213; September, 2000, Lody Auerbach, review of *Magic in Theory,* p. 333.

Library Journal, March 15, 2003, David Leonhardt, review of *The Luck Factor: Changing Your Luck, Changing Your Life: The Four Essential Principles,* p. 103.

Money, August, 2003, Jason Zweig, "R+U Lucky?"

O, April, 2003, review of *The Luck Factor,* p. 149.

Publishers Weekly, February 17, 2003, review of *The Luck Factor,* p. 63.

Skeptical Inquirer, May, 2000, Kendrick Frazier, review of *Magic in Theory,* p. 54.

Student BMJ, April, 2003, Clare Hughes, review of *The Luck Factor,* p. 126.

OTHER

"Interview: Dr. Richard Wiseman Discusses Luck" (radio transcript), broadcast on *Weekend Edition Saturday,* National Public Radio, 2003.*

*   *   *

WOLD, Donald J. 1945-

PERSONAL: Born 1945. *Education:* Trinity Evangelical Divinity School, M.Div.; University of California at Berkeley, Ph.D.

ADDRESSES: Agent—c/o Author Mail, Baker Books, P.O. Box 6287, Grand Rapids, MI 49516-6287.

CAREER: Pastor, counselor, and professor of Near Eastern studies.

WRITINGS:

Out of Order: Homosexuality in the Bible and the Ancient Near East, Baker Books (Grand Rapids, MI), 1998.

SIDELIGHTS: Donald J. Wold's first book, *Out of Order: Homosexuality in the Bible and the Ancient Near East,* uses Biblical passages and other primary sources from the ancient Near East to explain the Judeo-Christian position on homosexual practices. Wold examines Old Testament passages, such as the story of the destruction of Sodom, as well as legal strictures codified in Leviticus to support the theory that the ancient Hebrews felt homosexuality to be a violation of the natural order of God's world. The author finds a similar association between the notions of chaos and disorder and the practice of homosexuality in the New Testament. To quote Lori A. Burkett in her reading of the work for *Journal of Psychology and Theology,* Wold reaches the conclusion that "same-gender sexual relations are categorically forbidden in the Bible."

With his book, Wold has contributed to a growing body of scholarly literature on same-gender relationships in a Biblical context. James Beck noted in the *Denver Journal* that Wold "has made a valuable and substantial contribution to the current discussion among evangelicals regarding homosexuality." He added, "The book is best suited for understanding the Bible's condemnation of deliberate sins of homosexuality committed by adults. . . . This contribution is significant and noteworthy." Burkett declared *Out of Order* "a stimulating scholarly journey through the biblical texts of the Old and New Testaments as well as various historical data on the ancient Near East."

BIOGRAPHICAL AND CRITICAL SOURCES:

PERIODICALS

Denver Journal, Volume 2, 1999, James Beck, review of *Out of Order: Homosexuality in the Bible and the Ancient Near East.*

Journal of Psychology and Theology, summer, 2002, Lori A. Burkett, review of *Out of Order,* p. 170.*

WOLZ, Carl 1933(?)-2002

PERSONAL: Born c. 1933, in St. Louis, MO; died of cancer January 2, 2002, in New York, NY. *Education:* Attended Juilliard School; University of Chicago, B.A., 1959; University of Hawaii, M.A.

CAREER: Dancer, choreographer, and scholar, specializing in Asian dance. Dancer with Lucas Hoving Company, New York, NY, and José Limon Dance Company; University of Hawaii—Manoa, Honolulu, HI, faculty member and director of dance program, 1965-c. 1983; Hong Kong Academy of Performing Arts, member of organizing team, 1982, dean of dance, 1983-93; Japan Women's College of Physical Education, professor, 1993-98; taught at Washington University, St. Louis, MO, and Barnard College. Hawaii State Dance Council, founding member and past president; Asia Pacific Dance Alliance (now World Dance Alliance), founder, president of Asia-Pacific Division, c. 1988-2002, executive director, beginning 1995; organizer of dance festivals in Hong Kong. *Military service:* U.S. Navy (some sources cite Army); served during Korean conflict.

MEMBER: International Council of Kinetography Laban (fellow).

AWARDS, HONORS: East-West Center, fellow in Hawaii, 1962, Distinguished Alumni Award, 1992; Professional Achievement Award, University of Chicago, 1995; award for outstanding leadership in dance research, Congress on Research in Dance, 1995; award from Hong Kong Academy for Performing Arts.

WRITINGS:

Bugaku: Japanese Court Dance, with the Notation of Basic Movement and of Nasori, Asian Music Publications (Providence, RI), 1971.
(Editor, with Adrienne L. Kaeppler and Judy Van Zile) *Asian and Pacific Dance: Selected Papers from the 1974 CORD-SEM Conference,* Committee on Research in Dance (New York, NY), 1977.

Other writings include *Chinese Classical Dance.* Contributor to periodicals.

BIOGRAPHICAL AND CRITICAL SOURCES:

PERIODICALS

AB Bookman's Weekly, November 6, 1972, review of *Bugaku: Japanese Court Dance, with the Notation of Basic Movement and of Nasori,* p. 1382.

OBITUARIES

PERIODICALS

Honolulu Star-Bulletin, February 1, 2002.
Los Angeles Times, January 8, 2002, p. B9.
New York Times, January 12, 2002, p. A13.
Variety, February 11, 2002, p. 70.*

* * *

WOODGER, Elin 1954-

PERSONAL: Born June 24, 1954, in Port Chester, NY; daughter of Herbert A. (a drafter) and Carol (Magnusson) Woodger; married Norman Thomas Philip Murphy (a writer), October 6, 2001. *Education:* Attended State University of New York at Binghamton and State University of New York Empire State College. *Hobbies and other interests:* Reading (especially P. G. Wodehouse), long walks.

ADDRESSES: Home and office—9 Winton Ave., London N11 2AS, England. *Agent*—James Peters Associates, P.O. Box 358, New Canaan, CT 06840. *E-mail*—ewoodgerm@aol.com.

CAREER: Linguistics International, Boston, MA, operations manager and customer service manager, 1979-88; Massachusetts General Hospital, Boston, executive secretary, 1989-98; freelance writer and editor, 1997—.

MEMBER: Wodehouse Society (president, 1999-2001), P. G. Wodehouse Society.

AWARDS, HONORS: Cited among best reference sources of the year, *Library Journal,* 2003, Society of School Librarians International, Honor Book Award, 2004, both for *Encyclopedia of the Lewis and Clark Expedition.*

WRITINGS:

(With Brandon Toropov) *Encyclopedia of the Lewis and Clark Expedition,* Facts on File (New York, NY), 2003.

(With David Burg) *Eyewitness History: The 1980s,* Facts on File (New York, NY), 2006.

Coeditor, *Plum Lines,* 1996-2001. Also worked as ghostwriter for other authors.

SIDELIGHTS: Elin Woodger told *CA:* "I had long fancied myself a fiction writer until I realized that my talent really lay in nonfiction. In 1997 I began ghostwriting for Beach Brook Productions, which was a useful apprenticeship, as it not only gave me experience, but also helped me decide to quit office work and focus on writing. I also began editing, primarily assisting other authors with their works and sometimes also writing sections of their books for them. In 1999 I moved from the Boston area to Port Chester, New York, where, in addition to my writing assignments, I began doing copyediting work for New York-based clients. At this time I was working on the *Encyclopedia of Cold War Politics,* to which I made significant research and writing contributions.

"In the course of these years I discovered an affinity for topics in American history, in both my writing and my editing work. In 2001 Brandon Toropov, the official author of *Encyclopedia of Cold War Politics* as well as a friend and advisor who has given me numerous writing opportunities, asked if I would coauthor *Encyclopedia of the Lewis and Clark Expedition* with him. This was my breakthrough work, the first to be published under my own name, and it was a rewarding experience as I steeped myself in Lewis and Clark lore. The book has done very well in its market (primarily schools and libraries, but also retail), and I am proud to say that reviews have been universally good.

"In 2001 I married and moved to England. My husband is a retired British Army colonel who has written a number of books on P. G. Wodehouse, a history of London, and a logistics handbook for the North Atlantic Treaty Organization. In addition to being my biggest booster, he is also my severest critic and an excellent editor. I continue to work for U.S.-based clients, both writing and editing assignments, and my next book, *Eyewitness History: The 1980s,* is scheduled for publication in 2006. Being in London has not hampered my ability to research (thanks to the Internet and the British Library), and my work is very portable. Having found my milieu in academic publishing, I intend to continue my focus on American history and plan to return to college and get my degree in that subject.

"To aspiring nonfiction writers I would say: Be persistent and keep practicing your craft, writing on a variety of topics. Being able to write about *anything* is a big bonus!"

BIOGRAPHICAL AND CRITICAL SOURCES:

PERIODICALS

American Reference Books Annual, 2004, Mark A. Wilson, review of *Encyclopedia of the Lewis and Clark Expedition.*

Booklist, June 1, 2004, review of *Encyclopedia of the Lewis and Clark Expedition,* p. 1788.

Choice, April, 2004, J. Drueke, review of *Encyclopedia of the Lewis and Clark Expedition.*

Christian Library Journal, August, 2004, Donna J. Eggen, review of *Encyclopedia of the Lewis and Clark Expedition.*

Library Journal, December, 2003, Margaret Atwater-Singer, review of *Encyclopedia of the Lewis and Clark Expedition,* p. 102.

Library Media Connection, April-May, 2004, Lee Gordon, review of *Encyclopedia of the Lewis and Clark Expedition.*

School Library Journal, February, 2004, Grace Oliff, review of *Encyclopedia of the Lewis and Clark Expedition,* p. 94.

Voice of Youth Advocates, February, 2004, Cindy Lombardo, review of *Encyclopedia of the Lewis and Clark Expedition.*

*   *   *

WOODHOUSE, S(usan). T. 1958-
(Liz Carlyle)

PERSONAL: Born August 7, 1958, in Suffolk, VA; married; stepchildren: two. *Education:* Radford University, B.S. (journalism), 1980. *Politics:* Democrat. *Religion:* Episcopalian.

ADDRESSES: Agent—Nancy Yost, Lowenstein-Yost Associates, 121 West 27th St., Suite 601, New York, NY 10001. *E-mail*—lizcarlyle@aol.com.

CAREER: Author.

WRITINGS:

ROMANCE FICTION; UNDER PSEUDONYM LIZ CARLYLE

My False Heart, Sonnet Books (New York, NY), 1999.
A Woman Scorned, Pocket Books (New York, NY), 2000.
Beauty like the Night, Sonnet Books (New York, NY), 2000.
A Woman of Virtue (sequel to *A Woman Scorned*), Pocket Books (New York, NY), 2001.
No True Gentleman, Pocket Books (New York, NY), 2002.
(With Cathy Maxwell) *Tea for Two: Two Novellas* (contains Carlyle's "Hunting Season"), Pocket Star Books (New York, NY), 2002.
The Devil You Know, Pocket Books (New York, NY), 2003.
A Deal with the Devil (sequel to *The Devil You Know*), Pocket Star Books (New York, NY), 2004.
The Devil to Pay, Pocket Books (New York, NY), 2005.

Contributor of novella "Let's Talk about Sex," to *Big Guns out of Uniform,* Pocket Books (New York, NY), 2003, and "Much Ado about Twelfth Night," to *The One That Got Away,* Avon/HarperCollins (New York, NY), 2004.

SIDELIGHTS: S. T. Woodhouse, who writes under the pen name Liz Carlyle, is the author of historical romances that have received wide praise from critics who have admired the author's skill at characterization, setting, and original plotting. Carlyle worked in the corporate world for about eighteen years before writing her first novel, *My False Heart,* on a dare while she was between jobs. After a few years during which Carlyle struggled to find a publisher, the book was released in 1999 and hailed by romance novel reviewers as a promising debut. While keeping to many of the conventions of the romance genre, the

book, asserted *Romance Reader* contributor Lesley Dunlap, varies from the norm: "Countless romances have featured the classic plot of the degenerate rake who sees the error of his ways, reforms, and finds a lasting and true love with a good woman. Rarely, however, does the author provide much support for this personality change. Where Ms. Carlyle's book excels is in the how and why."

My False Heart features Elliot Armstrong, whose unfaithful fiancée's behavior leads to a broken engagement and his descent into a life of debauchery; his new love interest, Evangeline Stone, is a young artist who welcomes him into her home one stormy night, thinking that he is someone else. Elliot quickly becomes enamored by the beautiful Evangeline and does not reveal his true identity until a former mistress, who is also Evangeline's aunt, reveals Elliot's past. Although Dunlap felt the mystery subplot involving Elliot's ex-fiancée to be somewhat contrived, she found the love story convincing and entertaining.

Another *Romance Reader* reviewer, Jean Mason, was equally impressed with Carlyle's follow-up novel, *A Woman Scorned.* After Jonet Rowland's philandering husband is murdered, her brother-in-law, Lord James Rowland, is convinced that she is the killer, but he cannot prove it. He comes up with a ploy to hire his nephew Captain Cole Amherst, a former scholar who was injured in battle and was widowed while stationed in Portugal, to serve as tutor to Jonet's two children while also acting as his spy. Cole soon realizes that there are more secrets in the household than anyone suspected. In addition, Jonet and Cole are mutually attracted, but do not trust one another. Mason found the interweaving of mystery and romance to be effectively handled, concluding that "Carlyle's first book was very, very good. Her second is as good, or maybe even better."

A Woman of Virtue is a sequel to *A Woman Scorned* and includes Jonet and Cole in important roles. However, the main story features another tortured hero named David, whose illegitimate birth proves an impediment to his desire for Cecilia Markham-Sands. Throw in a number of murders, a scandalous rape, and a forced marriage and there are plenty of plot complications in *A Woman Scorned.* Although Dunlap, writing in *Romance Reader Online,* found some of

Cecilia's motivations less-than-satisfactorily explained, she complimented Carlyle on writing a historical romance that features not only upper-class characters but also glimpses into England's lower-class society. "David and Cecelia get to experience a vastly different segment of society," Dunlap commented, "and that makes for a more interesting story."

One of the minor characters readers meet in *A Woman of Virtue* is Constable Max de Rohan. De Rohan becomes the main character in *No True Gentleman,* which focuses on his forbidden love for Lady Catherine Wodeway, who is far above him in social status. In a tale *Library Journal* contributor Kristin Ramsdell predicted "will appeal to readers who like their mysteries with a little romance rather than the other way around," *No True Gentleman* is a Regency story that finds Max investigating an aristocrat's death. Carlyle juggles several plots, including Max's search for the killer, his relationship with Lady Catherine, and his troubles with his meddling grandmother in what a *Publishers Weekly* reviewer called "one of the year's best historical romances."

Carlyle began a new Regency romance series with *The Devil You Know* and *A Deal with the Devil,* though some of her previous characters still make appearances. In *The Devil You Know* Frederica D'Avillez is trying to forget a failed relationship when she meets the roguish Randolph Rutledge. One night of love leaves Frederica pregnant; Randolph convinces her to marry him, but Frederica soon learns that she will only find happiness in her new marriage if she is able to uncover Randolph's secrets. *A Deal with the Devil* begins as Aubrey Montford is hired by Major Lorimer to help him restore his castle, but when the major is murdered, his nephew comes to the castle to investigate and soon finds himself drawn to the mysterious Aubrey. Noting that "there's far more romance here than suspense," a *Publishers Weekly* critic was certain that "Regency fans . . . will be charmed." *Booklist* contributor John Charles even more enthusiastically called the novel "nothing short of brilliant."

Although not all of Carlyle's books have received such praise—the love story in *Beauty like the Night,* for instance, was deemed "predictable" by Mason in a *Romance Reader* assessment—the author's work has generally been found by critics to be a step above the average romance offerings. Nevertheless, Carlyle still describes herself as a struggling author. She is content, though, to continue following her current path, staying at home, writing, and occasionally traveling with her husband to England. "I truly enjoy what I'm doing," she told an interviewer for the *Road to Romance Web site,* "and I love working for [my publisher] Pocket. They have given me lots of latitude in terms of what I write, and they [have] been willing to take some risks. As you know, my novels are a little on the long side, and while they are very definitely Regency-era romances, they are quite sexually explicit and contain some darker elements. . . . So, while my books are not for everyone, I hope I'm filling a special niche for those historical romance fans who like a plot that's a little more intense."

BIOGRAPHICAL AND CRITICAL SOURCES:

PERIODICALS

Booklist, June 1, 2002, John Charles, review of *No True Gentleman,* p. 1693; September 15, 2002, Donna Seaman, review of *No True Gentleman,* p. 216; April 1, 2003, John Charles, review of *The Devil You Know,* p. 1383; March 1, 2004, John Charles, review of *A Deal with the Devil,* p. 1144.
Library Journal, May 15, 2002, Kristin Ramsdell, review of *Tea for Two,* p. 79; August, 2002, Kristin Ramsdell, review of *No True Gentleman,* p. 70.
Publishers Weekly, April 24, 2000, review of *A Woman Scorned,* p. 67; April 8, 2002, review of *Tea for Two,* p. 211; June 3, 2002, review of *No True Gentleman,* p. 71; January 19, 2004, review of *A Deal with the Devil,* p. 59.
Romance Reader, November 1, 1999, Lesley Dunlap, review of *My False Heart;* May 7, 2000, Jean Mason, review of *A Woman Scorned;* November 27, 2000, Jean Mason, review of *Beauty Like the Night;* March 20, 2001, Dunlap, review of *A Woman of Virtue.*

ONLINE

All about Romance Web site, http://www.likesbooks.com/ (December 3, 2002), Ellen D. Micheletti, reviews of *Beauty like the Night* and *A Woman of Virtue.*

BookBrowser.com, http://www.bookbrowser.com/ (August 15, 1999), Harriet Klausner, review of *My False Heart;* (November 14, 2000) Harriet Klausner, review of *Beauty like the Night;* (December 27, 2000) Harriet Klausner, review of *A Woman of Virtue;* (June 8, 2002) Harriet Klausner, review of *No True Gentleman.*

Liz Carlyle: Historical Romance Novelist Web site (home page), http://www.lizcarlyle.com/ (July 13, 2004).

Road to Romance Web site, http://www.roadtoromance. ca/ (December 3, 2002), interview with Carlyle.

Y-Z

YOOK, Wan-soon 1933-

PERSONAL: Born June 16, 1933, in Ch'ungju, Korea. *Education:* Ewha Women's University, B.A., 1956, M.A., 1961; attended University of California—Long Beach, 1971, and University of Illinois; Hanyang University, Ph.D., 1986; also attended Martha Graham School of Contemporary Dance, American Dance Festival, and Connecticut Summer Dance School, 1961-63.

CAREER: Orchesis Dance Company, founder, dancer, choreographer, and teacher, 1963-74; Korea Contemporary Dance Company, cofounder and artistic director, beginning 1975; Duljje (modern dance company; now TAM), founder, 1980; Modern Dance Promotion of Korea, founder, 1985. Lecturer at Ewha Women's University, Kyounghee University, Sookmyoung Women's University, Hanyang University, and Sangmyoung University, 1959-91. Performed as dancer on international tours, including appearances in New York, NY, Paris, France, London, England, Vancouver, British Columbia, Canada, and St. Petersburg, Russia, between 1975 and 1996; choreographer and director of dance performances for Olympic Games in Seoul, Korea, 1988; American Dance Festival, Seoul, host, beginning 1990; Environmental Arts Festival, copresenter, 1996; Seoul International Children and Youth Dance Festival, affiliate, 1997.

MEMBER: Modern Dance Association of Korea (founder, 1980).

AWARDS, HONORS: Seoul Cultural Award, 1981; Republic of Korea, Social Educator's Award, 1982, Award for Artistic Achievement, 1989; Christian Cultural Award, 1987; choreography award, 1988, for Olympic Games, Seoul; Appreciation Award, mayor of Los Angeles, CA, 1993.

WRITINGS:

Modern Dance, [Seoul, Korea], 1979.
Modern Dance Techniques, [Seoul, Korea], 1981.
Dance Improvisation, [Seoul, Korea], 1983.
Choreography, [Seoul, Korea], 1984.
(With Lee Hee-sun) *Curriculum in Dance Education,* [Seoul, Korea], 1992.

TRANSLATOR

Martha Graham, [Seoul, Korea], 1984.
History of Western Dance, [Seoul, Korea], 1986.
Letters on Dancing and Ballets, [Seoul, Korea], 1987.
(With Ha Jung-ae, Park Myung-sook, and Kwun Yoonbang) *Isadora and Esenin,* [Seoul, Korea], 1988.

BIOGRAPHICAL AND CRITICAL SOURCES:

BOOKS

International Dictionary of Modern Dance, St. James Press (Detroit, MI), 1998.*

*   *   *

YOUNG, Philip H(oward) 1953-

PERSONAL: Born October 7, 1953, in Ithaca, NY; son of Charles R. (a professor of history) and Betty (a librarian; maiden name, Osborne) Young; married Nancy Stutsman (a professor of dental hygiene),

446

August 18, 1979. *Education:* University of Virginia, B.A., 1975; Indiana University, M.L.S., 1983; University of Pennsylvania, Ph.D., 1980. *Hobbies and other interests:* Collecting rare books.

ADDRESSES: Home—4332 Silver Springs Dr., Greenwood, IN 46142. *Office*—University of Indianapolis, 1400 East Hanna Ave., Indianapolis, IN 46227. *E-mail*—pyoung@uindy.edu.

CAREER: Appalachian State University, Boone, NC, professor of history, 1980-82; University of Indianapolis, Indianapolis, IN, director of Krannert Memorial Library, 1985—.

MEMBER: Archaeological Institute of America, American Library Association.

WRITINGS:

Children's Fiction Series: A Bibliography, 1850-1950, McFarland and Co. (Jefferson, NC), 1997.
The Printed Homer: A 3,000-Year Publishing and Translation History of the Iliad and the Odyssey, McFarland and Co. (Jefferson, NC), 2003.
In Days of Knights (fiction), University of Indianapolis Press (Indianapolis, IN), 2004.

SIDELIGHTS: Philip H. Young told *CA:* "From childhood, I have been interested in studying and writing about the past, a love taught by my parents. My college years resulted in a bachelor's degree in history and a doctorate in classical archaeology, interests I have been able to continue alongside my work as an academic librarian. I love the written word and the pursuit of knowledge, and I am happy that I have been able to dabble in both, writing academic works and also fiction."

BIOGRAPHICAL AND CRITICAL SOURCES:

PERIODICALS

Booklist, June 1, 1997, review of *Children's Fiction Series: A Bibliography, 1850-1950,* p. 1750.

Library Journal, November 15, 2003, T. L. Cooksey, review of *The Printed Homer: A 3,000-Year Publishing and Translation History of the Iliad and the Odyssey,* p. 68.

*   *   *

ZHANG Yan 1938-
  (Xi Xi)

PERSONAL: Born October 7, 1938, in Shanghai, China.

ADDRESSES: Home—Hong Kong. *Office*—c/o Hong Kong University Press, 14/F Hing Wai Centre, Tin Wan Praya Rd., Aberdeen, Hong Kong.

CAREER: Novelist, short-story writer, and essayist. Primary school teacher, Hong Kong,1958-79; screenwriter, c. 1960s; *Damuzhi zhoubao* (literary magazine), editor, 1975-77; *Suye wenxue* (literary magazine), editor, 1981-84.

AWARDS, HONORS: United Daily (Taiwan) award, 1982, for "A Girl like Me."

WRITINGS:

Wo cheng [China], 1974, translated by Eva Hung as *My City: A Hong Kong Story,* Chinese University of Hong Kong (Hong Kong, China), 1993.
Jiao he, Xianggang wen xue yan jiu she (Xianggang, China), c.1981.
Chun wang (short stories), Su ye chu ban she (Xianggang, China), 1982.
Shao lu, Su ye chu ban she (Xianggang, China), 1982.
Shi qing, Su ye chu ban she (Xianggang, China), 1982.
Xiang wo zhe yang di yi ge du zhe, Hong fan shu dian, min guo 75 (Taibei Shi, Taiwan), 1984, translated by Stephen C. Soong as *A Girl like Me and Other Stories,* Chinese University of Hong Kong (Hong Kong, China), 1986, expanded edition, 1999.
Hu zi you lian (short stories), Hong fan shu dian, min guo 75 (Taibei Shi, Taiwan), 1986.
Marvels of a Floating City and Other Stories, translated by Eva Hung, Chinese University of Hong Kong (Hong Kong, China), 1997.

Fei zhan, [China], 1996, translated by Diana Yu as *Flying Carpet: A Tale of Fertillia,* Hong Kong University Press (Hong Kong, China), 2000.

Also author of *Aiado rufang* (tile means "Eleby for a Breast").

SIDELIGHTS: Zhang Yan, better known to readers as Xi Xi, is one of Hong Kong's foremost fiction writers. Her novels, beginning with *My City: A Hong Kong Story* first published in China in 1974, express the spirit and culture of modern China and, in particular, her hometown of Hong Kong. Her short fiction and essays have developed a simple and personal style that critics have connected to the Western literary genres of Magic Realism and Surrealism. Her works have been translated into English since the mid-1980s, expanding her audience from Hong Kong, Taiwan, and mainland China to the West.

Xi Xi was born in Shanghai into a Cantonese family in 1938. In 1950 the family moved to Hong Kong to distance themselves from the Chinese mainland, which had been taken over by the Chinese Communist party. She worked for twenty years as a primary school teacher, beginning in 1958, though for most of that period she also began working on her writing career, publishing short pieces in magazines and writing screenplays. During the 1960s she also wrote as a critic of film and art, and she wrote a newspaper column. Her first novel, *Wo cheng,* was translated as *My City.* It was among the first in Hong Kong literature to use the Cantonese dialect, a reflection of the complex culture of the Chinese city. The novel is also unique in its surrealist style, creating a world where walls, tools, and fruits can speak and have feelings. Hong Kong is depicted through the eyes of teenage characters Braids and Fruits, in a simple narrative style.

Reviewing *My City* for *World Literature Today,* Fatima Wu wrote that Xi Xi's "writing talents emerge in a complex tale wherein she, besides portraying the many facets of social and historical issues, is able to combine viewpoints of children and working men and women into a mosaic of surrealism, science fiction, and language games." Jeffrey Twitchell, in the *Review of Contemporary Fiction,* said, "It is above all the language that is the central protagonist of the novel. Xi Xi's subtle, childlike language is ever unpredictable, offering offbeat perspectives at every turn."

Toward the end of her teaching career Xi Xi also became the editor of one of Hong Kong's foremost literary magazines, *Damuzhi zhoubao.* In 1979 she retired from teaching so that she could concentrate on her writing. As she continued to be published, her reputation began to extend beyond Hong Kong. Her 1982 story "Xiang wo zhe yang di yi ge du zhe" ("A Girl like Me") won the *United Daily* award in Taiwan. The story also became the title piece for later English translations of her short fiction, first published in 1986, and in an expanded edition in 1999. *A Girl like Me and Other Stories* also contains excerpts from the autobiographical work *Aidao rufang (Elegy for a Breast),* about Xi Xi's experience with breast cancer in 1989.

Other stories that attracted an English readership are those written during the gradual conversion of Hong Kong back to China, finalized July 1997, and the negotiations preceding the transfer of power. Among these are the "Feitu zhen," or "Fertile Town," series, written between 1982 and 1996. This series includes the 1996 novel *Fei zhan,* translated as *Flying Carpet: A Tale of Fertillia.*

Xi Xi's *Flying Carpet* portrays the "fertile town" from the late nineteenth century up through 1995, addressing such issues as education, industrialization, and superstition through a web of fictional characters. Like her early novel *My City, Flying Carpet* captures something essential about the life of Hong Kong. Reviewing the book for *World Literature Today,* Fatima Wu wrote, "Being a native of Hong Kong myself, I travel back in time with the author into our grandparent's past lives. As the story moves into the modern period, I seem to see myself taking part in the city's growth and maturation."

Other stories written during the late 1980s include "Fucheng zhiyi" ("Marvels of a Floating City"), "Mali gean" ("The Case of Mary"), and the 1988 story "Yuzhou qiqu lu buyi" ("Delights of the Universe: A Supplement"). Three of these stories—"Marvels of a Floating City," "The Story of Fertile Town," and "The Fertile Town Chalk Circle"—were collected in the 1997 publication *Marvels of a Floating City and Other Stories,* translated by Eva Hung. The tales reflect the surrealism and magic realism at work in *My City.* "Marvels of a Floating City" is based on the surreal paintings of René Magritte, the author interpreting the condition of Hong Kong in the French artist's images.

In "The Story of Fertile Town" the soil of a poor town is magically transformed to sustain ever-increasing productivity.

Reviewing the collection for *World Literature Today,* Jeffrey C. Kinkley wrote that, "whereas the numerous books of speculative journalism and political analysis about the hand-over" of Hong Kong from Britain to China have become dated, "Xi Xi's images will live on."

Translator Hung, who created the English versions of *My City* and *Marvels of a Floating City,* summarized Xi Xi's career in the *Encyclopedia of World Literature,* noting that the author "is commonly recognized as Hong Kong's leading writer. Although she is remarkably versatile and covers most genres, she will be best remembered for her works of fiction. One of her major contributions is the sense of humor and fun that she brings to contemporary Chinese literature."

BIOGRAPHICAL AND CRITICAL SOURCES:

BOOKS

Encyclopedia of World Literature in the Twentieth Century, St. James Press (Detroit, MI), 1999.

PERIODICALS

Review of Contemporary Fiction, fall, 1995, Jeffrey Twitchell, review of *My City: A Hong Kong Story,* p. 243.

World Literature Today, summer, 1994, Fatima Wu, review of *My City,* pp. 634-635; spring, 1998, Jeffrey C. Kinkley, review of *Marvels of a Floating City and Other Stories,* p. 455; autumn, 2000, Fatima Wu, review of *Flying Carpet: A Tale of Fertillia,* p. 802.*